SOCIALIZING ARCHITECTURE

SOCIALIZING ARCHITECTURE
TOP-DOWN BOTTOM-UP

TEDDY CRUZ AND FONNA FORMAN

Hatje Cantz Verlag

The MIT Press
Cambridge, Massachusetts

Introduction: A Critical Spatial Practice at the US-Mexico Border 7

SECTION I: ESSAYS

1 CONFLICT IS GENERATIVE 14
2 INFORMALITY IS PRAXIS 22
3 CO-PRODUCING THE CITY WITH OTHERS 30
4 WHERE IS OUR PUBLIC IMAGINATION? 44
5 A PRACTICE OF MEDIATION: TOP-DOWN / BOTTOM-UP 56

SECTION II: PROJECTS

CLUSTERS:
1 CONFLICT URBANIZATIONS: VISUALIZING THE POLITICAL 68
2 URBANIZATIONS OF ADAPTATION: CROSS-BORDER
   MIGRANT FLOWS 158
3 IMMIGRANT NEIGHBORHOODS: HOUSING LABORATORIES 216
4 BOTTOM-UP PUBLIC: THE FUNCTIONAL DIMENSION OF
   PARTICIPATION 352
5 TOP-DOWN PUBLIC: DESIGNING URBAN JUSTICE 442
6 DECOLONIZING KNOWLEDGE AND DEMOCRATIZING
   THE CITY: THE UCSD COMMUNITY STATIONS 494

Notes 575
Image Credits 579
Acknowledgements 581
Colophon 584

This volume is the second in a two-volume series:
Spatializing Justice: Building Blocks
Socializing Architecture: Top-Down / Bottom-Up

The first volume, *Spatializing Justice: Building Blocks,* presents thirty provocations, or building blocks, that have shaped the research-based political and architectural practice of Estudio Teddy Cruz + Fonna Forman. The second volume, *Socializing Architecture: Top-Down / Bottom-Up,* manifests these commitments in spatial practice across five theoretical essays and six visual project clusters.

Introduction: A Critical Spatial Practice at the US-Mexico Border

We begin this second volume where the first left off, with *retooling ourselves*: seeing our own practices as sites of critical intervention. At key moments in the evolution of our practice, we have paused to construct what we call a "practice diagram"—to reflect on where we are, where we want to go, and to alter our priorities, tools and procedures to meet shifting geopolitical and sociospatial dynamics in the San Diego–Tijuana border region and beyond. Visually operationalizing in a diagram our evolving commitments and strategies to engage deepening social inequality and urban asymmetry has been an essential building block of our practice.

This critical detour always includes meditating on the state of our respective fields (Teddy in architecture, Fonna in political theory), their intersections, and the political and aesthetic positions we have taken over decades to engage social imperatives. Our shared dissatisfaction has always centered on a pervasive, beige professional neutrality in the face of global ecosocial crises. In the field of political theory, neutrality manifests as a rarefied conversation among defenders of abstract ideals that rarely engages the world. In architecture, neutrality has meant decorating urban inequality with veneers and dream castles. In recent years, we have been witnessing a grounded and solidaristic turn in political theory and a palpable social turn in architecture, with many design schools and cultural platforms demanding social and urban justice. For many, this is new terrain, because the neoliberal incentive structure since the early 1980s militated against social advocacy and public commitments in the design fields. These pivots are hopeful trends, and produce a very different professional design landscape than when we first launched our public interest practice two decades ago.

We believe architects and urban designers should take a position against inequality, accelerating climate change and the privatization of everything, and align our practices accordingly, continually checking ourselves: Why do we do what we do, for whom, when and how? We believe architects and urban designers should mobilize the tools of design to penetrate the drivers of injustice, exploitation and dispossession. Similarly, we believe that academics who think, write, debate and teach about these things should engage real-world inequality, listen to voices for whom these ideas reflect everyday experiences and co-produce new knowledge not only for academic audiences but for citizens and policymakers as well. Academic institutions that make it difficult for researchers to partner with communities, who erect barriers in the name of compliance, who denigrate community engagement as "service" rather than "research" and exalt academic publication as the holy grail of "research impact" need to change. They need to align their effusive narratives about "equity, diversity and inclusion" with actual protocols and policies that elevate institutional capacity to make positive change in the communities that surround them.

We see ourselves as urban curators, facilitating the movement of knowledges and resources across sectors and across urban borders. In this era of polarization, fragmentation and unprecedented privatization, we believe architects and urbanists can intervene in the gap between top-down institutions and bottom-up publics. While we understand the vulnerability of thinking dialectically about urban dynamics, for us thinking top-down / bottom-up has always been a point of entry into more experimental thinking "across." In other words, the contested power relations between oppositions has catalyzed fresh political and spatial thinking about horizontally traversing them. In our practice we partner closely with community-based agencies to mobilize bottom-up socio-spatial intelligence, to transform top-down policy and redirect institutional resources to support bottom-up agency.

As with any curatorial practice, this work demands epistemic humility and continual reflection on the ethical complexities of joining in solidarity with people struggling against injustice, from the privileged vantage of the academy, the cultural institution or other formal sites of power. We must avoid overconfidence in our capacity to know and say and do things that are relevant and faithful to real experiences. If we aspire even implicitly to advance justice, fairness and equity on behalf of people who are already marginalized, excluded, dispossessed and exploited, we inflict double harm by assuming that our urban and architectural dreams hold meaning for them, that our wishes for them align with their own.

Here we will demonstrate a model of "co-production" that entails *accompanying* struggles against urban injustice in real time, and seeking dialogue with people who are receptive to collaboration, weaving diverse skills, knowledges and experiences together into a richer account of struggle and more responsive strategies of resistance, advocacy and urban intervention.[1]

The Essays:
Theoretical Apparatus of a Critical Spatial Practice

The texts, diagrams and images assembled across these two volumes, *Spatializing Justice* and *Socializing Architecture*, follow a sequence: from *priorities* (building blocks), to *theories* (essays), to *projects* (project clusters). The priorities we presented in *Spatializing Justice* ground the theories and projects of our practice, which are elaborated in *Socializing Architecture* across five essays and six project clusters.

Essay 1 reinterprets urban conflict as a generative framework for design, and an essential backdrop to developing a grounded theoretical and research-based architecture practice. In our case, we radicalized the San Diego–Tijuana border as a global laboratory in which to engage the most intense urban conflicts of our time. Essay 2 investigates ingenious bottom-up practices of urban adaptation and solidarity that spring from conditions of urban conflict. In our practice, we seek to translate these emergent urban practices into new political economies and spatial strategies of equitable community development. Essay 3 elaborates the role architects can play, facilitating cross-sector experiments to *co-produce* the city. While architects typically wait for the client and the brief to design within a given site and budget, these conventional hierarchies have never worked for us. Over the years, we have co-produced the brief with communities, understood not as clients but as co-developers. And together we summon the resources that are needed, bottom-up and top-down, to actualize these projects in the absence of formal support. In essay 4, we connect this urban experimentation with cultivating a broader civic imagination in our cities. Our cultural aspirations are inspired by compelling cases of Latin American civic experimentation over the last decades. Essay 5 concludes with reflection on the ethical and epistemic challenges of doing research in places of marginalization and struggle, and an imperative to *retool ourselves* and expand the fields of design.

The Project Clusters:
Interventions of a Critical Spatial Practice

The second part of *Socializing Architecture* is organized across six project clusters, which assemble and visualize the projects and initiatives of Estudio Teddy Cruz + Fonna Forman over the last years. Project cluster 1 presents the geospatial armature of our embedded practice at the US-Mexico border, scaling down from global, to regional, to very local border neighborhoods where we work every day. Project cluster 2 presents the often invisible cross-border urban flows and circulations that we have documented over the years. Project cluster 3 presents our work on social and emergency housing, documenting two experimental projects we have co-developed with community-based agencies on both sides of the border wall. Project clusters 4 and 5 present a set of international collaborations that exemplify bottom-up and top-down urban ingenuity—project cluster 4, a sequence of bottom-up public space projects with communities across Buenos Aires, Madrid, Anyang and others; and project cluster 5, collaborations with top-down municipal institutions in Bogotá and Medellín to document and visualize the transformative civic and political processes that made these two Colombian cities global models of equitable urbanization in the late 1990s and early 2000s.

    Project cluster 6 concludes with a cross-border public initiative that manifests and integrates all of the provocations and theoretical commitments of our practice. The UCSD Community Stations are a physical infrastructure of public spaces across the San Diego–Tijuana border region where top-down and bottom-up knowledges and resources meet. Co-developed between our public university, UC San Diego, and community-based agencies on both sides of the border, the UCSD Community Stations are designed to spatialize justice in the border region and mobilize cross-border citizenship through cultural action.

***

As this book goes to print, the world is burning: pandemic and runaway climate change met with science denial; accelerating migration met with resurgent nativism and border building everywhere; dramatic social inequality met with disregard or tepid neoliberal antidotes; the return of fascism, populism and war in Europe; the dismantling of women's rights in the US; and undergirding everything perhaps, the dramatic unraveling of public trust. In every dimension, in every corner of the world, we are facing the consequences of polarizing private and public interests. It is difficult some days to stay optimistic, to resist the pull of defeatism, and feelings of inevitability and futility. And we reflect on the meaning of sharing this work now. But our community partners always help us recenter, reminding us every day that spatial practices can do more—must do more—than ride these waves of history. We hope that sharing this work, at this charged moment, will contribute to accelerating dialogue and commitment among architects, urbanists and design schools everywhere to resist injustice and ecosocial catastrophe, and to engage in solidaristic modes of operation.

1. CONFLICT IS GENERATIVE
2. INFORMALITY IS PRAXIS
3. CO-PRODUCING THE CITY WITH OTHERS
4. WHERE IS OUR PUBLIC IMAGINATION?
5. A PRACTICE OF MEDIATION: TOP-DOWN / BOTTOM-UP

CONFLICT IS GENERATIVE

Borders Localize Global Injustice

To remain neutral in face of social and economic injustice is to be complicit with the institutions and processes that perpetuate it. We challenge the hegemony of neoliberal urban development patterns across the world in recent decades, the damages it has inflicted to our collective economic, social and natural resources, and the gap it has widened between rich and poor.

    We live and work in a zone of conflict and disparity that divides two cities, two countries, two continents, two hemispheres. The border cities of San Diego, California, and Tijuana, BC, Mexico, share the Western hemisphere's busiest land crossing, with 100,000 crossings every day. Our region exemplifies the global dynamics of uneven urban growth of the last decades. From the start, our research-based architecture practice has forwarded the San Diego–Tijuana border region as a global laboratory for engaging the central challenges of urbanization today: deepening social and economic inequality, dramatic migratory shifts, urban informality, climate change, the thickening of border walls and the decline of public thinking. As the third decade of the twenty-first century unfolds, this region is the main site of arrival for people seeking asylum from Central American violence, poverty and the accelerating impacts of climate change. Global injustice is intensely local here.

    Our work localizes these global dynamics—"localizes the global"— from a *critical distance* to a *critical proximity*. It shifts focus and narrative from the abstraction of globalization "out there" somewhere to the here-and-now of the local physical territory and its sociopolitical dynamics. This does not mean privileging one scale over the other. Advancing egalitarian and multilateral forms of governance demands that we oscillate imaginatively across scales, and seek new critical correspondences between the global, the regional, the national and the local. In our practice, we engage the normative, institutional, territorial, spatial, social and environmental conflicts and ruptures generated by discriminatory zoning, the militarization of policing and the socioeconomic inequalities in today's neoliberal city. Our immediate social, geographic, environmental and political context has been our point of entry into these crises across the world, for understanding how global conflict shapes contested power relations inscribed in the everyday lives of people.

Border regions are a microcosm of the conflicts and injustices that globalization has inflicted on the world's most vulnerable people: poverty, environmental degradation, accelerating migration, labor exploitation, human trafficking, gender and racial violence, explosive urbanization, unchecked privatization, the decimation of public trust, etc. Global forces of division and control are amplified in critical thresholds across the planet, like the San Diego–Tijuana border, where we live and work. Racist political narratives continue to portray this region as a site of criminality and violence. A politics of fragmentation and division reinforce public perceptions of the border as a barrier separating hostile oppositions. In a time of global closure, this border is emblematic of anti-immigration panic everywhere, stoked by the xenophobic and protectionist agendas of Trumpism, Brexit and far-right movements across the world. Nativism shows its face with impunity, boldly fragmenting regional and local territories into archipelagos of exception, surveillance and exclusion, and physicalizing everywhere what can only be described as "urbanizations of fear."

But this is nothing new: convergences between militarization and urbanization are a perennial history. The spatial and political history of our region is another nineteenth-century story of annexation and partition, with a long legacy of violence and radical disparity. Throughout most of the twentieth century, the border wall between the US and Mexico performed like a line in the sand, with markers and light fences demarcating where one country began and the other ended. People in border towns moved quite freely back and forth to work, to visit family and friends. Children on both sides hopped the fence in play, and hopped back as easily. But over the last decades, the invisible line that was rendered arbitrarily at one point in history has hardened, thickened. The border has become militarized with massive force and surveillance infrastructure. A series of obelisks across the open landscape in the latter part of the nineteenth-century, a chain-link fence in the 1960s, a steel wall constructed with temporary landing mats discarded by the US military after Operation Desert Storm in Iraq in the 1990s, a concrete pylon wall crowned by electrified coils and panoptic night-vision cameras in the 2000s, and a proposed thirty-foot-high continental wall in 2016, which was erected in various places, demonstrate a deepening penetration of division and surveillance that have been part of everyday life for border communities in this region for the last 150 years. Now, the border performs more like a partition than a boundary because its purpose is less to demarcate than to separate, and to willfully obstruct the flows that have always defined life in this region.

The hardening of the border wall at San Diego–Tijuana physicalizes the erosion of public thinking in the US—the dismantling of the social welfare state and the expansion of economic austerity. A newly expanded border checkpoint in San Ysidro, California, has transformed San Diego into the world's largest gated community, subordinating collective life in this region to the fragmentation and privatization of our collective economic and social assets.

But we are not unique. The protectionist urge to build borders always intensifies when neoliberal agendas accelerate and hijack our politics. This is as true of Fortress Europe as it is at the US-Mexico border. Both are fueled by a collective obsession with sovereignty, national self-determination, security, economic greed and social paranoia against the "barbarian invasion," typically aligned with a populist commitment to market "freedoms." Instead of seeing borders as fluid zones of opportunity—their ideal of a "borderless" free market—these radically conservative cultural-economic agendas yield a rigid grid of global containment. The result is a global weakening of public institutions, geopolitical tensions—zones of overproduction, investment and excess on the one hand, and zones of scarcity, disinvestment and marginalization on the other—yielding dramatic socioeconomic disparities between rich and poor, between white and brown and between documented and undocumented, with new borders erected between them.

The Wall Is Everywhere

In a conversation many years ago, Mexican writer and social critic Carlos Monsiváis described the San Diego–Tijuana border wall as "portable." We carry the psychic wall within ourselves, he said, as we experience the physical wall from without, dividing our dreams and aspirations from the opportunities available to achieve them. This psycho-spatial rupture manifests perhaps most profoundly at a particular place along the wall's trajectory. As one travels alongside the border westbound, moving through the northernmost edges of Tijuana, one arrives finally at the Pacific Ocean. The wall continues its journey into the ocean for around 200 feet before it finally sinks, materializing the psychological landscapes of ambiguity and contradiction that define these border cities.

    The metropolitan identities of San Diego and Tijuana represent divergent socioeconomic and political universes. While San Diego calls itself "America's Finest City," Tijuana is viewed in Mexico as a decadent, transient world unto itself, distinct from and somehow inferior to the rest of the country. It is a region defined by radical disparity, where some of the wealthiest housing subdivisions in the United States sit only twenty minutes away from some of the poorest settlements in Latin America. It is a region of contrary attitudes to constructing the territory, side by side, overlapping and colliding, entangled in a double desire, between a shared destiny and a perennial divorce.

    San Diego is emblematic of an urbanism of segregation and control epitomized by the master-planned and gated communities that constitute its sprawl. The border wall itself symbolizes a puritan planning tradition grounded in principles of separation and exclusion, intended to neutralize the heterogeneity and social complexity of the contemporary city. The wall is a dam that keeps Tijuana's chaotic growth from contaminating San Diego's picturesque subdivisions. San Diego's periphery reveals a massive eradication of topography, as the bulldozers of private development flatten the ground to install one-dimensional pads for the construction of cheap, cookie-cutter housing projects. This top-down sprawl not only neutralizes the character of the ground and erases its historical, environmental, cultural and civic meanings, but also imprints on it, as Mike Davis has observed, an ecology of fear that ultimately flattens, along its path, a crucial sense of political will and social responsibility.[2] Tijuana's periphery, on the other hand, has mitigated distance by intensively urbanizing as a conurbation of informal, favela-like nomadic settlements. Tijuana's informal communities are growing faster than the urban core they surround, creating a different set of rules for development and blurring distinctions between the urban, the suburban and the rural.

From the perspective of borders, it is interesting that these radical contrasts that distinguish San Diego and Tijuana have diminished over time as the two cities and their urban growth patterns have begun to emulate and cross-contaminate one another. San Diego–style gated communities and signature mini-malls have sprung up on Tijuana's periphery, while Tijuana's random patterns of density and mixed use, along with its informal economies, have crept northward into many of San Diego's neighborhoods. In every global capital, an underdeveloped world exists, and every developing city replicates globalization. The global import-export processes that cause cities across the world to recycle symbols of progress suggest that, in fact, the periphery of the generic global metropolis is inspired by the suburban code of Southern California sprawl.

The wall, then, is portable and replicable. Local conflicts between density and sprawl, between formal and informal urbanizations, between wealth and poverty, mirror exclusionary urbanization across the world. Our border wall dynamics are replicated in cities and regions everywhere, as municipal, state and federal agencies compartmentalize territory through rigid jurisdictional boundaries that disrupt a fluid continuum of interdependences. What emerges is a global urban asymmetry, dividing enclaves of wealth and rings of poverty that surround and service them. In San Diego–Tijuana, discriminatory urban policies enable mega-scale architectural complexes, permitting special economic zones and gated communities to barricade themselves against the complexity and ambiguity of precarious zones and those who inhabit them—people who, through their labor, service the very neoliberal economy that excludes them.

Zones of Conflict:

Sites of Urban and Political Creativity

Only the most myopic politics will conclude that building walls across continents can solve our problems. Instead of wishing the "other" away with guns and fences, we should engage and cooperate with those most impacted by our policies, with whom we can imagine interdependent futures. A sense of mutual recognition and responsibility should guide US-Mexico relations and conversations, recognizing that the challenges of Mexico and Central America, are the challenges of the US too. Moreover, the border wall that divides the US from Mexico, while far from the daily lives of most Americans, is invisibly reproduced in neighborhoods across the US, from Ferguson to Chicago, where public divestment, marginalization, racism and inequality divide communities and institutions and enflame urban violence.

A capacity to think critically and politically in a world of flux and injustice was the touchstone of the historic avant-garde. Today, thinking critically and politically as an architect and urbanist means taking a position about where and when not to build, as much as where and when to build, for whom and why. These questions can shape a *critical spatial practice* to realign the ethical and the aesthetic in the architectural field. We are not interested in designing a more efficient or beautiful border wall; we do not want to participate in the spatialization of injustice. For us, shifting geopolitical boundaries, neoliberal patterns of development, explosive urban inequality, diversifying social and cultural demographics, the migration of labor and the redeployment of manufacturing centers across hemispheres have provoked us to reconsider our practice.

Over the last decades, we have been rethinking of the role of architecture within geographies of conflict, developing new conceptual frameworks as well as new procedures of engagement. Shifting one's gaze from privileged sites of development to peripheral zones of conflict demands a new praxis.

Countering racist political narratives that criminalize our region and its inhabitants, we mobilize different stories, counternarratives that are "grounded" in the voices of those who live here. In this sense, our work is deeply ethnographic and committed to practices of always listening.[3] Through this work over many years, we have encountered astonishing urban and political creativity across the border region, ingenious bottom-up strategies of coexistence and cooperation that regularly transgress the fixity of boundaries. As we see it, the most compelling examples of urbanization today arise not from within sites of stability and economic power but from within sites of crisis like ours, where the conflicts between top-down and bottom-up urban agendas are most profound.

For us, conflict is a creative tool. Exposing the drivers of urban inequality and challenging exclusionary policies is the first act in producing a more experimental architecture. Taking urban conflict as one's point of departure, as an operational tool, requires expanded modes of practice. We believe that architects can negotiate today's urban conflicts, can become interlocutors of institutional memory, can reimagine urban sociability and encounter, and can design new programmatic, formal and aesthetic categories that problematize relations between the natural, the social and the spatial. In other words, architects can engage critically the conditions that have produced our urban crises. We don't have to surrender professionally to the neutral and largely decorative enterprise of urban design and planning today, which typically bolsters and camouflages the greedy politics of urban development.

In our practice, architecture is not only or primarily about spatial-material intervention, but about constructing methods for visualizing the urban collisions between top-down policies of exclusionary urbanization and bottom-up social and ecological practices, and designing civic processes for creative mediation and intervention.[4] We believe that urban conflict can catalyze design. The San Diego–Tijuana border is the conflict zone where we work. Our practice is "embedded" here, but we are also committed to visualizing flows, correspondences and interdependencies between local, regional and global dynamics. Over time, we have curated a series of cross-border dialogues and nomadic public performances on both sides of the border wall to raise awareness of what's shared and what's at stake in refusing to collaborate. Ultimately, these dialogical community processes have been a point of entry for our practice, helping to rearticulate ideas of citizenship beyond the nation-state and seek new strategies of urban interdependence and regional collective action.

Our projects always begin with a *conflict diagram*, a research-based process that exposes, names and visualizes the contested political, social and economic dynamics that define a particular urban crisis, as a prerequisite for urban and architectural intervention. For us, this is a double project of critical research and action. It begins with engaging conflict dialectically and exposing hidden institutional histories in order to assemble a more accurate, anticipatory urban research and design intervention. This requires taking "detours" to engage diverse urban domains—social justice, ethics, law, economics, environment and politics—that have until now remained largely peripheral to design.

In other words, visualizing urban conflict becomes a method for generating propositions that are rooted in the controversies, contingencies and opportunities of a given site, an anticipatory framework that sets up the terms for intervention. In this sense, research-based processes help to expose complex vectors of power in any condition, but they become projective and operative, constructing a scaffold upon which "things can happen."

Visualizing the political does not stop at naming or "measuring" the conditions. At some point, critique must move toward proposition and action to avoid "analysis paralysis"—with the identification of strategies to uproot and challenge urban inequality, including cultural strategies to render the complexity of urban conflict more accessible to diverse publics. In our practice, we design programmatic frameworks to reorganize institutional protocols, knowledges and resources, as well as images, diagrams, storyboards and cartographies that can communicate urban complexity and increase community capacities for political action.

Risking professional suicide as architects, we maintain that building more equitable and democratic cities today is not about better buildings or even better infrastructure, but about fundamentally reorganizing the intersections of society, ecology, economy, politics and space. A critical understanding of urban conflict becomes the material for architects in our time, the most important tool we have for reimagining the city today.

Conflict Urbanizations

INFORMALITY IS PRAXIS

While the "global city" has been organized through top-down urban logics of consumption, leisure and display, the neighborhoods at the periphery that fuel these zones of economic power with cheap labor are sites of bottom-up economic productivity and urban resilience. At the periphery, alternative economies thrive; informal social, environmental and spatial configurations emerge to tackle conditions of scarcity. Emergent urban practices are redefining existing norms of ownership in the city today and shaping a new political economy of urban growth that is typically off the radar of those who define the formal categories of urban development. In our research, we are committed to engaging, understanding and translating these stealth urban practices of resilience and adaptation to challenge the formal protocols of urban development today.

What first brought us together, from the diverse vantages of political theory and architecture, was our shared interest in *informality*. We were both inspired by the bottom-up resilience and ingenuity of people who inhabit the periphery of cities in conditions of scarcity—how they assemble housing and infrastructure, markets of exchange, governance practices, and general strategies of collective survival and solidarity. We were both drawn to the emergent and the unplanned, inspired by unexpected genius and the endogenous springs of bottom-up collective action. We were both also critical of an obsession in architecture and urbanism with form and aesthetics for aesthetics' sake, and a neglect of the social, economic and political vectors that constitute urban space. The informal refers to the performative agency of people in conditions of emergency constructing their own spaces and economic relations in the absence of formal support, and constituting a set of bottom-up strategies that counter and transgress imposed political boundaries and top-down economic models. Ours has been a double task: while we visualize evidence that the informal emerges from urban injustice, we also partner with agencies that are mobilizing these energies as bottom-up power to spatialize social justice.

Revisiting the Formal-Informal Question:

From Binary to Dialectic

By formal urbanization, we mean the model of institutional planning that gives shape to the city from a macro perspective. Formal planning can be generated through government-led public agendas that organize the city through a deliberate civic armature (historically articulated by public space and infrastructure) that is subsequently infilled with private interventions; or, as is the case in recent years, in the absence of committed public leadership, through the dominance of private development interests. This second pathway frequently results in a highly deficient and exclusionary public realm.

By informal urbanization, we mean the social, economic and spatial conditions that evolve endogenously, organically from the bottom-up. Informal, everyday urban dynamics can be understood as extra-official since they are often invisible to formal institutions of planning. These stealth urbanizations often evolve as micro-strategies of survival to address the urgent needs of displaced or marginalized populations. Sometimes they manifest as bottom-up acts of collective defiance and resistance to the privatization and gentrification of our cities. Survival urbanization has intensified in recent years with the explosive growth of cities across the planet and the rapid urbanization of the world's populations produced by political instability, climate change, food scarcity and the neoliberalization of the world's economy.

Some scholars and practitioners have been uncomfortable drawing a distinction between formal and informal urban dynamics. The *informal* itself, as a concept, is problematic to those who suggest that formal and informal are not mutually exclusive, and that polarizing them undermines a more emancipatory consensus agenda for the city. While we accept their hybridity in practice, we believe the conceptual binary helps to convey power structures, disparities and counter-reactions in the neoliberal city. Formal and informal urbanization frequently clash, and this conflict physically manifests in the city as urban inequality. As long as social and urban inequality exists, the excluded will always devise scrappy, experimental strategies of resilience and adaptation that challenge unjust policies and agendas, and some will resist more overtly. We think it is time to reformulate the politics of difference as a tool to penetrate the drivers of inequality. Here, the dialectic between formal and informal systems becomes a device to visualize conflict, and to conceptualize new strategies that can mediate interfaces between top-down and bottom-up forces.

Designing a more socially and economically inclusive political economy of urban development requires the knowledges and resources of both domains. For example, we envision top-down institutions of development becoming more literate about informal urban conditions, designing more agile management systems to facilitate emergent dynamics in the contemporary city, negotiating large and small scales, public, private and collective gradations, and incremental adaptive growth. The eruption of informal urbanization today requires that planners recalibrate the totalizing abstraction of certain one-size-fits-all urban recipes. The shifting boundaries between top-down and bottom-up, formal and informal, private and public interests can demarcate a contested field from which to produce new urban and architectural paradigms.

Informal Lessons for the Formal City

Tensions between the top-down and the bottom-up take different shapes in the city. Historically, sites of wealth and power exist in relative proximity to sites of precariousness and marginalization. In recent decades, as urban asymmetry has intensified, slums, gated luxury condominium towers and special economic zones have come into closer adjacencies with each other. For example, La Limonada, the oldest metropolitan slum in Guatemala, is just minutes from the wealthy *zonas* 10 and 14; just as Villa 31, Buenos Aires's most noted slum, is adjacent to Puerto Madero, the newest luxury mega-development in the city. Uneven development often takes a syncretic shape, with the informal encroaching into formal urban systems, adapting the homogeneity of autonomous, closed-ended spatial frameworks into heterogeneous programmatic assemblages, where diverse uses coexist in unpredictable ways. Famously, this has been the destiny of many iconic urban and architectural projects in the Global South, such as Brasília and Chandigarh, whose formal organizational logics have been transformed on the ground through informal social and economic adaptations across time. Low-income neighborhoods in global capitals everywhere experience this same sort of alteration, reconfigured from the bottom-up by the hands of immigrants from Africa, Asia and Latin America, often fueled by remittances from abroad.

These bottom-up strategies of "encroachment" beyond the property line, and their informal economic circulations and spatial adaptations, can be reinterpreted as welcome strategies for tackling social-economic inequality and climate change today, a way to challenge closed-ended urban methods of top-down urban planning and demand new forms of accountability in our institutions. We believe there is much to learn from informal patterns of adaptation: about socializing infrastructure to anticipate inclusion, about social-ecological transformation and about the temporalization of space. Informal urban processes demonstrate the possibilities of reactivating productivity and social proximity in the city today. Architecture, as a material system, has long been an instrument of spatial colonization in conflict with ecological dynamics, freezing time and the destiny of the city into a fixed object at odds with the temporal social and economic contingencies of real life. Informal urban dynamics have hidden social and economic value that should be first recognized and then fully activated in strategies for more inclusive urban development. The informal is more than a romantic anecdote or *bricolage*. It is the physical evidence of urban creativity and intelligence that should be translated into a fresh urban language that challenges our clichés and public policies. What is infrastructure, housing, zoning? These formal categories are reinvented through human urgency in the informal sectors of the city.

In fact, we believe the most relevant urban practices and projects promoting social and economic inclusion today are emerging not from sites of economic power but from sites of scarcity and zones of conflict, where citizens themselves, pressed by socioeconomic injustice and necessity, are pushed to imagine alternative possibilities. It is from the sense of urgency that a new urban agenda is emerging, in which design and architecture are encroaching into the fragmented and discriminatory policies and economics responsible for producing inequality and marginalization. Again, we believe that a fundamental reorganization of social and economic relations—and not buildings—is the key to a more democratic and equitable city.

But informal urban practices are typically disregarded by planners, marginalized as something to avoid, to protect oneself from, to zone out of sight, to whitewash or clear, certainly nothing one would want to embrace or emulate or learn from. Through our work we challenge these biases, advancing informal neighborhoods not as sites of blight but of local productivity with important lessons for the "formal city." While we condemn the economic forces that marginalize people in slums, we believe that the most compelling practices of inclusive urbanization are emerging from within these peripheral sites of scarcity. Today, we must rethink the future of the city from the periphery, where alternative processes of urban growth are being shaped stealthily from the bottom-up. These nonconforming urban processes should not be marginalized from our "idea" of the city. The self-built logics, the ingenious practices of structural and spatial retrofit, adaptation and resiliency, the vibrancy of informal market dynamics, the solidarity of communities confronting scarcity and engendering new forms of collaborative local governance demonstrate other ways of constructing the city and challenge the hegemonic neoliberal paradigm of urban development today.

While our design methods are inspired by informal urbanization, the interface between the top-down and the bottom-up is our main site of intervention. Top-down urban planning is necessary to anticipate territorial organizational logics, the scaling up of sustainable urban-ecological interactions and the efficient management and distribution of resources. But macro planning must not underestimate the micro patterns of community development. The central questions here are: How do we mediate the planned and the unplanned? Can macro planning absorb the procedural intelligence of informal urbanization and its capacity to anticipate and negotiate the interface between spaces, resources, boundaries and the programmatic contingency of social density?

We are interested in translating the operative procedures of informal urbanization into new methods of urban intervention, curating a transfer of knowledge from the bottom-up to top-down institutions and policymakers. This means designing new systems of political representation that visualize the potential of these emergent and invisible urban practices from below and mobilizing this evidence to demand more inclusive urban public policy and to protect those who urgently need protection. Top-down public investment should support the spatial ingenuity of the bottom-up, reinterpreting informal urbanization as a mechanism for a more just and productive city. Urban zoning should not penalize alternative densities and transitional uses. It should be reconceived as a generative force to anticipate local economy and activity, and respond to emergent social and economic necessities. Housing affordability should be reimagined through the hidden value of community sweat equity and participation; urban infrastructure should be rearticulated as a hybrid, flexible and resilient framework for social integration. Just as global warming is forcing us to reimagine the city as a more porous and resilient urban ecology, accelerating global migration today should provoke us to reimagine urban infrastructure as a mechanism for inclusion and integration. In other words, urban infrastructure must be understood as more than freeways, bridges or other singular-use urban systems. Infrastructure must be able to absorb the migratory effects of climate change, poverty and political instability.

The Informal as Praxis

Engaging informal processes projectively, with an equitable public vision, suggests an expanded role for architecture in constructing the city today. We have been critical of the autonomous, self-referential language of the architectural field, articulating the city formally as a collection of discrete objects existing above a neutral speculative platform shaped by the forces of the market. Instead, we see the potential of architecture as a relational system that navigates complex historical, environmental, cultural, social, economic and political forces in the city, generating a more complex framework for urbanization itself. We investigate the spatial consequences of informal social and economic systems, whose design logics are not resolved *a priori*, but evolve incrementally, negotiating multiple and often contested metropolitan variables in real time. In informal settlements, buildings perform as anticipatory scaffolds. A house might begin with a pad and a frame. As resources emerge, so follow spaces; a second floor might evolve, threaded into the first. Habitation leads, spaces follow, nothing is wasted, everything is useful. This is why the exterior assemblage of informal houses resembles the interiors, as the aesthetic of the house is not determined by the resolution of an architectural object but reflects the memory of its own evolution.

Although many in the design and art worlds have recognized great aesthetic beauty in the ingenious *bricolage* of informal urbanization, we have focused on these environments not for what they look like, but for the ways in which they perform. They reveal a set of urban procedures, a political economy of urban cohabitation that holds clues for designing more equitable urban policy.

An important research agenda for us has been to produce new conceptions and interpretations of the informal. For us, the "informal" is not an aesthetic category or style but a praxis, referring to the social, political, economic and spatial processes that emerge extra-officially from the bottom-up. Instead of a fixed image, we see the informal as a set of urban operations that transgress imposed political boundaries and top-down economic models. In the context of thinking beyond "style," recall Christopher Alexander's theories of "pattern language" in the 1960s, and how they were hijacked by the field of architecture and reduced to a stylistic sense of regionalism and a folkloric idea of the vernacular.[5] A more critical reading of Alexander would recognize that language is less a fixed category than a performative system capable of reorganizing the political economy of building. Likewise, we are interested in translating the actual functions of informal practices into new strategies of urban intervention to challenge existing formal protocols of economic development.

Through this lens, we see the informal not as a thing but as a set of practices which detonates traditional notions of site specificity and context into a more complex system of hidden socioeconomic exchanges. We see the informal as the urban unwanted, that which is left over after the pristine presence of architecture with capital "A" has been usurped and transformed into tenuous scaffolds for social encounter. Because of our work in peripheral neighborhoods at the US-Mexico border, we also see the informal as a site from which to shape new interpretations of community and citizenship within divided territories.

In the border cities of Tijuana and San Diego, a context of rigid surveillance and exclusion, neighborhoods on both sides of the border wall have negotiated scarcity and public alienation by constructing alternative urbanisms of resilience and adaptation from the bottom-up. Informal settlements in Tijuana, for example, build themselves by repurposing urban waste from San Diego, transforming incrementally through time from emergency dwellings to permanent homes. As immigrants travel north in search of new opportunities, they bring into San Diego their own practices of urban retrofit and adaptation. An informal business operates from a garage or shed; a nonconforming granny flat is built in the backyard to support an extended family or a small business. These informal economies and patterns of density have fundamentally altered the urban fabric of many older, low-income American neighborhoods—the places where immigrants land.

These bidirectional transborder dynamics constitute an urban political economy of adaptation, retrofit and reuse; they suggest new ways of conceptualizing urbanization across this divided territory and challenge established top-down conceptions of belonging. In other words, these informal cross-border urban flows have also provoked us to reimagine the idea of citizenship as a creative urban practice, rooted in the bottom-up agency of the marginalized. Citizenship should mirror the formal and informal relations among people in everyday life. Belonging is an intensely practical matter, localized through the alteration and negotiation of boundaries, informal participatory governance, and the mobilization of informal economies and community development strategies.

We believe these bottom-up practices and interdependencies are the building blocks for a new kind of regional citizenship that has great significance for planetary urbanization as well. We see citizenship not as an identity designed and legitimated from above (the conventional way of thinking about citizenship), but rather as a set of performative urban actions from below that often connect people across the border through practices of flow and exchange. This bottom-up action can take the shape of emergent, everyday lived practices among marginalized communities, or more deliberate strategies of urban intervention designed to counter or resist exclusionary political and economic power.

A community is always in dialogue with its immediate social and ecological environment; this is what defines its political nature. But when this relationship is disrupted and its productive capacity splintered by the way jurisdictional power is imposed, it is necessary to find a means of recuperating its agency. This agency and activism often manifest in informal urbanization, which we see not only as an image of institutional alienation, poverty and exploitation but also as a set of everyday practices in marginalized communities, powerful evidence of bottom-up political and urban agency.

Informal urbanization is typically invisible to formal institutions, and it needs translation and political representation. In other words, informal urban practices need resources and mediating agencies that can represent their intelligence and demand accountability and support from top-down institutions. We do not celebrate informality to let formal institutions off the hook. While the creativity and emergent entrepreneurship in informal communities is compelling, truly awesome sometimes, we resist unwittingly conveying to governments that they are capable of sustaining themselves without public support and that institutions can therefore ethically unplug. Similarly, we have resisted gestures that give property titles to slum dwellers to "include" them in the official economy without protection mechanisms that guarantee social and environmental justice. Formalizing slums risks transforming these environments into laboratories of neoliberal economic tinkering and speculation, incentivizing the improvement and sale of parcels as commodities, without any assurances against exploitation by profit logics that neglect local communities and their social and economic well-being.

Our creative fields are well positioned to expand design into new urban strategies—translational, pedagogical and curatorial—to engage the informal and transform the political. Beyond architectural form, architects can be designers of political and civic processes to frame a more inclusive urbanization.

CO-PRODUCING THE CITY WITH OTHERS

Neoliberal "Urban Molotovs"

The metropolitan explosion of global cities across the world in the last decades was driven by a neoliberal political economy that prioritized deregulation, privatization, disinvestment and austerity. This unprecedented urban growth concentrated wealth in privileged urban centers and coincided with an equally unprecedented explosion of slums at the edges. This asymmetry lies at the heart of today's urban crises, a pattern that is consistent everywhere.

The combination of market-driven speculative urbanization and the erosion of the social safety net has exacerbated inequality in cities across the world. It is the same story everywhere: an "urban Molotov cocktail" comprised of unaffordable housing, stagnant wages, rising living costs and shrinking public support systems, forcing the displacement of many residents in urban communities. These disparities seem to be standardized, by-design. In the US, for instance, in the last decades, economic and land-use policies were connected to particular instruments of financialization and transformed many downtowns and other special economic zones into bubbles of wealth, enabling them to concentrate economic and political power through urban redevelopment corporations. For decades, tax-increment law enabled downtown San Diego, for example, to retain tax-revenue-generated urban development, effectively disenfranchising the diverse urban neighborhoods surrounding it, a border which is often demarcated physically with massive freeways—de facto infrastructures of segregation.

Even though the "return to downtown" was a welcome agenda in the early eighties after the postwar urban flight to the suburbs, its redevelopment strategies into the mid-2000s ended up accelerating gentrification at a massive scale. Accompanied by luxury condominium towers and hotels, sports stadia, convention centers and the ubiquitous corporate commercial franchises catering to tourism, these exclusionary economic development recipes foreclosed possibilities for residents of older communities, small businesses, alternative cultural agencies and young populations to remain downtown, as they had for decades when it was affordable to live there.

Ten years after the economic crisis of 2008, these asymmetric patterns of urban development had become the norm. Developer-driven revitalization is accelerating gentrification across US cities, bleeding into the edges of poor neighborhoods immediately adjacent to wealthy downtowns. Today, mega redevelopment projects are a formidable bubble of land speculation that inflate skyrocketing real-estate markets. Many of us thought this had finally imploded and would give way to new checks and balances and institutional reform across urban development industries. But recent federal economic policies like "opportunity zones" in both Democratic and Republican administrations cement the triumph of the private over the public, and exacerbate inequality and gentrification. "Opportunity zones" are effectively metropolitan tax havens for private developers, camouflaged as socially concerned, equitable urban development.

The Triumph of the Private

Today more than ever, the private developer is the chief protagonist in the development of the city, where free-market speculation and deregulation produce algorithms for building that undermine community benefit. This is the result of a weakened top-down public and the loss of a public urban framework within which buildings, even understood as commodities, could perform in more democratic and civic ways. Moreover, as cities compete to seduce the corporate headquarters of multinational corporations and their franchises to compensate for diminishing tax revenues, the public now *sponsors* the private, as many privatized urban behemoths siphon public subsidies to enable their development proformas.

    The emblematic case, as the second decade of the twenty-first century comes to an end, is Hudson Yards in New York City. This neoliberal urban stew is made of the same ingredients: tax-break-sponsored privatization, suburban theming and urban gating comprising millions of square feet of luxury housing, corporate office space and exclusive retail programs installed on an anti-street. A $1.5bn *tabula rasa* hovers above the ruins of public transportation infrastructure. This mega project physicalizes the concentration of economic and political power in urban development at the expense of a more distributive political economy that might lift all neighborhoods in the city. As *New York Times* architecture critic Michael Kimmelman described Hudson Yards: "at heart, [it] is a supersized suburban-style office park, with a shopping mall and a quasi-gated condo community targeted at the 0.1 percent."[6] The creation of this exclusive luxury palace at the expense of collective resources follows the same logics as the urban development processes we've witnessed in London, Istanbul, Buenos Aires and elsewhere over the last decades, where large swaths of public land were given to private developers in the name of economic growth.

Camouflaging Privatization with "Style" and "Innovation"

Beyond free-market fakes, we lack alternative approaches to a public urban reality.[7] Even seemingly innovative agendas such as "New Urbanism" and the "Creative Class" have become instruments for municipally endorsed privatization that exacerbates inequality. Dressing suburbia with facades of cityhood while suburbanizing center-city neighborhoods,

New Urbanist recipes typically prioritize historicist and form-based codes over social inclusion. In other words, New Urbanism has generally reduced the housing crisis to a question of "style" without addressing the foundational crisis: lack of affordability, community participation and public ownership. And while its more human-centric planning approaches were a welcome agenda for municipalities to retrofit the big-box, asphalt-covered suburbanization of the sprawling city of the 1980s and 1990s through notions of smart growth, walkability and livability, these urban mechanisms too often became rhetorical packages of urban "amenities" that camouflaged privatization.

Equally, the Creative Class agenda capitalizes on the aesthetics of a cosmopolitan hipster culture of arts, food and loft living, in which artists and cultural producers become reluctant brokers of gentrification. What the Creative Class agenda does not seem to advocate is affordable rents or mechanisms to incentivize bottom-up local economy as prerequisite to cultural development. As Ernest Hemingway reminds us in the opening pages of *A Movable Feast*, Paris became a magnet for writers and artists in the 1920s not because of its celebrated cosmopolitan aura and "bohemian atmosphere," but because of its affordable rents.

With their veneers of beautification and innovation, and often the commodification of the very cultures that have been priced out of the neighborhood, both of these neoliberal urban trends have accelerated gentrification and have done little to advance social or economic justice in the city. Adopted by many municipalities across the US, they do not rethink affordability or existing models of property ownership. They overlook entirely the value of social participation and the role communities might play in co-producing housing and redefining ownership in more inclusive, collective ways.

Adding to this portfolio of questionable progressive urban renewal agendas, even historic preservation has become a tool to camouflage private agendas as public benefit, resulting in the adaptive reuse of older urban fabrics as theme parks and exclusive economic zones, preventing local communities from benefitting from these improvements. As Michael Henry Adams laments regarding the gentrification of Harlem: "every new building, every historic renovation, every boutique clothing shop—indeed, every tree and every flower in every park improvement—is not a life-enhancing benefit, but a harbinger of a local community's own displacement."[8]

While often well-intentioned in their aspirations for restructuring a more egalitarian, middle-class urbanization, both New Urbanism and the Creative Class agenda fail to challenge the hegemony of neoliberal development, but instead camouflage it beneath a consumerist veneer of innovation and multicultural inclusion. Remaining neutral in their position on urban inequality,[9] they surrendered the kind of political advocacy necessary for social and economic justice—likely because they hoped the market would take care of "those things."

Exclusionary Lending and Zoning by Design

Gentrification is ultimately the result of deliberate economic and urban policies through which zoning and lending align to aggravate exclusion. While zoning should be an important framework for regulating unchecked, irresponsible urban speculation and guaranteeing social and environmental welfare, it has historically been the opposite: a design tool for segregating urban development, categorizing and dividing the metropolitan field and splintering everyday life. There is ample evidence that exclusionary land uses and real-estate economic modeling segregate by income and race, resulting in long-term urban and social decay. The urban ruins of redlining, for example, the radical institutional mapping process that targeted and racially profiled urban areas for disinvestment, are spatial evidence of these processes, and the foundation of current racist economic zoning policies that deliberately block denser, affordable multifamily housing across the city. This is especially important as climate change demands new models of inclusive densification to challenge irresponsible sprawl. In sum, when lending and zoning align to segregate by design, they become the most powerful drivers of structural inequality and exclusion.

Downtowns across the United States have remained bubbles of wealth, while the older neighborhoods that surround them have remained sites of disinvestment. These marginalized, low-income areas of the city become sanctuary spaces where immigrants settle. The cook, the janitor, the maid, the busboy, the nanny and the gardener live here. In other words, it is within these communities at the edges of the older metro areas that a ready-made blue-collar workforce awaits to service the luxury hotels and condominium towers of downtown and the McMansions of the new suburbs. These mid-city neighborhoods are service-sector communities supporting commodified lifestyles in adjacent zones of wealth.

What rents and housing markets will be available to this laboring class? What kind of affordability do these communities require to accommodate their low wages? What kinds of mixed uses will increase their capacity for entrepreneurship? There are currently not too many options. According to the 2019 housing census, San Diego has the second least affordable housing market in the US, with only eleven percent of households capable of affording the median-price home of $600,000.[10]

The marriage of immigrant labor and neoliberal urbanization has in many ways defined the histories of urban growth in cities across the world, reinforcing the proximity of precarity and wealth and exacerbating the crisis of housing affordability. The suburbs of Paris, for example, on the other side of the Périphérique—the border-like ring road that envelopes historic Paris—are dotted with old immigrant communities who have historically been ghettoized in social housing slabs to service gentrified Paris. Arab Emirate cities like Dubai and Abu Dhabi have built migrant labor housing camps to facilitate the construction of their dream castles in the desert, and many California cities and economies continue to depend on the cheap labor of Mexican migrants who have historically worked the agricultural fields of Imperial Valley and Central California, and supplied the majority of service-sector labor in San Francisco, Los Angeles and San Diego, where housing is scarce and expensive.

Affordable housing financialization has systematically prevented community-based agencies from taking a more meaningful role in co-producing housing. Currently, an affordable housing developer can qualify for tax credits only by partnering with a local nonprofit organization to ensure levels of engagement with the low-income community the project will serve and provide social programming for the residents who will live in it. While this requirement has its merits, ensuring at least the involvement of local agencies to facilitate community involvement, it reduces the role of these nonprofits to service providers with a minimal percentage of revenue in the development partnership, while the developers receive millions of dollars in tax credits to make their bottom-lines pencil out.

Besides the ownership disparity that characterizes this process of tax-credit allocation, these protocols do nothing to ensure that local communities truly profit from these interventions. The partnership between community and developer needs to be recalibrated to ensure a more meaningful role for community-based agencies as co-developers of housing. And the very definition of "community benefits" needs to be reconceived. Criteria for qualifying for tax-credit-based financing should include actual benefits, actual impacts on the social and economic fabric of the community. Currently, the criteria lack imagination, failing to demand evidence about how the so-called "benefits" will actually increase community capacities for social and economic sustainability: how they will increase access, civic participation and collaboration with local agencies. Community benefit should include fewer generic categories of mixed-commercial uses, oriented not only to consumption and burger-flipping, but also to generative community-serving uses organized around education, vocational training, entrepreneurship and local productivity.

Challenging the Regime of Bigness

The ongoing collision between top-down policies for urban development and bottom-up living conditions in low-income communities demands new, more equitable regulatory and economic policy strategies. Among the many negative impacts resulting from the alliance between punitive zoning and financialization is the erosion of policies that benefit small-scale mid-city development. In other words, affordable housing development policy does not support programmatically diverse, incremental development in small parcels in marginalized neighborhoods.

While larger projects are essential in metropolitan areas that require more density in downtown zones and transportation corridors, the institutions of development have not endorsed adequate financial and zoning incentives to facilitate the transitional small-scale development needed to assist many low-income mid-city neighborhoods at the peripheries of downtown. Consequently, only large private developers with enough equity and savvy to qualify for highly scrutinized lending become protagonists of urban development, yielding homogenized building envelopes and unit-counts that clash with the idiosyncratic patterns of everyday life and informal economies within culturally diverse inner-city communities. The mono-use and mono-economy of urban development ultimately deactivate an entire demographic of potential small actors in neighborhood redevelopment, such as residents who own their own parcels, community-based agencies, artists' collectives, architects, etc.

This was not always the case in the US. Mid-twentieth-century subsidy, lending and zoning mechanisms in cities across the US aligned in support of small-scale private development, in addition to large investments in public housing. This resulted in a proliferation of small-scale development in older neighborhoods adjacent to downtown, giving shape to new typologies, such as duplexes, triplexes, fourplexes, and even six-packs (dingbats), made popular in Los Angeles. This meant that small-scale actors in communities, facilitated by accessory-unit legislature, granny flats and other incremental density zoning incentives could qualify for an owner-occupied loan to develop two units on a parcel, where the owner could live in one and rent the one in the back to support a small mortgage. This small-scale, infill housing policy needs to be recuperated to support affordable housing in low-income neighborhoods today, to reenergize their economies and enable many other actors in communities to participate in the production of affordable housing.

Instead, we celebrate the gig economy today as the innovator of bottom-up entrepreneurship, forgetting that not so long ago it was progressive housing policy that curated gradations of scale and redistributed surplus value across the city through intelligent and inclusive zoning and lending. While airbnb has enabled people in neighborhoods to increase their financial capacity by renting their homes or small accessory units to customers (often at the expense of depopulating downtowns and neighborhoods of permanent residents), we cannot perpetuate the myth that only for-profit companies operating within market-driven dynamics can broker affordability, leaving urban public policy out of the equation, and with it, the ethical guarantees and protections against gentrification and labor injustice. Instead, new affordable housing policy and economy should be recalibrated to revive appropriate incentives for neighborhood-scale development, enabling local actors to partner in the production of housing stock and elevating community-based organizations, and not corporations, to manage their own modes of production and profit for more equitable neighborhood development.

Democratizing the Tools for Urban Development

Even the most enlightened developers cannot digress from the "available" development tools of the market. Notably, the feasibility studies that define what economic return means for their proformas are based on generic criteria that treat users as customers. Similarly, the demographic studies often fail to integrate the granular, everyday urgencies or capabilities of the communities these projects will serve. But the micro-urbanizations that are emerging within low-income and immigrant sectors of the city in the form of nonconforming spatial and entrepreneurial practices are forwarding a different idea of land use, density and economy. We have argued that a new economic proforma of development can be extrapolated from these stealth urban patterns. In conditions of social and economic emergency, peripheral communities and neighborhoods everywhere in the world are producing new social, cultural and environmental configurations, catalyzing a more inclusive political economy of housing and infrastructure.

This has convinced us that the future of the city will not be led by buildings alone, but will be defined by the urgent reorganization of socioeconomic relations. This also confirms that architects can have a significant role in designing alternative institutional protocols from which new architectures of social justice can spring up. In other words, this period of crisis represents an opportunity to rethink urban and economic policy to democratize community development. And this cannot happen without altering the exclusionary institutional financial protocols that have been monopolized by a few sets of urban actors and eliminating the siloing of knowledges and resources needed to produce the city. Confronting the drivers of social and economic inequality, recuperating the city and the neighborhood as sites of productivity and engines of local economy and job generation, requires that the top-down institutions of urban development make financing tools more accessible. A wider cast of bottom-up actors must participate in the co-production of the city, realigning zoning and lending to benefit communities by promoting small-scale, incremental urbanization.

Migrant Neighborhoods as Urban Laboratories

We question boilerplate urban strategies that organize the city through logics of consumption, commercialization and commodification. Our work aspires to *urbanizations of productivity* and focuses on the neighborhood as the urban laboratory of our time. Democratizing the city at large continues to be the ultimate project, but underserved neighborhoods are our unit of analysis and site of intervention to design a new political economy for inclusive urban development.

The bottom-up urban practices of resilience and adaptation in low-income and immigrant neighborhoods provide compelling challenges to discriminatory zoning and exclusionary economic development. Through the informal and entrepreneurial practices of alteration and retrofit, communities compensate for the lack of institutional support, appropriate infrastructural and spatial frameworks to support their idiosyncratic programs of use, and ultimately enact their right to the city. Small parcels are developed in nonconforming ways but with robust urban common sense to accommodate livable added densities and mixed uses. Small lots in mid-city metropolitan neighborhoods incrementally transform into micro social-economic infrastructures. What was once a single parcel with a single-family unit becomes a set of shared spaces to support extended families and micro-units that contain a variety of social and economic programs of use.

The value (cultural, social and economic) of this urban activism continues to be hidden from conventional, top-down planning institutions, and continues to lack formal support to increase these community capabilities. It takes grassroots organizations working within these emergent urban contexts to distribute support systems, while stitching together solidaristic practices at the scale of parcels into new forms of political representation. In other words, community-based agencies often organize and bundle the invisible social and economic entrepreneurship of the community and translate it into new policy proposals that represent the needs and urban imagination of the community, essentially lobbying for the transformation of discriminatory zoning and regulation. We believe these conditions can inspire an entirely different role for art, architectural and urban activist practices, moving beyond "style" and the metaphorical representation of spaces and people—in which only the community's symbolic image is rallied—to more operative social-economic models of urban and economic development, inclusive land-use categories and alternative financial proformas to support them.

To address the housing crises today, we must recalibrate the interface between housing policy and housing economy in relation to these stealth urban densities, informal markets and social contexts. In other words, more flexible regulatory frameworks are needed to pierce the homogeneity of totalizing zoning envelopes, catalyzing diversity and plurality. This means advocating for intelligent zoning to support bottom-up urban intelligence, promoting diverse scales and types of housing that cater to diverse economies and demographics, and intensifying incremental densities and mixed uses to sustain real life in urban neighborhoods. While this recalibration of urban policy and economy might not be appropriate for the city at large (we are aware that the mere mention of social density terrifies exclusive demographics and sectors of the city) we maintain that immigrant neighborhoods are already being transformed from the bottom-up by these informal urban processes, so why not elevate them to test new approaches to equitable urbanization?

This requires expanding the horizon of community participation in the field of urban development by summoning diverse actors and coalitions to co-develop housing. For us, this has meant partnering with local community-based agencies to experiment with new design processes of visualizing the invisible, representing local modes of productivity, bundling everyday social and economic practices into new evidentiary material for challenging exclusionary public policy—all while demanding new housing and infrastructural paradigms at the scale of the neighborhood with enough resolution to "trickle up" and transform urban policy. Having broader impact on the city will require new deliberative processes to promote shared urban interventions, negotiation and collaboration across agencies, institutions and jurisdictions, and incentives to summon diverse and heterogeneous proformas of economic development.

Summoning "Other" Developers

We realize that seeing marginalized neighborhoods as sites of economic productivity and development might make some activists nervous, leading them to detect in this formulation a complicity with privatization and disinvestment. The language of entrepreneurship, resilience and sustainability also resonates with neoliberal urban rhetoric. Part of the provocation here is to retake these concepts and reimagine them through more robust community-based strategies led by activists and communities themselves. What we propose here is to mobilize alternative economic proformas of development whose profits benefit the community and not private developers. We need to summon grassroots organizations, other actors, as developers of their own housing and neighborhood infrastructure.

We can all be developers. We believe that the developer's spreadsheet, the proforma, is a ripe site for intervention in our time. The proforma is the financial scaffold that gives form to most, if not all, buildings in the city. While it is the prelude to construction, it is architecture's economic envelope, giving form to any structure. The proforma is *architecture's financial plastic*, a site of design experimentation and intervention with potential to redistribute resources, spatialize inclusion and socialize profit.

More controversial: Can the developer's proforma become an instrument for constructing community, elevating the hidden value of informal urbanization, sweat equity, collaboration? We believe that a new political economy of urbanization can be constructed in which the bottom-up has a functional role, not merely a symbolic one. Can a community be a developer of housing, and be integrated into urban processes to co-produce the city? Can new alliances be forged between grassroots organizations and municipalities to co-develop municipal parcels? Can public institutions (universities, hospitals, schools) redirect their purchasing power to communities to promote neighborhood-based productivity and job generation? Can architects and communities collaborate to produce new economic models for small-scale urban development?

Affordable housing experiments in the US should be led by progressive, community-based nonprofit organizations. These agencies engage the everyday social and economic dynamics of mid-city neighborhoods, mediating between their bottom-up histories, identities and practices and the top-down planning policies that shape their neighborhoods. To democratize urbanization, it makes sense that these community organizations be incentivized as alternative developers of affordable housing and a new public realm at the scale of neighborhoods, and ultimately as curators of new paradigms of affordable housing. Their embedded social agendas provide the content to adapt the mathematics of the proforma, while translating neighborhood solidarity, volunteerism and programming into unique organizational and spatial strategies.

We also challenge the instruments of housing financialization themselves. The dominance of tax-credit-based financing as the only economic incentive to produce affordability ends up subordinating community agencies as symbolic partners, mere service providers and not elevating them as meaningful co-developers and co-producers of their own housing. Architects can collaborate to make co-development possible by activating the hidden value of their sweat equity. An architect's fee generally amounts to 10–15% of a project's construction costs, and this *undercapitalized asset* could be mobilized as collateral for development. Architects can become developers of their own projects, or collaborate with community-based investors who might own land or resources, even if not possessing the track record or liquidity needed to advance a development. Cities like San Diego and Berlin have become epicenters of architect-as-developer coalitions that pool resources and sweat equity of diverse actors to develop their own flats, reminding us that nothing should prevent us, as architects, from becoming developers of our own projects. By the same logic, nothing should prevent communities from doing the same.

Architects can lead the transfer of knowledge from the top-down to the bottom-up, translating the developer's economic logics and instrumentalizing them as alternative applications by other civic and community-based actors. Can we smuggle a community's bottom-up assets into the developer's proforma, such as the social programming of local nonprofits as equity for legitimizing new forms of mixed uses? Can architects act as facilitators, translating, representing and integrating the sweat equity of this bottom-up labor into a new model of shared urban development? By mobilizing the operational dimension of this stealth social and economic agency to alter the developer's spreadsheet, we can curate new partners and transform the proforma into a radical engine for community and urban development, ultimately redefining what we mean by an ownership society.

Collectivizing Ownership

The mythology of the American Dream is irrelevant in conditions of poverty. Unprecedented cyclical inequality demands that we rethink existing conditions of ownership. This means redefining affordability by amplifying the value of community participation: more than "owning" units, residents and community-based nonprofit agencies can also co-own and co-manage the economic and social infrastructure around them. Informal markets within communities can seed new models of financing that support unconventional mixed uses.

The absence of inclusive zoning and lending to support small-scale, neighborhood-based development amounts to "disinvestment by design," disempowering community representation in the creation of property and ownership. We need to complicate the meaning of property and diversify ownership models, primarily within zones of poverty, to prioritize housing as a collective right and not only as an individual asset vulnerable to market speculation. How can we design property models that promote racial and ethnic integration, that are inclusive of diverse housing economies—from private to public and collective—and that reinscribe ownership within a structure of social protection? The legislation to support such models exists but remains buried and deactivated because ideas about collective well-being and redistribution have been condemned as a "socialist agenda" and anathema to the American Dream—which is understood as a private dream and not a collective one.

We need to revive cooperative housing, community land trusts and other vestiges of collective housing legislation distributed across local, state and federal policy. We need to update the potential of "united housing federations" to safeguard long-term affordability; we need to rearticulate community land trusts as tools for community-based development in low-income neighborhoods to ensure local stewardship of land, property and services and prevent the social displacement produced by market fluctuation. While many of these examples are still open to examination and critique, they represent generative platforms for new strategies, methods of affordability and new conceptions of property.

Philanthropic foundations are also well positioned to become arbiters of ownership and affordability, acting as facilitators of alternative development processes by investing in the purchase of land with grassroots coalitions to secure its status as collective property. In fact, foundations and communities can co-develop affordable housing projects, together becoming interlocutors of institutional memory and advancing a new role for other civic actors in the co-development process.

Socializing Density and Zoning

Urban justice demands advances in urban policy and economy to assure inclusion, and this requires a new political language to complicate what we mean by density, zoning and property. Well-known clichés such as "equity," "walkability," "affordability" and "livability" are meaningless if they aren't specific about changes in policy and economy that are necessary to enact each of these well-intended aspirations.

In our practice, we have been committed to advancing a new critical language about urban density, and housing density specifically. We challenge the reductive institutional definition of density that measures the city in terms of bulk, or as a number of "units" or "people" per area. Social justice demands instead that we redefine density as an intensity of social exchanges per area. In this sense, density has less to do with buildings as objects than with spaces as stages for local social activity. Conventional planning similarly defines housing as an equation, as a number of "units." Both housing and density need to be reconsidered, not as singularities but as a set of spatial and economic relationships for social integration, deliberately threaded into public space and social infrastructure. In other words, housing and density need to be reimagined beyond units as a set of generative relational dynamics for constructing the city.

Zoning also plays a central role here, but not as a punitive system that prevents socialization, stupidly fragmenting the city into an archipelago of asphalted islands and big boxes. We challenge zoning that performs as a tool for disinvestment, perpetuating an unequal distribution of resources for civic infrastructure, affordable housing and public space, often erecting invisible borders between wealthy / white and low-income / black and brown communities. Zoning must be recalibrated as an intelligent, generative system that anticipates social and economic exchanges at the local scale, a flexible protocol that organizes activity, the interface between embedded and temporal land uses in a community. Zoning must be a site of intervention to advance architectures of social proximity and interdependence, and this requires a new political language that prioritizes and spatializes activity and exchange.

Conclusion: Surplus Value Is Not Evil

Co-producing the city with others is an antidote to urban inequality. And this will require new coalitions for urban development in which the sweat equity of diverse forms of labor can coalesce to produce new pathways for urban and economic development, appropriating the very systems of financialization that currently benefit only private interests. In this respect, we have argued that surplus value is not necessarily evil. What is appalling is the hoarding of urban profits by the very few at the expense of the many. We believe the task of any urban and political practice today is to reorganize, redistribute and redirect surplus, operationalizing its social value and its public meaning.

The bottom-up *praxis* of communities can be a tool for co-developing the city. Reassigning value to the skills and capabilities found in informal urbanization, aggregating this hidden value with the sweat equity of architects, cultural producers and community leaders, and connecting these to new municipal protocols for accessing public parcels becomes leverage to lift communities as co-developers of the city. This means including communities in cross-sector coalitions, bundling the programmatic and social capital of nonprofits and residents to create new partnerships for development with architects. In our case, this has also meant mobilizing the programmatic and economic power of universities as leverage for communities to develop their own housing and public spaces, and as guarantors for new cooperative revenue-generating business models. An imperative to co-produce the city should push us, as architects, to design physical spaces alongside their funding and management strategies, to devise curatorial mechanisms that ensure social inclusion and the sustainability of these spaces over time. Let's imagine a new proforma for urban development that integrates these strategies and redistributes the profits of our growing cities.

WHERE IS OUR PUBLIC IMAGINATION?

Decline of the Public

The *public* is collapsing as an ideal. Since the early 1980s, a powerful elite of individuals and global corporations has hijacked the public in the name of freedom, stewarding a steady regime of deregulation and privatization of public resources across the world. This shift of resources from the many to the very few, and the accompanying decline of public thinking, has undermined our public institutions at all scales. The welfare-state paradigm is faltering everywhere in a nationalist political climate obsessed with economic austerity and border-building.

The impact of neoliberal development on cities is dramatic. Across the US and elsewhere, municipalities have "unplugged" from neighborhoods at the margins, producing staggeringly uneven growth patterns, with centers of wealth surrounded by expanding peripheral territories of poverty and informality. Accelerating urbanization driven by poverty, political instability and climate change across the world is intensifying these dynamics. Urban development today takes direction from corporate power, with disastrous impacts on the city, where a public vision has been replaced by hyper-privatized, developer-driven urban speculation. Urban inequality, fragmentation and violence are a direct consequence.

These dynamics have been accompanied by an erosion of public trust in government and justifiable public cynicism about participating in the urban political process. While there are compelling examples of communities that have mobilized powerful resistance from the bottom-up, disengagement has deepened in many urban communities most impacted by public withdrawal—sometimes because marginalization produces a sense of futility, sometimes because people are preoccupied with the more urgent challenges of everyday life, and sometimes because they have been convinced by unscrupulous political messaging that their interests align with the very corporate interests that drive marginalization and displacement.

The neoliberal rhetoric of "job creation" continues to seduce working people and many marginalized demographics into believing that deregulating their employers is the safest path to social security. But, our own national history demonstrates that intelligent public investment, particularly in times of economic uncertainty, has stimulated economic growth and improved quality of life for all citizens, rich and poor alike. And yet, the ahistorical, arrogant agendas advanced in recent years by US and European governments are unraveling many of the advances of the last century and enflaming already volatile conditions in urban neighborhoods.

The depression of 1929 and the global economic implosion of 2008 were marked by a blatant consolidation of economic power and unprecedented income inequality. At these two moments, the unchecked economic logics of privatization and reduced taxation on the wealthy enabled the richest 1% to claim about one-third of US wealth, and 10% to own more than half of the nation's resources. Our situation today is even more dire, because the consolidation of power is protected by the largest corporate lobbying machine in history. The coordinated subordination of collective interests to individual interests has dramatically changed the terms of the game, polarizing institutions and publics, wealth and poverty, and radically misallocating our natural, social and environmental resources. The Supreme Court's decision in *Citizens United* exemplifies this shift, legitimizing unlimited corporate campaign spending and enabling wealthy elites to manipulate political opinion to benefit special interests. *Citizens United* is an overt blow to democracy because it undermines the political power of the collective by freeing wealth to dictate political priorities. It perverts our conception of the *demos*, privileging freedom over any sense of common values and shared responsibilities. By definition, the *demos* is meant to manifest the collective will of the citizens. How can the collective power of citizens be equated to the power of corporations and wealthy elites? A recent *New York Times* article exposed that half of all donations to Republican super-PACs for the 2016 election came from just 130 wealthy families, concentrated in seven exclusive neighborhoods across the US. How have we come to confuse citizens with corporations and a united imagination with the 1%?

Urban justice today must begin with a new public imagination. We urgently need to revive a sense of collective well-being, with special concern for people severely impacted by poverty, political instability and climate change. We need to increase public knowledge and forge new points of democratic access for marginalized people. We need to build collective capacity for civic and environmental action at local scales, and generate new experimental spaces, economic models and social programs for the city. We also must demand social protections that safeguard marginalized communities from gentrification, enabling them to control their own development and modes of production as well as to share in the profits of urbanization. The political "right" and political "left" too often coincide in their skepticism of government, claiming that "government gets in the way." We believe in the top-down public, and advocate for a radical reimagination and reinvention of what democratic urban governance can be, and what it means to elevate political leaders who are public servants, committed to producing more efficient, transparent, inclusive and collaborative local governance that connects top-down and bottom-up resources and knowledges. We believe that architectural and urban practices today can engage this political project head-on.

Reimagine Public Housing

Housing affordability is a major casualty of neoliberal urban development. Our policymakers have rejected redistributive models that tackle inequality by investing in underserved neighborhoods, essentially relinquishing the state's role as a developer of public housing. And society has acquiesced to the privatization of this public good, with a corporate lobby machine selling "home ownership" as the pinnacle of human happiness and freedom.

The evils of public housing were cemented in the American mindset in the early 1970s with the demolition of Pruitt-Igoe in Saint Louis, Missouri. Built in the fifties, by the time of its demise this massive public housing project had devolved into the urban slum it originally replaced, overwhelmed by poverty and crime. But this was not the fault of public housing *in se*. When this New Deal project was built, it was fortified with social support systems that only a robust welfare state could provide. Everything worked! Clean, bright and affordable units were framed by functional public amenities and social services, such as playgrounds, child and senior care, and vocational training. But as tax-based revenues began to erode because of neoliberal shifts in governance, displacing the common good with austerity and disinvestment, Pruitt-Igoe spiraled into decay.

The famous images of Pruitt-Igoe imploding solidified two American myths about public housing. One has been perpetuated by historian Charles Jencks: claiming that modern architecture was the culprit behind Pruitt-Igoe's demise, he declared the end of Modernism.[11] This eventually flung the doors open to a postmodern urban nightmare which coincided with the ascendance of neoliberalism in the early 1980s and propelled a culture of exclusionary private development, decorated with fake, populist historical props. Suggesting that the problem with Pruitt-Igoe was "aesthetics," Jencks demonized modernism only to unleash a politics of style to legitimize neoconservative historicist facades as the ubiquitous language of every strip mall and housing subdivision across the US in the years to come—with New Urbanism becoming its main political broker. The other Pruitt-Igoe myth was that its physical demolition officially announced the death of public housing in the US, inscribing in people's minds the equation that public housing = ghetto = crime. The strategic public relations campaign designed to demonize public housing was extremely effective, and by the mid-1980s the responsibility of producing affordable housing had shifted decisively from the public to the private, giving private developers and "the market" the "freedom" to determine their product and set the terms of affordability.

During the New Deal, housing authorities were supported by strong legislatures and tax-based revenue to ensure affordability for low-income working families, and to provide financial instruments that incentivize community-owned assets. In other words, the top-down public facilitated a more integrated process, in which design, funding and service provision were aligned, and architects were summoned to serve these public programs. But now, public housing is a forbidden word in the language of urbanization. Subsidies are called "tax credits" (essentially tax-exempt charity), and housing authorities have been relegated to a managerial role, coordinating permit bonuses and tax breaks for "affordable housing developers" and vouchers for families who qualify for housing, the affordability and accessibility of which is determined in turn by developers.

Both myths produced irreparable damage to the city. One focused on issues of "identity" (In what style should we build?) at the expense of social inclusion. The other perpetuated a fear of public housing and its inherent failure as an urban agenda, which still haunts us today.

We believe architects and urban designers can help to recuperate histories of successful public investment and housing practices to inspire new criteria and new mandates to tackle the crisis of affordability. We can learn a lot from housing policies from previous decades, including community trusts, community-based co-op housing, housing corporations and the best models of public housing. There are also decent examples of affordable, developer-driven housing projects across the US today, though these projects often lack the social programming necessary to support them. Private developers typically cannot integrate robust social amenities without compromising profits. Inclusive, affordable housing design today requires that we rethink the political processes and financial mechanisms within which affordable housing is produced and sustained. Fostering tax-credit-based financing as the main economic incentive to produce affordability has abandoned the right to housing to profit-driven market forces. Tax credits are essentially subsidies for private developers to generate affordable housing, enabling the private sector to render housing a commodity and neglect demographics in need.

Reimagine Governance

While we are inspired by moments of agile public management in US urban history, we do not wish to fetishize the top-down public. We recognize its very real limitations, opacity, byzantine inefficiency and corruption. But too thorough a critique of municipal bureaucracy is counterproductive because it begins to reinforce the neoliberal lie which holds that private markets manage public goods better than public institutions can—that they just need to be unshackled by regulatory frameworks, and somehow everything will fall into place. This claim is deceptive both pragmatically and from the vantage of equality. Public investment is not a drain on prosperity, but a stimulant that opens markets and ultimately produces more equitable economic growth. Moreover, a genuine commitment to social-democratic values demands investment in inclusive public infrastructure.

Tackling the housing crisis is not only an economic or political challenge; rebuilding a broad sense of public commitment and restoring trust in government is also, fundamentally, a cultural challenge. A key site of intervention is municipal bureaucracy itself. Cities need to rethink their fragmented and inefficient processes of public management. We witnessed this firsthand when we served as special advisors to the mayor of San Diego in 2013–14, who tasked us with designing a *Civic Imagination Lab* to recalibrate relations between the municipality and San Diego's underserved urban communities.[12] The planning department of the fifth largest city in the US had just been shuttered and its staff reassigned to "development services." Instead of being aspirational and projective through an intelligent and coordinated approach to public policy and regional planning, many municipal departments and city agencies remained managerial and preventive, conservative with a small "c," lacking coordination and curatorial agility to integrate fragmented resources and promote cross-sector synergies towards common goals. Most often the easiest path is taken: surrendering to boilerplate development recipes devised by private developers at the expense of community needs and neighborhood revitalization. We are certain that San Diego municipal planning and culture we witnessed is not unique.

How can we instigate more efficient, transparent, inclusive and collaborative forms of public management? We believe the design fields can help to curate new linkages between government and communities, social networks and cultural institutions, and help to reorient the surplus value of urbanization toward public interests and social priorities.

Even Adam Smith, the eighteenth-century "father of capitalism," understood that governments need to invest in public well-being, public goods and public culture.[13] Smith was alarmed by the conditions of the working poor in early industrial capitalism, devoting an entire section of his great book, the *Wealth of Nations*—indeed the longest section—to elaborating public provisions, progressive taxation and taxation on luxury goods. He spent dozens of pages elaborating the virtues of public education, essential to countering the dehumanizing effects of industrialization and cultivating a civic consciousness among the working classes. He worried about political apathy and encouraged modern people to keep an eye on unscrupulous political actors who would use government to their advantage. Workers and consumers needed to be citizens too. And he insisted that government needed to steward this process by investing strategically and judiciously in public goods and public infrastructure to ensure a basic quality of life for the least well-off, particularly when the market is not incentivized to do so. These inconvenient dimensions of Smith's thought were sidelined by his capitalist readers over the next two centuries.

Reimagine Urban Beautification

To democratize urban development, we need to focus less on "urban form," "beautification" and "lifestyle." We are not saying beautiful buildings don't matter. Any city benefits from them, and our commitment to beauty is something that architects, cultural producers and even politicians must embrace. But when the pursuit of beauty comes at the expense of collective well-being then it becomes a veneer. The city has become increasingly defined by urbanisms of beautification in which architecture wraps and camouflages exclusionary urban development with hyper aesthetics and forms, displacing communities for the sake of economic progress.

Our design fields are uniquely positioned to advocate for more experiential dimensions of beauty, based less on visual quality and more on social vibrancy, of encountering and coexisting with others—an aesthetic quality that embraces contradictions and risk and emerges from inclusiveness. This means engaging other actors than private developers to co-produce the city, imagining other forms of ownership and resource management, other financial arrangements to assure social and economic inclusion, and other mechanisms of institutional accountability. At bottom, we need to reclaim the public. The unprecedented urban inequality of the last three decades is all the evidence we need: the "free market" will never assure social and economic justice.

Urban Inequality as a Cultural Challenge

Neoliberal policies since the early 1980s have damaged our public infrastructure and deepened social inequality and exclusion in our cities and rural communities. While these correlations seem obvious, public acknowledgment and appropriate collective anger has been slow. Privatization has not ignited our collective imagination. Instead we proceed as if we are swept up in the inevitable flow of history, and within in it we must find our place.

Urban justice cannot progress without tackling public beliefs, without dismantling the erroneous assumption that individual and collective well-being are in conflict. We believe that the linkages between infrastructural defunding and inequality in housing, education, transportation, health access and vulnerability to climate change must be central in public debate today. We need to find new ways to communicate, to penetrate public perceptions with new heuristics that demonstrate the possibilities of a robust public sphere, and leaders who are committed to it. One strategy is to recuperate institutional memory and elevate histories of fruitful public investment in the US and across the world. For example, FDR's New Deal and the social-democratic urban politics of postwar Europe produced a surge of equitable urban strategies, enabled by progressive taxation and cross-sector investment in public infrastructure and social services.

In their pathbreaking study of twentieth-century American inequality, economists Emanuel Saez and Thomas Piketty demonstrate in highly accessible ways how decades of neoliberal public policy in the US have privatized the American Dream, destroyed our ethic of collective responsibility and accelerated inequality.[14] They investigated the peaks and valleys of American inequality across the twentieth century, moving pendulum-like, back and forth, between periods of investment and austerity, between public and private priorities. It turns out that America's moments of greatest socioeconomic inequality—the depression of 1929 and the economic downturn of 2008—were also its moments of lowest marginal taxation of the wealthy. Impressionistically, this diagram of inverted peaks exposes the hypocrisy of a "trickle-down" fantasy that lower taxation on wealth produces better outcomes for all. Clearly it has not done so.

Most interesting in the story that Saez and Piketty tell is the "valley" in the middle, when taxation increased and inequality flattened. These are the decades of FDR's New Deal and the Bill of Rights, through which government, civic philanthropy, the private sector, universities and communities convened across sectors to invest in the public. These decades produced unprecedented public investment in infrastructure, public housing, public health, public education and public art. During these decades "public" was not a forbidden word in our political language, and the US experienced the greatest economic boom it had ever known. Income rose across the board. The US was the global leader in education and employment. Arts and culture were mobilized as engines for growth, activating public spaces and institutions as the organizing systems for urban renewal. The design professions served not only the 10% but were also energized by a robust public agenda.

Where is the public today? Can we find compelling examples to rouse a new civic imagination?

We continue to find inspiration in a twentieth-century lineage of participatory urbanization in Latin America—cities that committed to tackling inequality through more inclusive and collaborative strategies of municipal governance, prioritizing public needs and mobilizing civic energy from the bottom up.

In Search of a New Public:
Latin American Inspiration

In recent years, we have investigated compelling case studies of equitable urbanization across Latin America, and how these cases can be translated into new paradigms of public housing, public infrastructure, property and even citizenship, inspiring experimental strategies of intervention in the contemporary city. In an era when urban development across the world tends to be controlled by an alliance among private developers, housing authorities and municipal governments, opening alternative points of access into urbanization might seem unattainable. But there are compelling examples of more democratic methods of urbanization and a commitment to urban justice over the last decades. Many cities across Latin America have experimented with inclusive political and civic processes, tapping into diverse social networks, informal economies and imaginative forms of public participation to stimulate civic consciousness and reorient the surplus value of urbanization from the private to the public.

Some of these cases have become mythical. From the participatory budgeting experiments in Porto Alegre, Brazil, in the 1980s, where communities deliberated and decided together how to allocate a percentage of the municipal budget; to the invention of BRT ("bus rapid transit") in Curitiba, Brazil, where existing bus lines and elevated stations were retrofit for lower-cost public transport; to Bogotá, Colombia, in the early 2000s, where BRT was perfected to become what was then the most advanced multi-nodal transportation system in the world, a tradition that still thrives in cities across the continent, from Medellín to La Paz, from Quito to Mexico City. We don't want to appear utopian—challenges remain in all of these cities—but we are inspired by this continental lineage of public commitment and urban creativity, and we will return to it at several points in this book. These Latin American cases have occurred at different moments in diverse political contexts, but together they have established a late-twentieth-century tradition of Latin American political and civic experimentation that powerfully counters the decline of public thinking across the world today. Ironically, some of these cities claimed inspiration in twentieth-century American progressivism—and now we find ourselves turning to them.

Bogotá and Medellín have been particularly compelling for us, notably during the mayoral administrations of Antanas Mockus in Bogotá (1995–97 and 2001–03) and Sergio Fajardo in Medellín (2004–08) in the two decades straddling the century mark. Both administrations prioritized reducing inequality, and tackled urban conflict and violence through experiments in collaborative municipal governance and planning, progressive taxation, and massive cross-sectoral investments in public infrastructure and social services in the poorest and most violent neighborhoods. They rejected "law and order" solutions to violence, which only perpetuate division and resentment. They both invested in cultivating a vibrant, participatory civil society—what Mockus called a "citizenship culture"[15]—and in rebuilding a sense of collective capacity and hope from the bottom-up. Bogotá especially became legendary for its methods of urban pedagogy and community engagement. Both cities forged cross-sector partnerships between progressive municipalities, community-based nonprofits and research universities to democratize knowledge and improve quality of life for the most marginalized populations. As Fajardo frequently points out, what ultimately transformed Medellín was not architecture or infrastructure, even though this is what the world sees and celebrates today. Medellín's transformation was fundamentally a "political project"[16]—to rethink governance as a collective activity, and to coordinate cross-sector alliances to mediate formal and informal dynamics in the city.

These Latin American cases exemplify what we call "civic imagination"—a way of thinking collectively about urban life that we have lost in the US, much of Europe and elsewhere in recent decades. Success is sometimes ephemeral. These cities still face corruption, poverty and violence. But they remind us that progressive municipalities can still exist, and that instead of turning our own justifiable dissatisfaction with government bureaucracy into a wholesale rejection of the top-down, we can reinvent governance with bottom-up sensibilities and knowledges.

Over the last decade, we have partnered with the main actors in these now fabled Colombian stories of urban transformation, carrying their lessons back with us to the San Diego–Tijuana border region. When we were summoned by the mayor of San Diego to develop an agile unit in his office to experiment with public space and civic engagement in marginalized neighborhoods, he was inspired by the Latin American stories we shared with him. The *Civic Imagination Lab* became a cross-sector municipal think tank modeled after Bogotá and Medellín—Bogotá for its strategies of changing social norms, and Medellín for its collaborative model of governance and spatialization of citizenship culture.

The commitments of Bogotá and Medellín have become increasingly relevant for us as we work to build solidarity among communities divided by the US-Mexico border wall. In this fragmented zone of conflict and disparity, we have been committed to rethinking citizenship itself from the bottom-up, opposing conventional jurisdictional and identitarian ideals with a more practical and cultural idea of belonging rooted in the norms, interests and aspirations shared by people on both sides of the wall.

Informal Public Demands

A society that is anti-tax, anti-public, anti-immigrant and that invests more in building prisons than schools commits civic suicide. As we do the collective long-term work necessary to restore the top-down public, what can be done right now, in the meantime, to alleviate the impacts of public defunding on marginalized communities? In our work, we envision a bottom-up public, with *informal public demands* that counter exclusionary political and economic power, from everyday acts of resistance and democratic agency in marginalized neighborhoods everywhere to bright spots of institutional courage in our cities. We are inspired by bottom-up tactics of opposition and resistance to the anti-public assaults that have descended upon us.

To change hearts and minds, informal public demands must begin as a social and cultural project. Urban activism should focus on increasing public knowledge, rejecting social norms that validate neglect, exploitation and dispossession in the city, igniting civic dignity, repairing public trust and restoring a belief in community agency at the neighborhood scale. Only then can top-down governance and spatial intervention produce meaningful change. In this light, we must demand a radical transformation of conventional advocacy planning protocols, which are too often box-ticking exercises that engage the same voices over and over again. These protocols typically are not inclusive, and they reproduce false perceptions that the majority of residents in neglected urban neighborhoods are disinterested, or unknowledgeable, or incapable of collective agency. It is an ethical imperative: municipalities must find ways to engage with demographics that have retreated, having been marginalized for so long from the city's scope of moral concern. Municipalities can restore public trust only by earning it—even if it takes time, even if it slows projects down. They need to stop coming in and rearranging the furniture.

The informal public demands below follow an incremental logic: they begin with a set of normative demands and cultural processes, followed by demands for more democratic and collaborative forms of governance, culminating in a set of policy demands focused on the equitable spatial transformation of the city:

→ Transform cultural practices of social exclusion and the corresponding denigration of public goods by cultivating new urban norms of human dignity and equality, and shame their violation.

→ Advance a language of "a right to the city" to stimulate a new sense of possibility in communities long marginalized from the privatized planning agendas of today's cities.

→ Enable more inclusive and meaningful systems of political representation and civic engagement at the scale of neighborhoods, tactically recalibrating individual and collective interests.

→ Design new forms of local governance to prevent gentrification, along with the social protection systems that provide guarantees for marginalized communities and secure their right to control their own modes of production and share the profits of urbanization.

→ Challenge existing models of property with a more inclusive idea of ownership that redefines affordability and the value of social participation, and augments the role of communities in co-producing housing and public infrastructure.

→ Mobilize social networks in new spatial and economic infrastructures that benefit local communities, beyond the short-term problem-solving logics of private developers or institutions of charity.

→ Create agencies that curate interfaces between top-down institutions (government, universities, foundations, cultural institutions) and the creative, bottom-up intelligence and sweat equity of communities and activists.

→ Close the gap between large-scale, abstract planning logics and the realities of everyday practices.

→ Challenge the autonomy of buildings and their indifference to urban socioeconomic temporalities, and instead engage the complex temporalization of space found in informal urban dynamics.

→ Question exclusionary logics of land use. Approach zoning not as a punitive deterrent to socialization but instead as a generative tool that organizes and anticipates local social and economic activity.

→ Politicize density. Measure it not as an abstract number of objects per area, but as the intensity of socioeconomic exchanges per area.

→ Retrofit the large with the small. The micro-social and economic contingencies of the informal will transform the homogeneous largeness of official urbanization into more sustainable, plural and complex environments.

→ Reimagine exclusionary logics that shape jurisdiction. Conventional government protocols give primacy to the abstraction of administrative boundaries over the social and environmental boundaries that informality negotiates as devices to construct community.

→ Challenge the idea of public space as a manicured site of beauty and leisure, and reclaim it as site of civic activity, urban pedagogy and cultural production.

A PRACTICE OF MEDIATION: TOP-DOWN / BOTTOM-UP

A Critique of Practice

Today's urban crises demand new theories, new forms of practice, different ways of knowing and doing. But urban institutions are typically conservative, protective, resistant to questioning their ways of thinking and orienting their resources around multilateral agendas to tackle complex, pressing priorities like climate change, public health and social-economic inequality. What can we do, as communities of practice and research, to support urban institutional change?

We want to revisit the old debate in art and architecture about what it means to be "critical" in the context of "crisis." On one end of the debate, some continue to defend the autonomy of art and architecture as a self-referential aesthetics, ultimately bolstered by a culture of private excess, distant from institutions and impartial to political forces. On the other end, some have sought to move beyond autonomy and engage the social, political and economic domains that have been conventionally peripheral to design.

Today's crises demand not "political architectures" but a new role for art and design in constructing the political itself—what we think of as a *critical proximity* to institutions—in order to transform them from the inside out, to produce new aesthetic categories that problematize relations between the social, the political and the formal. We seek to revive the central aspiration of the historic avant-garde: to reconnect artistic experimentation and social responsibility. This project is less about designing "things" and more about mediating processes that facilitate the transfer of knowledge between institutions, fields of specialization and publics. Knowledge that remains siloed and self-referential perpetuates existing power structures and disparities.

The Expansion of Practice

While our practice has focused on emergent, bottom-up urbanization, the ultimate goal of our practical work together in San Diego–Tijuana and cities elsewhere is to seek ways by which this knowledge can trickle upward to transform urban policy. We are wary of sending a message that informal dynamics are self-sustaining, and that top-down formal institutions can withdraw from them. We believe in robust social welfare and inclusive urban governance. We are inspired by design practices that are committed to mediating interfaces between the top-down and the bottom-up, and across divided institutions, jurisdictions and communities.

This public curatorial task pushes architecture and urban design into expanded fields of operation. We can do more than design buildings and things. We can design new platforms for dialogue and knowledge flow, problematizing what we mean by "experts" and finding new ways to speak with the other, new bridges and tunnels across divided sectors, between academia, community activism and public policy, piercing the compartmentalization of silos and fragmented institutions. This entails challenging conventional ideas of interdisciplinarity, moving beyond roundtable monologues and risking detours that recontextualize and "contaminate" our own partial worldviews and disciplinary techniques. Can social scientists begin to think spatially? Can architects spatialize human rights and dignity?

In many ways, conventional research-based academic culture is at odds with activist practices, which are, by their very nature, organic, diverse and trans-institutional. Can activist practices help academics rethink and reorient their pedagogic strategies? How can teaching and learning be more responsive to bottom-up knowledges? Architecture and planning schools too often camouflage exclusion with aesthetics, separating the conventional goals of architecture from activities that might advance more equitable and democratic outcomes in cities. Similarly, the social sciences refine their skills of measuring and exposing the mechanisms that produce social and economic inequality, but hesitate to partner with practitioners to translate that research into meaningful strategies for action and advocacy, to co-develop policy proposals and urban development strategies to advance social justice in the city.

Academic neutrality perpetuates social injustice, economic disparity and the erosion of civic thinking by fire-walling research from advocacy and political representation. Changing academic culture is a double project: exposing the institutional mechanisms that have systematically (and often through overtly racist and nationalist commitments) validated political and economic forces that perpetuate marginalization. We should also rethink the academic mission itself, breaking down silos that undermine holistic thinking and action, and validating more practical and proactive variants of research that advocate for and advance social justice. Today's social challenges are not confined to disciplines, nor can their solutions be. We believe universities should commit to teaching students how to engage communities with epistemic openness, to analyze social disparity through multiple lenses, to communicate across disciplinary language silos, and to collaborate with each other and with a diverse field of partners.

Curating Knowledge Transfer

Social justice today is not only about the redistribution of resources, but also about the redistribution of knowledges. A key site of intervention today is the widening gap between institutions of knowledge and the public. How can we mobilize new corridors of knowledge between the specialized knowledges of institutions and the community-based knowledges embedded in marginalized sites? This entails a critical intervention into our own practices and research protocols—learning how to listen and to recognize value in alternative ways of knowing, seeing and doing.

In our research-based practice, the pursuit of social justice entails mediating two-way flows of knowledge between the top-down and the bottom-up. In one direction, bottom-up urban activism and creative acts of citizenship can flow "upward" to transform top-down priorities and decision-making; in the other direction, top-down resources can be intelligently directed to elevate the creative intelligence of the bottom-up. We believe that an ethical circulation of knowledges across institutions and communities is an important step in constructing an engaged civic culture, more accountable public institutions and ultimately more inclusive urbanization.

Informal acts in the city—stealth spatial alterations, activist jurisdictional encroachments to activate urban leftovers and collective democratic actions—do not have to stop at the small-scale, but can be translated and carried in diverse directions to transform top-down policy. In San Diego–Tijuana, for example, border neighborhoods have constructed ingenious strategies of urban sustainability, resilience and adaptation —exemplary democratic creativity that is incommensurate with racist accounts of these urban neighborhoods that influence formal planning discussions. There is crime, it is true; poverty does that to communities. But there is amazing bottom-up democratic agency and cultural and economic creativity that needs documentation and translation.

We believe this journey from the bottom-up to the top-down can advance urban justice today. We need political leaders willing to listen, and to reimagine urban policy through the urgencies and practices of the bottom-up. We also need new urban curatorial practices that can help to facilitate these flows, to dismantle and decolonize vertical knowledge hierarchies that have perpetuated exclusion. We see this translational imperative opening creative spaces of operation for young artists and architects. Beyond the pursuit of form that manifests in buildings and objects, we can design civic processes, urban pedagogy, alternative economic models and collaborative networks across institutions and communities to advance equity and social justice. In our practice, this has entailed pursuing collaborations with community-based activist organizations to design more authentic mechanisms of neighborhood representation. Examples include: bundling the invisible sweat equity of labor and volunteerism into new strategies of collective governance and economy; designing new social contracts and safety-net protocols that protect the most vulnerable members of the community; visualizing and valuating nonconforming urban patterns in the neighborhood; curating pedagogic tools to increase public knowledge and collective agency; and facilitating cross-sector coalitions to collaboratively steward the public realm.

A New Public Knowledge

We have been critical of top-down advocacy planning methods and conventional community-engagement workshops, which tend to be biased towards conservative, form-based code. In a patronizing gesture, they elevate stylistic choice as the organizing criteria, packaging cultural identity into fixed iconic recipes that ignore social and economic processes. They too often lobby for consensus-building between developers and communities, and meticulously avoid the dangers of triggering public design imagination that might slide toward challenging unjust planning agendas and logics of development. For us, participatory planning demands new public knowledge: more complicated dialogical processes that invite dissensus and debate between the specialized knowledge of architects and the creative capacities of communities without subordinating each other's role.

Participatory urbanization requires new urban pedagogies to disrupt long-standing urban planning practices that are rooted more or less explicitly in racism, classism, ableism, sexism and anti-LGBTQ+ bias. At a time of division, polarization and disinformation, urban justice begins with equitable access to information, supported by education and critical methods of advocacy planning. Art and architecture can support these transformations, providing visual tools to help convey the complex histories and practices of injustice and ultimately to fortify the public sphere.

Public Space:
Where the Top-Down and the Bottom-Up Meet

We also need to rethink the spaces where diverse knowledges meet—how these spaces perform, and how they can be managed and programmed to assure accessibility over time. For us, public space is not a neutral space of leisure, or a magical platform where things can happen. We challenge conventions of public space as an urban commodity animated only by random encounter. To have civic impact, we believe public spaces should be rearticulated as a civic armature to reorganize the city, fortified with institutional support and inclusive public programming. Otherwise, public space is susceptible to being commodified, or privatized in urban "commoning" camouflage, or hijacked by the algorithms of digital capitalism, or dissolved into ephemeral gestures of resistance.

We believe that hybridizing top-down public resources with bottom-up, community-based social management and governance is the key to *civicizing* public space, producing sustainable, accessible, civically oriented public spaces in our cities today. This involves transforming often passive, neutral public spaces into active civic classrooms, spaces of knowledge, research production and local economy, which are co-curated by top-down and bottom-up civic actors to stimulate collective agency and a sense of "citizenship culture" in neighborhoods. We believe that neighborhood-scale civic education lies at the heart of inclusive urbanization.

Civic education is not about organizing allegiances or propagating tenets, but about increasing public knowledge through encounter, dialogue, debate, contestation and cultural action. Civic education in public space is about curating civic contact and increasing propinquity, equitable linkages, connections, flows and exchanges. It is about summoning diverse people to recognize themselves in the lives and struggles of others, and cultivating a more public and collective sensibility. Curating civic education and cultural activity in public space can unleash the collective agency and electoral power of young, immigrant and minority communities across our cities. Civicizing public spaces is an antidote to marginalization and exclusion, and it requires that we restore linkages between municipalities, social networks, cultural institutions and communities.

From the perspective of architecture and urban design, this civic model of public space requires simultaneously designing physical systems and the protocols for inclusion. It means designing both flexible physical infrastructure that can accommodate diverse social, economic and cultural activity, as well as cross-sector programming, management and maintenance protocols. Designing civicized public spaces means designing adaptable spaces that are richly programmed for dialogue, urban pedagogy, participatory design, climate action, cultural production, collaborative research and youth mentorship—as well as the financial mechanisms and maintenance protocols necessary to operate and sustain these activities.

Conclusion:

Learning to Speak to the Other

Chances are, many who are reading this agree on essential principles of inclusion and social equity, the importance of fostering public thinking, civic education and public space. But how do we engage those who don't? One school of thinking today says we should hunker down, stop trying to convince cultures of opposition—that the divisions are too deep, and are ultimately insurmountable. There is some wisdom here; it is important to know when to cut one's losses and focus energy on things capable of change. But viewing opposition simply as "the enemy" can result in political paralysis and hatreds between entire segments of society who may have more in common than trending political chasms and social media enable people to see. Ideology always confounds cross-purposes and shared interests, and dims possibilities for broader coalitions that demand accountability from power.

We believe ultimately in operating outside the parameters of consensus and beyond immediate, familiar audiences to engage cultures, stakeholders and institutions that disagree. Can a new civic dialogue be built through dissensus, confronting what has been silenced by the consensus politics of neoliberalism and nationalism? We need new civic practices that welcome contestation and a more incremental approach to social and political transformation that forces us all to challenge our own biases, clichés and platitudes.

SECTION II: PROJECTS

CLUSTERS:

1. CONFLICT URBANIZATIONS: VISUALIZING THE POLITICAL
2. URBANIZATIONS OF ADAPTATION: CROSS-BORDER MIGRANT FLOWS
3. IMMIGRANT NEIGHBORHOODS: HOUSING LABORATORIES
4. BOTTOM-UP PUBLIC: THE FUNCTIONAL DIMENSION OF PARTICIPATION
5. TOP-DOWN PUBLIC: DESIGNING URBAN JUSTICE
6. DECOLONIZING KNOWLEDGE AND DEMOCRATIZING THE CITY: THE UCSD COMMUNITY STATIONS

PROJECT: CLUSTER 1
CONFLICT
URBANIZA
VISUALIZI
POLITICA

ATIONS:
NG THE

CONFLICT URBANIZATIONS:
VISUALIZING THE POLITICAL

Project cluster 1 presents the territorial scaffold of our practice, a nested ecology that descends in geographic scales from the global border to the neighborhoods that flank the US-Mexico border at San Diego–Tijuana. We begin with *Political Equator: Linking Border Regions Across the World*, an experimental visualization of a global border that links contested geographic thresholds across the world. We descend closer to the ground in *Nation Against Nature* and *MEXUS: Geographies of Interdependence*, visualization projects that investigate conflicts between the nation-state and social and environmental ecologies across the continental border between the United States and Mexico. These conflicts and opportunities manifest powerfully in our region at a specific zone of conflict between San Diego and Tijuana, explored in the *Cross-Border Commons: A Transnational Land Conservancy*. Our visualization experiment *Radicalizing the Local: 60 Linear Miles of Cross-Border Conflict* further investigates a succession of local collisions between the top-down forces of urbanization and bottom-up socio-spatial practices and environmental systems.

1   Political Equator: Linking Border Regions Across the World
2   The Nation Against Nature
3   MEXUS: Geographies of Interdependence
4   Cross-Border Citizens: Border-Drain Crossing
5   The Cross-Border Commons: A Transnational Land Conservancy
6   Radicalizing the Local: 60 Linear Miles of Cross-Border Conflict

Political Equator:
Linking Border Regions Across the World

In the last decades, as societies of overproduction and excess barricade themselves against sectors of scarcity and poverty, a global border demarcated by inequality has been emerging across the hemispheres. The fortress mentality that once characterized the political fringe has gone mainstream, legitimizing bigotry and an urgency to build walls that are higher and stronger, and to protect national resources from an endless flow of "foreigners." Nativist dynamics and border mania have become ubiquitous across the globe, from the rise of Donald Trump to Brexit, "Fortress Europe" and the resurgence of far-right movements like Alternative für Deutschland in Germany, Le Front National in France, Lega in Italy and more.

In 2005, Thomas Barnett proposed a post 9-11 cartography which anticipated today's global closure. In his *The Pentagon's New Map,* he divided the hemispheres into the "Functioning Core"—parts of the world where "globalization is thick with network connectivity, financial transactions, liberal media flows, and collective security"—and the "Non-Integrating Gap"—"regions plagued by politically repressive regimes, widespread poverty and disease, routine mass murder, and chronic conflicts that incubate the next generation of global terrorists."[17]

With our *Political Equator* diagram, we wanted to elaborate on Barnett's cartography to visualize a walled world of isolationism and protectionism unfolding during the second decade of the twenty-first century. We animated two global flows depicted in Barnett's map. In one direction, unprecedented flows of migrants from the "Non-Integrating Gap" seeking the strong economies of the "Functioning Core." And in the opposite direction, the dismantling of industrial centers in cities across the world and concomitant shift toward service and banking economies and the politics of outsourcing, prompting the "Functioning Core" to seek the cheap labor markets of the "Non-Integrating Gap." In turn, as immigrants settle in the "Functioning Core," remittances flow back to the "Non-Integrating Gap," helping to build infrastructure and housing, a major urban investment that amounts to 30+ billion dollars annually in Mexico alone but remains largely unaccounted for in global development agendas.

Political Equator explores convergences between these global dynamics and local regions of conflict, and organizes many of the research agendas in our practice. The project also links border regions across the world to investigate what these regions can learn from each other about social, economic and environmental interdependence.

Taking the Tijuana–San Diego border as a point of departure, *Political Equator* traces an imaginary line along the US-Mexico continental border and extends it across a world atlas, forming a corridor of global conflict between the 30th and 38th parallels north. Along this imaginary border lie some of the world's most contested thresholds, including the US-Mexico border at San Diego–Tijuana, the most-trafficked international border checkpoint in the world and the main migration route from Latin America into the United States. Also included are the Strait of Gibraltar and the Mediterranean, the main funnel of migration from North Africa into Europe through which waves of migrants and refugees from North Africa and Syria flow across "Fortress Europe," thickened in recent years to contain the flow of refugees from Lampedusa into Italy and from Lesbos into Greece; the Israeli-Palestinian border that divides the Middle East, emblematized by Israel's fifty-year military occupation of the West Bank and Gaza[18]; India-Kashmir, a site of intense and ongoing territorial conflict between Pakistan and India since the British partition of India in 1947; the border between North and South Korea, which represents decades of intractable conflict, carrying Cold War tensions forward to the present day; and finally China's ambitions in the South China Sea, including Hong Kong and Taiwan.

When this political equator is visualized alongside the climatic equator, the convergence of environmental and social injustice across the world becomes evident. The ribbon between the two equators, give or take a few degrees, contains our planet's most populous slums, its sites of greatest natural resource extraction and export, and its zones of greatest political instability, climate vulnerability and human displacement. And when these parallel equators are applied to the Peirce quincuncial projection from above, the Arctic becomes a protagonist, with its melting ice caps detonating rising sea levels, dramatic coastal vulnerability and human displacement. Demographics most impacted by political instability often bear the disproportionate brunt of climate change. The collision of nationalism and border-building, climate crisis and massive human displacement is the global injustice trifecta of our age.

While *Political Equator* is a working diagram, emblematic of hemispheric divisions between wealth and poverty, a necklace of contested checkpoints across the world, it is ultimately not a "flat line" but a critical threshold that bends, fragments and stretches to reveal other sites of conflict where social, political, economic and environmental ruptures are manifested at regional and local scales.

Political Equator is a point of entry into many of these localities distributed across continents.

The Nation Against Nature

Global forces of division and control "hit the ground" in border regions. Descending from the *Political Equator* to the continental border between the US and Mexico, the global border is physicalized as a solid wall that bisects eight watershed systems shared by both countries, generating a collision between nature and politics that damages social, economic and environmental assets on both sides.

For those of us living along the US-Mexico border, the incremental hardening of this jurisdictional line has been part of everyday life: a chain-link fence in the seventies, a steel wall constructed with temporary landing mats discarded by the US military after Operation Desert Storm in Iraq in the nineties and a concrete pylon wall today, crowned by electrified coils and panoptic night-vision cameras. The specter of Trump's thirty-foot-high continental wall reignited worries about the delicate cross-border ecosystems it threatened, compromising the environmental health of human communities on both sides.

Eight $4 million border-wall prototypes were unveiled in 2018 in the border town of Otay Mesa, just east of San Diego. These massive objects were imposed on the rugged landscape and hovered ominously above the informal communities on the Tijuana side, a dramatic slap in the face to our neighbors and partners in this region. The prototypes exemplified the *Political Equator*'s architecture of violence and division, revealing a myopic fantasy that an inert object, a wall across the continent, will solve "our" problems while ignoring the damage this political artifact has already exerted on the bioregion. The Arizona-based Center of Biological Diversity sued the Trump administration for ignoring the environmental impact of the new border wall.

The Nation Against Nature is a visualization project that documents precise moments when the jurisdictional line of the nation collides with natural systems along the entire trajectory of the continental border. At these junctures, the border wall disappears momentarily as the complexity of these topographic systems challenges the one-dimensionality of the political artifact. Proposals to fortify the wall have threatened to close these gaps, further impacting binational ecologies and the shared destiny of border communities. We challenge the legitimacy of a rationalist, nineteenth-century line imposed on complex systems and seek to provoke a more ecological way of thinking about border spaces as well as a more inclusive idea of regional interdependence.

MEXUS:
Geographies of Interdependence

While public perception of the border has been shaped by fragmentation and division, it is actually the environmental, economic and social flows across the wall that have historically defined the resilient and hybrid identities of everyday life in this part of the world. The border is not simply a place where things "end." Our shared ecologies challenge us to consider a more porous border region instead of a flat line imposed on the territory. Instead of seeing border regions through a xenophobic lens, demonizing border communities as sites of crime and violence, we have been calling for cross-border collaboration and an idea of citizenship that reaches beyond nation, jurisdiction and identity toward more inclusive public imaginaries based on dynamic circulation and interdependence.

MEXUS is a visualization of the continental border region without the jurisdictional line, presented instead as a bioregion comprised of eight watershed systems shared by Mexico and the United States. By unwalling this thickened system of interdependencies, *MEXUS* provokes a pragmatic idea of citizenship based on coexistence, shared assets and cooperative opportunities across divided communities. *MEXUS* visualizes the conditions that a physical barrier wall along the political border cannot contain: watersheds, indigenous lands, ecological corridors and migratory patterns. This unrecognized geography of interdependence invites us to visualize the disruption that a jurisdictional border inflicts on the continental environmental commons.

As the nation retreats, the environmental systems of *MEXUS* become an organizing framework for bioregional thinking with corresponding cross-border opportunities and ethical imperatives. As development economist Amartya Sen argues, global ethics demands a "cross-border public framework" that includes not only voices within "our own" jurisdictional and territorial boundaries, but also the voices of those beyond our borders whom we impact through our decisions and actions.[19] By focusing on this swath of land as a *bioregion* rather than as a *border*, *MEXUS* reorients our ethical responsibilities to those beyond the nation state.

Cross-Border Citizens: Border-Drain Crossing

REGIONAL DISRUPTION:
INFRASTRUCTURES OF INSECURITY

The challenges and opportunities of *MEXUS* are explored more concretely as we zoom deeper into the westernmost watershed of *MEXUS*. Here, we find the Tijuana River watershed system, which is shared by the border cities of San Diego and Tijuana. Of this watershed, 25% is located in the US, 75% in Mexico. The construction of new border wall and surveillance infrastructure by US Homeland Security in recent years has obstructed many canyons that comprise this hydrological system.

Before the northbound canyons discharge into the Pacific Ocean, they navigate intense territorial conflicts between natural and administrative systems, between ecological and political forces. The contradictions are most profound at a specific juncture where the Laureles Canyon in Tijuana, an important finger of the binational watershed and home to an informal settlement of 92,000 people, crosses the border and culminates in the Tijuana River Estuary in southeast San Diego county. This sensitive federal environmental zone flanking the border wall has been impacted in recent years by US securitization activities, including the construction of a militarized "third border wall" and other infrastructures of surveillance and control.

The informal Tijuana settlement of Los Laureles Canyon sits in one of these canyons, in direct relation to the estuary. In this part of the world, water flows from south to north. Because the slum sits at a higher elevation, wastewater flows northward, carrying tons of trash and sediment with each rainy season and contaminating one of the most important environmental zones, the "lungs" of the bioregion. The wastewater, trash, sediment and pollution flowing from Los Laureles Canyon are accelerated by three interrelated forces: 1. As Tijuana became a global tax haven, many multinational factories arrived and established themselves along its edges to extract cheap labor, often ignoring environmental regulations and dumping industrial waste in the canyon streams where these slums are located; 2. As immigrant workers seek jobs in these factories, the slums have exploded with informal emergency housing, and this in turn has impacted the health of the landscape, eroding the topsoil of fragile hillsides, loosening fine sediment that is characteristic of this geography; and 3. As informal urbanization has exploded in the last years, intensifying as northbound migration flows accelerate, city services cannot keep pace. Inadequate sewer and water management infrastructure prompts heavy northbound flows of trash, sewage and pollutants towards the US estuary.

The newest section of border wall, with its concrete dams and drains, has accelerated these dynamics. Understood in these terms, the wall becomes an infrastructure of insecurity. This is not Mexico's problem only, but a problem shared by Tijuana and San Diego, a condition that must be tackled collaboratively by the two cities.

BORDER-DRAIN PERFORMANCE:
A PUBLIC "UNWALLING" EXPERIMENT

To visualize this cross-border conflict and raise awareness about the need for a binational approach to conservation and investment to protect bioregional assets in Los Laureles Canyon, we curated an unprecedented cross-border public action in 2011. We led a caravan across the border, traveling southbound through a sewage drain underneath a new section of the border wall located at the precise juncture where the informal settlement of Los Laureles in Tijuana collides with the estuary on the US side. With our community partners, we negotiated a special permit with US Homeland Security to transform the drain into an official port of entry for twenty-four hours.

This public performance was part of the *Political Equator Meetings*, which we have curated since 2006, a series of nomadic urban actions and debates, oscillating across diverse sites and stations between Tijuana and San Diego. These

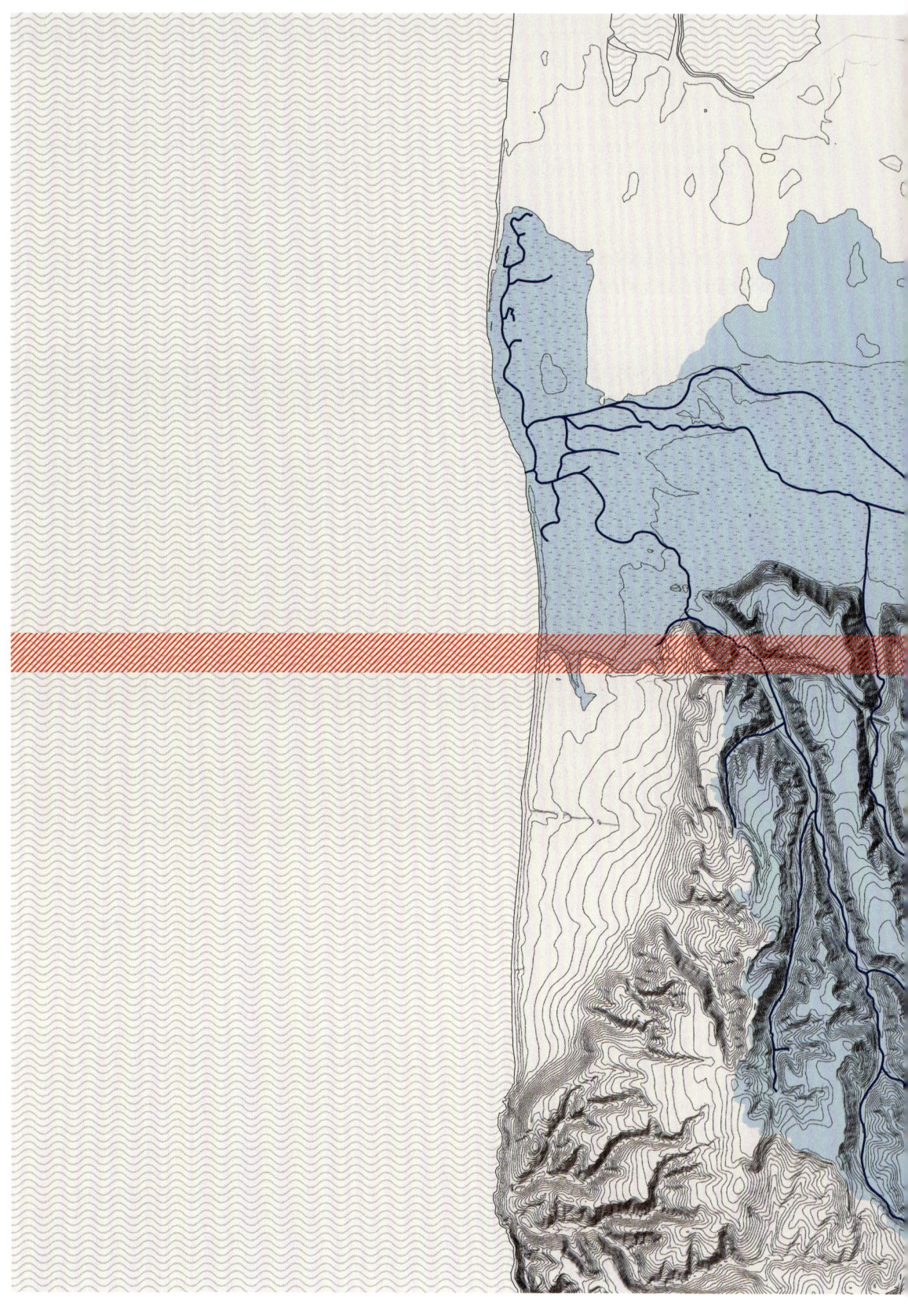

Tijuana's canyons colliding with the border wall

A memorial to stupid sovereignty

"conversations on the move" propose that debate should take place outside institutions and inside the actual sites of conflict, enabling the audience to be both witness and advocate. A strategic dimension of these itinerant border dialogues involves infiltrating zones of power with public works, performances and walks that serve as evidentiary platforms to recontextualize conversations among diverse publics and institutions that surround these conflicting territories.

The 2011 *Border-Drain Performance* consisted of two acts: a Forum and a Crossing.

The first act encroached into a site of exception, a 150-foot-wide corridor parallel to the wall that had been claimed by Homeland Security after 9-11. We declared it an open public space, and designated it as a site for a public forum about the future of the border region. We set up a tent in the center of this "no-man's-land" surveillance corridor a few meters from a newly built segment of the border wall. We summoned local, national and international activists, scholars and researchers, artists, architects and urbanists, politicians, border patrol and other community stakeholders who represented the many institutions that often conflict in this territory.

We curated a set of exhibits under this tent that enabled the diverse participants to visualize conditions that too often remain invisible and unaccounted for in public narratives about the border wall—invisible to both the communities who live adjacent to this site and the federal, state, municipal and military institutions tasked with managing and regulating the site. These visualizations ranged from physical models and projections that presented the topographic, environmental, social and economic assets of the site, to evidence of the negative impacts exerted by the existing border wall on binational social and ecological assets, to speculation about further damage that would be caused in years to come by proposed new border wall infrastructure. During the forum, we mobilized objects and images as evidence to organize debate, enabling diverse stakeholders to access the complexity of this particular territorial conflict and to recognize the binational collision between a vital environmental zone, surveillance infrastructure and informal urbanization in the Los Laureles Canyon settlement.

The second act involved the border crossing itself, which was through a nearby sewage drain under the wall. Preparations involved a long process of negotiation with both Homeland Security and Mexico's immigration officials, requesting a temporary recoding of this specific drain as a temporary but official port of entry that would enable the audience to slip uninterrupted from San Diego into Tijuana, and more specifically from the Tijuana River Estuary on the US side into Los Laureles Canyon in the western periphery of Tijuana. The public crossing was a performative device that visualized, and politically represented, the conflicts embedded in this site of collision, transforming this zone into a public space of contestation and debate. We wanted to create what Chantal Mouffe has described as a "vibrant 'agonistic' public sphere of contestation where different hegemonic political projects can be confronted."[20]

Homeland Security agreed to permit the passage when they confirmed that our goal was to *exit* and not *enter* the US. They also required that Mexican immigration officials wait for us at the south end of the drain to stamp our official documents. With passports in hand, 300 of us crossed the border drain southbound from the estuary to Los Laureles Canyon in Tijuana. As participants moved together under the wall against the natural northward flow of wastewater, we reached Mexican officers who had pitched an improvisational tent in Mexican territory on the south side of the drain. The strange juxtaposition of pollution seeping into the environmental zone, the stamping of passports inside this liminal space and the passage from pristine estuary to slum under a militarized culvert amplified the region's most profound contradictions and interdependencies. *Can border regions be laboratories to reimagine citizenship beyond the nation-state? Can citizenship be organized around shared interests in communities divided by a wall, rather than by nationalism and identitarian politics?*

Renewed investment in surveillance infrastructure along the US-Mexico border in recent years has further divided the communities adjacent to the wall, impacting the binational watershed systems that are essential to regional sustainability. The security regime exacerbates bioregional insecurity, as the myopic logics of division accelerate environmental and social-economic degradation. The *Border-Drain Crossing* exposed not only the dramatic conflicts between national security, environmental protection and the construction of citizenship, but also the need for urgent collaboration between these two border communities. *Instead of pouring billions of dollars into a new border wall, can we redirect some of this investment into the informal settlement in order to protect our binational assets? Can the Mexican slum protect the rich Tijuana River Estuary in the US?*

Reimagining the border through the logics of natural and social systems is the foremost challenge for the future of this bioregion, and for many border regions across the world. This is an important space of intervention that art and architecture practices can engage today.

The Cross-Border Commons:
A Transnational Land Conservancy

We facilitated the *Border-Drain Crossing* to raise public awareness of this conflict zone and open new channels of communication between the municipalities of San Diego and Tijuana, which typically ignore one another. But this border crossing was also an entry point into Los Laureles Canyon itself, gaining the trust of local activists and nonprofits in the informal settlement and initiating a new era of collaboration that has consolidated into an ambitious *cross-border environmental conservancy* initiative. This cross-sector project links the Tijuana River Estuary in San Diego with the Los Laureles Canyon settlements in Tijuana in a continuous political, social and ecological zone to protect the water and environmental resources shared by these border cities.

In the last decade, 70% of open space in Los Laureles Canyon has been lost to unregulated informal growth. Emergency housing, refugee camps and squatter dwellings have been built on the steep topographies of the canyon, encroaching into important natural and hydrological zones of the binational watershed. In this context, our work has assumed a double task. On the one hand, we have joined forces with planning activists to protect the remaining open spaces that have not yet been invaded by development. But we also engage informal urbanization processes with profound respect, and seek to translate creative social, spatial and material intelligence into new urban strategies that challenge top-down, mono-use infrastructure paradigms that accelerate displacement and disregard vital ecological systems.

The Cross-Border Commons "bundles" undeveloped parcels in the slum into an *archipelago of conservation* whose environmental programming protects and supports estuarine health beyond the border wall to the north. We are researching the role that each of these parcel-islands plays in the steady flows of waste and sediment, as well as their jurisdictional status, as they represent a mixture of private and public lands.

The first step has been establishing an institutional framework to formally designate a special transnational environmental zone, to found a land conservancy and community trust that can acquire land and sponsor sustainable conservation programming. This unorthodox cross-border land conservancy seeks to expand notions of conservation beyond isolating and protecting these parcels to activating them with environmental, pedagogical and social programming. Some of the smaller slivers of land are currently being transformed into social and pedagogical nodes that orient the community through environmental education and opportunities for participatory climate action. This necklace of public spaces will double as water and waste management infrastructure in order to mitigate flows of waste and sediment toward the border.

To steward *The Cross-Border Commons*, we have summoned a binational coalition of state and municipal agencies, grassroots organizations, communities and universities. We have designed two organizational bodies to focus on different scales of governance. The first is a cross-sector council that leads the broad coordination of the commons, negotiating its designation as a cross-border conservancy. This council is comprised of civic and community leaders on both sides of the border, representing institutions such as the State of California subcommittee on environmental assets; the mayor of Imperial Beach (the city that abuts the estuary in San Diego); the Tijuana Municipal Institute of Urban Planning (IMPLAN); the Municipal Office of Environmental Policy in Tijuana; the Tijuana River National Estuarine Research Reserve; the Center on Global Justice at the University of California, San Diego; the Colegio de la Frontera Norte in Tijuana; the religious organization Embajadores de Jesus in Los Laureles Canyon, Tijuana; and the nonprofits Divina Providencia in Los Laureles Canyon, Tijuana, and Casa Familiar in San Ysidro, California.

The second body is a smaller constellation that designs and stewards the programmatic agenda for each parcel on the Tijuana side, supported by a land trust that will be established as part of the Commons. In other words, these fragments of land will be adopted and programmed through a long-term partnership between universities, cultural and civic agencies, and environmental nonprofits to mobilize economic resources, stimulate community participation and curate conservation programming.

Radicalizing the Local:
60 Linear Miles of Cross-Border Conflict

Our descent from the global border to border neighborhoods culminates in a sixty-linear-mile cross-section, tangential to the border wall, between San Diego and Tijuana. We began this cartographic journey with *Political Equator*, a conceptual line that traverses the globe, and conclude now with a rhizomatic cross-section that traverses a variety of environments in two border cities, picking up along its trajectory a series of conflicts, all of which invisibly reproduce the border wall inside these two cities. Along this journey, we produce visual evidence that the forces of division and control manifest physically in the territory as urban borders. While this securitized binational conflict zone generates unique urban borders, we believe the conflicts we identify here resemble conflicts and borders in cities everywhere.

A sixty-mile section that crosses the border wall provokes dramatic challenges to our normative conceptions of architecture and urbanism. Along this trajectory, we find collisions between natural and artificial ecologies as well as between top-down forces of urban development and bottom-up social and ecological systems. These urban conflicts are spatialized by large freeway and military infrastructures that collide with watershed systems, gated communities that abut immigrant neighborhoods and formal urbanization pixelated with informal economies and densities—to give just a few examples.

"There is no such thing as a natural disaster," as landscape architect and theorists Anuradha Mathur and Dilip da Cunha declared in the context of their work on the Mississippi River.[21] Disasters happen, they suggest, when stupid urban development encroaches into natural systems. Every disaster that takes human life, every social-economic and environmental degradation, every instance of political strife, can be traced to a specific territorial conflict that emerges from collisions between jurisdictional and natural boundaries.

Our sixty-mile transborder cut begins thirty miles north of the border, at the periphery of San Diego, and descends sequentially southbound, ending with a thirty-mile dérive through Tijuana and its periphery.

CONFLICT BETWEEN TOP-DOWN DEVELOPMENT
AND NATURAL TOPOGRAPHY
Site 1: San Diego

San Diego's periphery is characterized by oil-hungry sprawl. The political economy of this expansionist suburbanization has made it cheaper to flatten the hills of San Diego's canyons rather than to negotiate the complexity of the topography. When we flatten topography, we flatten identity. Like a fingerprint, whose contour lines resemble topography, there are no two topographic conditions that are the same. As the bulldozers of private development flatten San Diego's canyons into an archipelago of voids, made of neutral berms and pads, the question of relations between civic identity and landscape, and thus between development and land use, is reopened. The massive eradication of topography in the periphery of San Diego supports the cheap construction of tract subdivisions and housing pads, homogenizing the ground and imprinting on it an ecology of fear that also flattens a sense of civic identity and political will.[22]

CONFLICT BETWEEN LARGE INFRASTRUCTURE
AND THE WATERSHED SYSTEMS
Site 2: San Diego

The main state highways in California run the length of coastal San Diego. Along their path, we find collisions with canyons, rivers and creeks that descend toward the Pacific Ocean. A necklace of territorial voids emerges from these territorial conflicts. As the politics of water and infrastructure defines the future of this region, the recuperation of these truncated natural resources is essential to anticipate metropolitan density. We've long maintained that the leftover spaces beneath California's freeways can become future nodes for public transportation and water conservancy.

CONFLICT BETWEEN URBAN SPRAWL AND SOCIAL LIFE
Site 3: San Diego

San Diego's homogenous sprawl of beige tract homes elevates a land use of exclusion into a sort of apartheid of everyday life, as gated communities retreat from the complexities of mixed uses and public transportation infrastructure, exacerbating unsustainable, car-centric growth. It is the ultimate irony that the pastoral, picturesque style of this oil-hungry suburban sprawl in edge-cities across the world has camouflaged an environmental disaster in the making. The ecological future of Southern California demands retrofitting mono-use suburban sprawl with plurality and difference.

CONFLICT BETWEEN MILITARY BASES AND ENVIRONMENTAL ZONES
Site 4: San Diego

The only undeveloped gaps within an otherwise continuous sprawl occur when the military bases that dot the edges of San Diego overlap with environmentally protected lands. This produces a strange tableau of housing subdivisions, natural ecologies and military spaces. The conflicts between military bases and environmental zones, and the juxtaposition of peripheral landscapes, systems of control, surveillance and gated communities have been recorded in the last decades in a series of strange scenes from everyday life: film footage of a tank leisurely moving through a housing subdivision (stolen from the nearby Miramar military base by a suburban man whose journey ended with a police bullet); a suburban house burning after the war-caliber weaponry stocked in its garage exploded; the strange montage of Humvees parked in front of super-size-me McMansions; and the mock-Arab villages built inside Camp Pendleton Marine Base as mini-Fallujah training sites, like movie sets equipped with hologram technologies to project Arab targets against the Southern California landscape.

CONFLICT BETWEEN FORMAL AND INFORMAL URBANIZATION
Site 5: San Diego

Across the older neighborhoods that comprise the first ring of suburbanization beyond San Diego's downtown, we find a different set of urban conflicts. The informal densities and economies produced by immigrants yield a sort of three-dimensional land use pattern that clashes with the one-dimensional, mono-use, exclusionary zoning that defines suburban tract subdivisions. Immigrant communities retrofit obsolete detached postwar bungalows with nonconforming uses: an informal economy in a garage, an illegal addition to a house that sustains an extended family, etc. The conflict between formal and informal patterns of development yields a new bottom-up political economy of urban growth that anticipates of the future of the city.

CONFLICT BETWEEN TWO BORDER CITIES
Site 6: The Border between San Diego and Tijuana

As we reach the border wall, the metal fence physicalizes the histories of conflict between the US and Mexico. Here, US investment in surveillance and control boldly announces its commitment to exclusion, exacerbating an "us" versus "them" mentality and transforming San Diego into the "world's largest gated community." The wall—an obelisk at the end of the nineteenth century, a chain-link fence in the 1970s, a steel wall in the 1990s and a wall of concrete pylons with electrified barbwire, buffered by a no man's land, in the 2000s—has hardened alongside deepening anti-immigrant sentiment in the US since 9-11, and the steady consolidation of economic power from the many to the few. While this partition has been part of everyday life of the border communities that flank it, Trump's failed proposal for a continental wall reopened questions about the environmental implications of imposing a thicker, higher property-fence on the delicate cross-border ecosystems essential to the life of these border cities.

CONFLICT BETWEEN THE BORDER WALL AND THE TIJUANA RIVER
Site 7: Tijuana

As we cross the international threshold into Tijuana, we witness a dramatic collision between the wall and the Tijuana River. Before crashing against the wall, the northbound river traverses the city as a large concrete channel. The only place where an otherwise continuous metal fence is pierced and opened is where the river meets the wall and its concrete infrastructure enters San Diego County.
A faint yellow line is inscribed on the dry river's concrete bed to signify the international line, a strange diagram that dramatizes this contested intersection between the administrative and the ecological. But as the channel moves beyond the fence and into San Diego's territory, the concrete gives way to landscape as the Tijuana River Estuary Reserve restores the natural river, allowing it to flow freely towards the Pacific Ocean. The San Ysidro border crossing, the most trafficked checkpoint in the Western hemisphere, represents the most intensified spot in this geography of conflict, because it is precisely here that river and wall, water and politics, intersect, dramatized by a matrix of border-patrol vehicles, US Homeland Security helicopters and electrified fences.

CONFLICT BETWEEN BORDER WALL, INFORMAL SETTLEMENTS AND NATURAL ECOLOGIES
Site 8: Tijuana

Many informal settlements crash against the border. In the minds of some San Diegans, the wall acts as a powerful dam, containing the chaotic density of Tijuana, preventing it from contaminating San Diego's picturesque sprawl. They never recognize the impact of the wall on binational ecologies.
   As these informal settlements grow, they encroach into the natural ecology of Tijuana's delicate topography, sprawling on the slopes of canyons that comprise the binational watershed, which is truncated by the border wall. Although these informal settlements are made of lighter architectures and lack the disruptive, top-down infrastructural colonization of other more official parts of the city, they nevertheless degrade delicate topsoil and accelerate sediment flows with each rain event. Nevertheless we have long argued that the ingenuity and scrappiness of these informal building practices can inspire new strategies for multi-scalar environmental infrastructure and watershed urbanization.

CONFLICT BETWEEN FACTORIES AND EMERGENCY HOUSING
Site 9: Tijuana

Tijuana's informal settlements are surrounded by NAFTA maquiladoras (factories). Over the years, Tijuana has become a global tax haven for multinational corporations to assemble parts into global commodities. Tijuana has become, for example, the television assembly capital of the world. The maquiladoras land on the edges of informal settlements to extract cheap labor, exacerbating the explosion of informal urban growth and drawing workers from all over Mexico and Central America. Yet, these multinationals remain unaccountable for the housing, education, health and transportation needs of their workforce. This conflict between factories, labor and informal housing is ubiquitous across Tijuana, intensified by private Mexican development corporations that capitalize on this unprecedented growth. Supported by public subsidies and benefiting from a vacuum of regulatory planning frameworks, they have built gigantic speculative housing subdivisions on the edges of the city without appropriate civic and transportation infrastructure. These housing developments represent Tijuana's version of homogenous suburban sprawl in the US, but without social support systems, they are quickly transforming into tomorrow's slums.

CONFLICT BETWEEN DENSITY AND SPRAWL
Site 10: Tijuana

Tijuana's massive, speculative eastward sprawl is seduced by the style and glamour of the master-planned gated communities of the US. The Tijuana version materializes as miniaturized replicas of typical suburban southern California tract homes, paradoxically imported into Tijuana to provide "social housing." Thousands of tiny tract homes called "mini-me's" now cover large swaths of Tijuana's periphery, creating a vast landscape of homogeneity at odds with this city's prevailing heterogeneous and organic metropolitan condition. These 250-square-foot (23-square-meter) single-family dwellings boast all the conventions of US tract homes, including gatehouses, model units and mini setbacks.

The conflict between formal and informal urbanization found in San Diego is reenacted here, as these mini tract homes quickly submit to adaptation by occupants. Residents have radically transformed them into micro social-economic engines to compensate for the lack of mixed uses and other social infrastructure. While the gated communities of Southern California remain closed systems due to stringent zoning that prohibits any kind of formal alteration or programmatic juxtaposition, residents in the Tijuana subdivisions occupy front yards with shops to support mixed uses and provide more usable space by building vertically and horizontally, often spanning more than one house. These transformations visualize the tensions and struggles between density and sprawl across the border region.

CONFLICT BETWEEN THE POLITICAL AND THE NATURAL
Site 11: Tijuana

As we reach the ocean on the Mexican side, we witness the most dramatic of all territorial collisions across this sixty-mile section of local conflict: where the metal fence finally sinks into the Pacific Ocean. As this militarized artifact descends into the depths of the water, the site is strangely poetic and hugely tragic, as two disparate urbanities meet and dissolve into the vastness of nature. As one stands on Playas de Tijuana, the beach neighborhood flanking the wall on the Tijuana side, witnessing the ocean water clash with steel pylons, one experiences what may be the most vivid manifestation of territorial collision between the natural and the political.

Architectural practice today needs to reposition itself in the midst of metropolitan and territorial conflict. No meaningful intervention can occur in the city before we first expose contested power relations, the political and economic forces that have produced the most profound collisions and contradictions of urban life. Each collision needs to be investigated and visualized to reveal the hidden institutional mechanisms that have produced it. The border zone is the laboratory of our practice for investigating the politics of migration, labor and surveillance, the tensions between sprawl and density, formal and informal urbanisms, and wealth and poverty. We have also designed processes of mediation that produce essential interfaces between top-down and bottom-up institutions and agencies that are impacted by and responsible for these transborder conflicts. This has entailed expanding and recoding conventional modalities of architectural practice. We have long argued that architects and urbanists can intervene in political and civic strategies to increase public knowledge, help build collective agency at local scales, and generate experimental spaces and social programs in the city.

A geography of conflict

THE POLITICAL EQUATOR
Extending a line from the Tijuana–San Diego border across a world atlas, between latitudes 30° and 38° north, we discover a corridor of a global conflict that links some of the world's most contested border zones. Regions most affected by poverty, violence, accelerating climate vulnerability and migration are situated between the Political Equator and the Climatic Equator. The collision of nationalism, environmental crisis, political violence and human displacement is the great crisis of our age.

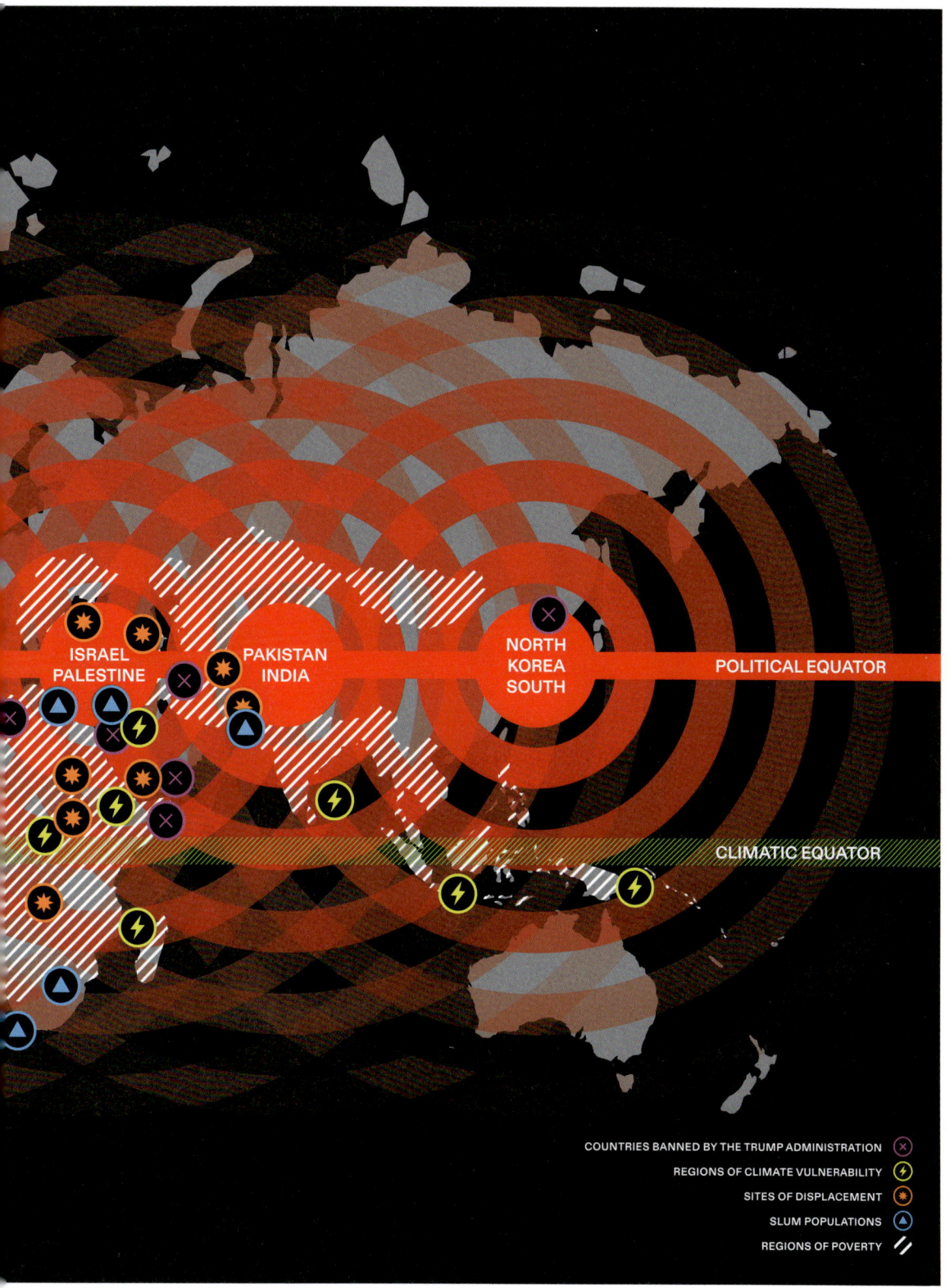

CONFLICT URBANIZATIONS: VISUALIZING THE POLITICAL

A WALLED WORLD
The Political Equator links San Diego–Tijuana, the most-trafficked international border checkpoint in the Western hemisphere, with the Strait of Gibraltar and the Mediterranean, where waves of migrants and refugees from North Africa and Syria flow across "Fortress Europe"; the Israeli-Palestinian border that divides the Middle East; the ongoing territorial conflict between Pakistan and India at Kashmir; and the border between North and South Korea, representing decades of intractable conflict and carrying Cold War tensions forward to the present day.

CONFLICT URBANIZATIONS: VISUALIZING THE POLITICAL

HEMISPHERIC ASYMMETRIES
The world is divided between enclaves of wealth, abundance and consumption, and sites of poverty, precarity and need.

UNEVEN URBANIZATION
The neoliberal urban explosion in global capitals coincided with the explosive growth of informal settlements across the world.

CONFLICT URBANIZATIONS: VISUALIZING THE POLITICAL

MIGRANTS GO NORTH

Cross-hemispheric flows across the Political Equator have particular socio-spatial implications in the San Diego–Tijuana border region, where these circulations "hit the ground." In the last years, we have witnessed unprecedented flows of migrants moving northward seeking asylum and the more stable economies of the Global North, as they seek to escape violence and political, economic and environmental strife.

RIVERS OF HUMANITY
Calling this flow of immigrants a "caravan" dehumanizes the individual and her family. When she is depicted within a mass of others, her stories, her struggles are obliterated. It has been particularly devastating in recent years to witness the emotional impact on children.

REMITTANCES GO SOUTH
When immigrants settle in cities across the Northern hemisphere their labor unleashes gigantic economic flows in the opposite direction, across the political equator, in the shape of remittances. In Mexico alone this amounts to more than 20 billion dollars per year in recent years. These informal economic flows help to reduce poverty in cities across the Global South.

10 LARGEST REMITTANCE OUTFLOWS, 2019
REGIONS OF POVERTY

REMITTANCE-ARCHITECTURES
These informal cross-hemispheric economic flows are spatialized in villages across the Global South. Remittances enable US-style McMansions to spring up in rural zones of Guatemala and Mexico, for example, as migrant workers in the US export their strange homage to the American Dream.

OUTSOURCING THE NORTH TO THE SOUTH
As migrant laborers move north multinationals seek the cheap labor markets of the Global South.

TERRITORIES OF LABOR
The Global South is home to most assembly factories in the world, where wages are low and child labor is rampant. These maquiladoras service corporate production chains, headquartered in global capitals across the world, and cater to their consumerist economies.

VACCINES GO NORTH
The COVID-19 pandemic exposed inequality across the world. As vaccines became available, doses were concentrated in the Global North. In January of 2021, there were 10 vaccine doses per eligible person in the US and Europe, while only 1 vaccine per 10 people in the Global South.

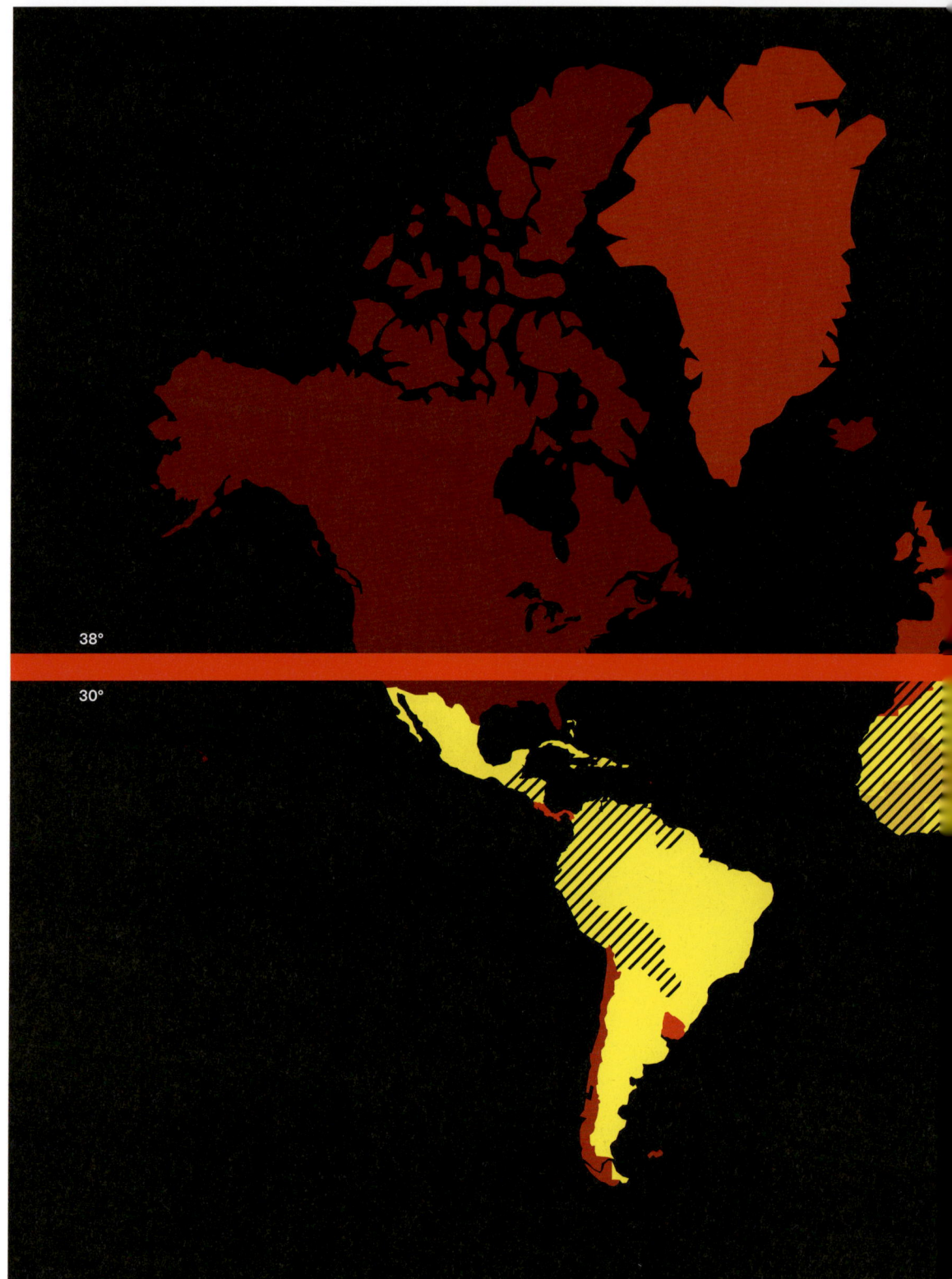

CLIMATE INJUSTICE
In red: greenhouse gas emissions by country. In yellow: negative climate change impact on human well-being. The richest one billion people on the planet are responsible for about 50% of greenhouse gas emissions, while the poorest three billion, without access to affordable fossil fuels, are responsible for about 5%. In contrast, the "bottom 3 billion" suffer the greatest harms associated with climate change.[23]

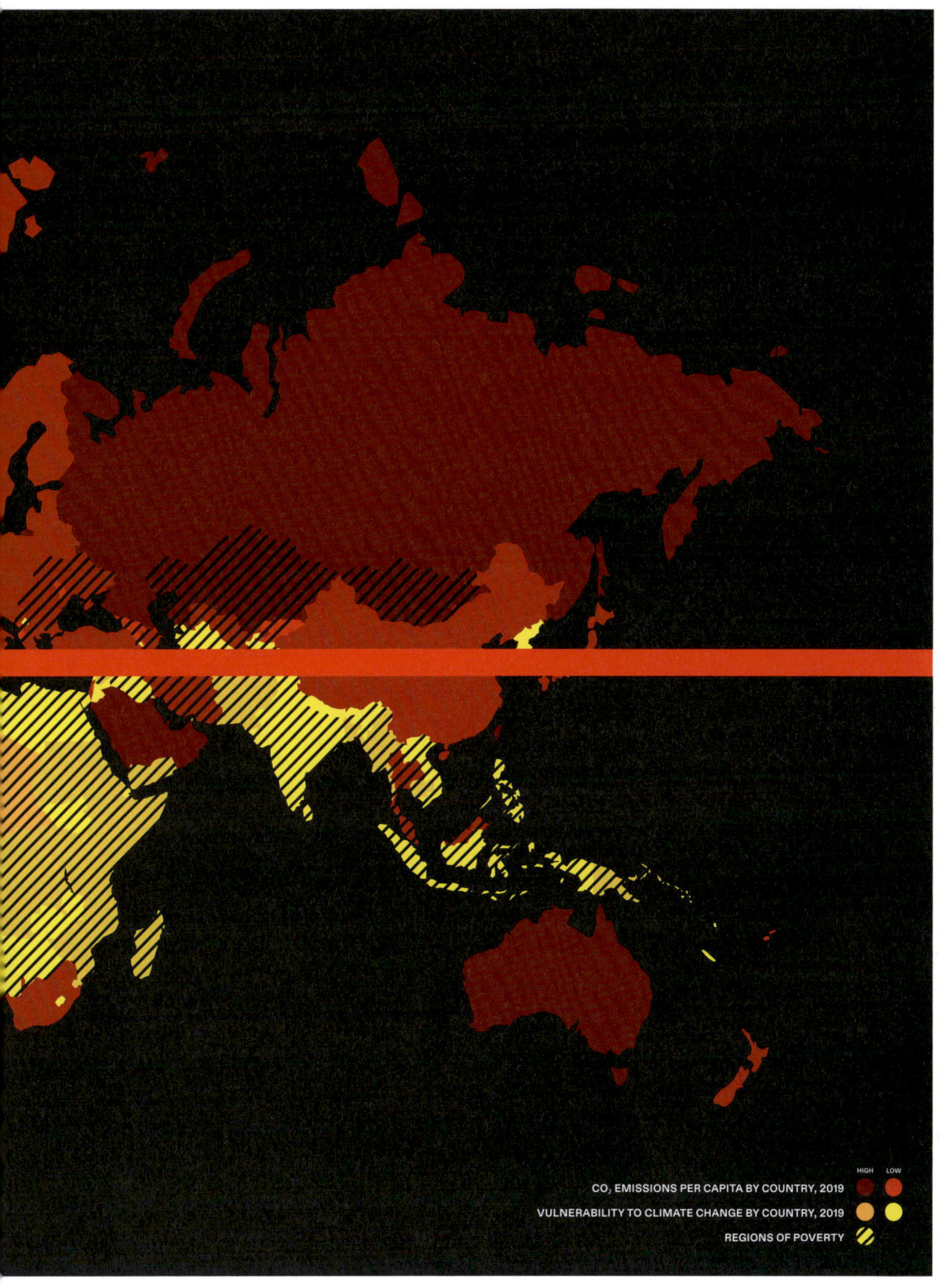

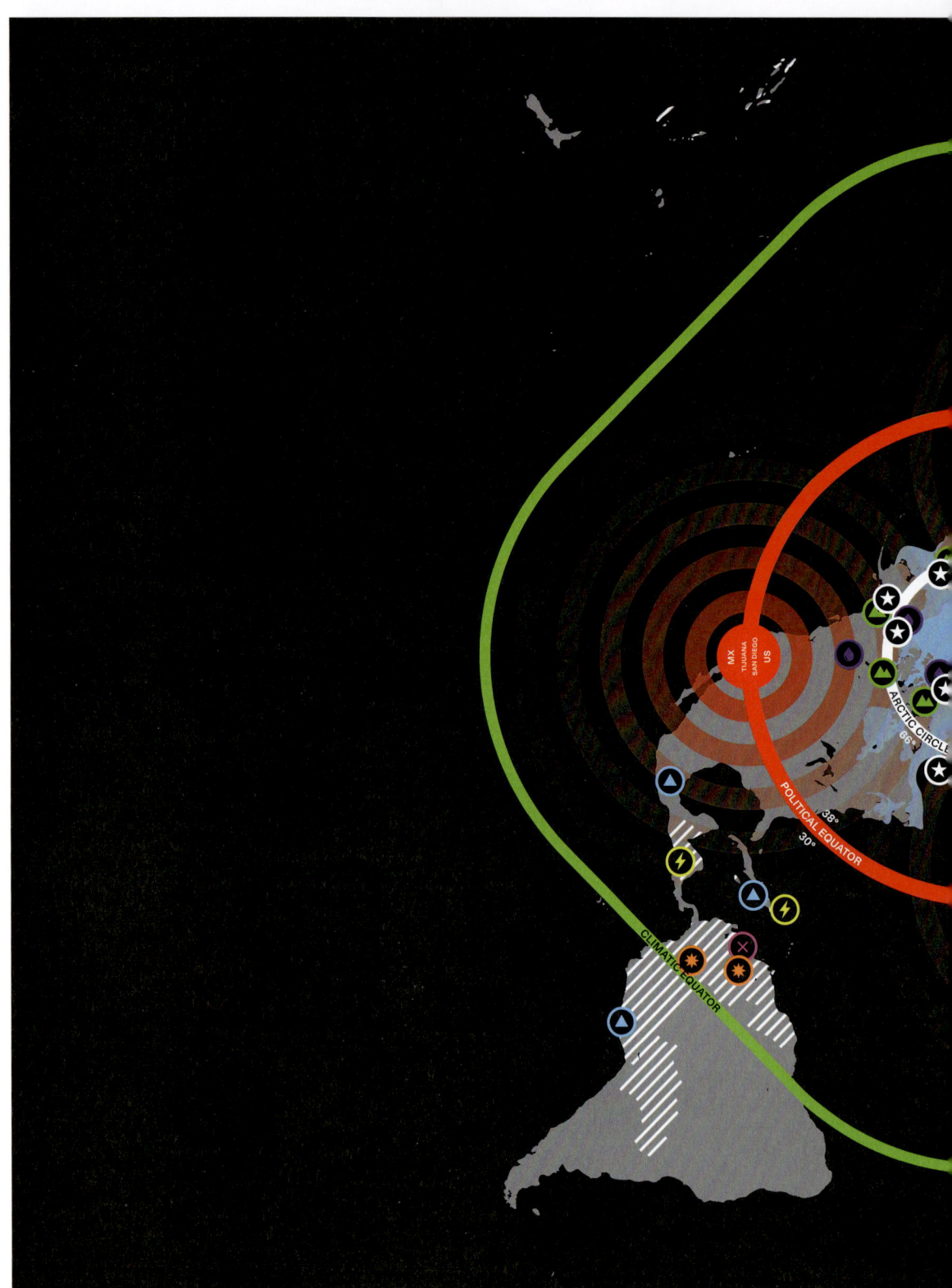

CLIMATE CHANGE IS A FORCE MULTIPLIER
When the climatic and political equators are applied to the Peirce quincuncial projection of the earth, the North Pole becomes protagonist, with its melting ice cap detonating sea-level rise, dramatic coastal vulnerabilities and human displacement.

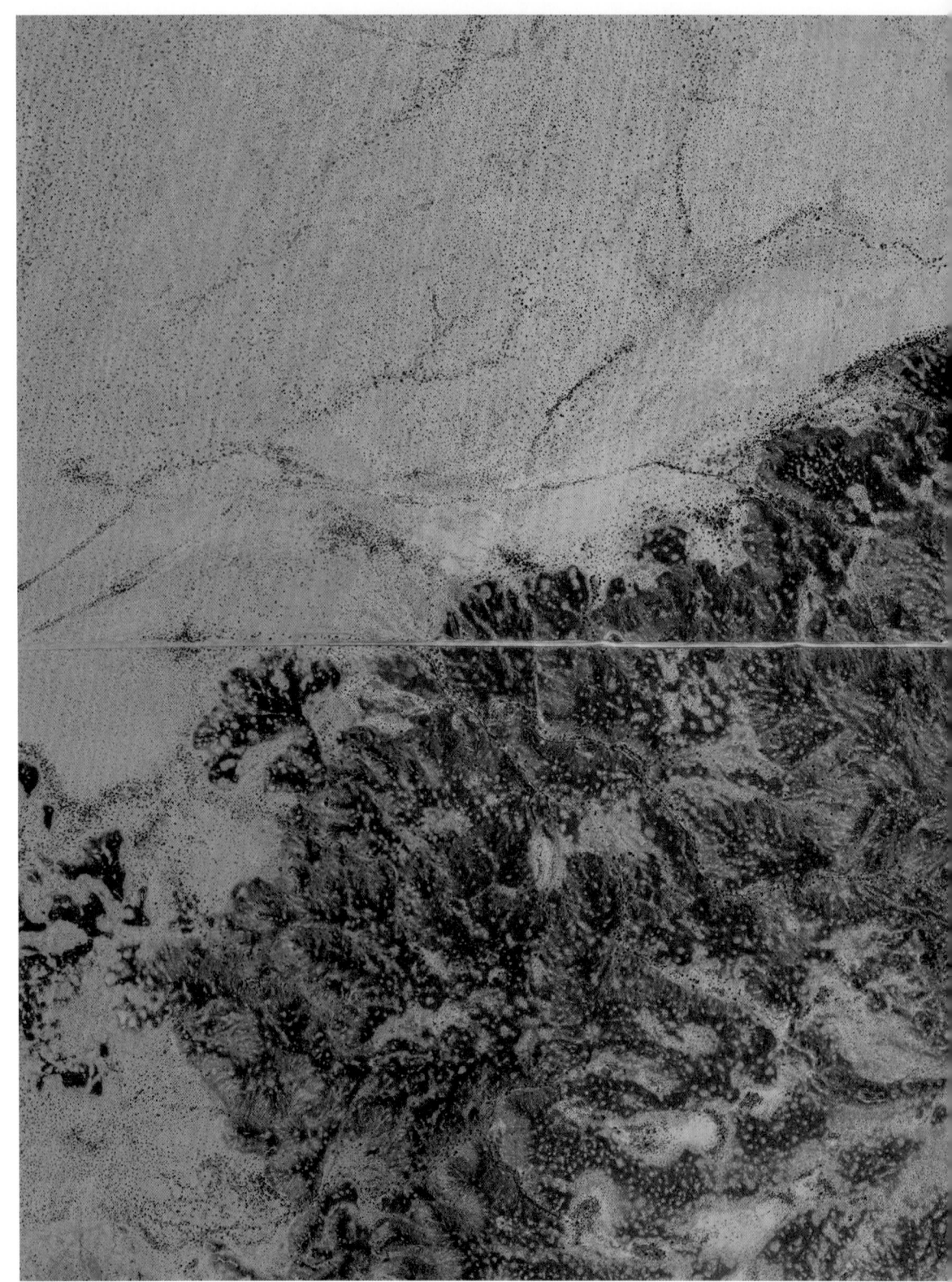

THE NATION AGAINST NATURE
The Political Equator is physicalized along the US-Mexico border. By building a new border wall against the "other," the United States violates its own natural resources, and those of Mexico.

"DUMB SOVEREIGNTY"
Archived aerial images depicting moments of collision between natural systems and the political line along the entire trajectory of the continental border, transforming the wall into a self-inflicted environmental wound.

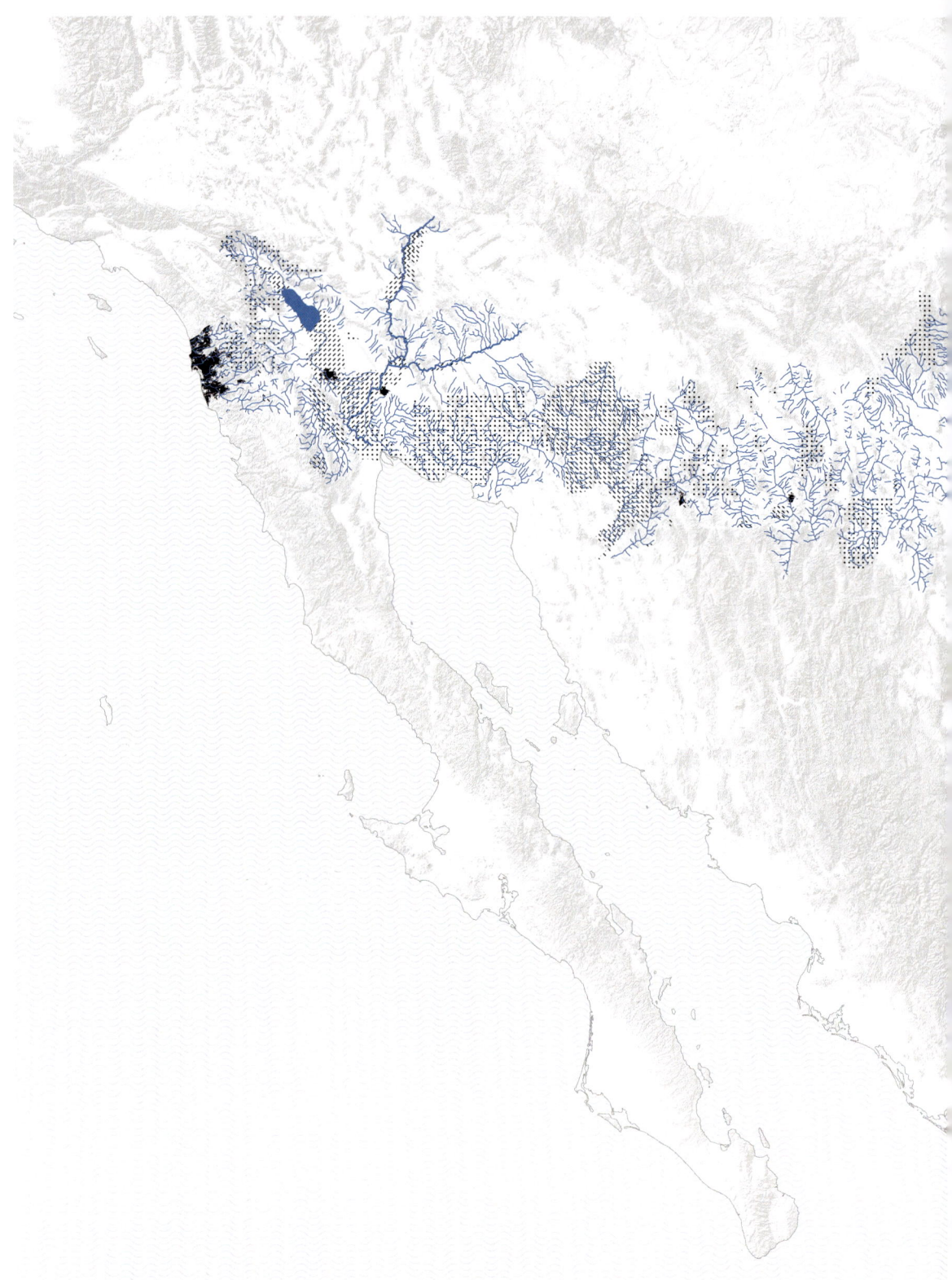

MEXUS: A GEOGRAPHY OF INTERDEPENDENCE

Instead of a flat line imposed by the nation onto complex territory, *MEXUS* presents the US-Mexico border as a 410,000 km² bioregion, a thickened set of ecologies whose shape is defined by the eight binational watershed systems that are shared between the US and Mexico. We have visualized the border as a shared region made of water, comprised of what walls cannot contain: hydrographic basins, indigenous lands, ecological corridors, wildlife corridors and migratory patterns.

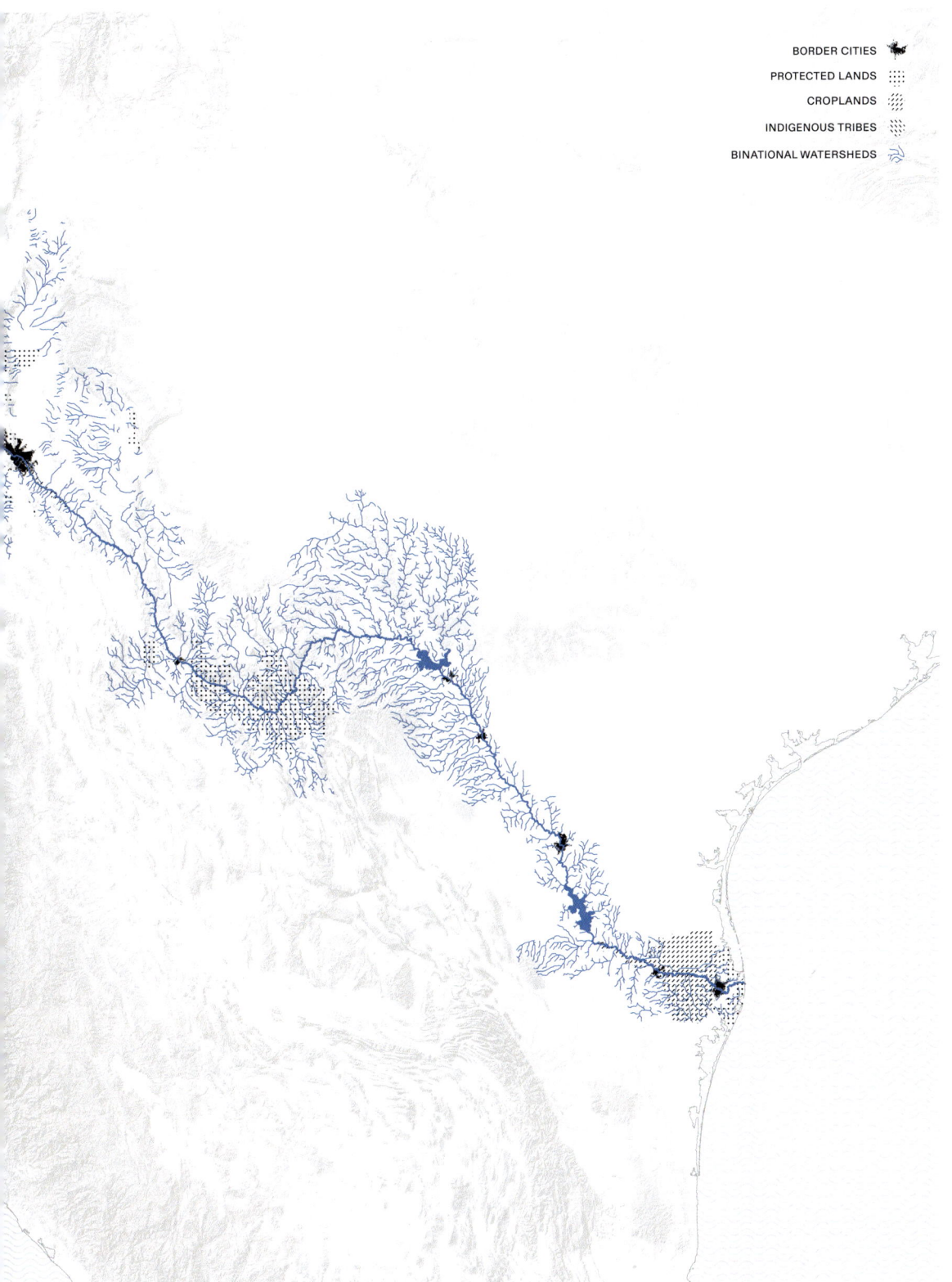

MEXUS: A Geography of Interdependence was exhibited in *Dimensions of Citizenship*, in the US Pavilion at the 18th Venice Architecture Biennale in 2018.

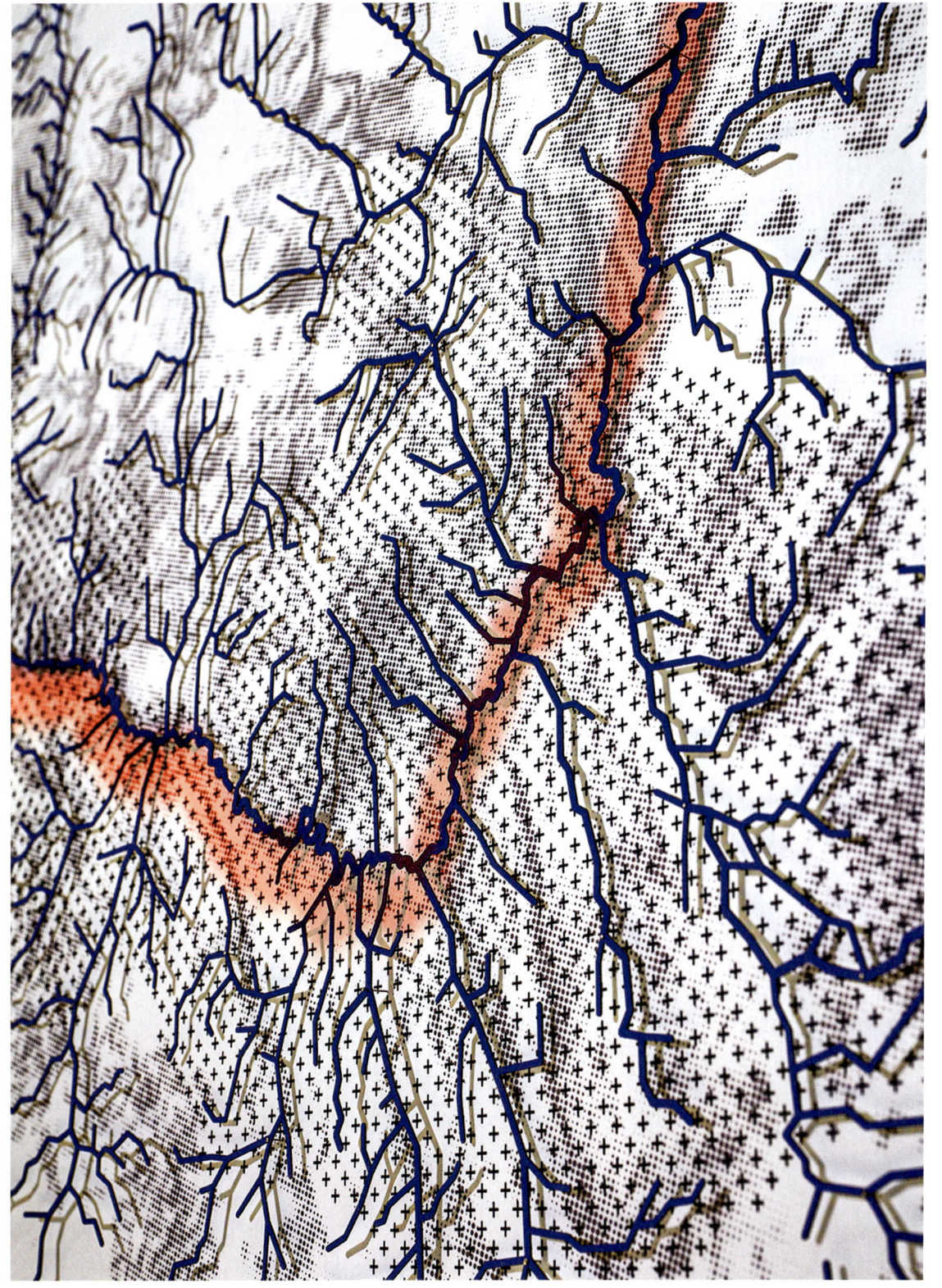

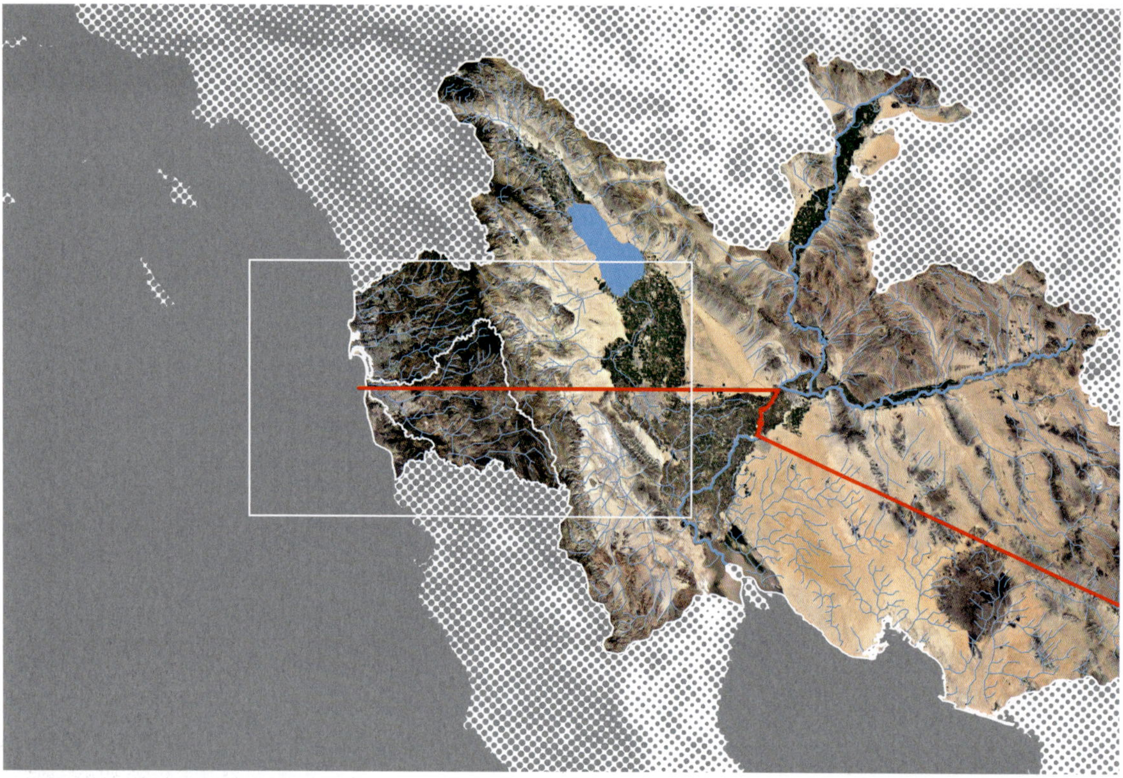

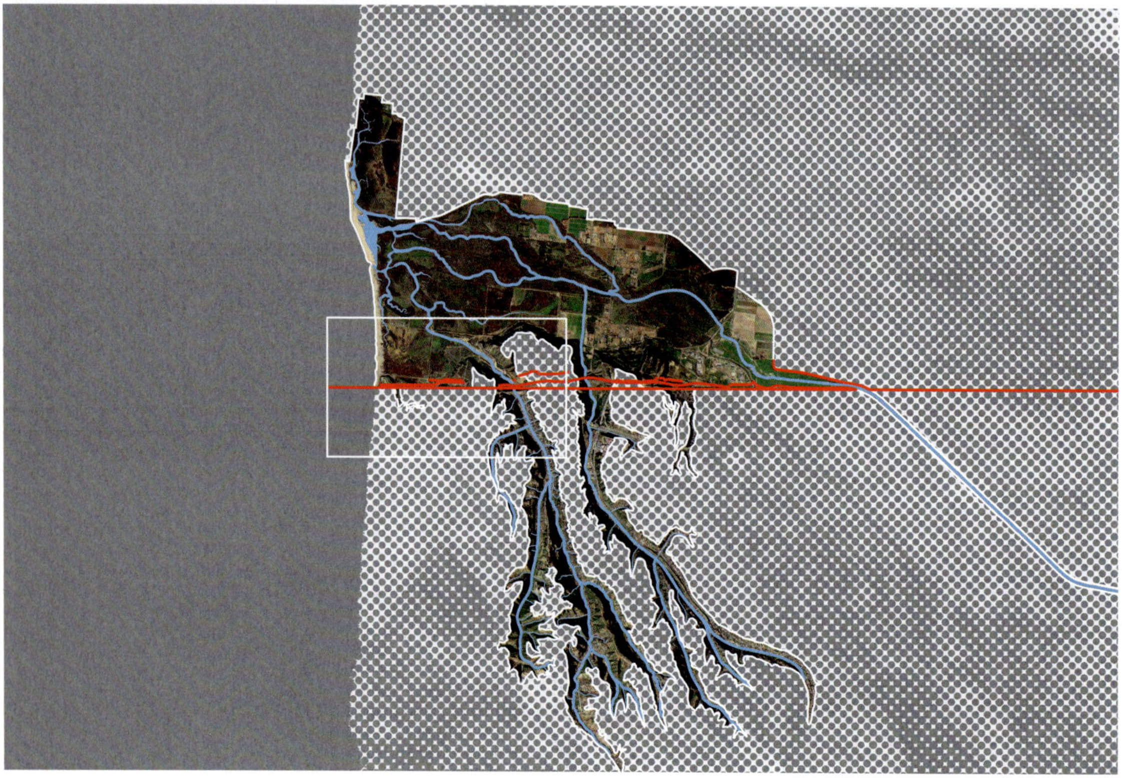

LOCALIZING *MEXUS*
Above: Zooming deeper into MEXUS, we arrive at the westernmost watershed, the Tijuana River watershed in the San Diego-Tijuana region.
Below: At this juncture, the topography of Tijuana's canyons clashes with the border wall before spilling into the estuary valley below. Here, the collision between ecological and political priorities is profound.

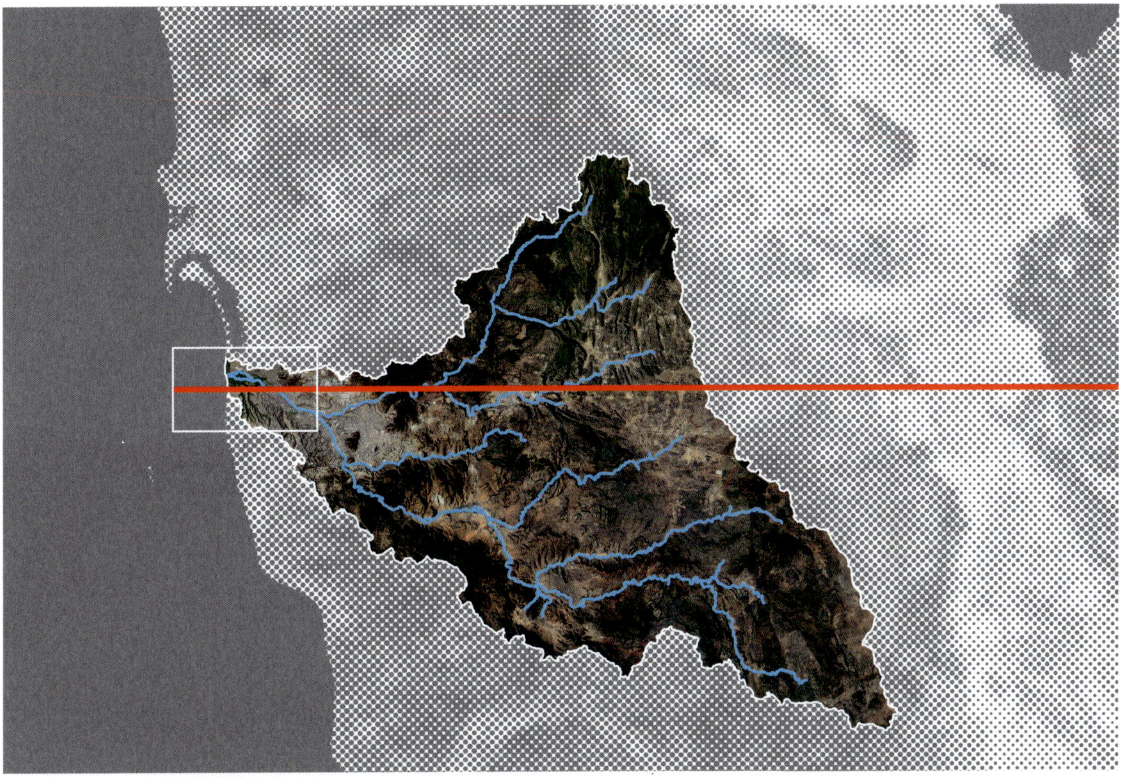

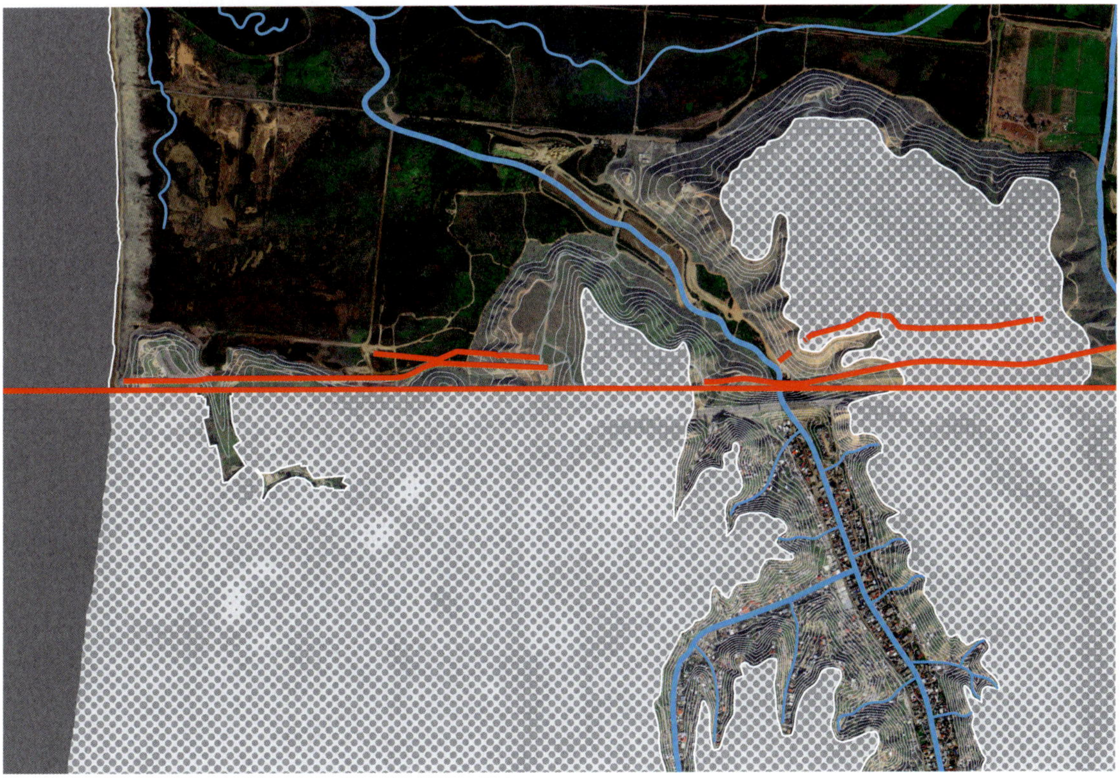

Above: The Tijuana River watershed system is bisected by the wall.
Below: As we zoom in further, we witness a collision between the US estuary, the border wall and an informal Tijuana settlement of 92,000 people.
(The red lines show the multilayered border walls built by the US in recent years)

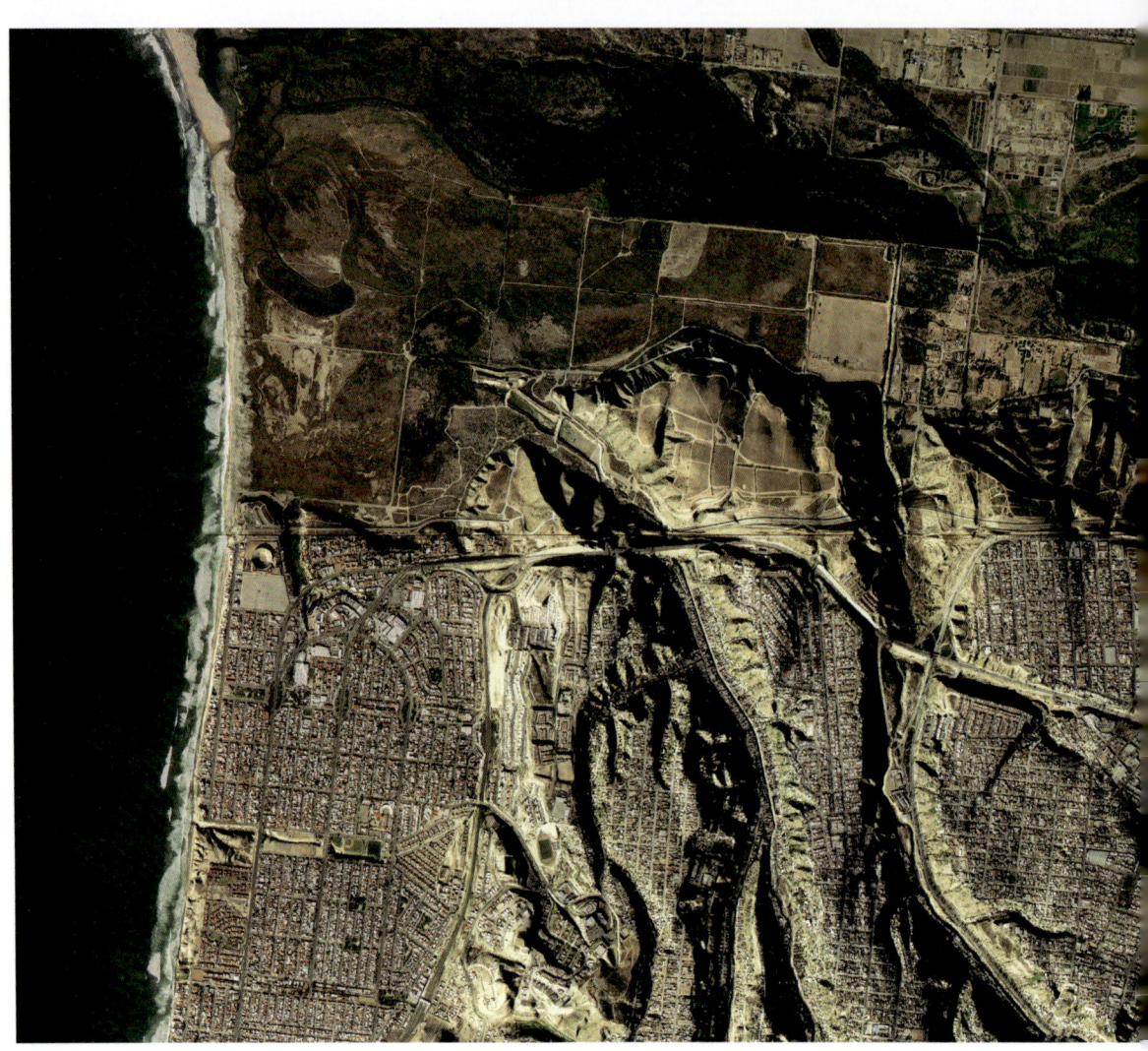

BROKEN NATURE
The conflict between the natural and jurisdictional.

A CONFLICT OBSERVATORY

Standing high on a promontory overlooking Tijuana's Los Laureles Canyon and the border wall, one witnesses the intersection of poverty, urban informality, migration, militarization and environmentalism—localizing global conflicts across the Political Equator.

INFRASTRUCTURES OF INSECURITY

With the construction of the new border wall and its concrete dams and drainage systems, the US has further truncated the canyons that travel northward from Tijuana. This has accelerated the water flows from the upper informal settlement basins into the valley and the estuary below, syphoning tons of trash and sediment with each rainy season and contaminating the "lungs" of the bioregion. Here, the border wall is an artifact of environmental insecurity.

CONFLICT URBANIZATIONS: VISUALIZING THE POLITICAL

COMMON PROBLEMS: MUTUAL RESPONSIBILITIES?
The Mexican settlement lacks water and waste management infrastructure, and dump sites are distributed across the Los Laureles Canyon sub-basin. Border building in recent years has intensified ecosocial and economic impacts, exacerbated by a lack of collaboration between San Diego and Tijuana to manage these cross-border flows.

CONFLICT URBANIZATIONS: VISUALIZING THE POLITICAL

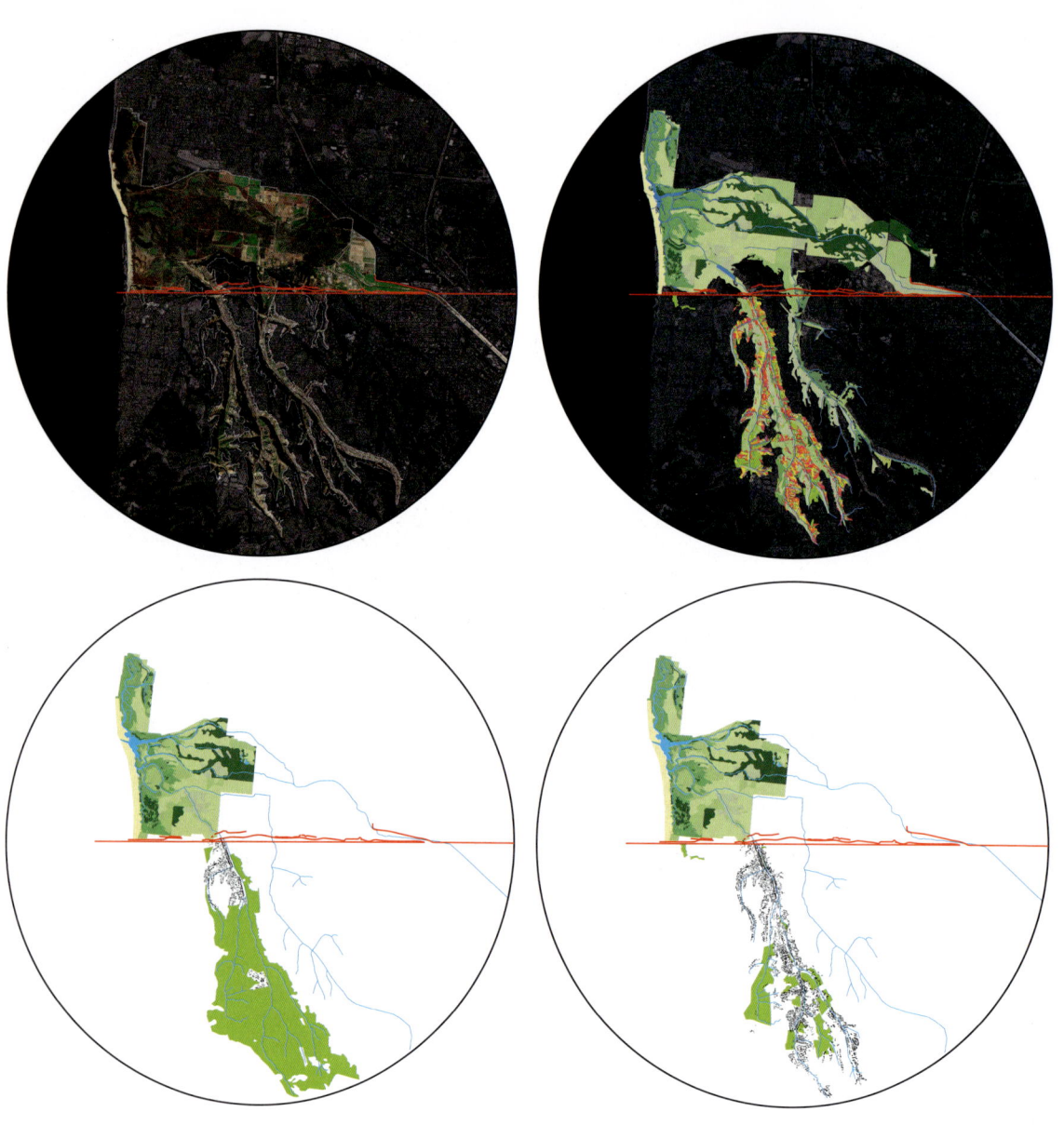

AN ARCHIPELAGO OF CONSERVATION

In the last decades, 70% of the open lands in Los Laureles Canyon has been lost to irregular urban growth. With our partners in Tijuana, we are identifying and bundling remaining undeveloped lands in the informal settlement that can still be rescued in order to secure them as an *archipelago of conservation*.

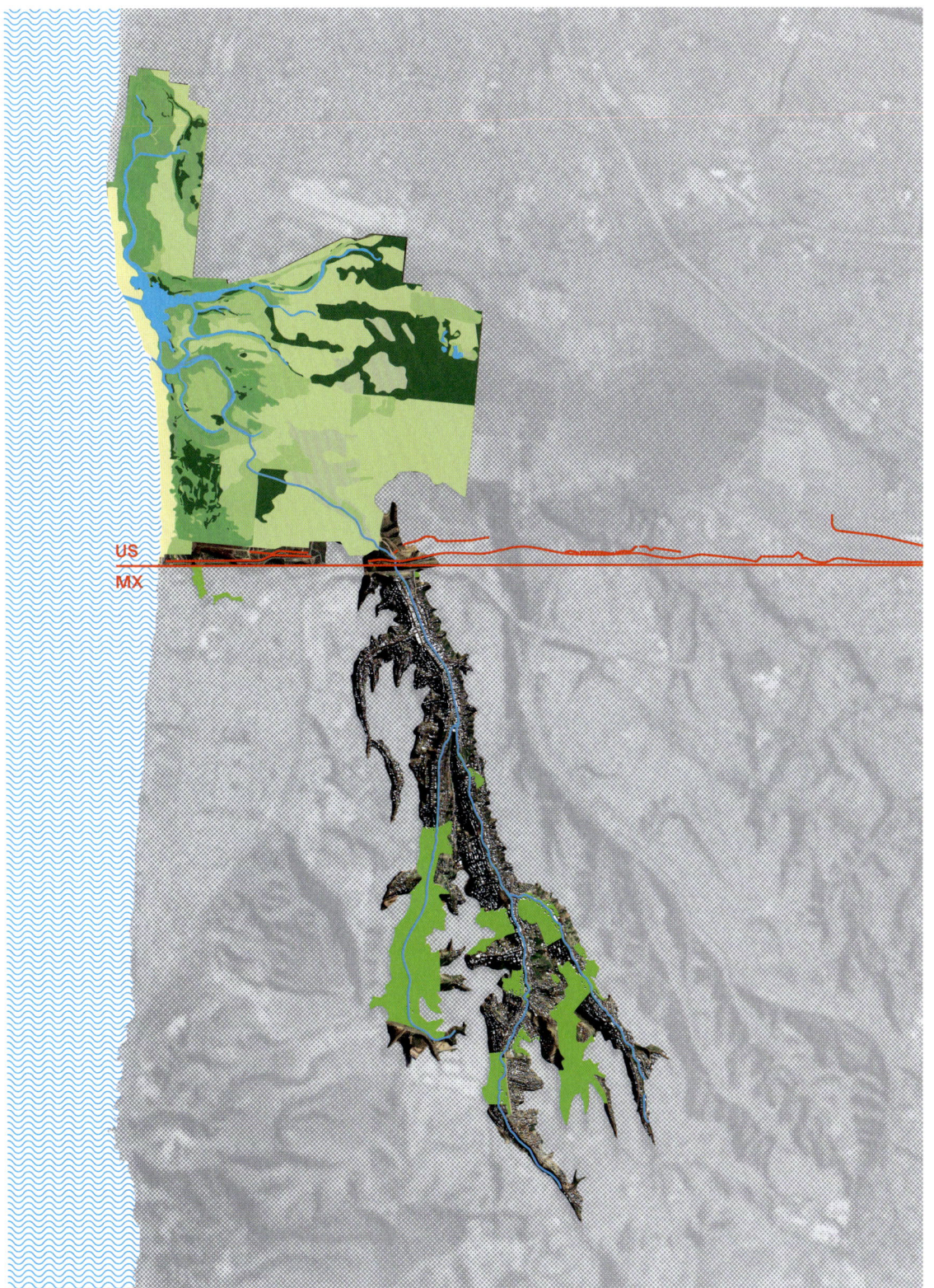

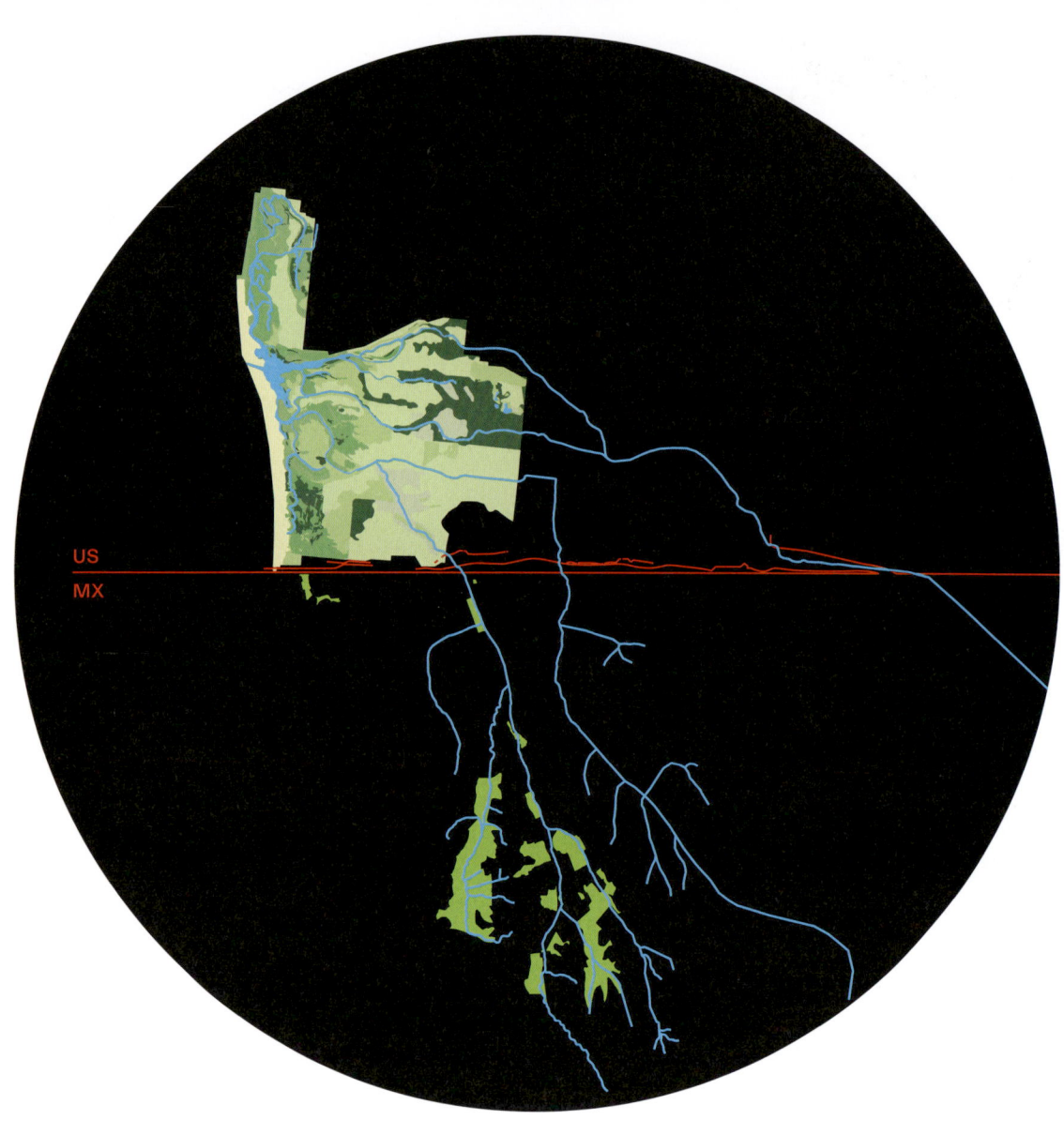

THE CROSS-BORDER COMMONS
With our partners in Tijuana, we are stewarding a transnational environmental conservancy initiative that links the estuary in San Diego with the archipelago of conservation in the informal settlement in Tijuana, forming a continuous social-ecological system.

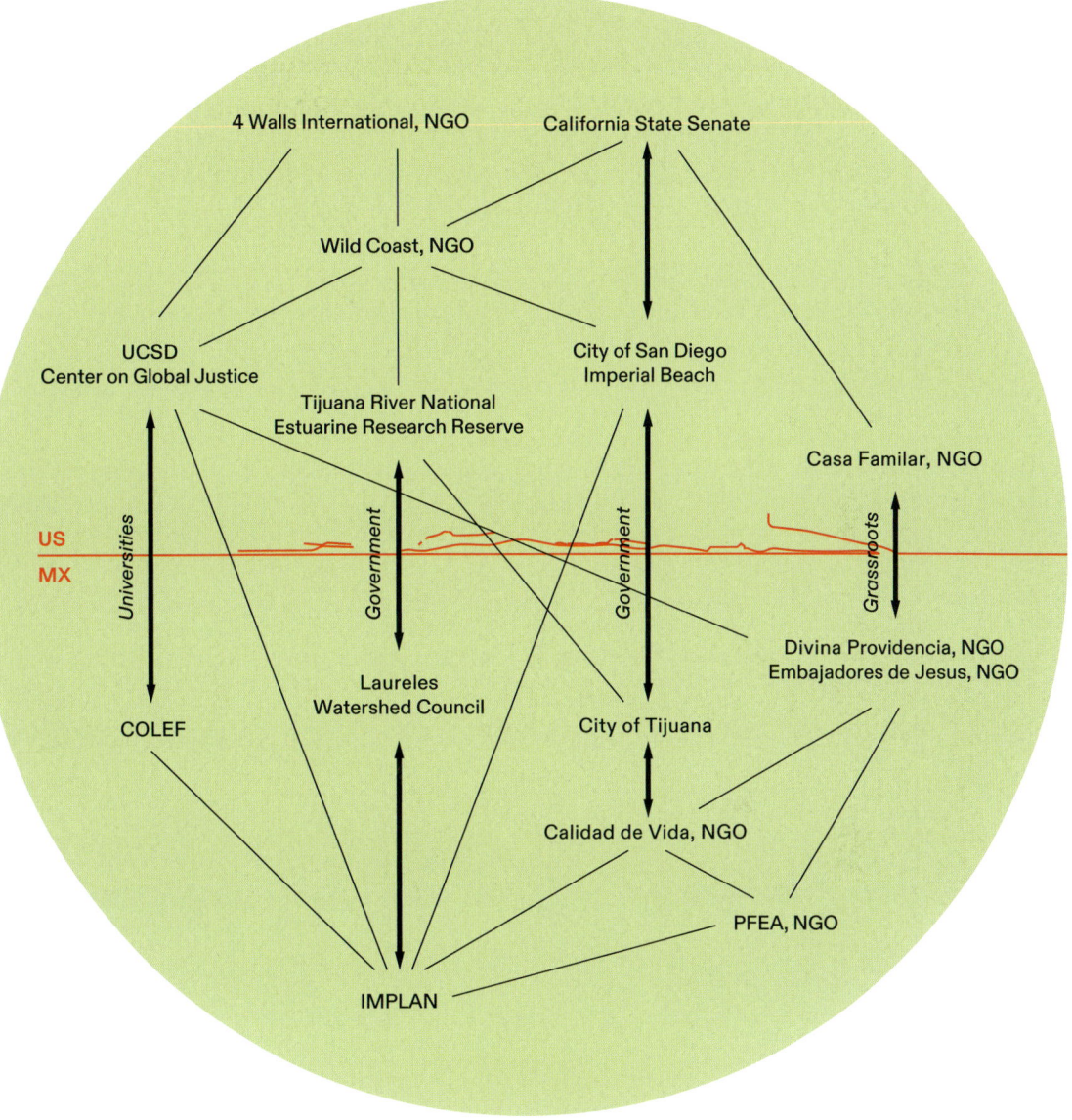

INVESTING IN A COMMON DESTINY
We are summoning a coalition of state and municipal agencies, grassroots organizations and universities on both sides of the border to collectively invest in environmental programming to sustain this shared cross-border commons.

GREEN CROSS-BORDER STITCH
This unorthodox binational land conservancy expands notions of conservation beyond protection, activating green infrastructure with specific environmental, pedagogical and social programming. With local community groups, we are co-developing some of these slivers as public spaces with a double function: water-waste management infrastructure and pedagogical nodes, to protect the shared hydrological-environmental resources of the bioregion.

CLIMATE ADAPTATION FROM BELOW

This has included bottom-up socio-ecological planning to inject many of the archipelago's islands with nature-based solutions, eco-strategies and eco-technologies to restore the habitat and support biodiversity. These include: native plant restoration, reforestation and deep root planting on slopes, water catchment and stream daylighting, erosion control along water routes, constructed mini-wetlands, gray water hydro-filtration channels, swales and kumeyaay rock drop infrastructure, rewilding through revegetation, gabion terracing and eco-technologies for slope stabilization, topsoil regeneration and activation, native plants seed propagation for pollinators, removal of high-risk non-native species, establishing and reinforcing biodiversity corridors and support systems for bird and animal migration.

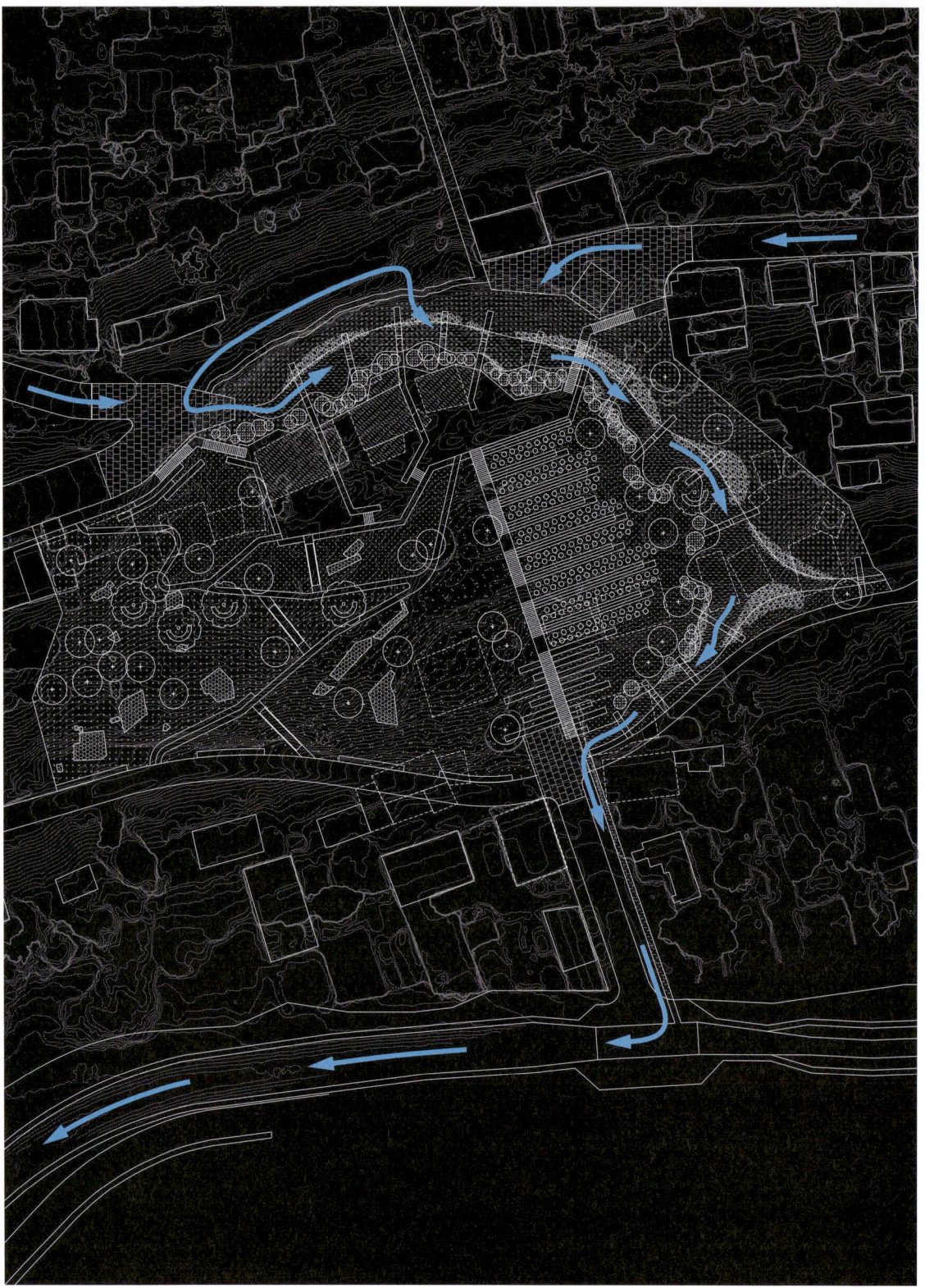

MIRAMAR HYDRO-PEDAGOGIC PARK
The Municipality of Tijuana granted access to a parcel destroyed in 2015 by a landslide. In collaboration with the nonprofit Proyecto Fronterizo de Educación Ambiental (PFEA) we are advancing a regenerative hydro-pedagogic space for the Miramar community, restoring pedestrian circulation and directing rain runoff towards an open-air channel in the lower part of the canyon. The is the first prototype in the archipelago of conservation, part of the Cross-Border Commons.

CONSERVATION COMMUNITY BRIGADES

The topographic scar of the landslide became a dump site. We are transforming it into a hydrological promenade, a natural biofiltration channel designed to mitigate the risk of landslides and erosion; it also doubles as an ecological-educational walk. Miramar is both a green sponge and a node of conservation awareness, designed for the participation of local residents. We launched "community brigades" to steward the site.

60 LINEAR MILES OF CROSS-BORDER CONFLICT

From this geography of conflict, where informal settlement, border wall, and estuary collide, we trace a geographic cross-section between these border cities to visualize how the border wall and its jurisdictional rigidity is reproduced inland. Along this "local equator" trajectory lie a sequence of urban collisions, critical junctures, between natural and artificial ecologies, top-down forces of urban development and bottom-up social and ecological systems.

0 miles
san diego - tijuana: conflict between two border cities

10N miles
san diego: co

CONFLICT URBANIZATIONS: VISUALIZING THE POLITICAL

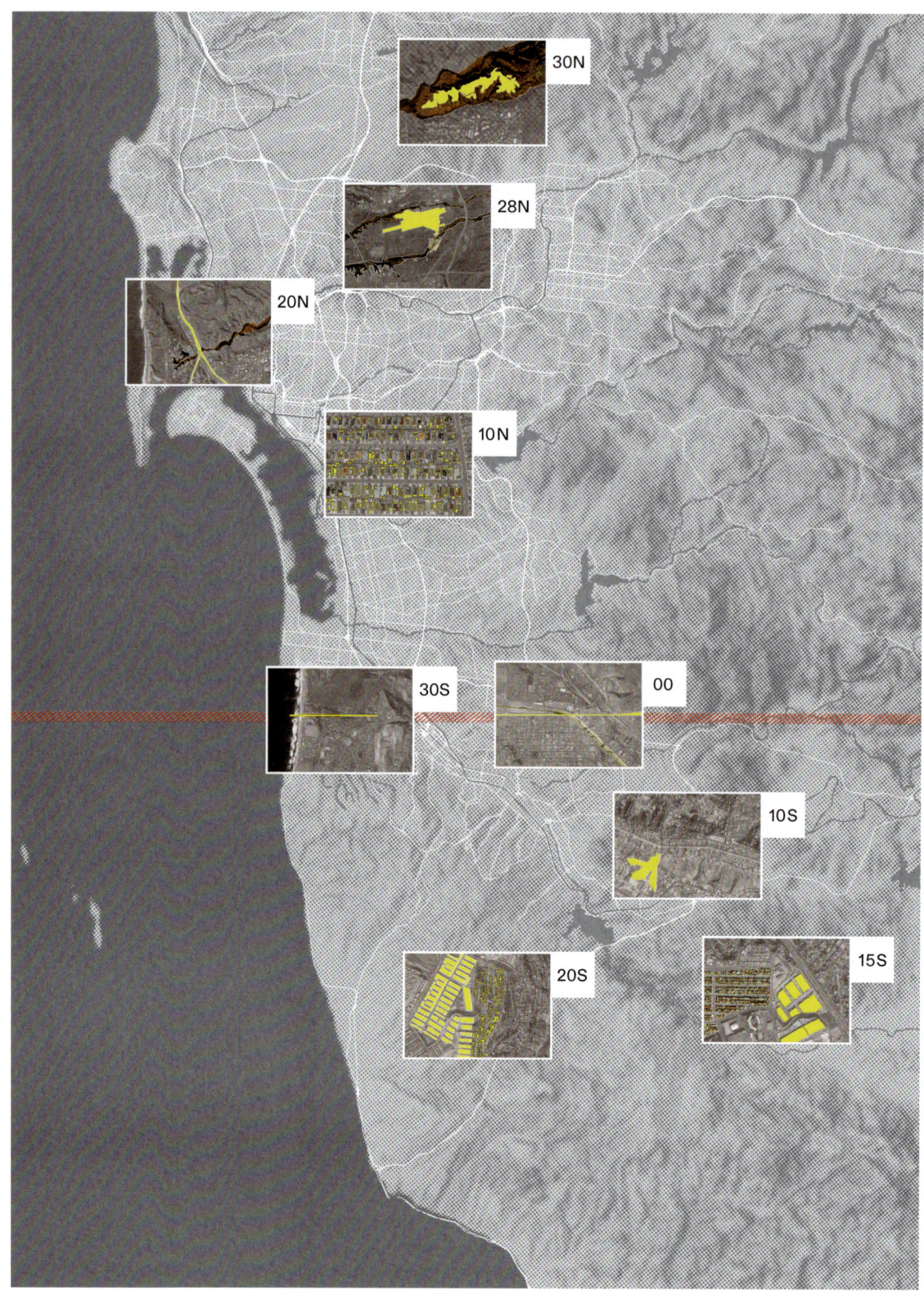

RADICALIZING THE LOCAL
We begin this transborder "cut" 30 miles north of the border, at the periphery of San Diego, and move southward across diverse urban borders. Then we enter Tijuana and meander 30 miles south of the wall, ending where the border wall sinks into the Pacific Ocean.

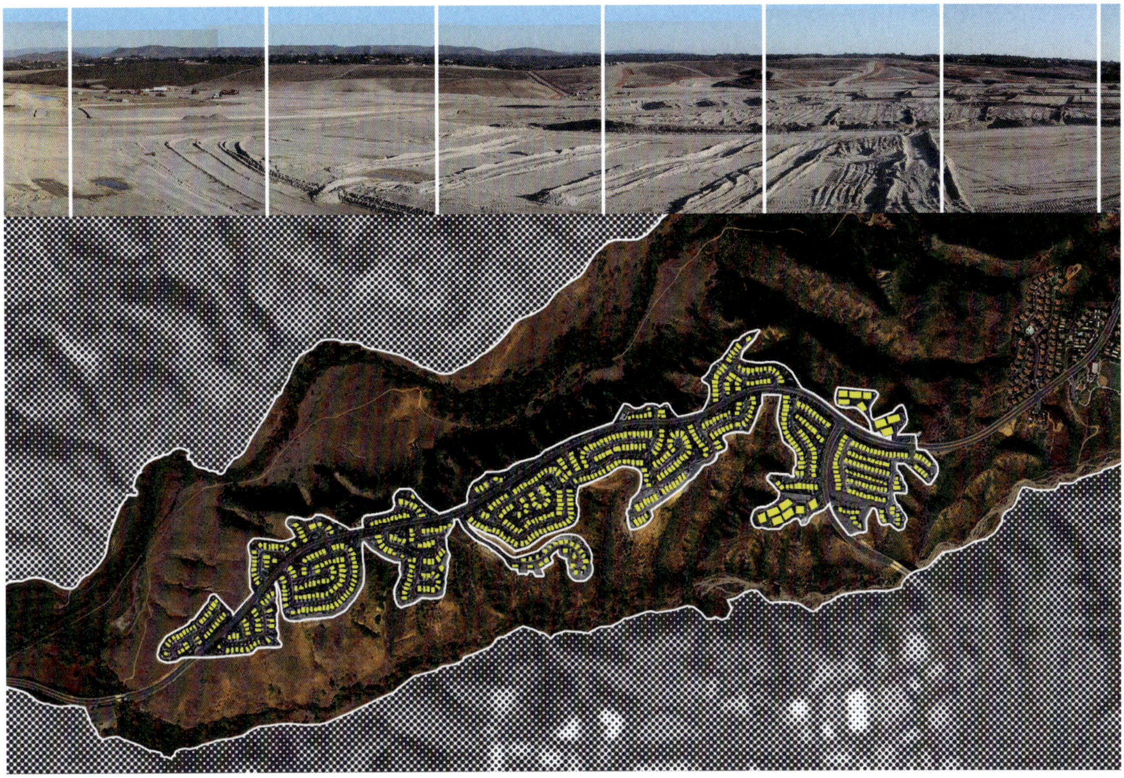

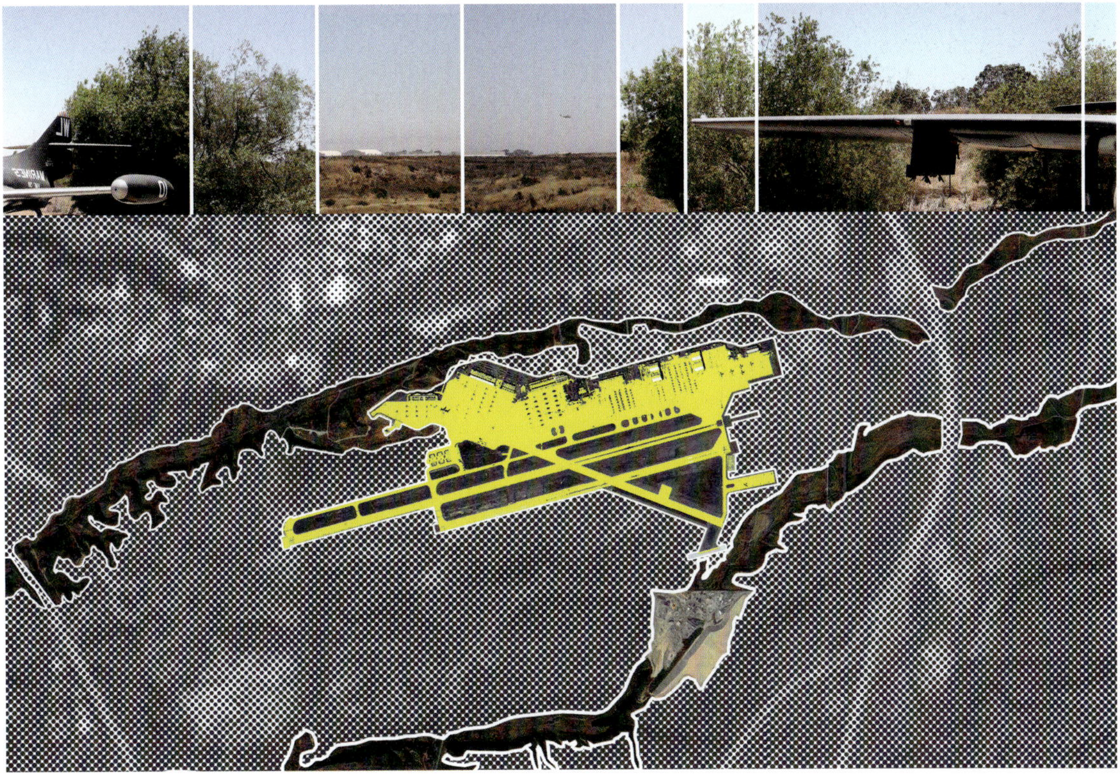

Above: Conflict between Top-Down Development and the Natural Topography
Below: Conflict between Military Bases and Environmental Zones

139

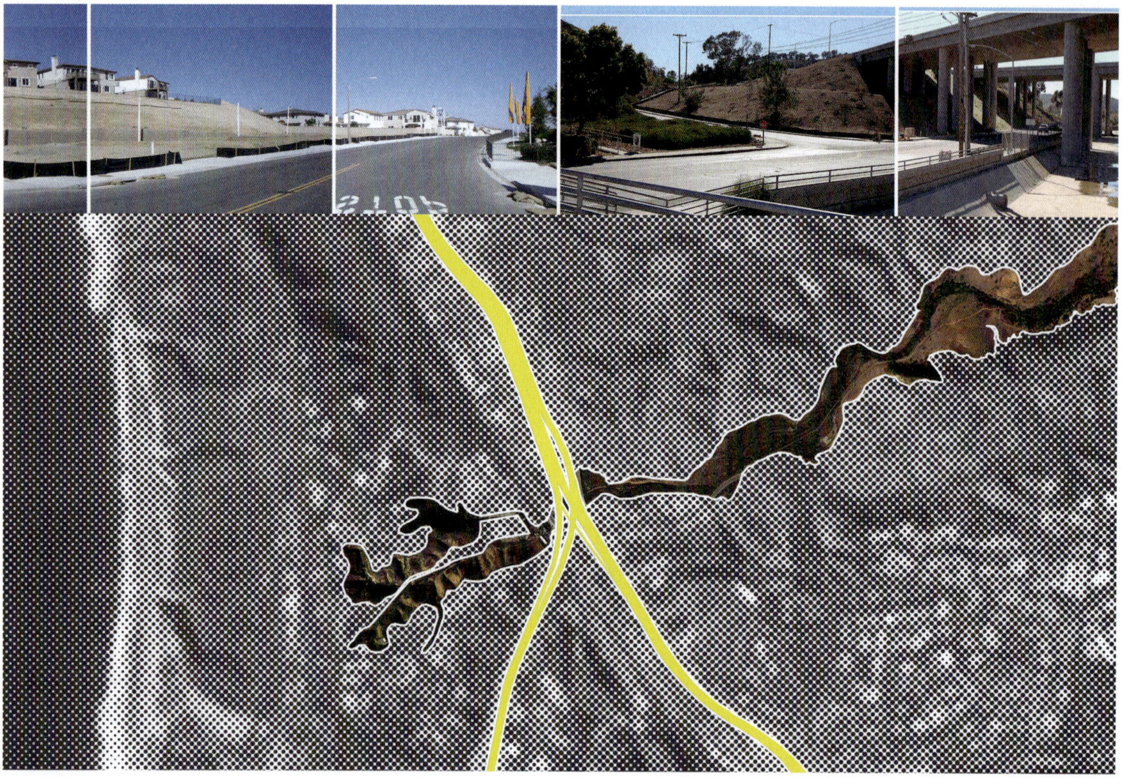

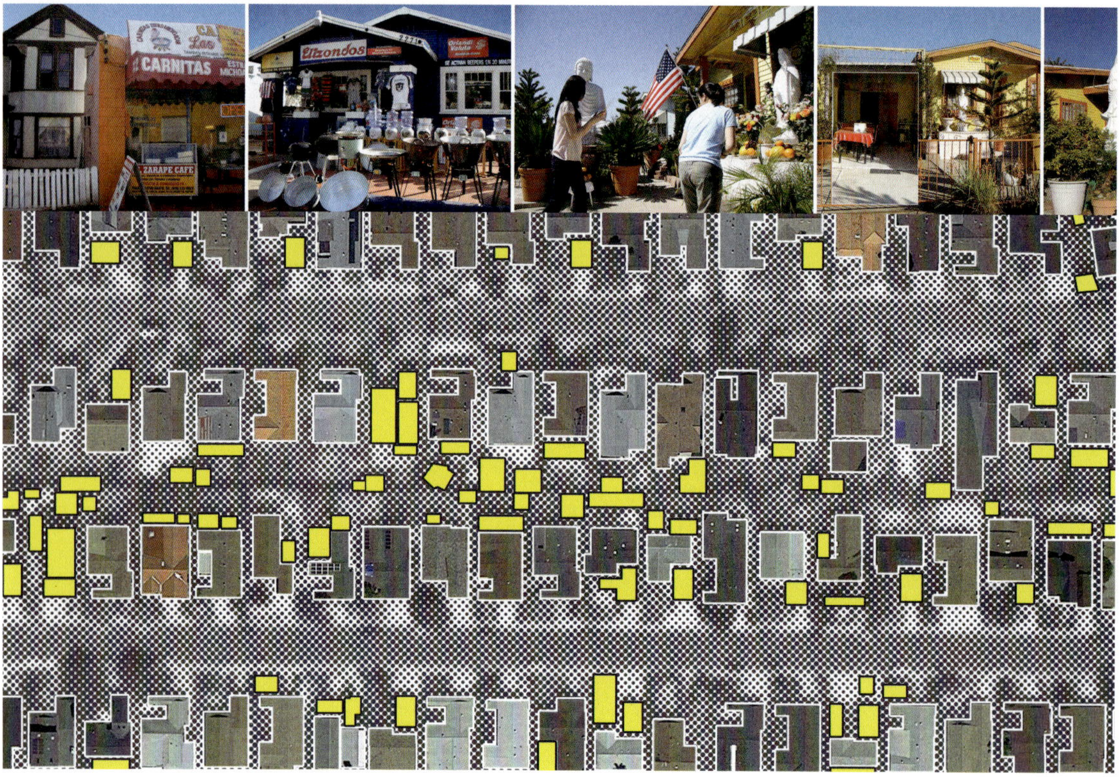

Above: Conflict between Large Infrastructure and Natural Hydrological Systems
Below: Conflict between Formal and Informal Urbanizations

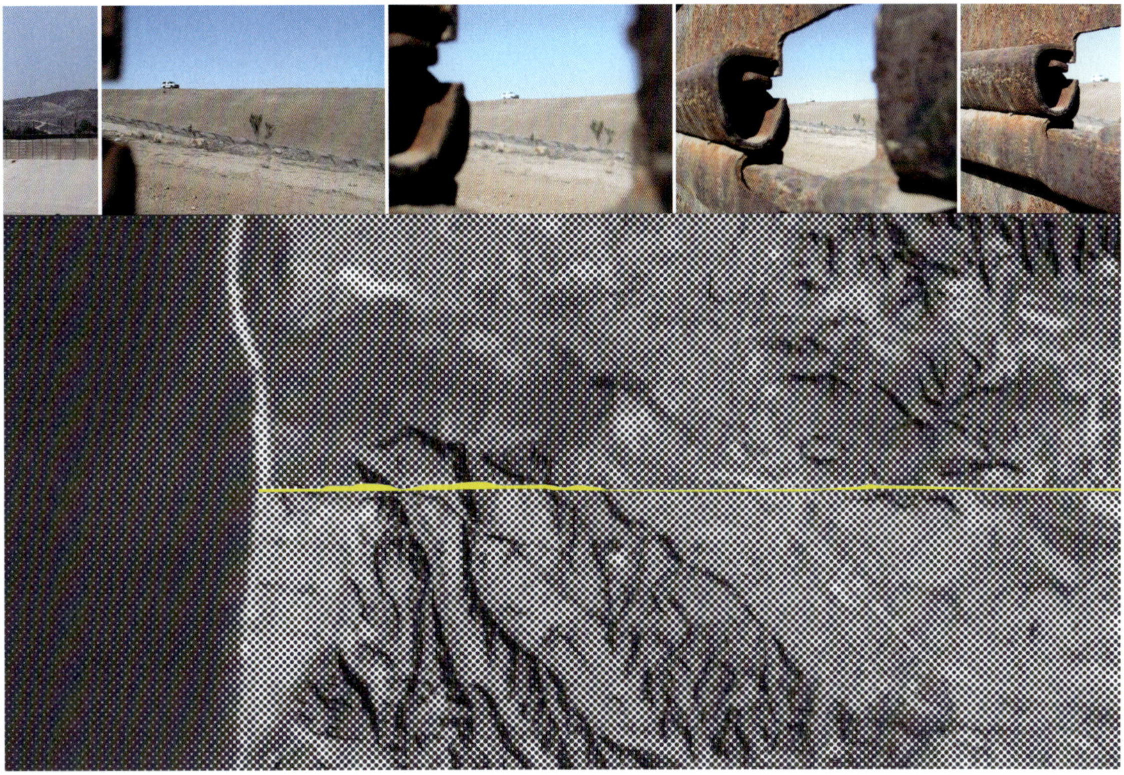

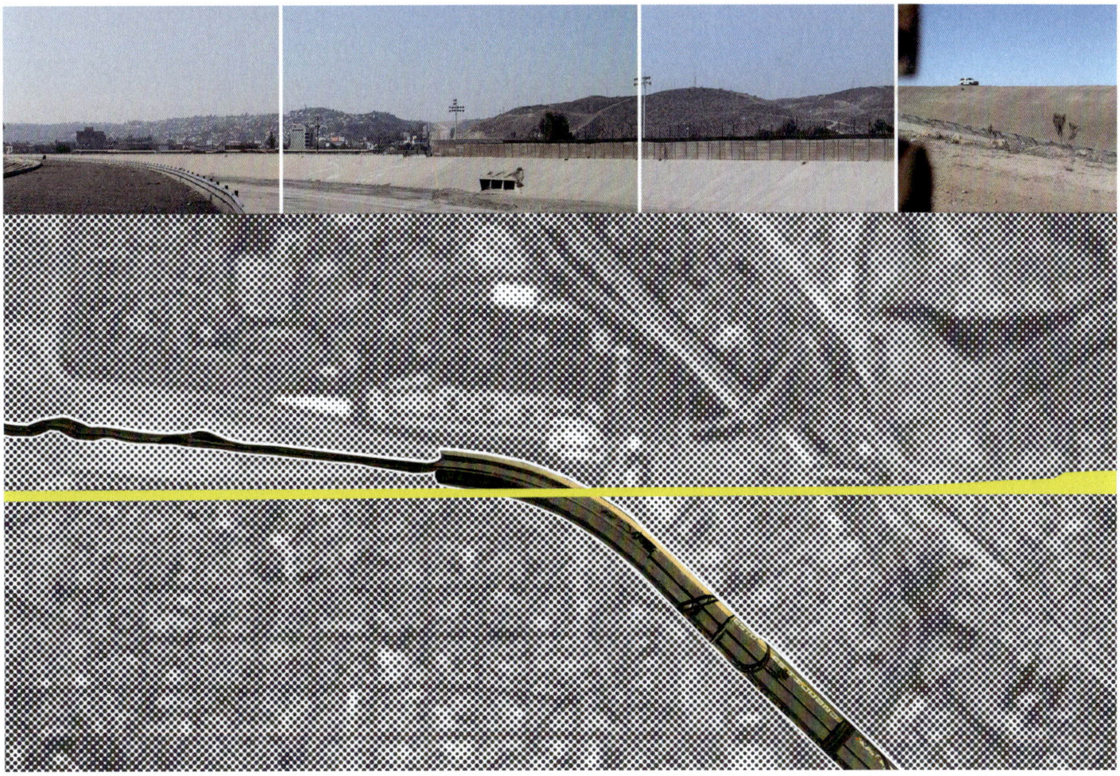

Above: Conflict between Jurisdictional and Topographic Boundaries
Below: Conflict between the Tijuana River and the Border Wall

141

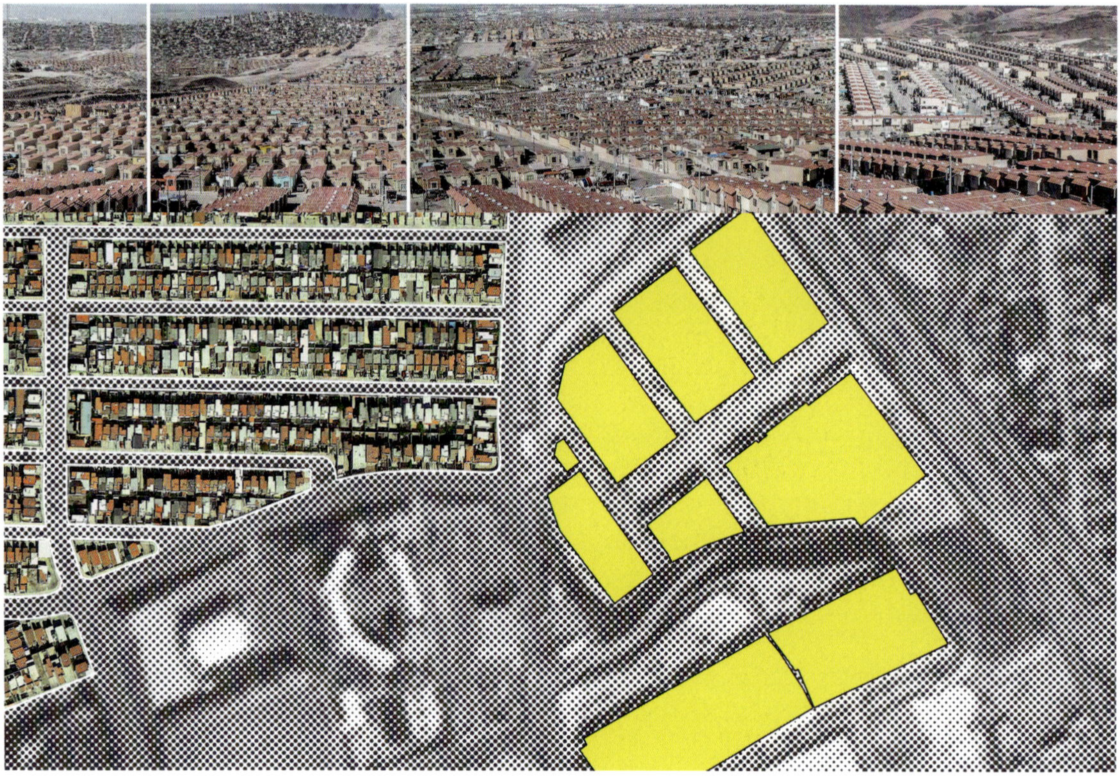

Above: Conflict between Informal Settlements and Natural Ecologies
Below: Conflict between Multinational Maquiladoras and Emergency Housing

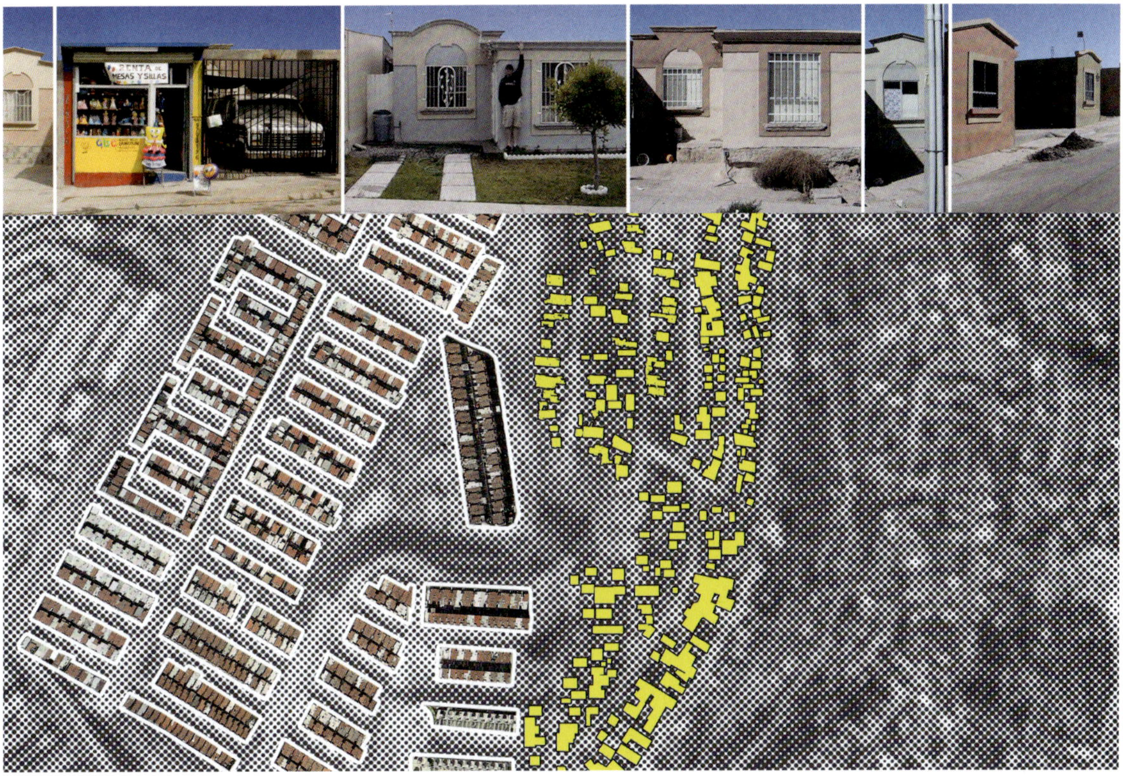

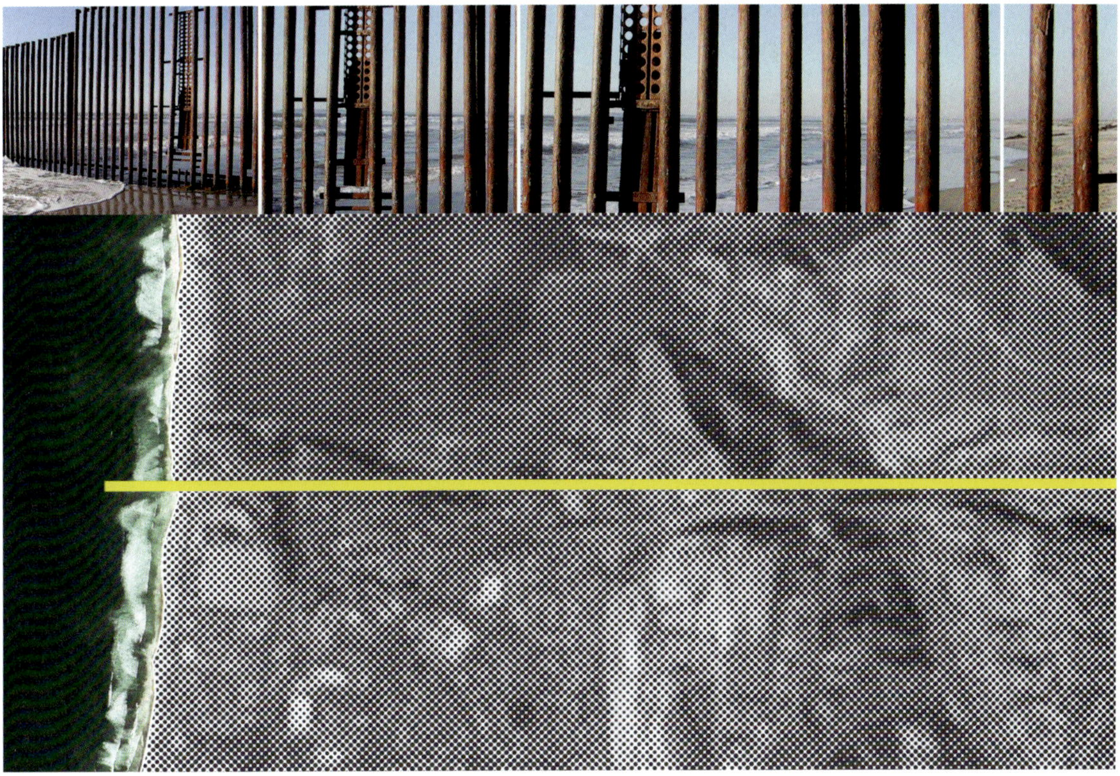

Above: Conflict between Density and Sprawl
Below: Conflict between the Political and the Natural

The *60 Linear Miles of Cross-Border Conflict* visual narrative was installed on the facade of the US Pavilion at the 2008 Venice Architecture Biennale, the very month the global economy collapsed and the Bush administration enforced its final wave of border securitization

CONFLICT URBANIZATIONS: VISUALIZING THE POLITICAL

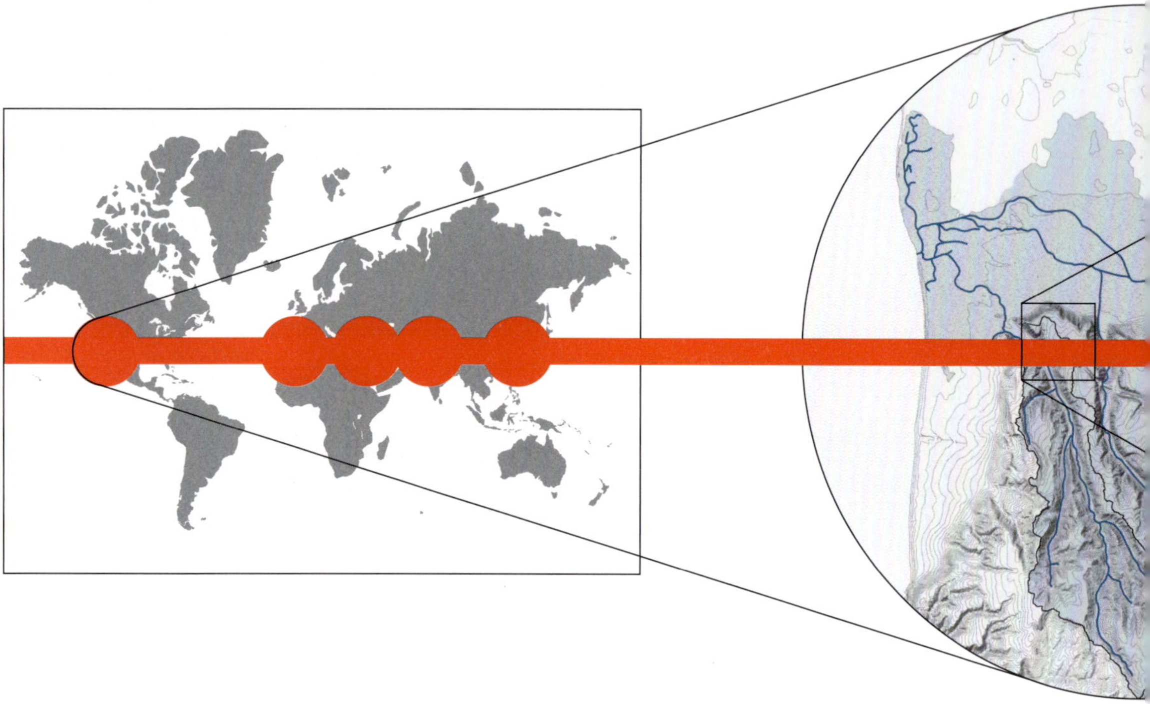

A PUBLIC ACTION AT THE BORDER

Our descent from the global border to the border neighborhoods, across planetary, continental, regional and local scales, culminates in the communities themselves that are divided by the border wall. In 2011, we curated an unprecedented cross-border public action, in collaboration with grassroots organizations that flank the border wall, at the intersection of the informal settlement in Tijuana and the estuary in San Diego. This public action was comprised of two acts: a Forum and a Border Crossing.

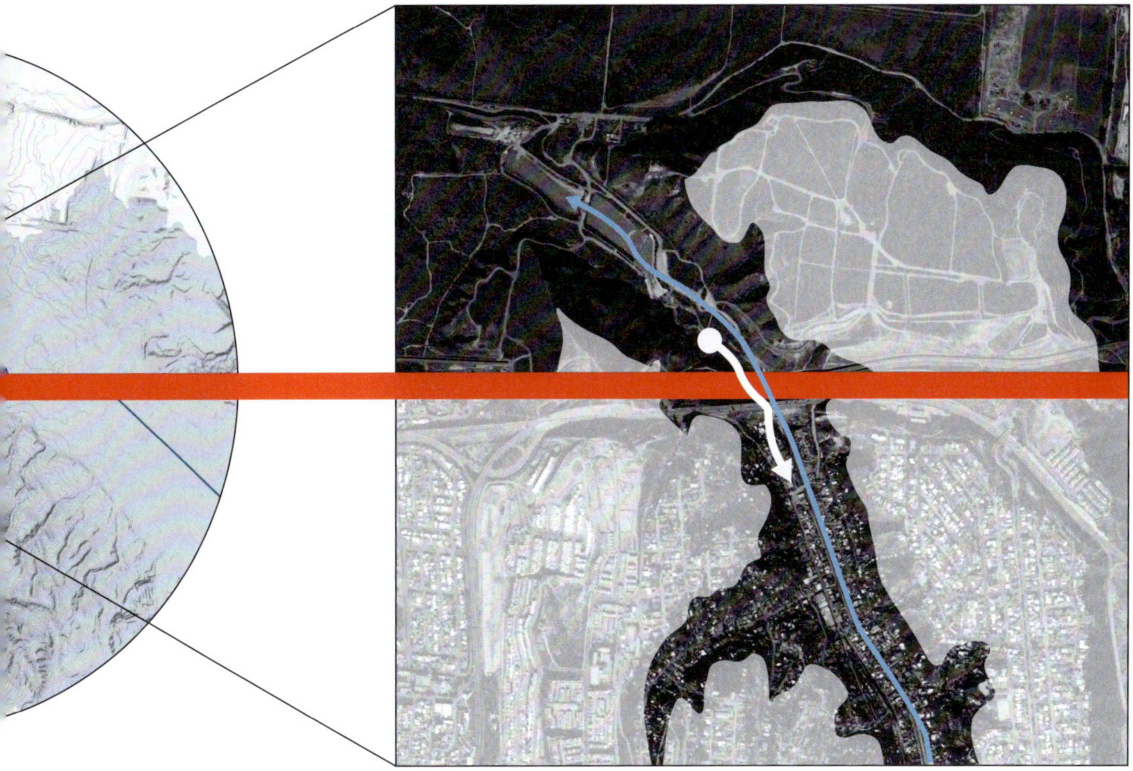

CONFLICT URBANIZATIONS: VISUALIZING THE POLITICAL

A BORDER FORUM
We pitched a tent-forum in the middle of a surveillance corridor on the US side, a few meters from a newly built segment of the border wall. We summoned diverse local and global actors from civil society, academia, government, arts and culture to discuss the impacts of wall building on local communities and the entire bioregion.

A BORDER WALK
With our community partners, we negotiated a special permit with US Homeland Security to transform an existing drain under the wall into an official port of entry for twenty-four hours. After the forum, we moved toward the wall to collectively witness the conditions we had debated, exposing conditions that remain invisible, too often unaccounted for in public narratives about the border wall.

BORDER-DRAIN CROSSING
We crossed the border through an existing sewage drain beneath a new section of the wall, located at the precise juncture between the informal settlement and the estuary. US Homeland Security permitted the passage when they confirmed that we had engaged the Mexican immigration authorities to wait at the south end of the drain to stamp our documents.

A PUBLIC "UNWALLING" EXPERIMENT
The strange juxtaposition of pollution traveling northward and the passage from pristine estuary to informal settlement under a militarized culvert amplified the region's most profound contradictions and interdependencies. *Can border regions be the laboratories for reimagining citizenship beyond the nation-state? Can citizenship be organized around shared interests in communities divided by a wall?*

THE POLITICAL EQUATOR MEETINGS

This public performance was part of the *Political Equator Meetings*, which we have curated since 2006—a series of nomadic urban actions and debates that oscillate across diverse sites and stations between Tijuana and San Diego. These "conversations on the move" propose that interdisciplinary and cross-sector debates take place outside the institutions and inside the actual

sites of conflict, enabling diverse constituencies to experience urban conflicts together. Our itinerant border dialogues infiltrate zones of jurisdictional power, with public works, performances and walks, serving as evidentiary platforms to recontextualize debates and conversations among diverse publics and institutions that surround these conflicting territories.

LOCALIZING THE GLOBAL

From the global Political Equator, we arrived at the political inscribed in the local territory, performed through concrete actors and specific sites. Ultimately, *unwalling experiments* are tools to visualize embedded conflicts, the invisible cross-border urban flows and migrant architectures that define this border region.

CONFLICT URBANIZATIONS: VISUALIZING THE POLITICAL

PROJECT: CLUSTER 2

URBANIZA[TION] OF ADAPT[IVE] CROSS-BO[RDER] MIGRANT[S]

ATIONS
ATION:
ORDER
FLOWS

URBANIZATIONS OF ADAPTATION: CROSS-BORDER MIGRANT FLOWS

Project cluster 2 presents our research and visualization of the invisible cross-border flows that transgress the wall dividing Tijuana and San Diego. We focus on two migratory currents that have been conceptually generative for our design practice: from south to north, the positive impact of immigrants in the transformation of American neighborhoods; and from north to south, the recycling of urban fragments from San Diego in Tijuana that creatively transforms informal settlements into laboratories for incremental urbanizations of adaptation.

1. **South to North**
   Nonconforming Suburbs:
   Tijuana's Encroachment into San Diego's Sprawl

2. **North to South**
   Suburbs Made of Waste:
   San Diego's Levittowns Are Recycled into
   Tijuana's Informal Settlements

Our practice is embedded in the neighborhoods that flank the San Diego–Tijuana border wall. These sites reveal at local scale broader social dynamics of structural racism, exclusion and inequality as well as rich bottom-up urban activism and resilience. Through long-standing partnerships with agencies in these neighborhoods, we have developed new paradigms of civic infrastructure and social housing, and solidaristic imaginaries of a cross-border future for this region.

The hardening of the US-Mexico border wall in recent decades has prompted a multitude of insurgent responses. In conditions of scarcity and displacement, border communities have produced alternative modes of encounter, dialogue and circulation, sharing resources and infrastructure, recycling the fragments of these two cities and constructing bottom-up social practices of adaptation, overlap and encroachment that resist and challenge top-down forces of economic privatization, marginalization and exclusion.

These insurgent "off-the-radar" urbanizations confirm that no matter how high the border wall becomes, the everyday flows and circulations of goods and services, social norms and everyday practices, dreams and aspirations will always find their way around, over, under and through the barrier. In an age of wall building, these cross-border urban flows become an antidote to global closure. As long as regional inequality exists, the excluded will always devise bottom-up, experimental strategies of resilience and adaptation that transgress unjust policies, agendas and structures. Some will resist overtly, at great personal risk.

Our research has centered on recognizing and visualizing these invisible urban flows and circulations, which often manifest as stealth penetrations from north to south and from south to north, through which informal architectures and bottom-up urban practices enter and transform neighborhoods on both sides into laboratories for more flexible and inclusive land uses, spaces and economies. We find profound urban lessons in the collective agency and creative intelligence that drive these informal cross-border dynamics, and we have committed our practice to investigating, understanding and translating them. We believe these practices register important bottom-up alternatives to the formal patterns of uneven urbanization everywhere. In our practice, we have committed to communicating these lessons to top-down institutions that govern urban and economic development in the border region, advocating for a more equitable distribution of resources to support these processes.

LOCALIZING GLOBAL FLOWS: SOUTH INTO NORTH, NORTH INTO SOUTH

Thomas Barnett's *The Pentagon's New Map* proposes a post 9-11 cartography for the globe in which the hemispheres are divided between the "Functioning Core," the financially interconnected, neoliberal, strong economies of the global north, and the "Non-Integrating Gap," regions of the global south defined by poverty, political violence and precarity. Through our *Political Equator* project, we carried Barnett's cartography into the second decade of the twenty-first century, characterized by nationalism, border building, hateful anti-immigration policy and protectionism across the world.

As we descend from the global border to border neighborhoods in San Diego–Tijuana, these global flows are localized. Our border region presents flows in both directions: the accelerating flows of migrants from the global south seeking jobs and security in the north, and the north seeking extractive opportunities and cheap labor markets in the south. In one direction, migrants arrive at the San Diego–Tijuana border in search of livelihood and safety in California, one of the strongest economies in the world. In the opposite direction, US manufacturing has moved south into Mexico in search of a tax haven, lax environmental and labor regulations.

These cross-border circulations yield two different yet interdependent political economies of urban development and divergent land-use patterns and economies. Migrant workers flowing from Tijuana into San Diego in one direction, and "infrastructural waste" moving in the opposite direction as Tijuana builds its slums with recycled urban "leftovers" from San Diego. These south-to-north and north-to-south circulations inspire new ways of conceptualizing housing and density, and continue to inspire our architectural and political practice.

Nonconforming Suburbs:
Tijuana's Encroachment into San Diego's Sprawl

Millions of migrants have flowed northward in the last decades, escaping violence, political instability, poverty and more recently the disruptions of climate change. Accelerating waves of immigrants from Southern Mexico and Central America have had a major impact on urbanization in cities across the US. The city of Los Angeles, for example, is home to the second largest concentration of Latin Americans outside the major Latin American capitals. Demographic studies predict that Latin Americans will become the majority of California's population in the next decades. This demographic shift will have significant implications for the physical transformation of American cities in the years to come.

While a social legislation of fear continues to criminalize the 11 million undocumented immigrants presently in the US, we have always seen migrant communities as creative engines of urban practice. The immigrant neighborhoods where they live and work are sites of critical investigation and partnership in our urban and architectural research. Our work emphasizes the positive impact of immigration on the American city, advancing more socially inclusive and environmentally sustainable urbanizations.

In San Diego, immigrant communities are concentrated in the so-called "first ring" of suburbanization, in the mid-city. It is no coincidence that these older inner-city San Diego neighborhoods have been marginalized over decades in processes of neoliberal urban redevelopment, as developers and city officials focused entirely on two main areas: the redevelopment of downtown with a wealthy project of gentrification one the one hand, and an expansive project of suburban sprawl comprised of high-priced real estate and big-box consumerism, supported by oil-hungry freeway infrastructure, on the other. The older neighborhoods of San Diego's mid-city remain depressed and ignored. It is here, in the first ring of suburbanization, that immigrants from Central America, Asia and Africa have settled in recent decades, unable to afford the high rents of downtown's luxury condos and the expensive McMansions of the new suburbs. They conveniently become service providers to both.

Fifty years ago, these older mid-city neighborhoods didn't look much different than the new rings of suburban sprawl that began to metastasize at the edges of San Diego. The urban DNA of these older subdivisions followed the same Levittown logics of homogeneity and standardization, similar to today's master-planned gated communities. But today, the scale has exploded with "super-size-me" development sprawling to the edges of sanely buildable space—and even beyond in some cases. These new rings of suburbanization are like *Levittowns on steroids*, and even the first ring of suburbanization is rejecting older housing typologies as obsolete. Postwar bungalows are unable to accommodate the currently enlarged housing market. In some cases, private developers buy them up in their drive to displace and gentrify urban neighborhoods at the edges of downtown. But in other cases, the obsolescence of the old produces an economic void in these underserved zones of the city, filled by the temporal, informal economies and densities of immigrant arrivals, fundamentally retrofitting the homogeneity of mid-city Levittowns into more complex networks of social and economic activity.

Imagine a binational land-use map of San Diego and Tijuana that visualizes these shifting urban dynamics. What we would observe is a contrast in attitudes towards land use and density. San Diego is comprised of large zones of tract subdivisions, bedroom communities devoid of mixed uses, flanked by mega-mall developments that appear as large commercial islands and surrounded by equally vast and fragmented leftover spaces. These large blocks of diverse colors on the map represent overregulated, exclusionary zoning—maximum space with minimum complexity, where uses are separated and spread in horizontal, wasteful sprawl that antagonizes physical and ecological systems. To the south, in Tijuana, these same colors of housing, commerce and open space are highly pixelated, representing more compacted densities and fearless approximations of multiple uses—minimum space with maximum complexity. This confetti-like fragmentation of use represents the myriad nonconforming uses which, while in need of regulatory oversight, become unwitting experiments in more layered and vertical land uses that thrive through contact and not separation. In this binational land-use visualization, the contrast between the different sizes of color zones and their divergent spatial organization north and south delineates a *practical* border line—quite literally demarcated visually by urban land use.

This cross-border map is not static. If we animated it across time, we would notice that

Tijuana's confetti of alternative uses have been seeping northward beyond the border line into the largeness of Southern California's land uses, pixelating San Diego's monochromatic zones of use with a more compacted and pixelated set of colors. In other words, when these confetti "hit the ground," they alter the mono-use and monoculture of many parcels in San Diego's mid-city neighborhoods, layering these older postwar urban fabrics with alternative uses and social densities, a phenomenon that we have called the "retrofitting of Southern California's Levittowns." Upon examining these areas parcel by parcel, block by block, what emerges is a multicolored land-use condition reflecting the gradation of use and scale produced by the diverse social composition, nonconforming small businesses and social exchanges that characterize these culturally intensive areas of the city. We would also find three-dimensional zoning based not on adjacencies but on juxtapositions, as dormant infrastructures are transformed into usable semipublic spaces and larger-than-needed parcels are illegally subdivided to accommodate extra dwelling units.

Of course, each pixel of color in this visualization represents countless urban anecdotes of adaptation. As the Central American diaspora travels northward, it inevitably alters and transforms the fabric of San Diego's subdivisions. Immigrants bring with them diverse social-cultural attitudes and sensibilities regarding the use of domestic and public space as well as the natural landscape. In these neighborhoods, multigenerational households of extended families shape their own programs of use, taking charge of their own microeconomies in order to maintain a standard for the household, generating nonconforming uses and social densities that reshape the fabric of the residential neighborhoods where they settle. An informal economy is plugged into a garage; housing additions in the shape of illegal companion units are plugged into existing suburban dwellings to provide affordable living; next-door neighbors negotiate their property line to generate a shared space. Alternative social spaces begin to spring up in parking lots; informal economies such as flea markets and street vendors appear in vacant properties; and underutilized alleys become zones of cultural exchange and pedestrian circulation, blurring private and public boundaries. Urban survival strategies in immigrant communities generate new spatial configurations that thrive through solidarity and resilience, anticipating new paradigms for shared urban infrastructure.

We have documented many stories of urban adaptation in these underserved San Diego environments. An emblematic case is the *nonconforming Buddha*. A group of Vietnamese monks acquired two adjacent parcels, each containing a small house, located in the City Heights neighborhood of San Diego, one of the most demographically diverse communities in the city. Over the last twenty years, these tiny postwar bungalows have been transformed from single-family residences into a Buddhist temple.

The monks incrementally altered the small parcels, adapting them into a micro social-economic infrastructure for the neighborhood. The small decorative lawn that once filled the front yard has been hardened into a fake, shiny marble plinth that serves as altar for a huge white statue of Buddha that encroaches illegally into the front setback. The driveway has become a dining room leading into an interior altar, meditation space and community room. The old setbacks that defined the separation of these houses have now been filled with small sheds to accommodate other programs related to the temple. From far away, though, this small bungalow resembles any typical house.

While the spatial alterations of these parcels are compelling evidence of the incremental and extra-official retrofitting of space in these neighborhoods to accommodate diverse land uses and everyday practices, this story also revealed to us not only the urban processes of physical adaptation themselves, but also that these houses have become a social agency inside the neighborhood, facilitating social relations, pedagogical programming, cultural support and economic exchange.

Community-based agencies like the Buddhist temple become urban facilitators that compensate for the lack of public support for social, economic and educational services for these immigrant communities. In other words, the story of the "nonconforming Buddha" suggests the need for "mediating agencies," neighborhood-based social platforms that curate the interface between institutions and communities, top-down resources and bottom-up intelligence. These neighborhood-based agencies (spiritual and religious groups, nonprofit organizations, arts collectives, community activism alliances) serve as urban curators, able not only to adapt the spaces of the neighborhood to generate new civic infrastructure at small scales, but also to organize and bundle the invisible social and economic agency embedded in these immigrant communities, translating it into new policies and economies that can increase their collective capacity and improve quality of life. This interface between the physical and the curatorial has been central to our research on expanding design processes that give form not only to objects and spaces, but also to protocols that enable management, economy and governance to assure access to the spaces.

THE DOUBLE DESTINY OF LEVITTOWN
The cookie-cutter bungalows in San Diego's Levittown-like subdivisions have been adapted and retrofitted by immigrants, but many of them have also been recycled into Tijuana's informal settlements.

LEARNING FROM TIJUANA'S NONCONFORMING USES

A car-garage conversion for urban theorist and political activist Mike Davis was an early experiment to adapt a generic garage in mid-city San Diego. An accessory building was inserted on the garage roof as a sleeping porch, and the garage was transformed into a writer's studio.

The idea that one residence can become a multi-faceted social agency suggests that our normative idea of density should be questioned. The micro-heterotopias emerging in immigrant communities through informal spatial practices are redefining density and land use. Making visible the invisibility of these nonconforming forces and their operational potential to bridge the formal and the informal, the wealthy subdivisions and the urban enclaves of poverty, is a point of departure for imagining more democratic ideas of density, resilience and sustainability. We need to engage new conceptual and representational models that allow us to transcend the reductive understanding of density as an abstract number of objects / units / inhabitants per acre, and see it instead as the intensity of social interactions and economic exchanges per acre.

Therefore, altering conventions of representation to communicate these often-ambiguous forces remains the essential task in negotiating between the formal and the informal city, the top-down and the bottom-up. The hidden value of these informal transactions across bottom-up cultural activism, economies and densities continues to be off the radar of top-down institutions of planning. They are typically uninterested in and unable to interpret the ingenious logics of the informal social and economic dynamics at play in the city—incapable of navigating the multiple forces that shape the politics of the territory or resolving tensions between the macro, top-down urban strategies of official development and the micro, bottom-up tactics of community resilience. Our practice dwells in this space of connection, mediation and facilitation.

The question for our practice, however, is not only *what* we represent, but also *whom*. We are interested in what we call "visualizing citizenship"—assembling the evidence of immigrants reinventing spaces and situations, adapting monocultural and mono-use urban contexts into more heterogeneous and plural urbanizations of retrofit. Visualizing and translating these stealth alternative patterns of urban development requires new intersections between ethnography, sociology, architecture, urbanism and visual culture. What emerges is a powerful strategy of political representation that demands changes in discriminatory urban norms and policies.

Our work in San Diego has focused on translating social, cultural and economic intelligence embedded in marginalized immigrant neighborhoods in order to propose more inclusive land-use and economic categories to support new forms of sustainability. These bottom-up urban transformations ultimately demand an overhaul of zoning that prohibits alternative densities and transitional uses that directly respond to the needs of communities navigating scarcity and inequality. How do we accelerate creative urbanization beyond the property line? How can we validate and support the collective agency and creative intelligence embedded in migrant communities? How can we amplify these practices as a critical armature for rethinking the future of the city? The mutation of these older bedroom communities from rigid, monocultural, one-dimensional environments into informal, multicultural and cross-programmed communities ultimately opens a fundamental question: How do we anticipate density? If the first ring of suburbanization in San Diego transformed so radically in the last fifty years, will the third and fourth rings of sprawl in the exurbs submit to the same forces of urban adaptation in the next fifty? Will the super-size-me McMansions in the exurbs eventually be retrofitted to become multifamily and mixed-used environments?

We believe that the future of urbanization in Southern California and cities across the world is smallness. To achieve social and environmental resilience, this future will depend on the adaptation of big-box and exclusionary urban development by pixelating the fixity of largeness with small alterations and more agile conditions of land use and spatial organization. The micro social and economic contingencies of informal urbanization will transform the homogeneity of the official city into more sustainable, plural and complex environments.

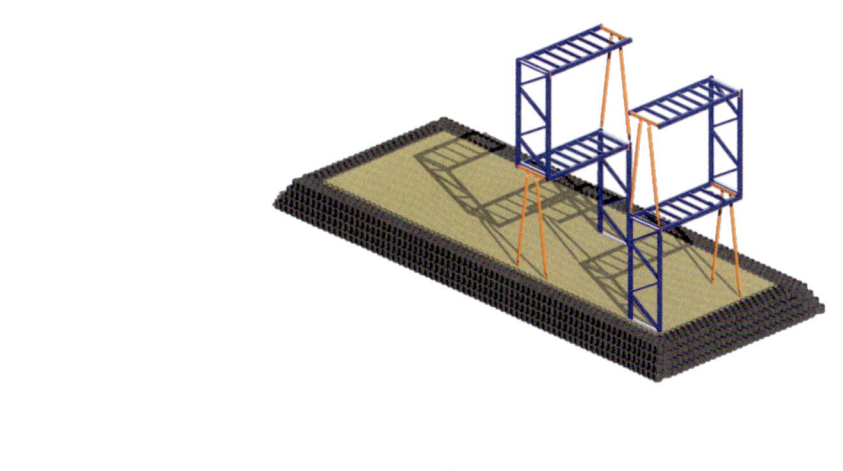
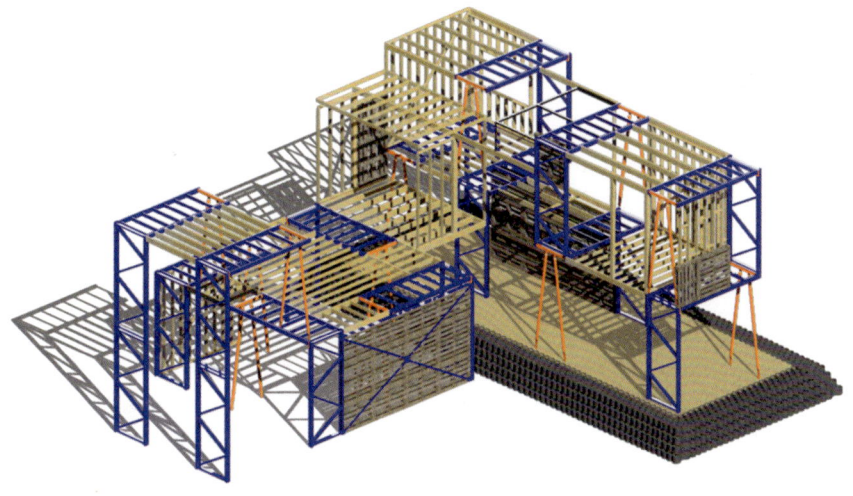
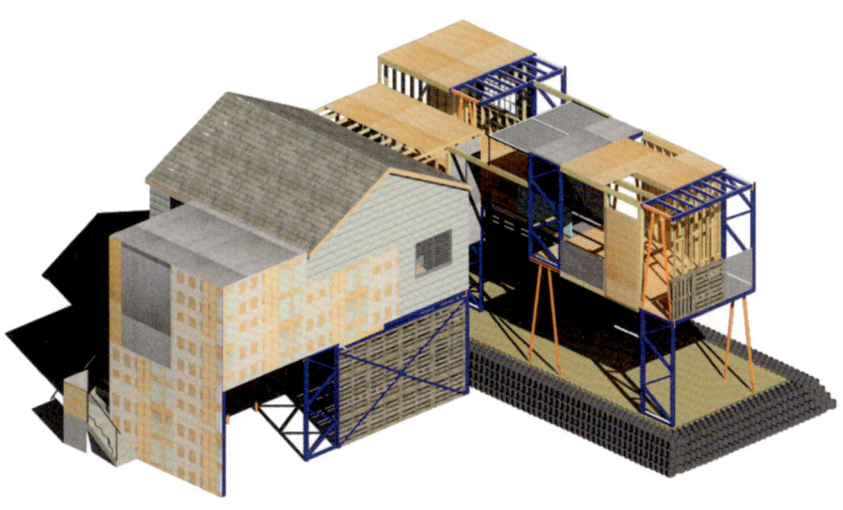

SCAFFOLDS FOR INFORMAL HOUSING

Maquiladora-made framing systems support the recycling of San Diego's urban waste into Tijuana's incremental architectures made of parts to build emergency housing. Recycled houses, garage doors, pallet racks, discarded framing and other urban debris from San Diego is reassembled in Tijuana.

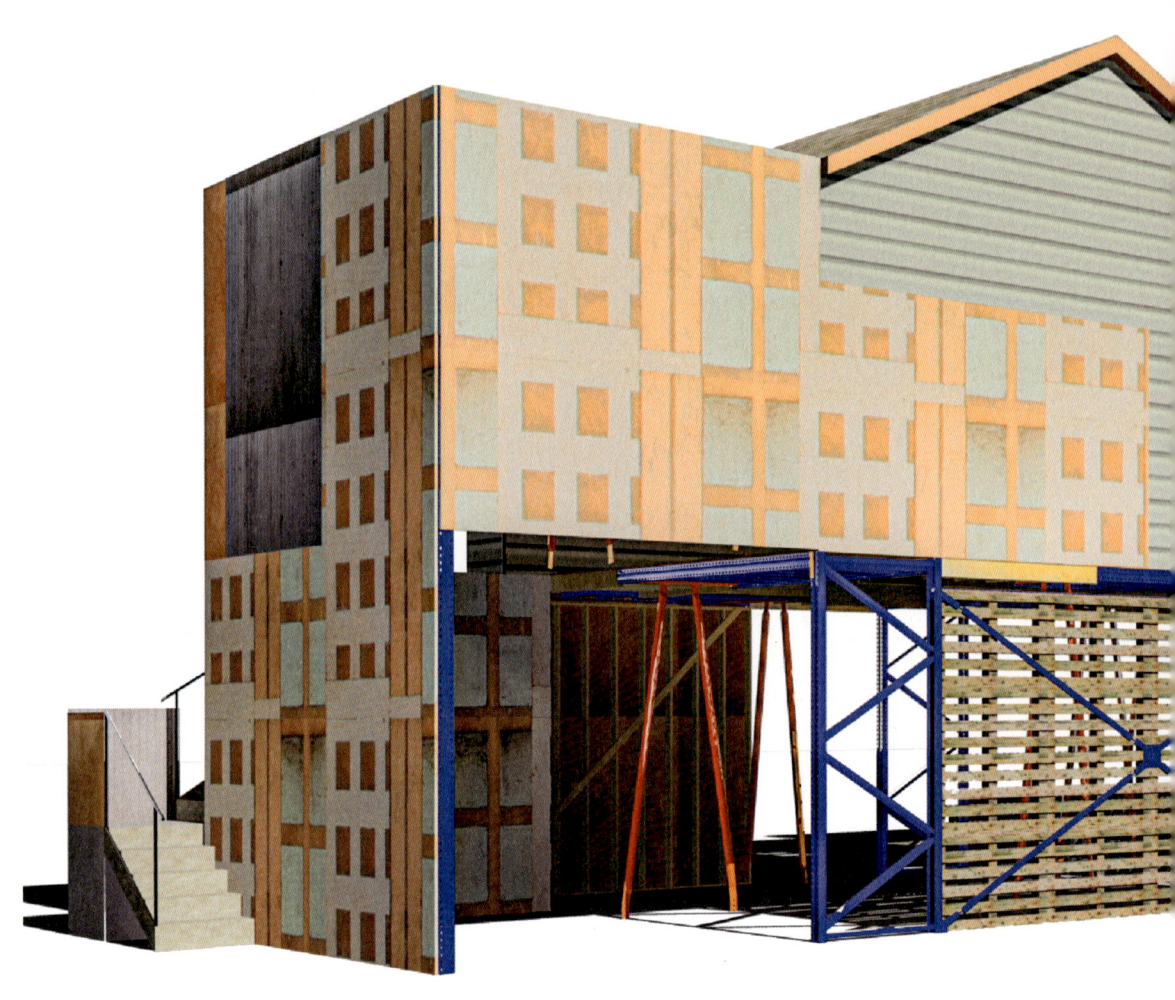

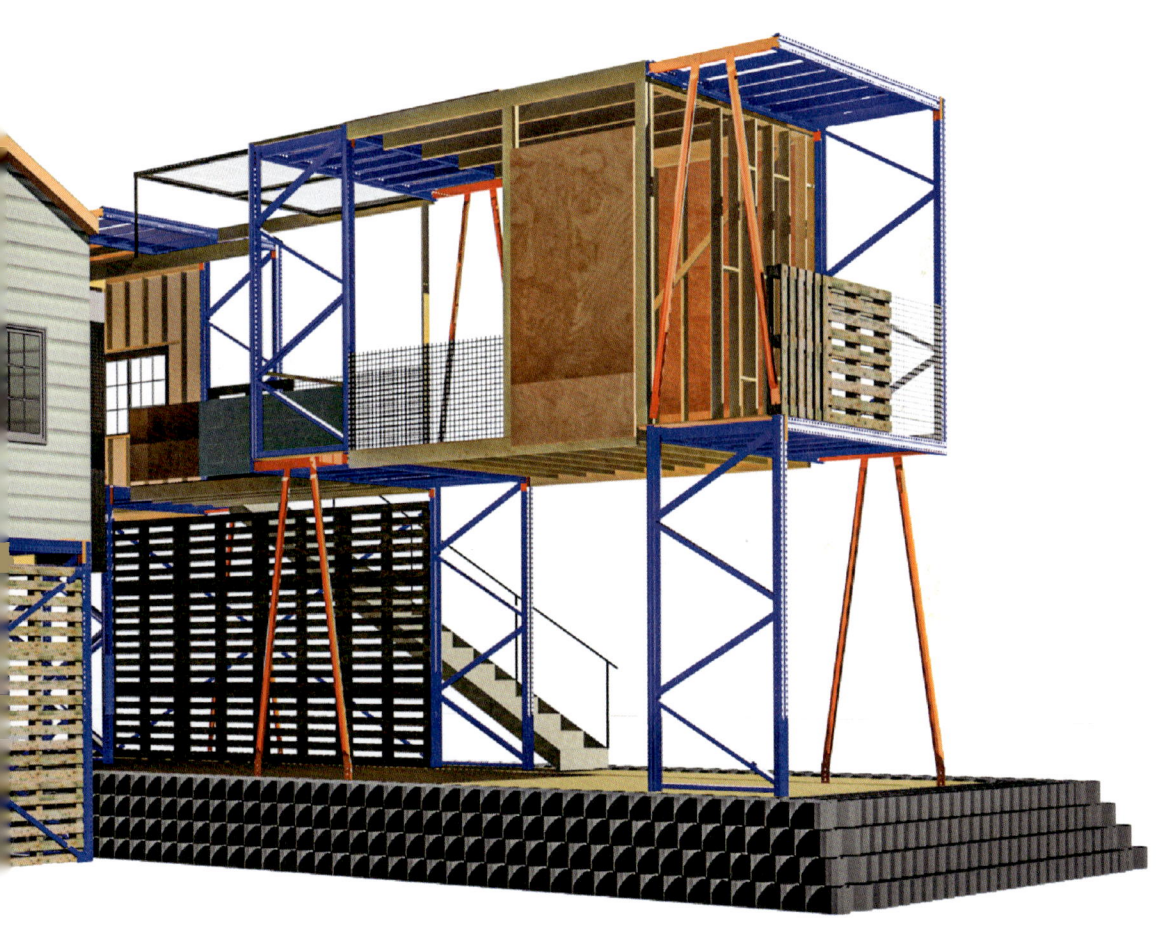

Suburbs Made of Waste:
San Diego's Levittowns Are Recycled into Tijuana's Informal Settlements

While migrants go north, urban waste from San Diego flows southward to construct an urbanism of emergency in Tijuana's periphery, which has primarily evolved as a collection of informal, favela-like settlements. These start-up settlements gradually evolve, or violently explode, from conditions of social emergency and are defined by the negotiation of territorial boundaries, the ingenious recycling of materials and human resourcefulness. The multiplicity of recycled materials and systems brought from San Diego and reassembled in Tijuana gives primacy to the layered complexities of these sites over the singularity of the object. By bridging the planned and the unplanned, the legal and the illegal, the object and the ground, Tijuana's informal urbanism anticipates the patterns of density and programmatic intensity that are already redefining the American metropolis and contemporary notions of housing and urbanism worldwide.

Just as the master-planned communities of San Diego's periphery physicalize an atomized version of the American Dream—as promised by neoliberal urban agendas that focus on individualism and privatization at the expense of public resources—Tijuana's slums erupt as the underbelly of exclusionary neoliberal global economic policies that have turned cities like Tijuana into tax-free factory-cities, where multinationals set up shop to take advantage of cheap labor and benefit from zones of exception to avoid any sort of regulation against human and environmental exploitation. As such, slums are the embodiment of global inequality. Our research in Tijuana investigates the relationships among informal settlements, emergency housing and the politics of labor, as maquiladoras (NAFTA factories) settle in the midst of these slums, typically investing nothing in return.

What distinguishes these peripheral settlements in Tijuana from urban informality across the world is that they abut the US and build themselves with the urban waste of San Diego. To contextualize this invisible north-to-south flow, imagine another dynamic map that juxtaposes urban growth patterns in San Diego and Tijuana over the last century.

Today, San Diego and Tijuana have roughly equal populations, making the region among the largest binational conurbations in the world. But in the last decades, San Diego has sprawled approximately six times the size of Tijuana, spreading itself indiscriminately across the territory, while Tijuana has remained significantly more compact. There are, of course, many factors that contribute to these contrasting growth patterns, including divergent economic development capacities, topographic limits surrounding their main zones of growth and, potentially the most important, contrasting attitudes and sensibilities towards density and urban infill.

Ultimately, San Diego's dramatic sprawl is emblematic of market-oriented planning strategies, which rely on oil-hungry infrastructure to support private *tabula rasa* approaches to development, making older suburbs obsolete through disinvestment in order to build the next ring of suburbanization, and the next, and so on. This expansionist car-centric agenda never considers building incrementally through alteration and adaptation, through urban infill, appropriate densification and conservation, before exploding amorphously into the edges. This image, which contrasts regional growth patterns oriented by density and sprawl, visualizes one of the most pressing challenges for our binational region and many other cities across the world: How can we reverse unsustainable patterns of urban growth and the social and economic asymmetries they engender? How can we challenge the urban and economic policies, design and planning practices that continue to misallocate our natural, social and financial resources?

The temporalities of suburbanization in San Diego and Tijuana are also divergent. As large suburban subdivisions spring up at the edges of San Diego, Tijuana's periphery is dotted with dense informal settlements, typically located on precarious canyon hillsides. While San Diego's vast sprawl of loosely planned housing is incrementally supported by gigantic, planned freeway infrastructure, dense inhabitation at Tijuana's edges happens first and incremental small infrastructure follows.

As the city expands outward, entire San Diego neighborhoods are disenfranchised. They begin to erode and physically implode, and their marginalization is refurbished by the urban aspirations of immigrant communities. In Tijuana, city officials continue to ignore the potentialities of retrofitting slums to redefine the future of the city, dreaming instead of importing San Diego models to pave the periphery into replicas of US-made gated communities. Meanwhile, as San Diego's suburban construction continues to explode, relying on unsustainable oil-based materials—from vinyl to plastics to asphalt—and generating huge quantities of urban deconstruction waste—including rubber tires and other discarded or obsolete materials—this urban debris is carried across the border and recycled inside the slums of Tijuana.

The contrasts between San Diego and Tijuana are profound, but it is also important to recognize that differences between these border cities dwindle as their contrasting urban logics overlap across the border zone. San Diego–style gated communities and signature mini-malls spring up on Tijuana's periphery, while Tijuana's random patterns of density, mixed-use and informal economies have erupted in mid-city San Diego neighborhoods. In every first-world city, inevitably a third world exists, and every third-world city replicates the first. The global import-export processes that cause cities across the world to recycle symbols of progress begin to suggest that, in fact, the periphery of any global metropolis is being incrementally shaped by the suburban code of Southern California's sprawl: archipelagos of atomized single-family subdivisions. In the early 2000s, this phenomenon manifested in the dramatic images of a development outside Beijing built as a pleasure enclave for the Chinese *nouveau riche*. The private developers of this gated community faithfully replicated a master-planned community from Orange County, California, importing authentic Southern Californian plastic stucco, foam detailing and fake Mediterranean clay tiles. A suburb in a box!

In the midst of these contradictions at the border, where conditions of difference and sameness collide and overlap daily, we have been investigating the flow of urban waste from north to south: one city recycling and rebuilding itself from the waste of the other. Tijuana's slums are built with the demolition debris of San Diego's master-planned communities. As San Diego's older suburbs erode, private developers demolish the older housing stock in order to install new condominium projects and larger versions of cookie-cutter houses. Some old bungalows are adapted *in situ*, like the Buddhist temple in San Diego. Some are demolished, disassembled into their prefabricated parts, and their pieces given away to speculators. Leftover parts—framing, joists, connectors, plywood, aluminum windows, garage doors—are disassembled and recombined on the other side. Once in Tijuana's periphery, these parts are reassembled into fresh scenarios, creating a housing urbanism made of waste to mitigate social emergency and housing shortage. This is how San Diego's urban waste becomes an asset to Tijuana as an affordable set of reusables.

Some of the postwar bungalows are left intact and sold cheaply to speculators who carry them whole across the border. The little houses are loaded onto trailers and required to clear customs before making their journey south. One sees small houses on flatbeds waiting in line to cross the border, just like cars and pedestrians. When they enter Tijuana, they are mounted on top of one-story metal frames that leave an empty space at the street level to accommodate future uses. These floating houses define a space of opportunity below that will be filled, through time, with more housing space, a taco stand, a car repair shop, a garden. One city profits from dwellings the other discards, recombining them into fresh scenarios and creating countless possibilities open to the unpredictability of time and programmatic contingency.

The transformation of San Diego's mid-city, in constant flux between demolition and adaptation, presents the strange triple destiny of Levittown: to be demolished and upsized, to be retrofitted by immigrants in San Diego or to be recycled into Tijuana's slums.

The border cities perform a strange mirroring effect: while housing stock in San Diego is inaugurated as permanent, it turns disposable from one decade to the next; Tijuana's informal housing, by contrast, begins as an ephemeral gesture but aspires to become permanent. Tijuana recycles the leftovers of the other into a sort of *secondhand urbanism*, transforming its informal settlements into laboratories for rethinking the relationship between infrastructure, sociability and temporality. The informal settlements of Tijuana are open-air housing factories, built temporally through human agency, sweat equity and social organization. This incremental layering of physical and social systems presents an alternative paradigm for building the city.

Undeniably, these precarious environments are also shaped by the contested power dynamics found in the official city. Informal settlements begin as sites of urban crisis, where people in conditions of social and economic emergency squat in underutilized territory and high-risk topographic zones on the slopes of canyons to create their own housing. This scrappy nomadic urbanism is supported by a sophisticated social choreography of individual and family survival, neighborhood participation and often slum-lord exploitation.

This process begins with deliberate "tactics of encroachment," as we call it, when dozens of squatters called "paracaidistas," (parachuters) collectively invade large, vacant, public (sometimes private) properties. As these urban guerillas descend into the hills of Tijuana's canyons, they are organized and choreographed by what are commonly called "urban pirates." These characters are either individuals who bring their families to find an available site to begin a shelter, or housing activists who bring a few families in need, defending their rights to emergency housing. In the worst case, they are slum lords who accumulate small, empty parcels to provide housing to people in need. At times this process is controlled by urban developers, who, through corrupt politicians, gain illegal access to larger plots of land to carve an array of small parcels without water or sewer infrastructure, and to sell these plots to vulnerable people seeking housing.

Regardless of the particular squatting process, people in need are ultimately left to their own devices. Here, practices of social organization, activism and informal building begin to emerge. Through improvisational tactics of construction, distribution of goods and ad hoc services, a process of assembly begins by recycling San Diego's urban debris. Garage doors are used to make walls (entire houses are made with San Diego garage doors as the main structural and exterior skin); rubber tires are cut and dismantled into folded loops, clipped and interlocked, creating an inventive, functional retaining wall; wooden crates become armatures for other imported surfaces, such as recycled refrigerator doors, etc.

In slums, buildings *spatialize process*. Informal environments are not shaped *a priori* by an architect freezing concept into shape. Buildings in slums are not static objects but performative systems that evolve incrementally, anticipatory scaffolds negotiating with topography and transforming continually as human needs and capacities evolve, and as resources become available. In slums, architecture *performs*, socializing urban theorist Stan Allen's definition of infrastructural urbanism: "form matters not for what it looks like but for what it does."[24]

After months of physical construction and social organization, community representatives begin to request municipal services. There are municipal planners whose task is to research, identify and begin negotiations with new zones of informal squatting so that they are included in the official maps of the city. It is important to mention here that what differentiates informal Mexican urbanization from other places across the world where slums proliferate, from India to Brazil, is that Mexican law protects squatters from eviction. An agrarian reform dating back to the Mexican Revolution of 1910, which gave land to peasants to form collective ownership of lands, called *ejidos*, also legislated the protection of squatters through a political process that enables them to negotiate land tenure through time. It does not matter whether the squatted land is public or private. In the latter case, eminent domain enables this process.

Land-title agencies serve as curators of this process, mapping new informal neighborhoods within new administrative boundaries and setting in motion a payment plan for squatters to receive their property deeds. Throughout this process, small payments are exchanged for layers of light infrastructure, and municipal services begin to trickle down, initiating a complex dance between the planned and the unplanned to incrementally solidify this temporary urbanization over time. The city sends trucks to deliver water at certain locations, and electricity follows as the city installs *one* official power line, anticipating that the community will steal the rest via a tangle of illegal cable clippings called *diablitos* (little devils). In the early days of the informal process, one can see entire areas of the slum roofed by hundreds of electric wires.

In Tijuana's eastward expansion, "social housing" has bypassed informal bottom-up processes. Seduced by the style and glamour of the master-planned, gated communities of San Diego, developers build their own version: miniaturized replicas of typical suburban tract homes. Thousands of tiny tract homes are scattered across the periphery of the city, a vast landscape of homogeneity and fragmentation at odds with the prevailing complex heterogeneity of informality surrounding Tijuana's urban core. These diminutive dwellings come equipped with all the US suburban clichés and conventions: manicured landscaping, gatehouses, model units, banners and flags, mini setbacks, front and back yards and the ubiquitous beigeness.

Mexican housing authorities from the second half of the twentieth century acted as developers of public housing, coordinating economic and social programming but also design and planning processes at higher densities. But after the neoliberalization of the banking industry in Mexico (and the world)—and with it the diminishing role of public agencies to lead the way—social housing was outsourced to private developers who retreated from the vertical densities of mid-century public housing in order to embrace the more horizontal, US-inspired, commodified single-family subdivisions. So these miniaturized master-planned communities are now the new social housing paradigm for edge cities across Mexico, and incrementally across Latin America. While they are subsidized by the Mexican government, as housing authorities provide vouchers for customers who qualify, these housing units are built by private developers and speculators who do not invest in public transportation or any essential social, economic and cultural amenities for the long-term sustainability of these communities. They are effectively the worst version of US-style bedroom communities, without any proper supportive infrastructure. Isolated from social services, these communities typically spiral rapidly into decay and violence.

While the gated communities of San Diego remain closed systems due to stringent zoning that prohibits any kind of formal alteration or programmatic juxtaposition, these housing tracts in Tijuana quickly submit to informal transformation by occupants who are little hindered by comparatively permissive zoning regulations. Occupants customize their tract houses—filling in setbacks, occupying front and back yards as well as garages with more construction and overlapping programs—mirroring strategies common to older, informal communities of the city. Even if designed by developers following a fixed stylistic recipe, these tracts are quickly adapted by their occupants into open systems, activating improvisational higher densities and mixed uses. A small shop appears in the front yard, a second floor springs up to become a live-work unit, and two houses might merge into a larger container for multiuse activity, even a supermarket, a temple or a school. Incrementally, these developer-driven, top-down formal systems are forever transformed by informal alterations of space and program, reminiscent of the retrofitted lives of San Diego's Levittowns.

WHAT CAN WE LEARN FROM BOTTOM-UP CROSS-BORDER URBANIZATIONS?

Tijuana's informal communities and San Diego's older subdivisions are densifying faster than the urban cores they surround, creating a different set of rules for development and blurring the distinctions between the urban, the suburban and the rural. In contrast to unsustainable *urbanizations of consumption* in global cities across the world, local neighborhoods at the margins of economic power remain sites of social and economic creativity and productivity.

In these peripheral neighborhoods, new bottom-up dynamics give the local and the peripheral a more critical role in rethinking globalized urban dynamics. Contexts of scarcity and adaptation present us with alternative social, cultural, economic and political practices, and can inspire more inclusive public policies to promote sustainable patterns of equitable urban growth and economy worldwide. We argue that these "tactics of encroachment" in immigrant neighborhoods across San Diego and Tijuana might prefigure the fate of urban densification in cities around the world, where redevelopment has been driven by privatization and homogenization.

While these immigrant neighborhoods that flank the border wall reveal ingenious spatial and social processes of survival, adaptation and economic productivity, this invisible urban praxis urgently needs conceptual interpretation and political representation. In our practice, we believe these bottom-up procedures need top-down recognition and support, and we are committed to advocating for this knowledge and bridging this resource divide. Our focus on informality is not meant to weaken the demand for robust, accountable public institutions.

We also believe that this bottom-up agency can help the contemporary city rethink resilience and equity, and transform urban policy. At a time of unprecedented social and economic inequality, climate disruption and anti-immigrant fervor, it is more urgent than ever that we translate these procedures into new urban strategies. Informal urbanization as a *civic practice* through which critical spatial and social tactics aggregate can trickle upwards to transform the institutions of urban development.

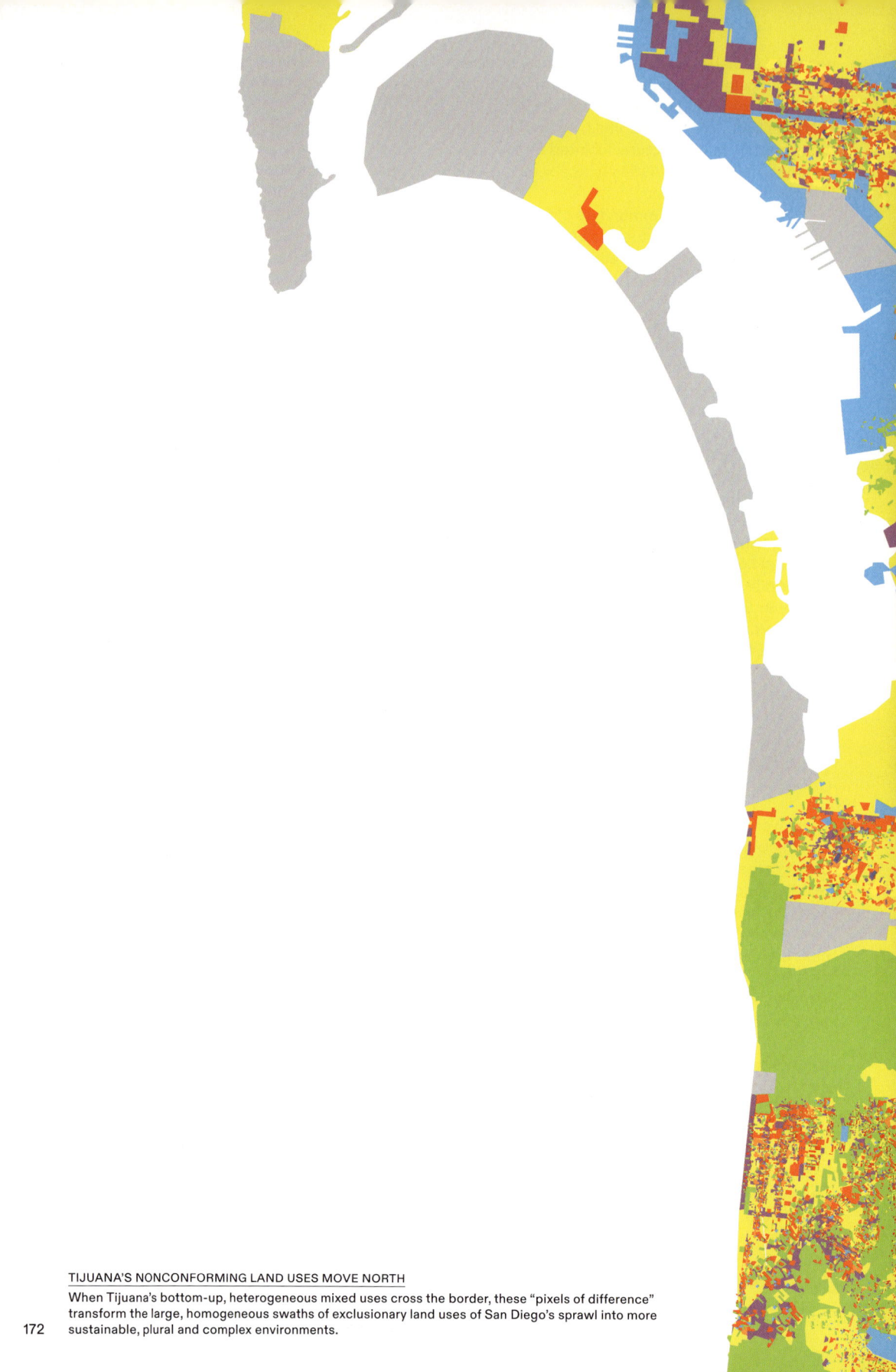

TIJUANA'S NONCONFORMING LAND USES MOVE NORTH
When Tijuana's bottom-up, heterogeneous mixed uses cross the border, these "pixels of difference" transform the large, homogeneous swaths of exclusionary land uses of San Diego's sprawl into more sustainable, plural and complex environments.

SOLIDARISTIC LAND USES

When Tijuana's "confetti" of nonconforming uses "hits the ground" in San Diego, it alters existing mono-use parcels across mid-city neighborhoods into more complex social, economic and cultural environments.

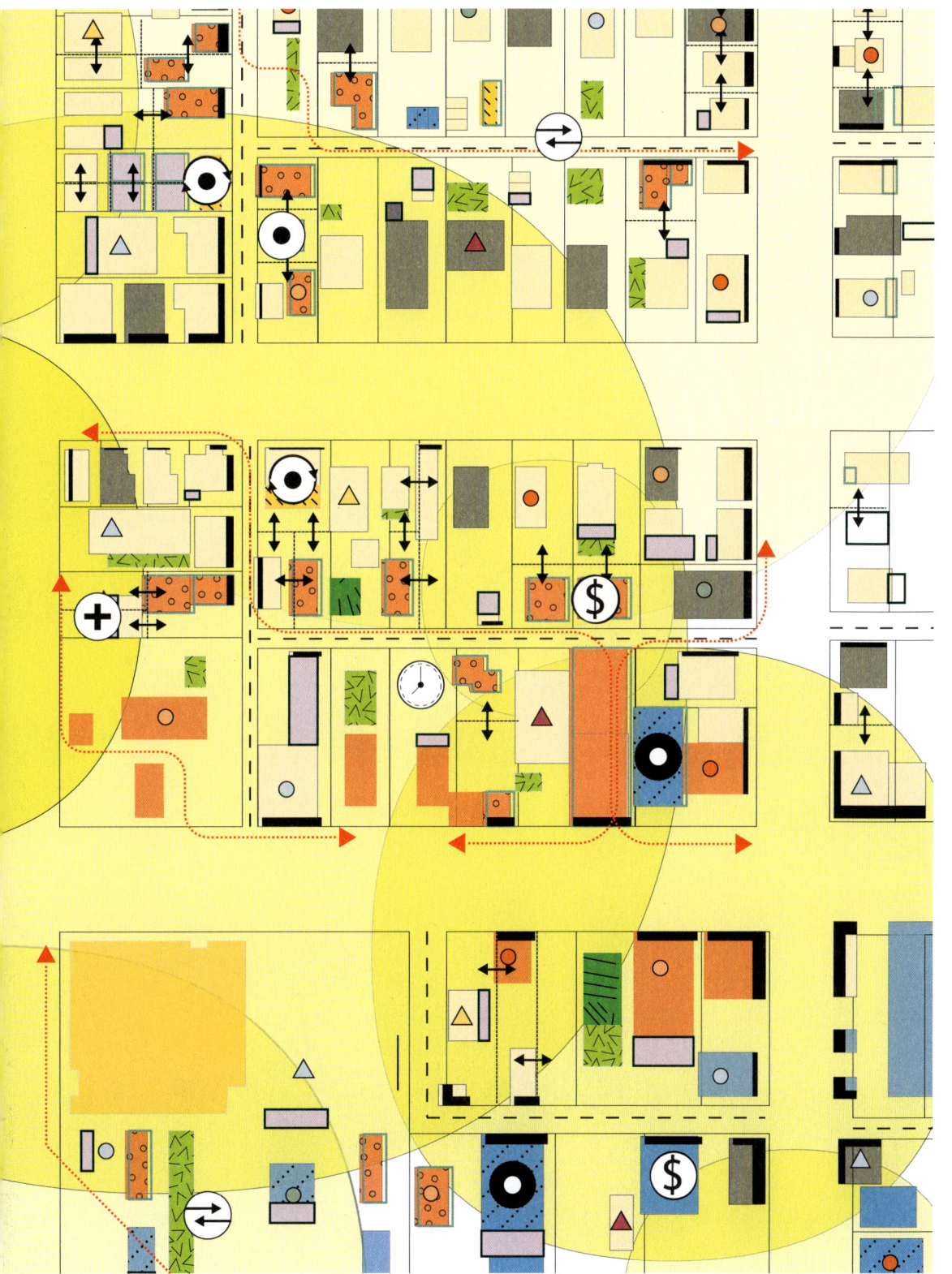

URBANIZATIONS OF ADAPTATION: CROSS-BORDER MIGRANT FLOWS

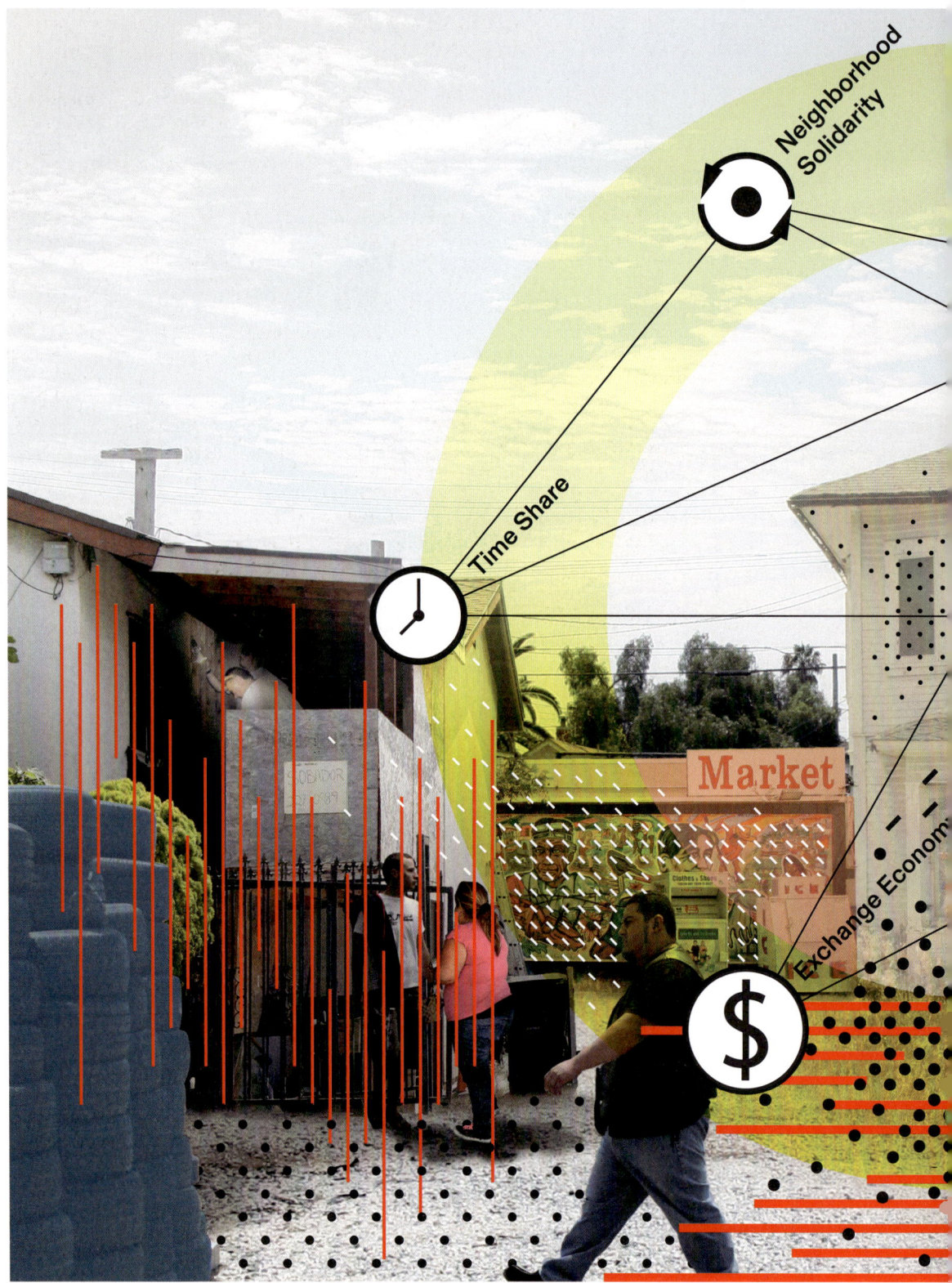

COMMON SENSE CITY
The visualization and translation of incremental, bottom-up tactics of urban adaptation can mobilize the hidden value of informal economy and social density into new paradigms of community and economic development, spatial reciprocity, skills exchange, informal economy, neighborhood collaboration, solidaristic programming and social resilience.

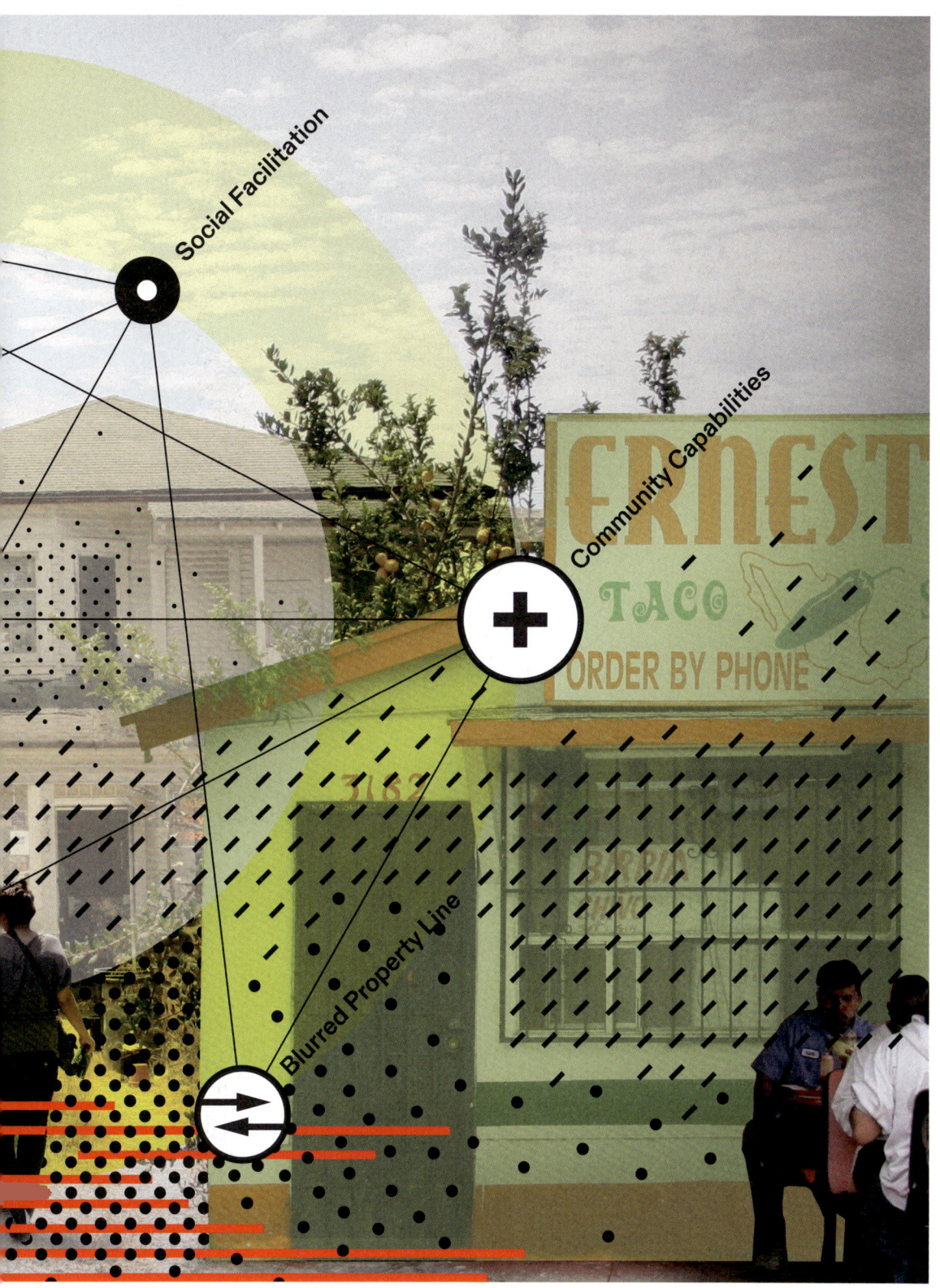

URBANIZATIONS OF ADAPTATION: CROSS-BORDER MIGRANT FLOWS

URBANIZATIONS OF ADAPTATION
San Diego's mid-city neighborhoods are adapted into alternative mixed uses and bottom-up spaces of socialization and economy. These informal acts of retrofit are a material manifestation of everyday survival practices in migrant communities, negotiating boundaries, spaces and resources.

URBANIZATIONS OF ADAPTATION: CROSS-BORDER MIGRANT FLOWS

LEVITTOWN RETROFITTED
Who would imagine that the postwar American Dream, exemplified by the detached single-family suburban dwelling, would be retrofitted over time by the entrepreneurial energies of migrant communities, who thread small parcels in neighborhoods into socio-spatial fabrics?

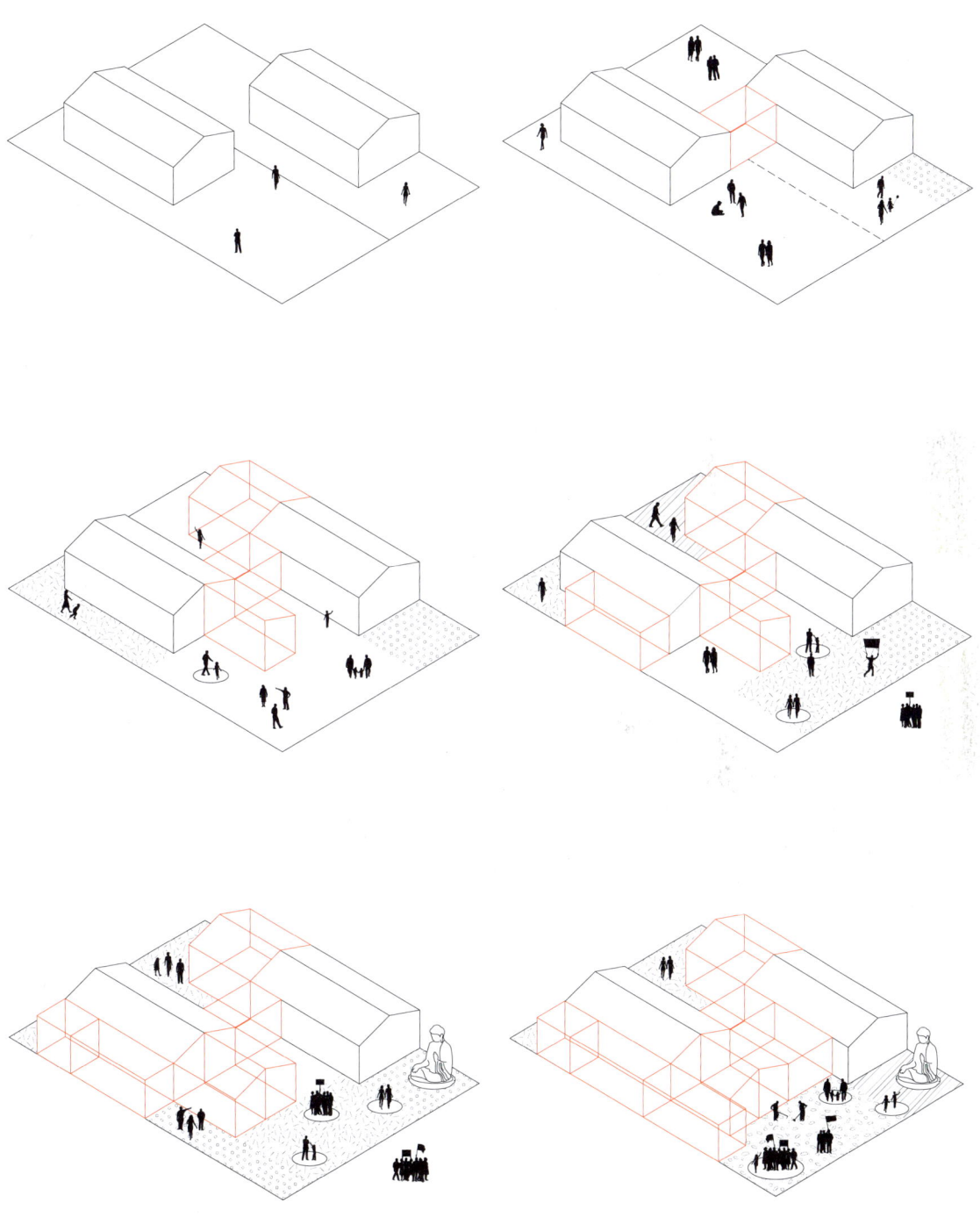

URBANIZATIONS OF ADAPTATION: CROSS-BORDER MIGRANT FLOWS

SPATIALIZING CITIZENSHIP

182   In the San Diego neighborhood of City Heights, a mid-city, postwar bungalow was transformed into a Buddhist temple.

URBANIZATIONS OF ADAPTATION: CROSS-BORDER MIGRANT FLOWS

THE NONCONFORMING BUDDHA MANDALA
Community groups become mediating agencies to facilitate linkages between top-down institutional support systems and bottom-up community agency, bundling local economic capabilities and coordinating a social safety-net at the scale of the neighborhood.

URBANIZATIONS OF ADAPTATION: CROSS-BORDER MIGRANT FLOWS

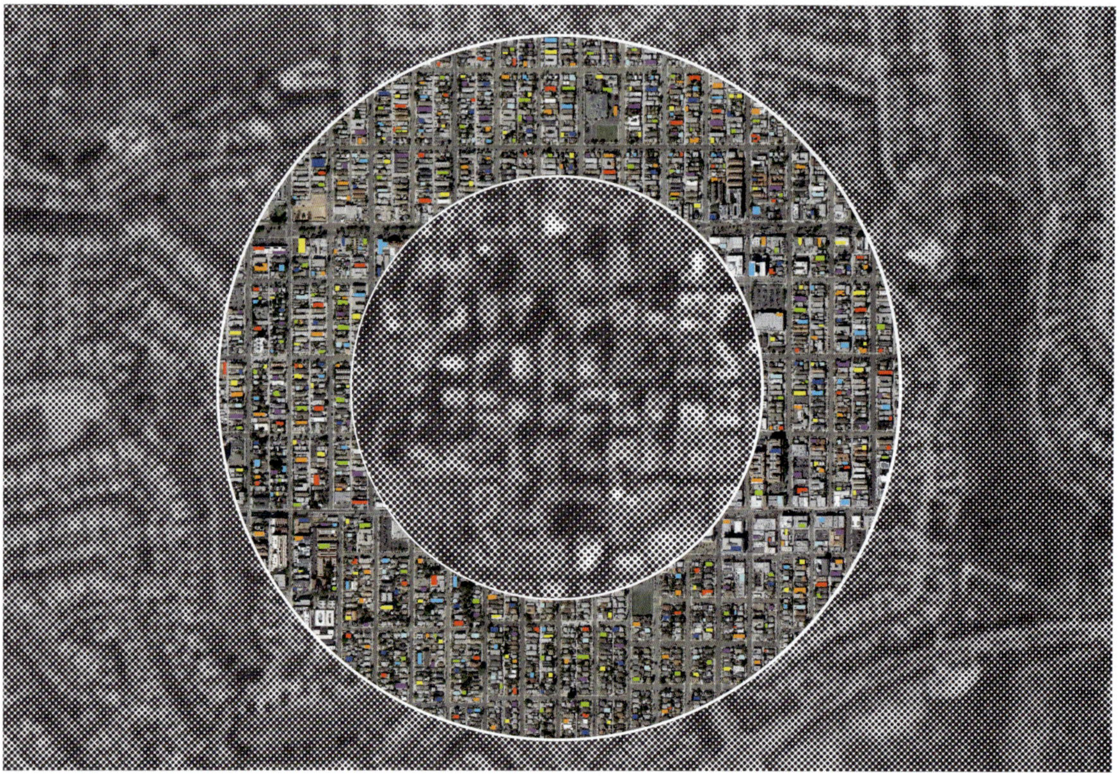

PIXELATING THE LARGE WITH THE SMALL
The last decades of urban growth in San Diego have focused on two main areas of development: 1. The redevelopment of downtown into a gentrifying bubble of wealth; and 2. The expansive project of sprawl comprised of equally high-priced real-estate projects across the second and thirds rings of suburbanization. The older mid-city neighborhoods of the first ring remain depressed and ignored.

Waves of immigrants have settled in the mid-city, unable to afford the high rents of downtown's luxury condos and the expensive McMansions of the new exurbs, and they pixelate these older subdivisions with alternative land uses and densities. If the first suburban ring of San Diego transformed so radically in the last fifty years, will the third and fourth rings of sprawl submit to the same forces of urban adaptation in the next fifty?

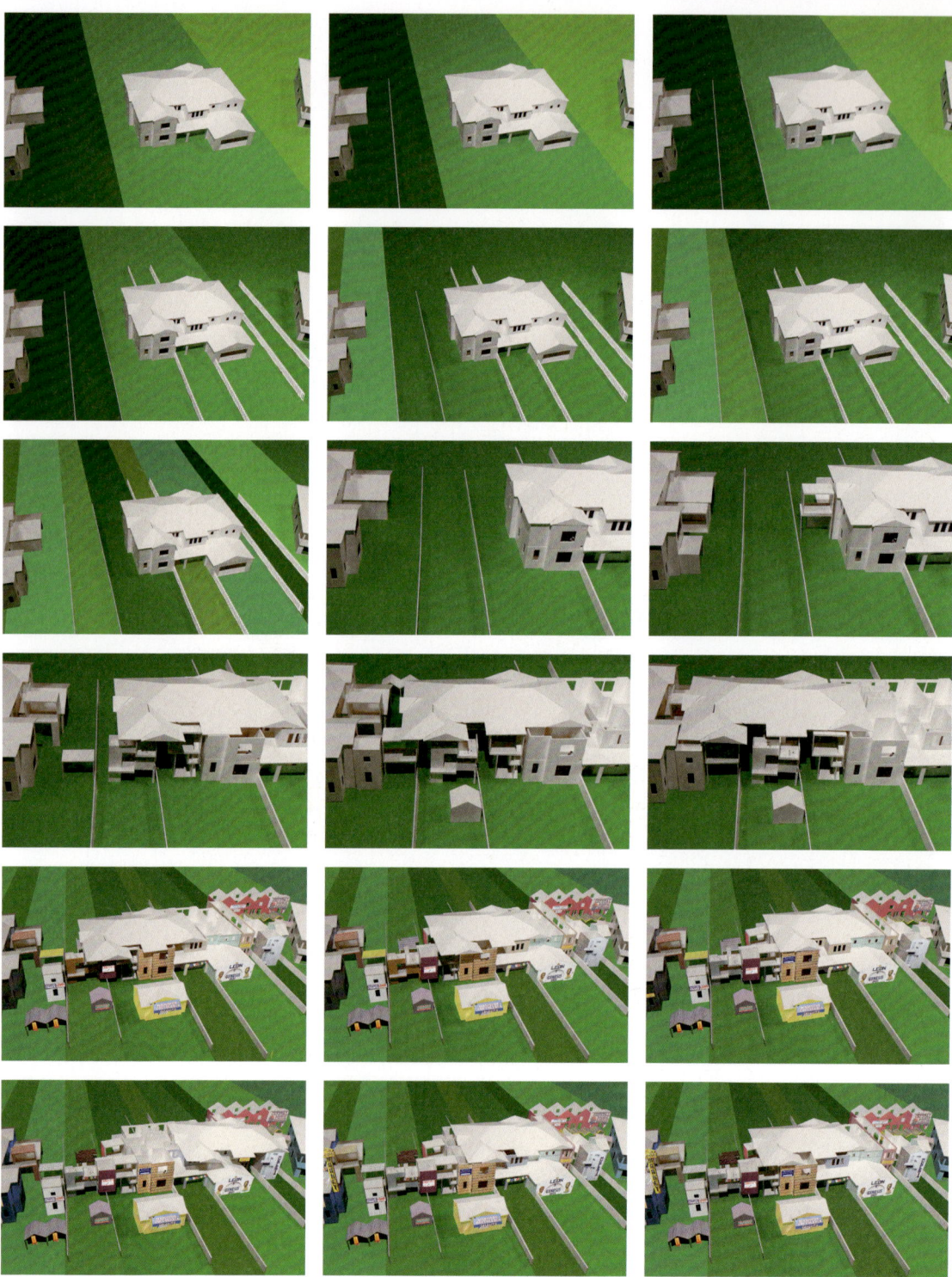

MCMANSION RETROFITTED
Speculating how a generic 9,000 sq ft Mc Mansion is adapted with nonconforming additions, informal economies and diverse demographics, and transformed through time into a full-on neighborhood.

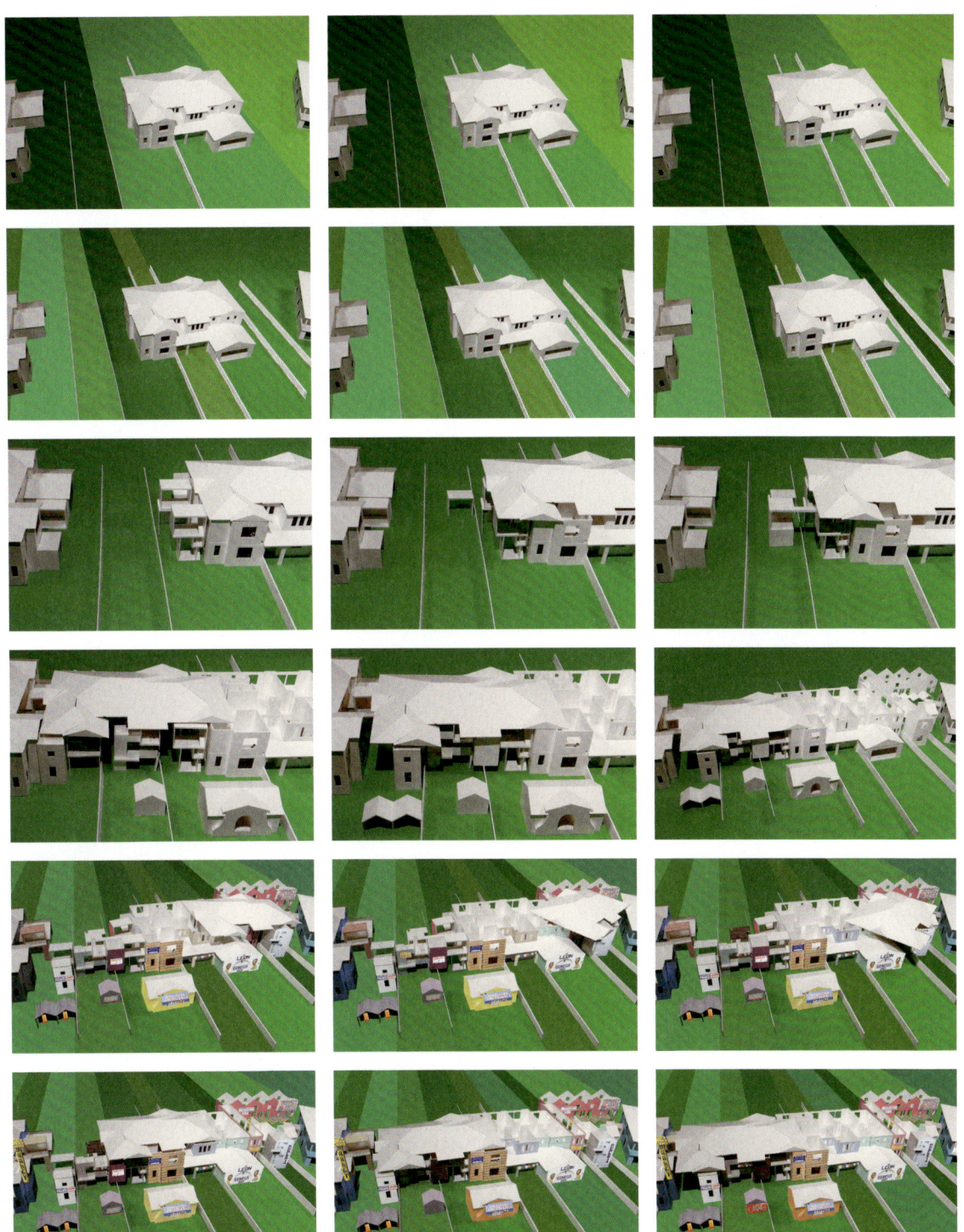

URBANIZATIONS OF ADAPTATION: CROSS-BORDER MIGRANT FLOWS

NON-STOP SPRAWL
Inspired by Archizoom's *Non-Stop City*, this installation at the MAXXI museum in Rome assembled the McMansion retrofitted models and visualizations, together with immigrants' stories of urban adaptation.

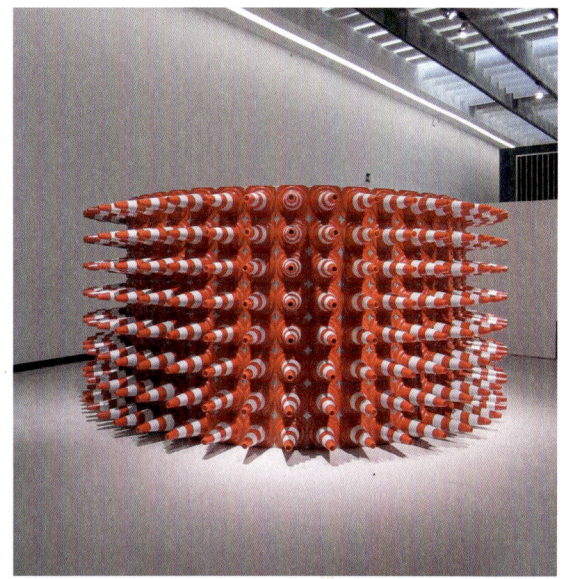

SAN DIEGO'S URBAN DEBRIS MOVES SOUTH
While migrants go north, urban waste from San Diego flows south to construct an urbanism of emergency in Tijuana's periphery.

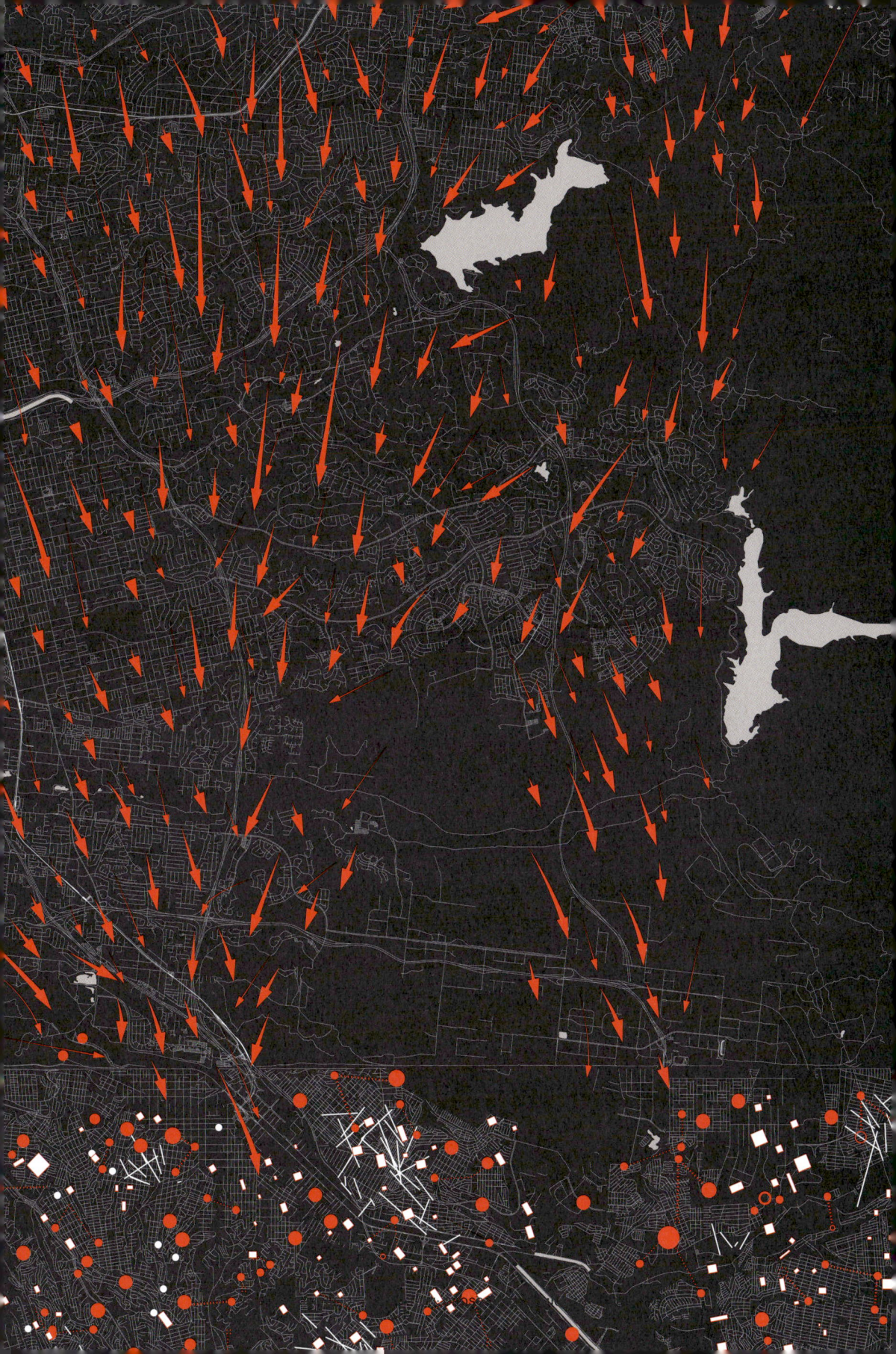

ONE CITY RECYCLES THE WASTE OF THE OTHER
The multiplicity of recycled materials and systems imported from San Diego and reassembled in Tijuana give primacy to the layered complexities of these sites of emergency over the singularity of buildings.

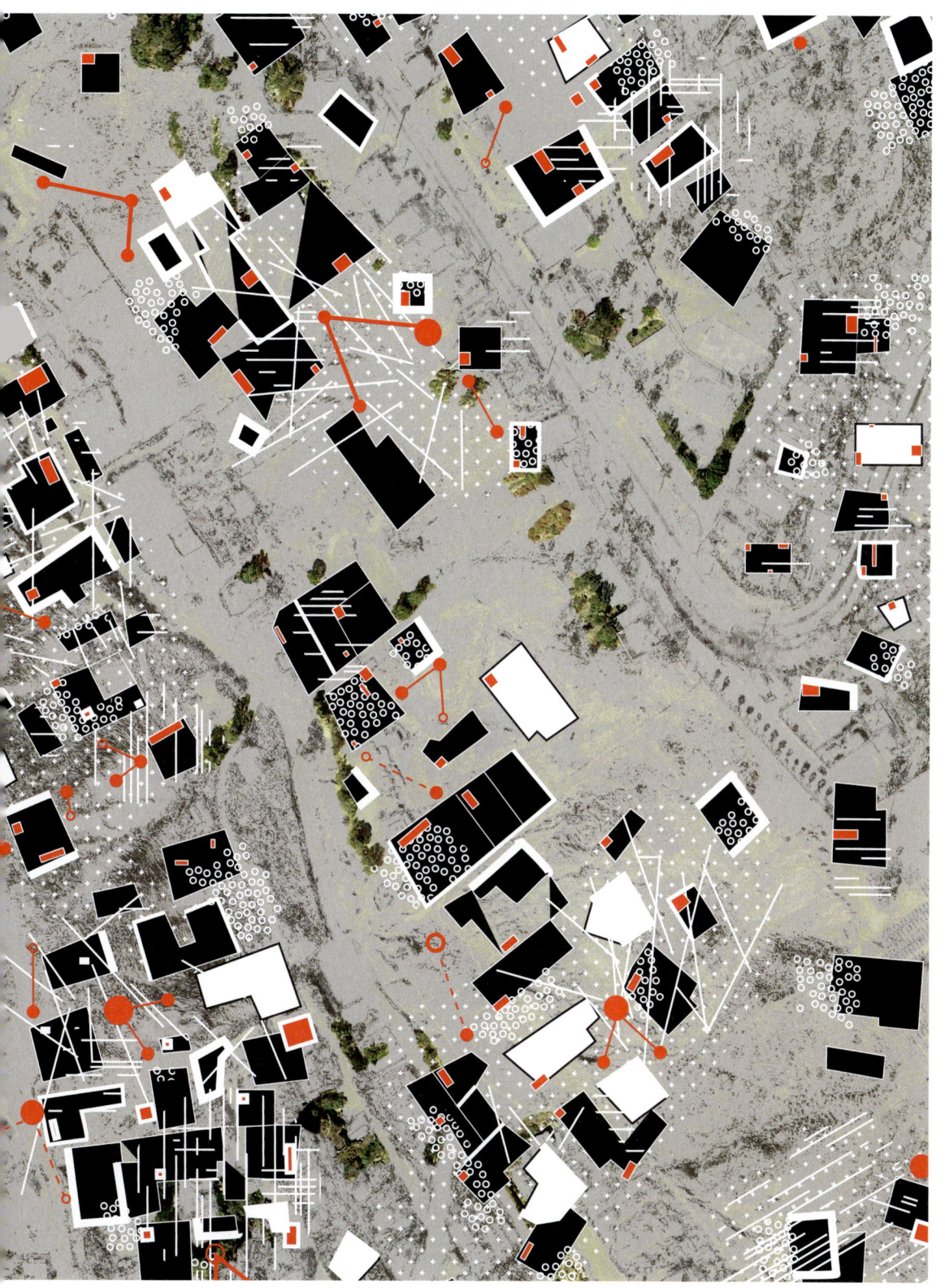

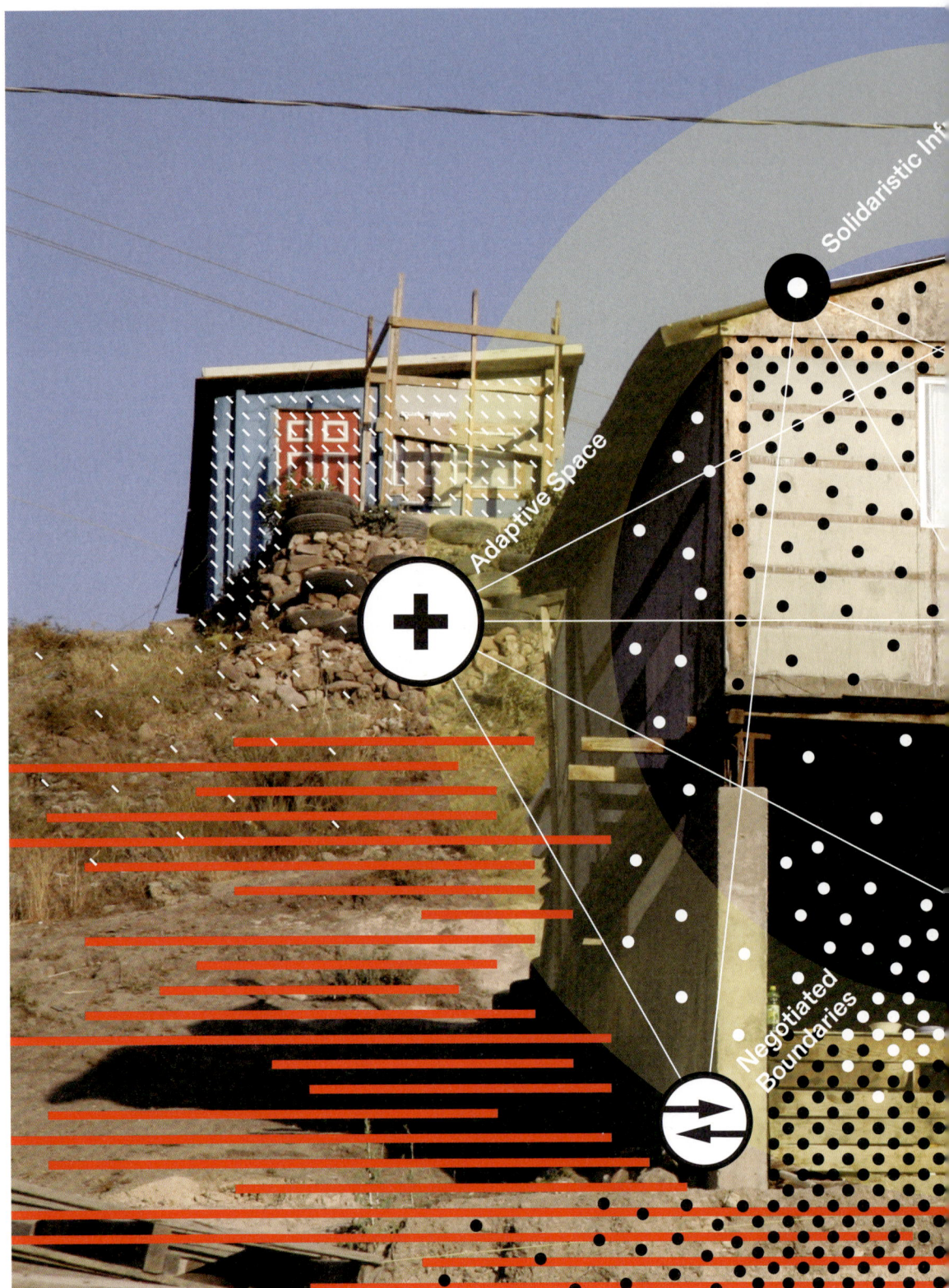

NOTHING IS WASTED, EVERYTHING IS USEFUL

The informal settlements of Tijuana are built with the urban waste of San Diego, recycling architectural parts to construct habitation and infrastructure. Bridging the planned and the unplanned, the legal and the illegal, the object and the ground, informal settlements in Tijuana are socio-spatial laboratories of self-built urbanization, anticipating the patterns of density and programmatic intensity that are already redefining the American metropolis and problematizing contemporary notions of housing and infrastructure across the world.

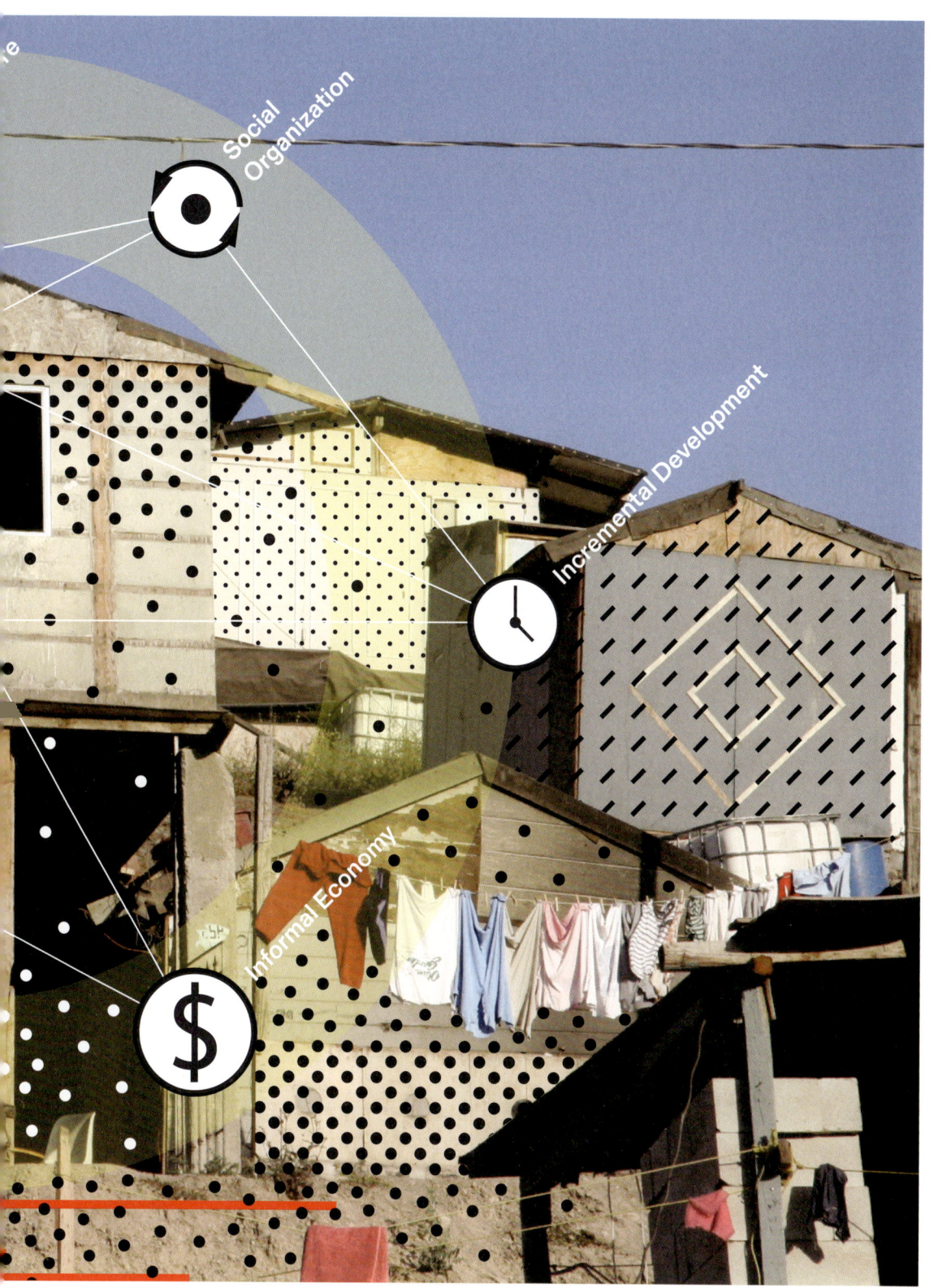

URBANIZATIONS OF ADAPTATION: CROSS-BORDER MIGRANT FLOWS

SECOND-HAND URBANIZATION
Tijuana's urban speculators travel to San Diego to rescue little postwar bungalows slated for demolition. They load them onto trailers and import them into Tijuana, where they are mounted atop one-story metal frames, leaving empty spaces at the street level to accommodate future uses. Retaining walls are built by resassembling rubber tires into looped and interlocking systems to maximize efficiency. San Diego's discarded garage doors become the new skins of emergency housing.

URBANIZATIONS OF ADAPTATION: CROSS-BORDER MIGRANT FLOWS

MEXICAN DREAM
Seduced by the lifestyles of master-planned communities, private developers in Tijuana import suburban recipes from San Diego. Thousands of tiny developer-driven tract homes metastasize across the periphery to provide subsidized social housing. Compensating for a lack of social and economic availabilities, these housing tracts are quickly transformed as occupants fill in setbacks, occupying front and back yards as well as garages with more construction and overlapping programs.

URBANIZATIONS OF ADAPTATION: CROSS-BORDER MIGRANT FLOWS

TIME IS MATERIAL

In a case study we documented, a metal frame appeared from one day to the next. In a couple of months, recycled materials began to thread the spaces. In the next weeks, an informal house emerged. We are not suggesting replicating this precarity in the official city, but we want to learn from this creative intelligence and the incremental building practices of informal urbanization—an urban promiscuity through which one thing can become many.

URBANIZATIONS OF ADAPTATION: CROSS-BORDER MIGRANT FLOWS

CONSTRUCTING FRAMEWORKS FOR THINGS TO HAPPEN

Informal urban processes challenge the autonomy of buildings, often conceived as self-referential systems that benefit the one-dimensionality of the object and are indifferent to socioeconomic temporalities of the city. How can we learn from and engage the complex intersections of time, people, spaces and resources found in informal urbanization?

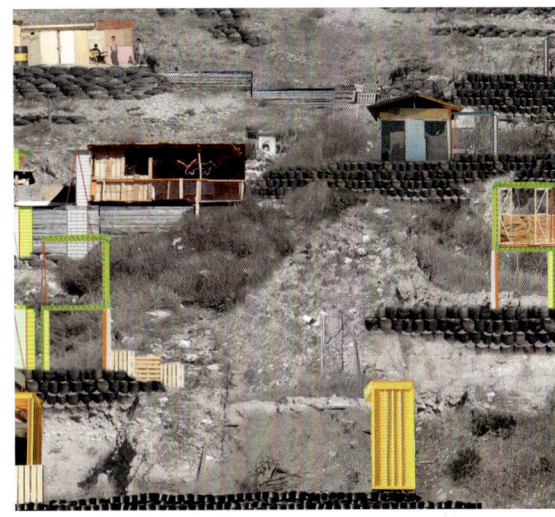

URBANIZATIONS OF ADAPTATION: CROSS-BORDER MIGRANT FLOWS

MANUFACTURED SITES
In Tijuana, we have investigated a new model of anticipatory infrastructure, proposing prefabricated acupunctural scaffolds to frame and choreograph incremental informal housing.

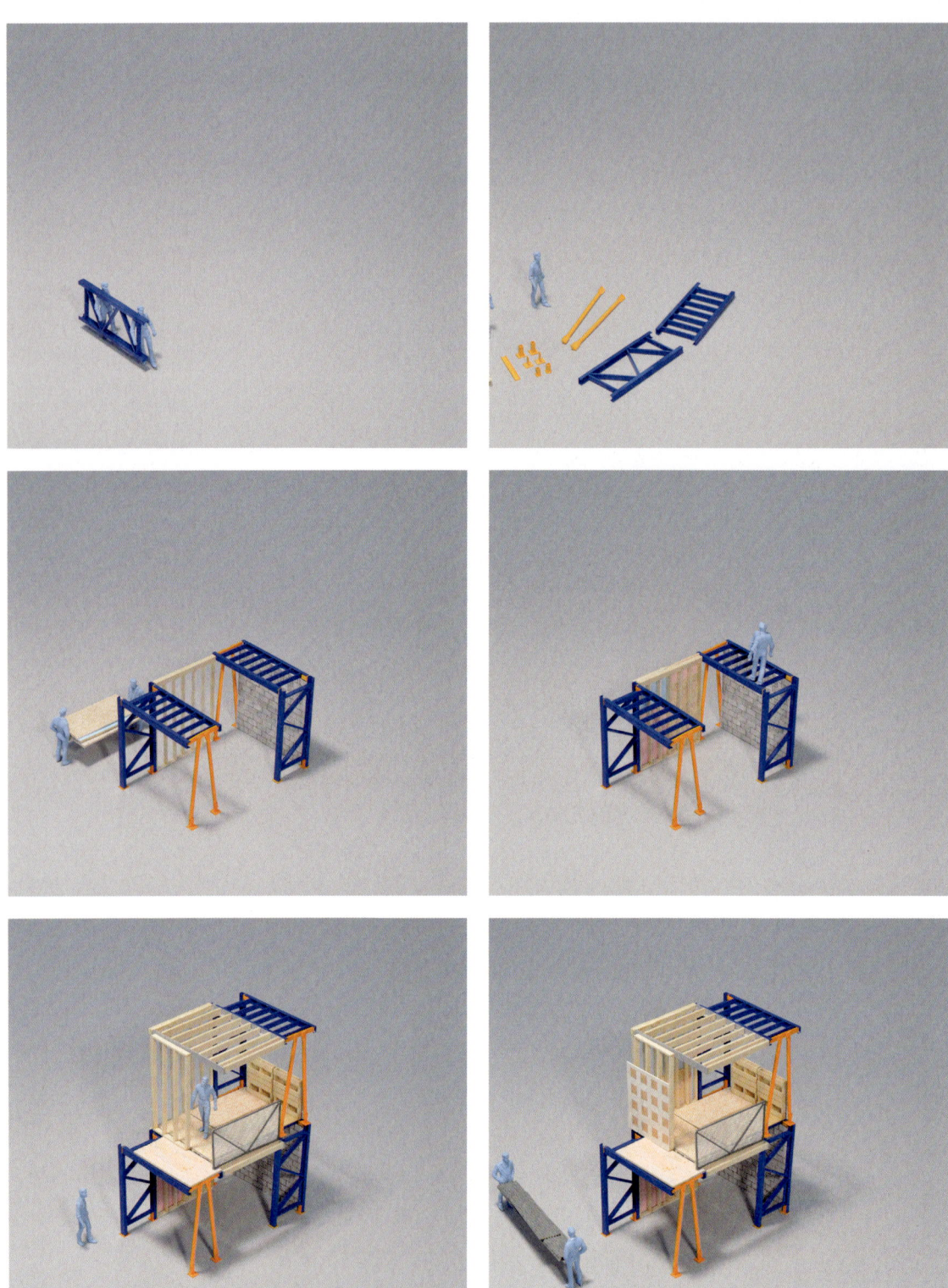

TRANSITIONAL INFRASTRUCTURES
Over the years, we have proposed adapting prefabricated systems made by NAFTA factories to structurally mediate the recycling of waste, supporting the transition from ephemeral spaces into established neighborhoods.

PROJECT: CLUSTER 3

IMMIGRA[NT] NEIGHBO[RHOOD] HOUSING LABORAT[ORY]

NT
RHOODS:

ORIES

IMMIGRANT NEIGHBORHOODS:
HOUSING LABORATORIES

We see housing as public infrastructure, and a tool for social integration in the city. Project cluster 3 presents our work on the social, economic, political and cultural dimensions of housing. Bottom-up urban dynamics on both sides of the US-Mexico border generate different ideas of density and land use from which to reimagine affordable housing. We tell the stories of two social housing case studies that have emerged from our cross-border research and our collaborative work with border communities to seek new cohabitation strategies for social justice. These two projects are the culmination of lengthy social and political processes, embedded in the micro-scale of migrant neighborhoods, from which, we argue, a new civic imagination can be reconstructed.

1   San Diego Case Study: Living Rooms at the Border

    Urban Conflict:
    The War Between Developers and Communities

    Designing Process:
    A Social-Economic Micro-Policy for Housing in San Ysidro

    Urban-Architectural Intervention:
    Small Parcels as Social-Economic Infrastructure

2   Tijuana Case Study: Santuario Frontera

    Urban Conflict:
    Conflicts Between Factories, Migrant Labor
    and Emergency Housing

    Designing Process:
    A Social and Economic Micro-Policy for Social Housing
    in Los Laureles Canyon

    Urban-Architectural Project:
    Refugee Camps as Infrastructures for Inclusion

Our research on the informal urban flows across the San Diego–Tijuana border region has provoked a dual approach to urban intervention, two radically different approaches to constructing the city. On the San Diego side, our work has focused on intervening within suburban contexts, where top-down logics of sprawl and fragmentation divide the city, misallocating resources and exacerbating consumption and waste. Here we have been interested in *informalizing the formal*, just enough to maximize social densification, economic plurality and climate adaptation—in other words, injecting complexity into highly homogenized, unsustainable environments.

On the Tijuana side, we partner with community agencies to intervene in informal settlements, where bottom-up urban organizational logics generate programmatic and spatial mixing, plurality and adaptation, but lack resources to scale up and perform to their full capacity. Here we have been interested in *formalizing the informal*, just enough to maximize its infrastructural capabilities for spatial evolution and economic agency—in other words, injecting modular frameworks to organize heterogeneity.

This dual approach to urban intervention problematizes formal / informal binaries. In our work, we mediate the interface between them in particular urban contexts on both sides of the border, where immigrant communities have already set in motion urban procedures from which to reconceptualize housing and public space, and give us clues about scaling up. We believe informal immigrant neighborhoods are the housing laboratories of our time, where top-down and bottom-up urban and architectural knowledge can meet to produce new housing policy and economy and new spatial typologies of public housing.

Here we present two case studies of affordable housing that emblematize this dual approach to urban and architectural intervention on both sides of the US-Mexico border. Each of these projects emerged from urban processes that were carefully choreographed through years of research in partnership with community-based organizations rooted in the sites where the projects are built. The design of these social, economic and political processes yielded particular spatial resolutions and a set of concepts that we believe are reproduceable and scalable to low-income communities across the border region. One project is in San Diego, located in the border neighborhood of San Ysidro, the first community one encounters when crossing the San Ysidro international checkpoint from Tijuana into the US. This urban neighborhood is emblematic of many older mid-city urban fabrics where immigrants have settled in the last decades. The second project is located barely five miles away across the border, in Los Laureles Canyon, an informal settlement at the western periphery of Tijuana, often referred to as the *last slum* of Latin America, literally crashing against the border wall.

San Diego Case Study: Living Rooms at the Border

URBAN CONFLICT:
THE WAR BETWEEN DEVELOPERS AND COMMUNITIES

The death of public housing in the US was cemented in 1995 by the Faircloth Amendment, which severely curtailed the development of public housing established by the New Deal's 1937 Housing Act. Since then the housing agenda has morphed from social systems into isolated units, from housing to houses, bringing about a sprawling recipe of radical fragmentation that scatters millions of objects across the territory indiscriminately in a way that is socially and environmentally unsustainable. In conditions of poverty, Section 8 vouchers given to individuals have replaced our collective investments in housing as a public good, placing the production of affordable housing and its profits in the hands of private developers. Social housing has become commodified and subjected to the vulnerability of market forces, and neither developers nor governments have been able to produce new paradigms of affordability. In fact, during the last decades, thousands of public housing units were demolished, millions of mortgages were foreclosed and, more recently, millions of people have faced post-COVID-19 eviction, making a new social economy of housing more urgent than ever.

But the current political climate suggests that large-scale public housing will not return any time soon. In the meantime, can other scales and configurations of affordable housing be explored that incrementally infill, adapt and retrofit the vastness of market-based sprawl? The cookie-cutter architecture of today's amorphous suburbs and exurbs, transforming housing into commodified objects, things floating on an undifferentiated territory, only divorces housing from a differentiated *civic ground*, where public infrastructures of mobility and sociability would otherwise stitch these fragments within a deliberate set of interdependencies to sustain affordability. Current municipal planners collude with private developers, whose market-driven redevelopment schemes only lead to gentrification. But ironically, as developers and municipal planners aspire to *citify* the suburbs into more civilized urban cores, dressing up suburbia with a fake facade of urbanity, they continue to redevelop downtowns across American cities by importing into them the very suburban recipes of homogenization, privatization, gating and theming, rendering both the suburbs and city centers sites of gentrification. The zones that continue to be ignored are the spaces in between, the mid-city, where older neighborhoods have remained sites of disinvestment. These are the sites where we work.

DESIGNING PROCESS:
A SOCIAL-ECONOMIC MICRO-POLICY FOR HOUSING IN SAN YSIDRO

Developers had their chance. It is time to produce a new public housing agenda, led by communities and supported by restructured modes of governance and planning that can advance housing through a more holistic, integrated management of resources and programs within which affordable housing can be embedded. The most experimental work in housing in the United States should be in the hands of progressive, community-based, non-profit organizations. These agencies engage the social dynamics of mid-city neighborhoods daily, mediating between their bottom-up histories and identities and the top-down planning policies that too often unjustly shape their destiny. It seems appropriate that these organizations become the future developers of affordable housing within a new public realm, because their sociocultural agendas and deep community knowledges can translate into unique organizational and spatial strategies.

Working in the neighborhood of San Ysidro, so close to the militarized border checkpoint, we reflect on ideas of sovereignty at the scale of neighborhoods. In neighborhoods as diverse as Ramallah, San Ysidro and Boyle Heights, we have come to believe that a community's civic freedom rests in creatively stewarding civic culture and local modes of social and economic productivity. Can a more critical orientation to sovereignty be shaped at the neighborhood scale in the way a community participates in the construction of its own housing stock, its own public spaces and infrastructure? Can the border neighborhood of San Ysidro be a site of exception and experimentation where new forms of local governance are designed and tested?

A MICRO-POLICY AT NEIGHBORHOOD SCALE

It became clear to us at some point that entering the politics of affordable housing in San Diego required partnering with community-based organizations, because they are highly effective at community mobilization and have the trust and capacity to summon the community and understand its urgencies. Architects too often undervalue partnership with communities. We sometimes think our expertise can solve urban problems without realizing how little we actually understand about the histories and embedded knowledges of communities, essential to making real progress on affordable housing today.

For more than thirty years, Casa Familiar has been deeply rooted in the community of San Ysidro, with fifty-two programs focused on community engagement and well-being. *For decades,* Andrea Skorepa was Casa Familiar's executive director, an urban activist who became the matriarch of this small and forgotten Latinx border community. We partnered with Skorepa to research a new approach to redevelop her neighborhood, with the idea that before designing form, we would design the social and economic processes that would make the housing forms sustainable, and would instigate a change in existing municipal policy. It is interesting to note that some of the most progressive community-based leaders across the United States are powerful women, a phenomenon that highlights the intersection of gender politics and spatial justice.

We began by denouncing the stigmas of criminality and poverty cast on low-income immigrant neighborhoods like San Ysidro. Instead, we sought to elevate a more complex idea of community and spatial organization, a complexity we needed to translate and make accessible to frame the terms of an alternative housing policy. Across these neighborhoods, housing is informally operationalized as a relational socio-spatial system. Our process with Casa Familiar began by declaring the neighborhood of San Ysidro a site for housing experimentation from which to investigate specific, not abstract, economic and spatial tactics that could mobilize dormant sources of funding and blur obsolete boundaries between public and private resources. This is one of the reasons this collaboration has been recognized internationally:

Living Rooms at the Border: constructing the site

Living Rooms at the Border: interlocking living units with social space

together we forwarded the possibility that in times of crisis, communities can become sites of political and spatial experimentation, with new zoning and density typologies organizing spaces for sociability and programs for small-scale economic productivity. Moreover, a new paradigm emerged from our work together, through which housing becomes an armature to support public culture and infrastructure, redefining sustainability as the integration of environmental, social and economic justice agendas.

The San Ysidro Micro-Policy advocated for a new role for neighborhood nonprofits to co-develop housing, like community-based *informal city halls*. This included mediating and translating otherwise invisible neighborhood dynamics, connecting tangible housing needs to specific community participants, and supporting new economies through social and vocational services, sometimes embedded in social housing itself.

Agencies like Casa Familiar can mobilize latent entrepreneurial and activist civic energies in the neighborhood towards a more localized political economy. We understood that challenging housing policy requires partnering with a community agency because they are already attuned to the particular social-economic agendas and spatial organizational logics in the neighborhood. Collaboration is essential to proposing a new zoning policy to the local municipality—emerging not from the planners' table, but initiated by the community, represented politically by the community agency, spatialized and visualized by architects like us, and supported by enlightened urban governance willing to accommodate more inclusive and complex neighborhood-scale development.

Our development of the Micro-Policy began with documenting all stealth, nonconforming additions, micro-units and small informal economies distributed across the neighborhood. The goal was to legitimize and protect them, and advocate for the formal approval of a new, affordable housing overlay zone for the neighborhood to increase allowable densities from one to two or three units per parcel, if desired by the occupant. Skorepa called it "common sense urbanization," illustrating how an existing single-family residence could easily coexist on one parcel with two nonconforming micro-units to sustain an extended family or a small business.

With this research-based mapping of nonconforming but generative patterns of development, the second stage of our political process was to co-design a pedagogical strategy with Casa Familiar through a series of community dialogues and workshops. These became a monthly forum, *San Ysidro Sin Limites,* which still thrives today and at which community issues are presented and deliberated to increase community awareness of existing urban policy and advocate for new policies and regulatory frameworks that accommodate the community's own patterns of informal development. What defines a residential unit? The kitchen. What defines a bedroom? The size of a window. What defines density? A sterile number of people per area.

We learned that a meaningful participatory design practice needs to challenge conventional practices of community-engaged design in urban redevelopment in the US, which typically reduces community engagement to symbolic box-ticking gestures, with options constrained by the agendas of developers and municipalities, too often in collusion with one another. This process is too often co-opted by a *politics of consensus* in which iconographic architecture is pandered to a reified portrait of neighborhood "identity" to grease the wheels for private development. In what *style* should we build? These processes typically ignore critical social and economic considerations and the role that everyday practices already play in negotiating boundaries and resources, producing alternative spaces for sustainability and fostering coexistence. Often these processes pave the way for gentrification and dispossession.

Our Micro-Policy became a tool for igniting a politics of information in the neighborhood, for increasing public knowledge. In other words, *designing sustainable, affordable housing must advance in tandem with new systems of community pedagogy to cultivate a new political language. This is ultimately why we are interested in the mediating role that nonprofit organizations play in immigrant neighborhoods, because they become the representatives of the invisible. They become curators that bundle the agency of everyday practices into cohesive forms of political representation, from which new modes of local self-governance can emerge.*

Our pedagogical models included visualization tools, models and cartographies designed to problematize what we mean by the public, density, housing, infrastructure and property. For example, we designed a tabletop game to facilitate a conversation about the topic of density and to demystify mutual misconceptions. The meeting with neighborhood activists and residents began with the provocation: What is density? We designed *The Density Game,* a board representing the generic parcels of an existing neighborhood block accompanied by colored wooden blocks representing housing units, trees and cars. We set up the game at a community table. The facilitator, a neighborhood youth mentored to lead the workshop, explained what the board and blocks represented. He announced to the group: "We are going to explore the idea of density. A developer usually says: let's build so many units on this block ... but how many units can we really place in these parcels?"

Doña Maria, an elder community leader, made the first move: she placed one piece of wood in one parcel, another piece in another parcel, and so on. In effect, she reproduced the existing reality of her own block, one house per parcel. But then someone pushed two blocks against each other: "What if two owners collaborate and join their houses [in a zero-setback condition] to generate extra space in the parcel, allowing for an extra unit? Or a shared space?" Very soon, everyone began to place multiple blocks of wood in the parcels, and Doña Maria exclaimed: "Now I remember! When I was a young girl in Guadalajara, Mexico, I used to live in an older neighborhood near downtown, and those blocks were not made of individual buildings, but they were a continuous building. There were doors against the street, and you would open a door and find patios inside...." Another person asked: "Can density be about spaces rather than buildings?" Doña Maria punctuated the moment: "I cannot believe our houses are selfish! Maybe density can be about neighborhood collaboration."

The *Density Game* was a mediating tool that enabled anecdotes and experiences to challenge conventional ideas of density. This exercise also challenged conventional municipal- and developer-driven community workshops organized around style and the packaging of identity into metaphorical tropes: buildings that look like Aztec pyramids, or Mediterranean villas. While respectful of iconographic histories and cultural signification, with our community partners we wanted to move past "façadism" and explore the everyday performance of existing blocks, where spaces are in flux, activated through nonconforming uses and negotiations of private and public boundaries.

This dialogical experiment also enabled the community to recognize the hidden value of their everyday social and economic entrepreneurship. Neighborhood stories of informal economic activity led to speculation about how to translate these stories into new policy configurations, through which Casa Familiar, our community partner, could act as facilitator. Take the example of two women, responding to lack of childcare in the neighborhood, who rent a three-bedroom apartment and transform it into a small day-care facility to help other

Living Rooms at the Border: housing porches surround an adapted historic church

working families. They are recognized by Casa Familiar, which supports them with economic resources, channeling and redirecting subsidies and other cash flows while maintaining their invisibility. Some will dismiss this activity as "illegal," but we would like to recognize its potential in the absence of state support—scaling it up, formalizing it along with other bottom-up practices in the neighborhood in order to bundle local-scale economic and social creativity. We want to frame the agency of these stealth practices as an operative tool to rethink economic development at local and small scales, and ultimately to help the city reimagine typologies of housing and public space.

With all of this evidence, the third area of design within the Micro-Policy for San Ysidro proposed partnerships between Casa Familiar and property owners of nonconforming parcels with undocumented micro-units. These are neighborhood residents who own their parcels but do not have the resources or knowledge to leverage their real-estate equity. At this point, the idea of new social contracts emerged, which could enable the community to produce a new shared ownership model, new interpretations of community trusts. In a sense, this amounted to bundling nonconforming parcels into a distributed community trust. Broadly speaking, community trusts assure the collective ownership of particular land by a particular community-based organization, even if the buildings built on that land will be leased to individual actors. This assures protection against market speculation and locks community benefits into place. What can happen when many small parcels are bundled into a collective model of ownership, to assure equitable distribution of resources and profits?

This bundling and protecting process ultimately mounted a major challenge to existing models of housing financialization. During one of the community meetings, the question emerged: Why wasn't a single affordable housing project built in San Ysidro during the economic boom of the 1990s to the mid-2000s? Since the early 1980s, expensive luxury housing developments proliferated across downtowns and other privileged urban zones, while few affordable housing projects were built in underserved communities across the US. The reasons are clear. For a private developer to secure profits in the development of affordable housing in many mid-city, low-income neighborhoods in dense

American cities, they need to rely on tax-credit subsidies (tax breaks). To qualify for these competitive subsidies (it is ironic to realize that even the word "subsidy" has been whitewashed in the economic development glossary), the development needs to produce at least fifty units of housing. This kind of density is prohibited by zoning in many mid-city neighborhoods—while in wealthier communities, that kind of density and the mere mention of affordability connotes images of a barbarian invasion. But this is not only about punitive zoning. To connect these affordable housing projects more meaningfully with the local community to prevent gentrification, their development proformas would need to propose land uses that benefit local residents, increasing their capacity for small business and economic development. But existing land uses in many of these neighborhoods prohibit mixed uses, and because of the stratification of subsidy lending that polarizes residential and commercial uses, many affordable housing developers focus solely on housing *units,* undermining the urban innovation needed to advance interfaces between residential units, mixed uses, public spaces and local business. Finally, because of the high costs of urban development, exacerbated by heavy municipal bureaucracy and myopic administrative processes, there is no economic incentive for developers to promote affordability or demographic and economic diversity at local scales. How can affordable housing developers be held accountable for innovation when even the municipal boilerplate requirements from housing authorities tasked with securing affordability correspond with median income brackets that belie the reality on the ground, where poverty and marginalization are rampant?

After the community dialogues increased awareness of possibilities, and with the social contracts in motion to experiment with diverse forms of economic development, the San Ysidro Micro-Policy was proposed to the municipality of San Diego as a shared model of public management, through which Casa Familiar would become a facilitator to represent residents. We co-designed a catalogue of small building typologies and housing additions, combining them in a variety of imaginative scenarios that were resonant with community resourcefulness and scrappy ingenuity.

We then co-developed a package of construction drawings with a compendium of micro-units to replace old ones that lacked structural stability. In the design process, we recuperated dormant legislation from the 1960s regarding accessory units—granny flats or "companion units," as the municipality called them. To understand their potential, imagine accessory units as the airbnbs of the New Deal. Accessory units as a typology can support small-scale urban development when plugged into the backyards of older mid-city parcels, occupying a small percentage of the existing area of the house. According to planning code, accessory units require a small kitchen, but *accessory buildings* do not. And if an accessory building is no larger than 120 square feet (around 12 square meters), it does not require a permit. Imagine a small shed of 10 by 12 feet given a high ceiling, fitted with a small bathroom, a utility sink and a big window. What emerges is a functional studio for a local artist, or countless other uses. Since it does not need a permit, it can be built by the community. With examples like these, our San Ysidro Micro-Policy advocated affordable housing as a neighborhood-scale economic engine, incentivizing jobs within communities.

Taking these hidden assets into account, the Micro-Policy proposed a tactical new zoning policy for San Ysidro: new transitional densities and spaces linking existing patterns of everyday use to a small network of micro units distributed through the neighborhood. This demanded a more imaginative model of community-based economic development. We designed a strategy with Casa Familiar to fund these new distributed micro-units by "piggybacking" on existing models of affordable housing subsidy. We proposed that the neighborhood would serve as developer of its own housing to prevent gentrification, challenging conventional developer-driven protocols of tax-credit-based financing. In our vision, the City of San Diego would enable Casa Familiar to officially prepackage and facilitate construction permits to replace the existing precarious, nonconforming dwelling units, as well as allow for a new typology of tax-credit subsidy to support the designation of these small units as affordable housing. This meant that Casa Familiar could break apart and distribute the fifty-unit density equation which formerly prevented San Ysidro from qualifying for tax-credit subsidies, as long as all of the fifty units would be built at the same time, distributed across parcels in the neighborhood, and as long as Casa Familiar could centralize management and liabilities on behalf of the community. In contrast to conventional community trust agendas, the land (parcels) here is individually owned, while the ownership and revenue streams of this array of extra affordable housing units would be shared collectively, between Casa Familiar and all participating residents.

The prepackaging of design systems, permits and lending by bundling and synergizing resources, social contracts, political representation and new cross-institutional collaborations between top-down planning agencies bottom-up neighborhood ingenuity amplifies the essential mediating role played by agencies like Casa Familiar. The Micro-Policy presented a new approach to community-engaged urban development; it opened up a small-lot ordinance process in San Diego that aimed to infill transitional and suburban areas of the city with small, community-led development. This momentum provided fertile political ground from which alternative hybrid projects and their sources of funding could emerge, and opened more imaginative channels of engagement between the City of San Diego and neighborhood-based, local nonprofit organizations. Most importantly, the San Ysidro Micro-Policy boldly provoked: Can communities become developers of their own housing stock? Can embedded, neighborhood-based nonprofits facilitate alternative urban processes to co-produce the knowledges and co-own the resources of development, becoming long-term choreographers of social and cultural programming for housing and public infrastructure at the scale of the neighborhood?

URBAN-ARCHITECTURAL INTERVENTION:
SMALL PARCELS AS SOCIAL-ECONOMIC INFRASTRUCTURE

We designed the Micro-Policy with Casa Familiar as a general policy framework for experimental small-scale urban interventions in San Ysidro and beyond, and also to launch a proof-of-concept case study called *Living Rooms at the Border*. This multi-year, research-based, ultimately built project has been important for us because it illustrates a key political position we have taken as a political and architectural practice: that to achieve social and economic justice in the city we need to co-produce projects with communities. Designing architectures that can spatialize more solidaristic urban processes entails a double task: designing the physical spaces as well as the protocols for inclusion. This means developing conceptual and programmatic content to reorganize spatial, social and economic relations.

While *Living Rooms at the Border* began with a robust community-based process, it lacked the economic resources and development support systems necessary to realize any architectural project within conventional time frames and development protocols. These weaknesses became our site of intervention, within which we agreed, together with our partners, that we would not summon a developer to assist the project, but that Casa Familiar would present itself as an alternative developer of affordable housing. Architects conventionally wait for the client and the brief in order to design within a given site and budget. But the language of "client" and conventional hierarchies of practice don't work for us. Over the years, we have *co-produced* the brief with communities, understood not as clients but as co-developers. And together we summoned the bottom-up constituencies and top-down institutions needed to realize these projects in the absence of formal support. This has always entailed designing economic proformas that assure inclusion and long-term sustainability.

This pilot project emerged, then, from collaborative research that observed how people in San Ysidro thrive, and these existing patterns of use became our point of departure to propose architectural solutions that rendered obsolete existing housing planning policy, lending and subsidy structures. *Living Rooms at the Border* became a political tool through which Casa Familiar was able to push against regulatory constraints in San Ysidro, as well as to propose new densities and mixed uses.

THE BUILDING BLOCKS FOR AFFORDABLE HOUSING

The physical design of *Living Rooms at The Border* incorporated elements of the San Ysidro Micro-Policy and our cross-border urban research to challenge conventional definitions of affordability, housing, density, zoning and land use. This is a summary:

1.
To promote local nonprofits as developers of affordable housing in their own neighborhoods.

2.
To bundle the sweat equity of architects and the landownership and programmatic capacity of non-profits to co-develop housing to improve the quality of architecture and neighborhood planning. This also means elevating nonprofits as local experts, epicenters of urban and political creativity.

3.
To challenge normative definitions of "density." In neighborhoods like San Ysidro, density is not sustainable if understood as the number of objects / people per area. Density must be redefined as intensity of social and economic exchanges per area. The operative dimension of everyday bottom-up practices—informal economies that spring up in residential parcels, generating alternative mixed uses; solidaristic programming led by neighborhood agencies to compensate for lack of public support—should provoke new meanings of densification.

4.
To challenge conventions that see affordable housing solely as cheap residential units to "rent" or to "own." Instead, affordable housing should be reimagined as an economic and social engine for producing new kinds of property and ownership. In conditions of poverty, units cannot be expected to thrive in a social vacuum. They need to be embedded within an infrastructure of social and economic support.

5.
To diversify the actors and sectors involved in urban development. Housing projects are typically produced by a single developer, one architect and a construction company, whose proforma articulates a homogeneous housing typology, style and material choice, bypassing community partnerships and stifling the diversity and everyday

heterogeneity inherent in vibrant neighborhoods like San Ysidro.

6.
To decriminalize zoning, which too often prevents local, economic and social development. Zoning should be a generative device to elevate rather than stifle the many bottom-up entrepreneurial social and economic activities in the neighborhood. Zoning should position housing to become a central neighborhood asset.

7.
To challenge the minimum parcel size in mid-city neighborhoods, which in Southern California have remained hugely mono-use and suburban, requiring five thousand square feet for a single-family home. Mid-city parcels can be activated as economic and social engines if diverse small-scale building typologies are encouraged rather than discouraged.

8.
To rethink housing affordability. More than "owning" or "renting" units, residents benefit from the immediacy of accessible social infrastructure and revenue-generating opportunities, including access to higher education. There is great hidden value in community participation and access to social and economic programming designed to build capacities and skills.

CRITICAL LOCATION

San Ysidro is among the poorest, most marginalized neighborhoods in San Diego, uniquely situated next to the busiest border checkpoint in the western hemisphere. With a population of 30,000, 90% of which is Latinx, median household income is $27,943, 60% below city averages. The *Living Rooms at the Border* project site is located in the historical center of San Ysidro, less than a mile from the US-Mexico border wall. San Ysidro lacks adequate pedestrian and public infrastructure. While many parcels remain vacant, it has the largest deficit of affordable housing and public space in the city. *Living Rooms at the Border* is located in a small parcel within a historic twenty-block grid of small parcels checkered by a network of alleys. This particular parcel contains a small and largely abandoned but beloved historic church building, built in 1927, which Casa Familiar acquired many years ago. It later became the generative architectural anchor for this pilot project.

As city, state and federal resources have been reoriented toward surveillance and control across the border region, San Ysidro remains largely off the radar of political, regulatory and economic institutions. But despite poverty and persistent social challenges, a distinctive feature of San Ysidro is the close social ties among its residents and their willingness to come together around issues of common concern. Much of this community energy has been cultivated by the social programming of Casa Familiar over the past thirty years. Through our collaboration, this social capital has generated spatial propositions for alternative urban design strategies of resilience and adaptation.

DESIGN STRATEGIES

The informal negotiation of boundaries and spaces in San Ysidro inspired incremental design solutions that could have a catalytic effect on the urban fabric. We wanted to spatialize these existing patterns of neighborhood use within conventional parcels, learning from the improvisational appropriation of the public right-of-way by residents, who blur the boundary between private lots and the street, transforming alleys into complex, informal networks of pedestrian and economic activity. Everyday community life also includes provisional, multi-program and hybrid uses of space, such as informal markets.

We especially wanted the parcel to extend and strengthen the existing network of old alleys surrounding it. The small parcel was organized as a series of linear "strips," demonstrating that conventional parcels can be retrofitted into different gradations of property and pedestrian circulation, housing economies and social interactions, promoting organic and flexible development through time. Some of these strips are small linear buildings, some are interstitial landscape spaces that support informal uses, and others serve as circulation pathways threading the neighborhood together, from alley to street.

In a parcel where existing zoning allows only three units of housing, we negotiated density bonuses and proposed an alternative mixed-use spatial system that included ten affordable housing units, threaded by community spaces for cultural, educational, social and economic activity. What follows are the main design, programmatic and economic strategies for the incremental development of *Living Rooms at the Border*:

1. Designing Social-service Infrastructure for Affordable Housing

Advancing the idea that affordable housing is not sustainable as "units" only but needs to be embedded within an infrastructure of social support, *Living Rooms at the Border* was designed as a double project: affordable housing conceptualized as a spatial system programmed with social, cultural and economic activities.

The social service infrastructure is conceptualized as a series of functional public spaces, curated with activities and funding streams for sustainability:

Community Theater:
The historic church is transformed into a small community theater, called *El Salon*, to serve as a cultural asset for the neighborhood. The community theater extends outward through a shaded balcony stage to animate a small plaza for outdoor performances.

Civic Classroom:
The Community Theater is flanked to the south by *Casa Patio*, a shaded open-air civic classroom-pavilion to support outdoor civic and educational activities.

Social Service Pavilions:
The Community Theater is flanked to the north by seven small accessory buildings designed to house Casa Familiar's social service programming. These small buildings have utility sinks and large windows, enabling a variety of uses: an artist's studio, a café, a clinic, an office for migrant support services. The accessory buildings serve as demonstrations of small-scale development framed by the San Ysidro Micro-Policy, an illustration that can be reproduced across the neighborhood.

This social, educational and cultural infrastructure anchors ten units of affordable housing at both ends of the parcel.

These housing units are designed to be subdivided according to the different needs of their users. One-, two- and three-bedroom units, for example, can be subdivided into smaller studios sharing kitchens to enable affordability, transitional housing, extended-family living and live-work scenarios.

Housing Type 1:
Small units are dedicated to young couples and single mothers with children.

Housing Type 2:
Live-work units allow the exchange of rent for social service. Artists and Casa Familiar choreograph pedagogical and cultural interfaces with children and families.

Housing Type 3:
Larger three-bedroom units are dedicated to large families who live with grandparents. Casa Familiar partners with families to promote economic entrepreneurship through catering and food-based initiatives.

Housing Type 4:
Accessory buildings serve as alternative housing. These small sheds become flexible spaces for extended families. For example, a nephew studies at a local community college and rents studio and living space; a niece, recently married, rents a studio temporarily and uses a small shed for office space; or Casa Familiar subsidizes a room for a gardener who collaborates with residents to maintain the project's landscape.

All housing typologies and community spaces in the small parcels are mediated by pedestrian walkways. Designing linear housing units linking streets and alleys supports existing circuits for pedestrian and landscape corridors across the neighborhood.

2. <u>Designing the Programmatic Interface between Public Space and Housing</u>

Affordable housing takes on a different meaning when it is deliberately threaded into a service infrastructure, where "units" are embedded in social programming, summoning residents to participate in the development of local economy and cultural production. A conventional affordable housing developer generally maximizes residential units and minimizes social infrastructure. *Living Rooms at the Border* does the opposite: we calibrated interfaces between units and social infrastructure to maximize social and economic exchanges, while proposing mid-density housing to provide a model of incremental densification of suburban subdivisions. For each housing unit, there is a deliberate ratio for social programming.

The tactical programming is choreographed by Casa Familiar and other cultural partners. The community spaces are designed to be adaptable, accommodating diverse uses: a gallery, a stage, an arts workshop, a market.

To support these spaces with specific programming and funding, we conceived a unique partnership model that links the resources and knowledges of immigrant communities and the University of California, San Diego, where we teach and where our practice is based. The *UCSD Community Stations* are a network of field stations on both sides of the border, where universities and communities collaborate on cultural and educational activities, and a model of shared urban intervention and community development (see project cluster 6). We see urban justice as a redistributive concept, entailing not only the redistribution of resources, but also the redistribution of knowledges. *Living Rooms at the Border* is now the home of the *UCSD–Casa Community Station*. At Casa Familiar we curate the "meeting of knowledges," promoting circulations between the university and San Ysidro residents, connecting university students, curators and researchers with community-based youth, community activists and cultural producers. This partnership also produced channels for political representation, mobilizing bottom-up research initiatives into neighborhood advocacy for transformations in public policy.

A Day in the Life of Living Rooms at the Border, a fellowship from the *UCSD–Casa Community Station*, enables a local artist to collaborate with script writers from the UCSD theater department. Engaging Casa Familiar's commitment to improving air quality in San Ysidro, a script begins to emerge that addresses environmental justice. Orientation meetings and rehearsals occur under *Casa Patio*, the open-air civic classroom, culminating in a play performed in the Community Theater, where neighborhood youth and residents enact the story of environmental injustice in San Ysidro before the community. To coordinate these social interfaces and activities, Casa Familiar dedicates one of its housing units to a community curator, who exchanges rent for social service, supporting and facilitating the cultural life of the parcel.

3. Designing the Economic Proforma and Funding Mechanisms

The organizational design of the parcel through a system of linear strips was a deliberate strategy to mobilize diverse financial streams to support the different building typologies. In other words, the diversification of buildings and programs in low-income neighborhoods demands creative diversification of lending brackets, philanthropic and foundation support, and other mechanisms. If the project remains mono-use, mono-scale and large in its deployment, it reduces opportunities for incremental development and limits potential sources of funding, whether private lending, public subsidy, social impact investment or others.

New approaches to inclusive and equitable urban development demand robust cross-sector coalitions. As we established the *UCSD Community Stations* to support social housing, we discovered that this platform for collaborative knowledge production could be deployed as a new model of shared urban intervention, in which the economic and programmatic power of the university becomes leverage for communities to develop their own public spaces and housing, placing education at the center of community and economic development.

The financing process began when Casa Familiar and UCSD joined forces to pursue philanthropic support to renovate and transform the abandoned church into a Community Theatre. The Mellon Foundation had already committed funds to support educational and cultural programming at the *UCSD–Casa Community Station* (understood in those early years as a partnership that utilized the existing spaces of Casa Familiar). Casa Familiar and UCSD developed a compelling narrative to leverage these programmatic commitments and deployed significant community enthusiasm to secure capital investments to build out the social spaces of *Living Rooms at the Border*. The NYC-based PARC Foundation, led by artist David Deutsch, and ArtPlace America, a consortium of US-based foundations committed to equitable place-making, generously agreed to fund renovation of the church as the Community Theater / *El Salon* and construction of *Casa Patio* (the open-air classroom) and the social-service accessory buildings.

This social infrastructure then *seeded* the affordable housing component. Conventional affordable housing developers seek to balance their proformas by maximizing profitable housing space and minimizing social amenities to the greatest allowable extent. We turned this model on its head. Our commitment to social spaces led the project, and housing spaces then followed. Philanthropic investment in the Community Theatre, outdoor classroom and accessory buildings enabled Casa Familiar, performing as a developer of affordable housing, to qualify for a $9M New Markets Tax Credit development package facilitated by Civic San Diego, the development agency that manages the municipality's investments in low-income communities. New Market Tax Credits are a funding typology not typically utilized by conventional affordable housing developers since these subsidies are designed to support community-serving mixed uses, reducing private benefit. Although the categories of mixed use typically supported by these subsidies are large-scale interventions such as hospitals or libraries, we made a case for advancing arts, culture and educational activities through the partnership between the university and the community as an alternative small-scale, mixed-use category at the scale of the neighborhood. As part of this strategy, UCSD committed to paying leases for the spaces of the new *UCSD–Casa Community Station* site.

Additionally, it was agreed that housing units in this first San Ysidro pilot project would be offered as affordable rentals, with the idea that subsequent projects would explore diverse models of ownership through alternative community trust arrangements.

As part of this hybrid financial proforma, Casa Familiar decided not to rely on conventional tax-credit-based financing for affordable housing. (New Market Tax Credits are different, as they are directed to community-based mixed uses.) Tax credit subsidies come with burdens and constraints that ultimately do not benefit local communities. These include limiting the community agency's capacity to allocate housing to local residents. Often, subsidy structures require that housing be offered through a "first come, first served" arrangement, creating a list of customers in a city-wide speculative process. For Casa Familiar, it was important not only to build housing, but to build community in the process. Casa Familiar sought a more flexible arrangement to make the project accessible not only to people urgently in need of housing, but also to people eager to participate in the construction of community, connecting civic participation to affordability. Casa Familiar designed an open and democratic process with local residents to design a selection process based on need, demographic and generational diversity, and willingness to participate in community efforts. This also enabled Casa Familiar to set up its own brackets of affordability beyond the boilerplate equations of median income established by housing authorities in every city, which do not address the levels of poverty found in communities like San Ysidro.

In sum, *Living Rooms at the Border* is the story of a creative development proforma, shaped collaboratively by architects, community and a public university, synergizing philanthropic investment, social impact investment, municipal resources and private lending, as well as robust community assets related to management and participation. What makes the model unique is that Casa Familiar performed as an alternative developer of housing for San Ysidro, assuring that the project's profits would remain in the community, for the benefit of its own productivity and sustainability. For Casa Familiar, this formula is the antidote to gentrification.

Tijuana Case Study: Santuario Frontera

URBAN CONFLICT:
CONFLICTS BETWEEN FACTORIES, MIGRANT LABOR AND EMERGENCY HOUSING

A CITY OF FACTORIES

Tijuana is a city of factories, a tax haven for multinational assembly plants, called *maquiladoras*. Maquiladoras were first set up in the 1960s through the border industrialization program and became ubiquitous across Mexico in the 1990s after the ratification of NAFTA (the North American Free Trade Agreement) and the liberalization of international trade. Maquiladoras are manufacturing enclaves that benefit from tariff-free and duty-free economic arrangements, lax labor laws that enable low wages and lax environmental regulations that relieve companies of environmental accountability to the local communities that surround them. Even with the expansion of global outsourcing to other Asian and Latin American cities, maquiladoras in Tijuana remain the largest industry at the border, employing thousands of workers and attracting migrant labor from Central Mexico and further south.

The adjacency of Tijuana's maquiladoras to San Diego demonstrates the intersection of geopolitical borders, migrant labor and informal urbanization, with close adjacencies between slums and special economic zones. It also dramatizes the proximity of Tijuana's labor inequities to the US, a function of outsourcing from one city to the other. Minimum-wage US workers earn in an hour what Mexicans earn in a day. The vicious cycle of planetary overproduction, consumption and waste, extractive transnational economies, resource exploitation, labor abuse, social marginalization and environmental negligence manifests at very local scales in Tijuana.

EMERGENCY HOUSING

As a special free-trade zone and a destination for Mexican, Central American and more recently Haitian migrants seeking work, this border city has experienced a dramatic population explosion along with informal growth, exacerbating social and environmental challenges and the crisis of social housing. These northbound migratory patterns are driven primarily by poverty and violence, political instability and the agricultural ravages of climate change. Much of the migration to Tijuana is motivated by the hope of low-wage work in the maquiladoras. Much of it is motivated by a desire to enter the US, to join family or simply to seek a better life. And among this latter group, many are denied asylum but decide to remain in Tijuana rather than return to an uncertain or dangerous life in their home countries.

While housing availability is a critical challenge for Tijuana, the crisis of housing affordability is a national problem for Mexico, just as it is in San Diego and the US. The Mexican Housing Authority estimates that soon 35% of Mexico's population will lack housing.[25] Also, similar to the US, government-sponsored social housing in Mexico has been replaced by private, developer-driven speculation. Social housing is by definition an exercise in mass producing units through top-down development models intended to address housing for the masses, which, in the best of cases, is conceived within a framework of public infrastructure and support. However, state-driven efforts to fulfill Mexico's enshrined right to *vivienda digna* in the wake of fiscal austerity and the shift towards neoliberal, market-driven development have resulted in a housing crisis of another kind. We find mass housing comprised of individual houses in subdivisions sprawling at the edges of every major Mexican city, increasingly sufficient in numbers perhaps, but utterly deficient in the support systems that create robust, connected communities. In other words, in Tijuana, as in the rest of the world, the shift from public to private housing management has resulted in an atomization and commodification of social housing, as people in need now have to qualify for market-based vouchers rather than units supported by a social safety framework.

In the absence of social housing alternatives, many people in Tijuana squat in canyons, on hillsides and in vacant sites across the periphery. As we have written before, the informal settlements in Tijuana are built with urban waste from San Diego, resulting in a recycling of architectural parts to construct habitations and infrastructure. As such, informal settlements absorb the deficits of social housing, becoming endogenous laboratories by default for new paradigms of self-built social housing. While our work in San Diego focuses on how the imported heterogeneity and juxtapositions found in Tijuana "contaminate" the formal urban fabric, the energies that drive our housing work in Tijuana seek to mobilize an acupunctural urbanization that can inject services and small infrastructures into the precarious conditions in these endogenous peripheral settlements. The central challenge is access to basic, technical infrastructure to support incremental housing processes, in which nothing is ever really final. Everything is always becoming, layered, still to be improved and expanded, diversified one day when time, labor and materials make it possible. We think of infrastructure, housing and social agency as an integrated socio-spatial system. The informal settlements of Tijuana are open-air housing factories, built temporally through human capacity, sweat equity and social organization. And this incremental layering of physical and social systems presents a different paradigm for building the city through housing.

We have researched how maquiladoras position themselves strategically adjacent to Tijuana's informal settlements for easy access to labor with little formal regulation or accountability to the fragile communities surrounding them. As foreign factories capitalize on the low-wage Mexican labor market to benefit global markets, local environmental impacts are often disastrous—dumping, suburbanization and sprawl. So, as we investigate the modest tactics of retrofit and alteration that transform Tijuana's informal settlements into open-air social housing factories, we have also researched the factory itself as a site of potential engagement. While we want to solve the housing problem immediately to relieve human distress, we resist perpetuating the conventional dynamics of architectural charity in which housing is built top-down as boxes for shelter without infrastructure for community or the political representation needed for these communities of labor to advocate for institutional reformation to tackle the roots of the problem.

While our work in San Diego detoured from conventional architecture design to rethink the developer's proforma, to propose more sustainable interfaces between affordable housing and public space at the scale of low-income neighborhoods, our detour in Tijuana took us to the maquiladoras as a site of intervention, to see if we might redirect their materials to support emergency housing and public space in the informal settlements adjacent to them. We wanted to advance a new approach to spatial and infrastructural design that elevates rather than replaces or obliterates the existing temporal dynamics of recycled urbanization. We wanted to link factory-produced prefabricated materials with the sweat equity of local, self-built housing, and establish a protocol of mutuality and reciprocity, an ethical loop between the maquiladoras and the marginalized labor communities that surround them. We designed a Micro-Policy to tackle the conflicts between maquiladoras, informal settlements, emergency housing and labor. Utilizing the factory's prefabricated systems and material production, we proposed a reciprocal investment of resources among factory, government, university and the community-based agencies we work with in the informal settlement of Tijuana's Los Laureles Canyon.

DESIGNING PROCESS:
A SOCIAL AND ECONOMIC MICRO-POLICY FOR SOCIAL HOUSING IN LOS LAURELES CANYON

BEYOND HOSPITALITY

The pursuit of *resilience* and *sustainability* is ubiquitous language in urban planning today, but these concepts remain symbolic in an age of dramatic global migration if they don't include the capacity of our cities to anticipate social emergency. Building higher walls is one response to deter the migrant, but inconsistent with a long history of international human rights norms. We ought to reject it on ethical grounds, and we have long argued that architects and urbanists become complicit when they participate in the design, construction or decoration of walls. Protecting the human rights of migrants and refugees demands just asylum laws that protect human beings in crisis. But asylum has a spatial dimension too, and we believe urbanists and architects must place themselves at the front lines of these spatial imperatives.

Between 2016 and 2020, thousands of Haitian and Central American migrants seeking asylum in the US arrived in Tijuana, escaping violence, poverty, political instability and the impacts of climate change. They were met with public anger, demonized by both the US and Mexico as an unruly mob, repelled with tear gas and forced to find refuge in wet, makeshift camps distributed in the interstices of the city. This humanitarian crisis prompted us to reflect on the relationship between human rights and what Henri Lefebvre called "the right to the city."[26]

We resisted the language that referred to this flow of humanity as a "caravan," because it de-individuates, dehumanizes the individual and her family, transforming the particularity of human struggle into an abstract movement, a "barbarian invasion" to be grasped in its magnitude from above. When the immigrant is depicted aerially within a mass of others, she loses her own story. Her reasons become invisible; her rights become easier to violate. The more strident voices among her group can jeopardize her claims in the court of public opinion. One rock thrown, and the claims of thousands dissolve into a narrative about the "criminal immigrants threatening to infest our nation."

Today, protecting migrants from political repression and public reprisal means intervening in the very sites of contact between the nation and the other: *the arrival city*. Just as climate change forces us to reimagine the city, dramatic migration demands that we design resilient housing infrastructure that anticipates social inclusion. Tijuana's informal settlements have provoked us to rethink urban infrastructure beyond single-use physical systems, conceiving it instead as hybrid, flexible and adaptable infrastructure, able to absorb accelerating migration. Hospitality must be the first gesture, an essential charitable opening. Asylum-seekers have immediate needs of food and water, medicine and shelter—urgent needs of the body. Providing these needs is the proper, charitable response of an ethical society. But we need to problematize and expand the meaning of hospitality. Needs become more complex over time, and charity is not the appropriate model for building a just society in an age of accelerating migration. Immigrants must be integrated into the civic, social and economic life of the city. They must have opportunities for education, and psychological and spiritual health. The urban challenge is how to escalate hospitality towards inclusion, both normatively and spatially. Cultivating new social norms of equality and respect has a physical dimension; it must be accompanied by inclusive spaces and programming. In other words, protecting human dignity in the host city has an urban and architectural mandate. It is a process through which human rights are spatialized in the host city, through which "we" transform alongside "the other." This prompts an idea that refugees should have rights to remain, should they so choose.

As we write this, thousands of Central American and Haitian migrants wait at the wall for asylum that never comes, reviled by the Mexican public as a nuisance, a drain on scarce public resources. Many of them found refuge in the informal settlements at the edges of Tijuana. Our case study unfolds in the informal settlement of Los Laureles Canyon, where 92,000 people live in conditions of precarity immediately adjacent to the US-Mexico border wall. This environment occupies the slopes of a canyon within the binational watershed system, whose tributaries directly shed sediment and waste into an environmentally protected estuary in San Diego. Because of its binational significance, Los Laureles Canyon is the epicenter of our work in Tijuana. Our research investigates how the informal urban processes of recycling and adaptation, resiliency and solidarity can help us rethink social and environmental infrastructure in this precarious environmental zone.

A MICRO-POLICY FOR AN INFORMAL SETTLEMENT: ETHICAL LOOPS BETWEEN FACTORIES AND A SANCTUARY NEIGHBORHOOD

Analogous to the cross-sector collaboration we curated with Casa Familiar in San Ysidro in order to produce a Micro-Policy and zoning strategy to realize *Living Rooms at the Border*, we embarked similarly on a process to design a Micro-Policy for Los Laureles Canyon that would support more sustainable social housing configurations. *It also became clear that to enter into the politics of social housing in Tijuana, the first step is to partner with a community-based organization rooted in these informal neighborhoods that is already addressing the multiple challenges of its marginalized populations.*

Embajadores de Jesús is a religious organization located in the Alacrán canyon, a particularly craggy sub-basin of Los Laureles Canyon, led by pastor / economist Gustavo Banda Aceves and *pastora* / psychologist Zaida Guillén. With limited resources, they began construction of a refugee camp to provide shelter, food and basic services to hundreds of Haitian and Central American refugees as they navigated prolonged and inconsistent asylum procedures in the US and Mexico. The shelter began in 2016 when Banda Aceves met a group of Haitian men whose wives and children were granted US asylum, leaving them waiting on the Mexican side of the wall. These men were skilled in construction; together they built a warehouse structure at the Embajadores site in Alacrán to house dozens of tents as they awaited the next flow of immigrants. As migration accelerated over the next years with the arrival of thousands of Central American migrants, Embajadores opened its doors, and occupancy began to swell. What began as a single structure evolved incrementally through necessity, ingenuity and self-built logics into a distributed set of informal houses and public spaces of varying sizes and configurations, threaded into what seems like impossible canyon topography. This was all well underway when we began working together. When we met, Embajadores was receiving no formal institutional support of any kind, but a cohesive core of migrant men and women were dedicated to the life and future of the refugee camp.

We established a partnership with Banda and Guillén to elevate their housing capacity and to co-develop a *sanctuary neighborhood*, framed by a Micro-Policy and a sustainable migrant housing prototype. In the course of our work together over time, the Alacrán canyon became home to our fourth UCSD Community Station: *The UCSD-Alacrán Community Station*.

Our process began by challenging the stigma that informal settlements are sites of danger, places not to intervene because of their topographic complexity, their facades of poverty. These biases prompt conventional institutions of urban development to look the other way and build in the periphery, on *tabula rasa* environments. Our Micro-Policy for Los Laureles Canyon began by declaring informal settlements as urgent sites of intervention, not only because of ethical commitments, but also because the human capacity, the incremental and layered, self-built processes of bottom-up urbanization turn these precarious environments into living laboratories of transitional infrastructure, sites for rethinking emergency and social housing.

The Micro-Policy for Los Laureles Canyon included a pedagogical process that engaged local residents in conversation about the significance of their own strategies of recycling, retrofit and adaptation. With our partners we elaborated a variety of best practices in the construction process, amplifying the social capital, the hidden value of sweat equity and creative urban intelligence behind these processes. This was evidence that the community was already involved in producing social housing, and that their entrepreneurship deserved validation and top-down support. We wanted to visualize the urban political economy of waste, demonstrating that recycling dynamics in the canyon constitute micro-economic loops that transform San Diego's urban waste into affordable building materials not otherwise available for the construction of housing.

In one of our community workshops, a municipal representative in Tijuana stood up and asked: "Who are *you* to say (referring to our partners and our team, guiding the dialogue) that these people want to be building with waste? I am sure if you ask them many would rather live in a large tract home in the suburbs of San Diego." An older man, a resident from the informal neighborhood, quietly responded before we had a chance: "That might be true, but when will we be able to live in that large house? Next week? Next year? Next decade? What do we do in the meantime?" This launched a debate about the function of infrastructure as an *anticipatory* framework, to support the transition from ephemeral spaces into established neighborhoods, through which housing emerges as an engine for urban evolution and social change—from the ephemeral to the permanent, from the invisible-emergent to the visible-established, the recognized, included and represented.

This process of recognizing and validating the social and economic value of bottom-up processes within informal settlements included visualizing the proximity of the maquiladoras, located along the edges of these canyons. Most maquiladora labor comes from these informal settlements, evidenced physically in the trails left by workers as they circulate up and down the hillsides between canyons and the factories on the mesas above.

Another dimension of the Micro-Policy for Los Laureles Canyon was to conceptualize a process through which maquiladoras that benefit from easy access to cheap labor could reciprocate with subsidized, factory-made material systems to support incremental construction practices. By mobilizing the production capacities of the maquiladora industry to address local social and ecological challenges, the Micro-Policy merged mainstream notions of factory-based prefabrication with geopolitical and economic realities of conflict, migration, labor and informality.

We designed an ethical loop between factories and communities, negotiating with maquiladoras to redirect their surplus value to Tijuana's informal settlements. We proposed an unorthodox relationship between Tijuana's maquiladora industry and informal housing, where prefabrication can play an important role within these precarious environments, linking top-down resources and bottom-up entrepreneurship while advancing the reproducibility of self-built housing. Prefabrication is ubiquitous in the building industry, and reinvented every few decades. In our region, people in conditions of social emergency recombine the detritus of prefabricated suburbs in Southern California, essentially operationalizing the ubiquity of prefabrication to rethink social housing. Adapting these disjointed and repurposed architectural parts into new subsidized, prefabricated structural environments produces a unique opportunity to reimagine the relationship between community processes, prefabrication and social housing. The Micro-Policy is a protocol that intensifies the relationship between the factory-made and the handmade. It has been important for us to emphasize that prefabrication cannot be separated from human resourcefulness, from the potential to respond to the idiosyncratic conditions of the world.

The final dimension of developing the Los Laureles Canyon Micro-Policy was designing an economic model for circulating materials between the factory and the migrant community for the construction of their own housing. To sustain the construction process over time, we designed a pilot for linking self-built community processes and jobs. Similar to *Living Rooms at the Border*, the housing project in San Ysidro that embeds housing within an infrastructure of social service and cultural production, we proposed to embed migrant housing units within an infrastructure of fabrication. With our Tijuana-based community partners, Embajadores de Jesús, we designed a *sanctuary economy*, conceived to transform the refugee camp into an incubator of community and economic productivity, where permanence and belonging become an option for migrants and their children. To achieve this, we proposed spaces for vocational training, fabrication and small-scale economic development. This resulted in a community-owned cooperative business model to connect factory systems with the sweat equity of migrant residents. It was seeded by a coalition of universities, social impact investors and grassroots partners.

The Los Laureles Canyon Micro-Policy became the social and economic foundation for building *Santuario Frontera* 1500 yards from the border wall. Our larger goal is to move the spatial conversation about refugee housing *beyond shelter to inclusion*—to reinvent the refugee-camp model from an ephemeral space of hospitality to a durable incubator of environmental and economic-productivity, where the option of permanence becomes real. While the conversation around refugees today is framed by intolerance and xenophobia, and they are often seen as a drain on the societies and economies that host them, the Micro-Policy presents refugees as change-agents producing public goods, housing and public space infrastructure, relieving pressure on already-stressed regional resources, improving the quality of life in the surrounding communities, and ultimately transforming public perception and promoting social inclusion.

URBAN-ARCHITECTURAL PROJECT:
REFUGEE CAMPS AS INFRASTRUCTURES FOR INCLUSION

BUILDING BLOCKS TO TRANSLATE INFORMAL URBANIZATION STRATEGIES INTO HOUSING

The Los Laureles Canyon Micro-Policy in Tijuana generates of a set of building blocks that are essential to our research on bottom-up urbanization and housing within informal settlements. In summary:

1.
To co-develop housing with migrant communities requires interlocutors to democratize the instruments of economic development, enabling access for vulnerable communities to the tools for increasing productive capacities. Can architects and migrant communities collaborate to decentralize economic and political power, and produce a new model of neighborhood-based economic development through social housing?

2.
To pursue detours, engaging top-down institutions that "surround" the problem to negotiate how their material and organizational logics can be redirected to support bottom-up communities in need. Architects can curate new partnerships between industry and community activists. In our work, we have reconceived prefabrication not as an autonomous, universal system, but as a particular assembly protocol that links industries and their surrounding communities, whose informal building logics can penetrate design and production processes.

3.
To operationalize informal urbanization as a set of practices to be scaled. Bottom-up spatial dynamics give primacy to the layered complexities of informal sites over the singularity of the object. Through these processes, incremental architectural systems facilitated by prefabrication can be devices to augment localized forms of industry, governance and economy. The informal is not about isolated objects built into the territory, but about the webbing of spaces and the anticipation of transformation.

4.
To link housing "unit counts" to jobs. Can we reimagine the equation as "number of jobs per unit" rather than "number of units per area"? This new reformulation recalibrates the relationship between urban density and social housing as a scaffold for job generation. It also transforms the production logics of emergency housing as mono-use shelter units into an idea of social housing that increases local capacities and economic mobility.

5.
To temporalize space. The incrementalism of informal building practices allows for fine-grained programmatic adaptations in which space, activity and economy merge. Time itself becomes material. Our work amplifies the right of informal communities to develop themselves through time, against the *tabula rasa* approaches that devalue and undermine local entrepreneurial dynamics. We believe there is much to learn from informal settlements as we reimagine the transformation of US sprawl in the next decades. Informal building practices anticipate scenarios for the future retrofitting and adaptation of Levittowns across America.

6.
To expand affordability through the low-cost layering of informal housing. We translate the informal juxtaposition of material skins into new assemblages, where prefabrication becomes an armature for organizing sequential, affordable material envelopes and hybridizing standardized systems with vernacular construction methods. Self-built housing in Tijuana constructed by local, unspecialized labor make these informal settlements transitional zones for urban development, absorbing the deficits of affordable housing in the city and mitigating the high infrastructural costs of formal social housing.

7.
To socialize housing economy by integrating migrant building practices and sweat equity, enabling people in conditions of struggle to benefit from their own labor. In Tijuana, construction workers are mostly self-taught, and residents in informal neighborhoods become communities of labor as they build their own infrastructure. People build their houses themselves, lowering costs and producing a sense of ownership and feelings of agency and dignity.

CRITICAL LOCATION

As the US dismantled its asylum protocols in the last years, thousands of Haitian, Central American, West African, Yemeni, Southeast Asian and most recently Ukrainian refugees found themselves waiting at the wall. By default, Tijuana becomes home for many refugees, a city itself already struggling with pervasive poverty, inequality and environmental upheaval.

Santuario Frontera: Scaffolds for inclusion

Santuario Frontera is located inside Los Laureles Canyon in Tijuana, home to an informal settlement of 92,000 people. This canyon is part of the Tijuana River binational watershed system, whose tributaries crash against the US-Mexico wall before spilling into the Tijuana River Estuary located in San Diego—a binational public good, essential to the environmental and economic sustainability of the border region. We have been researching the critical eco-social interdependencies between the informal settlement of Los Laureles Canyon in Tijuana and the Tijuana River Estuary in San Diego. In the last decades, 70% of the open lands in Los Laureles Canyon have been lost to irregular urban growth. The impacts on natural ecosystems are dramatic. The cross-border Tijuana River is a source of pollution and disease. Trash and plastics clog wastewater infrastructure, triggering massive sewage spills. Explosive informal development at the city's periphery erodes topsoil, washing tons of fine-sand sediment and waste northbound into the estuary with each rainy season. Regional governments spend millions of dollars mitigating these environmental damages.

Our refugee housing prototype sits at heart of these catastrophic flows, in the Alacrán canyon, the most rugged, precarious and polluted sub-basin of Los Laureles Canyon. The site is a critical component of the *Cross-Border Commons*, a transnational environmental conservation initiative that links the estuary in San Diego with Los Laureles Canyon in Tijuana to form a continuous administrative, social and ecological system (see project cluster 1). The *Cross-Border Commons* operates as an archipelago of conservation inside the informal settlement, bundling parcels that can still be protected into a network of public spaces co-developed with community partners to mitigate the impact of pollution flows in the border region and serve as hydro-pedagogic hubs for community engagement.

DESIGN STRATEGIES

The physical design is an extension of our research project called *Manufactured Sites*—producing a maquiladora-made prefabricated frame as a hinge mechanism to mediate the multiplicity of recycled materials and systems imported from San Diego and reassembled in Tijuana. This frame becomes a larger, interwoven and open-ended scaffold that helps to stabilize precarious terrain without compromising the improvisational dynamics of self-made environments. Here, prefabrication not only frames social housing as objects, but also becomes an acupunctural system to support incrementality, adapting to space and territory, generating infrastructure, urbanism, landscape.

The Micro-Policy provides social and economic tools to design a participatory process for cross-sector collaboration, a foundational act to anticipate physical design. It is a complex story, but as we began to design and assemble resources for the project, we engaged the maquiladoras that surround Los Laureles Canyon. We approached Mecalux, a Spanish maquiladora that produces lightweight metal shelving systems used in warehouses across the world. It was an agonistic impulse: Can Mecalux become partners in social housing? Could they contribute with subsidized material systems to improve the quality of life in the informal settlements that provide affordable local labor for their global production chains?

With our partners we assembled a set of protocols to frame the design process for the incremental physical, programmatic and economic strategies for the *Santuario Frontera* housing project.[27]

1. Designing Inclusive Infrastructure for Migrant Housing

Mecalux agreed to explore possibilities and participate in our proposal to adapt its prefabricated metal shelving systems into structural scaffolds as armatures for informal housing, while structurally supporting the sustainable waste-recycling processes of Tijuana's bottom-up building practices. Their willingness brought us inside the factory—a small achievement in itself—to negotiate how its material systems and technical expertise could support the project, and whether a subsidy could be arranged. We collaborated with Mecalux CEO, Angel de Arriba, and David Felix, his chief production engineer, who understood the meaning of investing in the communities they inhabit and the value of facilitating small infill infrastructure for start-up housing settlements. Mecalux suggested we review their factory catalogue of parts. We studied their material systems and adapted our design to minimize impact on economies-of-scale at the assembly plant. We requested one minor adjustment to existing catalogue parts. We discovered that changing the angle of the shelving system's base would allow us to create an "A" frame as the structural core of the system, while allowing other prefabricated parts to structurally interlock, shaping a butterfly roof, extending outward from the core. It was similar to the prefabricated system that Jean Prouvé created for his *Maison Tropicale* in postwar France.

Unlike specialized, large-scale, industrialized and modular social housing, Prouvé's approach linked mass production to small-scale assembly. Only a few people would be needed to assemble an "architecture of parts." For Prouvé, the relationship between factory-made pieces that can be transported easily to the job site and assembled locally according to a predetermined manual of connections re-energized relations between industry, prefabrication and social housing in local contexts.[28] Expanding on his thinking, our Embajadores housing design proposal mobilized prefabrication not as an idealized form that is brought to the factory for replication, but as a way of working through what already exists, reorganizing materials, procedures and resources to take the field to a realm of operation and performance oriented to social justice. We designed a new catalogue of modular structures that could be embedded in the promiscuity of construction systems and spaces that define this city's temporal, flexible and adaptable informal urbanization, mobilizing participation among people who are already invested in the incremental building of their communities. In other words, we designed a *mediating infrastructural system* which connects a factory-made structural frame that is easy to assemble, and into which formal parts can be added without difficulty by those with the informal skills and scrappiness of Tijuana's inhabitants. Here prefabrication negotiates the generic and the idiosyncratic, the general and the specific.

We designed Embajadores as both refugee housing infrastructure and as the seed for an evolving sanctuary neighborhood, to be infilled through time by the migrant community, led and coordinated by our activist partners. Let's imagine the buildings as social housing factories whose envelopes would be built first, leaving the interiors as *planned open systems*, built incrementally by residents and equipped with interior utilities to support evolving live-work configurations. The design was developed in layers, embedding migrant housing within an infrastructure of fabrication and economic development.

Layer 1:
Housing as Water- and Waste-management Infrastructure

With collective resources, seed grants from foundations and the adoption of dormant slivers of land owned by the municipality, we began to acquire a series of parcels adjacent to the refugee camp, stitching them together to anticipate the evolution of a sanctuary neighborhood. As we described earlier, the site is impacted by the flow of trash and sediment from the dump sites that surround it. The first layer of intervention was to design a new *ground* for the project, to heal a parcel excavated illegally by a previous land speculator. We wanted to restore the hillside topography with terracing, gabion walls and swales, transforming the site into a water- and waste-management system. Similar to the *Living Rooms at the Border* housing prototype in San Ysidro, the *Santuario Frontera* site is articulated as a series of linear pedestrian circulation systems, threaded through the terraces as biofiltration promenades. The integration of migrant housing and ecological infrastructure demonstrates that social and environmental justice can be advanced through migrant housing, yielding both sanctuary spaces for cohabitation and production, and the rehabilitation and restoration of the of the local landscape.

Layer 2:
Vernacular Post and Beam Infrastructure

Concrete columns and beams are ubiquitous construction systems across the informal settlement, built throughout the topography to support lighter wood and metal framing structures above them, leaving the spaces beneath open-ended for evolving programs and additions. This system is widely adopted across the canyon because of its economy and the building capacities of the canyon's residents. It was a logical extension of these local practices that the migrant population and the local community would be eager to participate in the construction of a foundational grid of columns and beams emerging from the gabion walls and terracing that defines the perimeter of two containers.

Layer 3:
The Mecalux System

We increased production of the Mecalux frames and installed them on top of the vernacular, exposed concrete grid, creating a hybrid system between factory-made and handmade scaffolds. The metal frames defined an upper layer that allowed flexibility for installing light roofing and shading systems, while the concrete columns below grounded the building to its foundations and the more landscape-oriented surfaces of the ecological systems, synergizing temporal and permanent materials.

Layer 4:
Lightweight Envelopes and Utility Infrastructure

The scaffolds define two main structures, two containers, each of which has two wings flanking a central pedestrian alley which operates as an arcade offering protection from the rain. Once the scaffolds are completed, a skin of lightweight plastics, sandwiched with shading and insulation, will enable an affordable envelope to protect interiors from the rain while minimizing investment in expensive waterproof detailing. This envelope will contain sliding-door systems for cross ventilation, completing the perimeter of the scaffolds. Once this exterior layer is completed, collective bathrooms and kitchens will be installed inside the envelopes to anticipate the first phase of habitation.

Layer 5:
From Transitional Tents to Construction Workshop into Housing

The housing envelopes are designed to contain the economic incubator, a construction workshop equipped with wood and metal fabrication machines, plastic presses and a tool library. Since the buildings are designed with two wings, one wing is used in the first phase of occupation to house immigrants in temporary tents, coordinated by our activist partners. The other wing houses the construction workshop. Training sessions are organized to initiate construction of the lighter interior architecture, composed of both formal and informal, recycled materials. At this stage, the residents will develop a diverse ecology of housing environments and furniture, ranging from family units to single rooms for women and children, and collective spaces for men, transforming the previously shared bathrooms and kitchens into gradations of private and public use. Note the environmental benefits of an architecture of parts that encourages local reuse and recycling patterns in the development of housing, rather than relying solely on the production of new housing materials. Once the first wing is finished and people move into the units, the second wing, now without tents, will begin construction.
    The project broke ground in March 2020.

2. Designing Economic Incubators for Inclusive Refugee Housing

Reimagining refugee camps as an infrastructure for inclusion means designing spaces and programs that integrate migrants and their children into the civic, social and economic life of the city. Advancing our commitment to embedding social housing in systems of support, the *Santuario Frontera* housing project is an infrastructure of productivity. The construction workshop provides tools, trucks, tractors and skills-training to the migrant community to accelerate its own productive capacity. In addition, we are exploring the feasibility of an industrial laundry facility for community use to support public health, but also as a revenue generator for the informal settlement, which still lacks small business opportunities. *Santuario Frontera* is an anticipatory housing infrastructure, designed to facilitate transition from an ephemeral to a permanent neighborhood, where the building process itself becomes a tool for constructing community through social integration and job generation. The *UCSD Community Stations*, the cross-border platform for collaborative education, research and cultural activity that we founded at the University of California, San Diego, is activated here to support social programming with resources, programmatic capacity, training and education.

3. Designing a Sanctuary Economy and Funding Mechanism

Conditions of social emergency demand reorganizing resources, institutional accountability and collaboration. The Mecalux frame was cross subsidized by the Spanish maquiladora, and supported by social impact investment from foundations and philanthropy to seed the project, with the idea that the project would generate revenue to sustain itself into the future. Seed capital for site development and foundational housing scaffolds for housing was provided by philanthropist-scholar Robert Rubin and Stéphane Samuel, whose ongoing collaboration on this project expands their commitment to the prefabricated social housing of postwar French architect Jean Prouvé. Rubin and Samuel sold a vintage Prouvé chair at Sotheby's in New York City in December 2019, committing all proceeds to the first phase of this project as homage to the legacy of Prouvé and his commitment to prefabrication and social justice through housing.[29]

With our partners we have designed a business model to further embed the housing units in spaces of fabrication, training and small-scale economic development by seeding refugee-owned cooperatives and parallel economies that capitalize on the sweat equity of people living and already working in the informal settlement. By collectively owning the means of production, the migrant community is able to undertake construction-related jobs across the informal settlement, sustaining themselves while producing revenue for programming in the sanctuary neighborhood. This can help increase a sense of belonging, psychological security and pathways towards permanent resettlement.

With capital funding from David Deutsch and his New York City–based *PARC Foundation*, we established a community-owned cooperative, *The Embajadores Construction Cooperative*. This cooperative will finish the interior architecture of the housing units and then remain intact to take on other for-profit construction projects across the canyon, with a focus on mitigating waste-and-sediment flow, and ultimately producing environmental, health and economic benefits for Tijuana and San Diego and the informal settlements of Los Laureles Canyon, where the sanctuary neighborhood is located.

With our partners and a small coalition of binational agencies—including Proyecto Fronterizo de Educación Ambiental, The Tijuana River Estuarine Research Reserve, and 4 Walls International, we will generate revenue streams for the cooperative—what we think of as a *sanctuary economy*. Structured by a cross-border funding loop conceived by our partner 4 Walls International, the undertaking will redirect millions of dollars spent by regional governments to mitigate the environmental damages caused by decades of solid-waste contamination from plastics, foam, tires and sediment that flow northward from Tijuana into the Tijuana River Estuary every year. We argue that these economic incentives can support the restoration of habitats on the Tijuana side of the border, as well as other bottom-up transitional infrastructure, such as public spaces that double as waste-management infrastructure and pedagogical nodes to help prevent pollution from the settlement from traveling north to the estuary. Recognizing the value of migrant sweat equity, an inclusive economic model emerges, opening opportunities for migrant communities to become informal developers of their own housing as well as environmental infrastructure that benefits the region. The language of social and economic *sustainability* becomes operational—and a force through which a new paradigm of social housing can advance new civic narratives about the collective benefits of migration.

 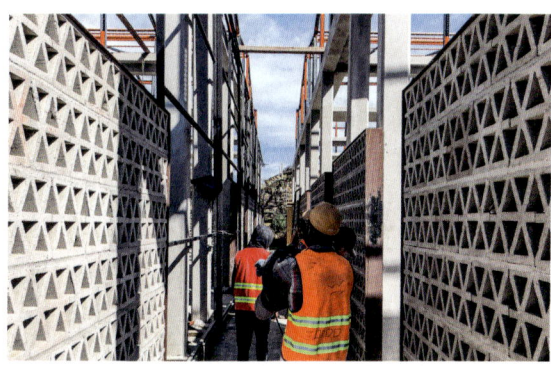

Top four images are Living Rooms at the Border under construction; bottom four images are Santuario Frontera under construction.

1 URBANIZATION OF RETROFIT

2 SOCIAL PRACTICES OF ADAPTATION

The future of the city depends on pixelating the large with the small

Architects and NG
top-down resource

DESIGNING A POLITICAL PROCESS: A SAN DIEGO CASE STUDY
There can be no advances in affordable housing design without advances in housing policy and economy. This includes transformations in exclusionary land-use and zoning policy, and a new political economy that can support the alternative social densities, transitional uses and shared economies found in informal urbanization. What is needed is a political process that recognizes the social and economic dynamics embedded in communities as foundational to reimagining social housing.

3 THE NEIGHBORHOOD AS POLITICAL UNIT

4 SPATIALIZING CITIZENSHIP

1 Translating the Informal

2 Community forums

3 Community as developer

4 Distributed community trust

Designing policy and economic frameworks for sustaining housing in the long term

In low-income neighborhoods, housing units need to be embedded within social support infrastructures at the scale of parcels

DESIGNING A COMMUNITY PROCESS: A MICRO-POLICY FOR SAN YSIDRO
With Casa Familiar, we designed a neighborhood protocol for local governance and community development. The Micro-Policy advocates a new role for NGOs in low-income neighborhoods as "informal city halls" to co-develop housing—connecting tangible housing needs with specific community participants, and supporting emergent economies by embedding enhanced social services into housing.

MEDIATING THE INTERFACE BETWEEN INSTITUTIONS AND COMMUNITIES

Casa Familiar is a 30-year-old, community-based social service organization located in the border neighborhood of San Ysidro, California. Casa Familiar exemplifies a local agency that facilitates interfaces between top-down resources and otherwise invisible bottom-up neighborhood dynamics and needs.

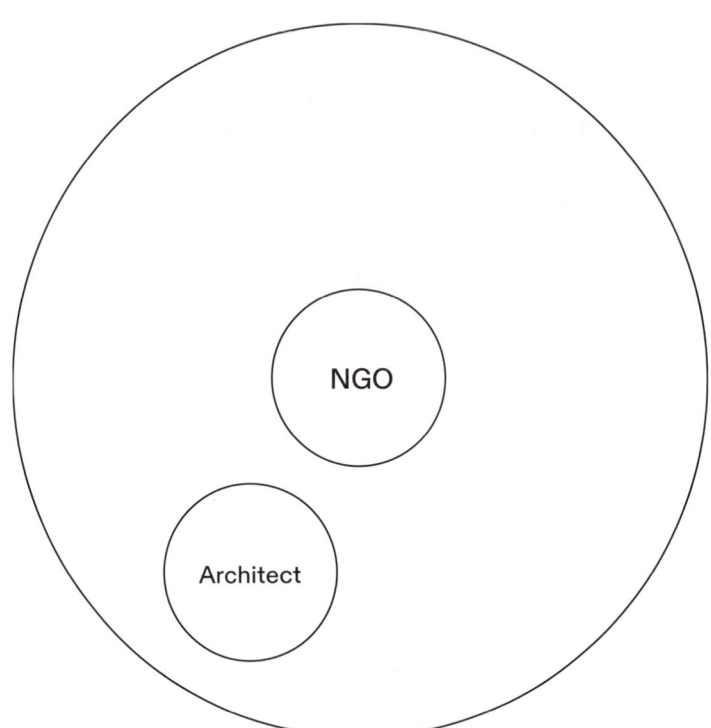

MICRO-POLICY STAGE 1: VISUALIZING EVIDENCE
Documenting all nonconforming, informal additions, micro-units and small informal economies sprinkled across the neighborhood to legitimize and protect their existence. With this new evidence, the NGO advocates for a new affordable housing overlay zone for the neighborhood to increase densities from one, to two or even three units per parcel when appropriate.

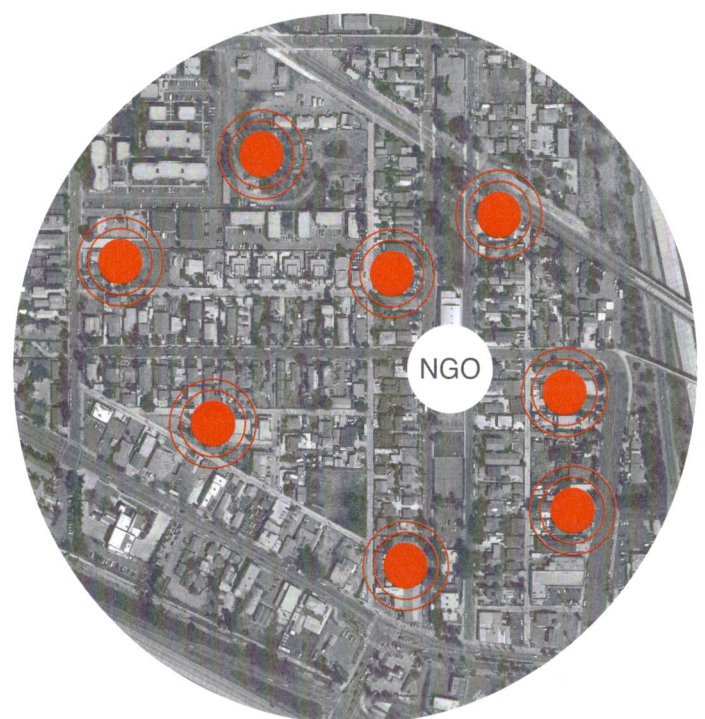

IMMIGRANT NEIGHBORHOODS: HOUSING LABORATORIES

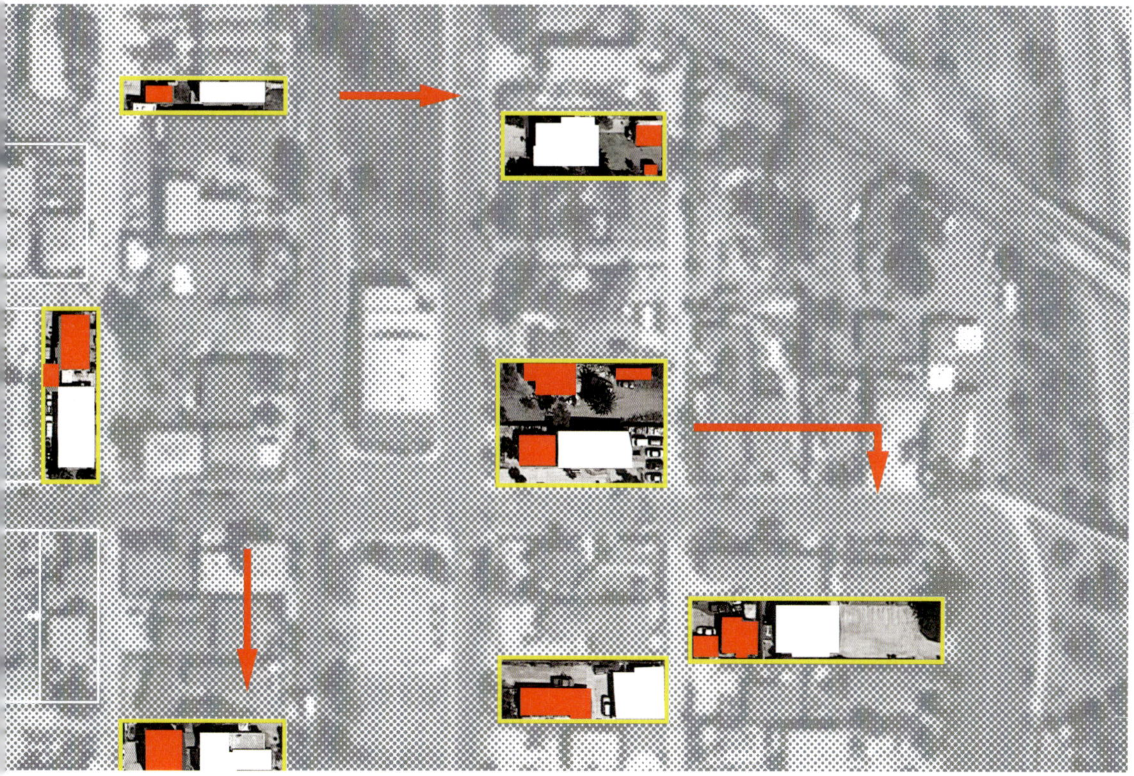

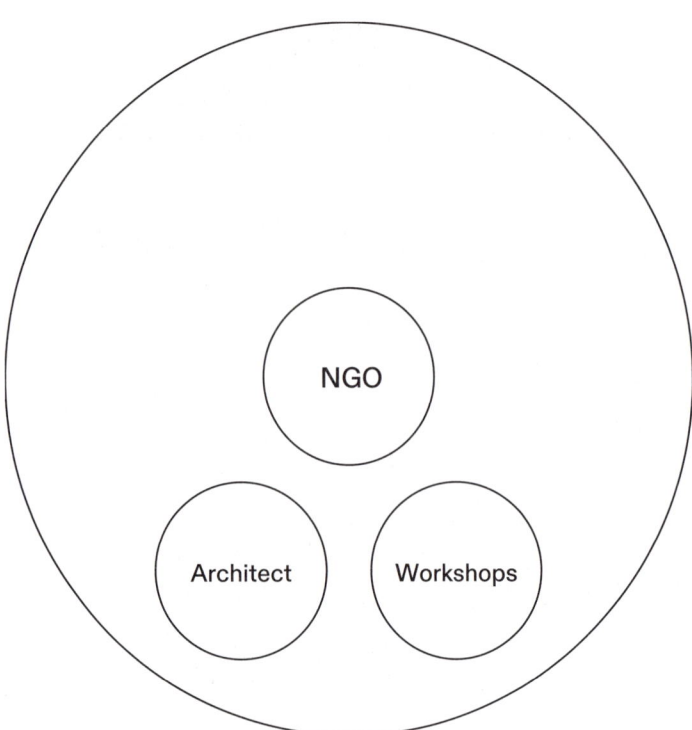

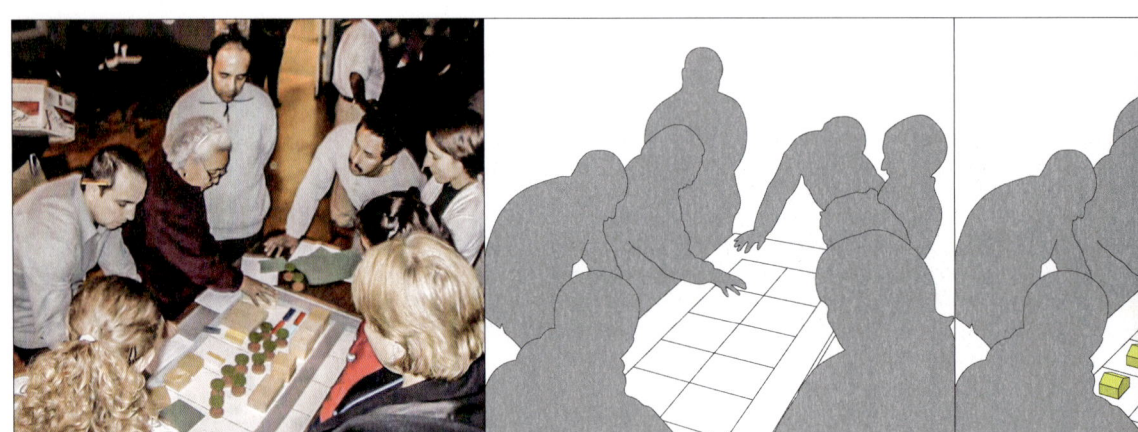

MICRO-POLICY STAGE 2: NEW TOOLS FOR COMMUNITY ENGAGEMENT
Affordable housing must be developed in tandem with methods for more meaningful community engagement. This entails designing urban pedagogical tools and visual systems that organize dialogues and knowledge exchanges to enable community access to the complexity of urban policy, and to mediate community processes and new forms of political representation.

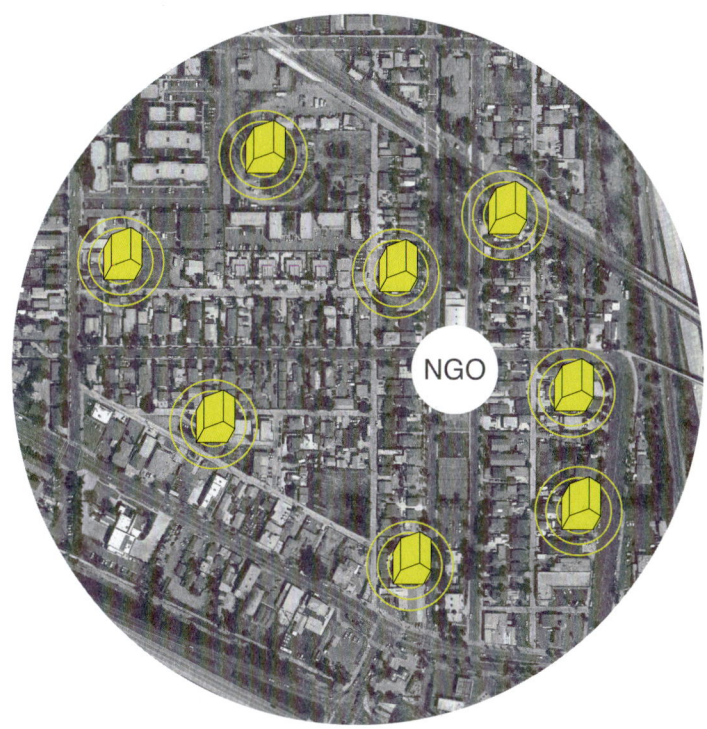

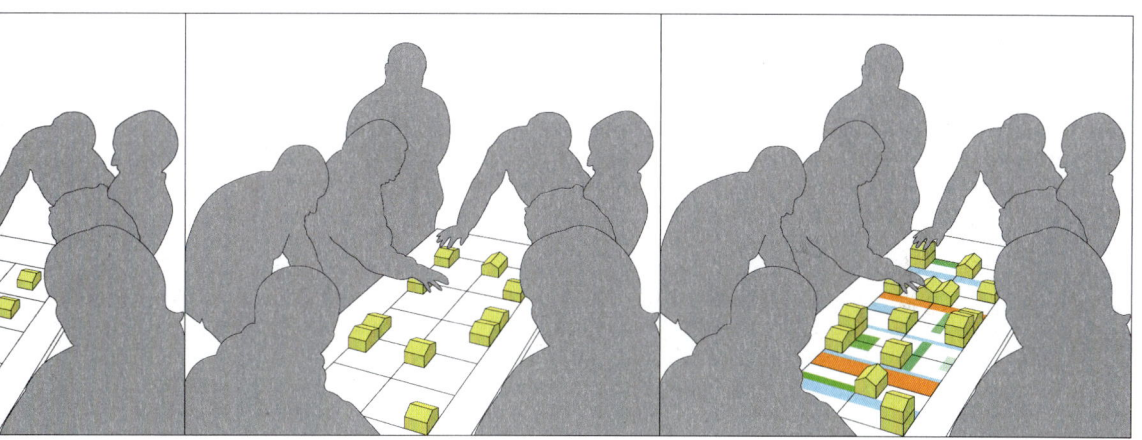

1. Designing the density game: a board that represents the parcels of an existing neighborhood block, accompanied by wood blocks representing housing "units," trees and cars.

2. The game is set up at a community table, where residents participate in the conversation: "We are going to explore the idea of density. A developer usually says: let's build so many units on this block. How many units can you really place in these parcels?"

3. Doña Maria makes the first move: she places one piece of wood in one parcel, another piece in another parcel, and so on. She reproduced her own block, one house per parcel.

4. Then someone places two pieces of wood against each other: "What if two owners collaborate and join their houses to generate extra space in the parcel, allowing for an extra unit? Civic imagination is sparked, and soon everyone begins adding wood to the neighborhood block."

5. Doña Maria exclaims: "Now I remember! When I was a young girl in Guadalajara, I used to live in an older neighborhood near downtown, and those blocks were not made of individual buildings, but they were a continuous building. There were doors against the street, you would open a door and find patios inside...." "Can density be about spaces rather than buildings?" someone asked. "I cannot believe our houses are selfish!" Doña Maria exclaimed, "Maybe density can be about neighborhood collaboration."

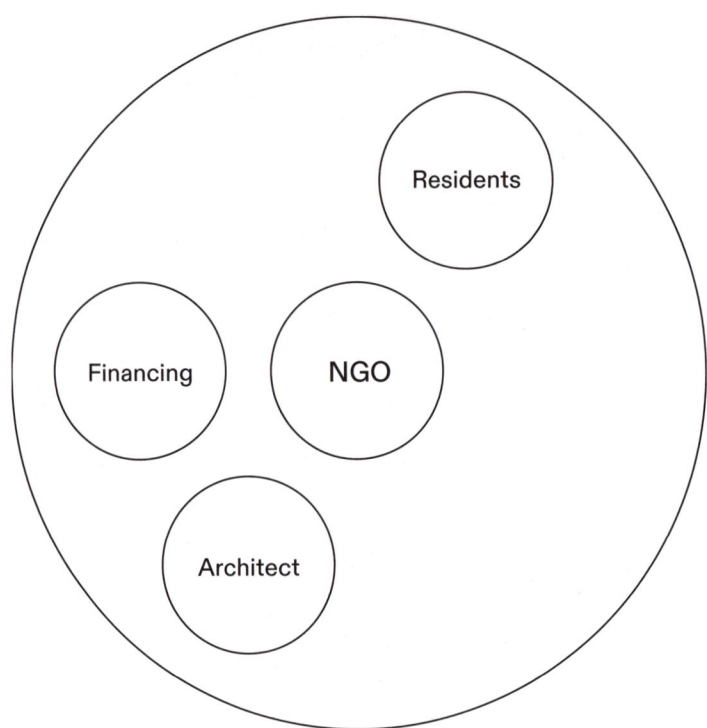

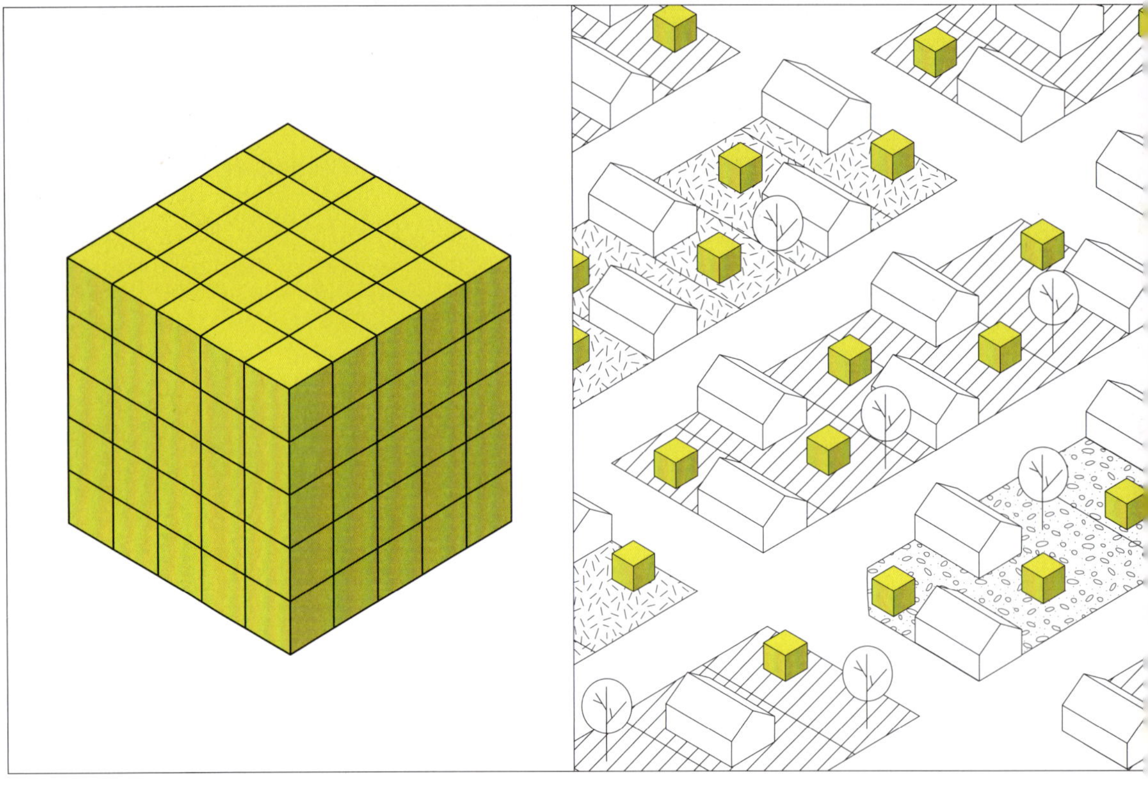

MICRO-POLICY STAGE 3: RETHINKING TAX-CREDIT BASED DEVELOPMENT
Problem: For private developers to secure profits in the development of affordable housing, they rely on tax credits. To qualify for these competitive subsidies, the development typically needs to generate at least 50 units of housing. But this kind of density is prohibited by zoning in many mid-city neighborhoods. It is not surprising there is so little affordable housing in so many low-income, mid-city neighborhoods.

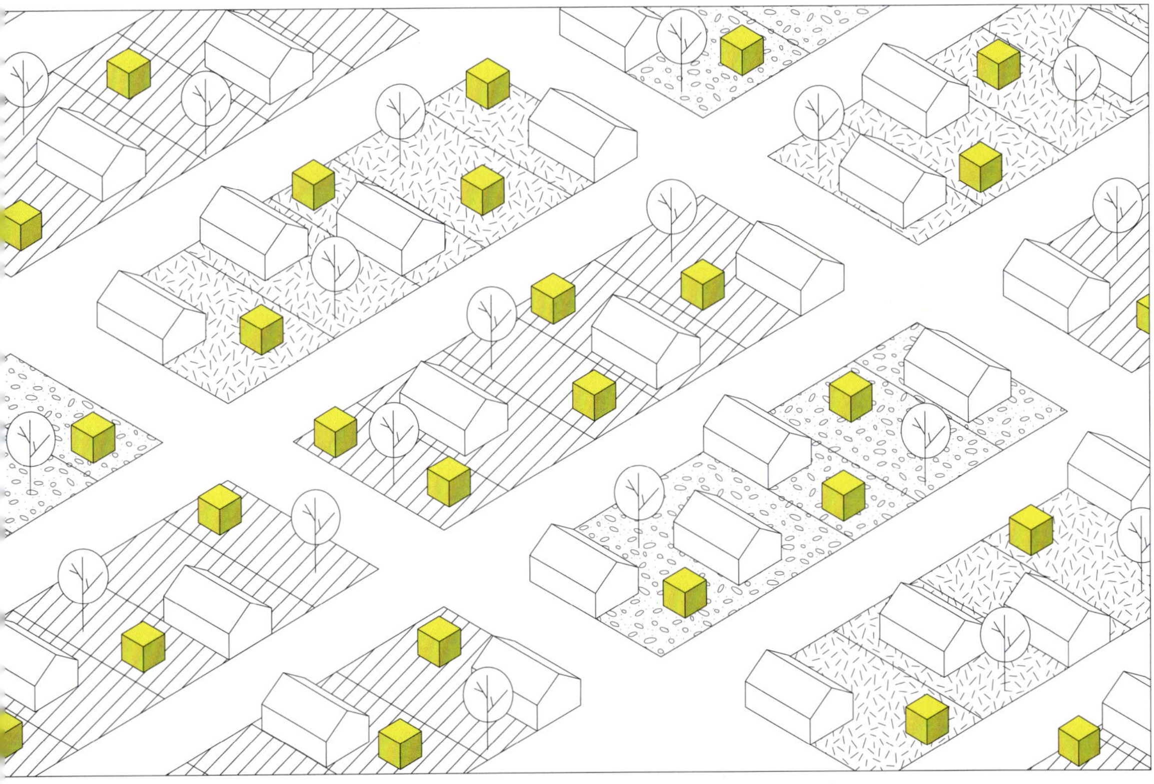

OPPORTUNITY: THE COMMUNITY AS DEVELOPER

Instead of pursuing a large building which is prohibited by zoning, we proposed breaking apart the generic 50-unit project into small buildings, and distributing them as accessory units throughout the neighborhood. As long as these 50 distributed units are built at the same time and their management is centralized, our community partners can qualify for tax-credit based financing, acting as guarantor for the development project.

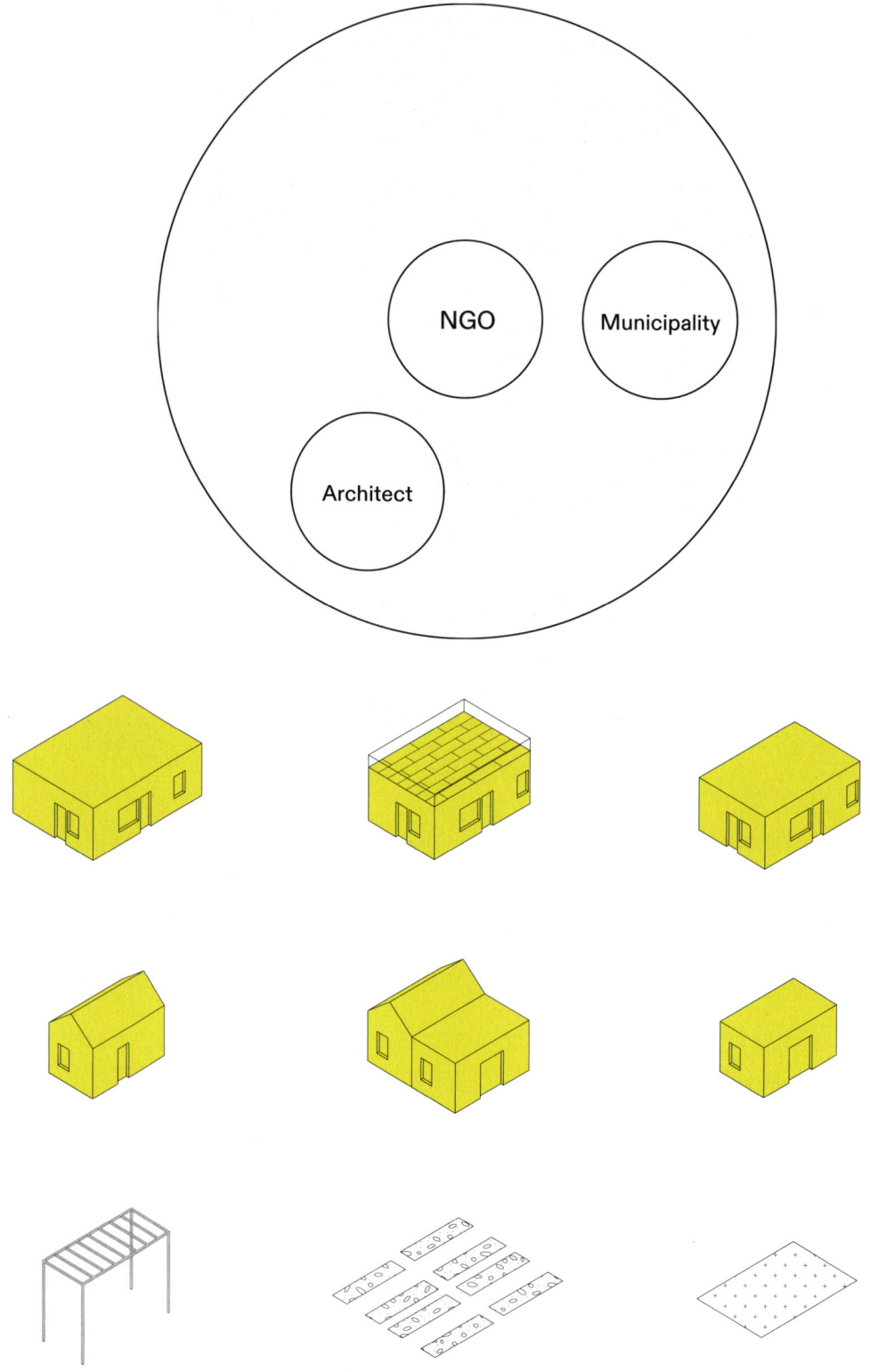

MICRO-POLICY STAGE 4: DISTRIBUTED ACCESSORY DWELLING UNITS

Accessory buildings and accessory units are powerful tools for advancing a neighborhood-based development proforma. According to code, accessory buildings are small sheds that can accommodate a variety of flexible uses, such as a play room, a painting studio, storage. If no larger than 120 sq. ft. they don't require a permit. Accessory units are companion units, often called granny flats, that can be built in backyards.

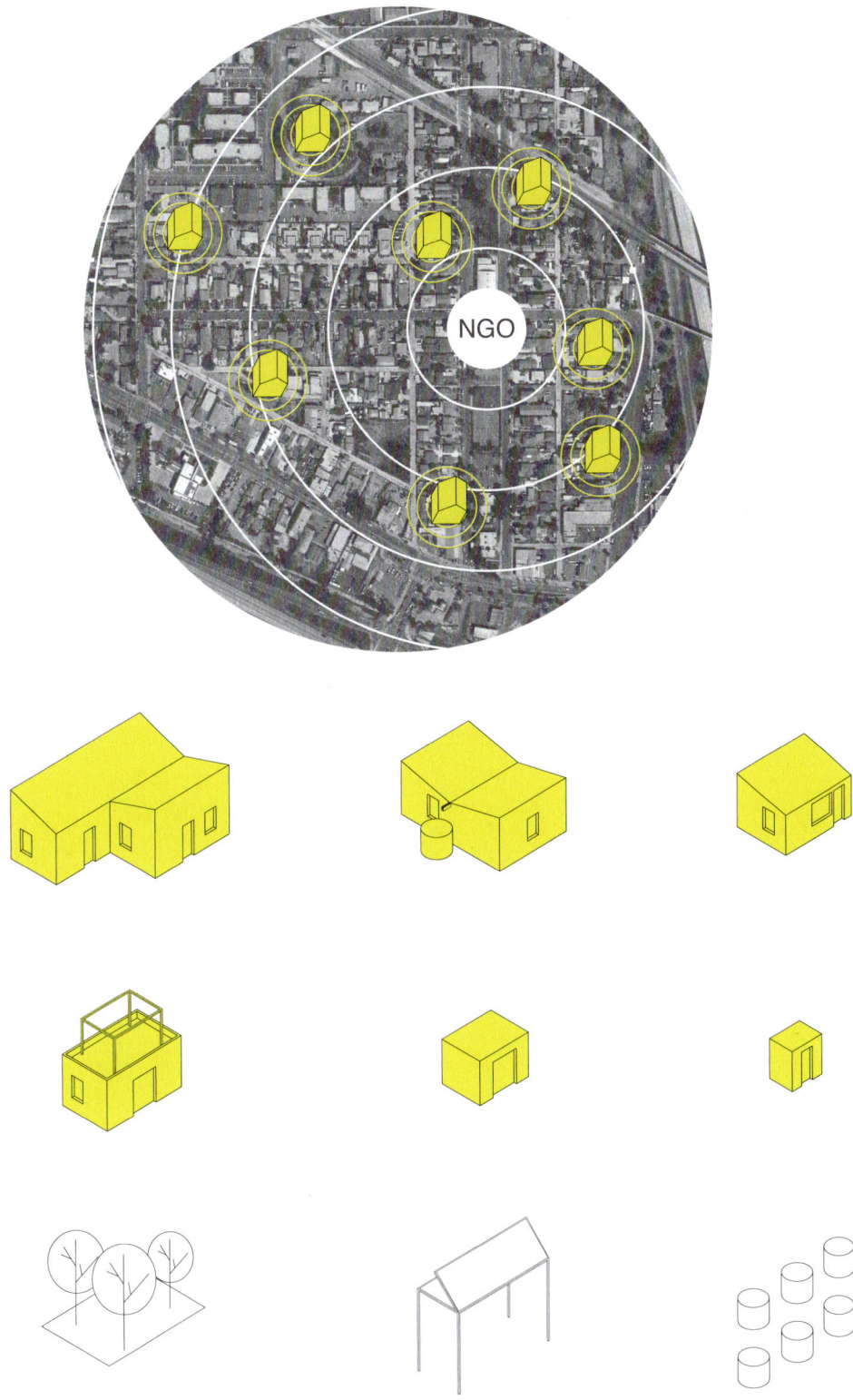

PREPACKAGING PERMITS AND MICRO-LENDING
Our nonprofit partner works directly with the municipality to prepackage building permits for a portfolio of accessory unit and accessory building typologies. They also prepackage the lending structure, taking liability for construction loans and tax-credit-based financing. Casa Familiar becomes a facilitator of political and economic processes, representing residents and assembling a catalogue of small building typologies, housing additions and support systems.

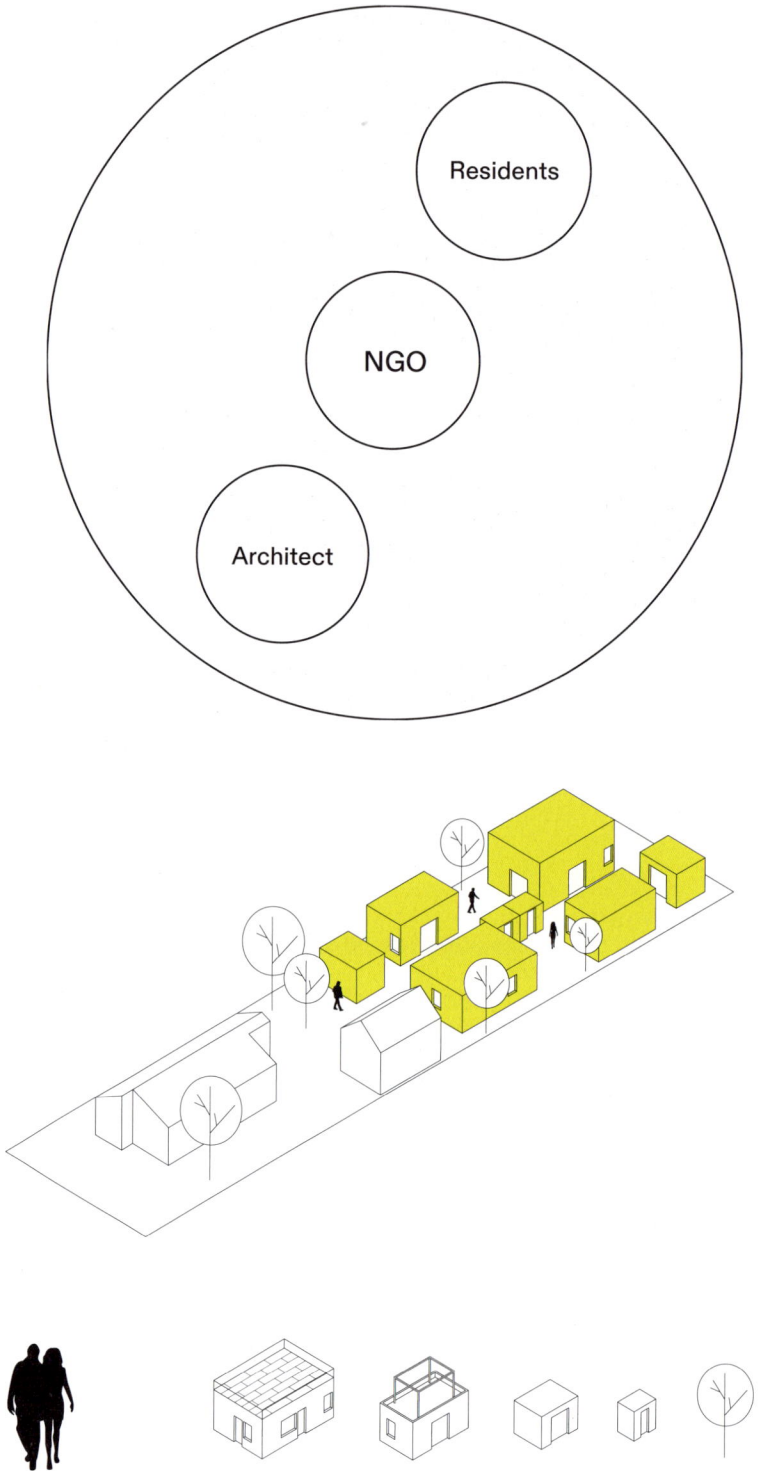

MICRO-POLICY STAGE 5: DISTRIBUTED COMMUNITY TRUSTS
We proposed partnering with willing property owners and bundling a set of parcels across the neighborhood. These are long-time neighborhood residents who don't have resources to capitalize on the equity of their land. Here we proposed a distributed community land trust through which neighborhood residents and Casa Familiar partner as co-owners and co-developers of these new units.

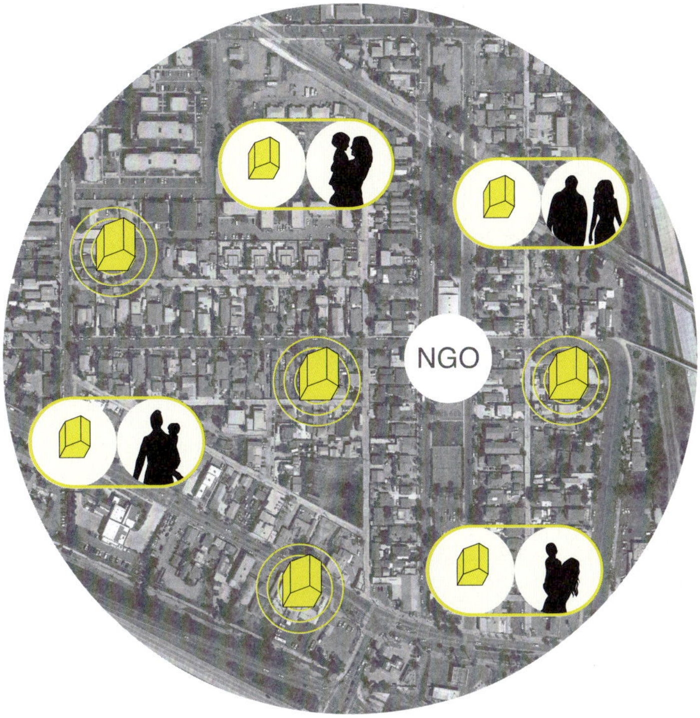

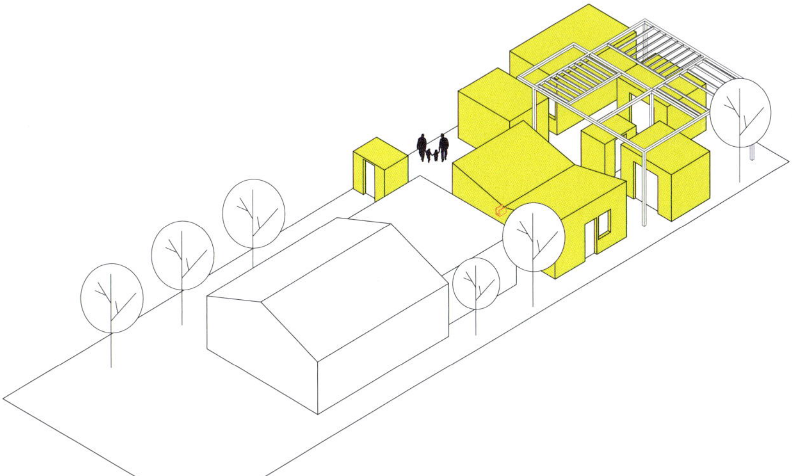

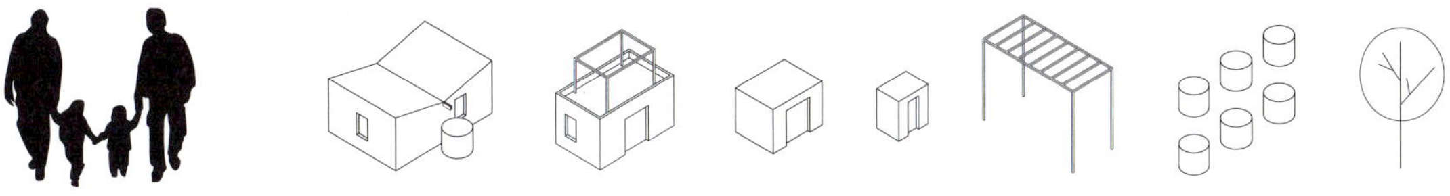

URBANIZATION AT THE SCALE OF A PARCEL

Participating residents choose from a catalogue of options—i.e., one bedroom, studio, accessory shed, trellis structures for water and energy systems, agriculture garden, combining them into a variety of spatial scenarios that are then assembled by human resourcefulness within the community. Some of these spaces are extensions of their homes or rental units to support informal economies.

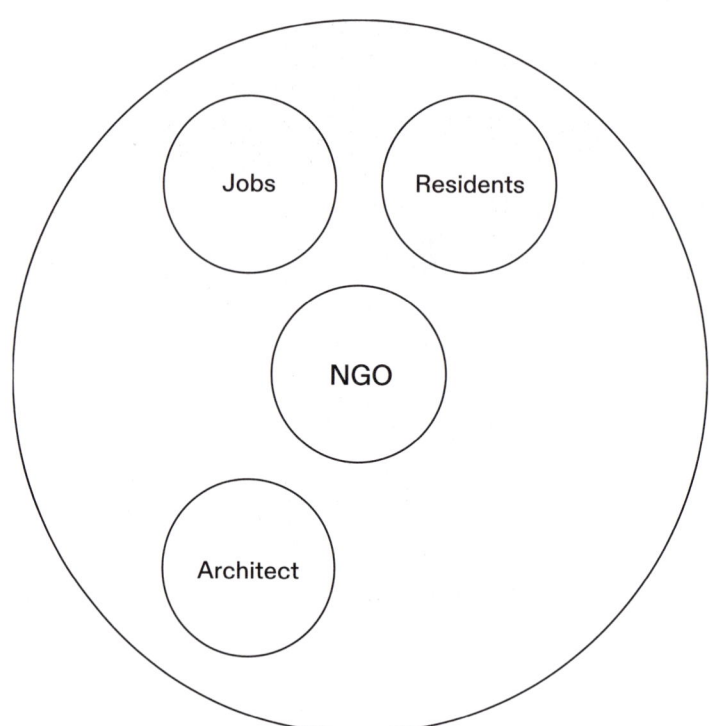

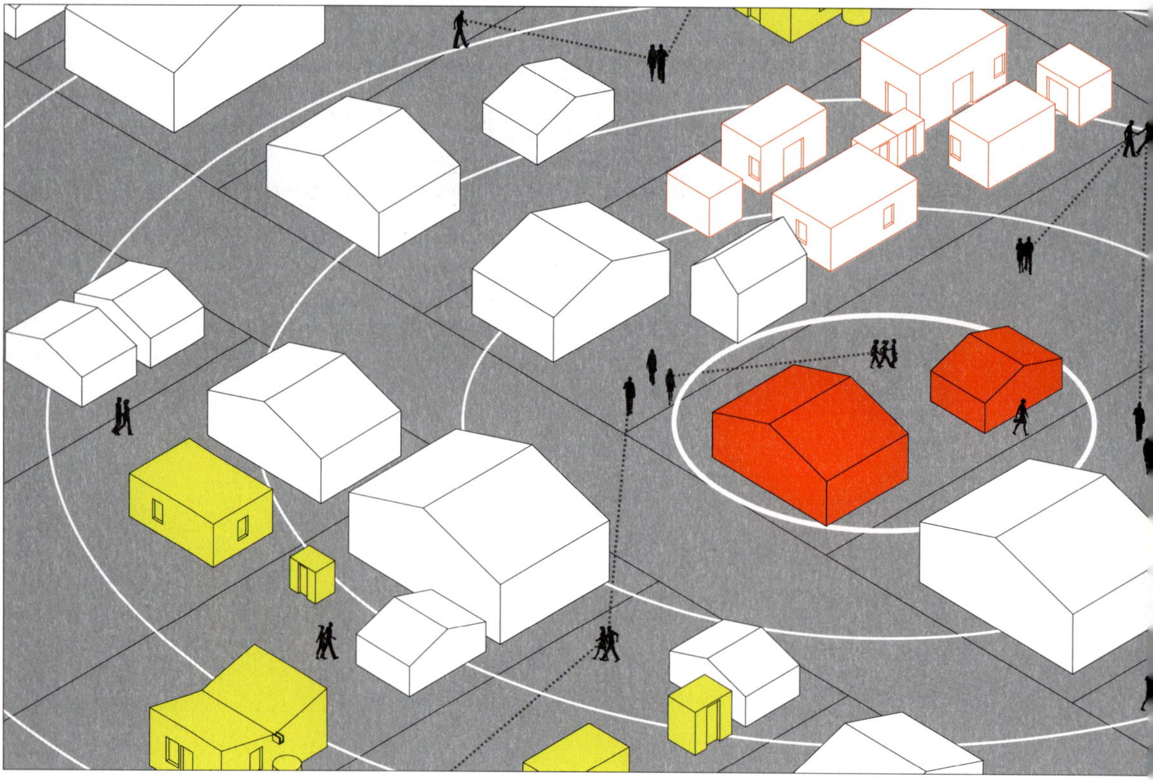

MICRO-POLICY STAGE 6: SOCIO-SPATIAL CONTRACTS
An important part of the process was producing new social contracts in the community to produce shared ownership with appropriate social protection mechanisms to prevent land speculation and gentrification. The Micro-Policy promotes incremental densification, advocating affordable housing as a neighborhood-scale economic engine, to incentivize job creation, while elevating community-based ownership and revenue streams.

IMMIGRANT NEIGHBORHOODS: HOUSING LABORATORIES

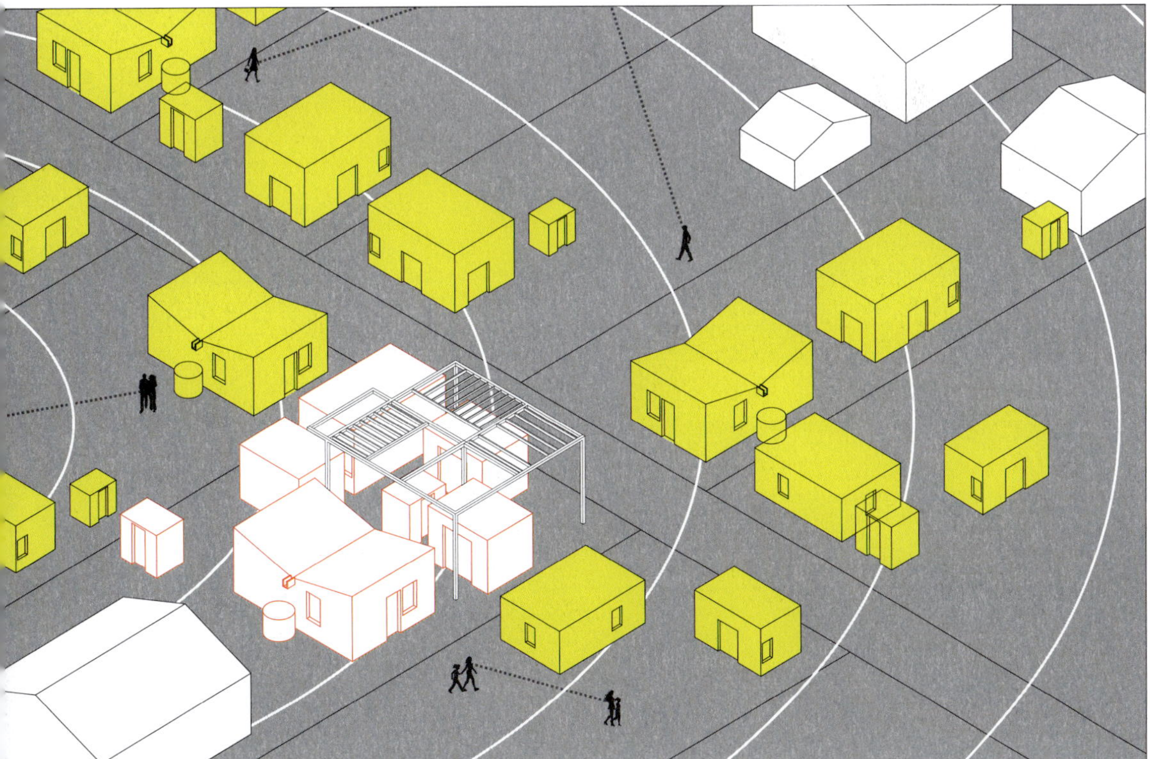

1 TIJUANA RIVER ESTUARY

2 BORDER WALLS AND DRAINS

3 INFORMAL SETTLEMENT

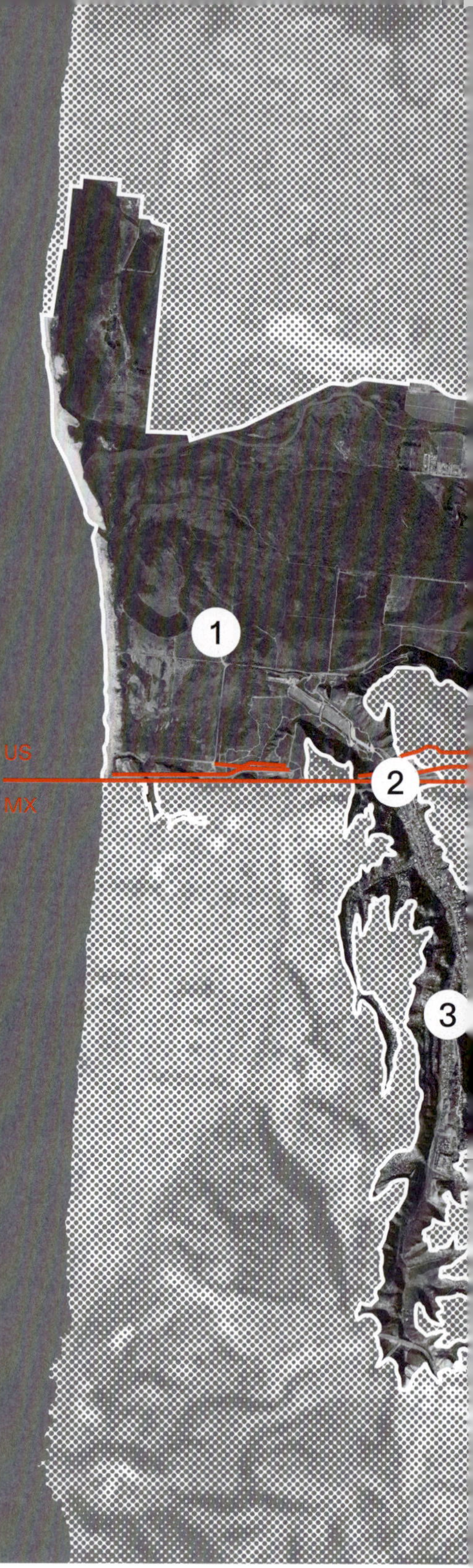

SAN DIEGO CASE STUDY / CONTEXT: SAN YSIDRO

We designed the Micro-Policy with our partners, Casa Familiar, as a framework for urban interventions in the border neighborhood of San Ysidro, a marginalized neighborhood uniquely located at the busiest land crossing in the Western hemisphere. It is 90% Latinx, with some of the highest unemployment rates, lowest median household income and worst air quality in San Diego County.

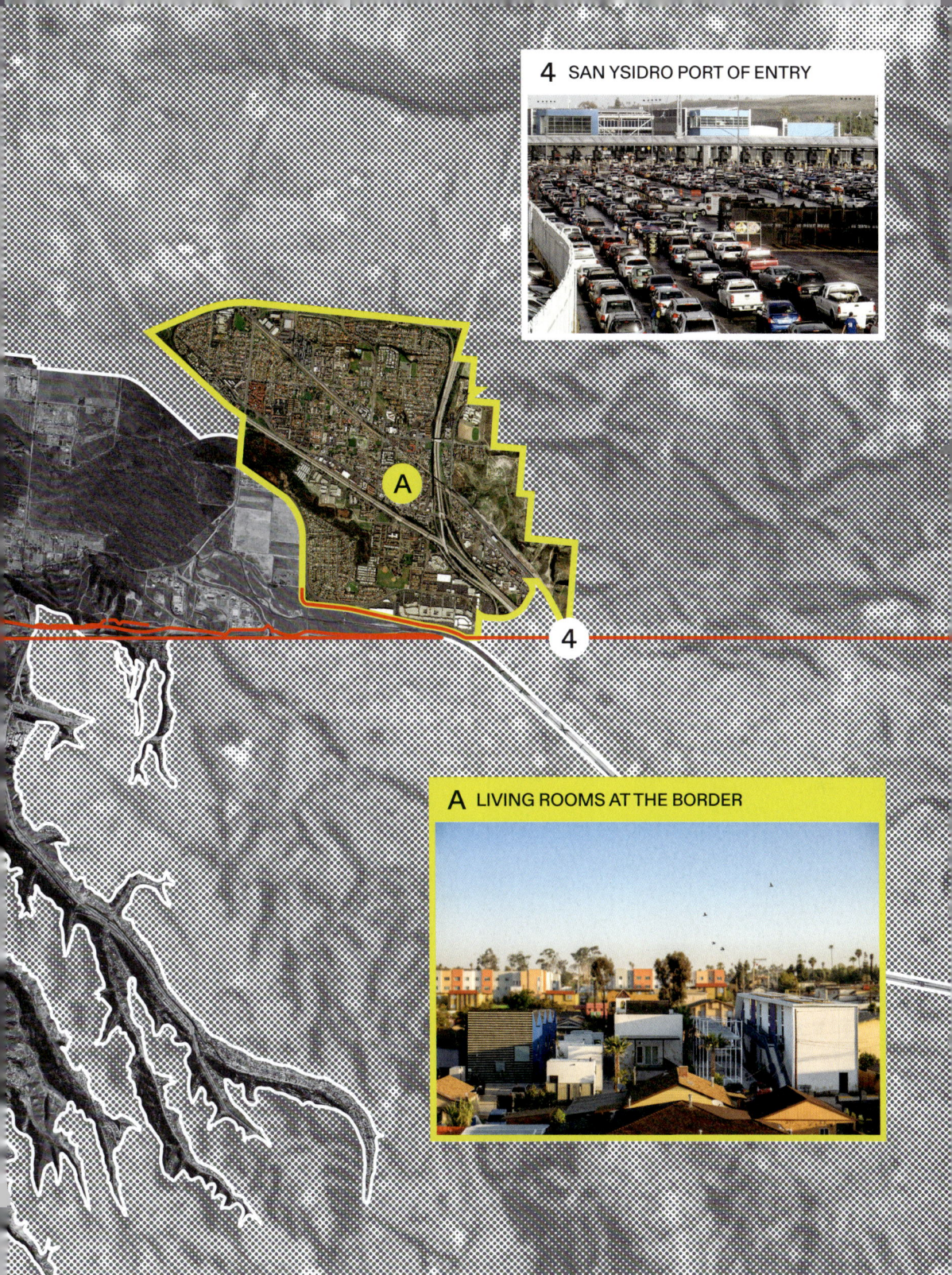

4 SAN YSIDRO PORT OF ENTRY

A LIVING ROOMS AT THE BORDER

IMMIGRANT NEIGHBORHOODS: HOUSING LABORATORIES

SAN DIEGO CASE STUDY / PROJECT: LIVING ROOMS AT THE BORDER
Led by Casa Familiar, we engaged the community of San Ysidro to develop a proof of concept, an affordable housing case study called *Living Rooms at the Border*.

ADAPTIVE REUSE AS CATALYST

The heart of *Living Rooms at the Border* is a beloved historic church that sat for decades in disrepair, which we were able to rescue through this project. During construction, the building had to be lifted for installing new foundations. During times of so much political violence inflicted on this border community, the surreal image of the church levitating with Tijuana's informal settlements in the distance inspired a sense of hope within the community

SMALL PARCELS: SOCIAL-ECONOMIC INFRASTRUCTURES

Living Rooms at the Border is a pilot proposal for affordable housing to spatialize a local Micro-Policy, presenting small parcels in low-income neighborhoods as infrastructure for social, economic and cultural production.

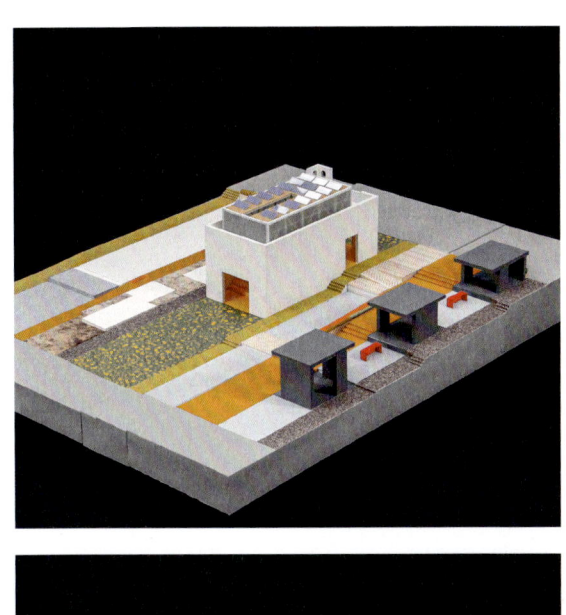

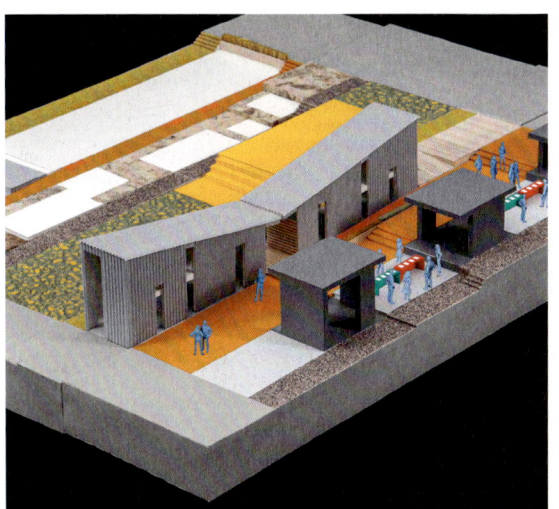

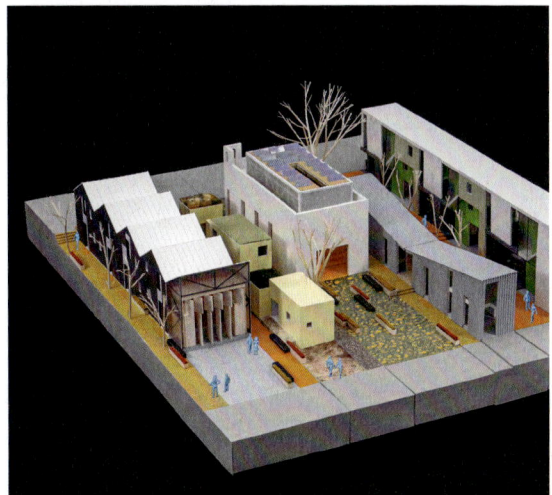

IMMIGRANT NEIGHBORHOODS: HOUSING LABORATORIES

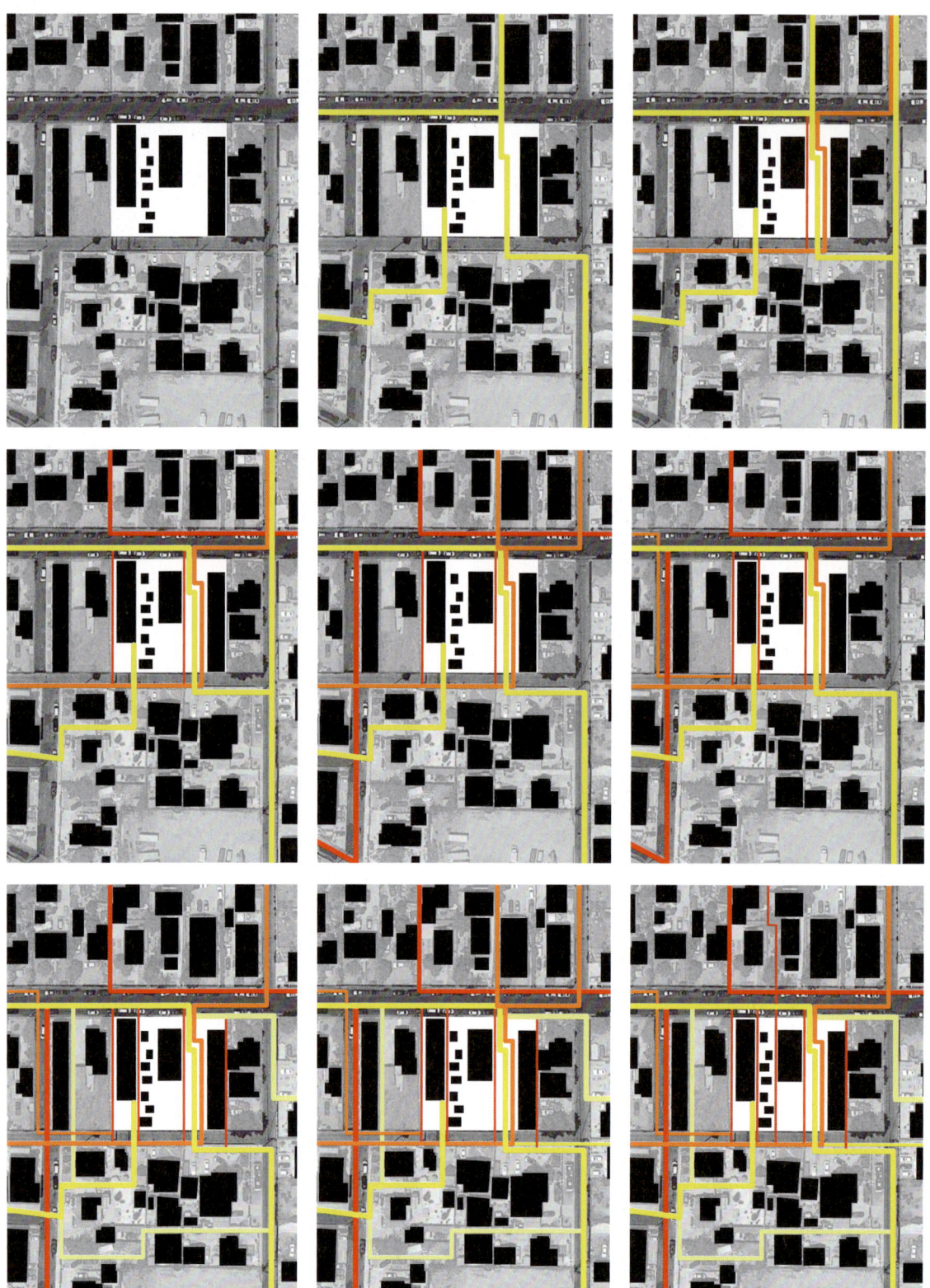

INFORMAL PEDESTRIAN CIRCULATIONS AS FRAMEWORK

The project began by strengthening and expanding an existing network of old alleys that are used by local residents as informal pedestrian corridors.

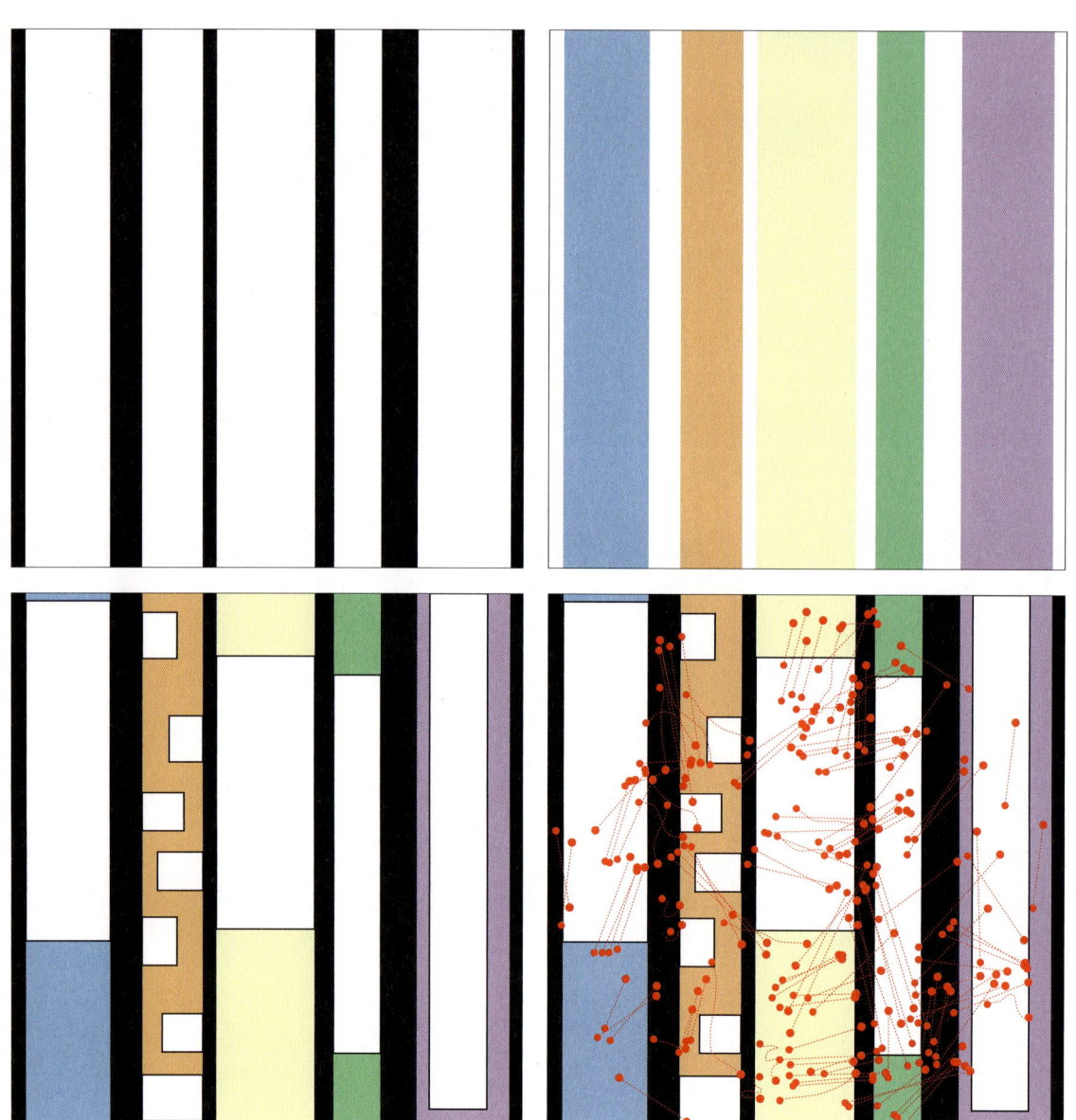

ANTICIPATING THE NEGOTIATION OF PRIVATE AND PUBLIC BOUNDARIES
The informal circulations through alleys helped to organize the small parcel as a series of linear "strips," some of which take the shape of small buildings, some landscape-interstitial spaces for informal uses, and some circulation pathways between them.

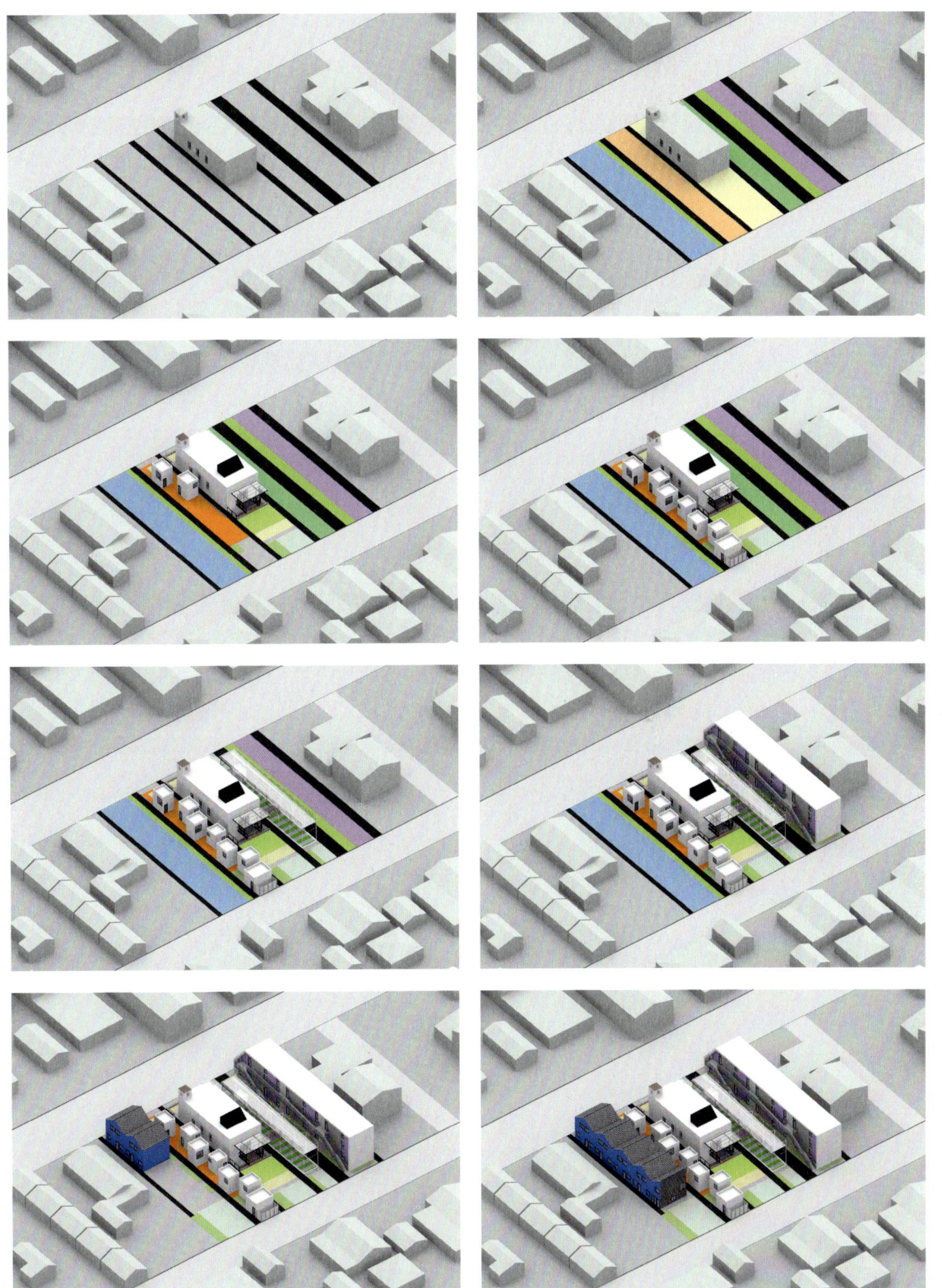

SOCIALIZING SMALL-SCALE URBAN FABRICS IN SUBURBAN NEIGHBORHOODS
The project advances a scalable prototype for small-scale development in low-income neighborhoods, where buildings collaborate to transform small lots into social housing infrastructures. We argue that community-led, incremental small-scale development democratizes urbanization.

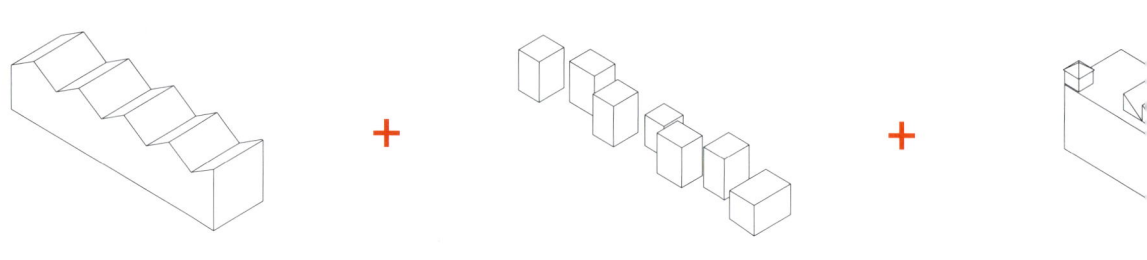

Large units for families Social service accessory buildings Historic church as

AFFORDABLE HOUSING CANNOT BE SUSTAINABLE ON ITS OWN

We designed *Living Rooms at the Border* as a double project: A parcel-sized social infrastructure made of spaces for cultural and economic activity, co-developed between Casa Familiar and UC San Diego, is flanked by affordable housing. Affordable housing is not sustainable as "units" only, but needs to be embedded within an infrastructure of social support, a fabric of community spaces programmed with resources for sociability, jobs and access to education.

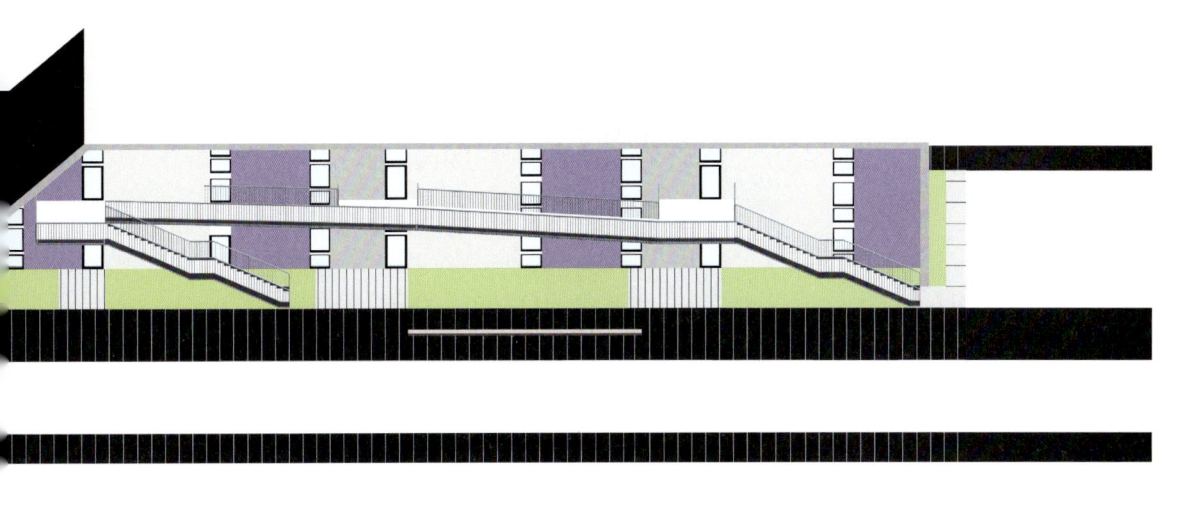

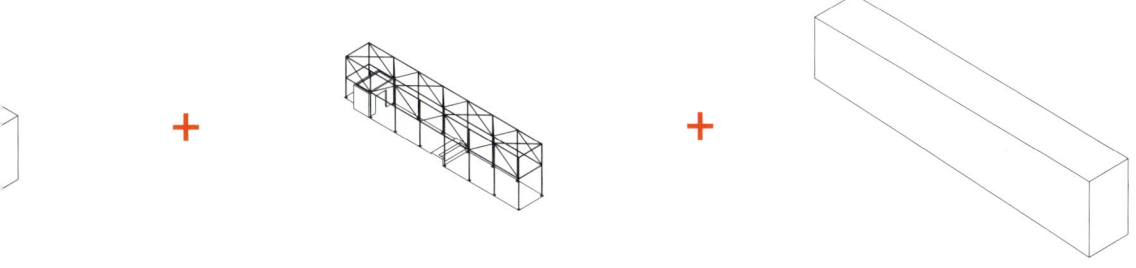

ity theater   Open-air civic classroom   Small flexible units

The organizational design of the parcel through a system of linear strips with a variety of small-scale buildings performing different roles was a deliberate strategy to mobilize diverse financial streams. In other words, the diversification of buildings and programs enabled support from diverse funding sources, hybridizing private lending, municipal subsidy, social impact investment, and support from foundations and the public university to benefit the community.

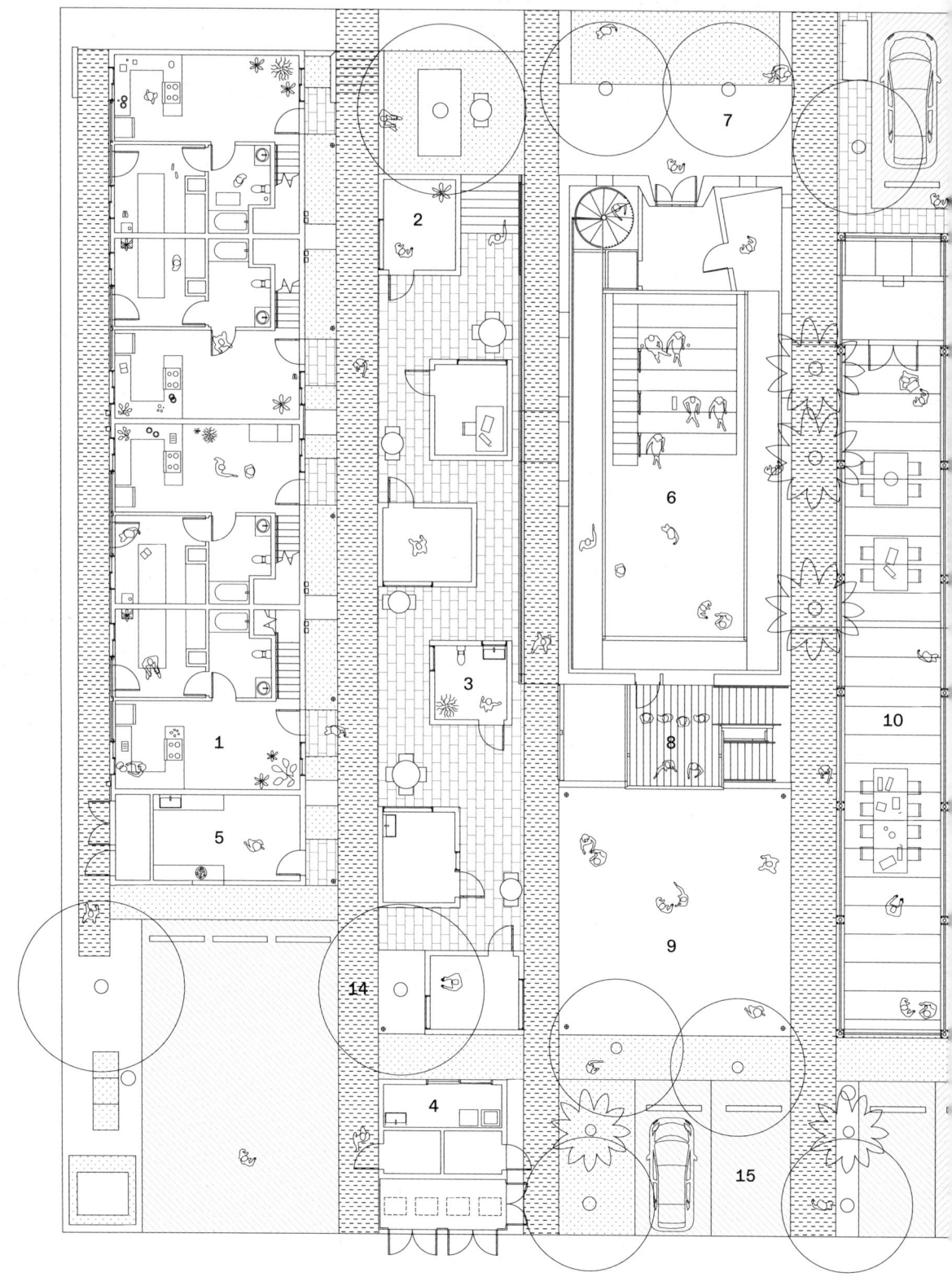

DESIGNING THE INTERFACE BETWEEN HOUSING AND PUBLIC SPACE

We renovated the historic church (6) into a community theater with an outdoor stage (8). This performance space is flanked on one side by a series of small accessory buildings for Casa Familiar's social programming (2, 3), and on the other side by an open-air civic classroom-pavilion (10). This social, educational and cultural infrastructure anchors ten units of affordable housing, at both ends of the parcel (1, 10, 11), all mediated by pedestrian walkways.

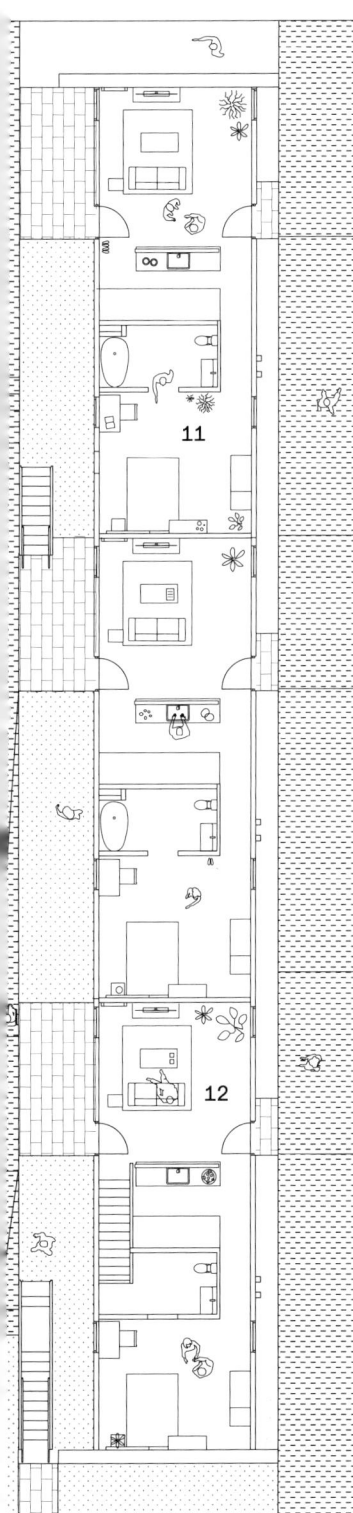

1. Housing for families with grandmothers
2. Accessory buildings for Casa Familiar social programs
3. Accessory buildings for artists' studios
4. Accessory building for community laundry
5. Small cafe training program
6. Community theater
7. Theater plaza
8. Outdoor music and performance stage
9. Outdoor commons
10. Open-air civic classroom pavilion-porch
11. Housing for couples / single mothers with children
12. Live-work unit
13. Catwalk above for circulation and viewing
14. Pedestrian walkways
15. Parking

CURATING THE SPACES BETWEEN BUILDINGS TO ANTICIPATE INTERACTION

This is an integrated socio-spatial system programmed by university and community (see project cluster 6). Affordable housing takes on a different meaning when it is deliberately threaded into spaces for social programming, summoning residents to participate in the development of local economy and cultural production, synergizing spaces, programs, resources and people.

TOP-DOWN / BOTTOM-UP

IMMIGRANT NEIGHBORHOODS: HOUSING LABORATORIES

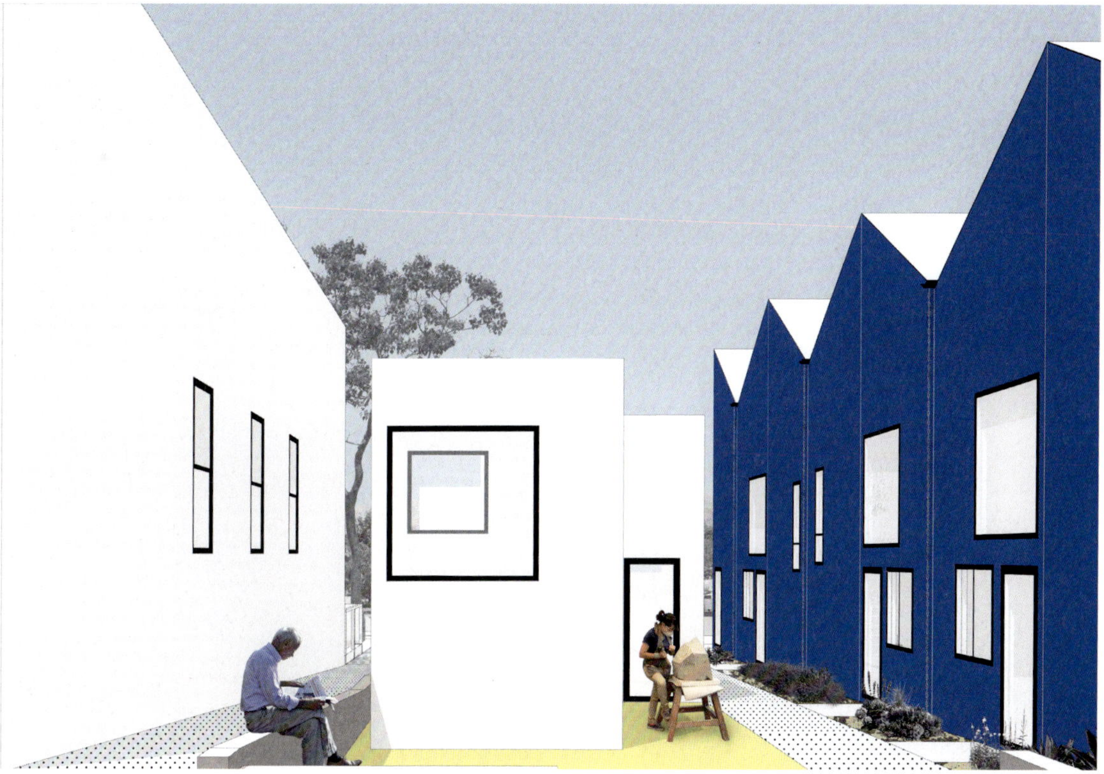

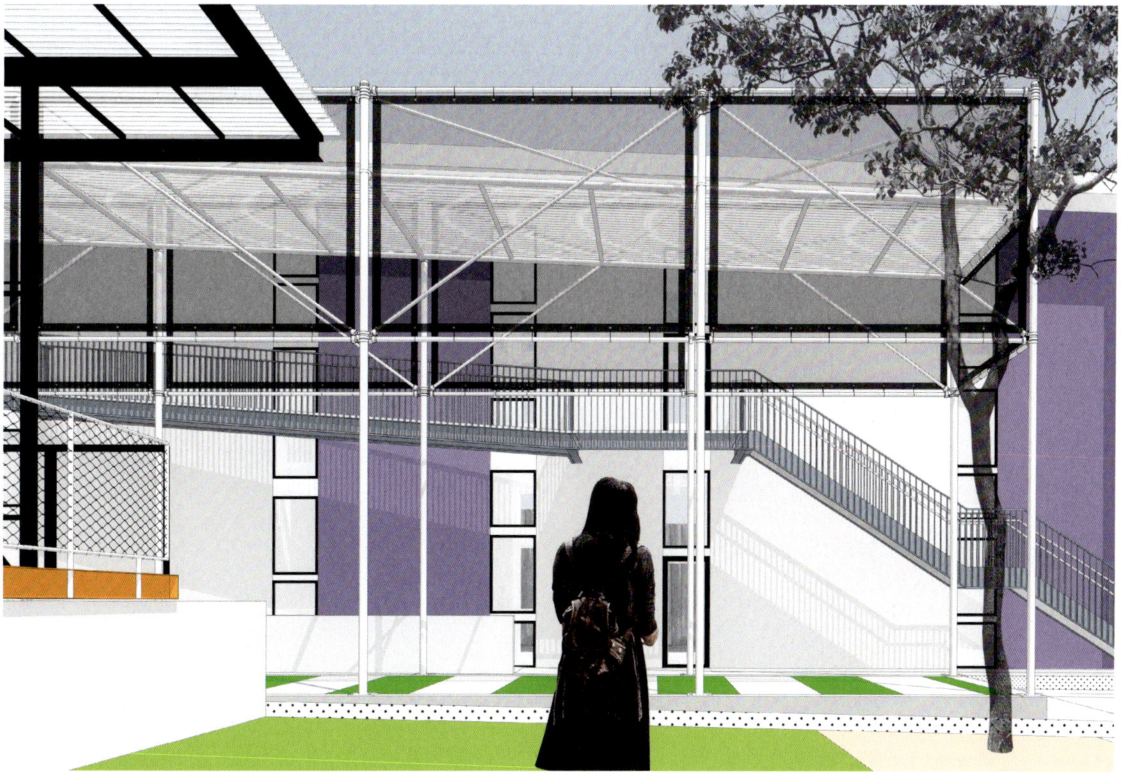

IMMIGRANT NEIGHBORHOODS: HOUSING LABORATORIES

SPACES FOR SOCIAL PROXIMITY

We completed construction of *Living Rooms at the Border* in February 2020 just before COVID-19 hit, and the residents moved in. We never imagined that a site built for social proximity, and choreographed for social flows between indoor and outdoor spaces, would become a community asset during a pandemic.

IMMIGRANT NEIGHBORHOODS: HOUSING LABORATORIES

IMMIGRANT NEIGHBORHOODS: HOUSING LABORATORIES

IMMIGRANT NEIGHBORHOODS: HOUSING LABORATORIES

NEIGHBORHOOD-SCALE URBANIZATION

Casa Familiar has become an alternative housing developer, reimagining civic infrastructure at neighborhood scale with a variety of housing prototypes, and social and cultural hubs. Their leadership assures that urban profits will remain inside the community, benefitting local modes of social and economic production—a safeguard against gentrification.

1 URBANIZATION OF ADAPTATION

2 HOUSING MADE OF WASTE

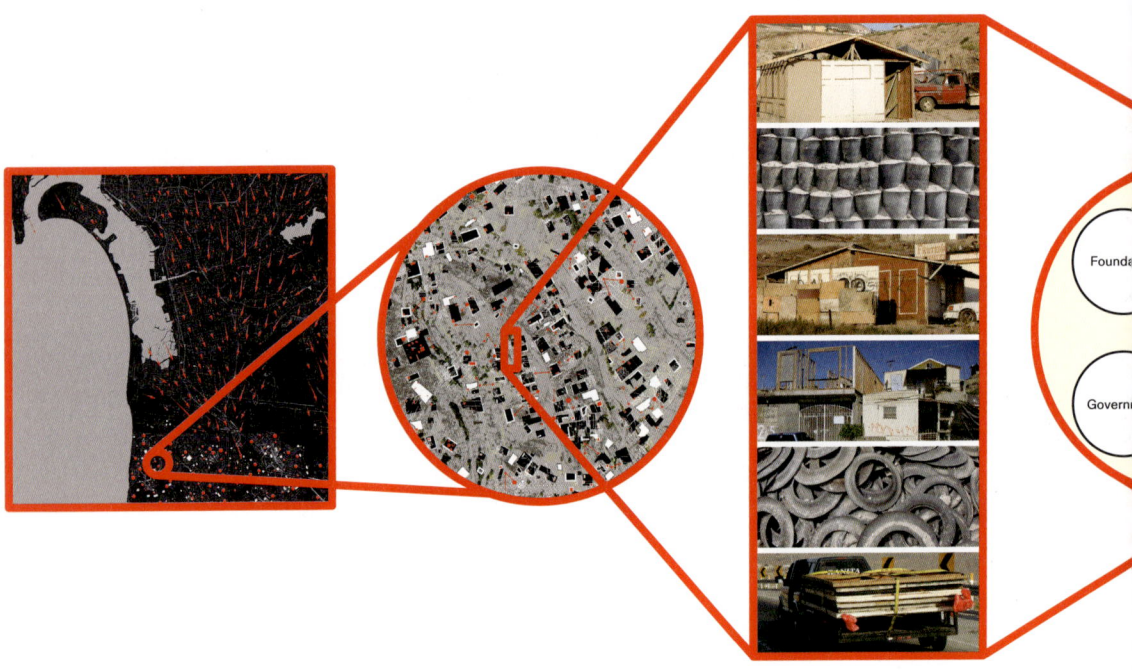

Tijuana's informal settlements recycle urban debris from San Diego

Linking factory ar

DESIGNING A NEW POLITICAL ECONOMY OF HOUSING: A TIJUANA CASE STUDY

Tijuana's informal settlements are open-air housing factories, as people recycle discarded architectural parts from San Diego to construct habitation. We have advanced new approaches to spatial and infrastructural design that are inclusive of these temporal social-economic dynamics of informal urbanization. We connect prefabricated material systems from global factories surrounding these settlements to the sweat equity of self-built housing. What emerges is a new political economy of waste in the informal settlements of Tijuana.

3 THE FACTORY AS SITE OF INTERVENTION

4 TRANSITIONAL INFRASTRUCTURE

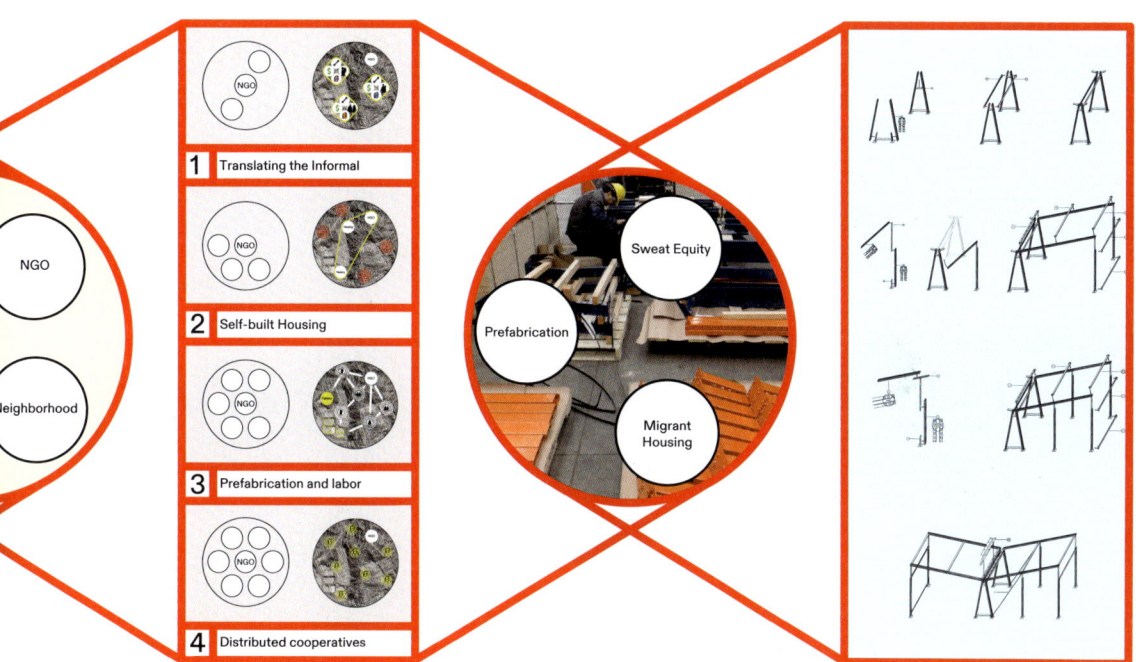

1 Translating the Informal

2 Self-built Housing

3 Prefabrication and labor

4 Distributed cooperatives

Prefab frames for informal housing

IMMIGRANT NEIGHBORHOODS: HOUSING LABORATORIES

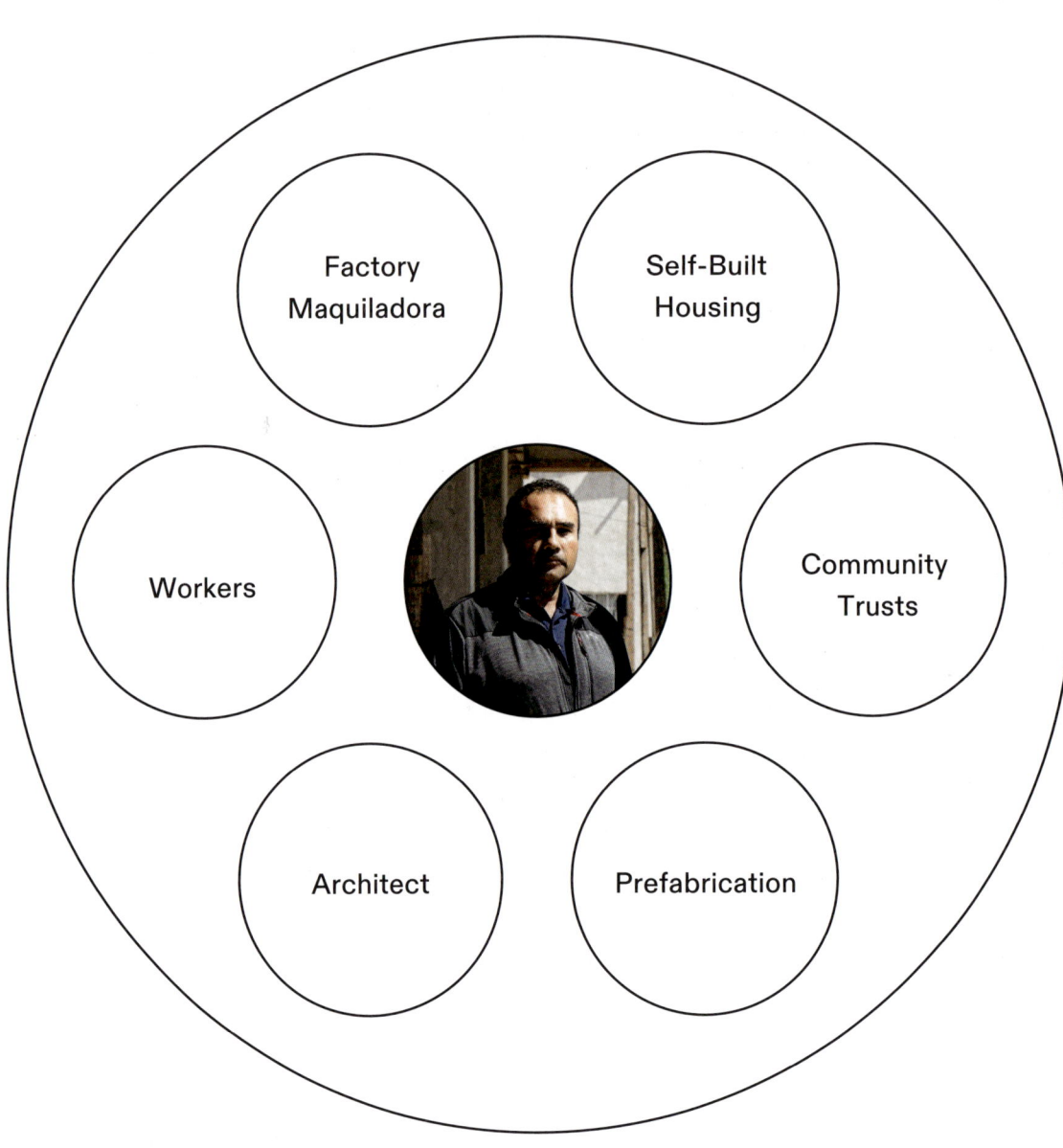

DESIGNING A COMMUNITY PROCESS: A MICRO-POLICY FOR LOS LAURELES CANYON
Tijuana is both a city of multinational factories and a geopolitical destination for refugee-migrants from central Mexico and Central America more broadly. With Embajadores de Jesús, our community partner in Los Laureles Canyon, we are mediating the conflicts between maquiladoras, informal settlements, refugee housing and the politics of labor, with a protocol of reciprocity between the maquiladoras and the marginalized labor communities that surround them.

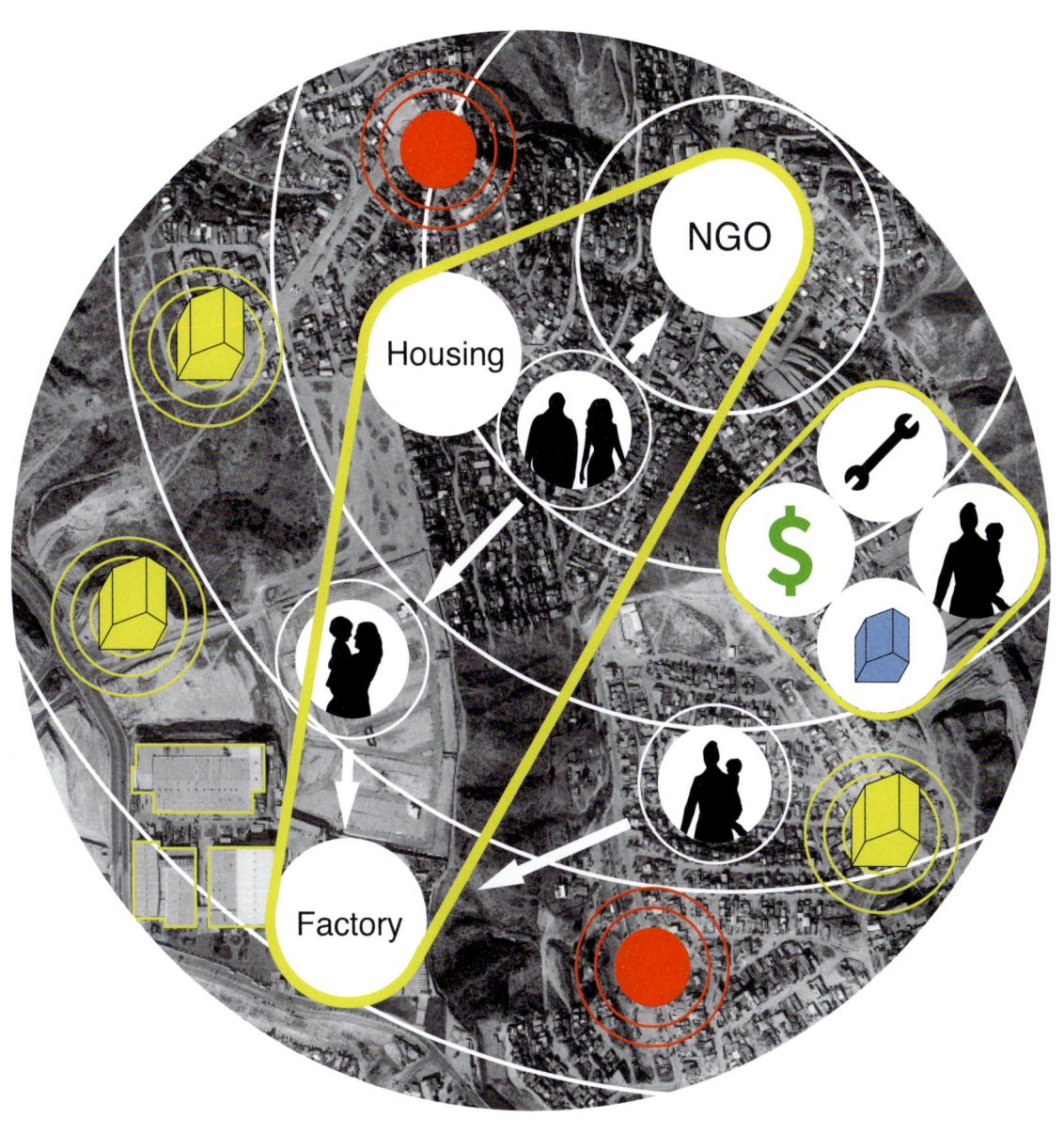

MEDIATING THE INTERFACE: HOUSING-LABOR-PREFABRICATION

Embajadores de Jesús is a religious organization led by activist-pastor-economist Gustavo Banda Aceves and *pastora*-psychologist Zaida Guillén. They began construction of a refugee camp to provide shelter and basic services to hundreds of Haitian and Central American refugees navigating unjust asylum processes in the US and Mexico. The Micro-Policy in Los Laureles Canyon proposes an ethical loop in which factories invest in emergency housing, mobilizing prefabrication through human agency to support the adaptive processes of informal urbanization.

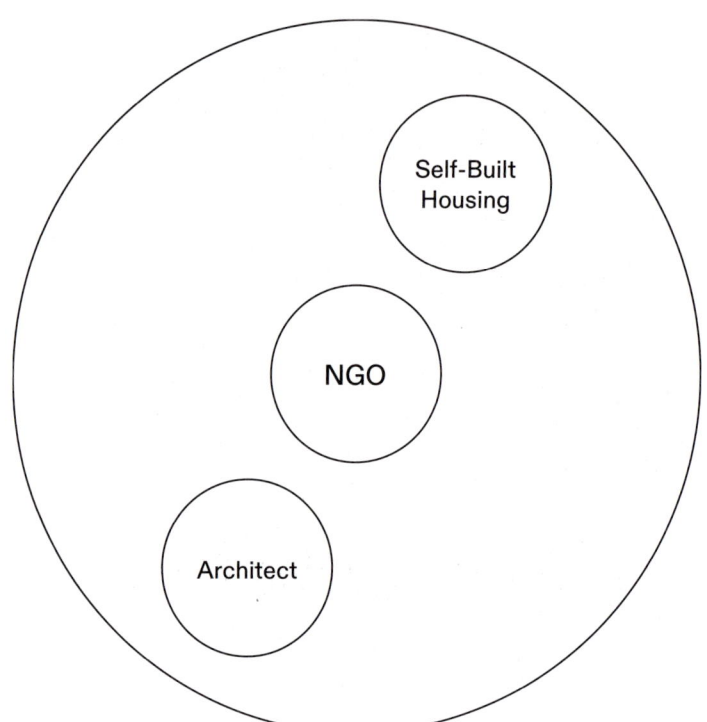

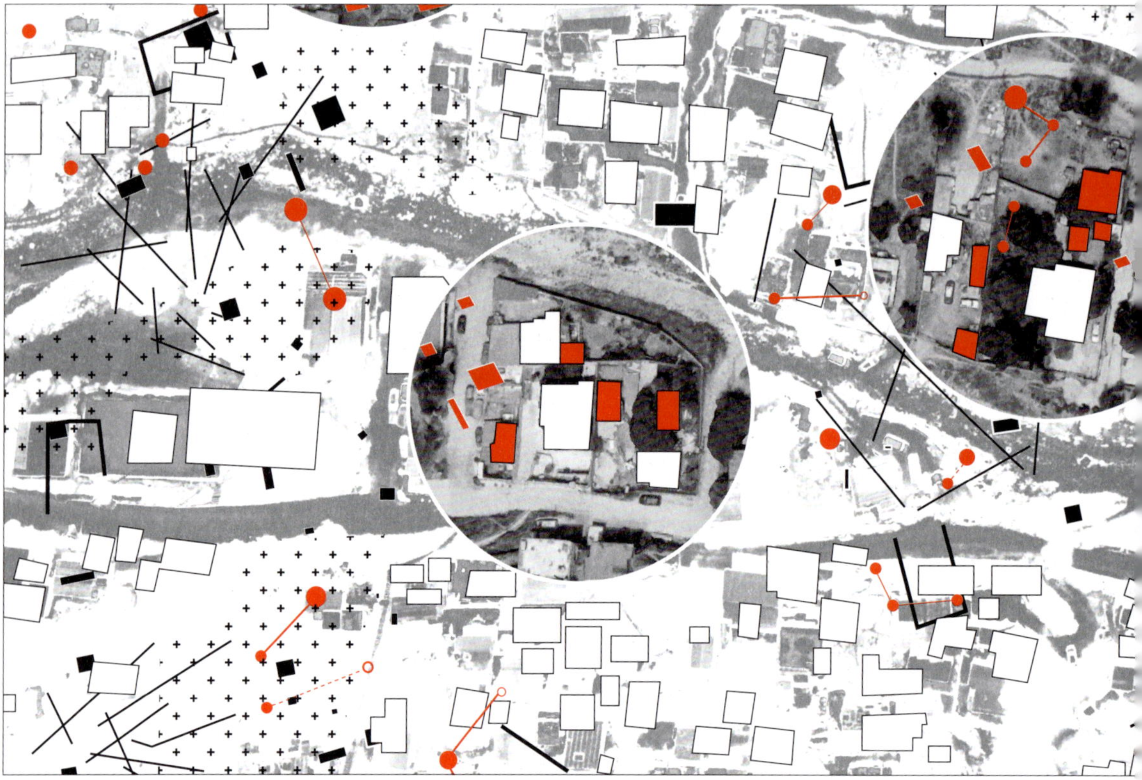

MICRO-POLICY STAGE 1: VISUALIZING EXISTING CAPABILITIES

The Micro-Policy declares informal settlements as urgent sites of intervention—for ethical reasons, and because the ingenious self-built processes of urbanization and the political economy of waste need top-down subsidy and support. These processes are typically invisible to institutions, and often to communities themselves. The Micro-Policy begins by increasing recognition of the hidden value of informal processes that merge material systems with human agency.

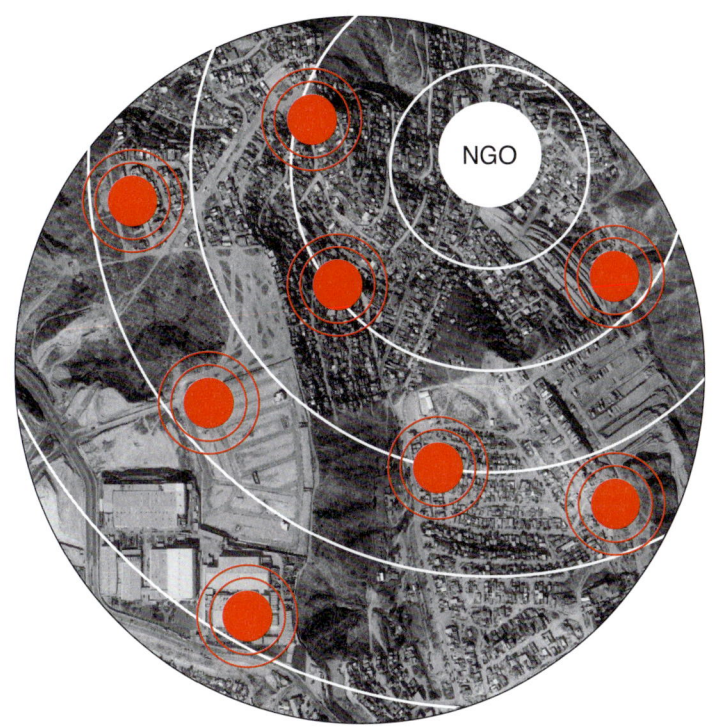

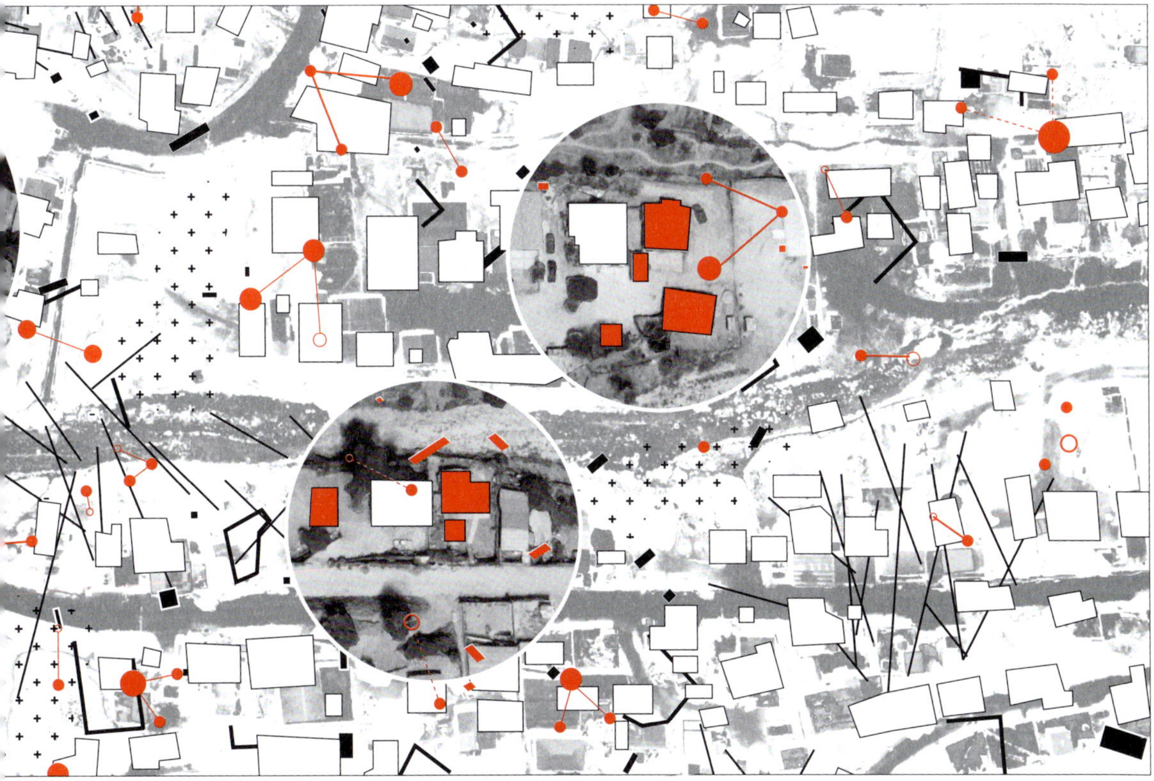

AN URBAN PEDAGOGY OF WASTE
We engage local residents in conversations about the significance of their own recycling strategies, amplifying the social capital and creative urban intelligence that characterizes this "second-hand urbanization."

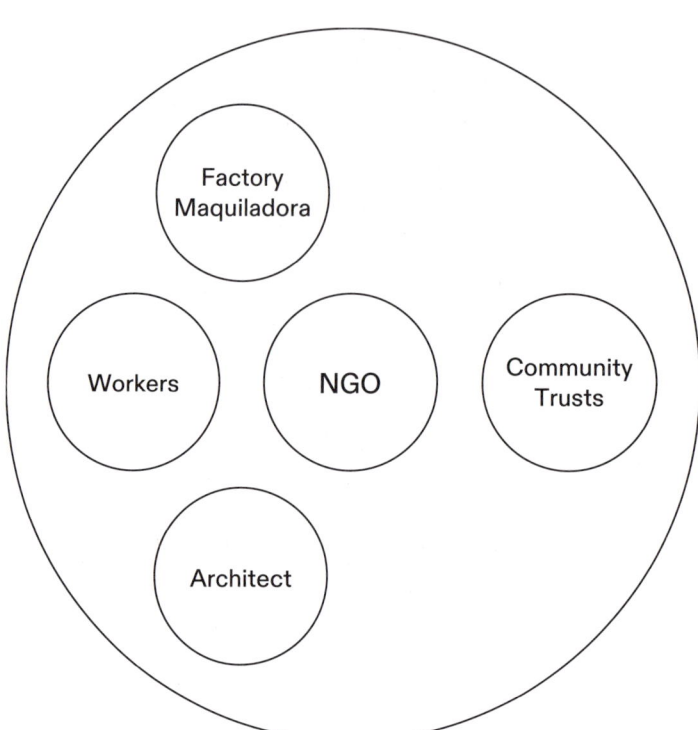

MICRO-POLICY STAGE 2: LINKING FACTORY WORKERS AND SELF-BUILT HOUSING
Multinational maquiladoras position themselves strategically adjacent to Tijuana's informal settlements to benefit from easy, unregulated access to cheap labor. These communities-of-labor produce their own social housing, and their entrepreneurship demands top-down support.

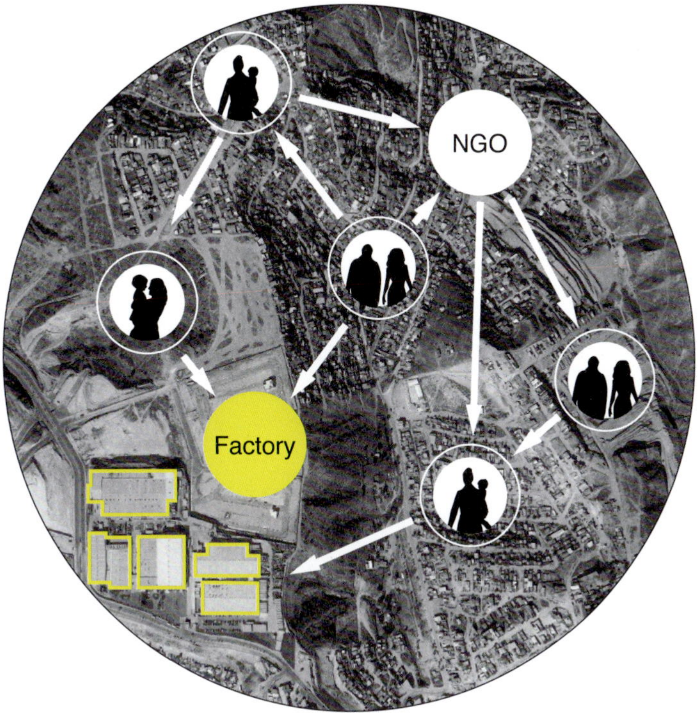

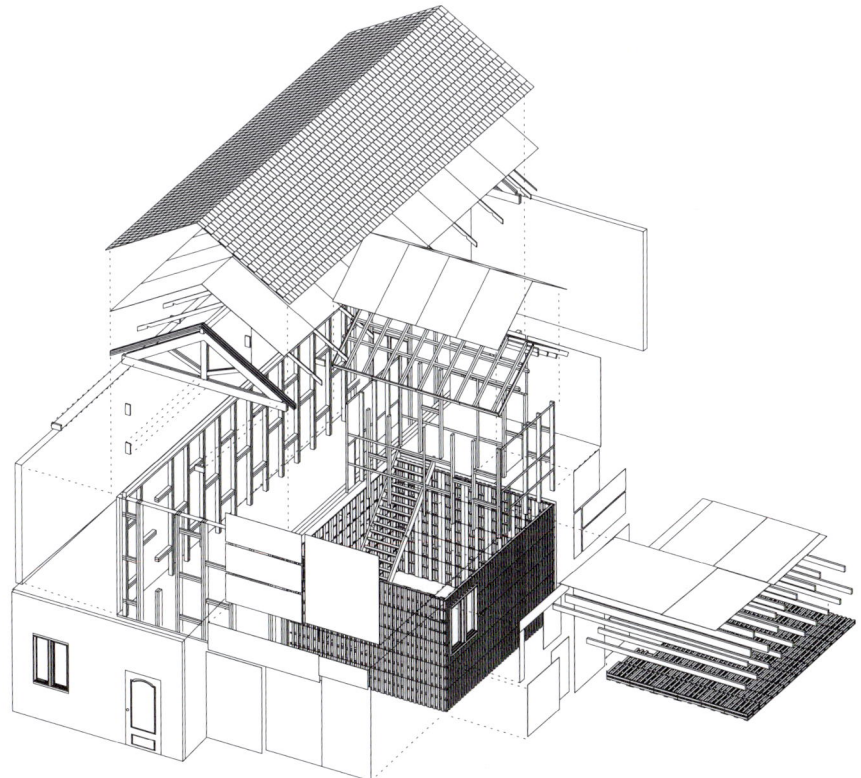

VISUALIZING A POLITICAL ECONOMY OF WASTE

To recognize and validate the social and economic value of these bottom-up informal processes, we visualized the proximity of multinational factories to these informal settlements and catalogued diverse best practices in the recycling and retrofitting of material systems. Visualizing this political economy of waste was essential to securing agreements with the factories to support the housing needs of their workforce.

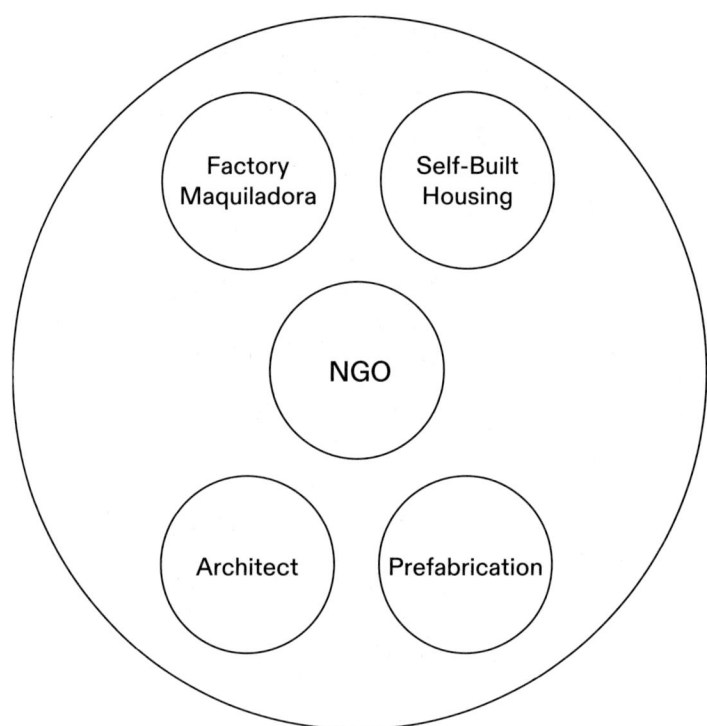

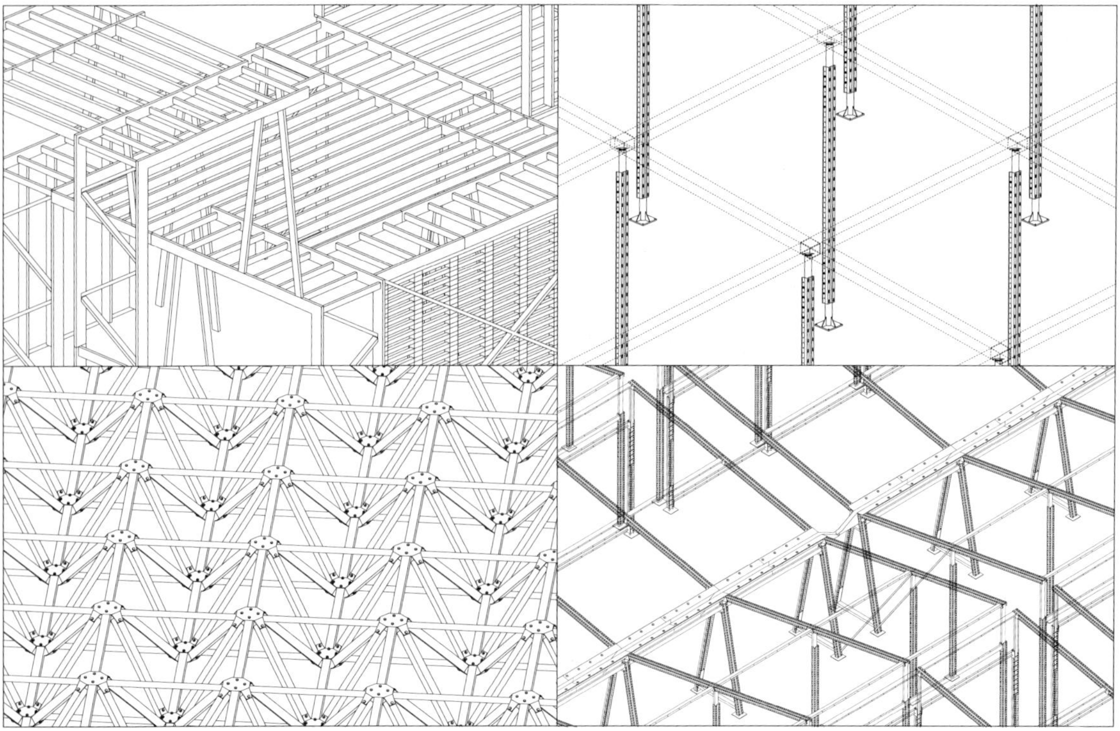

MICRO-POLICY STAGE 3: DESIGNING ETHICAL LOOPS
We proposed an ethical loop in which factories invest in emergency housing, linking factory-made prefabricated parts with the local sweat equity of self-built housing, establishing a protocol of reciprocity between the maquiladoras and the marginalized labor communities that surround them.

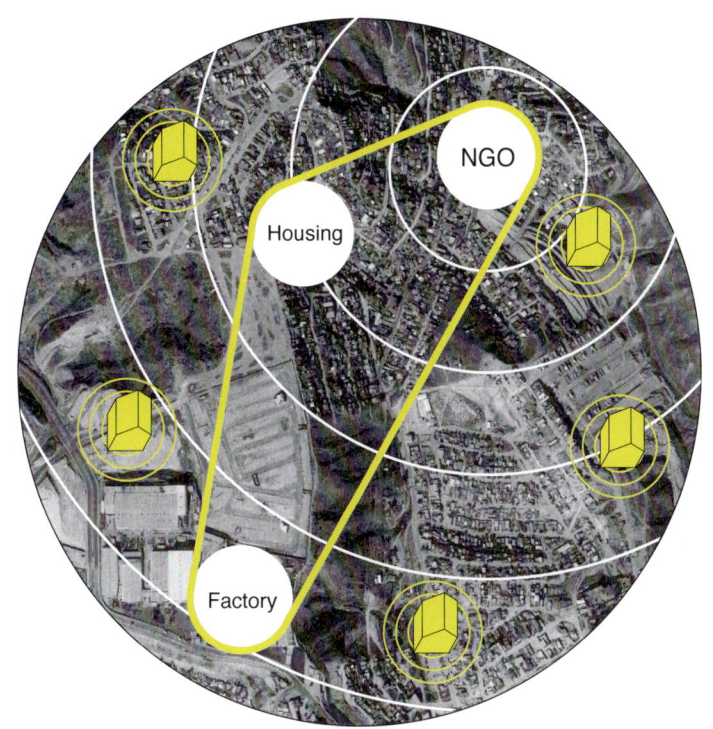

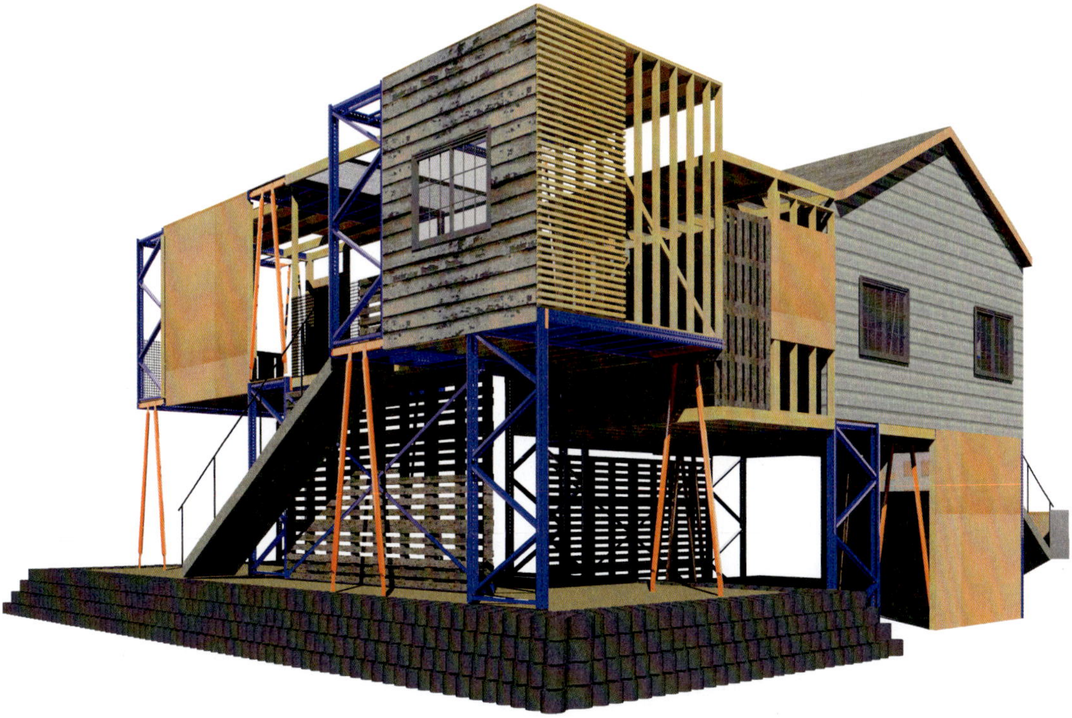

FRAMES TO ANTICIPATE TRANSFORMATION

Over the years we have experimented with methods to structurally mediate the recycling of waste, speculating how factory-made prefabricated systems can serve as structural scaffolds for informal housing. This ethical loop enables a relationship between the factory-made and the handmade. The Los Laureles Canyon Micro-Policy posited that prefabrication cannot be separated from human resourcefulness, from the emergent human capacity to respond to the idiosyncratic conditions of the world.

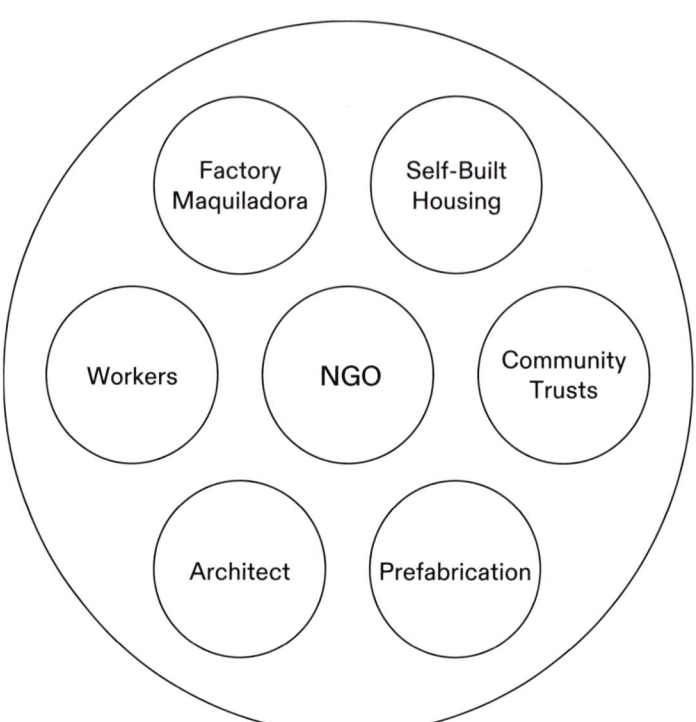

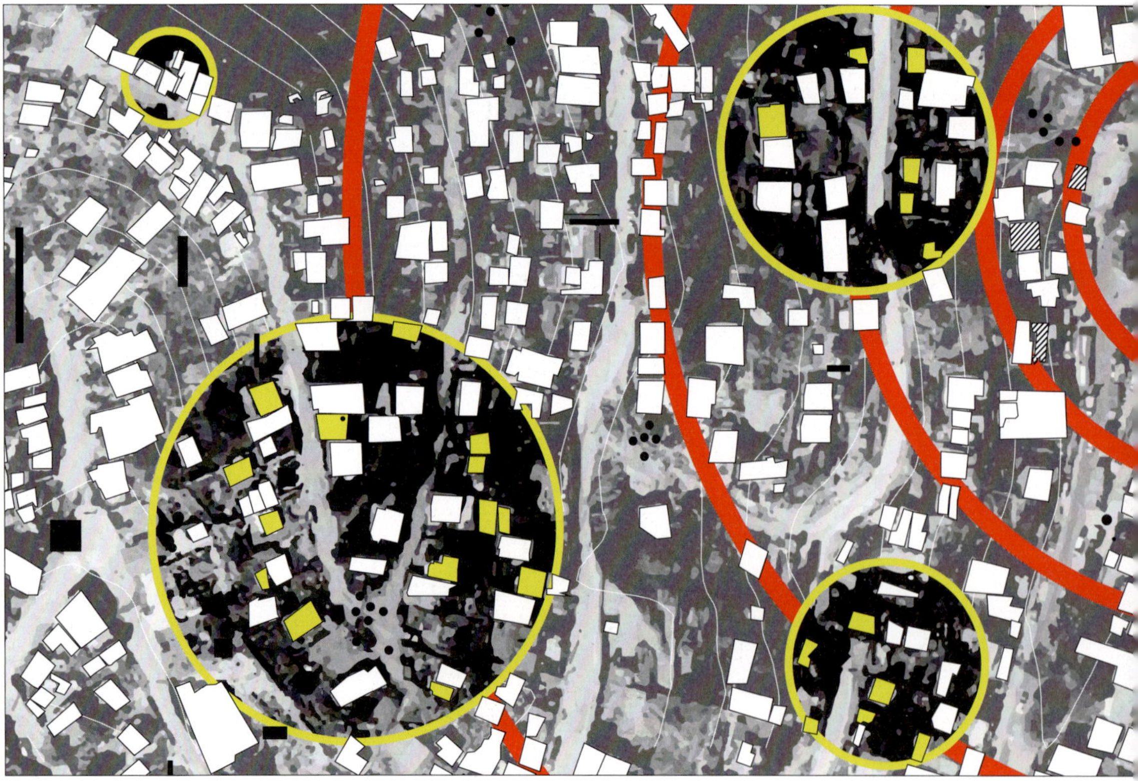

MICRO-POLICY STAGE 4: AN INFORMAL COMMUNITY TRUST

The Los Laureles Canyon Micro-Policy is also an economic model for sustaining material circulations between the factory and the migrant communities surrounding it. This entails a cooperative model that connects factory systems and the sweat equity of migrants, seeded by a coalition of university, social impact investment and our nonprofit partners.

MICRO-*EJIDOS*
To sustain construction capacity over time, the Micro-Policy proposes a model of co-development between the nonprofit and the residents of Los Laureles Canyon, linking self-built community processes and jobs. A construction cooperative is seeded, equipped with fabrication infrastructure, summoning coalitions of local residents into small *ejidos* (clusters of collective property) to adapt and restructure existing housing, and build new housing units co-owned by an informal community trust.

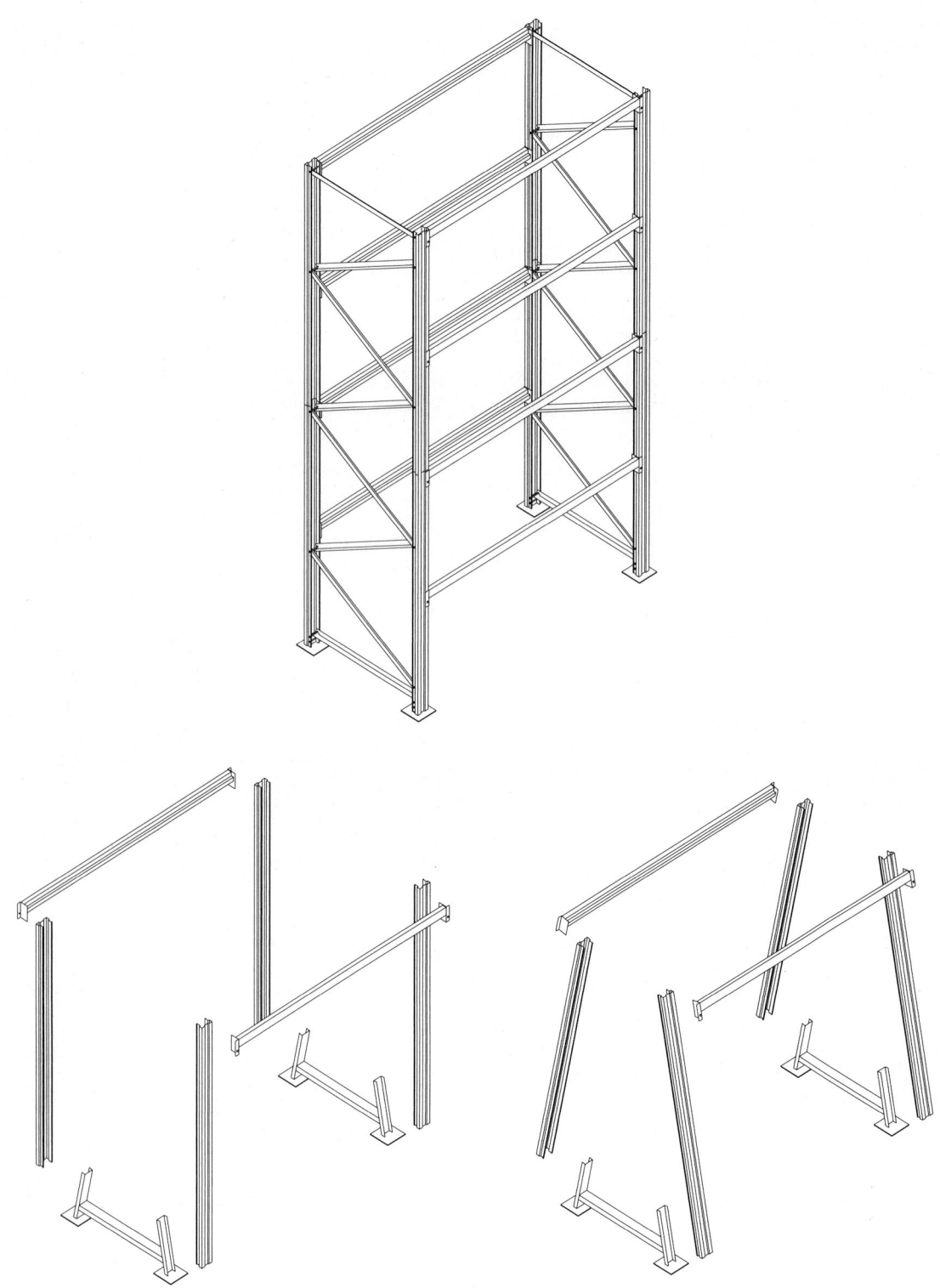

OPERATING INSIDE INSTITUTIONS, REDIRECTING SURPLUS VALUE

The maquiladora became a site of intervention. Here we are inside of Mecalux, a Spanish maquiladora that produces lightweight metal shelving systems for global export. We began a special collaboration to adapt its prefabricated parts into acupunctural systems to support incremental housing. To maintain the economy of the interlocking parts and the assembly line, we adapted only the angle at the base of the system.

PIGGYBACKING INDUSTRY
We have reimagined the relationship between industry, prefabrication and emergency housing. We discovered a factory CEO who was willing to subsidize parts to support communities in need. We designed a catalogue with the factory's engineers to test a variety of prototypes and configurations, and made this resource available to residents in the construction process.

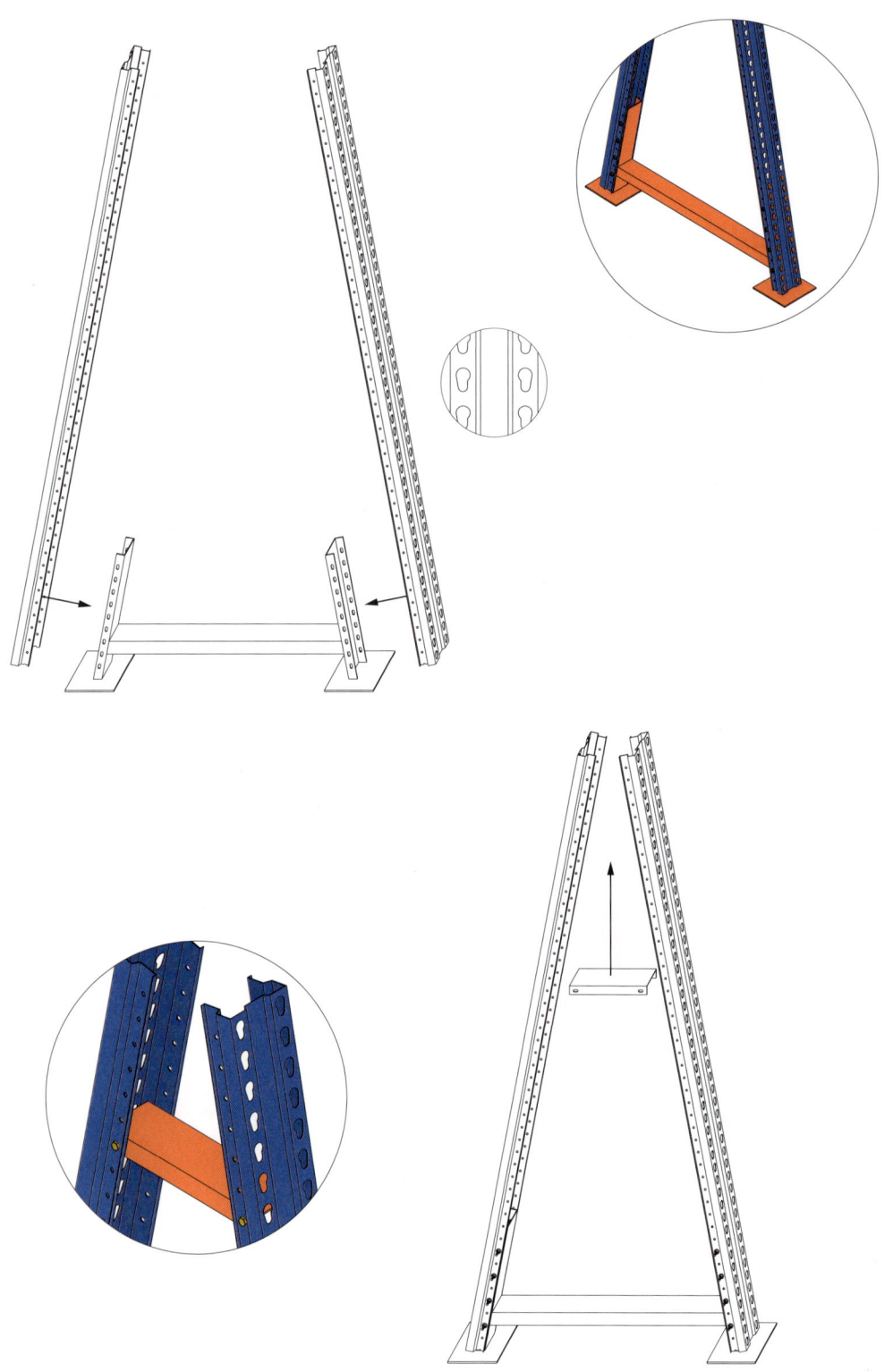

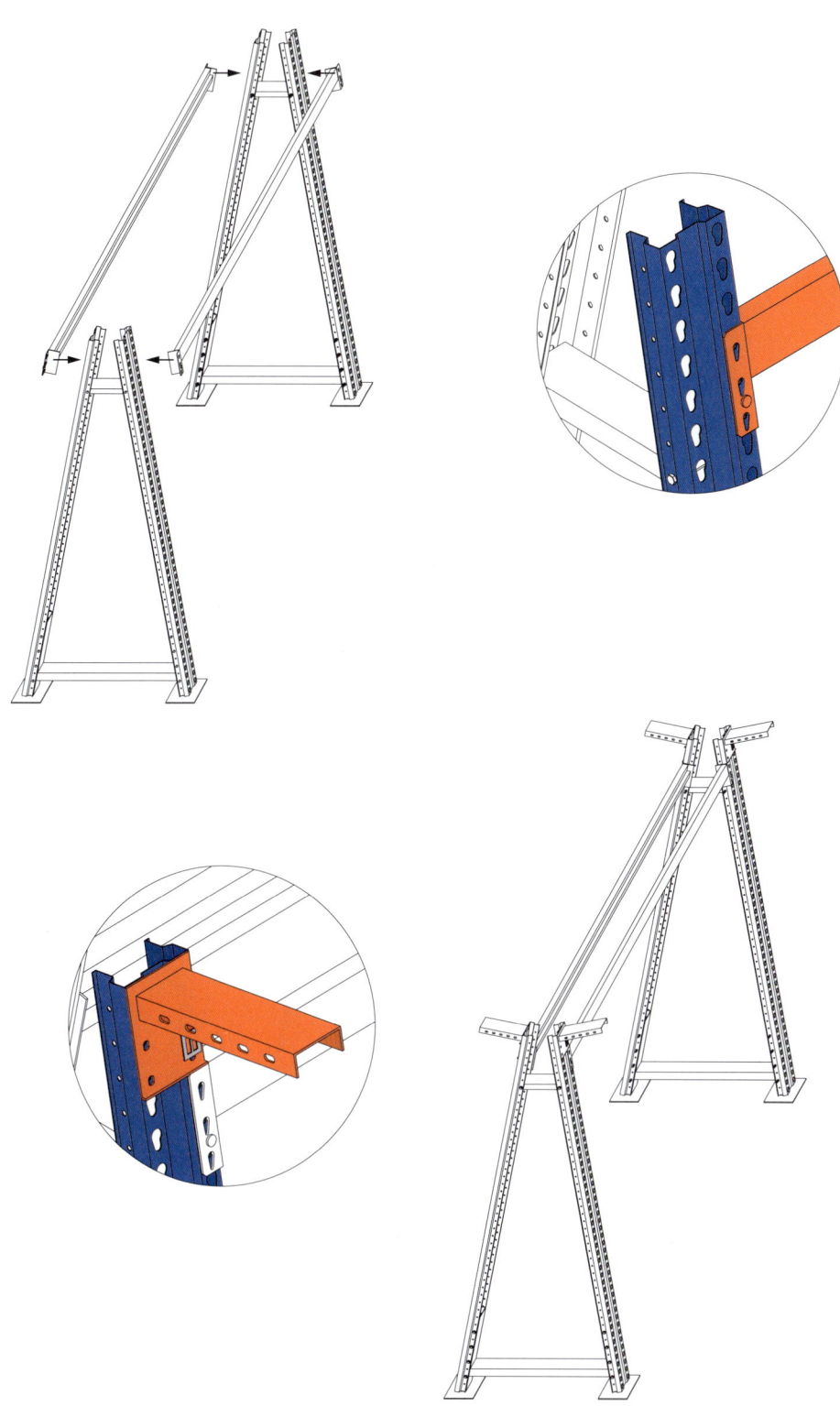

IMMIGRANT NEIGHBORHOODS: HOUSING LABORATORIES

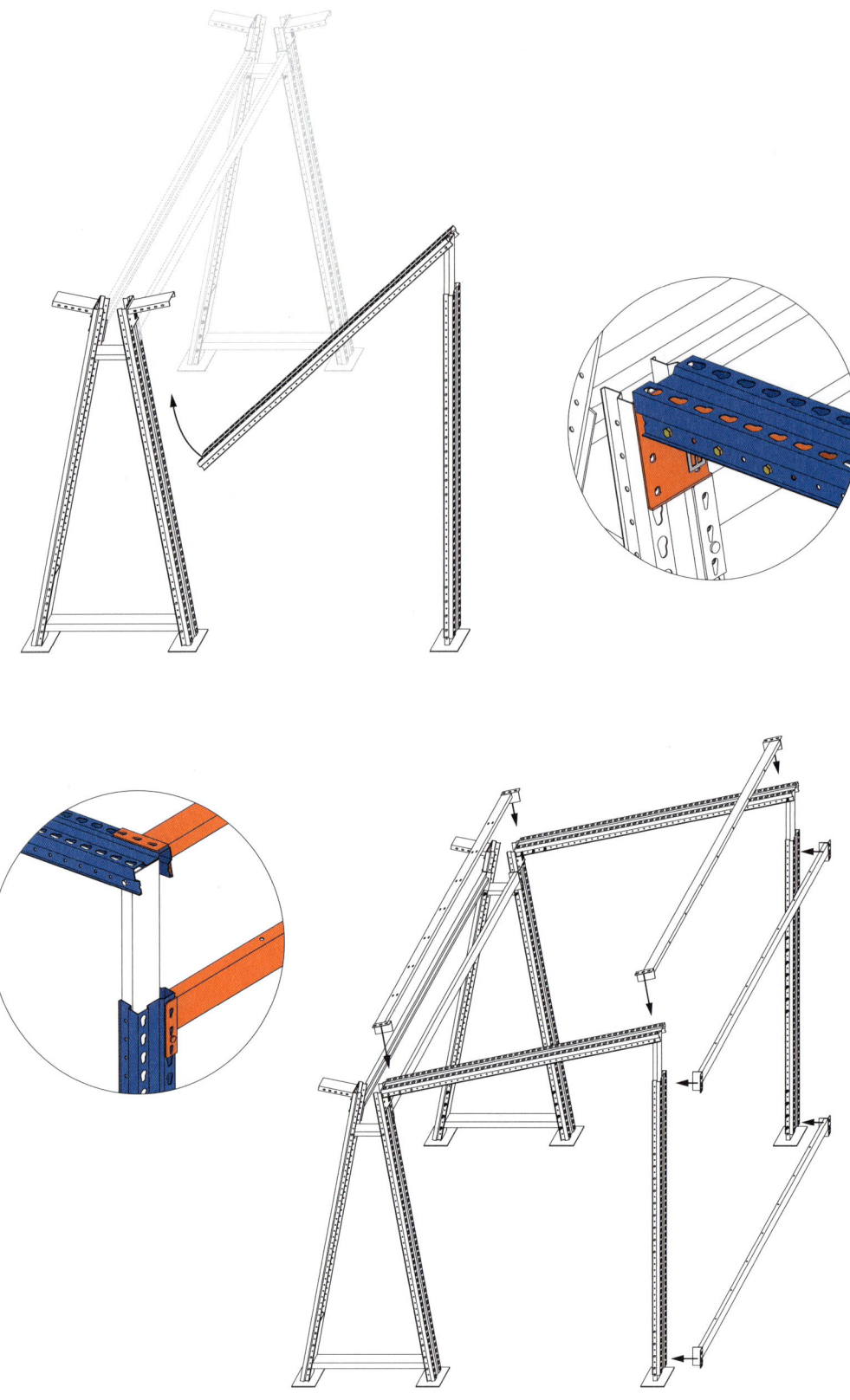

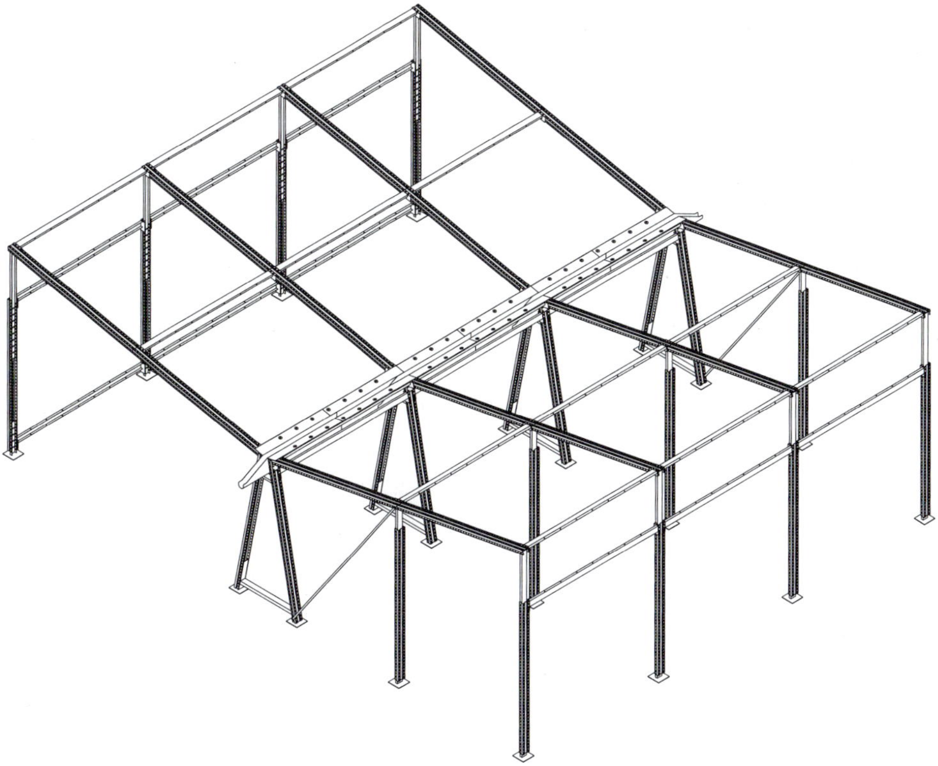

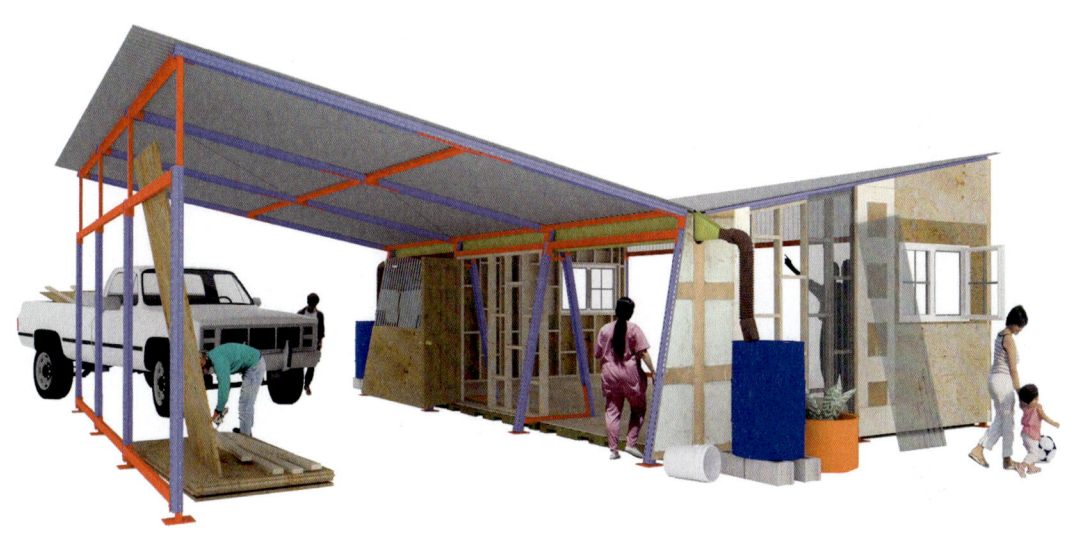

THE MECALUX FRAME
We built the first prototype inside the Mecalux factory. Being inside the maquiladora, redirecting its material systems and subsidy to sites of emergency, was an important milestone in our research-based practice

1 POLLUTION AT THE ESTUARY

2 BORDER FENCES

3 LOS LAURELES CANYON

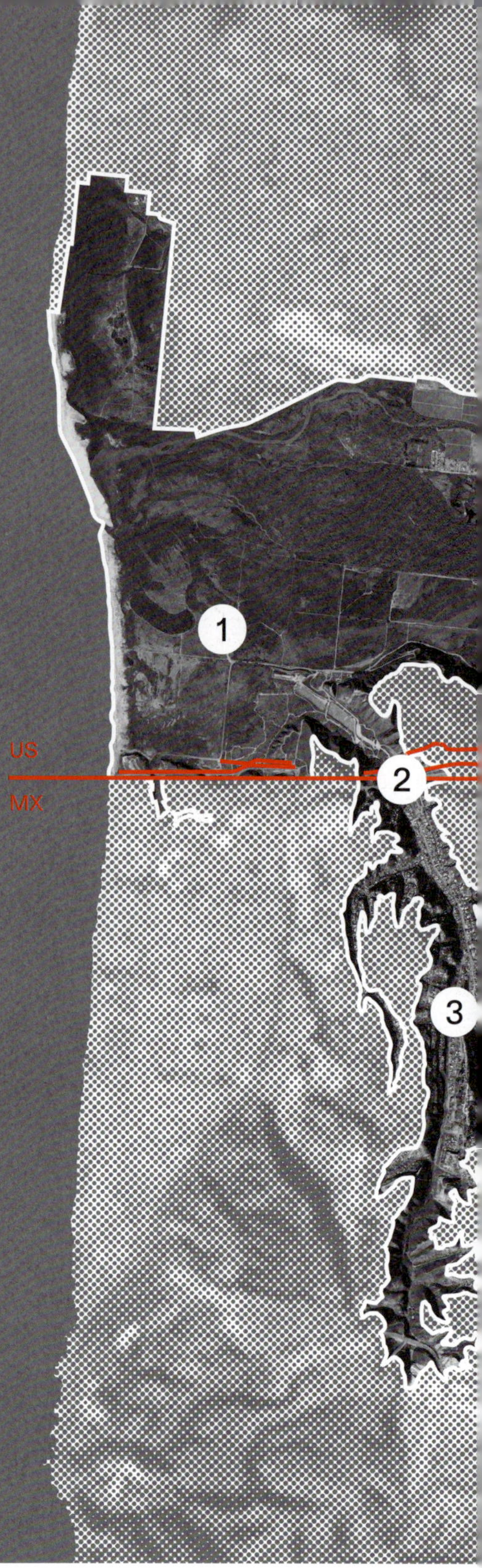

TIJUANA CASE STUDY / CONTEXT: LOS LAURELES CANYON

The Tijuana case study is located in the Alacrán canyon, the most rugged, precarious and polluted sub-basin of Los Laureles Canyon, an informal settlement that is home to 92,000 people. Alacrán is further impacted by flows of trash and sediment from the dump sites that surround it.

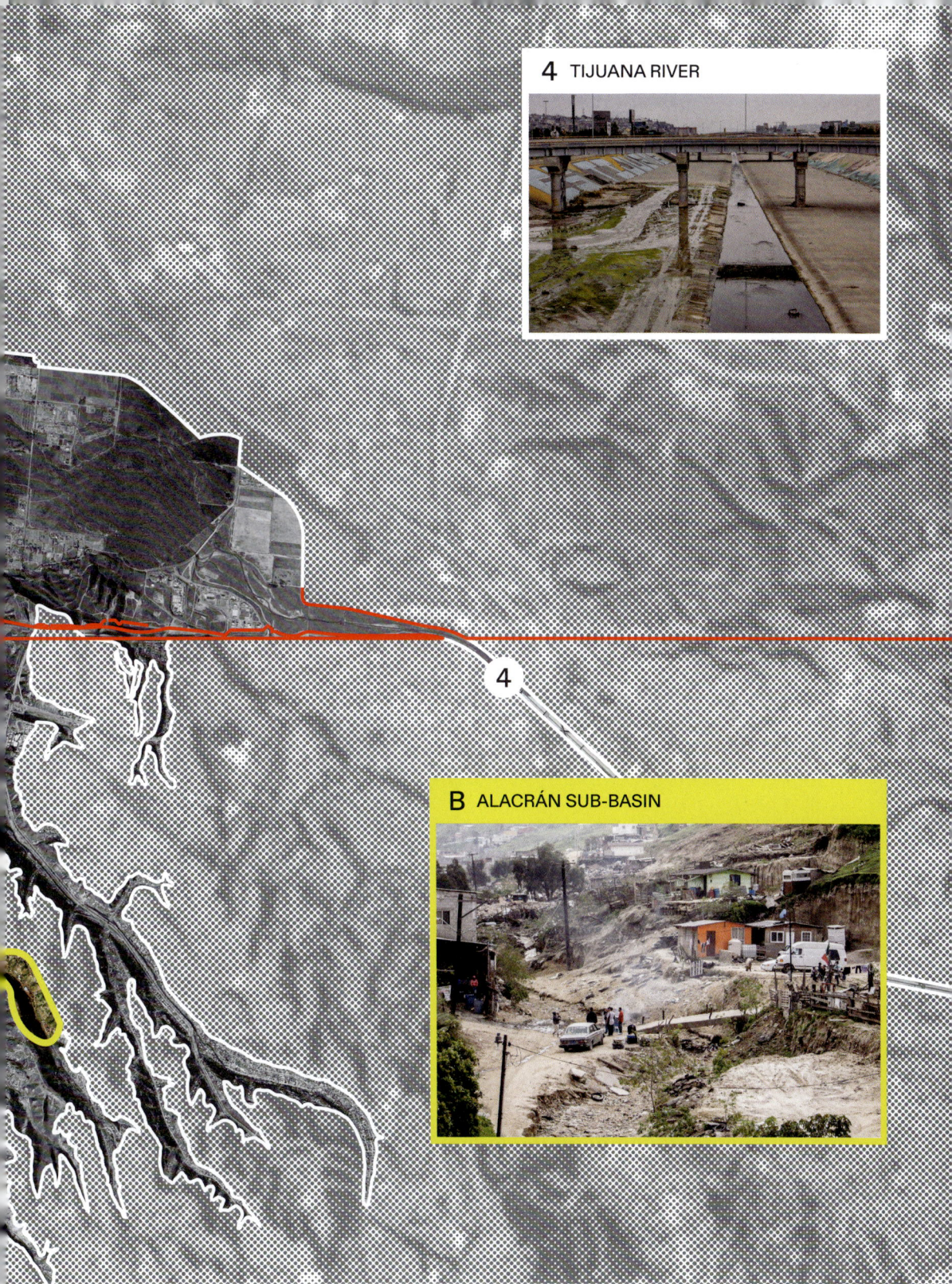

4 TIJUANA RIVER

B ALACRÁN SUB-BASIN

IMMIGRANT NEIGHBORHOODS: HOUSING LABORATORIES

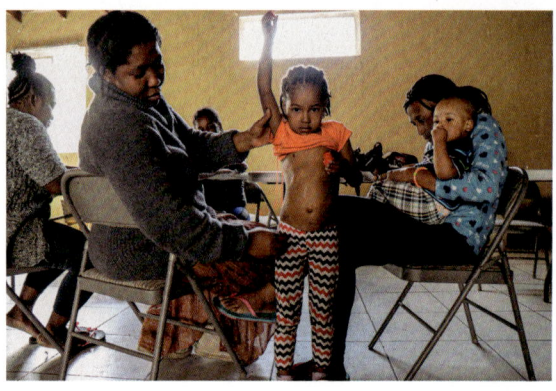

TIJUANA CASE STUDY / PROJECT: SANTUARIO FRONTERA

Embajadores de Jesús began construction of *Little Haiti*, a migrant refugee shelter. With the help of skilled migrants they began expanding their emergency housing capacity.

MIGRANT HOUSING AS INFRASTRUCTURE
The refugee housing project occupies an illegally excavated parcel on a steep canyon hillside, restoring the topography with terracing and biofiltration promenades. The site now doubles as a water- and waste-management system, and becomes the seed for an evolving sanctuary neighborhood.

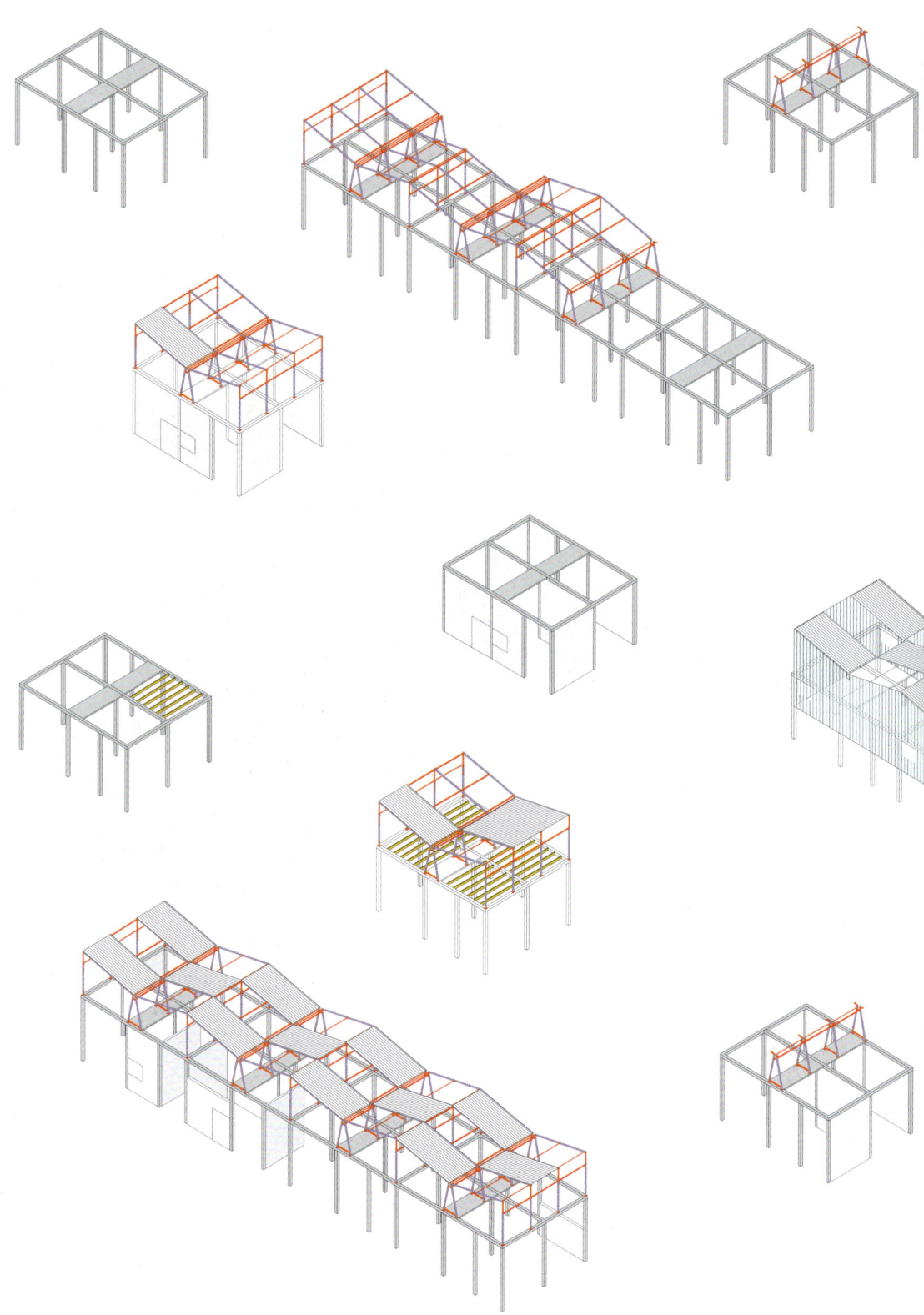

LINKING PREFABRICATED AND VERNACULAR CONSTRUCTION SYSTEMS
We are accelerating production of Mecalux frames and installing them on a vernacular concrete post and beam grid to increase refugee housing capacity.

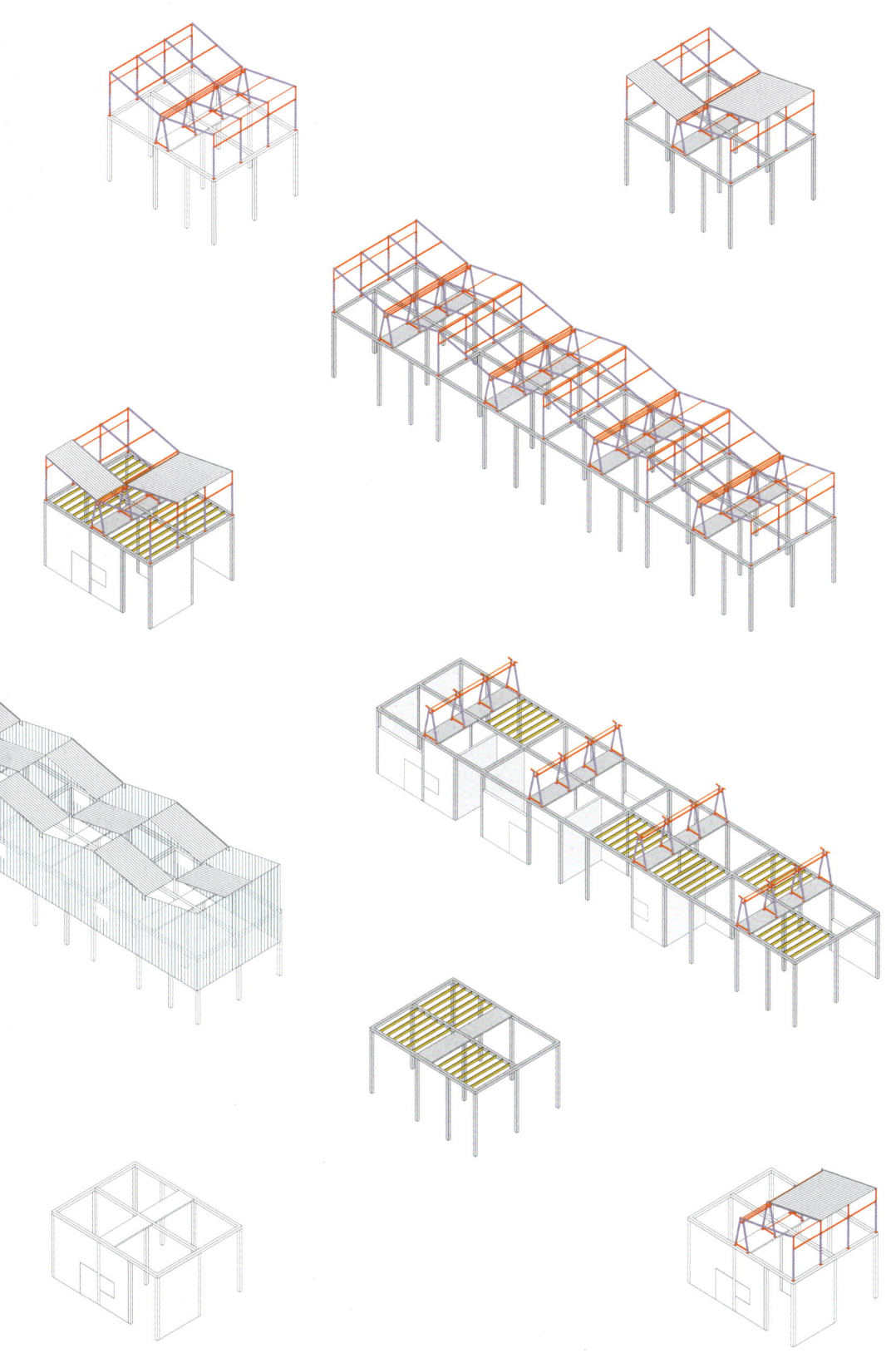

SANTUARIO FRONTERA: SCAFFOLDS FOR INCREMENTAL MIGRANT HOUSING
The housing "scaffolds" will be built first, leaving the interiors as "planned open systems," equipped with utilities to support live-work configurations. Roofed by lightweight plastics, shading and insulation, the scaffold will transform through time into a diverse ecology of housing environments and working spaces, infilled incrementally by migrants.

IMMIGRANT NEIGHBORHOODS: HOUSING LABORATORIES

HOUSING: AN ECONOMIC ENGINE
Migrant housing can be a mechanism for generating jobs. To sustain the construction process over time, we are designing a community-owned economic model. We embed refugee housing in spaces of fabrication, training and small-scale economic development.

EMBEDDING HOUSING IN SPACES OF PRODUCTIVITY
Economic incubators frame a covered pedestrian alley: a tool workshop, an industrial laundry, a health clinic.

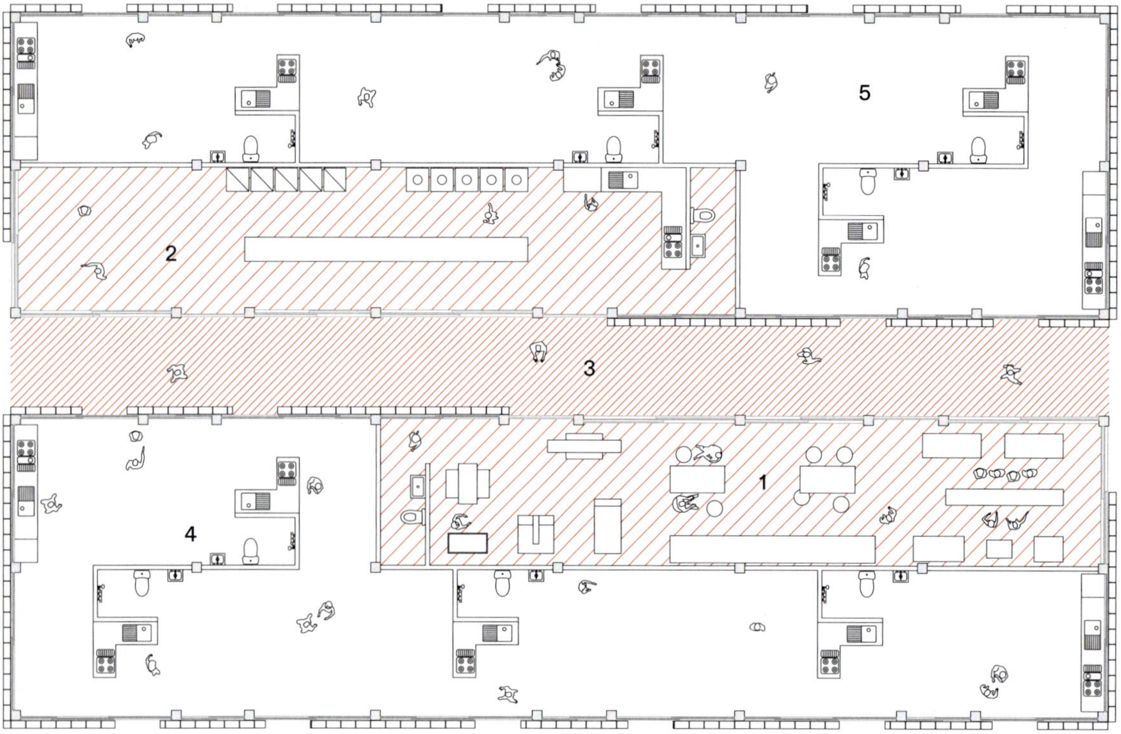

TOP-DOWN / BOTTOM-UP

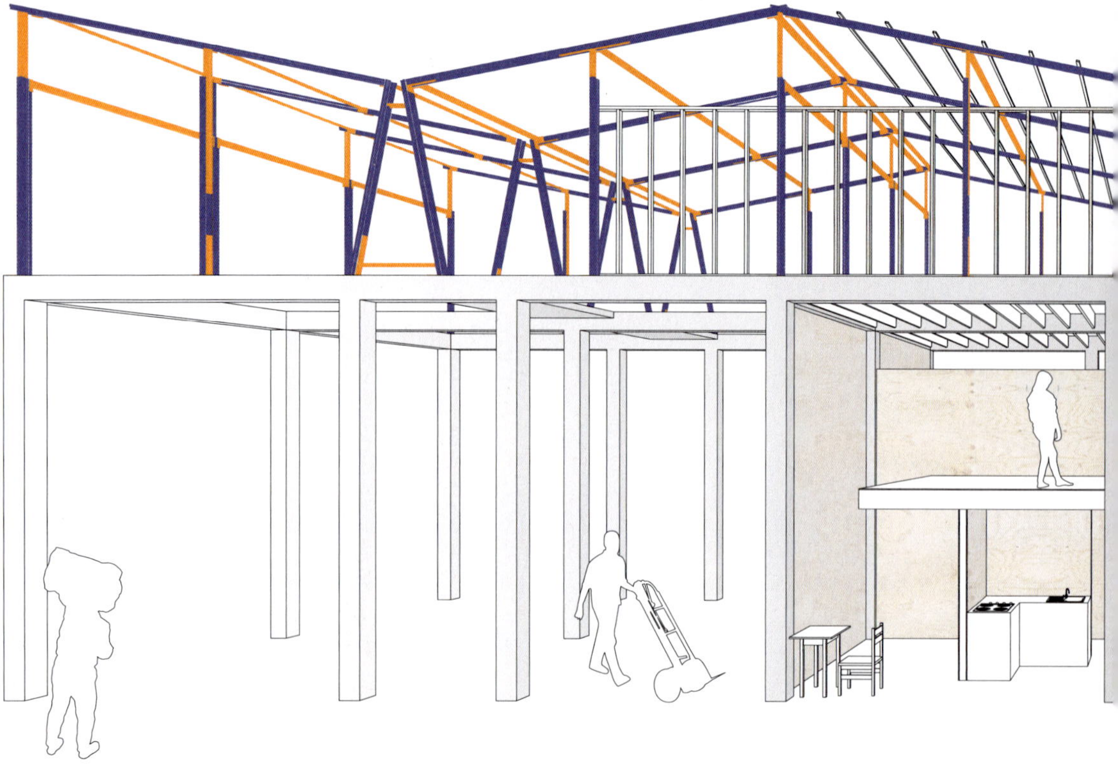

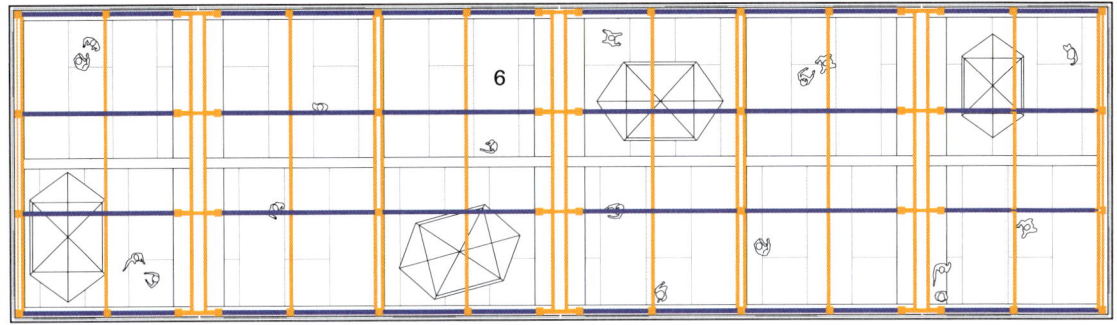

1 Fabrication shop
2 Industrial laundry
3 Internal street
4 Utility infrastructure
5 Spaces for housing infill
6 Typical upper housing mezzanine

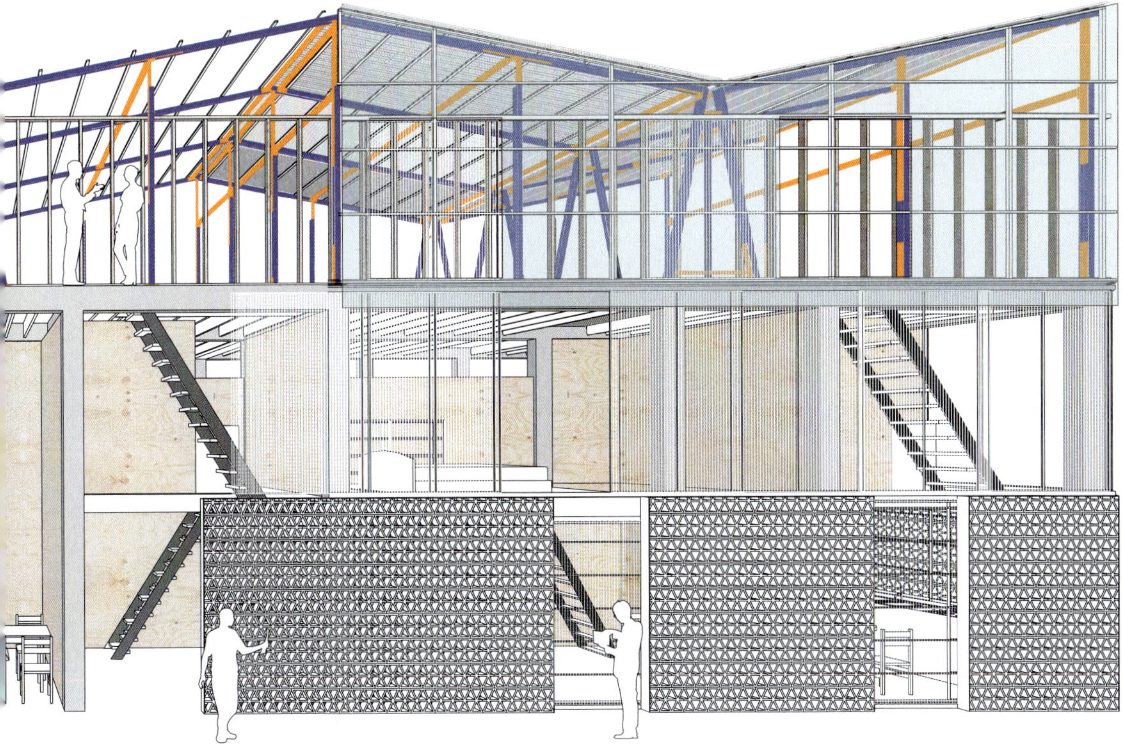

IMMIGRANT NEIGHBORHOODS: HOUSING LABORATORIES

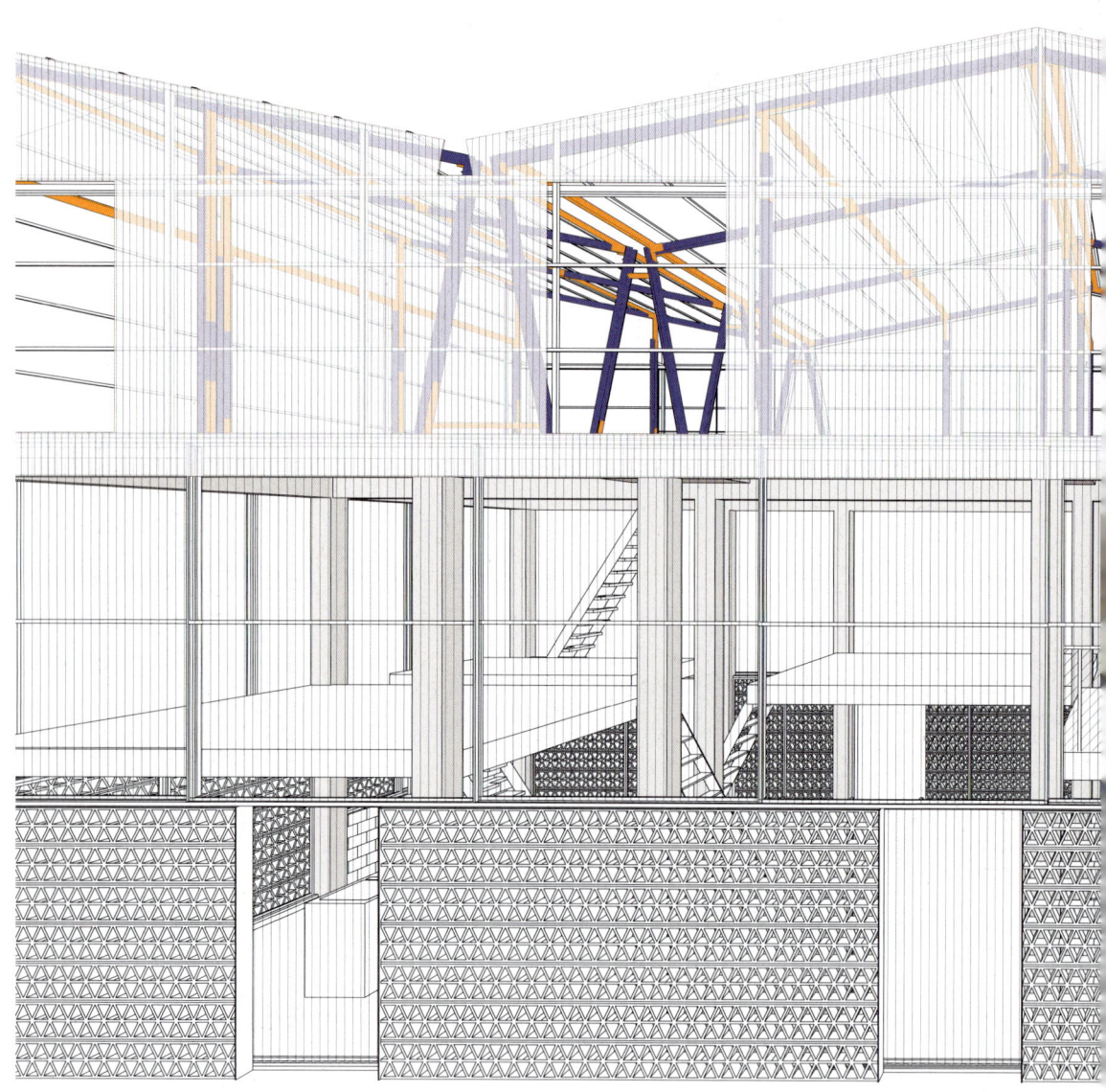

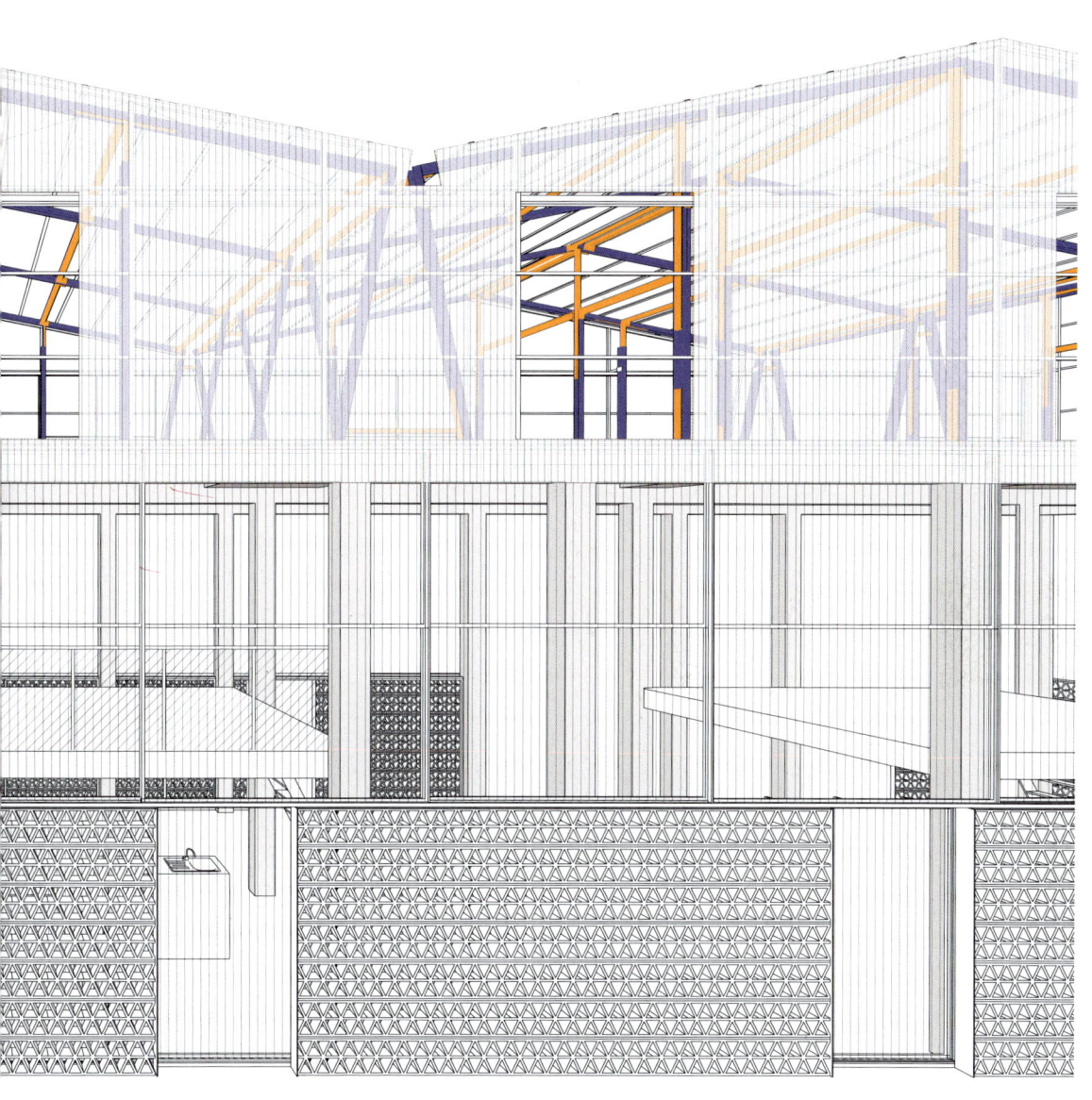

AN HOMAGE TO JEAN PROUVÉ

Santuario Frontera began construction in the summer of 2020, during the COVID-19 lockdowns. The migrant community living together were able to work safely on-site. The project began with seed capital provided by NY-based philanthropists Robert Rubin and Stéphane Samuel, whose collaboration on this project expands their commitment to the prefabricated social-housing logics of postwar French architect Jean Prouvé. The construction shop incubator was seeded by NY-based artist David Deutsch and the PARC Foundation.

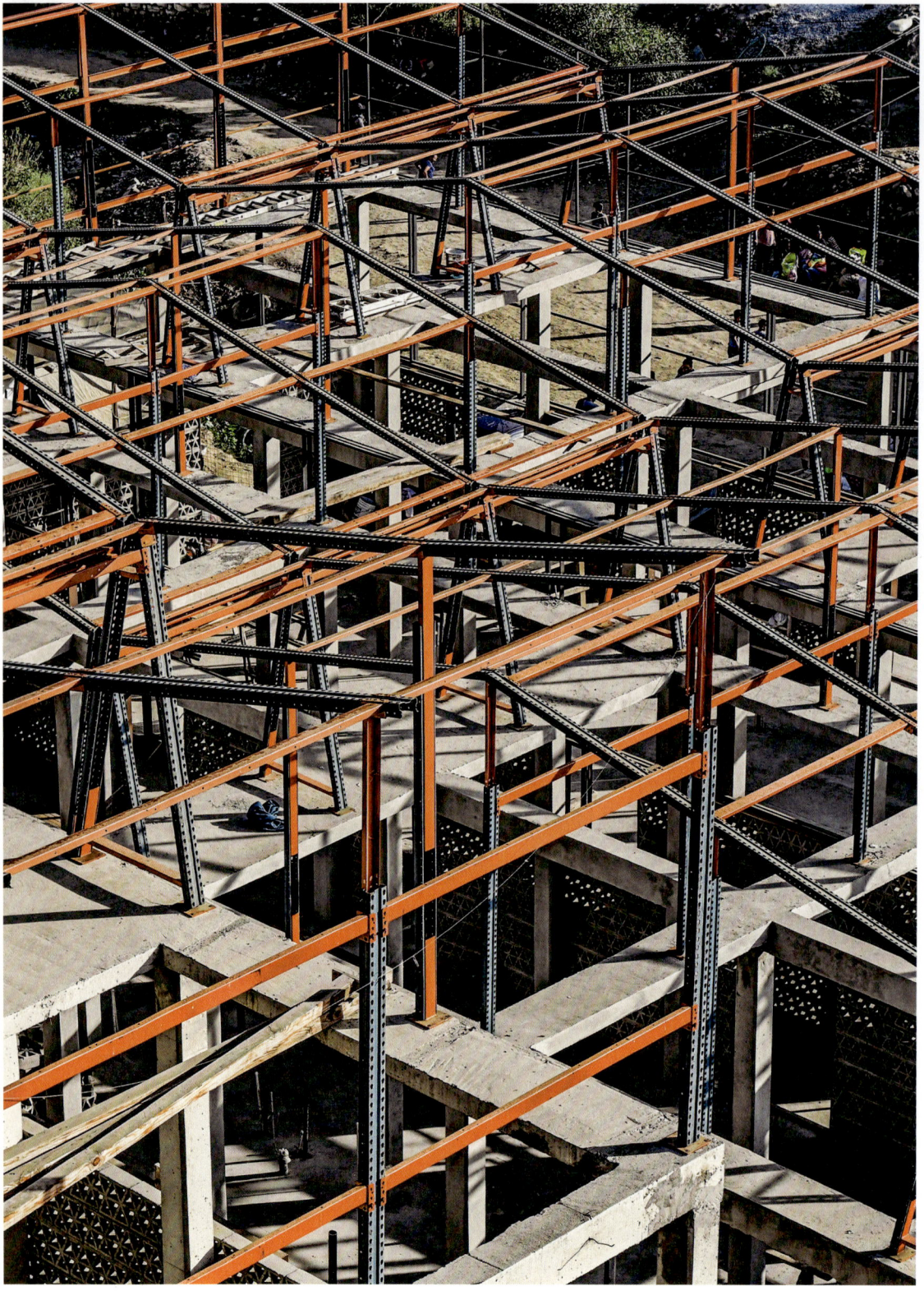

IMMIGRANT NEIGHBORHOODS: HOUSING LABORATORIES

IMMIGRANT NEIGHBORHOODS: HOUSING LABORATORIES

PROJECT: CLUSTER 4

BOTTOM-U
THE FUNC
DIMENSIO
PARTICIPA

P PUBLIC:
TIONAL
N OF
TION

BOTTOM-UP PUBLIC: THE FUNCTIONAL DIMENSION OF PARTICIPATION

Project cluster 4 presents a set of public cultural interventions that we have curated to amplify collective agency as material for design. These projects illustrate that art and culture can be mobilized as tools for mediation and social organization. They demonstrate agonistic models of intervention in the public domain that facilitate critical interfaces between institutions and communities. New communities of dissent operationalize bottom-up resistance and participation into active urban processes that can transform not only widely held beliefs, but also unjust top-down policies and institutional practices. The procedural dimension of the bottom-up also has spatial implications, challenging generic notions of public space.

1   Curating Communities of Practice
    Introduction
    Rethinking Participation: *The Washington Street Skateboard Park*

    Act 1:
    Buenos Aires, Argentina
    Villa 31: Co-producing Evidence

    Act 2:
    Madrid, Spain
    "How Is Your Art Going To Help Us?"

    Act 3:
    Anyang, South Korea
    The Future Neighborhood: Conversations on Coexistence

2   Nomadic Frames for Sociability

    InfoSite:
    Migrant House, Portable Public Space

    Urban Rooms:
    Scaffolds for "Things to Happen"

    Retrofit *Gecekondu:*
    Prefabrication as Social System

Curating Communities of Practice

INTRODUCTION
RETHINKING PARTICIPATION: *THE WASHINGTON STREET SKATEBOARD PARK*

We see citizenship as a creative act from below. We are inspired by the journeys of marginalized people—migrant communities, low-income neighborhoods, disenfranchised youth—who challenge institutions, policies and norms that exclude and violate them. In our practice, we document and visualize the complex social processes through which marginalized people respond to and resist injustice—from collective gestures of protest to stealth urban acts, like designing spaces of exception, informal economies and collective democratic processes to protect themselves from violence, and to carving out livelihoods when formal pathways are closed to them. We are inspired by activist processes and urban scripts that reorganize lives and priorities, challenging unjust power while adapting the spaces and practices of everyday life in the city.

Antanas Mockus, former mayor of Bogotá, told us many years ago that the erasure of the *anecdotal* in cities today is a form of social injustice.[30] In some ways, we see ourselves as urban ethnographers, seeking to understand and visualize urban anecdotes of injustice and resistance in the city. As we have written, the "informal" is not just an aesthetic category, but a set of practices, procedures and protocols that we seek to understand, interpret, translate and ultimately represent politically to top-down institutions that lack information about informal processes when they make decisions that impact marginalized people. In our urban research, we archive "chronicles of transgression"—the anecdotal dimension of bottom-up urban transformation—harvesting lessons from these stories to construct a new civic imagination. Through stories that might seem trivial to some, we learn about the everyday, which contains powerful lessons that instigate new ways of thinking about, researching and practicing as architects and urbanists eager to advance justice in the city. We often develop cartographies to accompany stories we encounter to enable others to visualize the narrative, the chronology of processes and the array of actors, spaces and conditions.

A CHRONICLE OF INVASION

Many years ago, San Diego helped us define a set of priorities for our research-based practice. It is a story about the role that vacant land can play to advance inclusion and social justice in the city. First, some context: we had been mapping the city without buildings to visualize an *archipelago* of empty spaces across San Diego County. These included abandoned brownfields, setbacks, easements, paper streets, dead-end streets, forgotten canyons, watershed systems and more. We recognized that these spaces are remnants of a deliberate political fragmentation achieved through segregationist urban planning that divides the city into islands of development, big-box commercial suburbanization, housing subdivisions, highways and parking lots, all separated by huge voids.

This *archipelago of voids* is ultimately the result of planning policy that refuses to imagine the territory through natural boundaries and public infrastructure, but succumbs to the power of jurisdiction and distance separation. We discovered that many of these islands of emptiness were not as empty as we thought. Paper streets (streets not built by the municipality due to costs incurred by topographic conditions), dead-end streets (streets that emerge because of transportation planning discrepancies), and even freeway underpasses and utility easements have been taken over and occupied by activist practices, often transforming these spaces into productive gardens, markets, alternative public spaces and emergency housing. We decided to explore a few of these spaces for stories of encroachment, adaptation and alteration. One stood out: the site, a freeway underpass in San Diego. The agents, a group of teenage skateboarders. We interviewed them and together began to map their chronology of encroachment and spatial transformation of a freeway underpass.

In 2007, the teenagers decided to organize themselves in response to a lack of skateboard parks in the city. One night, armed with shovels, they invaded an underpass under Interstate 5, a typical site of collision between freeway and neighborhood. The teenagers began to dig, to build their own park. After two weeks the police stopped them, expelled them and barricaded the space. The teenagers decided to organize a process to confront the city, and to demand a park. Their first task was something we seldom do as designers: they wanted to understand the jurisdictions that defined the seemingly neutral territory, to map the political interests embedded in that juncture. They discovered they were lucky since they had not begun their digging in Caltrans territory—the state agency that administers transportation infrastructure. It would have been virtually impossible to negotiate any deal with the keepers of Southern California's holy transportation ground! In our first interview, they explained that they began to dig unknowingly under an arm of the freeway that belonged to the municipality. They also discovered that their location was a sort of "Bermuda triangle" of jurisdiction—between port authority, airport authority, two city districts and the Pacific Coast Highway Review Board. With red lines traced onto a city map, the teens visualized the hidden jurisdictional power inscribed in that otherwise vacant and abstract space. With this information, they designed a strategy to engage the many political institutions and agencies implicated in this jurisdictional map.

They decided to organize themselves as skater-citizens, to negotiate with city officials, the city attorney and the city council. Once at the municipality, they were advised that to continue the process of negotiation, they had to form an NGO. They did not know what an NGO was, so they sought help from a group of skateboarders in Northern California who had gone through a similar experience. This marked an interesting moment, a transfer of procedural knowledge across urban activist practices. After conferring with their allies to the north, the teenagers realized that they had "to get their act together," as they put it: to fundraise, to engage a public lawyer, to get construction insurance, to organize their budgets, to find "evidence" that justified their case for reform, and to navigate the countless permits and faulty definitions that blocked community action. One such faulty definition, around which they organized much of their case against the city, is the way "public space" was defined in the municipal planning code. The existing language was extremely reductive, explained as "green, undifferentiated space," without any reference to the diversity and multiplicity of urban spaces, communities, and cultural and generational uses in the city.

They felt compelled to challenge the neutrality of the policy in order to reclaim that vacant site under the freeway, transforming it into a specific public space to support youth skating activity and temporary uses.

They also researched existing legislation and regulatory frameworks to advance their proposal. For example, they discovered that existing permits, such as the Right of Entry Permit, the Public Event Permit, the Removal Permit and the Temporary Encroachment Permit could become devices to redefine land-use categories at that location. In other words, they realized that they, as urban activists, could produce new definitions of zoning and public space to enable ephemeral and transitory uses, and different types of activities and programs beyond the generic and fixed "green space" categories conventionally drafted by city officials. After researching and connecting these disparate pieces of legislation, as well as the municipal resources and loopholes to benefit their cause, the teenagers officially requested access to the space. They proposed to assume all liability and to ensure maintenance, coordination and operational activity in the space, making it function as a public asset, but with a semi-private management structure. In other words, the NGO would manage the space and assume all liability for the site.

By transferring liability from the public to the newly founded semi-private agency, the city permitted use of the site for one cent per year, entering into a social and political contract to manage vacant public land through self-initiated social-economic programming. This unorthodox lease agreement to activate the abandoned site under the freeway was an instrument to subsequently construct *The Washington Street Skatepark*. The teens won rights to the space, not just through placards and protest, but by designing and mobilizing a political process. They constructed *the political* itself to transform legislation to benefit their community. They organized themselves as activists, researched evidence, reorganized and consolidated fragmented resources and knowledges inside the institutions governing urban development and asserted a new definition of public space in the city.

This story helped clarify an essential commitment in our own urban research: that an informal act of encroachment like this one, which goes beyond the jurisdictional property line, does not have to stop at the small and symbolic gesture. Bottom-up urban resistance can trickle upwards to contest and then reconstruct urban policy and urban spaces. The tenacity of the teens inspired us. Their story contains the DNA for rethinking conventional paradigms. One is the meaning of "community." What is a community? More often than not, ideas of community are deployed gratuitously, but this particular assemblage constructed itself out of urgency. It became a *community of practice* oriented around shared representation of specific spatial possibilities and committed to a process of transformation.

The marginalized teens also embarked on a double project: simultaneously designing physical systems, and essential protocols for inclusion. When designing physical spaces as architects, we rarely ask: Who will maintain the public space? Who will assure inclusion and programmatic sustainability? Nor even the more fundamental questions the teens asked as they embarked on their journey: Whose territory is this? Who owns these resources? By exposing and visualizing the conditions of conflict they encountered, the teenagers began to reorganize resources and knowledges as well as the invisible jurisdictional boundaries that disabled these spatial assets as public availabilities. Thus, the teenagers not only designed physical space, but simultaneously designed the protocols of inclusion, and the systems of shared management that would assure economic and social sustainability. This story of adaptation taught us that public spaces should not be conceived as neutral commodities for leisure, assuming that people somehow will magically "show up" because they are "beautiful." Public spaces, particularly in marginalized zones of the city, need to be designed to anticipate social encounter through more deliberate choreographies.

The ultimate provocation for us was to rethink community participation. In conventional participatory processes organized by municipal planning offices, or even communities themselves, participation is reduced to a symbolic endeavor through which community members testify and voice concerns, needs and preferences. Sometimes participation entails responding to a survey or questionnaire devised by planners and developers, or appearing as witnesses to support a particular agenda, often reduced to issues of façadism, aesthetics and style. We found that this micro *community of practice* constructed by the teens had effectively moved "participation" from being a passive, box-ticking endeavor to a more operative performance of democratic agency that ultimately transformed policy and space. Here the participants acted as agents of the change they demanded and did not stop at the rhetorical argument or demand.

We need to rethink civic participation as an active, more functional set of strategies to co-produce the city—to open alternative points of access and pathways to economic and social development. We believe this opens an expanded role for artists, architects and urban researchers, who can retool themselves as interlocutors and translators of urban praxis, facilitating stories of urban survival and adaptation into new possibilities for urban intervention, linking the procedural intelligence of the bottom-up with new mechanisms of institutional support.

In our practice, we often co-curate projects with communities of practice that reimagine public space and participatory processes. Among these projects in the last decades, three stand out as exemplary. Our role as architects was to link what is divided and mediate the gap between institutions and communities, resources and processes, research and practice, academia and activism, artistic experimentation and social responsibility. The projects are unique because they were threaded into a continuous process, and moved across the world in three diverse locations: Buenos Aires, Argentina; Madrid, Spain; and Anyang, South Korea. We mobilized a set of urban anecdotes from one city to the next. Within each setting we partnered with communities of practice to choreograph a particular process of community participation, linking sites, institutions, resources and knowledges. People's stories were the material to mobilize the projects, and the knowledge transfer from one geography to the next established corridors of solidarity between institutions and communities in new, distributed forms of political and cultural representation. This ensemble of projects was organized in three acts, as follows.

ACT 1: BUENOS AIRES, ARGENTINA
VILLA 31: CO-PRODUCING EVIDENCE

The first project emerged as part of an urban workshop in December 2009 at the Centro de Investigaciones Artisticas (CIA) in Buenos Aires. The participants in this workshop were primarily artists and architects. As it is often the case when we conduct workshops with cultural institutions around the world, we begin the conversation with local participants by exploring sites of conflict in their immediate urban field that might motivate more social and political forms of artistic and architectural production. The urban hotspots we focus on are typically complex scenarios that even some local actors have not recognized or experienced—often *urban borders*, characterized by the clash of jurisdictions that fragment urban territories at odds with one another and divide social and cultural demographics. These are *conflict urbanizations* that have been exacerbated by discriminatory urban regulations and economic development patterns. These urban zones, often adjacent to each other, have dissimilar and incommensurate structures of political and cultural representation that rarely converge to negotiate their roles. These become internal communication barriers in the city, preventing knowledge flows, exchanges and mutual recognition. This indifference and ignorance about what happens on the other side gives rise to persistent prejudices and hostilities.

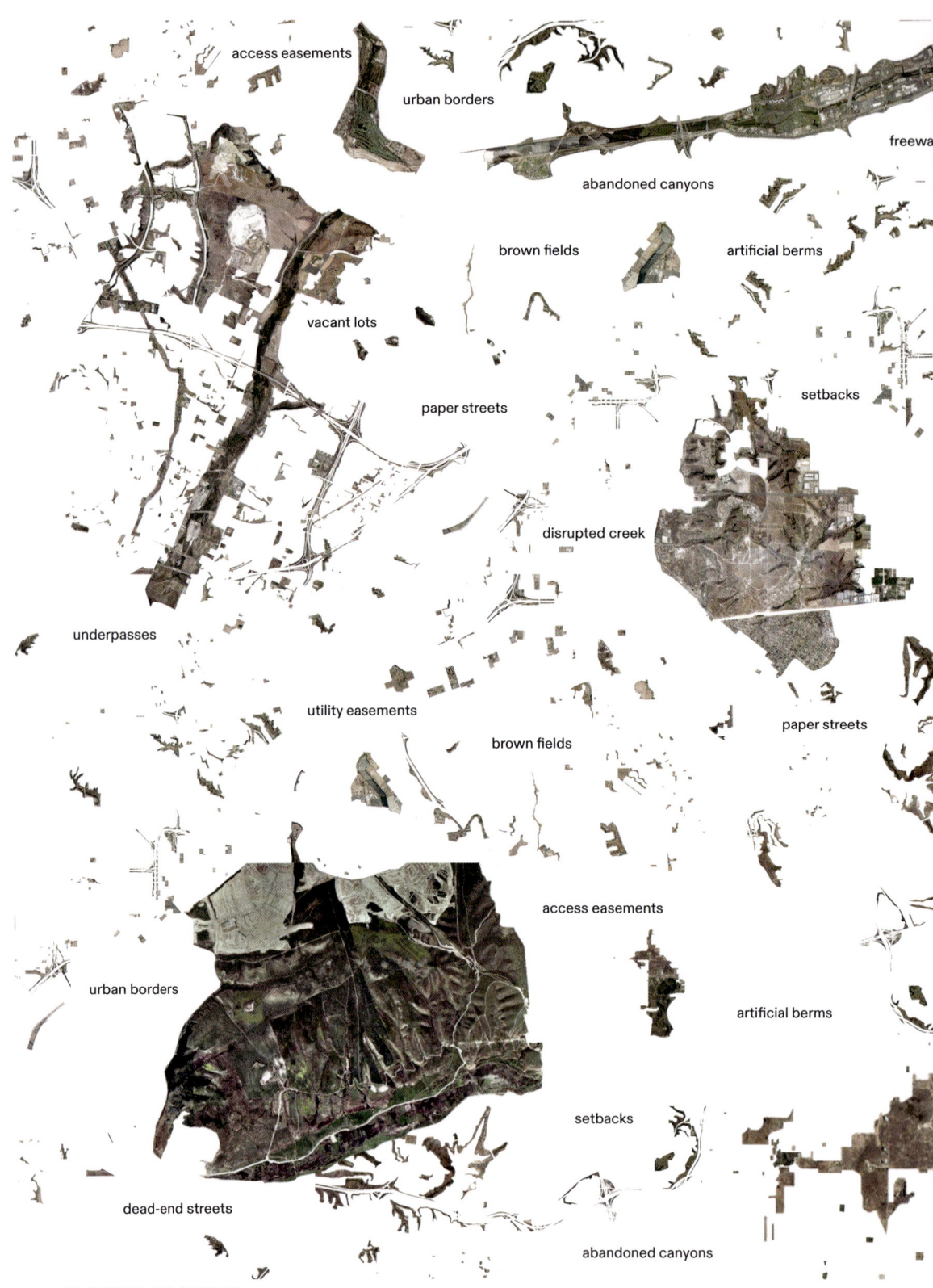

AN ARCHIPELAGO OF VOIDS

The fragmentation of the city reflects the fragmentation of institutions, jurisdictions and policies in the city. These vacant spaces are the political remnants of segregationist urban planning policies that divide the city into islands of development, big-box commercial suburbanization, housing subdivisions, highways, parking lots and other isolated fragments separated by voids. These fragments emerge from "splintering" regulation, such as setbacks, easements, dead-end streets, forgotten canyons, brownfields and ignored watershed systems.

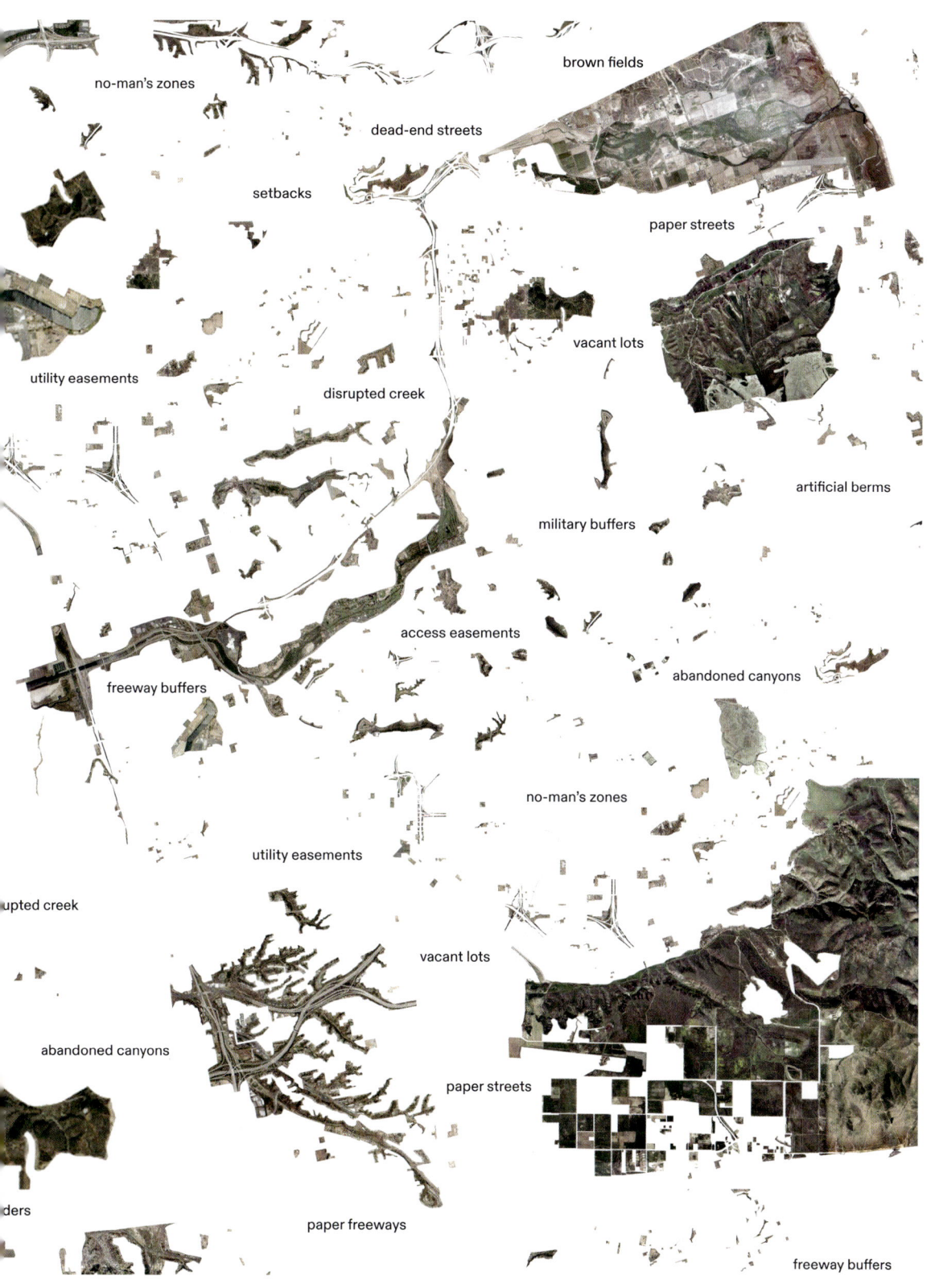

BOTTOM-UP PUBLIC: THE FUNCTIONAL DIMENSION OF PARTICIPATION

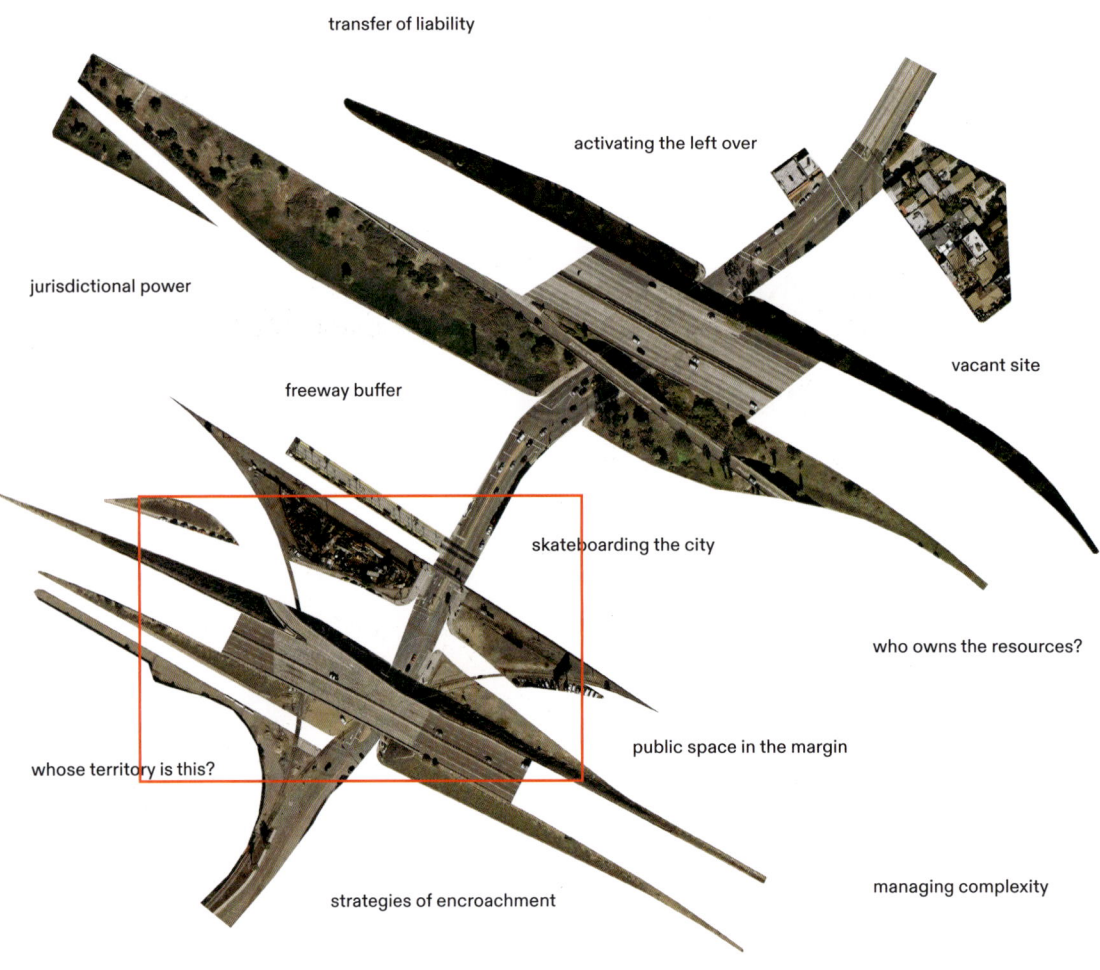

A CHRONOLOGY OF ENCROACHMENT

Many of these islands of emptiness are not as empty as they seem. Many have been taken over by activist practices, and transformed into productive urban gardens, alternative public spaces, even emergency housing. We "descended" into one these islands, a highway under-pass, where we discovered a story of urban adaptation and alteration by a skateboard community.

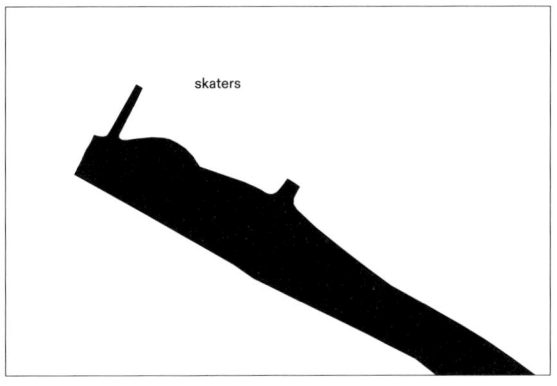
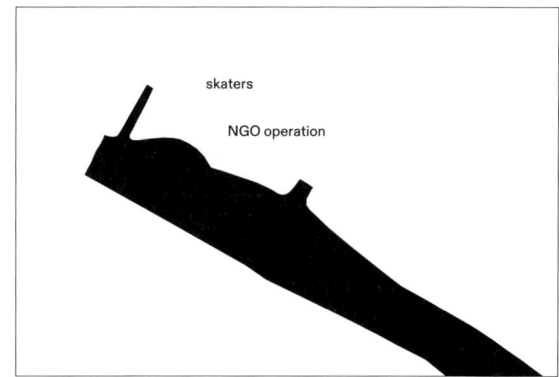
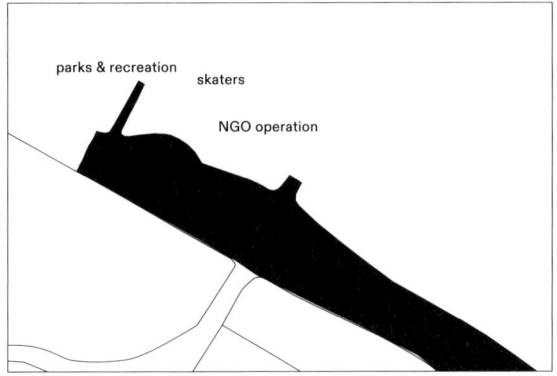
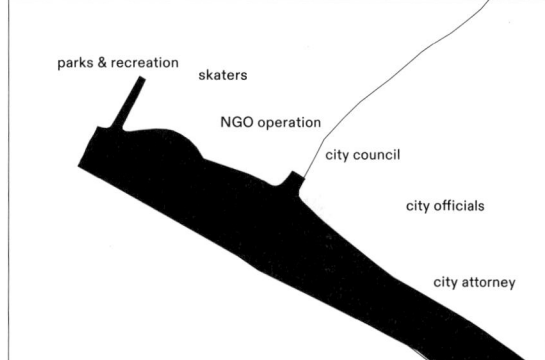
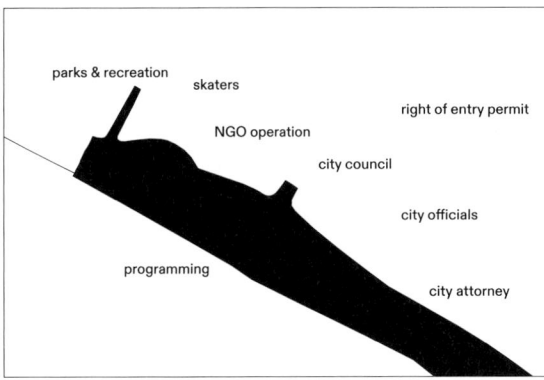
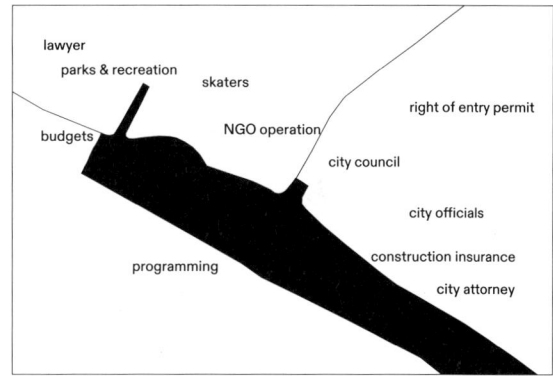
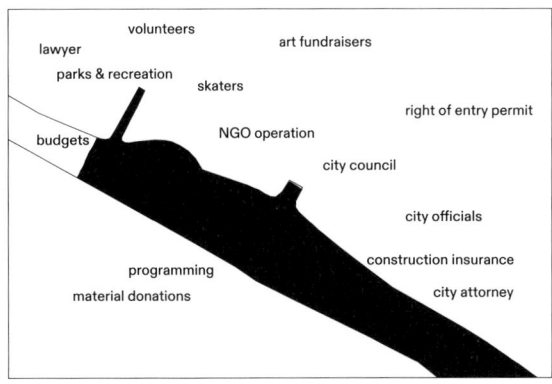
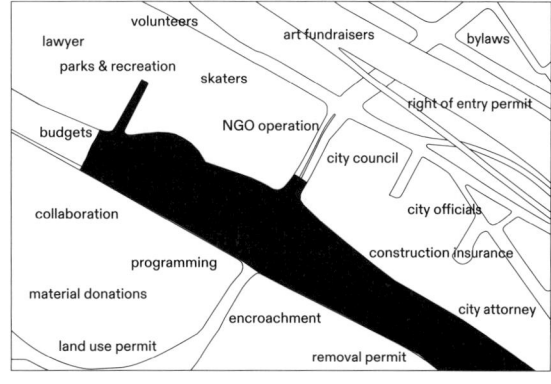

DESIGNING A PARTICIPATORY POLITICAL PROCESS

The teenagers began to dig under the freeway to build their own skateboard park. The police evicted them from this abandoned public space, and they fought back, engaging the municipality in a process of negotiation to reclaim the space as a functional skateboard park. They designed a political process that triggered a municipal "Transfer of Liability" allowing them to take ownership of the site, committing to its management and programming.

TRICKLE-UP URBANIZATION
This story of adaptation helped to clarify an essential commitment of our urban research: that an informal act of encroachment beyond the jurisdictional property line, like this one, does not have to stop at the small, symbolic gesture. A performative, participatory urban act can trickle upwards to construct a political process to transform top-down policy.

THE JOURNEY FROM THE BOTTOM-UP TO THE TOP-DOWN AND BACK
It is urgent today to journey from bottom-up gestures to negotiate with top-down institutional processes.
This is what we mean by a more "functional" dimension of participation.

With the participants of this workshop we discussed a gradual approach to one of these controversial urban spaces in Buenos Aires, known as Villa 31, currently called Barrio Carlos Mugica. This dramatic urban favela, home to around 40,000 people, is barely a mile away from some of the wealthiest enclaves in the city, such as the historic Retiro neighborhood and the newly gentrified Puerto Madero, a site of typical luxury condominium high-rises. In a pedagogical sense, the proposal consisted of provoking the participating artists to encounter "other" spaces, "other" demographics in the city, which were largely invisible in their work as cultural producers. As a point of departure, we attempted to operationalize, in our own terms, Bruno Latour's *actor-network theory* by engaging an embedded voice within the conflict.[31] Opening a dialogue begins a "funnel in reverse" to reveal and map the shifting networks of relationships, controversies and problematics within their immediate social situation and geographic context.

Alejandro López, assistant to the workshop, established contact through the internet with the activist Liliana Da Silva. Liliana had written an open letter on the internet, a cry for help that had not been heeded until Alejandro responded. We met Liliana on the edges of Villa 31, and she led us into the world of her community. Liliana told us how she had stumbled on a moment of crisis when a group of newcomers to the informal settlement, a group of Bolivian and Ecuadoran immigrants, were about to be evicted by the local police. She was passing by when she witnessed the harassment and unjust treatment by the officers, and without hesitation, she rushed to the scene to defend the group of vulnerable families. She became an accidental activist, she told us.

She told us stories about the housing problems in the area, the social organization of her neighbors, their processes of working together, and the dynamics and characteristics of the property system that governed their homes. She took us to meet the residents of Villa 31's Block 107, the block of approximately 300 square meters squatted by the small immigrant group who had just arrived in Buenos Aires. With Liliana as our facilitator, the neighbors received the group very kindly but were somewhat baffled. We sat together, some on improvised chairs, others on the dirt floor. At some point during our conversation an immigrant member from the community asked us: *"How is your art going to help us?"* This question provoked us and ignited a process of collaboration. It prompted internal debates among the group of artists to reflect on their practices, their work, leading to other questions and other debates: What is the role of the artist-researcher in this context? Is it about being a facilitator, an enabler, an interlocutor, a spokesperson? A co-producer? Or nothing at all?

The situation was complex when we first made contact with the residents of Block 107. They had already been entangled in several conflicts with the city government, which began when the municipality of Buenos Aires tried to demolish any house with more than one floor as "dangerous." They also wanted to demolish houses located in Block 107 nearest the road, since they "interfered with the future urbanization plans for the zone." This generated discussion between city officials and neighbors, and it was during this period that a new Urbanization Law of the Polygons Villas 31 (No. 3343) was passed. The law provided for the creation of a "Multidisciplinary and Participative Management and Planning Table" comprised of public officials from the national and city governments, academics and neighborhood delegates who wished to present a proposal for the urbanization of their space. This opening became a potential space for intervention and collaboration between our CIA group and the Villa 31 community. Together we planned to attend several of these crucial meetings as part of the "Planning Table."

In principle, we speculated that one of the functions of the artist-researcher may be to instigate a conversation as a means of activating the actors. Art can mediate, become a tool to access the complexity of urbanization, helping to translate the often-invisible forces of marginalization and exclusion. As a vehicle of information, it can transcend urban borders. With the group we speculated about how to curate a flow of information between the social actors of Villa 31 and the experts constructed through particular artistic gestures. Art, in turn, we debated, can become evidence, providing missing pieces of information—the processes and histories that had unfolded at that particular site of conflict. Art can be a tool for political representation, a system to visualize the alienating political structures that marginalize the other. In this way, the artist's political practice becomes an experimental act in space, in collaboration with others.

By this time we had been in Buenos Aires for a week, and the formal period of the workshop was coming to an end. We remembered the words that Arjun Appadurai had shared with us years earlier regarding his critique of artistic festivals that come to cities to intervene momentarily, ephemeral acts that disappear after the festival ends. He suggested that the task of the artist might be instead to *leave a trace*, a platform for increasing capacities, mobilizing the agency of local people beyond the "happening," establishing roots for an evolving institutional collaboration. Before we departed, we signed a "social contract" between CIA workshop participants and the residents of Block 107. Both actors committed themselves to a set of future activities, including the creation of an online informational platform and a small research library dedicated to the history of the Block 107 project. Seed money from CIA enabled the purchase of a computer, which Liliana and the artists used to co-curate an archive of memories and film-related projects based on the storytelling of the neighbors.

Liliana recounted her own initial work with the Block 107 community:

> I cried a lot, they asked me many questions, none of them had an answer! So I made up my mind and began to look at a piece of land that was not used, I began to study it, to plan how to take it for the community, and place in it those families who really needed it! It was very, very cold that day, when I shared my idea to the others, and even though they were a bit afraid they joined in the decision to take that place, and we did. We made a small collection to buy flour to mark the small parcels of land for each one. With the flour in hand, we went out! The women with their children in their arms, and I leading the group; the security guards gave notice and whoosh, the police on patrol cars showed up. But all of us were determined! Nothing would make me turn back. When I looked at babies and children, it seems that God gave me more strength. They intimidated us, they harassed us, but we could not hear anything. The need was greater. But what a surprise, we began to be joined by more and more people with children and older people, and we could not say no! We marched ahead. All day we sat on the ground, each one taking care of her place, I remained there with the women. More patrollers came, then the infantry. The sun was strong, and the other municipal delegates, everyone against us! Of course! They are already safe with their houses and their profit from their rents ...

Participants who remained working with Liliana after we left included architects Pio Torroja and Mauricio Corbalán from m7red, and artists Eduardo Alcon Quintanilha, Laura Códega, Leopoldo Estol, Renata Lozupone and Paula Massarutti. As part of their social contract with the activist Liliana and the Villa 31 community, they decided together to create a collective called the *Cooperativa Guatemalteca* to expand their work into similar invisible, marginalized urban contexts. The work was characterized by what they called "ritual practices"—making journeys within contexts of urban conflict, accompanying local processes of protest and resistance. The issues of concern and opportunities appear "in the process" through encounter and conversation. Ultimately, one no longer speaks in terms of "conflict resolution" but in terms of the management or generation of opportunities through the conflict itself. The m7red organization links various disjointed actors, curating forums and assemblies of experts and non-experts to produce an "interlocution" between territorial and technical actors, so that the information can be channeled and concretized.

The first concrete action carried out jointly between the *Cooperativa Guatemalteca* and the neighbors of Block 107 was a historical reconstruction of the violent act of eviction by the police—a reenactment in which artists and members of the community took center stage in a double sense: to act and perform together, but to also co-produce evidence. A video entitled *La Toma Resiste* (*The Squatting Resist*) was co-produced to document what happened and make it part of the debates in the Planning Tables as well as to visualize and publicize the housing challenges in the City of Buenos Aires.

The report of the Planning Tables was presented on May 31, 2011. The report acknowledged that places like Villa 31 need different development logics, some guided by the "informal" development patterns of the neighborhood—and that these informal dynamics can provide new and important knowledge about the city. From 2010 to the present, the space has been modified, new land has been occupied and other structures have been built. There were also changes in the dynamics of the actors. Working cooperatives were created, comprised of residents who carry out neighborhood-scale tasks, such as repairing the streets (paving stones) or developing the sewage system. The experiences of CIA and their subsequent work as *Cooperativa Guatemalteca* reflects a more functional and operative dimension of civic participation. Their intervention in complex scenarios like Villa 31 instigated creative processes and concrete actions, and also provided new political and organizational spaces for the co-production of the city. Members of the *Cooperativa Guatemalteca* continue to work in the neighborhood to influence urban policy.

ACT 2: MADRID, SPAIN
"HOW IS YOUR ART GOING TO HELP US?"

In collaboration with Mauricio Corbalán (m7red) and Iago Carro (Ergosfera)

We carried the question "How is your art going to help us?" from our conversations with the immigrant residents of Block 107 in Buenos Aires to Madrid, Spain, to participate in *Madrid Abierto*, an international public art event that transforms Madrid into an urban laboratory for rethinking the relationship between public space and social networks. We invited Mauricio Corbalán from m7red, the architecture collective that had worked with us in the CIA Workshop. The idea was to create linkages between the processes advanced in Buenos Aires with the community of Block 107 in Villa 31 to construct a second act, an evolving set of strategies for community participation and urban justice.

We were invited to intervene in the facade of *Casa de America*, an important Spanish museum and cultural institution that focuses on Latin American art. *Madrid Abierto* takes place during ARCO, the most important international art fair in Spain. The facade of this neoclassical building, located on a prominent traffic roundabout called La Cibeles in the heart of Madrid, has been a prominent space of intervention by artists in previous versions of the event. Taking advantage of this visual exposure, widely seen by the busy traffic along this important parkway, and in conjunction with the international traffic of artists through Madrid's art fair, we decided to print Villa 31's question on a very large yellow billboard covering the facade.

Different than previous works on this frontal face of Casa de America, whose visual protagonism was based on grand sculptural installations, we proposed the provocation: "How Is Your Art Going to Help Us?" We transformed the facade of this iconic cultural institution into a site of cultural production. Our impulse was to extend our Buenos Aires investigation and adapt it to the context of Madrid to establish contact with a local, marginalized neighborhood. We saw it as an opportunity to open a *corridor of cultural exchange* between a major top-down arts institution and a bottom-up cultural initiative in a Madrid neighborhood, home to the Latin American diaspora. Instead of focusing on the visual aspect of the facade as a focal point, we wanted to make it perform, to make it operative —literally to open it, to infiltrate the institution. As in Buenos Aires, we would assume the role of *cultural brokers*, mediating and negotiating the interface between institutions and communities of practice to support unrecognized bottom-up creativity.

With Mauricio Corbalán and Iago Caro, we researched areas in Madrid with a high concentration of bottom-up social-cultural initiatives, small activist groups, and NGOs working to tackle social and economic urgencies within Madrid's marginalized populations. As in Buenos Aires, our investigation led us to a few social actors whose work in this case was concentrated in the neighborhood of *Puente de Vallecas*, located at the edges of the city, just 4.9 kilometers from Casa de America. We chose Puente de Vallecas as the neighborhood in which to operate because of its significant immigrant population, its history as a critical threshold at the margins of the urban structure of Madrid, and because of its activist networks. Inside this neighborhood, we began conversations with a network of social actors and their activist agencies in Vallecas: Juan Carlos Rios and Juana Molano of *AESCO*, an association that works with the Colombian and Latino population in general, human rights, gender violence and initiatives for Latin American culture; Esperanza Camarasa of *Asociación Abierto Hasta el Amanecer*, a cooperative that provides service-grant loans to projects that generate employment, promote cooperativism, associations and social economy; Lucia Ruiz of *Radio Vallecas*, a neighborhood-based radio station, home of the program Nosotras en El Mundo; Juan Rodrigañez and Pablo Perez of *Asociación Al Alba*, a film association focused on video-histories of Vallecas; and Gonzalo Sarmiento of *Asociación Cultural de la Kalle*, an agency dedicated to advancing socio-pedagogical actions in the neighborhood.

Instead of intervening only upon the facade of Casa de America, the group expressed interest in working inside of it, literally penetrating and activating it with a work program, a platform of collaboration with social activists in Vallecas. We debated collectively the merits of the project, as we did not want to suggest the need to use the top-down institution to legitimize the powerful work that these bottom-up agencies were already doing on the ground. But we were surprised when many of the local cultural leaders shared with us that they had already in fact "knocked on the door" of this particular cultural institution to ask for support for neighborhood-based activities, and they had not been heard. We agreed to co-curate and facilitate a conversation about circulating neighborhood-based social actors and networks in Casa de America, and, likewise, institutional resources to advance cultural projects in Puente de Vallecas. To accomplish this we advanced a contingent proposal: that we would indeed transform the facade of Casa de America into a cultural threshold for *Madrid Abierto*, but through this, we would conceptualize and generate a parallel project, to be enacted once the *Madrid Abierto* ended. In other words, we wanted to produce an event-after-the-event to ensure a redistribution of resources back to the neighborhood.

THE OPEN FACADE

The physical intervention on the facade was minimal: a text and a ladder.

1. A text contextualizes the intervention in an emblematic way. By posting on the facade the question posed by a Paraguayan immigrant to our Buenos Aires–based CIA group, "How is your art going to help us?," we intended to provoke an urgent investigation of more functional relations between research, artistic intervention and the co-production of the city.

2. A ladder enabled us literally to enter the facade through a large window, allowing direct access to the institution through a symbolic *back door*. In other words, the ladder enabled the artists to penetrate the facade while activating it internally, gaining access to a prominent Baroque salon immediately behind the facade called the *Salon Inca*. This ornate room became the site for conversations between neighborhood activists, diverse publics and the institution to develop programs that would activate the entire Casa De America and bring resources to Vallecas after the event.

THE ARCHITECTURE OF A CONVERSATION

We wanted to curate two-way flows between the institution and the neighborhood, and also to construct the dialogical content of these conversations to advance debates about institutional accountability. We curated a question that would become essential to our work at the San Diego-Tijuana border: How can we construct a *productive* conversation among actors who are not often in contact with each other, and whose views about cultural production and the meaning of art as a social tool were at odds? How can we design the scaffolds for an agonistic intervention in public space?

Generative topics included: the role of artistic practice in relation to the current real-estate crisis and the shortage of social-economic resources and investments in public space and infrastructure; the possibility of participatory budgeting; the possibility of generating seed capital from *Madrid Abierto*'s own cultural budget to support an artistic intervention in Puente de Vallecas; and the possibility of connecting this resource to other public resources, linking public policy and urban imagination inside and outside the state. This set of provocations included creating a process to locate dispersed resources and recalibrate budgets for diverse spatial and temporal dynamics. We hoped the architecture of the conversation would use the facade of Casa de America as a platform for thinking collectively in real time about the transformation of the city.

Meetings took place inside the building, behind the facade, among the artists and activists of Vallecas, who also choreographed exchanges with publics in their own neighborhood. The meetings were inaugurated by climbing up the exterior ladder and entering the facade through a large window. During the meetings, the *Salon Inca* was opened from the facade to invite diverse groups of people, some chosen by the actors, others institutionally affiliated and others from diverse cultural sectors. During these meetings, a variety of activities and performances occupied the space, transforming the *Salon Inca* into a satellite public space of the Vallecas neighborhood. These actions included inviting a neighborhood council meeting to take place inside this room in Casa de America and discussions about participatory budgeting and the redistribution of cultural support systems. The room was also transformed into a neighborhood radio station to disseminate the activities and conversations taking place to wider publics. As these activities unfolded, neighborhood-based cultural activities were brought to Casa de America. The local Vallecas agencies co-curated a program of activities inside the museum, using their auditorium and galleries to present music performances and other actions as part of the official programming of this cultural institution.

Like the Buenos Aires project, which seeded this effort in Madrid culturally, it was essential to us all to leave an institutional trace once *Madrid Abierto* concluded. During our meetings in the *Salon Inca*, we also conceptualized a post-event initiative that took the shape of an online knowledge-exchange platform and archive for the many agencies involved in the project—an architecture for collaboration among the activist groups inside this critical Madrid neighborhood. For many of the participants, an archive that visualized resources, common values and shared interests would trigger the true beginning of *Madrid Abierto* and elevate the neighborhood of Vallecas as a site of cultural, social and economic production.

ACT 3: ANYANG, SOUTH KOREA
THE FUTURE NEIGHBORHOOD: CONVERSATIONS ON COEXISTENCE

In collaboration with Mauricio Corbalán (m7red)

The third act in this research-based triptych of community participation practices and their operative effects on the urban field focused on marginalized neighborhoods as places of social and economic performance. We were invited by urban curator Kyong Park, director of the biennial APAP-2010 in Anyang, a large satellite city at the edges of Seoul, South Korea. Park's intention was to push the conventional biennial beyond the typical public art event through which artistic interventions tend to camouflage gentrification, and often are operationalized by governments in collusion with private developers. The premise for the event was to question the future of the neighborhood at a moment of accelerating urban growth in Anyang, when municipal agendas of redevelopment had prompted demolition of older neighborhoods in order to build higher density housing towers called *New Towns*.

With the recent experiences from Buenos Aires and Madrid, we brought our partner Mauricio Corbalán from m7red to collaborate with us once again to engage diverse communities and constituencies in Anyang. Our first meeting took place at office of the mayor of Anyang, along with curators and other project participants. We were presented with the current planning agenda of the city, which announced major transformation efforts including demolition of five older neighborhoods, to be replaced in the following years by the typical top-down project of high-rise redevelopment.

Our Buenos Aires project began by entering conflicts between informal settlements, emergency housing and the forces of urban exclusion; the Madrid project expanded these issues, exposing the gap between top-down institutions and marginalized neighborhoods and forwarding the decentralization and redistribution of economic and cultural power. The third act in Anyang elevated the neighborhood as the physical manifestation of bottom-up social and economic exchanges and the spatialization of communities of practice. As the City of Anyang aspired to densify through conventional top-down housing redevelopment with towers, it proposed to erase its older neighborhoods, demolishing along the way the complexity of local social and economic relations and the everyday activist practices that are endogenous to South Korean society.

At the mayor's office, we saw a poster depicting the *New Town*, a homogeneous tower complex surrounded by meandering lawns and parking lots, which would replace District 7, an old, mid-density neighborhood that was home to an eclectic array of small businesses, incremental densities, spaces and situations. Coming from Southern California, where urban growth prioritizes homogenous, horizontal sprawl, we knew immediately in Anyang that we would tackle the conflict between the vertical and the horizontal. We found the same recipe but rendered upward, through vertical sprawl. The approaches are linked in their destruction of the street as a stage for multiple and heterogeneous modes of social and economic intersections. It became clear that these new developments all over Asia were imitating the worst recipes of US-style suburbanization without consideration of the embedded cultural and social practices that have shaped older communities across time. It was also clear that many cities across the world had failed to reconcile vertical and horizontal densities, producing new hybrids between them. How can the vibrancy of street culture be reproduced across scales? How can community values of activism, solidarity, collective property, cooperation, bottom-up entrepreneurship—in sum, the economic and associative fabrics of everyday life—be preserved and transferred? And how can these performances organize the future neighborhood physically and programmatically.

In Anyang, we reproduced the collaborative models from Buenos Aires and Madrid to advance the project in association with actors in the city. We summoned sectors that were at odds with one another in the urban redevelopment wars. Here, as at the previous sites, we began by intervening in the communication gap between government and community, the lack of transparency in the process of redevelopment. We also saw a need to produce new interfaces with diverse publics across new informational and communicational systems, conveying to our partners that community participation is meaningless when the critical questions are not being asked or problematized: How do we tactically intervene in the debate, questioning existing consumer tendencies as they are co-opted by politics and economics of speculative housing developments *(New Towns)*? How do we intervene in the hegemony of exclusionary development and its systems of perception and representation?

We met with housing activists who were fighting the bulldozers. While we were impressed with their amazing courage in resisting these forces, we found that their project was concentrated on organizing the community to protest in front of the municipality but short on strategies to politically represent the informal economies, spaces, housing typologies and modes of exchange under threat—in essence, the public and social capital that the city would destroy in the process of erasing those older neighborhoods. In other words, they hadn't mobilized a political and economic language to quantify the opportunity costs, the externalities these faulty redevelopment logics would impose on their own community. We saw here an opportunity to collaborate, to discuss how to represent neighborhood resources and knowledges against generic advocacy planning processes which silence meaningful, critical discussion in search of consensus, relying on community passivity to camouflage the conflict between large urban developments and small neighborhood communities. We discussed how art and architecture can produce tactical disruption of the mythologies that perpetuate public desire for vertical sprawl. We agreed to cooperate in a knowledge-production process, to stimulate recognition of what already exists in District 7, visualizing hidden value and the qualities that are lost in processes of ostensible improvement.

We also met with other stakeholders in the conflict, including city officials, private developers, university professors and even the Catholic Church, which is aligned with the activists, defending their right to affordable housing. It became clear that we wanted to intervene in the debate in the midst of these polarizing forces. We proposed a mediating protocol and a new cross-sector civic conversation to visualize and debate the vulnerabilities of redevelopment, the controversies, contradictions and inconsistencies within both top-down and bottom-up strategies, and potentially to arrive at a common language, an unexpected urban script that might reveal new strategies of coexistence between the vertical and the horizontal.

We organized foundational workshops with the housing activists of District 7. We shared with them the memory of our visit years earlier to the *City Museum of Paris*, where we saw physical models of all the small neighborhoods that Haussmann had demolished in the mid-nineteenth-century. We discussed how the models remained in the public consciousness of Parisians as evidence of what had been destroyed. Could we also build physical models of the Anyang neighborhoods that were slated for demolition in the next years? And could these models, besides being fragments for a memory archive, become mediating tools to advance a cross-sector conversation about the issues of concern? A performative archive of operational social practices and spaces? We embarked on designing a process with our community partners to build the physical models, both as a research-based project to gather the evidence of how their district performs as a community, and as a mediating tool to represent and discuss with others, including planners and decision-makers, how these social and economic relations were physicalized in the neighborhood, and how they might be preserved.

DESIGNING CIVIC PROCESS

1. Research and Documentation

From Anyang's thirty-one redevelopment zones, we selected five neighborhoods that had become most controversial. Through interviews with local residents, we focused on the most meaningful, active areas of the neighborhood, places filled with social and economic activities. We proposed a collaborative educational effort involving engineering students from Anyang University through a special research-based seminar we taught with local academics called *Urban Information Engineering*; an educational program geared to local elementary school students titled *Imagining the Future Neighbor*; and a council comprised of community activists representing these neighborhoods. Together, we embarked on a process to build the physical models and a visual and oral archive containing narratives of bottom-up social and economic practices unrecognized by the institutions of planning.

We co-curated the guidelines for an urban pedagogical process, an educational neighborhood kit, a manual with provocative questions and prompts, experiments and narratives to be performed by citizens from the five different neighborhoods. These didactic tools were tactically constructed to expose both conflicts and controversies between official top-down planning information and stealth bottom-up neighborhood activity, and also to explore a refreshed community awareness of their immediate environment. The manual of provocative questions given to the dwellers of District 7 was the provocation for discussions at the scale of the unit, the block and the neighborhood. Through this process, we launched a generative conversational model of interface with the community to play conceptually with existing top-down mythologies of housing in Anyang, summoning citizens to participate in a parallel urban planning process to co-produce bottom-up *counter-myths* that emerged from their own practical everyday realities. These anecdotal exchanges and performances took place in tandem with physical model-making as a backdrop to recognizing and reflecting on the qualities of their surroundings, revealing the unexpected cultural, social and economic value embedded in their own neighborhoods.

2. Models as Evidence

Small coalitions of university students, elementary schoolchildren and activists organized a sequence of field trips to produce a photographic and drawing archive of the neighborhoods, street by street, block by block, recording small details and textures of buildings and everyday life. Each group was organized around a particular block and conducted micro-workshops with its residents. Together, through conversation, observation and debate, they built a 1/8" handmade 3-D model of that particular block.

These field trips and workshops introduced the group to a reading of the city from the scale and vitality of the street, challenging protocols from the normative urban planner's bird's-eye view with the scale usually navigated by citizens. Through these neighborhood walks, groups took account of the many socioeconomic programs and spaces that are off the radar of official municipal surveys and statistical data of top-down institutions. These unrecognized patterns of neighborhood activity were visually registered to produce a new level of awareness of the spatial performance of these places. Through photography and narrative, and by classifying their spatial features and through conversations with residents *in situ*, we began a process of archiving the everyday programmatic performance within these informal environments, such as micro-farming zones, alternative social spaces and cooperative economic initiatives.

Initial study models were conceived as a first approach to capture the basic configuration of the study area. But as the models absorbed the idiosyncratic textures of many blocks, they were also used as mediating tools for conversations with groups of neighbors and individuals. They were often displayed at the center of the table during informal meetings with activists to provide spatial references and evidentiary material. Somehow, the models became cultural mirrors, enabling neighbors to recognize themselves and their daily lives as a part of a bigger entity: the city of Anyang. The models became instruments for identifying value in existing socio-spatial and economic resources, essential dialogical instruments for empowering communities facing eviction. The students and activists became aware of the necessary reciprocity between the top-down view of the city and the urban agency of the street.

3. The Neighborhood Performs

While the 3-D models of these neighborhoods became a record of what would be erased physically, they also became a legitimation of intangible collective qualities under threat: community rituals, cultural exchanges, the social and economic entrepreneurship of informal urbanization. This opened the question of how to measure a space's performance—and the amount, type and role of stakeholders that activate and manage it. The group asked: Who or which organization or group is responsible for activating the common spaces of particular areas? Are these common spaces considered "public"? Who represents them? Have they emerged as alternative life-support systems in the absence of municipal investments? Or as acts of resistance to exclusionary regulation from the government? These questions evolved into conversations about how spaces in the neighborhoods negotiate diverse informational flows representing different constituencies. For the real-estate agent, the city is made of strategic areas, square meters and market prices; for the urban planner, it is made of plans, surveys, statistics and regulations; for the local recycler, it is made of waste materials and supply routes; and for the neighborhood volunteer and activist, the city is made of special zones to be cared for.

So, in tandem with the construction of the physical models, which took place on neighborhood streets (a display of images, maps and modeling materials were provided to the neighbors and occasional passersby), we conducted a series of video interviews with local activists and community entrepreneurs to share their stories. The initial scripts focused discrepancies across different perspectives and priorities, between redevelopment agencies and local citizens. We found that spaces considered "abandoned" by urban planning agencies are often considered by local residents to be spaces charged with social energy for community gatherings and filled with potential for small entrepreneurial initiatives. To capture this discrepancy in perspectives, we documented a variety of bottom-up social and economic projects and spaces inside the neighborhood. The documentation of these stealth initiatives would inform the models (many of these programmatically charged neighborhood spaces happened on rooftops, hidden alleys, behind facades, etc.), but they also enabled us to develop a compendium of video testimonies together with our community partners, featuring the diverse community actors who had advanced these initiatives and involving them in the process of defending their sustainable practices from erasure.

One emblematic case study was an interview with a man who, with his neighbors, had co-developed a snail farm across five rooftops within a single block. The residents blurred their property lines to produce an economic cooperative, setting up the protocols for local governance. These few small parcels were bundled to become an alternative political and economic unit to produce sustainable revenue and a system of sociability.

4. Conversations on Coexistence

Through these interviews, debates and conversations, residents across these neighborhoods were asked to share memories of their homes and neighbors, recognizing the psycho-geographic value of the places where they interact daily. While this process opened a forum for residents to express their desire to stay or leave the area, more fundamentally, it gave residents an opportunity to express the significance of their everyday practices, and through this awareness imagine future directions their community-based entrepreneurship could take if they participated in the planning of New Towns. Because the top-down urban planning company's interpretation of "community," "public space" and "social density" is quite different from that of the residents, this process enabled the construction of new information to be shared with stakeholders in the redevelopment processes who operate outside the neighborhood.

As visiting artists invited by Anyang's municipality to participate in the city's *Public Space Biennial*, we chose to facilitate the movement of this bottom-up information to the top-down institutions of urban development. This opened an important reflection in our practice: the task that architects and artists can perform in politically visualizing and representing, while protecting, invisible social and economic relations in communities. We transported the physical models and their testimonies, and displayed them inside the institutions of public planning and private development at Anyang's municipality and other top-down venues. We organized dialogues, using these models as a medium for communication between residents and experts, and with public institutions, including the mayor's office, the architects of the *New Towns* and the city planners. We presented the physical models as evidence to facilitate a new language to reimagine the "Future Neighborhood in Anyang." The city planners acknowledged the value of bottom-up social and economic initiatives; private developers were surprisingly open to experimenting with scenarios about mixed uses and alternative spatial scales and rates of development to accommodate idiosyncratic community-serving uses; the residents understood the need for increased densities and urban growth but demanded options and inclusion in sharing revenues. In sum, there was a common understanding that the Future Neighborhood needed to physicalize a more complicated idea of "community" and "local economy,"

and that a heterogeneous set of social and spatial performances demanded more choices, many more housing typologies, conditions of property and temporalities beyond the homogeneity of the ubiquitous *New Town* towers that were appearing everywhere across the city.

5. The Rights to the Neighborhood

At a special ceremony at Anyang's municipality we presented the findings of this common language in a *Bill of Rights for the Neighborhood*. We translated and represented the many conversations across stakeholders to shape ten central rights that Anyang's older neighborhoods should have in the context of urban growth. The idea of designing protocols for inclusion as a prerequisite for urban intervention has been foundational for our practice and emerges from these research-based interactions with low-income communities across the world. This protocol also contained a proposition for the City of Anyang: to scale up the impact of these physical models and accompanying archive of memory by creating a nomadic City-Lab museum where all neighborhood and institutional narrative proposals could be woven together into an integrated vision. This nomadic public forum would disseminate a new urban pedagogy in which maps, models and archives stitched together a more comprehensive image of the city at the interface between the top-down and the bottom-up, and framed by the *Bill of Rights for the Neighborhood*:

The right to access diverse economies of housing
The right to develop incrementally at different rates of growth
The right to transform through retrofitting additions instead of demolitions
The right to share the profits of urbanization
The right to develop local modes of productivity
The right to zoning and land-use policy that support local entrepreneurship
The right to inclusive participation in the decisions of redevelopment
The right to prioritize social value in the equations of economic development
The right to infrastructure that mediates large- and small-scale development
The right to improve the neighborhood without gentrification

Nomadic Frames for Sociability

The three urban actions in Buenos Aires, Madrid and Anyang were developed over two years of work in collaboration with dozens of social actors and institutions, and tackled a variety of urban crises. Their intersections generated an array of bottom-up strategies and community processes that have inspired our work at the San Diego–Tijuana border. These three projects explored the role architects can play in designing civic processes in which community knowledges, capabilities and participation become the material for reconfiguring social, economic and spatial relations. We confirmed the importance of curating and facilitating cross-institutional interfaces to prepare the political ground for architectures of social justice. Ultimately, these experiences taught us to question existing models of advocacy planning. Social justice in the city requires activating communities-of-practice as co-producers of the city, and this demands new, more functional, strategies and methods of civic participation. By "functional" we mean that community participation in urban redevelopment processes should be not only about expressing a point of view or stylistic preference, but about including community members as active urban agents, co-developers of policy, and beneficiaries of the profits of urbanization.

These experiences were formative, as we continued to explore new territories of operation for architects and artists in urban design today. They helped to solidify a core commitment in our practice: that the future of the city today depends not only on buildings, but on the recalibration of social and economic relations—and that architects can design social and economic processes as a prerequisite to building in underserved places. These emergent insights have inspired us over time to imagine new kinds of public spaces, where community processes and performances are supported by flexible scaffolds to enable diverse nomadic and programmatic configurations. Three of our public space interventions in recent years illustrate these commitments and demonstrate how lessons from Buenos Aires, Madrid and Anyang continue to inspire new strategies to activate often passive public spaces into dynamic, civicized urban systems for sociability and economy.

INFOSITE: MIGRANT HOUSE, PORTABLE PUBLIC SPACE

This public space project was commissioned by *InSite*, a cross-border art biennial project that invited diverse international artists to propose site-specific installations on both sides of the San Diego–Tijuana border. By 2005, the project had expanded its curatorial strategies beyond site specificity and normative notions of art in public spaces, calling instead for artistic interventions in the cross-border public domain. Can art be distributed through invisible cross-border urban-social flows and networks? Artists were invited to co-produce their work with diverse communities, institutions and associations.

We were asked to design *InfoSite*, a temporary information station that encroached into an underutilized parking lot in San Diego, infusing it with alternative cultural programming. We thought of this station as a nomadic platform for the exchange and dissemination of information within the increasing privatization and homogeneity of the public realm, a temporary research library for cross-border publics to accompany the artists and their processes and projects during the event. We wanted to insert this public space project into dynamics we had documented over the years, such as the invisible cross-border urban flows of discarded, leftover bungalows from San Diego that are recombined in Tijuana into fresh housing scenarios, creating countless new urban opportunities in the informal settlements in the city.

We used the project as an excuse to engage these cross-border tactics of recycling by exposing the often-invisible processes of transferring a discarded San Diego house into the informal urbanization of Tijuana. *InfoSite* was conceptualized as an artificial nomadic site for assembling the scaffolds and architectural parts of a house composed of ready-made structures, including off-the-shelf systems and materials, such as truck beds, pallet racks, tents and traffic cones. They were assembled in a variety of environments that encroached into the underutilized parking lot, transforming it temporarily into a site of knowledge exchange. Once the event ended, the wooden armatures of the house were mobilized as a *portable public space* across the border in Tijuana, where they were absorbed and altered by an informal neighborhood at the periphery of the city. It was a gesture intended to amplify mutual recognition of the urban exchanges, interdependences and shared regional destiny of these divided cities.

URBAN ROOMS: SCAFFOLDS FOR "THINGS TO HAPPEN"

We have always resisted the idea of public space as a neutral site devoid of programming that assures social inclusion. In our practice we see the activation of public space as a "double project" that includes designing flexible physical infrastructure to enable activity and transformation across time, accommodating diverse social, economic and cultural activities, as well as deliberate strategies for shared programming and management of space to assure longevity and inclusive civic participation. We proposed such a double strategy when we were invited to adapt and retrofit an existing, under-utilized public space in San Jose, California. The project was a collaboration between MACLA (Movimiento de Artes y Cultura Latino Americano) and the City of San Jose Office for Arts and Culture.

A small public plaza across the street from MACLA remained underutilized because of a lack of shading and cultural programming. The process of adapting and retrofitting this vacant site began by establishing a co-production model between MACLA, whose main galleries are across the street, and the City of San Jose, constructing a curatorial project that would assure a choreography of arts and cultural programming throughout the year as instruments for civic participation, as well as engines to incentivize new neighborhood-based economies to improve the quality of life in San Jose's low-income neighborhoods. Designing these protocols for inclusion generated a sustainable funding and programmatic architecture for the physical space.

We transformed the amorphous scale of the plaza by distributing four scaffolds, simple ready-made steel structures, across the open space to configure four *Urban Rooms* that threaded a series of shaded zones and areas for activity that would be programmed by MACLA and the City of San Jose. Each steel armature was clad in layered vinyl-coated chain-link systems with varying degrees of opacity to provide shade and texture. Each *Urban Room* was equipped with movable urban furniture to accommodate flexible uses, and demountable shading curtains that could be stored and maintained across the street at the MACLA site. These nomadic tools transformed the *Urban Rooms* into a variety of spatial and programmatic configurations, including small tiendas for local artist-led economic projects, open-air civic classrooms, forums for community-based projects and open stage platforms for cultural performances and activities throughout the year, including skateboarding, arts fairs and concerts.

RETROFIT GECEKONDU: PREFABRICATION AS SOCIAL SYSTEM

Finally, we include a public space experiment we developed in collaboration with the Berlin-based housing activist collective, Kotti & Co. We were brought together by co-curator Jesko Fezer as part of the international housing exhibition *Wohnungsfrage* at the Haus der Kulturen der Welt (HKW) in *Berlin.* The exhibition paired five architectural practices across the world with five grassroots social initiatives on the ground in Berlin to reimagine social housing.

Our contribution to the exhibition began with circulating knowledges between our practice advancing affordable housing at the San Diego–Tijuana border and Kotti & Co, an activist practice in Berlin challenging the housing crisis in that city. Sandy Kaltenborn, a graphic designer and activist representing Kotti & Co, and Christian Hiller from the HKW met with us in our San Diego studio, and we embarked on a series of conversations-on-the-move, journeying to some of the sites and communities we work with in Tijuana, Mexico. During these visits we shared our own research on incremental housing and building practices in the informal settlements of San Diego, where people construct their own shelter in layers over time. We also shared our knowledge of how the multinational maquiladoras surrounding these informal settlements typically benefit from easy access to cheap labor, and how over the years we had experimented with factory-made material systems to structurally mediate the recycling of waste.

Soon after this field visit to Tijuana, it was our turn to travel to Berlin to meet Kotti's activist community, composed of local, largely Turkish immigrant tenants who risked rent increases and eviction from a social housing complex in the heart of Berlin's Kreuzberg neighborhood. We arrived at Kotti & Co's headquarters, a small, precarious salon called the *Gecekondu*, named after the bottom-up dwellings that spring up informally in Istanbul's periphery. The group of tenants had built this structure years earlier in the plaza of the housing complex as part of their protest campaign to call for public awareness, municipal and federal attention to housing affordability and creeping gentrification, and to engage the political dimension of housing, demanding transformations in housing policy and economy. In this process, the tenants formed a neighborhood platform for knowledge exchange and bottom-up planning over debates with tea. Over time, the *Gecekondu* become a beloved public space in the shape of a *people's house* in which these debates could occur. The structure became the community's forum for debating and exposing the social, economic and political dynamics often missing from the housing question. In our minds, Kotti & Co's temporary *Gecekondu* physicalized a notion that had been fundamental to our work at the Tijuana–San Diego border: the rethreading of public space and housing, demonstrating that housing can be more than dwelling units. It can also carve heterogeneous spaces for political representation, socialization and debate.

The circulation of knowledges between Kotti & Co and our practice resulted in a proposal that connected informal urbanization, nomadic public space and social housing, driven by a practical and concrete goal to elevate Kotti's process in Berlin while advancing our work with informal housing in San Diego. We entered into each other's histories through the idea of the *Gecekondu*. Our dialogues with the activist tenants engaged the housing question today, not only through questions about "housing design" but also primarily by infiltrating the politics and economics of housing with the idea that affordability must be connected to the politics of labor—in Berlin, in Tijuana and everywhere. We ultimately proposed a global circulation that linked these critical issues in Germany and at the US-Mexico border, advancing a new housing policy that embeds social housing within public space infrastructure to incentivize local economic productivity—a new social economy of housing seeded by public space.

A major point of contact between Kotti and our practice is the notion of "urban retrofit"—adapting housing with social, economic and material support systems. Just as Kotti's *Gecekondu* was an act of retrofit in an underutilized public space to anticipate social exchange, most of our housing projects and processes at the US-Mexico border are defined by urban tactics of adaptation. We learn from the recycling strategies and incremental, layered growth of Tijuana's informal settlements and from San Diego's immigrant neighborhoods, where the homogeneous housing of Southern California is adapted into diverse spatial and programmatic ecologies. The mutual housing question, then, focused on how to connect social housing to bottom-up community capabilities and on "retrofitting" processes to carve new spaces of socialization and job generation within the mono-use and mono-economy of existing slab housing buildings in Berlin and around the world.

We proposed to begin the project in Tijuana and then circulate it to Berlin and back to Tijuana, a convergence of global and local dynamics. With Berlin's HKW budgets, the exhibition narrative and our public university's institutional representation, we approached Mecalux, a Spanish maquiladora that produces lightweight metal shelving systems in Tijuana for global export. We negotiated a subsidy to adapt the factory's prefabricated shelving systems into structural scaffolds as armatures for informal housing. We designed a catalogue with the factory's engineers to test a variety of prototypes and configurations and the first "Mecalux housing typology" was born. We then shipped the parts to build two Mecalux housing frames to Berlin. One would be exhibited in the museum as part of the *Wohnungsfrage* exhibition to visualize these sociospatial and material dynamics to the general public, and the other would be installed in Kreuzberg, next to the *Gecekondu*, as an adapted extension of the existing public space. The idea was that Kotti & Co could then transform the structure into a nomadic forum for disseminating their housing agenda across the city.

The Mecalux-*Gecekondu* became a nomadic public space, a light infrastructural system easily transported and assembled. Since the frame was essentially a scaffold made of recombined off-the-shelf elements, it was open to adaptations with locally available materials. Can we imagine an "architecture of parts" to anticipate diverse spatial configurations according to local needs, an architecture not of housing "units," but a platform to anticipate the construction of diverse self-help housing additions: an assembly hall, a small street market—or a temporary urban parliament, which is the program Kotti & Co advanced during the period of the exhibition and beyond.

Back in Tijuana, a multi-year collaboration was launched with the Mecalux factory. In recent years, as thousands of Central American migrants have arrived in this border city seeking asylum, the local housing crisis has intensified. We are now expanding production of the Mecalux frame to increase refugee housing capacity in the informal settlements where we work (see project cluster 3). The frame has been transformed into housing "scaffolds" equipped with utilities to support incremental live-work configurations. These housing envelopes are the seeds for an evolving sanctuary neighborhood, to be infilled through time by the migrant residents themselves.

In the end, these bottom-up public space projects convey a commonsense idea: that designing sustainable and inclusive cities today demands a deliberate investment in public spaces that are dedicated to social programming that synergizes spaces, programs, resources and people. In our experience, integrated socio-spatial systems can emerge in today's neoliberal cities only through curated interfaces between top-down resources and bottom-up participation, where institutions and communities agree to share responsibilities to build a more inclusive public realm.

AN ATLAS OF PARTICIPATORY PRACTICE

We have advanced initiatives and projects to explore "functional" civic participation, partnering with communities-of-practice to reimagine public space and public domain intervention. Among these projects three stand out—a set of three consecutive acts moving across the world in three diverse locations: Buenos Aires, Argentina; Madrid, Spain; and Anyang, South Korea. Each story set the terms for the next, shaping a sequential process of knowledge exchange.

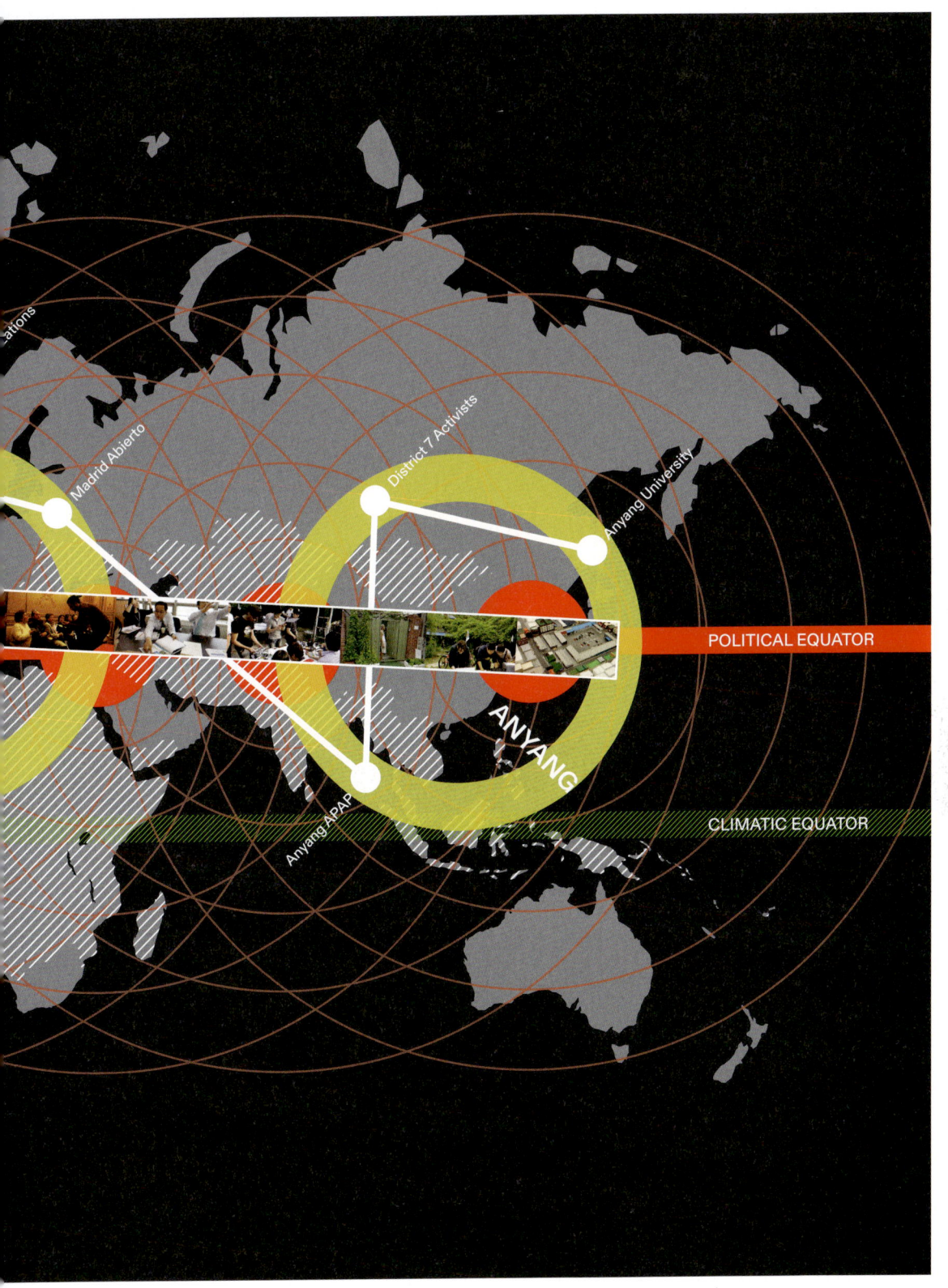

¿COMO
A AY
CON SU

ACT 1: VILLA 31: CO-PRODUCING EVIDENCE, *BUENOS AIRES*
This story begins with an urban workshop in Buenos Aires. We provoked the participating artists to encounter "other" spaces and demographics, off the radar from their work as cultural producers. This took us to Villa 31 (now called Barrio Carlos Mugica) a controversial informal settlement in the city. During our conversations, a newly arrived immigrant family in Villa 31 asked: "How is you art going to help us?" This question detonated a process of collaboration.

NOS VAN
UDAR
ARTE?

Bernardo,
Inmigrante Paraguayo
Villa 31- Bis
Manzana 107
Buenos Aires

VILLA 31

The largest, most populous informal settlement near downtown Buenos Aires, overlaid on a decomissioned rail line.

CIA

Centro de Investigaciones Artisticas, an experimental artistic laboratory in Buenos Aires.

TRANSGRESSING URBAN BORDERS

With local participants we explored sites of local conflict to motivate more social and political forms of artistic and architectural production. These are urban hotspots and borders that local actors often have not recognized or experienced, characterized by the clash of jurisdictions and social-economic demographics. Urban adjacencies often have dissimilar structures of political and cultural representation, and multiple actors do not converge to negotiate and co-produce their own city.

PUERTO MADERO

One of the most expensive redevelopment projects in Buenos Aires, fitted with luxury housing, commercial malls and next to an important protected environmental zone.

BOTTOM-UP PUBLIC: THE FUNCTIONAL DIMENSION OF PARTICIPATION

LOCAL ACTORS

We contacted an "embedded" actor within the urban conflict, opening a dialogue, a "funnel in reverse," to reveal the shifting networks, controversies and problematics within her immediate social and geographic context. We found Liliana Da Silva online. She had written a letter, a cry for help, that had not been heeded until we responded. We met Liliana on the edges of Villa 31, and she led us into the crises of her community.

MEETING OF KNOWLEDGES
Liliana took us inside Villa 31 to meet the residents of Block 107. They shared stories about their squatting, the housing problems in the area, their processes of working together, the characteristics of the property system that governed their homes and the specter of eviction. We sat together, some of us on improvised chairs, others on the dirt floor. At some point a member from the community asked us: "How is your art going to help us?"

VISUALIZING RIGHTS
We speculated that art can be a tool to visualize the complexity of urbanization, translating the often invisible forces of injustice, marginalization and exclusion, and bringing ethical scrutiny to alienating political structures that marginalize the "other." We co-produced a script with the community as a tool for political representation, visualizing missing information, the social processes and histories that unfolded at that particular site of conflict.

CO-PRODUCING EVIDENCE

This process resulted in a visual archive, constructed with the residents of Block 107 to accompany local processes of protest and resistance, establishing an evolving media platform to increase community capacity for political representation. The first project included a visual documentary, a historical reconstruction of the violent act of eviction by the police—a reenactment in which artists and community members took center stage, "acting" and "performing" together, to co-produce evidence.

ACT 2: "HOW IS YOUR ART GOING TO HELP US?", MADRID
This question posed by a Paraguayan immigrant in Buenos Aires became a provocation in *Madrid Abierto*, an international public art event that transforms the city of Madrid into a laboratory for rethinking public space, demanding more functional relations between civic participation, artistic intervention and the co-production of the city.

CASA DE AMÉRICA

The most important museum in Madrid dedicated to Latin American Arts and Culture.

PUENTE DE VALLECAS

CORRIDORS OF CULTURAL EXCHANGE

We extended our Buenos Aires investigation across similar urban borders in Madrid, contacting local conflicts, top-down institutions and marginalized neighborhoods. The goal was to open corridors of cultural exchange between official arts institutions and bottom-up cultural initiatives across Madrid's immigrant neighborhoods, such as the neighborhood of Puente de Vallecas.

A working-class Madrid neighborhood on the edges of the city, home to many Latin American immigrants and known for its social activism.

THE OPEN FACADE
Our intervention took place on the facade of Casa de America, an important Spanish museum and cultural institution focused on Latin American art. We proposed to literally open the facade, to make it perform, to infiltrate the institution with an alternative cultural program to circulate resources and knowledges between the institution and the neighborhood of Puente de Vallecas, a few kilometers (but worlds) away.

CURATING COLLABORATION
A ladder enabled us to literally enter the facade through a large window into a Baroque salon called the *Salon Inca*. This was a symbolic provocation for the institution, but also an operative act that summoned cultural activists from Puente de Vallecas to co-curate and facilitate two-way circulations between neighborhood-based cultural networks and Casa de America.

BEGIN WITH A PROVOCATION

"How Is Your Art Going to Help Us?" was printed on a large yellow billboard covering Casa de America's facade, widely visible from a prominent traffic roundabout called La Cibeles during ARCO, the most important art fair in Spain. The question detonated a performative social process, transforming the facade of Casa de America into an actual site of cultural production.

THE ARCHITECTURE OF A CONVERSATION
We summoned social actors and their activist agencies working in Vallecas on a range of issues including human rights and gender violence, cooperativism and social economy, socio-pedagogical action and neighborhood radio. We curated an agreement to co-curate and negotiate the interface between institutions and communities-of-practice, bundling top-down resources to support unrecognized bottom-up cultural activism.

OCCUPY THE MUSEUM (OPERATIONALLY)

A schedule of meetings took place inside the facade, occupying Casa de America to choreograph diverse activities and performances. These actions included hosting a neighborhood council meeting in *Salon Inca* broadcast by a neighborhood radio activist group to discuss participatory budgeting and the redistribution of cultural support systems from institutions to marginalized communities.

CULTURAL TRAFFIC BEYOND BORDERS
Vallecas programming took place inside the museum's auditorium and galleries, including art and music performances by neighborhood youth that circulated between Vallecas and Casa de America.

BOTTOM-UP PUBLIC: THE FUNCTIONAL DIMENSION OF PARTICIPATION

ACT 3: THE FUTURE NEIGHBORHOOD: CONVERSATIONS ON COEXISTENCE, ANYANG
The Madrid project exposed the gap between top-down institutions and marginalized communities, forwarding social justice as a redistributive concept: how to decentralize economic and cultural power to sites of need. We arrived in Anyang, South Korea, and these questions were rearticulated, reformulated. How can communities-of-practice and bottom-up social and economic exchanges in Anyang's older neighborhoods, slated for demolition, be preserved, elevated to spatialize social justice?

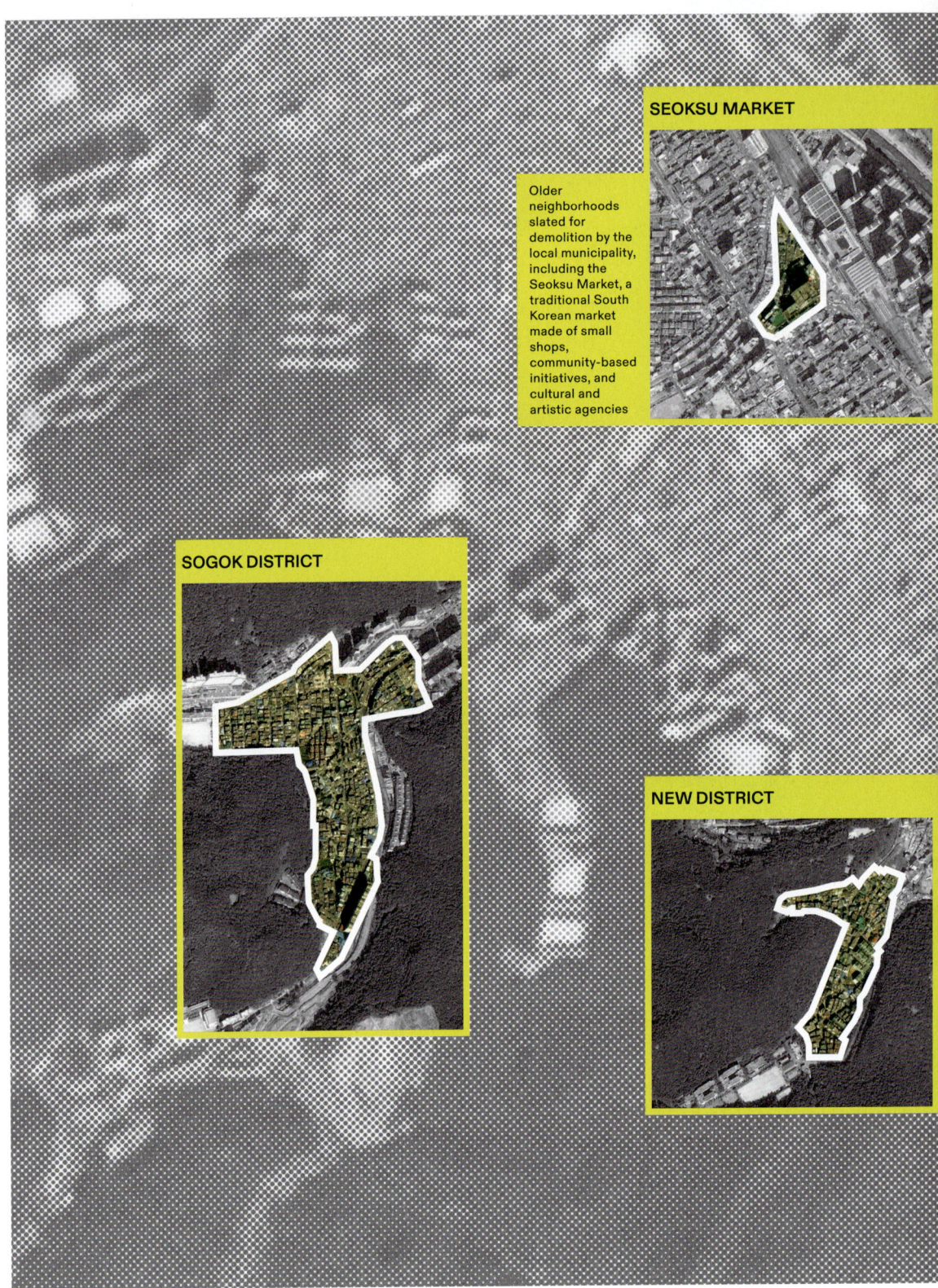

THE ERASURE OF NEIGHBORHOODS
We moved from Spain to South Korea to participate in Anyang's International Public Space program APAP, curated by Kyong Park. As we arrived, the office of Anyang's mayor announced radical urban transformation agencies that would demolish diverse older neighborhoods in the city and replace them with "New Towns" made of homogenous, high-density housing towers.

OLD RAILROAD

While Southern California's suburban subdivisions are emblematic of a ubiquitous horizontal sprawl of sameness, many New Towns in South Korea are now emblematic of an equally homogenous vertical sprawl everywhere.

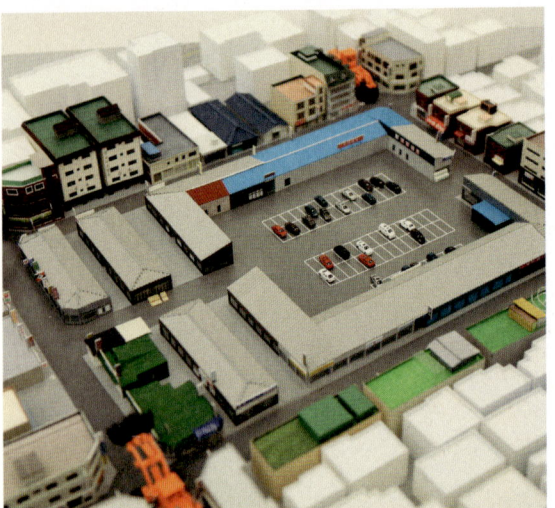 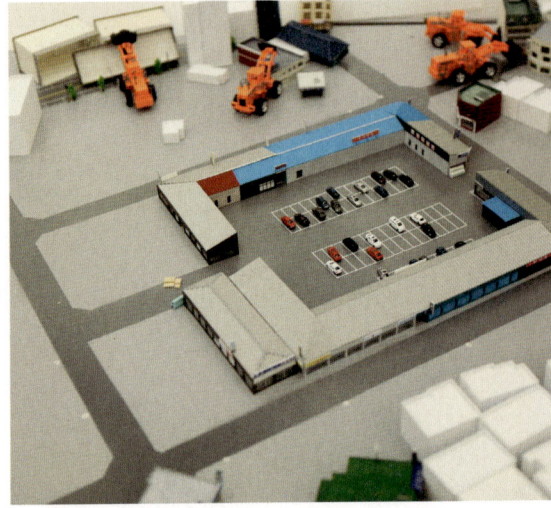

MODELS AS EVIDENCE
This specter of erasure inspired us to construct physical models of these old neighborhoods, performing as both objects of memory and evidentiary tools. As a municipality erases older communities, they also risk demolishing the embedded complexity of local social and economic relations, and the everyday activist practices which are endogenous to these communities. We summoned activists, students, children and residents to build these models.

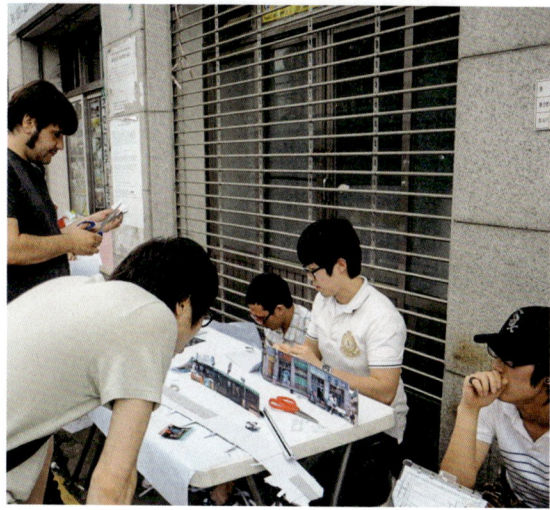

THE CONFLICT BETWEEN VERTICAL AND HORIZONTAL
We organized a series of field trips to produce an archive of neighborhood photographs and drawings, block by block, parcel by parcel. Often, the models provoked reflection on before-after scenarios, opening debates about conflicts between the "vertical and the horizontal" (In efforts to densify, cities are often unable to reconcile vertical and horizontal densities to produce new hybrids between them.)

CO-PRODUCING KNOWLEDGE
We met with housing activists who were fighting the bulldozers. While their project was focused on protest, they weren't politically representing the neighborhood's diverse informal economies, spaces and housing typologies—the public and social capital—that the city was planning to destroy. We agreed to cooperate in a knowledge production process to recognize what exists, visualizing hidden value, quantifying what will be "lost" in the process of "improvement."

NEIGHBORHOODS PERFORM
We linked the physical models with visual-oral testimonies, gathering evidence of the social and economic practices that were not recognized by the institutions of planning, and how these performances should organize the future neighborhood physically and programmatically. For example, a group of neighbors co-developed a snail farm on 5 rooftops, blurring property lines, establishing local governance and cooperative revenue at the scale of the block.

 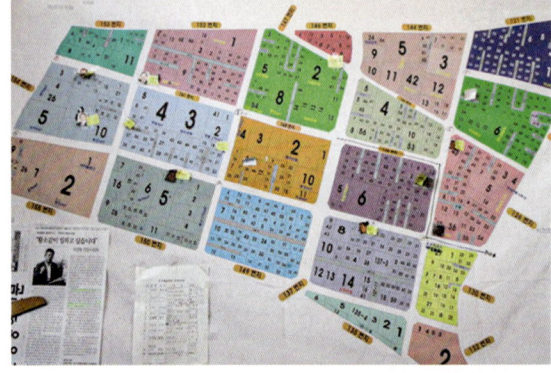

THE RIGHTS FOR THE NEIGHBORHOOD
We transported the physical models and their testimonials across institutions and communities. We organized dialogues using these models as mediating tools between residents and experts, including *New Town* developers and planners. With our activist partners we presented a *Bill of Rights for the Neighborhood*. We discovered that many of these dialogues contained a common language supporting the values of activism, solidarity, shared property, cooperation and bottom-up entrepreneurship.

The right to access different econom

The right to develop incrementally at

The right to transform through retrofi

The right to share the profits of urban

The right to develop local modes of p

The right to zoning and land-use poli

The right to inclusive participation in

The right to prioritize social value in t

The right to infrastructure that media

The right to improve the neighborhoo

of housing

ferent speeds of growth

g additions instead of demolitions

tion

ductivity

hat support local entrepreneurship

cisions of redevelopment

equations of economic development

large- and small-scale development

without gentrification

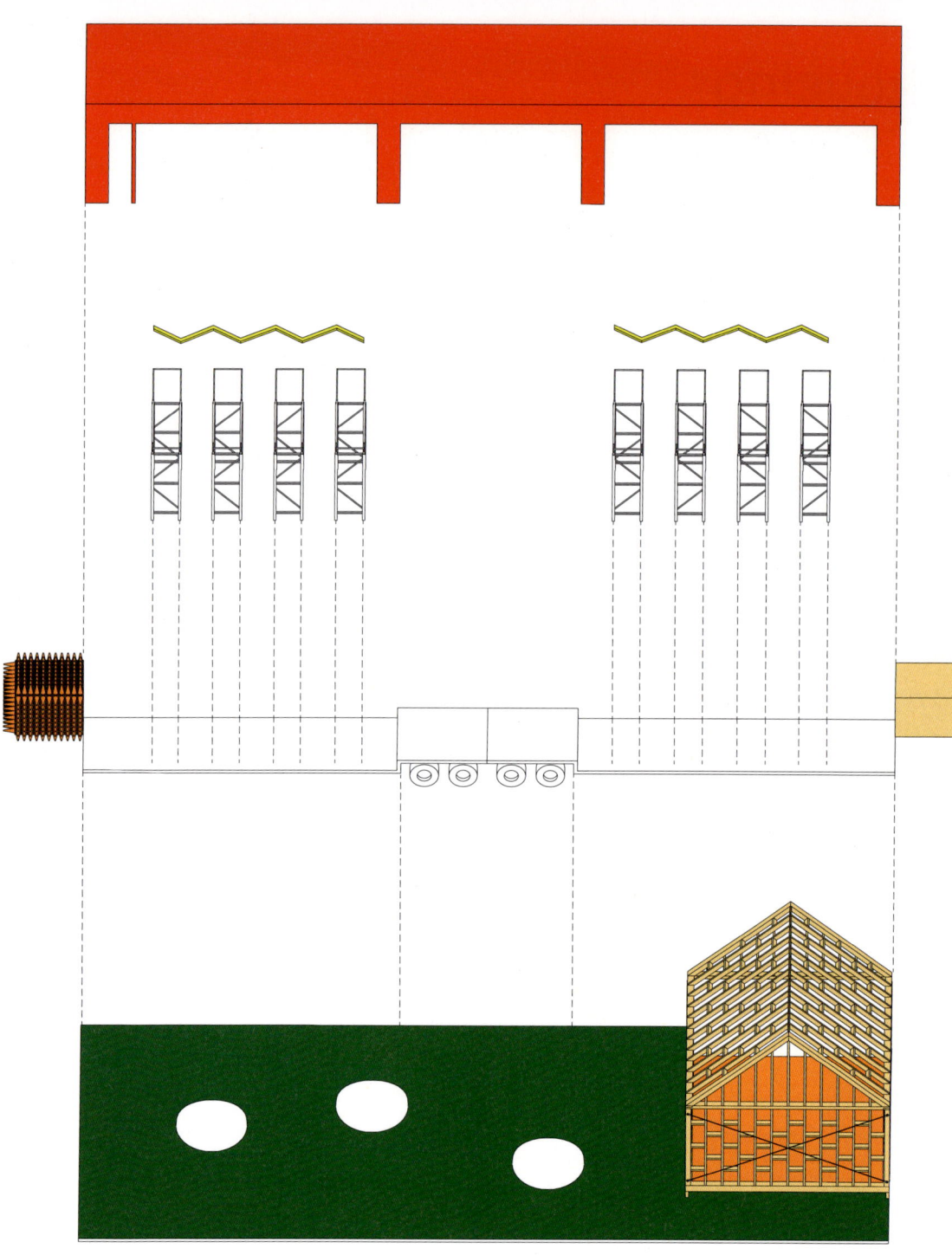

INFOSITE: *NOMADIC PUBLIC SPACE*

The act of facilitating social and economic processes as a prerequisite for building has provoked us to reimagine spaces to support political and cultural action. Here we conceptualized public space as a stage where these dialogical processes can be spatialized and performed, supported by flexible scaffolds that enable a variety of nomadic and temporal community programs.

THE MIGRANT HOUSE
A temporary research library for cross-border publics to accompany the research-based arts projects of InSite, a San Diego–Tijuana Art Biennial. This project referenced the invisible cross-border flows that we have researched over the years, exposing the often invisible recycling processes through which discarded San Diego houses end up in the informal settlements of Tijuana.

READY-MADE SITES
InfoSite was conceptualized as an artificial nomadic site, stationed temporarily in a San Diego parking lot and assembled with ready-made, off-the-shelf systems and materials, such as truck beds, pallet racks and the architectural parts for a house that would later travel to Tijuana.

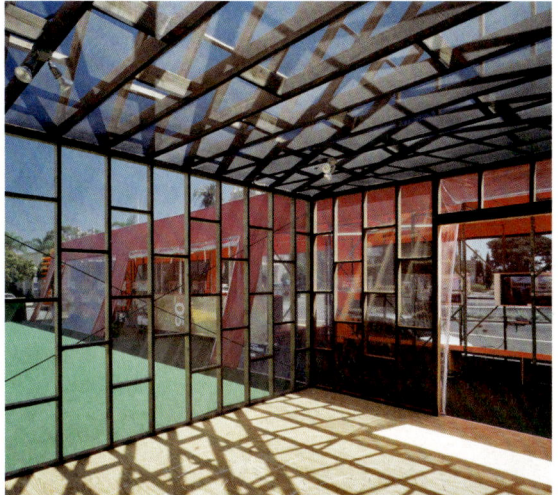

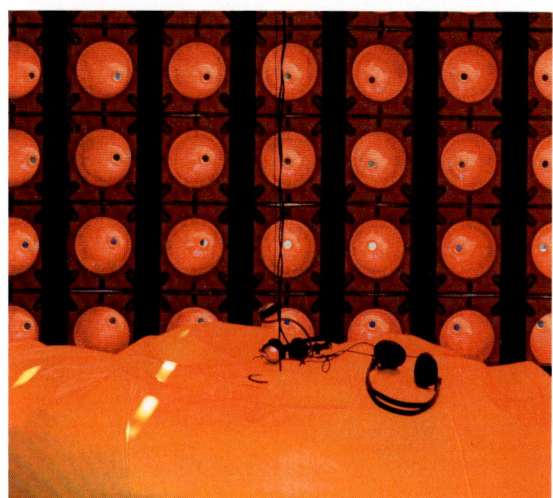

ANTICIPATING TRANSFORMATION

These ready-made systems were assembled in a variety of environments, covered by vinyl and traffic cones, and framed by pallet-rack scaffolds to support plastic bookshelves and a tent. Once the Biennial event ended, the housing armature and systems of the "portable public space" moved across the border into Tijuana to be metabolized and altered by an informal neighborhood at the periphery of the city.

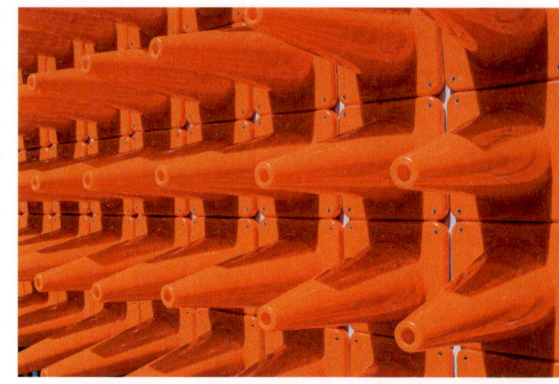

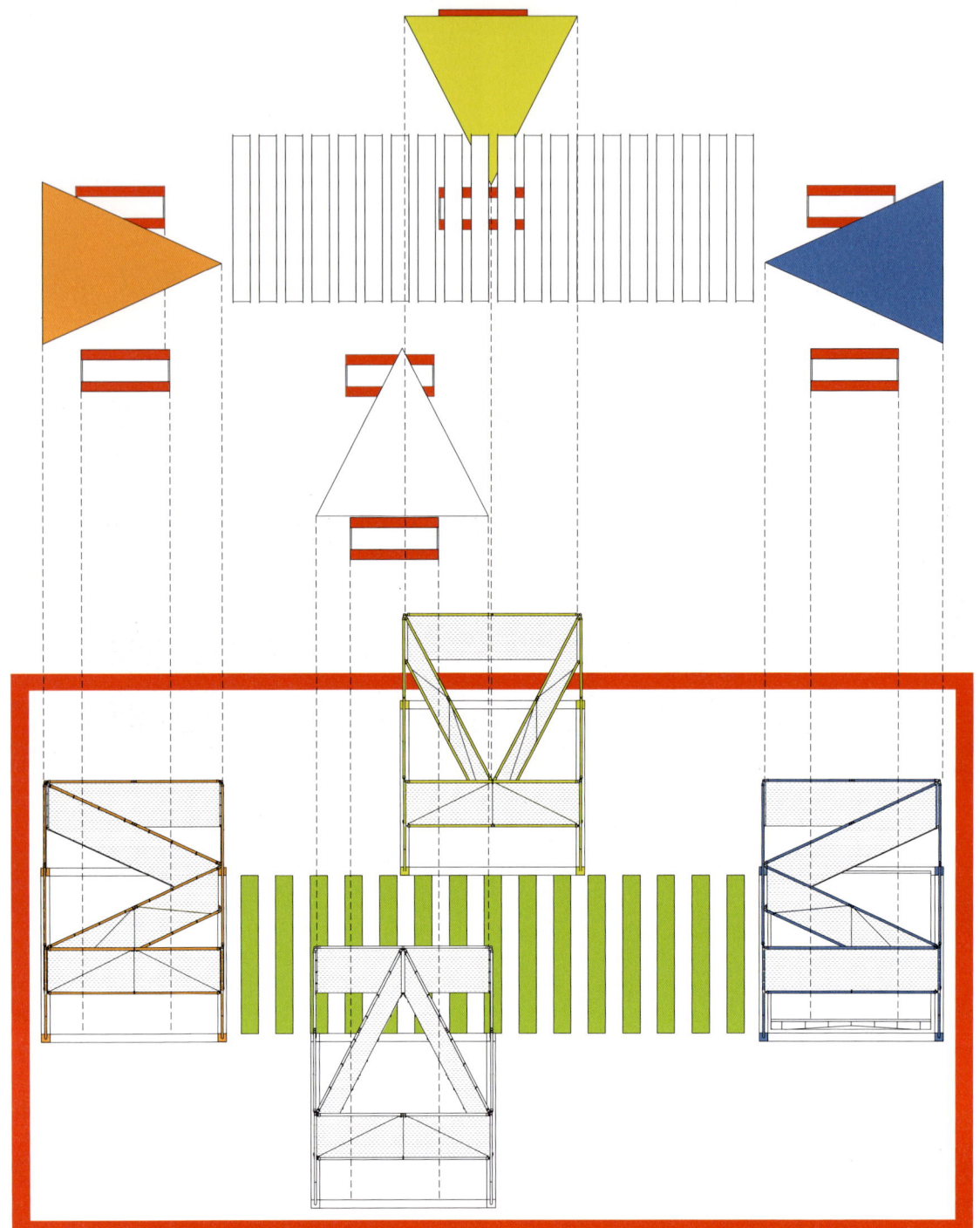

URBAN ROOMS: *SCAFFOLDS FOR "THINGS TO HAPPEN"*

We challenge the idea of public space as a neutral site, devoid of programmatic content and management protocols to assure sustainability and social inclusion. We see public space as a flexible physical infrastructure that enables transformation across time, accommodating diverse social, economic and cultural activities.

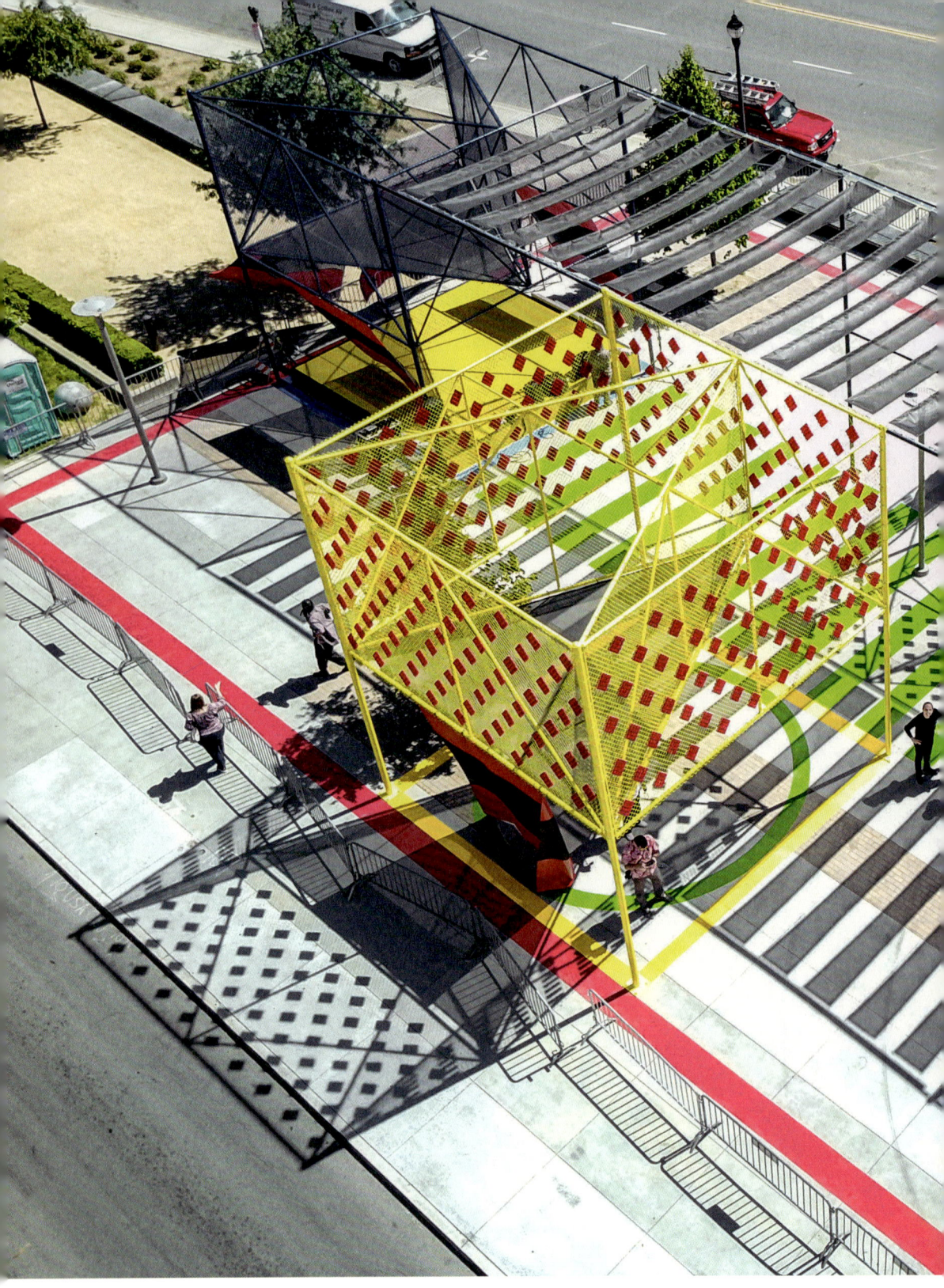

SPACES FOR CULTURAL PRODUCTION

Urban Rooms is a collection of light structures, shading systems and painted surfaces that activate a vacant and undifferentiated public space in San Jose, California. These scaffolds, including stages, urban furniture and curtains, support the choreography of social, economic and cultural events co-organized by the local community and civic institutions.

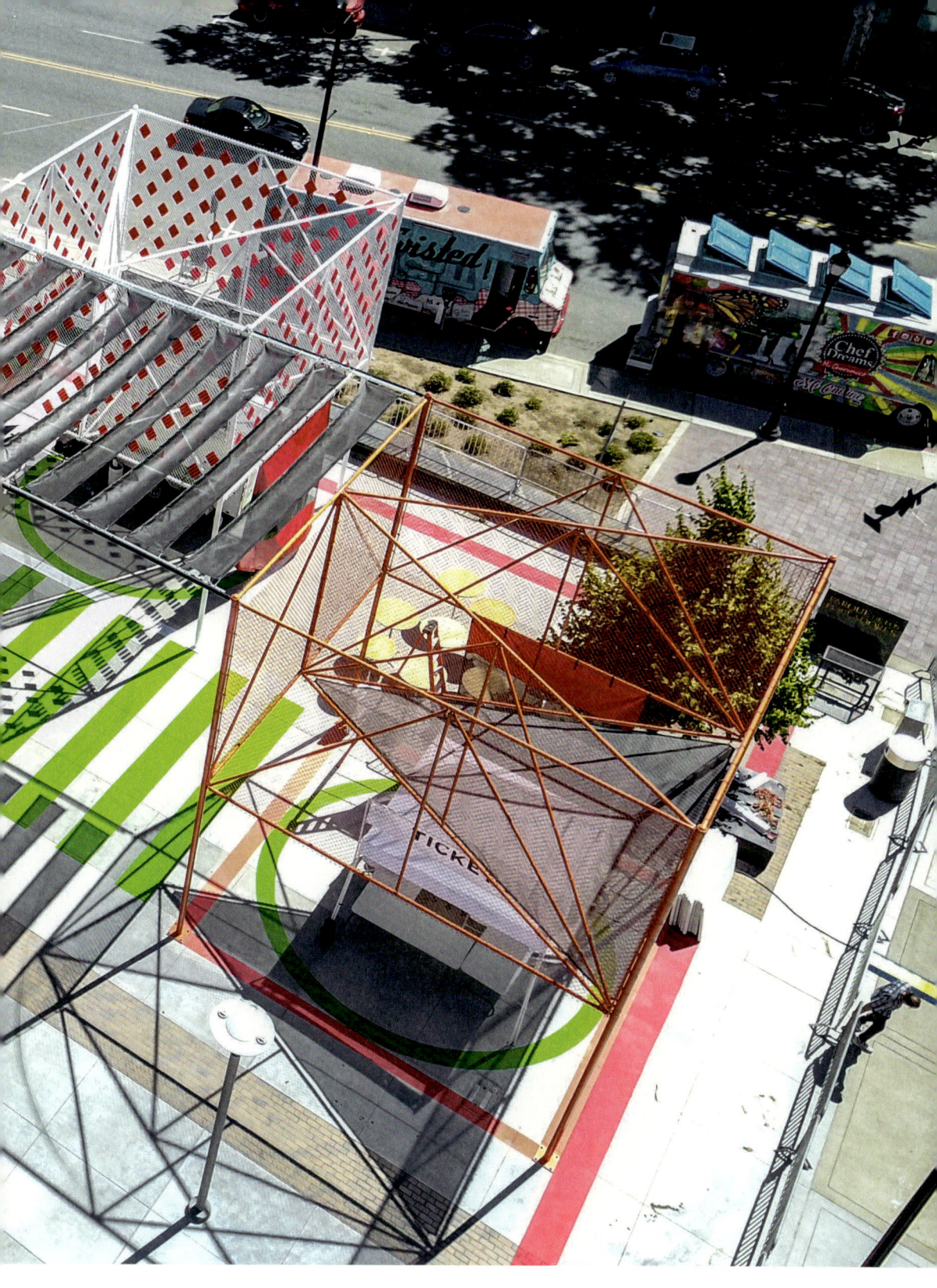

STAGING DIFFERENCE
We distributed colored chain-link scaffolds across the open space to configure four "urban rooms" that thread a series of shaded zones and areas for activity. The physical site was designed with protocols for shared management and cross-sector cultural strategies.

CURATING THE INTERFACE
The project is co-curated by MACLA (Movimiento de Artes y Cultura Latino Americano), whose main gallery spaces are across the street, and the Office for Arts and Culture of the City of San Jose. Together they will assure sustainability and social inclusion by sharing responsibilities for programmatic support systems, funding and civic participation.

425

BOTTOM-UP PUBLIC: THE FUNCTIONAL DIMENSION OF PARTICIPATION

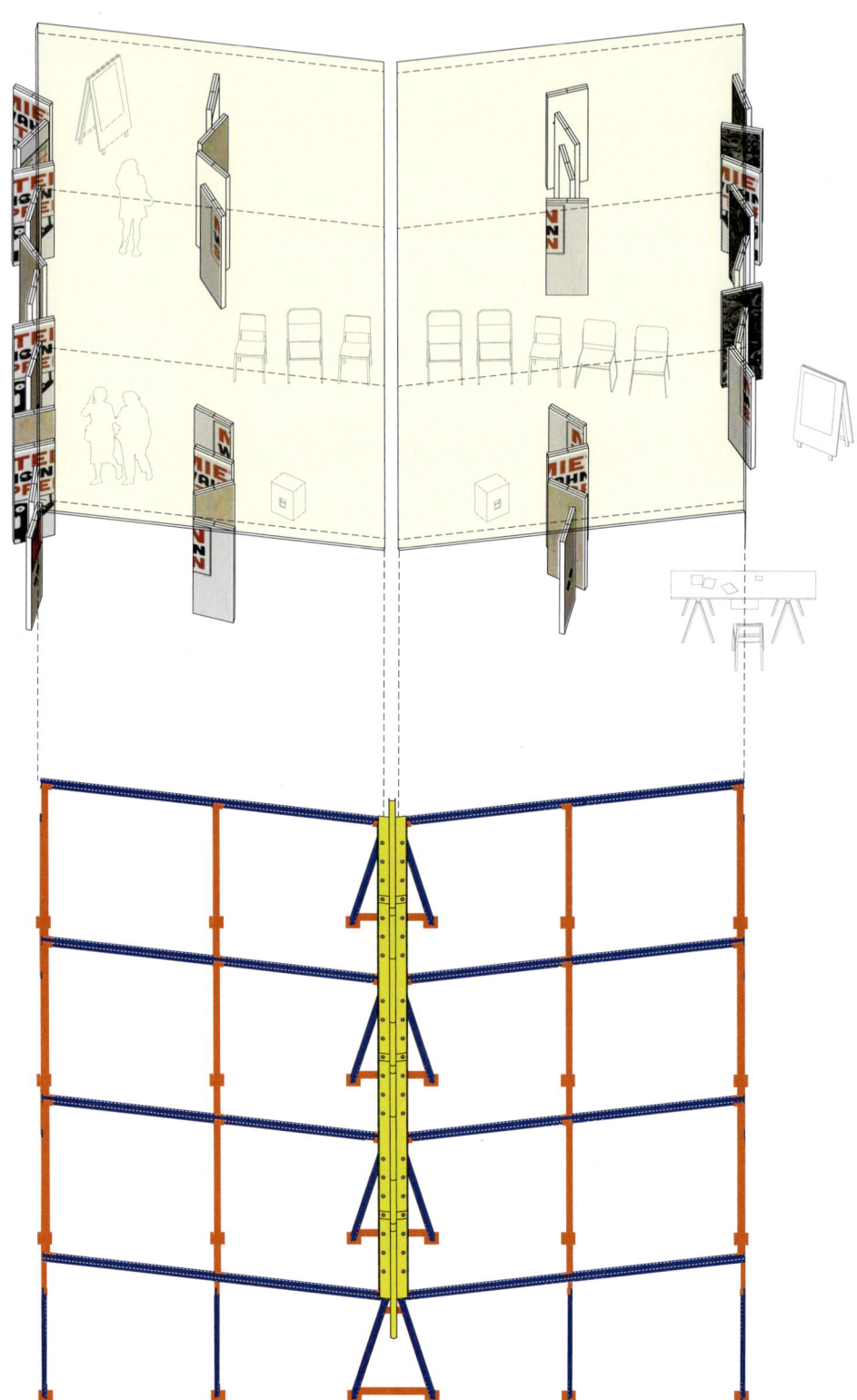

RETROFIT *GECEKONDU*: PUBLIC SPACE AS THE SEED FOR SOCIAL HOUSING

A project developed in collaboration with the Berlin-based activist housing collective, Kotti & Co to explore the relationship between informal urbanization, nomadic public space and social housing. Public space became a site for knowledge transfer, unfolding through a two-way exchange of urban procedures: to elevate Kotti's housing activism in Berlin, while advancing our work on informal housing in San Diego–Tijuana.

PLATFORMS FOR BOTTOM-UP PLANNING
This project was part of the international housing exhibition *Wohnungsfrage* at the Haus der Kulturen der Welt (HKW) in Berlin, threading together "performative" public space and social housing. We wanted to demonstrate that housing can be more than dwelling units. It can also carve new heterogeneous spaces in the city for political representation, socialization and debate.

BERLIN INTO TIJUANA

Sandy Kaltenborn of Kotti & Co and Christian Hiller of HKW traveled to the San Diego–Tijuana border to visit the sites and communities we work with. We shared our research on the multinational maquiladoras that surround informal settlements in Tijuana, and that we had been experimenting with factory-made systems to structurally support informal housing processes.

TIJUANA INTO BERLIN

We then travelled to Berlin to meet Kotti & Co, a collective of local tenants, many of whom are Turkish immigrants who live in a social housing complex in the heart of Berlin's Kreuzberg neighborhood. We arrived at their headquarters, a small, informal salon built on the street, called the *Gecekondu*, named for the bottom-up dwellings that spring up in Istanbul's periphery. They shared stories about shaping a neighborhood platform for knowledge exchange and bottom-up urban planning through community debates over tea.

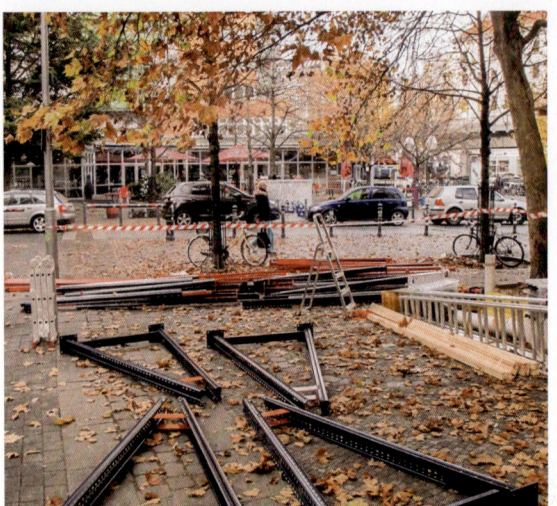

ADAPTED PUBLIC SPACE

We concluded that the notion of urban "retrofit" was a point of contact between our practices—the adaptation of housing with social, economic and material support systems. We negotiated with Mecalux, a Spanish maquiladora in Tijuana that produces lightweight metal shelving systems for global export, to adapt its prefabricated shelving systems into structural scaffolds. We installed the Mecalux frame as a "retrofit" to Kotti & Co's *Gecekondu*. It became a nomadic forum for disseminating their housing agenda.

A SITE OF DEBATE AND CONTESTATION
Kotti & Co organized a series of performances and dialogues to raise public awareness and demand municipal and federal attention to housing affordability and creeping gentrification. Housing is more than "units." It is a platform to anticipate inclusion and coexistence, and can transform along with community needs into an assembly hall, a small street market or a temporary urban parliament.

A NOMADIC FORUM FOR HOUSING JUSTICE

The Mecalux *Gecekondu* became a platform for Kotti & Co's activist social programming. Assembled and furnished informally with chairs, a video-beamer, speakers, and an energy-hub, plus a tea-maker and blankets for the cold, the frame supported a variety of uses: sometimes a public cinema for collective viewing to inspire neighborhood organization, sometimes a flea market to sell neighborhood goods or distribute info materials on housing availability.

A TEMPORARY URBAN PARLIAMENT

Most often, the frame transformed into an assembly room for 80 people or more, equipped with foldable chairs and info boards for posters and printed material. The tent also served as a workshop space for local craftsmanship, youth engagement and protest organization.

PROJECT: CLUSTER 5

TOP-DOW
DESIGNIN
URBAN JU

N PUBLIC:
G
STICE

TOP-DOWN PUBLIC:
DESIGNING URBAN JUSTICE

Project cluster 5 presents our research on case studies of progressive urban governance in Latin American cities over the last decades, contrasting the decline of public institutions across the US and Europe over the last fifty years, where austerity, isolationism and unchecked privatization have eroded public thinking. We have been inspired by the cities of Medellín and Bogotá, Colombia, where the top-down public was transformed through inclusive and collaborative strategies of municipal governance, and targeted investment in social and civic priorities, including a massive mobilization of civic energy from the bottom-up. Here we elaborate two projects that we developed in dialogue and collaboration with former Colombian mayors Antanas Mockus (Bogotá) and Sergio Fajardo (Medellín), in which we visualized the civic and political processes that made two Colombian cities once defined by violence and conflict global examples of equitable urbanization and civic experimentation. We believe these cases contain the DNA for reconstructing a new civic imagination everywhere.

1   Learning from Bogotá: *The Cross-Border Citizenship Culture Survey*
2   Learning from Medellín: *The Medellín Diagram*

Over the last decades, as the attention and envy of the world was focused on sites of abundance, the most interesting cases of urban experimentation were emerging in sites of conflict and scarcity, particularly in Latin America. Challenging entrenched neoliberal urban logics of development based on top-down privatization, homogeneity and exclusion, visionary mayors in cities such as Porto Alegre, Curitiba, Bogotá and Medellín were activating new institutional protocols, new interfaces with publics and unorthodox cross-sector collaborations to rethink infrastructure, housing and density while mediating top-down municipal intervention and bottom-up social organization.

While inventive mayors and municipalities played a crucial role in stimulating a new public culture in many of these Latin American cases, it is the emergent civic practices of citizens that has carried and sustained this momentum over the last decades. Latin America is arguably the most vibrant scene of participatory urbanization in the world today, manifesting at unprecedented urban scales what David Harvey, following Henri Lefebvre, calls the "right to the city"[32]—or what James Tully calls "civic freedom."[33]

No other continental region in the world has produced so many living laboratories of civic imagination, led by municipalities in partnership with communities in pursuit of more equitable and sustainable ends. Latin American cities have produced dozens of experimental projects in recent years, marked not only by a *redistribution of resources* through massive investment in public infrastructure and social service, but also by a *redistribution of knowledges*, rethinking the role of the public in co-producing the city. Many of these stories of unorthodox urban transformation and experimentation are now legendary, from Porto Alegre's "participatory budgets" to Curitiba's urban acupuncture, Bogotá's citizenship culture interventions and Medellín's social urbanism. These well-known cases have democratized our urban imaginary, demonstrating that communities can participate in shaping the city of the future. They also demonstrate that municipalities can help to recover collective agency among citizens whose civic sensibilities have been squashed into acquiescence through centuries of imperialism and domination.

Latin America has taught us about local municipal and civic processes designed to produce more equitable forms of urbanization. These cities are committed to simultaneous cultural, institutional and spatial reform: partnering with neighborhood agencies to cultivate civic engagement among the marginalized, transforming municipal bureaucracy into a more efficient, transparent and accountable system, and advancing public works projects and educational infrastructure in the poorest, most violent and most neglected zones of the city.

Medellín and Bogotá have been particularly compelling for us—Bogotá for infiltrating civic dysfunction with performative gestures designed to change social norms and belief systems from the bottom-up, and Medellín for its collaborative model of governance and intervention as well as its spatialization of citizenship culture in public space. In the last decade, we have partnered with the central political actors in these remarkable urban stories—the former mayor of Bogotá, Antanas Mockus, and his research team at Corpovisionarios, and the former mayor of Medellín, Sergio Fajardo, and his director of urban projects, Alejandro Echeverri, who was responsible for many of the city's most important interventions. The catalyst for our own partnership, in fact, was our long connections with these Colombian cities. Translating and adapting their political and civic lessons has been essential to the evolution of our research and practice.[34]

Here we will introduce our research collaborations with both—with Mockus to produce a *Cross-Border Citizenship Culture Survey*, designed to identify and visualize a cross-border citizenship culture in the San Diego–Tijuana border region, and with Fajardo and Echeverri to produce the *Medellín Diagram*, a relational cartography of the political, civic and ultimately spatial processes that enabled dramatic, equitable transformation in that city.

Learning from Bogotá:
The Cross-Border Citizenship Culture Survey

CITIZENSHIP CULTURE

When philosopher Antanas Mockus became mayor of Bogotá, Colombia, in 1995, the city was in a free-fall of urban violence, poverty, infrastructural failure and choking air quality—the worst anywhere on the continent. People referred to Bogotá at that time as the most dangerous city on the planet. Rejecting the conventional law-and-order response to urban violence, Mockus came with very different ideas. He saw the city as a classroom, and became legendary for the distinctive ways he partnered with artists and cultural producers to intervene in the behavioral dysfunction of urban Bogotá to dramatically reduce violence and lawlessness, reconnect citizens with their government and with each other, conserve scare natural resources, and ultimately improve quality of life for the poor. From the start, he committed his administration to an idea of justice rooted in social equity and the redistribution of wealth. As he described his mandate: "Those who have come to the world at a disadvantage, those who live in extreme poverty and lack the means to have access to health services, or to adequate nutrition and education, have an inalienable right to a minimum standard of living. These minimum conditions must be sufficient for each to be able to begin building their own life as they imagine and desire it."[35]

But his strategies went beyond providing social service and public infrastructure from the top-down. While public provision was essential to reducing poverty and restoring human dignity in the urban periphery, Mockus argued that the production of a more just and equitable city must simultaneously engage public culture. Urban transformation, he believed, is as much about changing patterns of public trust and social cooperation as it is about changing urban policy, service provision and infrastructure. His provocation for urbanists is that before transforming the city physically, we must first transform social norms—intervene in the belief systems that perpetuate an acceptance of dramatic inequality, violence and corruption in the city. He targeted not only those with resources and power, but more essentially, the marginalized and the poor, who through decades of neglect had come to accept their condition as natural and resistant to structural change. Drawing on the emancipatory pedagogic theories of the Brazilian educator Paulo Freire, designed to reclaim the humanity of the colonized, Mockus believed that restoring urban dignity, a sense of possibility, a right to the neighborhood and a belief in collective agency are essential to a just and equitable urban agenda.[36]

Political leadership was a critical part of the story. Mockus emphatically declared the norms that should regulate social relations in the city: that human life is sacred, that radical inequality is unjust, that adequate education and health are human rights, that gender violence is unacceptable. He reoriented public policy to nurture a new "citizenship culture" in Bogotá, grounded in a shared commitment to human dignity: that all human beings, regardless of formal legal citizenship or race, deserve respect and basic quality of life. In other words, social norms that degraded human dignity needed to be changed, harmonized with moral norms that honored and respected human life. Meeting urban violence with stricter penalties will not work. Law-and-order solutions don't interiorize new values among the public. What Mockus's work demonstrates is that informal social norms can only be reoriented at the urban scale through top-down municipal intervention. As mayor of Bogotá, Mockus enacted a distinctive kind of egalitarian political leadership.

But Mockus also understood that new human rights norms could only take root and thrive in a participatory civic culture. As he put it, "The foundation here is the respect for life itself, as common ground. But this needs specific cultural strategies of intervention."[37] To achieve this, he designed an urban pedagogy of sometimes outrageous performative interventions to reorient social norms to harmonize with these moral norms, inspiring generations of civic actors, urbanists and artists across Latin America and the world to think more creatively about transforming urban norms and behavior.[38]

One of his very first acts in office was the distribution of "citizen cards" depicting a large thumb, which were designed to be used performatively to communicate approval or disapproval. Placards were distributed to the residents of Bogotá, who were encouraged to use them as they moved through the city. A pro-social act would earn a thumbs-up; an act that violated one's sense of civic decency, a thumbs-down. Through this performative gesture, people began to look at each other again and recognize the reciprocal impact of urban behavior—that one's behavior has an impact on others and vice versa. Without realizing it, they were deciding together the kind of city they wished to inhabit. From the bottom-up they began to construct a new "citizenship culture" based on the shared expectations they had of one another and their collective responsibilities to the city.

The impact on quality of life in Bogotá during Mockus's first administration was truly remarkable: murders were reduced by seventy percent, traffic fatalities by fifty percent, tax collection nearly doubled and water consumption decreased by forty percent, even as water and sewer services were extended to nearly all households. As civic bonds were re-established and life improved across the city, people began to recognize that a different sort of politics was taking place. Mockus restored public trust in Bogotá, inspired a new sense of urban pride and collective identity, and paved the way for Enrique Peñalosa's celebrated infrastructural interventions (Cyclovia, TransMilenio) during his succeeding term as mayor of Bogotá.

BINATIONAL CITIZENSHIP CULTURE

After Mockus left office, he established *Corpovisionarios*, an agency that consults municipalities across Colombia, Latin America and the world on how to build citizenship culture. Every intervention begins with a diagnostic survey, called the *Citizenship Culture Survey*, designed to evaluate public trust (understood vertically between publics and institutions) and civic capacity (understood as horizontal capacities for collective action) in a city. Corpovisionarios has applied their *Citizenship Culture Survey* in sixty cities across Colombia and dozens of cities across Latin America and Europe, typically multiple times in each site. It has also developed an impressive database of comparative urban research on issues ranging from legal culture, behavior regulation systems, mobility, tolerance, tax culture, public safety, sexual violence, civic participation, public trust and victimization.

In 2013, we invited Mockus and Corpovisionarios to San Diego–Tijuana to reflect on citizenship culture in the border region, and the moral claim that human beings, regardless of formal legal citizenship, regardless of race, have dignity and deserve equal respect and basic quality of life. Together, we decided design a special *Cross-Border Citizenship Culture Survey* for the binational region of San Diego and Tijuana. In early conversations with Mockus, he was eager to explore *cultura ciudadana* in a context like ours, where the designation "citizen" is frequently deployed as a divisive patriotic device, often wrapped in the flag of "us versus them," to separate and marginalize people, allegedly to protect Americans from the encroachment of the other. In Bogotá, citizenship was mobilized as a unifying cultural tool to integrate what had been fragmented by conflict, and to signify collective ends. Just after our cross-border survey was completed, Mockus shared his thoughts about the essential differences between US and Latin American conceptions of citizenship, drawing on actual survey results to illustrate his point: "Something that impressed me a lot is that defense of property as a justification for illegal behavior is much higher in San Diego than in the rest of Latin America.... I believe the concept of citizenship in the US is behind the times as compared to Latin America."[39]

Funded by the Ford Foundation, our *Cross-Border Citizenship Culture Survey* was an instrument to measure "cross-border citizenship culture" in the San Diego–Tijuana border region. Working with the municipalities of San Diego and Tijuana, as well as cross-sector stakeholders from both sides of the border, we spent nearly a year designing a survey that was responsive to the needs and challenges, resources and aspirations, of this distinctive binational region.

Our San Diego–Tijuana survey produced entirely new challenges for Corpovisionarios. They had always done single-city surveys with comparative aspirations, and had never done a survey of two border cities that are intimately intertwined across a militarized wall. The challenge in our case was to design a survey that would investigate the interpenetration and interdependence of these two cities, and identify the presence of a citizenship culture that transgressed formal national boundaries. Our claim had always been that the wall ultimately cannot disrupt the informal normative, social, economic and environmental flows that define the border region, and we were eager to document this. In collaboration with Corpovisionarios, we designed a special "binational" module to accompany the standard city-based survey they typically use when assessing citizenship culture in cities across Colombia and Latin American. The purpose of the binational module was to identify and document formal and informal interests and aspirations shared by residents of these two cities divided by a wall.

We also envisioned that a binational module of the survey might be adapted to other cities straddling the US-Mexico border, as well as other

SÃO PAULO SESCS 1946 CURITIBA 1974 PORTO ALEGRE 1989

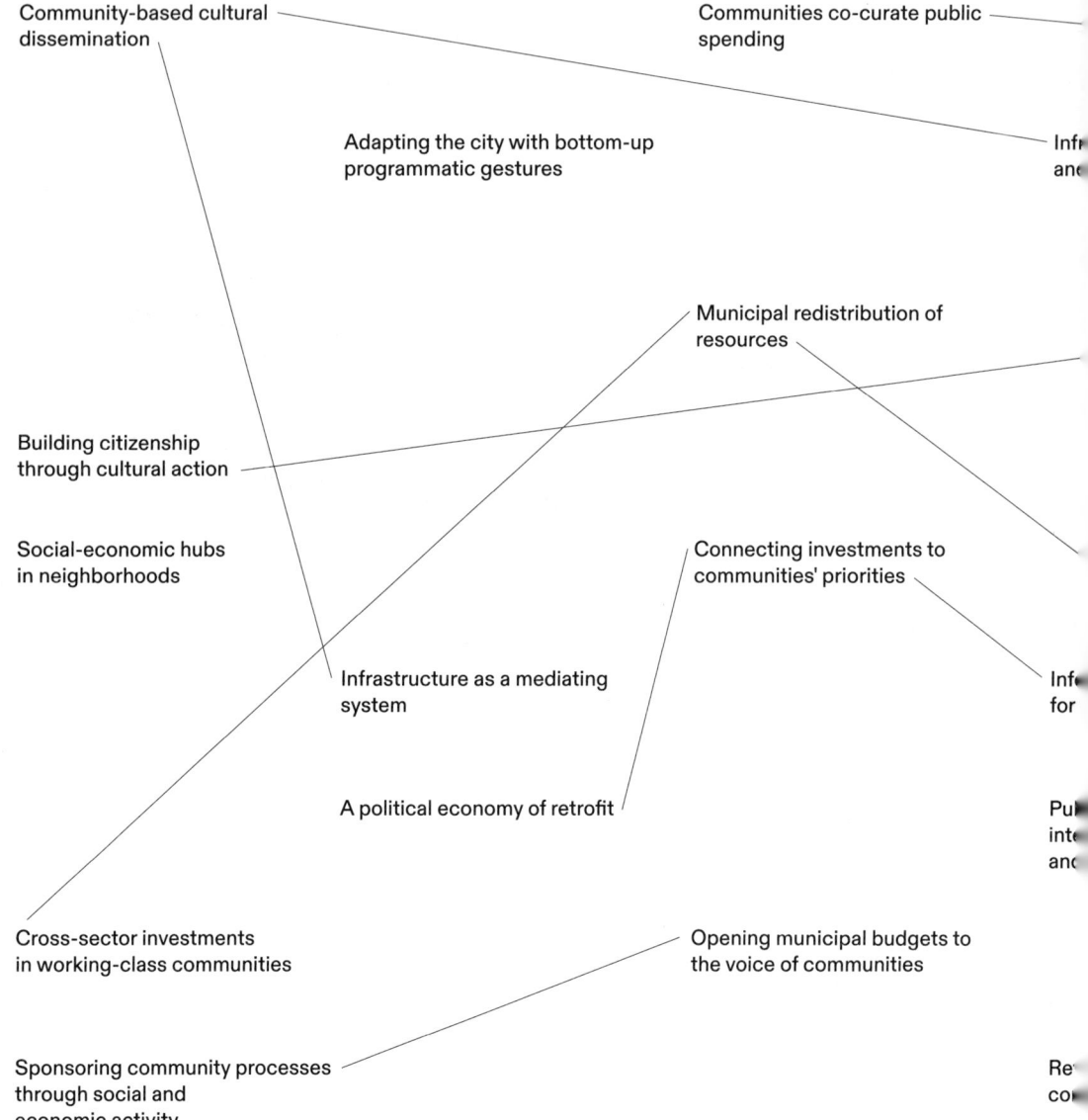

An acupunctural urbanization for public transport

Community-based cultural dissemination

Communities co-curate public spending

Adapting the city with bottom-up programmatic gestures

Infr
an

Municipal redistribution of resources

Building citizenship through cultural action

Social-economic hubs in neighborhoods

Connecting investments to communities' priorities

Infrastructure as a mediating system

Inf
for

A political economy of retrofit

Pu
int
an

Cross-sector investments in working-class communities

Opening municipal budgets to the voice of communities

Sponsoring community processes through social and economic activity

Re
co

WHO ARE THE INTERLOCUTORS OF INSTITUTIONAL MEMORY?
In the last decades, many Latin American cities challenged neoliberal austerity, privatization and exclusion by mobilizing public investment and cross-sector collaborations to tackle urban inequality head-on. Even though these urbanizations of social justice from Brazil to Colombia are widely recognized, much information remains missing about their processes of political and civic transformation.

| BARRIO 1995 | BOGOTÁ 1995–1997 | MEDELLÍN 2012–2016 |

| | "The need for mutual regulation and reciprocal expectations is a prerequisite for dialogue. In fact, I proposed that all citizens could participate in the transformation of their own behavior…" Antanas Mockus | "What transformed this city was not architectural or urban interventions; it was first a political project…" Sergio Fajardo |

Rebuilding reciprocity and trust by reattaching citizens to each other

Curating cross-institutional and cross-sector collaboration

…s for integration

Urban pedagogy as the generative tool for rethinking infrastructure

The municipality is transformed into an urban think-do tank

Before transforming the city physically, we must transform social norms

The validation of transparent public management

Constructing a citizenship culture is the prerequisite for a just city

The construction of a social-political and economic democracy

Art is a tool for community engagement and disrupting harmful behavior

Designing the rights to the city

…ements as laboratories …anization

"But here, art also meets pedagogy, their collaboration is required today to construct a new social contract…" Antanas Mockus

Tackling urban conflict by summoning a new civic conversation

…ructure at the …ween the formal

Democratizing infrastructures of mobility

The root of violence is inequality

"An advanced society is not where the poor have cars but where the rich ride public transport." Enrique Peñalosa

Public space educates

…roperty as a public

"The foundation here is the respect for life itself, as common ground. But even this needs specific cultural strategies of intervention, requiring the mobilization of strategic planning, cross-institutional coordination organized around specific objectives and performances, cemented in people's minds through public communication, consistency, transparency and trust…" Antanas Mockus

TOP-DOWN PUBLIC: DESIGNING URBAN JUSTICE

contested borders across the world, where everyday practices, social and economic exchanges, and spatial flows are invisible or undervalued. We have always maintained that identifying and visualizing these flows can provoke a more practical idea of coexistence and belonging in the ruptured civic spaces of border zones. Our aspiration was that our cross-border survey could help make the invisible visible, that in fact a regional citizenship culture was already latent in our practices, but unrecognized in our deeply entrenched culture of mutual neglect, physicalized by the metal wall and surveillance infrastructure that separates us.

The ultimate aim of the survey was to stimulate a new era of public self-knowledge and cross-border civic collaboration. Over the decades, mayors in San Diego and Tijuana had signed agreements, promising to collaborate on shared concerns such as environment, economy and regional resilience. But these agreements were always largely symbolic, lacking specificity, springs of action and meaningful public buy-in. They also always glossed the dramatic inequalities that characterize the border region, aspiring to "regional economic development" without inserting ideas about equity anywhere in this formulation.

In February 2015, Henry Murraín, Executive Director of Corpovisionarios, stood before a room of fifty diverse San Diego bureaucrats, business leaders, community activists, academics, artists and civic philanthropists, who had convened in the conference room of a local foundation to witness the results of the survey.[40] A similar configuration that included Tijuana's mayor, Jorge Astiazaran, had convened in Tijuana the day before. The city-based surveys contained much information that reinforced what most of us already knew or suspected about ourselves: people in San Diego tend to drive cars; people in Tijuana tend to mistrust public officials; people in San Diego tend to keep to themselves; people in Tijuana have a more participatory civic culture. The city-based surveys presented a reality that was familiar to us—though there were some outliers, such as Tijuana's disturbing cultural acceptance of domestic violence and homophobia (both were more severe than any other Latin American city studied by Corpovisionarios). We were also intrigued that people in Tijuana are far more receptive to law and behavioral regulation than people in San Diego, and particularly when it comes to protection of private property—a finding that surely reflects the liberal biases of American political culture.

In the binational module, however, we learned very new things about our region, results that had potential to change the way these cities saw each other, their identity as participants in a larger urban region with common interests and values, and their aspirations for a shared future. People in San Diego, it turned out, overwhelmingly trusted Mexicans and respected residents of Tijuana, far more than we had expected—far more than people in Tijuana trusted and respected citizens of the US and of San Diego, and sadly far more than people in Tijuana even seemed to trust and respect themselves—possibly a function of marginalization, pervasive corruption and economic insecurity. There is much to say about Tijuana's challenges and the city-based results of Tijuana, which demonstrated low levels of citizenship culture, not uncommon in a great majority of the Latin American cities surveyed by Corpovisionarios.

But the San Diego results were surprising to all. This finding of trust for people in Mexico and Tijuana undercut deep assumptions about racial and socioeconomic biases on the San Diego side, reinforced by immigration politics and the intensification of drug violence in the past decades. It revealed an arguably more tolerant and egalitarian sensibility in San Diego, and more readiness to collaborate than we would have expected. This readiness was confirmed by perhaps the most exciting result of all: that roughly sixty to seventy percent of respondents in San Diego believed that the cities had an interest, and should be collaborating, on issues ranging from border wait times and immigration to public health and environment. A final intriguing result was that respondents in both cities demonstrated a desire for collaboration on issues of mutual interest, but indicated a lack of trust in conventional institutions to facilitate it. Both sides placed more faith in civil society to make progress on these issues.

The *Cross-Border Citizenship Culture Survey* confirmed what we already suspected: that we are united in this divided region by a "cross-border citizenship culture," an idea of belonging that is guided not by the nation-state or identitarian politics, but by shared values, social norms, common interests and aspirations. These findings became a mirror for the region, and an important resource for our practice, a "script" for future civic and architectural interventions. The UCSD Community Stations initiative that we will explore in the next project cluster (see project cluster 6) was inspired directly by our partnership with Antanas Mockus and the results of the *Cross-Border Citizenship Culture Survey*.

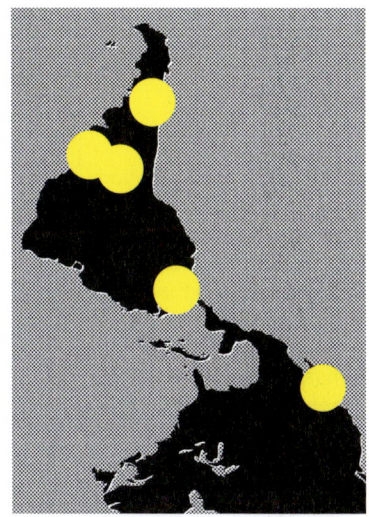

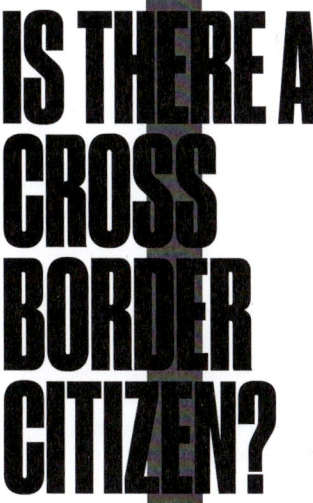

THE CROSS-BORDER CITIZEN
Posters developed for the exhibition *Visualizing Citizenship* at the Yerba Buena Center for the Arts in San Francisco, 2017. They tell the story of Bogotá, Colombia, the unconventional mayoral administration of Antanas Mockus, and our collaboration on the *Binational Citizenship Culture Survey* at the San Diego–Tijuana border.

Learning from Medellín: *The Medellín Diagram*

> What transformed this city was not architectural or urban interventions; it was first a political project...
> —Sergio Fajardo

Medellín, Colombia, is arguably the most comprehensive case study of Latin American civic experimentation over the last decades. Medellín was once widely regarded the world's most violent city—home of cocaine kingpin Pablo Escobar, a battleground of drug lords, paramilitaries and left-wing guerillas, with murder rates as high as 6,300 in 1991 alone (a staggering 380 per 100,000 people) and a site of severe unemployment and poverty.[41] Imagine Medellín's topography: bowl-shaped, with the urban center at the bottom and informal *comunas* sprawling into the peripheral hillsides, typically so steep that they were once effectively cut off from the urban center, marginalizing their inhabitants geographically, socially and economically. The isolated terrain of informal urban density was an ideal setting for the cartels to operate, enlist their armies and maintain their own ruthless mix of patronage and social order. Through the late eighties and early nineties, Medellín's homicide rate was the highest in the world. After Escobar was killed in 1993, his Medellín Cartel quickly lost power. But the city was left in chaotic disarray, with neither the order nor resources that the cartels had provided.

Fast-forward two decades: the city became a site of urban transformation so compelling that it captured the attention of urbanists, architects and planners across the world. Medellín's determination to reduce violence and poverty and improve public health and education was activated through strategies of collaborative municipal governance and planning, a campaign to cultivate a vibrant, participatory civic culture, and the coordination of massive cross-sector investments in public infrastructure and social services in the poorest and most violent *comunas* in the city. Here again, political leadership was essential. When mathematician Sergio Fajardo became mayor in 2005, he declared: "We will not build down here (in the wealthy center), but up there (in the periphery, where the necessities are)."[42] Public infrastructure was the physical manifestation of civic commitment to a just city, spatializing Antanas Mockus's idea of citizenship culture and Freire's critical pedagogy. Fajardo committed to transforming Medellín into "the most educated" city in Colombia, insisting that social justice depended not only on the redistribution of resources but also on the redistribution of knowledge. Medellín is a story of civic freedom, remarkable not only for its dramatic public architecture, but more fundamentally for its collaborative municipal processes and the emergent participatory civic culture that it enabled.

Even though much has been written about important civic experiments throughout Latin America, and many have come to see Medellín as emblematic, most descriptions of Medellín focus on the physical interventions themselves—the buildings, the innovative transport systems.[43] It makes some sense, since the infrastructure, buildings and public art are beautiful, designed by world-class architects and artists. But too often, admirers disregard the political and civic processes that enabled rapid urban transformation on such a massive scale. Note, for example, this account of Medellín's successes in 2012 as the Urban Land Institute awarded Medellín its "Innovative City of the Year" prize:

> Originally distinguished for its progress and potential, the winning city found new solutions to classic problems of mobility and environmental sustainability. Today, gondolas and a giant escalator shuttle citizens from steep mountainside homes to jobs and schools in the valley below. As a result, travel time for the majority of its citizens has been cut from more than two hours to just a few minutes. In this city, a modern underground metro system has eased pollution and crowding in the city's main arteries above, and glistening new museums, cultural centers, libraries and schools enrich the community. ... Connections create innovation, and it is no wonder that our winning City of the Year has achieved great success in bringing its residents together to assure opportunities for all.[44]

But how did governance transform to enable these massive public interventions? What was the role of Medellín's citizens? Were they merely passive recipients of municipal investment, liberated from isolation to commute to work and consume like good cosmopolitans? Was it really the infrastructure that restored hope and agency amidst intransigent conflict and deprivation, or does this get the story backward? What were the transactions, exchanges and negotiations that took place

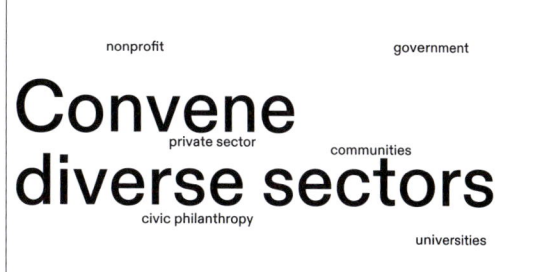
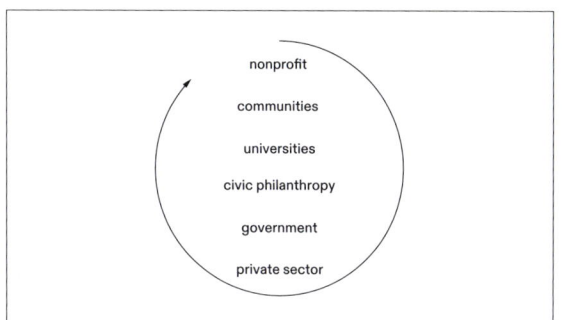
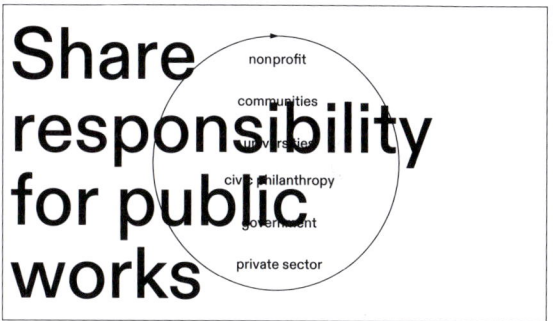
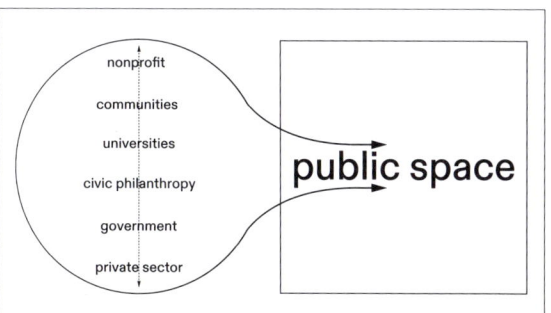
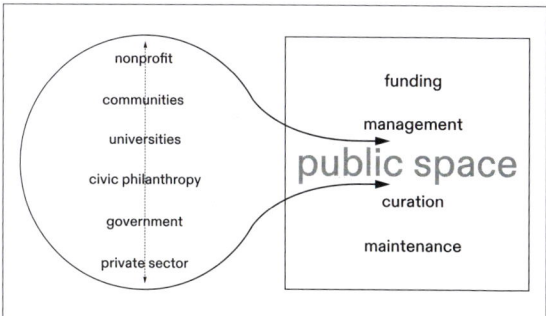
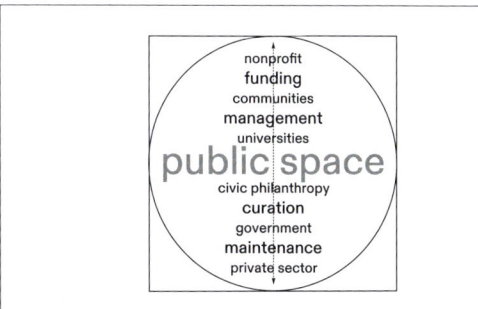

THE MEDELLÍN DIAGRAM
Video scenes from the Medellín Diagram, prepared for the exhibition *Diagrams of Power* at the Ontario College Museum of Art, Toronto, Canada, 2018.

across institutions and communities that enabled the projects to materialize and succeed?

Medellín's transformation was grounded in socioeconomic and political paradigms that challenged dominant conceptions of public and private. While the public welfare state paradigm was losing ground worldwide to neoliberal growth, Medellín committed itself to a very different public imaginary to reinvigorate civic culture and commonwealth from the bottom-up. The ULI award (underwritten by Citibank and *The Wall Street Journal*) sees only the linkages between infrastructural investment and economic progress, articulated in a smooth neoliberal narrative about innovation that masks Medellín's civic resistance to the dominant top-down paradigms and patterns of twentieth-century urbanization across the world.

THE MEDELLÍN DIAGRAM: VISUALIZING POLITICAL AND CIVIC PROCESS

Medellín is remarkable not only for its public architecture and infrastructure, but for the egalitarian vision that grounds them and the innovative political and civic processes that enabled them. To appreciate how Medellín might become a political and civic model to be translated and adapted to other contexts, it is essential to understand just *how* the city managed to reorient resources on such a massive scale toward sites of greatest need. What must a city do? What must political leadership entail? How does government need to transform? What kinds of institutional intersections are necessary? How can these interventions be funded? What is the role of the bottom-up in enabling these interventions to succeed and be sustained over time? These are the processes we wanted to pursue and translate, so that Medellín might become intelligible, not only as a set of buildings, structures and spaces—but primarily as an imaginative set of political and civic processes.

In 2011 we joined forces with Fajardo and Alejandro Echeverri (former Director of Urban Projects of Medellín, responsible for many of the city's most iconic urban interventions) on a multi-year research project to visualize the political and civic processes that enabled Medellín's rapid transformation. We wanted to design a diagram useful to the citizens of Medellín as an archive of institutional memory to guide future interventions, and to municipalities elsewhere eager to emulate Medellín's achievements. Ultimately, it is not by emulating buildings and transport systems that cities across the globe can approximate the inclusive urbanization that transformed Medellín, Colombia, over the last two decades. The key is to understand *process*. We began by conducting interviews with dozens of local political and civic actors, since what happened there was a complex process of negotiation and collaboration across institutions and publics. We interviewed the mayors and their staff, the business leaders and urban designers, the civic leaders and academic researchers, the grassroots organizers and the cultural producers. We translated and stitched together stories and anecdotes, identified connections and mapped the way ideas and actions evolved across time to visualize their complexity. What emerged was *The Medellín Diagram*, designed in partnership with graphic designer Matthias Görlich.

The Medellín process, as we present it in the Diagram, is comprised of three broad elements, each essential to the emergence of a new citizenship culture in which the inhabitants of Medellín found their collective voice and asserted their rights to the city:

Positions
1. Constructing the Political: Medellín confronted urban inequality

Processes
2. Designing Governance: Medellín committed to collaborative public management

Interventions
3. Spatializing Citizenship: Medellín built performative infrastructures of inclusion

1. CONSTRUCTING THE POLITICAL

Fajardo reminds us that the Medellín model did not begin as an architectural initiative to beautify the city with world-class design. It was primarily a political project, driven by a radical repositioning on urban violence: that violence was rooted in systemic inequality. When Fajardo took office as Mayor of Medellín in 2003, he declared a distinctively "political moment" and committed the municipality to a new era of "social urbanism."

For Fajardo, the foundational act of urban transformation was "taking a position" against entrenched social and economic inequalities that had prompted decades of alienation, vulnerability, fragmentation and violence across the city. "Taking a position" and following through meant reframing entirely the role of municipal governance and its response to urban violence. Like Mockus, Fajardo rejected police repression and committed instead to cultivating civic dignity and collective agency, and helping to reconnect the public with the future of the city. He believed that public space, and massive investment in public works, would play an essential role in this fundamentally political and cultural agenda of restoring a sense of collective destiny in Medellín.

Fajardo began symbolically with the *comuna* of Santo Domingo, which was the stronghold of Escobar's Medellín Cartel, and the most violent and isolated neighborhood in the city. Fajardo's directive was clear: "We will not build down here, but we will build up there." This "shifting of the gaze" from the center to periphery was a political act, a paradigm shift, moving the priorities of urban development from the predictable zones of investment to the most marginalized and traditionally underserved zones. Fajardo's coordination of massive cross-sector investment in the city's poorest and most violent neighborhoods is arguably the finest example of equitable urbanization in the world of urban planning.

While increased municipal investment in public works was essential to Medellín's process, these interventions must be understood within a long civic tradition of progressive cross-institutional collaboration. Industrialists like Ricardo Olano in the 1920s, for example, were among the first to propose planning education in the city's universities; they established entities like the *Sociedad de Mejoras Publicas de Medellín* (Medellín Public Works), which linked natural systems with social spaces and cultural institutions. During the same period, painter, sculptor and civil engineer Pedro Nel, director and professor of the *Academia de Bellas Artes de Medellín*, produced fantastic political murals, along with plans for modernizing Medellín that included creative interfaces between civil society and government.

While Medellín's vibrancy was notoriously interrupted by years of drug violence, threads of civic consciousness wove through that tragic period, focused primarily on resolving armed struggle and a transition to social reform. The work of *Corporación Región* is exemplary in mediating conflict and stewarding transition toward a pluralistic, rights-bearing sociopolitical and economic democracy. Their exemplary methods of civic engagement paved the way for progressive policies produced by mayors committed to a post-violence civic era, which reached its apex with Fajardo's administration. The Medellín model demonstrates the importance of resuscitating civic lineages embedded in a city's institutional memory to support civic projects.

2. DESIGNING GOVERNANCE

Medellín designed a new model of city management, rejecting opaque, labyrinthine bureaucracy in favor of flexible, agile and inclusive governance and transversal relations across city departments, across sectors and between top-down institutions and bottom-up community dynamics. Fajardo's mayoral office became an urban laboratory where intelligent, experimental modes of urban intervention were conceived and enacted. This process began with the consolidation of fragmented policies and agendas, summoning divided constituencies and institutions, and integrating the knowledge and resources of government, universities, civic philanthropy and communities in a shared commitment to implementation. It was a strategy of simultaneous centralization and decentralization, a new model of management that strategically integrated diverse knowledge and resources only to redistribute them more intelligently towards sites of marginalization.

The municipality became an urban think-and-do tank, summoning university researchers, design professionals, urban activists and cultural producers to reimagine the future of the city. Fajardo activated architect and urban designer Alejandro Echeverri, our partner in the *Medellín Diagram* project, as the "urban curator" who could facilitate these exchanges of knowledge. The municipality became the place where new political and civic processes could be aligned with urban design criteria and financial frameworks to execute projects —simultaneously engaging the scales of territory and neighborhoods, the abstraction of large planning logics with the specificity of everyday practices in communities.

Bringing design innovation into municipal thinking to create new urban processes, criteria and demonstration projects also brought with it an expanded role for urban design. The mayor's office became an engine of creativity that shaped a community-based urban vision, transforming informal settlements into laboratories of local governance and socioeconomic development, forging new corridors of knowledge exchange between government and communities, mediated through partnership with locally rooted organizations, and ultimately reimagining public space and infrastructure, mobility, neighborhood-based planning and regional socioeconomic development.

Redesigning governance also entailed redirecting economic flows. People naturally inquire how Medellín was able to pay for such comprehensive urban interventions. *Empresas Publicas de Medellín*, EPM (Medellín Public Works) remains an essential economic engine for these achievements.

This municipal agency owns telecommunications, water and energy services, and directs forty percent of dividends directly back into public infrastructure. In the United States, this would amount to "socialism." In Medellín, and Latin America at large, EPM is considered an exemplary public agency with private organizational logics in terms of transparency, efficiency and the capacity to redirect surplus value for socially responsible urban development. Ultimately, Medellín's successes represent a radical departure from top-down models of urban development endorsed by autocratic governments in China and the United Arab Emirates, and from the urbanisms of gentrification through which private developers everywhere have homogenized cities under the banner of "democratizing happiness."

3. SPATIALIZING CITIZENSHIP

The cultivation of a new civic sensibility and the design of new modes of governance and management were followed by a commitment to excellence in public architectural and infrastructural design. But Fajardo challenged conventional public design imperatives when he asked: Can public space educate? The former professor of mathematics insisted that education was the key to a better future, and that every investment in infrastructure should further this mandate: "Medellín, the most educated."

The famous *Library Parks* project challenged conventional ideas of public space as neutral amenities and committed to a deliberate, curated democratization of space. Beautifying a space or plaza with foliage and murals will not magically assure civic engagement and inclusion. Fajardo insisted that that social justice rests not only on the redistribution of resources but also on the distribution of knowledges; each park and public space was curated with pedagogical systems to support diverse and historically underserved publics and communities, animated by education, arts and cultural programming, and vocational training, designed to cultivate pride and collective agency. Public spaces were designed in tandem with civic programming and the cross-sector management structures necessary to assure sustainability over time. The ultimate legacy of the Medellín model is that public spaces need to be curated and nurtured by a collective imagination where buildings and protocols meet to perform citizenship.

Moreover, Medellín's urban interventions engaged the complexity of the *existing real*. They were critically positioned to expose and penetrate entrenched urban borders. For example, while observers admire Alejandro Echeverri's *Parque Explora* and Camilo Restrepo's *Jardín Botánico de Medellín* as discrete pieces of architecture, they need to be understood as a relational urban system that performs as an urban thread, stitching together the marginalized community of Moravia with cultural institutions, public spaces and other support systems. The *Jardín Botánico de Medellín* is an extension of *Parque Explora*, which is situated in the margins of the city between the wealthy older subdivisions and the precarious Moravia neighborhood, a previously informal settlement with a strong tradition of activism. The ensemble of architectural and programmatic interventions moves from the large to the small as it threads through the neighborhood. The system begins with *Parque Explora,* which connects directly with the metro system at the border between these urban zones, continues with the *Jardín Botánico,* connects with *Moravia Cultural Center* and its more localized cultural programming and ends deeper in the social fabric with *Casa Amarilla,* a smaller cultural venue whose arts and culture programming is co-curated by the local community. Public infrastructure becomes a mediating system for socioeconomic inclusion, between objects and fields, large and small buildings, where the interface between things is what matters, and not the autonomy of stand-alone buildings. Moreover, each of these cultural spaces is charged with specific programming that assures longevity and accessibility, supported by cross-sector public-private coalitions.

While these successes make Medellín a unique model of urbanization in the world, it would be inaccurate to declare Medellín's crises "over" or "resolved." In fact, citizens regularly voice irritation when confronted with superficial, rosy accounts of their city's "successes" amidst undeniable urban problems today. News stories and global prizes celebrating Medellín's miraculous transformation are typically met with skepticism, as locals point to persistent poverty, unemployment, drugs and street crime—noting as well that Antioquia remains the most inequitable region in all of Colombia. Medellín is a living, breathing urban experiment in civic freedom that sometimes experiences frustrating lapses in its transformational momentum. Nevertheless, while Medellín remains a work in progress, as so many Latin American cities are, experiencing setbacks, often struggling to stay on course, the eighty-percent decrease in homicide and dramatic rise in all major public health indicators in recent decades is impressive by any standard. What makes Medellín ultimately important from the perspective of participatory democracy and social justice is that the there are few urban projects in the world of this scale where a municipality made a deliberate choice to confront inequality and urban conflict, not by mobilizing law and order but

TOP-DOWN PUBLIC: DESIGNING URBAN JUSTICE

with massive investments in civic culture and public works in the most marginalized zones of the city. Medellín reimagined public space and infrastructure as mediating systems for socioeconomic inclusion, connecting top-down municipal interventions with bottom-up civic participation.

Bogotá and Medellín are part of a long experimental lineage of "social urbanism" across the continent, led by mayors who committed their administrations to reducing poverty, cultivating civic participation and stewarding cross-sector investment in public well-being. In both cases, these municipalities became think tanks, problem-solving laboratories facilitated by urban curators who mediated convergences between academics, the private sector, grassroots organizations and cultural producers to transform urban norms, design new strategies and spaces for civic engagement, and new processes for public management. Both Bogotá and Medellín invested massively in public infrastructure and transportation projects to shrink distance and stimulate movement and flow. Both cities concentrated investment in their most marginalized zones, building schools, library parks infused with cultural amenities and social services, and extending water and sewerage services to nearly all residents. But fundamental to all of this was cultivating new bonds of public trust, new corridors for cross-sector collaboration, and a sense of urban dignity and collective ownership of the city. These are the Latin American lessons that we wanted to carry back to our own distinctive context at the San Diego–Tijuana border.

As we write today, in the long tail of the COVID-19 pandemic, we are witnessing a distinctive spiraling back across Colombia to an era of polarization. We are reminded how ephemeral urban transformation can be, and how susceptible cities are to geopolitical forces and political transition. As history unfolds, our greatest hope is that Colombia can learn from its own past and recuperate the institutional memory of Bogotá and Medellín that so inspired the world.

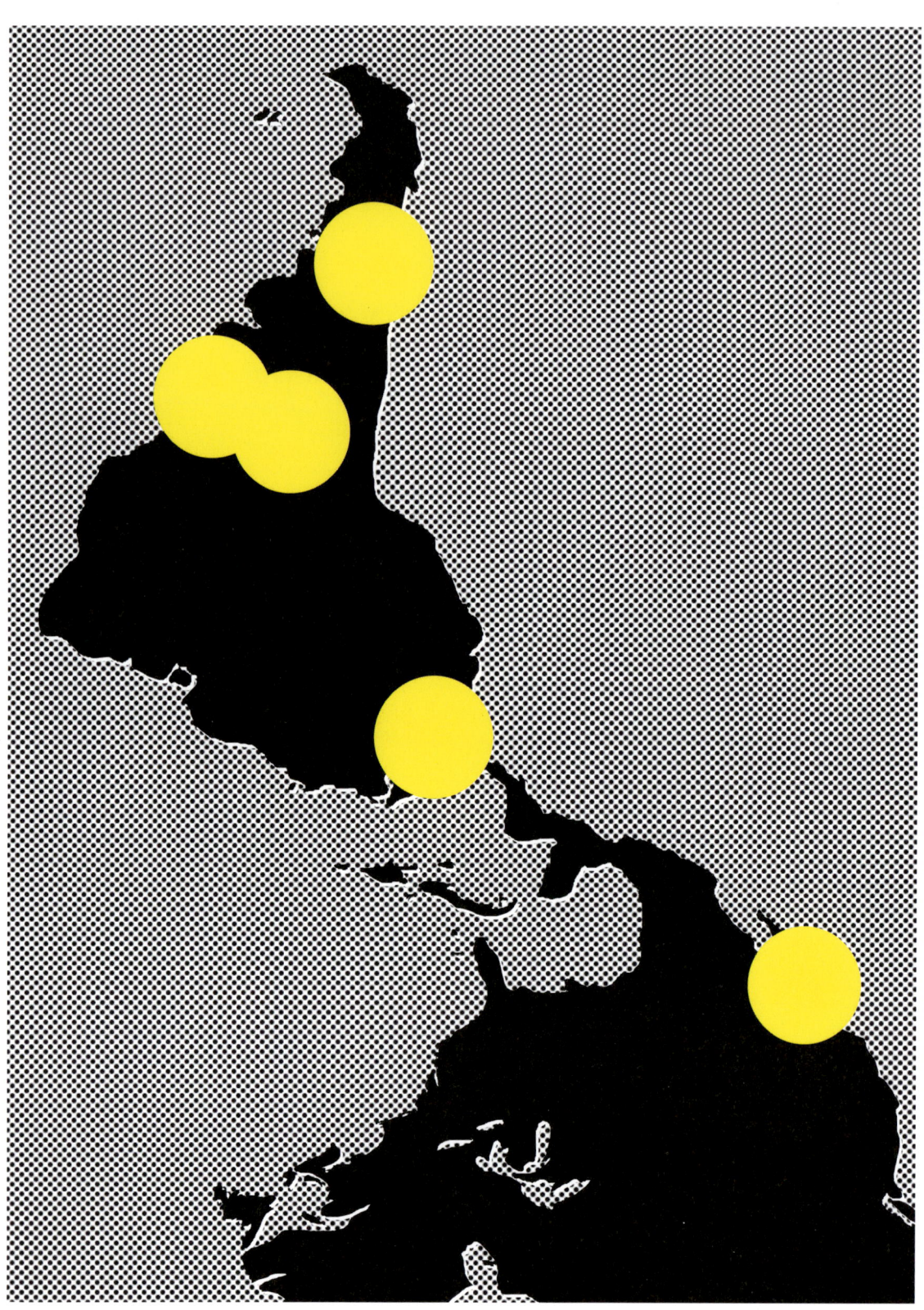

LEARNING FROM LATIN AMERICA
In our search for alternative ideas of citizenship, we have been inspired by Latin American cities that have transformed themselves over the last decades through a renewed commitment to collective life, civic participation and public investment.

THE PHILOSOPHER MAYOR
In the 1990s, Bogotá, Colombia, was described as "the planet's most dangerous city." When Antanas Mockus became mayor, instead of coming with guns and tanks, he proposed to change the hearts and minds of citizens: that human life is sacred, that radical inequality is unjust, that gender violence is intolerable, that education and health are inalienable human rights, and that paying ones taxes and conserving natural resources are duties of citizenship.

PERFORMING VULNERABILITY
In one of Antanas's first public appearances as mayor, he emerged wearing a bullet-proof vest with a hole in the shape of a heart. It was a radical gesture of vulnerability, trust and commitment to his community.

THE *PERINOLA*: CHOOSING MORAL ACTION
Play was always an essential tool for Mockus. With the spin of a *perinola*, he demonstrated to the citizens of Bogotá that human beings are not always motivated by selfishness, but are frequently motivated by social and collective aspirations. The art of governance, he said, is to cultivate the social dimension of human choice-making.

THE THUMBS: PERFORMING CITIZENSHIP CULTURE
Mockus distributed placards across the city with the image of a thumb that could be displayed either up or down. Citizens were encouraged to use the thumb as they moved through the city to communicate approval and disapproval toward one another. A thumbs-up to acts of civility and urban dignity; and a thumbs-down to behavior that violated civil coexistence. Through mutual recognition and responsibility, people performed the kind of city they wished to inhabit.

THE MIMES: SOCIAL ACCOUNTABILITY
Mockus replaced Bogotá's corrupt municipal traffic police with a troupe of mimes, who stood on street corners of downtown Bogotá and shamed drivers and pedestrians for traffic violations. With bells and whistles, and comedic play, the mimes disrupted a dangerous urban norm of ignoring traffic signage. While critics thought the intervention was silly, the proof was in its impact: traffic fatalities in Bogotá decreased by 50% during Mockus's first term.

VISUALIZING THE PROBLEM
Mockus launched a water conservation campaign by pouring gallons of drinking water into a toilet to demonstrate the water wasted with every flush. To advance water conservation, he believed we need to see the problem. This campaign also mobilized 4,000 children and youth into a group called Aqua-Civics.

SUPER CITIZEN
As mayor, Mockus created a *super citizen* persona who would appear suddenly in different parts of the city, to provoke questions: Was he the mayor or a citizen? Does cultural change begin at the top or the bottom?

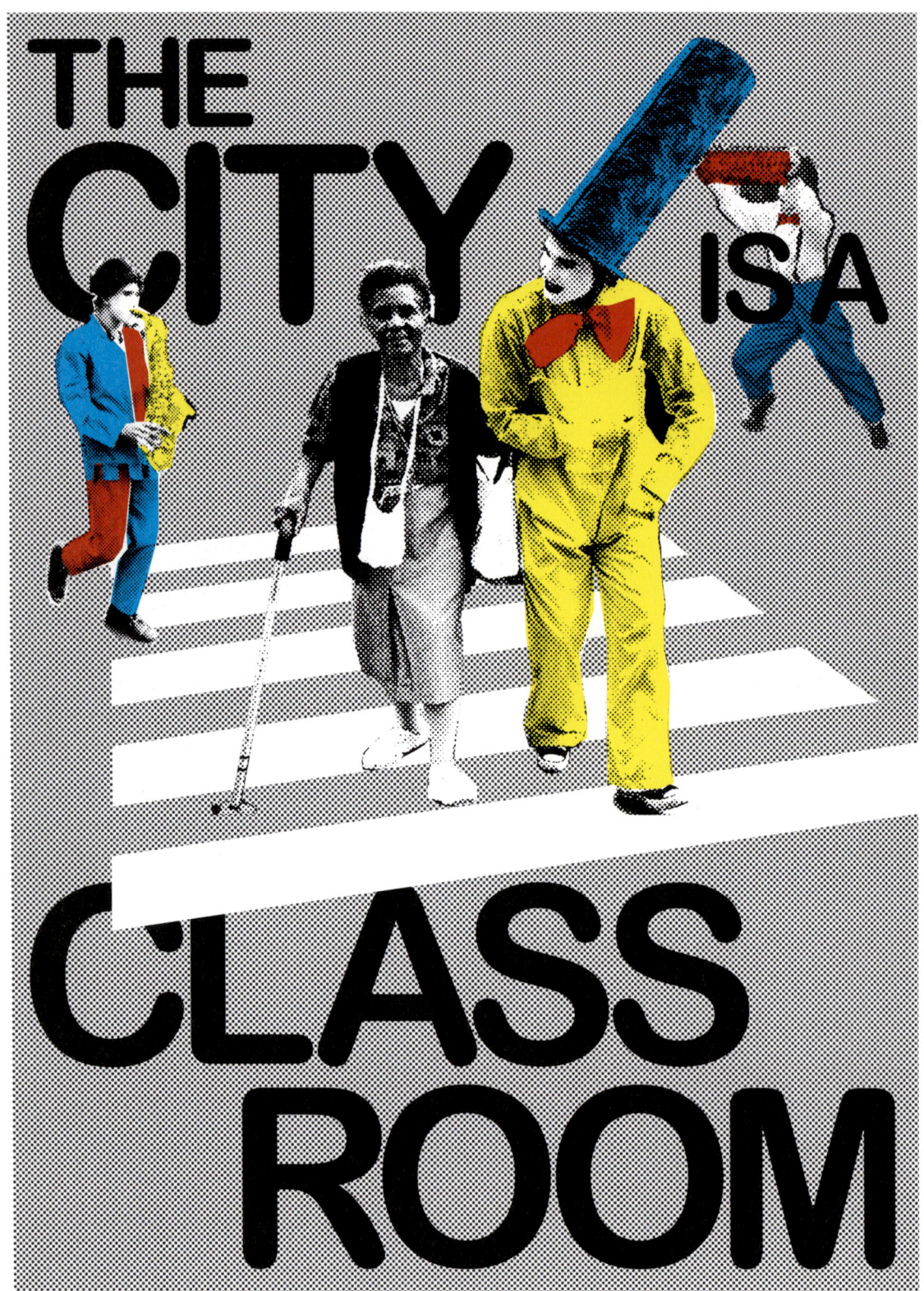

THE CITY AS CLASSROOM

"As mayor I assumed a fascinating pedagogical task: learning and teaching in a community of seven million people. I decided to confront the culture of the city, its languages, perceptions, customs, clichés and especially people's excuses." —Antanas Mockus.

CIVIC LESSONS:

-  **Before transforming the city physically, transform social norms**

-  **Better to fight violence with community process than with "law & order"**

-  **Arts and culture are engines of civic engagement**

LESSONS LEARNED
Mockus inspired generations of civic actors, urbanists and artists across Latin America and the world to think more creatively about transforming urban norms and building citizenship though cultural action.

THE CITIZENSHIP CULTURE SURVEY

Mockus established Corpovisionarios to consult municipalities on citizenship culture. Every urban intervention begins with a *Citizenship Culture Survey* (CCS), a sophisticated social science instrument designed to measure public trust and civic coordination in a city. Corpovisionarios has applied its CCS in 55+ cities across Latin America and beyond. The survey is a mirror of urban self-knowledge, and becomes a script for action, identifying zones of vulnerability and opportunity in public policy.

CITIZENSHIP CULTURE AT THE BORDER?
In 2015 we brought Mockus to San Diego–Tijuana, to help us explore the notion of a "cross-border citizen." In Bogotá, citizenship had been deployed as a cultural device to integrate what conflict had divided. Mockus was eager to think about citizenship culture across two cities fragmented by an international border wall—a place where citizenship denotes division, separation between "us" and "them."

CROSS-BORDER CITIZENSHIP CULTURE SURVEY
We spent a year working with Mockus to design a *Cross-Border Citizenship Culture Survey* to identify the presence of a citizenship culture across the border region—an idea of citizenship organized around the shared values and common interests of divided communities. Corpovisionarios had never done a survey of two border cities.

IS THERE A CROSS-BORDER CITIZEN?

A CATALYST FOR CROSS-BORDER COLLABORATION
The survey was designed to instigate a cross-border, cross-institutional civic dialogue, summoning sectors seldom in conversation with one another. How do we disrupt the mythologies of public opinion perpetuated by xenophobic fears of the "other"? How do we facilitate a new conversation between institutions of power and diverse communities on both sides of the border?

SURVEY IS A MIRROR: CURATING DIALOGUE
During the design and execution of the survey, we convened the mayors of San Diego and Tijuana, as well as government agencies, cultural institutions, foundations, the private sector, university researchers, community-based and civic organizations across issues of public health, environment, immigration, and arts and culture. The survey became a mirror of regional self-knowledge, enabling participants to recognize their interdependence. The results were unveiled in 2015 to publics in San Diego and Tijuana.

1 PERCEPTIONS OF TRUSTWORTHINESS

7 out of 10 San Diegans feel that people from Mexico can be trusted. Tijuana residents are more distrustful in general but a near majority say that San Diegans can be trusted.

2 PERCEPTIONS OF COMMONALITY

A majority of respondents in both cities felt that San Diego and Tijuana have some or a great deal in common

3 DESIRE FOR COOPERATION

Perceptions of commonality increased desire for collaboration among a majority of respondents in both cities. Conclusion: increasing cross-border understanding of shared interests is essential.

4 HOPE IN GRASS-ROOTS ORGANIZATIONS

In both cities there is significant lack of trust in civic institutions and governments at all scales. Conclusion: underlying mistrust of government opens an important space for non-governmental organizations to steward cross-border initiatives.

DIVIDED CITIES / SHARED FUTURE
The survey revealed a cross-border public, communities willing to collaborate, ready to reimagine a shared destiny, and receptive to new civic mechanisms for activating it.

TRUST
In general, can people from the neighboring country be trusted?

EXPECTATIONS
Thinking about the situation of the city, what comes closer to your mind?

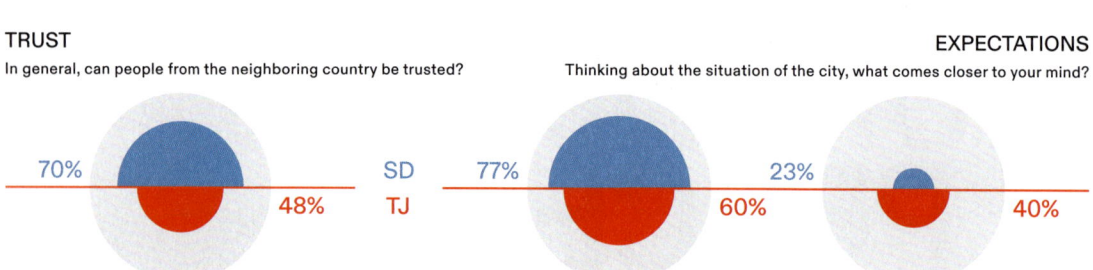

70% SD   77%   23%
  48% TJ   60%   40%

         Things will get better   Things will get worse

PARTICIPATION
In the past year, have you participated in any of the following activities?

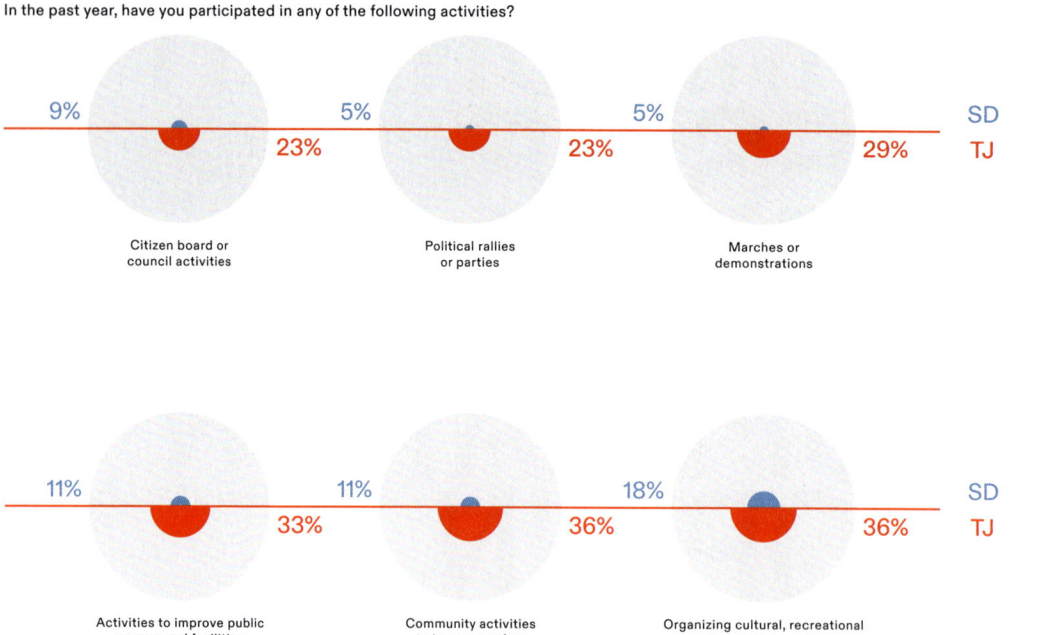

9%   5%   5%   SD
  23%   23%   29%   TJ

Citizen board or   Political rallies   Marches or
council activities   or parties   demonstrations

11%   11%   18%   SD
  33%   36%   36%   TJ

Activities to improve public   Community activities   Organizing cultural, recreational
spaces and facilities   to increase safety   or sporting events

A GENERATIVE SCRIPT FOR URBAN INTERVENTION BEYOND WALLS

The survey became evidence to challenge hateful, racist claims that would unfold in the following years. The period 2016–2020 escalated a politics of fear that transformed the border into an epicenter of American nativism and nationalism. The survey results remained a curatorial script to organize priorities and shape our cross-border projects and initiatives to tackle institutional violence against the "other."

JUSTIFICATIONS FOR DISOBEYING THE LAW
To defend property or belongings

OBSTACLES
Major obstacles that require Tijuana and San Diego to work together

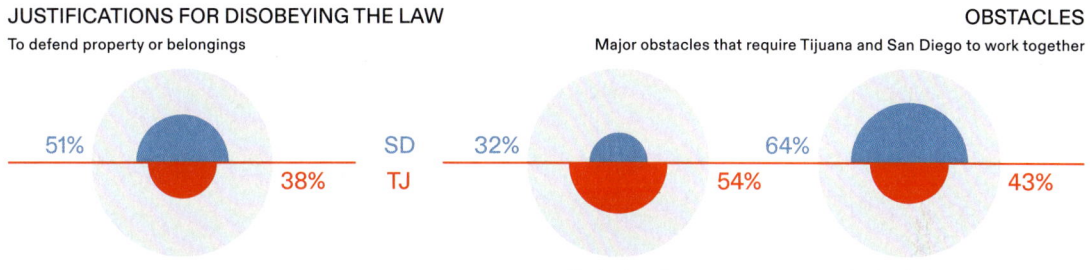

51% SD
38% TJ

32% / 54% — The border wall
64% / 43% — Immigration issues

COOPERATION
Importance of the following issues of cooperation between San Diego and Tijuana

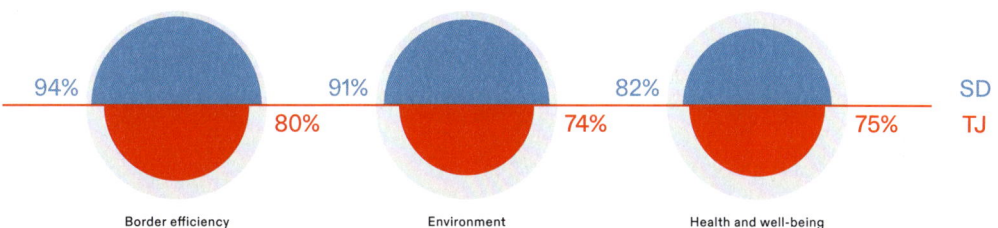

94% / 80% — Border efficiency
91% / 74% — Environment
82% / 75% — Health and well-being

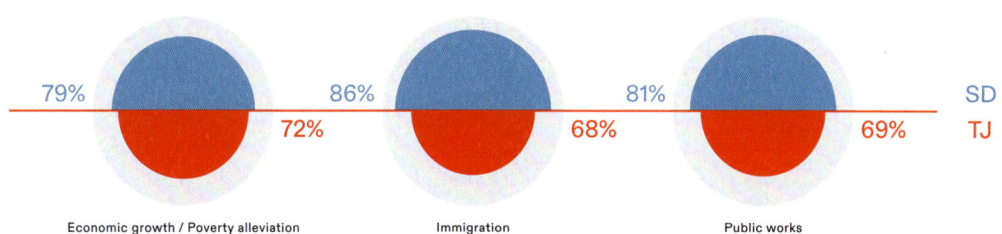

79% / 72% — Economic growth / Poverty alleviation
86% / 68% — Immigration
81% / 69% — Public works

TOP-DOWN PUBLIC: DESIGNING URBAN JUSTICE

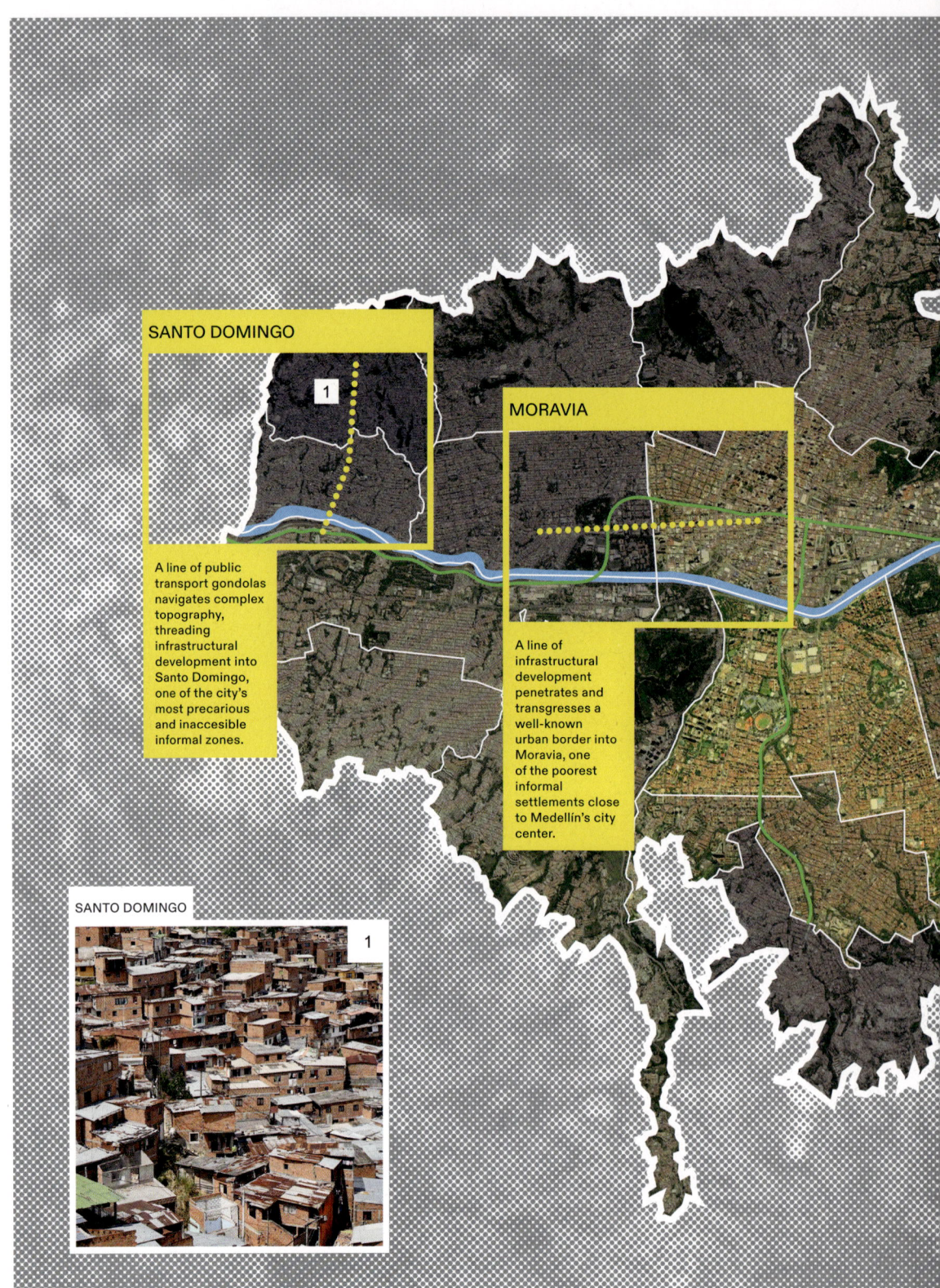

THE TRANSFORMATION OF MEDELLÍN
Medellín, Colombia is arguably the most comprehensive case study of equitable urbanization in Latin America in the last decades.

POBLADO

WEALTHY

POOR

RETHINKING THE CITY FROM ITS PERIPHERY
During the late 1980s and early 1990s, Medellín was among the most violent cities in the world. By the mid-2000s, and especially during the administration of Mayor Sergio Fajardo, the city became a model of equitable urbanization, exemplifying a commitment to progressive municipal governance. Medellín prioritized two goals: to transgress urban borders and to narrow the gap between wealth and poverty.

SITE 1: MORAVIA: TRANSGRESSING URBAN BORDERS

The emblematic architectural interventions in Medellín are discrete objects. They were a choreographed urban strategy, performing as a necklace of public spaces, threaded by transportation and connected to peripheral neighborhoods. Moravia for example: Carabobo Boulevard pierces an urban border with a Botanical Garden and the *Explora Science Museum*. *Moravia Library Park*

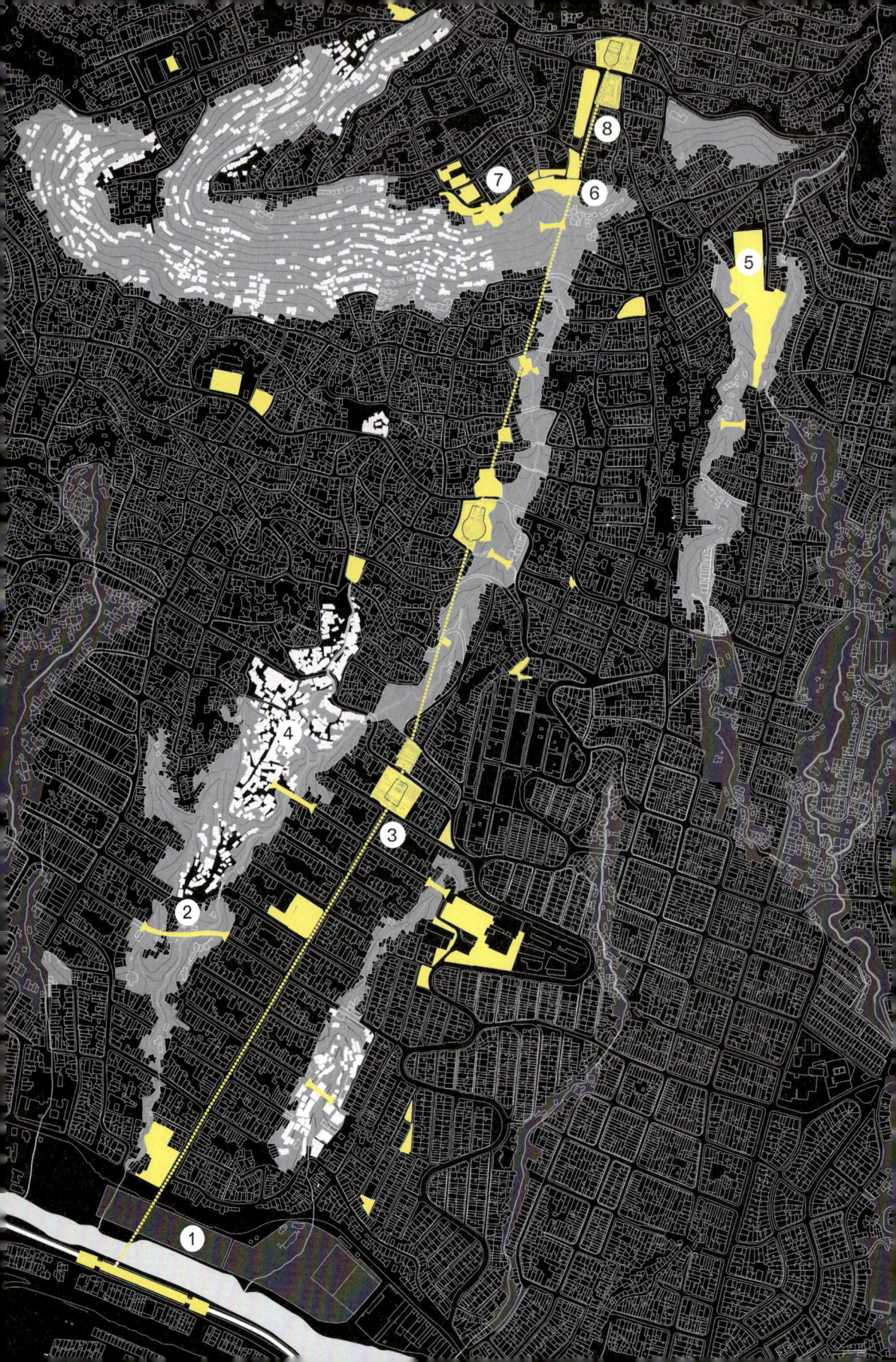

SITE 2: SANTO DOMINGO: SHRINKING DISTANCE, EXPANDING ACCESS

Santo Domingo was the poorest district in Medellín, the site of extreme cartel violence. Topographically splintered from the city, this is where the celebrated gondola transportation system was built. New bridges connect divided neighborhoods; public spaces are threaded through the topography; new schools are installed at the edges; the iconic *Santo Domingo Library Park* crowns the integrated system as a social balcony. The once marginalized community is now visible to the city.

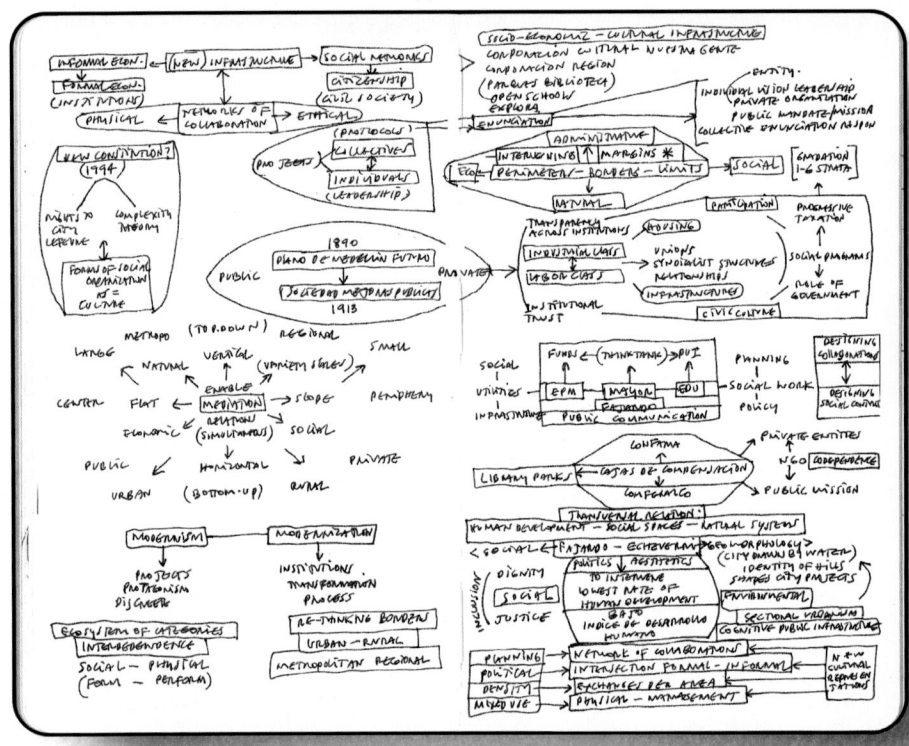

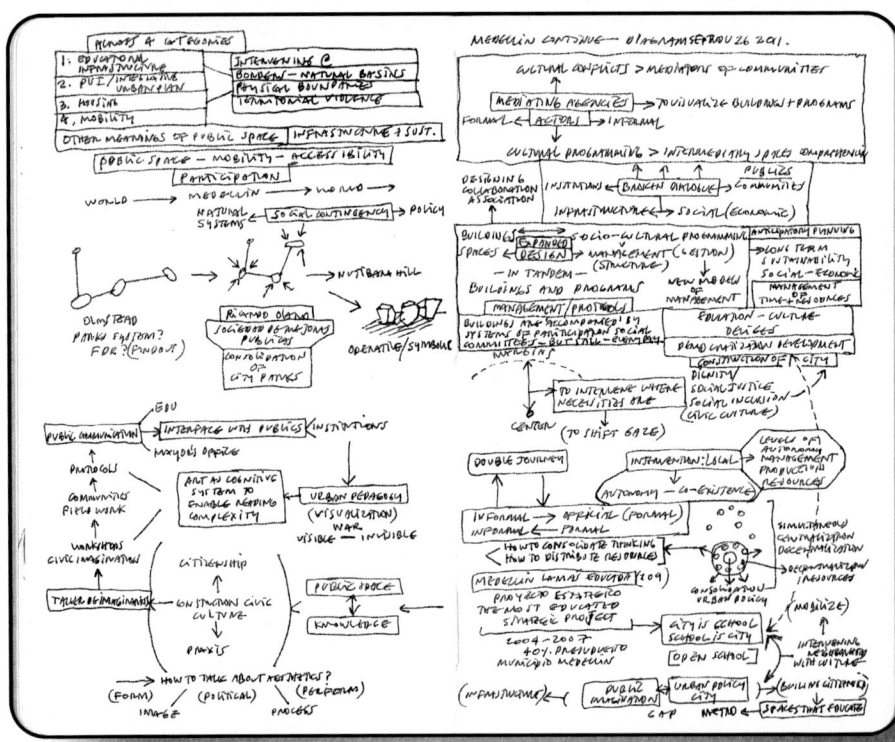

THE MEDELLÍN DIAGRAM

The international urban and architecture community tends to focus on the architecture projects. But as Mayor Sergio Fajardo emphasizes, Medellín's transformation was not an architectural project, but a political one. We arrived in Medellín to research and visualize the political and civic processes that made these transformations possible. We interviewed dozens of actors across sectors who participated in this transformation.

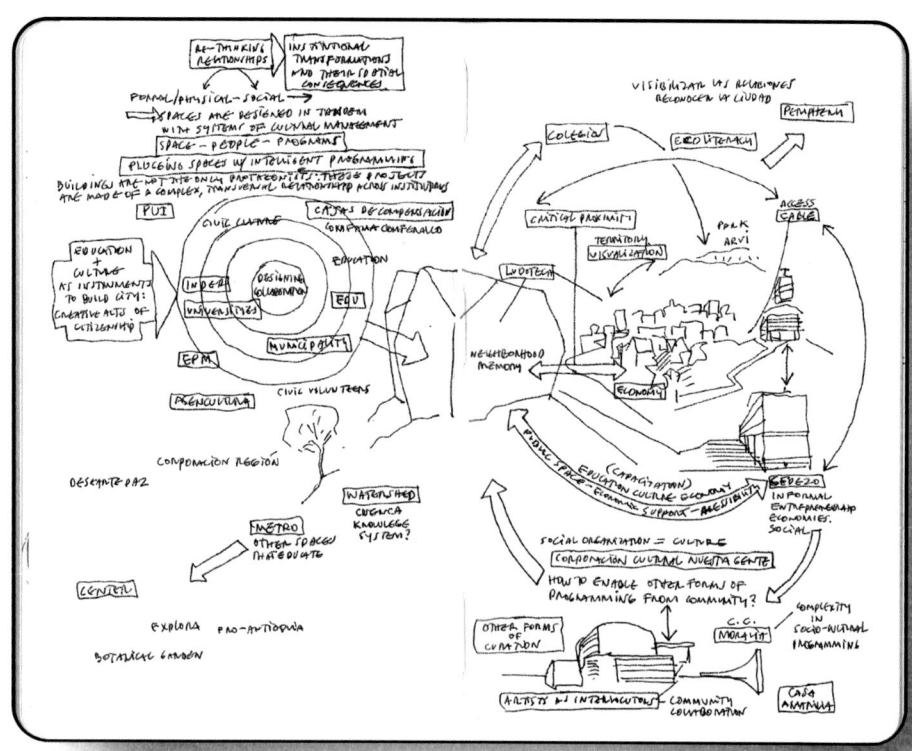

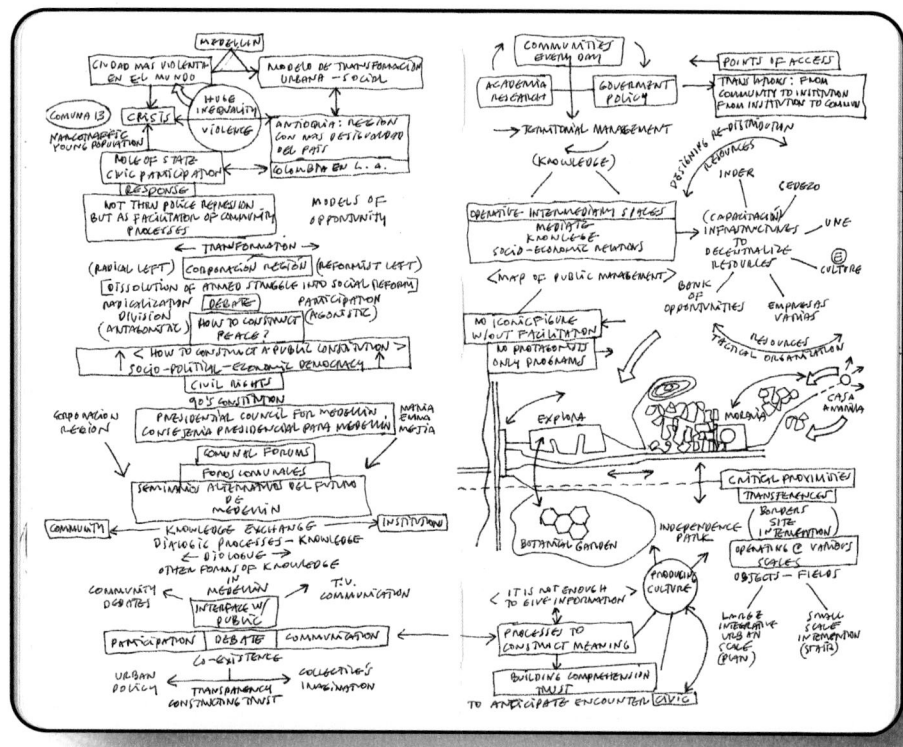

WHAT REALLY HAPPENED HERE?

Interviews and focus groups were organized in collaboration with Medellín's former Director of Planning Alejandro Echeverri, and his URBAM program at EAFIT University in Medellín. We extracted the most compelling concepts from these interviews and stitched together a relational map to visualize civic priorities, institutional procedures and urban strategies, and to reflect on their procedural replicability in other sites of urban conflict.

PRIORITIES

1.
Putting Inequality First

Medellín constructed a new political agenda

PROCESSES

2.
Designing Gove[rnment]

Medellín transformed municipa[l...]

1.A Committing to zones of poverty

1.B Mediating urban conflict

1.C Cultivating a new civic imagination

2.A Assembling transparent and inclusive public management

2.B Inte[grating] redis[tribution,] know[ledge, and] reso[urces]

1.A	1.B	1.C	2.A	2.B
1.A.1 Medellín was first and foremost a political project, not an architectural one	**1.A.2** Medellín chose a new political leadership committed to confronting inequality	**1.A.3** Medellín declared that violence is rooted in poverty	**1.A.4** Medellín sought to narrow the gap between wealth and poverty	**1.A.5** Medellín reimagined the city from its periphery	**1.A.6** Medellín identified sites of urgency and invested in the poorest zones of the city	**1.A.7** Medellín built public trust with small-scale interventions while planning a long-term urban vision	**2.A.1** For Medellín, urban equality demanded a transformation of government bureaucracy	**2.A.2** Medellín studied the best models of municipal governance from across Latin America	**2.A.3** Medellín tackled institutional corruption
1.B.1 Medellín visualized urban conflict as point of departure	**1.B.2** Medellín pursued social order not through police repression but through community processes	**1.B.3** Medellín embraced empathy as a pathway to inclusive urbanization	**1.B.4** Medellín created spaces for mediation and conflict resolution	**1.B.5** Medellín mediated divergent perspectives and challenged polarization with constructive dialogue	**1.B.6** Medellín facilitated understanding between marginalized communities and institutions	**1.B.7** Medellín constructed a new social contract to guarantee peace and democracy	**2.A.7** Medellín increased transparency through public communication and accountability	**2.A.8** Medellín repaired public trust across institutions	**2.A.9** Medellín embraced progressive taxation as the foundation for equitable urbanization
1.B.8 Medellín summoned artists to resuscitate urban memory	**1.C.1** Medellín cultivated respect for human dignity	**1.C.2** Medellín prioritized public thinking	**1.C.3** Medellín learned from examples of participatory urbanization across Latin America	**1.C.4** Medellín imagined a new era of civic participation	**1.C.5** Medellín developed strategies to restore collective agency	**1.C.6** Medellín facilitated community forums to discuss the future of the city	**2.B.2** Medellín reconceived public management as a transversal curatorial project	**2.B.3** Medellín transformed the mayor's office into an urban laboratory for cross-sector problem solving	**2.B.4** Medellín mediated interfaces between top-down institutions and bottom-up agency
1.C.7 Medellín summoned diverse civic actors to collaborate	**1.C.8** Medellín designed new platforms for public communication	**1.C.9** Medellín awakened its own institutional memory	**1.C.10** Medellín recovered its own lineages of civic commitment	**1.C.11** Medellín resuscitated a history of collaboration between labor and industry			**2.B.8** Medellín encouraged public input into municipal resource allocation	**2.C.1** Medellín did not "outsource" urban design	**2.C.2** Medellín summoned the design professionals to collaborate "in house"
							2.C.6 Medellín connected planning logics with the everyday practices of communities	**2.C.7** Medellín transformed informal settlements into laboratories of urban policy	**2.C.8** Medellín designed urban frameworks to navigate the topographic complexity of the city

---

THE MEDELLÍN DIAGRAM TABLE OF CONTENTS

From the interviews and focus groups, we constructed a table of contents to diagram the Medellín model, an archive of institutional memory for Medellín itself and for those eager to learn from its political and civic processes. This table was accompanied by a series of video narratives that explored central concepts.

INTERVENTIONS

3. Spatializing Citizenship
Medellín built performative infrastructures of inclusion

2.C Bringing design intelligence into public policy			3.A Transgressing urban borders			3.B Creating public spaces that educate			3.C Bringing design intelligence into public policy
2.A.4 Medellín prioritized bureaucratic efficiency and agility	2.A.5 Medellín revised its org-chart to facilitate collaborative aspirational planning	2.A.6 Medellín designed municipal structures and procedures for participatory governance	3.A.1 Medellín identified target zones for integrated urban design intervention	3.A.2 Medellín penetrated into marginalized communities with public works	3.A.3 Medellín shrunk distance between wealthy and poor zones to increase accessibility	3.A.4 Medellín orchestrated diverse social encounters in urban space	3.A.5 Medellín democratized the city through new systems of mobility	3.A.6 Medellín took a position against tabula rasa approach to urbanization	3.A.7 Medellín mobilized urban strategies of space alteration and adaptation
2.A.10 Medellín invested public utility dividends into public infrastructure	2.A.11 Medellín created new public institutions tasked with social and economic inclusion	2.B.1 Medellín committed to collaborative municipal governance	3.A.8 Medellín conceptualized natural systems as a framework for integrating the city	3.A.9 Medellín prioritized natural boundaries over jurisdictional ones	3.A.10 Medellín imagined a watershed urbanization, adapting public infrastructure to natural topography	3.B.1 For Medellín, social justice was not only about redistributing resources but also redistributing knowledges	3.B.2 Medellín committed to incentivizing local economy and knowledge	3.B.3 Medellín advanced the rights to the city through a new public space agenda	3.B.4 Medellín viewed public infrastructure as the armature of progressive governance
2.B.5 Medellín summoned cross-sector priorities, knowledges and resources	2.B.6 Medellín redistributed cross-sector priorities, knowledges and resources	2.B.7 Medellín redirected public resources toward socially responsible development	3.B.5 Medellín understood that buildings are not static objects but spaces that perform as urban systems	3.B.6 For Medellín, public space is a space of knowledge	3.B.7 Medellín intervened into public space to reorganize social norms	3.B.8 Medellín advanced citizenship as a creative act that transforms everyday urban practices	3.B.9 Medellín elevated urban pedagogy and education to democratize the city	3.B.10 Medellín activated community-based arts to build citizenship through cultural action	3.B.11 Medellín cultivated a new citizenship culture, mediated by arts and education
2.C.3 Medellín engaged local universities to rethink urban policy	2.C.4 Medellín co-produced the city with communities	2.C.5 Medellín integrated "large-scale" territory with "small-scale" neighborhoods	3.B.12 Medellín elevated art as a tool for publics to comprehend urban complexity	3.B.13 Medellín connected citizenship to a visual awareness of the territory	3.B.14 Medellín reconceived artists as urban curators and 'facilitators' of cultural service	3.B.15 Medellín incentivized local knowledge and economy	3.C.1 Medellín introduced specific tactical programming into abstract open space	3.C.2 Medellín designed spaces, programs and protocols simultaneously	3.C.3 Medellín promoted dialogical spaces and social processes
2.C.9 Medellín conceptualized infrastructure as a platform for social density			3.C.4 Medellín empowered citizens to be curators of process	3.C.5 Medellín assembled cross-sector coalitions to support socio-economic and cultural processes	3.C.6 Medellín linked urban stewardship, civic society and government	3.C.7 Medellín promoted collaborative programming that assured sustainability over time			

REDISTRIBUTE KNOWLEDGES AND RESOURCES

PUBLIC SPACE EDUCATES

DON'T PRIVATIZE!

LOCAL PROCESSES FOR RE-THINKING GLOBAL URBANIZATION
Six diagrams constitute a compendium of Medellín's urban processes for knowledge transfer across cities.

MEDIATE TOP-DOWN AND BOTTOM-UP

TRANSGRESS URBAN BORDERS

REDESIGN GOVERNANCE

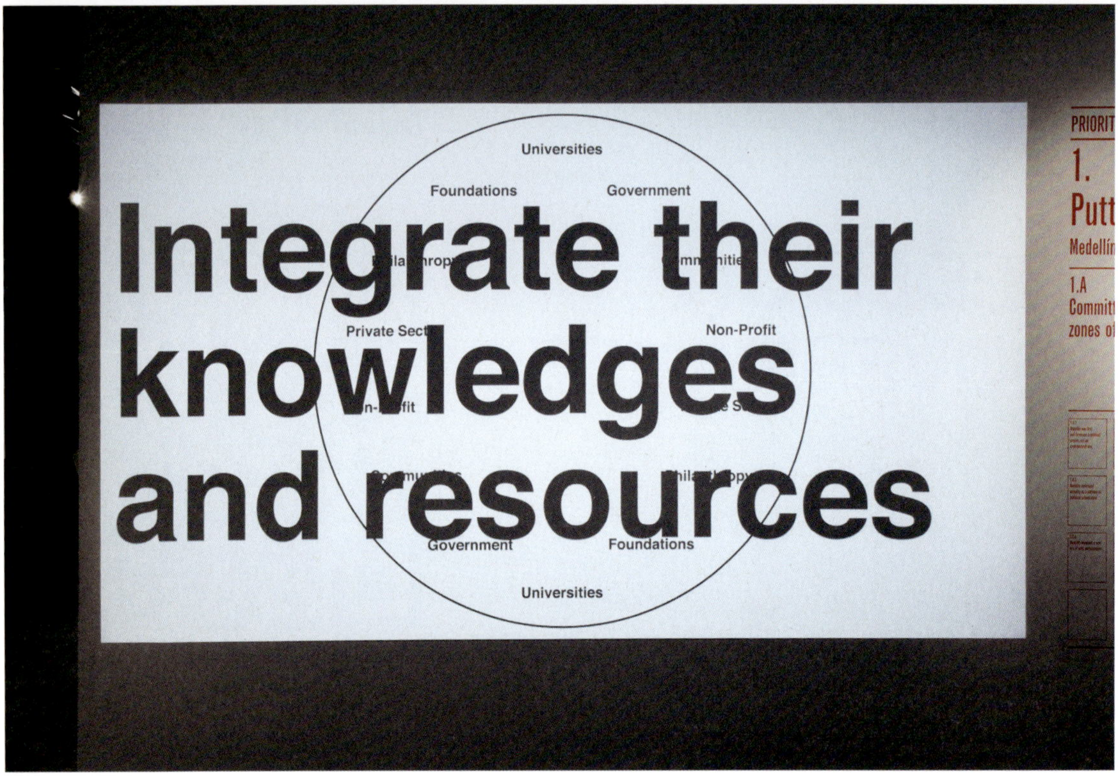

DIAGRAMS OF POWER
The *Medellín Diagram* in the exhibition *Diagrams of Power* at Ontario Museum of Art, Toronto, Canada, 2018.

TOP-DOWN PUBLIC: DESIGNING URBAN JUSTICE

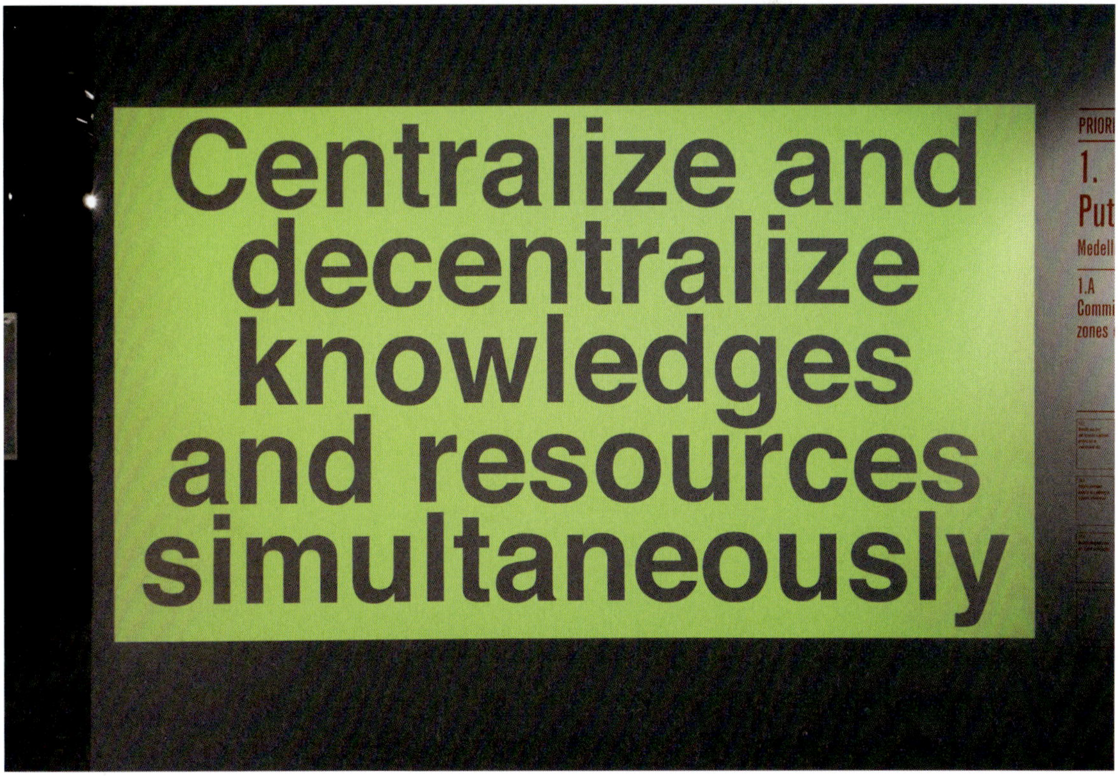

VISUALIZING CITIZENSHIP

The Cross-Border Citizen and the *Medellín Diagram* in the exhibition *Visualizing Citizenship* at the Yerba Buena Center for the Arts in San Francisco, 2017.

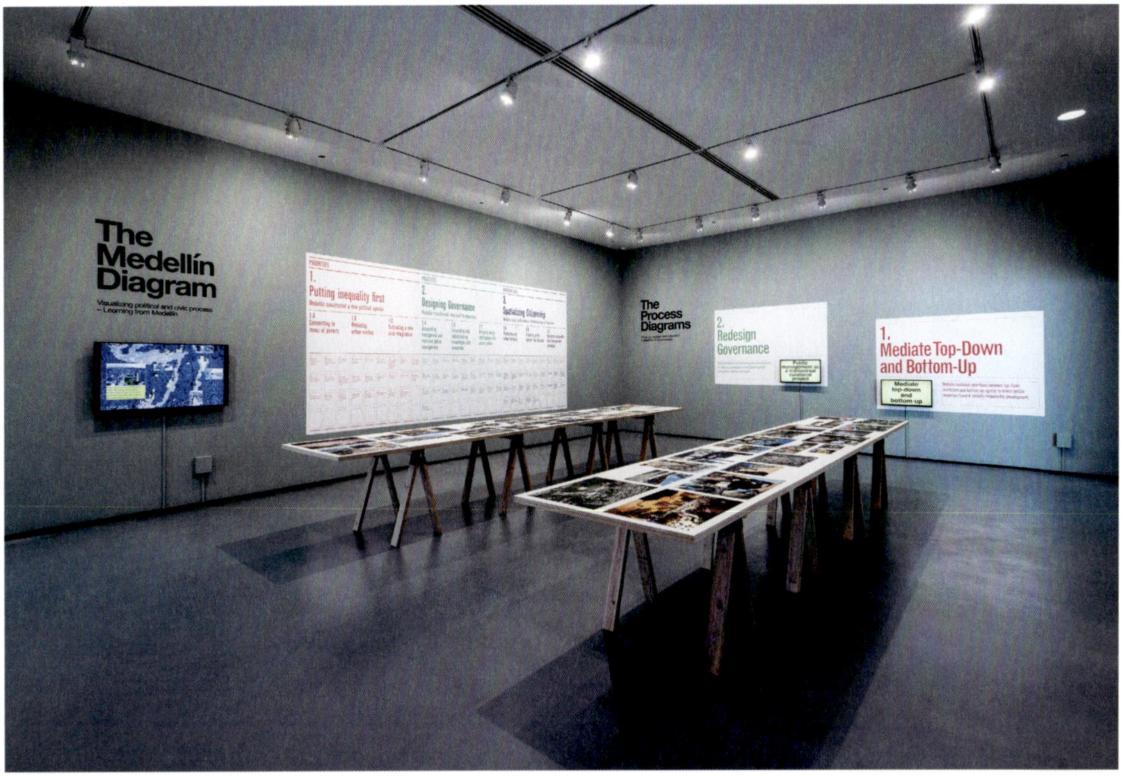
The Medellín Diagram
1.
Putting inequality first
2.
Designing Governance
The Process Diagrams
2.
Redesign Governance
1.
Mediate Top-Down and Bottom-Up

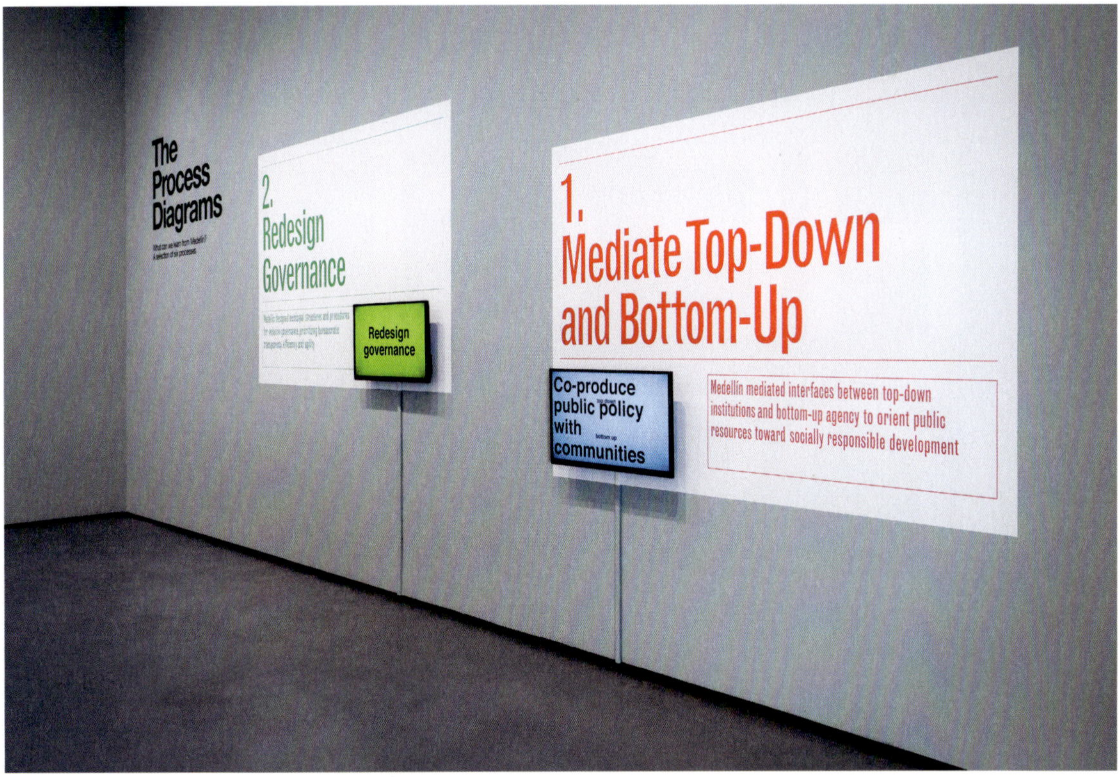
The Process Diagrams
2.
Redesign Governance
Redesign governance
1.
Mediate Top-Down and Bottom-Up
Co-produce public policy with communities
Medellín mediated interfaces between top-down institutions and bottom-up agency to orient public resources toward socially responsible development

PROJECT: CLUSTER 6

DECOLON[IZING]
KNOWLED[GE,]
DEMOCRA[TIZING]
THE CITY: [THE]
UCSD CO[MMUNITY]
STATIONS

IZING

GE AND

ATIZING

HE

MMUNITY

DECOLONIZING KNOWLEDGE AND DEMOCRATIZING THE CITY: THE UCSD COMMUNITY STATIONS

Project cluster 6 presents a project that integrates all the diverse research strands elaborated in this book. Here we present the UCSD Community Stations, a network of public spaces located in vulnerable neighborhoods on both sides of the wall, where education, research and cultural agendas are advanced collaboratively between community activists and our campus, the University of California San Diego. The UCSD Community Stations are designed to transgress the border wall, spatialize social justice and mobilize cross-border citizenship through cultural action. As the field-based social-engagement arm of our research-based design practice, the UCSD Community Stations are designed for the exchange of diverse knowledges, to facilitate new interfaces between top-down and bottom-up energies in the city, and to democratize urban development. They demonstrate a model of urban co-development, in which the economic and programmatic resources of the university serve as leverage for community agencies to develop their own neighborhood infrastructure, housing, and experiments in economic and cultural production. The UCSD Community Stations manifest our commitment to thinking structurally about the drivers of inequality and injustice across the San Diego–Tijuana border region, and strategically about cultural, institutional and spatial transformation.

The UCSD Community Stations

1. The UCSD-EarthLab Community Station
2. The UCSD-Casa Community Station
3. The UCSD-Divina Community Station
4. The UCSD-Alacrán Community Station

Our work advances ideas and practices of "interdependence." Even if we risk seeming romantic or utopian in this time of global closure, polarization and division, we are drawn to the possibilities of mutual recognition among people on opposite sides of territorial struggle, who typically possess insurmountable differentials in power and capacity, and often radically conflicting religious, cultural and ideological commitments and agendas.

We have always begun with the premise that the future of San Diego depends on the future of Tijuana, regardless of the physical wall that arbitrarily divides the territory. Moreover, we have observed through many years of grounded practice that interdependence is most acutely experienced in local contexts, where populations endure the consequences of recklessly fragmented environmental, economic and social ecologies.

In recent years, the injustice of border dynamics in our region has attracted artists and cultural producers from around the world to engage in acts of performative protest. While these gestures by visitors are often creative and provocative, we have been mostly critical of this uptick in ephemeral actions that dip in and out of the conflict. They are often extractive in their processes, and their impact on public consciousness as fleeting as the Instagram posts they generate. What happens the day after the happening? Who will steward the longer-term work necessary to transform top-down policy, and the parallel political representation and economic investments essential to improving the quality of life in border communities impacted by the forces of surveillance, control and radical exclusion?

Inspired by our research in Colombian cities, we have been advocating for a longer view of resistance and more strategic thinking about cultural, institutional and spatial transformation in the border region. In the last years, we have committed to a more rooted, long-term infrastructure of cross-border partnerships with grassroots organizations. To enable this longer-term work, we developed the UCSD Community Stations, a cross-border infrastructure of partnerships and sanctuary spaces designed for community-engaged pedagogy and civic action. Inspired by Bogotá's commitment to rallying "citizenship culture" as the foundational gesture to improving quality of life in the city, and by Medellín's commitment to mobilizing citizenship through cultural action in public space, the Community Stations spatialize regional solidarities. Through long-term civic partnerships, coalitions of knowledge and spaces of radical reciprocity, we are committed to horizontal practices of co-production with communities to generate counternarratives of interdependence that reflect the everyday cross-border flows and circulations in our region. The Community Stations are the social-engagement arm of our research-based architectural practice, enabling a cross-border knowledge loop between our practice, the public university campus where we work, and the border communities we partner with.

THE COMMUNITY STATIONS: SPATIALIZING SOLIDARITY

The UCSD Community Stations are a reciprocal knowledge platform, a network of field stations located in vulnerable neighborhoods on both sides of the border wall, where the public university and marginalized communities meet to share knowledge and resources, and advance research, education, cultural, urban and environmental agendas. Blurring the line between research and activism, we have committed to grounding our claims about the border region through horizontal practices of engagement in which university researchers and community activists assemble as partners to learn from each other, and ultimately co-produce new narratives, new strategies, new alliances and new forms of solidarity to tackle injustice and propose more equitable projects in the city. We believe urban justice demands both the redistribution of resources and the redistribution of knowledges. We designed the Community Stations to link the resources and knowledges of universities and communities on both sides of the border wall, and ultimately to forge channels of political representation to connect bottom-up urban research with top-down policymaking.

Spatializing solidarity, then, is a double project: designing transgressive physical spaces that are flexible and adaptable sites for knowledge production, contestation and debate, and infusing them with support systems, resources and tools to assure sustainability and inclusion. In other words, like Medellín, we co-develop the spaces along with the protocols and programs that can increase public knowledge and community capacity for political and environmental action. We envision these public spaces as sites where citizenship is constructed through cultural mobilization, where programmatic content helps to reorganize spatial, social and economic relations.

The Community Stations are also a new model of urban co-development between public universities and community organizations to democratize the city. Universities can support communities in becoming developers of their own social housing, public spaces and neighborhood infrastructure.

Communities can own the means of productivity and generate revenue to advance their own programmatic agendas. This strategy of neighborhood-based urban and economic development lies at the heart of our research and practice, and the projects we have been fighting for over the years.

PUBLIC SPACES THAT EDUCATE: THE COMMUNITY STATIONS MODEL

We have a set of core commitments, which together comprise the Community Stations Model. We believe they are highly replicable.

1.
We localize the global, which in San Diego means recognizing our regional interdependence with Tijuana. Despite the wall and the ugly political rhetoric designed to divide us, we are a binational ecology of flows and circulation, and our future is intertwined. Air, water, waste, health, culture, money, hope, love and justice—these things don't stop at walls. We have always resisted the idea that global injustice is something that happens "out there" in the world somewhere. Living and working where we do, we don't need to send our students far away to learn about territorial conflict, migration, poverty and climate justice. We are minutes away from an international border in crisis, and this enables an amazing proximity between campus and field, between theory and practice—what we think of as a critical proximity.

2.
We build trust bridges, long-term embedded partnerships between the university and community organizations on both sides of the wall. The Community Stations are designed, built, funded, programmed and managed collaboratively between campus and community. We're not like so many university programs that dip in and out, diagnosing crises and then disappearing. We don't disappear. Our investment in Community Stations infrastructure quite literally cements campus commitment to our community partners. We are there for the long haul, and aspire to long-term impact. Communities are justifiably skeptical of research universities who often suddenly appear with requests, plant their flag and then disappear just as abruptly once they get what they need. Often times, it doesn't even occur to researchers to share their research and publications with their community "subjects."

3.
We decolonize knowledge by co-producing research, cultural activities and urban interventions with communities. Academic culture is filled with vertical assumptions that we know more than others, that we are trained to solve the world's problems (if only they would listen to us). We are committed to horizontal practices of co-production. We engage communities not as universities often do—as sites from which to extract data, but as participants with knowledge and agency. Everyone brings something to the table, everyone learns, and we do things together in the border region that neither partner could have done alone. We don't figure out solutions in our campus studios and labs, and then descend to test them out, like applied researchers do. We also don't do charity. When we teach our students the skills and methods of collaborative research, we do not see this as "service learning," but as an opportunity to revitalize our languages and research strategies through engagement with Indigenous epistemologies and other activist knowledges and practices.

4.
We curate two-way flows: inside-out, and outside-in—un-siloing the campus, and inviting activists and community leaders to teach with us. Today's social challenges are not confined to disciplines or sectors, nor can their solutions be. We are a platform for deep intersectionality—not as an end in itself, but because the problems we tackle demand that we un-silo our thinking. This means curating an inclusive epistemic ecology beyond the walls of the university, in collaboration with "others."

5.
We manage complexity. We made a commitment long ago that the university must never become a burden on already-stressed community partners. Given the complexity of Community Stations partnerships and programming, and regular, frequent movement back-and-forth across a militarized border wall, we have designed an unconventional social infrastructure of actors to manage the complexity of resource and knowledge circulations, including Bridge Curators, who keep one foot on campus and one foot in our partner organizations, beholden to both, managing flows of money, people and materials, and coordinating our collaborative research and programming. Additionally, all student field research is supervised by seasoned Field Coordinators, who understand the complexities of field research and know how to navigate border

dynamics accompanied by student teams. Our Bridge Curators and Field Coordinators are incredibly agile and committed people, capable of navigating both university bureaucracy and the delicate social ecologies of community-based work.

6.
We validate community investment. Universities too often take for granted the resources communities invest when they work with us—time, space, social capital, labor, knowledges. As a matter of epistemic justice and labor equity, these contributions need to be validated and compensated. We designed a second unconventional role called Public Scholars, essentially community leaders who serve as trust bridges to residents and youth. These individuals don't have conventional academic credentials, but their knowledge and labor are essential to co-producing the research and cultural activity that we do.

7.
We are also rethinking equity, diversity and inclusion—goals that should be primary in every educational mission today. Diversifying campus demographics and culture is the essential foundational commitment, but we are also accelerating campus commitment to partnering with local communities of color to cultivate skills of empathy, respect, listening and collaboration in our research and teaching—skills we believe are best learned *in situ* through practice—and to forging accessible pathways to higher education for underserved youth of color across the border region.

8.
Based in a public institution, we are committed to high-impact public research and teaching on issues that most impact our community partners: migration and inclusion; affordable and emergency housing; environmental justice and clean energy access; climate adaptation; health and well-being; educational access; human rights and social justice; and political and environmental mobilization. In this light, we challenge the conventional trinity of academic merit: "research, teaching and service." Co-producing research with communities integrates all three, but is often misunderstood by academic reviewers as "service," which can discourage young researchers and designers from pursuing community-engaged work.

9.
The Community Stations open possibilities of co-developing the city with communities. We have designed a new model of urban co-development between public universities and community organizations to fight the creeping gentrification of border neighborhoods. Our process is a model of shared urban intervention in which the economic and programmatic power of the university, the sweat equity of architects, cultural producers and community leaders, and municipal protocols for accessing public parcels become leverage for communities to develop their own neighborhood spaces and social housing, placing education at the center of community-based development.

10.
Finally, we believe public space detonates community power. We reject conventional strategies of urban beautification and innovation that turn our public spaces into sites of leisure and consumption. We question the agendas of the creative class and their pop-ups, which too often accelerate gentrification, appropriate arts and culture for private ends, and become an apology for the absence of more substantial public investment in the city. We believe public space must become civicized, to use James Tully's beautiful concept[45]—must become a site of dialogue and contestation infused with resources and tools to increase public knowledge and community capacity for political and environmental action.

The UCSD Community Stations

Imagine the Community Stations as a distributed campus, an infrastructure of field stations that connect the University of California San Diego with diverse communities at the edges of our border region. With our community partners, we have co-developed four Community Station sites, two in San Diego, two in Tijuana. Each station is a robust partnership between the university and a community-based agency governed by an MOU. Each is co-designed, co-funded, co-built, co-programmed and co-managed by university and community.

This project cluster is a narrative and visual tour of the four UCSD Community Stations sites, moving from north to south:

THE UCSD-EARTHLAB COMMUNITY STATION

EarthLab is a partnership with the environmental justice nonprofit Groundwork San Diego–Chollas Creek and the San Diego Unified School District. This station is located fifteen miles from the border wall in Southeast San Diego, in the underserved, primarily Black and Latinx neighborhoods of Encanto, characterized by high unemployment, low educational attainment, food insecurity and cyclical poverty.

The Community Station occupies a four-acre parcel owned by the San Diego Unified School District (SDUSD) and granted to our partnership in a forty-year lease to increase educational capacity and enrich environmental content for the eight public schools within walking distance of the site. Access to this public parcel became leverage for assembling a unique cross-sector collaboration between the region's major public research university, a local school district and a community-based agency to co-develop space. The SDUSD provided the land and funded the physical construction of the site; UCSD funds sustainable educational programming, research and management in collaboration with Groundwork San Diego, which stewards community participation.

Together, we are developing the site into an open-air climate action park, designed for outdoor experiential education and neighborhood-scale climate justice for underserved youth and their families. The UCSD-EarthLab Community Station is equipped with a variety of landscape-based environments that include energy, water and food learning stations and conservation infrastructure, all wrapped by Indigenous Kumeyaay knowledges and environmental practices. It is designed to perform as an outdoor environmental design lab.

With our community partners, UCSD researchers, teachers and local environmental activists, we have designed an educational method—a portfolio of programs, lessons and activities that expand learning and experiential environmental education, serving as a model for other low-income communities to bridge the achievement gap, elevate socio-emotional well-being and develop environmental empathy. Racial and environmental justice demand enhanced outdoor learning opportunities for low-income youth in neighborhoods lacking green spaces and historically underserved by the educational system.

More than 3,000 kids circulate through the EarthLab each year. During COVID-19, the space continued to operate as an outdoor, socially distanced classroom. As families join their children, the effort has become a holistic, community-based economic development project, opening doors to higher education and vocational training while advancing community-based participatory climate action and promoting youth as stewards of their own community.

THE UCSD-CASA COMMUNITY STATION

Moving nine miles southward toward the border, the UCSD-Casa Community Station is a partnership with the sixty-year-old social service agency Casa Familiar, located in the border neighborhood of San Ysidro, a few blocks from the busiest international land crossing in the Western hemisphere. With 100,000 crossings every day, the neighborhood is fragmented by freeway and surveillance infrastructure, and under continual surveillance by US Homeland Security. This community is ninety percent Latinx; many are DACA and many are undocumented.

The UCSD-Casa Community Station was conceptualized as a cultural seed for social housing. We designed it as a parcel-size infrastructure of cultural and social spaces, anchoring ten diverse units of affordable housing, called *Living Rooms at the Border* (see project cluster 3). This infrastructure organizes a collection of small buildings: a renovated church adapted into a community theater, accessory buildings housing social, immigration and health services, and an open-air civic classroom led and managed by Casa Familiar, UCSD and residents.

Our research and programming at the UCSD-Casa Community Station focuses on arts and culture. Imagine a small coalition of local artists, promotors and youth collaborating with university curators, theater script writers and visual artists, who come together twice a year to co-produce a play that explores an urgent issue facing the community, enacted by local youth in the community theater. These artistic productions are rooted in neighborhood stories and become bottom-up evidentiary material to increase public knowledge.

Moving southward across the border, our two UCSD Community Stations in Tijuana are located in Los Laureles Canyon, an informal settlement of 92,000 people that literally crashes against the border wall on the western periphery of Tijuana. This precarious zone is forty minutes from our campus and demonstrates the dramatic proximity of wealth and extreme poverty in our region. Los Laureles Canyon is highly susceptible to erosion and flooding, and lacks water and waste management infrastructure. Much of the trash, along with tons of sediment, flow upstream, ending in the protected Tijuana River Estuary and causing pollution and health issues for residents of southern San Diego County. It is an important case study of regional interdependence.

THE UCSD-DIVINA COMMUNITY STATION

This Community Station is located in the Divina neighborhood of Los Laureles Canyon and managed in partnership with the A.C. Colonos de la Divina Providencia, a community agency that provides meals for youth and seniors, a weekly health clinic and environmental literacy classes. Activist Rebeca Ramirez, our Tijuana partner, inherited the land on which the agency's current building is located from her mother, who secured it as a public space by sitting on a makeshift basketball court site to protect it from squatting. Access to this parcel has been negotiated with the municipality through a special liability transfer, allowing our community partners to program the site for social purposes.

At the UCSD-Divina Community Station we work closely with our partners to lead education and adaptation efforts focused on social protection from landslides, floods, ecological restoration and estuarine health. We lead programming on soil erosion that helps young people understand zones of vulnerability in their own neighborhoods and the ecological conservation of species and habitat restoration. We also lead community-based behavioral interventions related to the dumping and burning of trash. At the UCSD-Divina Community Station, our programming tends to focus on environmental programming for youth. We elevate children here as the "cross-border citizens" of the future.

Behavioral interventions in Los Laureles Canyon, where our Community Station is located, can have a significant positive impact on environmental health upstream. For this reason, the pedagogic activities of the UCSD-Divina Community Station are central to our longer-term binational conservation efforts in the Cross-Border Commons, a binational land conservancy initiative to protect the Tijuana River Estuary in the US from sedimentation and pollution flowing northward from this Mexican canyon settlement (see project cluster 1).

For the moment, our collaborative programming at the UCSD-Divina Community Station utilizes the agency's existing community center, a small two-story structure with an adjacent basketball court and pedagogic garden. New physical infrastructure will be developed in layers as funding becomes available. We are designing a perimeter ambulatory for vendors and a social garden equipped with movable pavilions for social service. A plinth will be built to support a flexible sports court and event space, flanked by classrooms and a children's library. These porous and multiuse environments will be enveloped by subsidized Mecalux maquiladora-produced prefabricated systems and covered with affordable plastic and shading systems (see project cluster 3). The Community Station building will accommodate a variety of informal programs, such as weekly neighborhood markets and economic incubators. It will also contain a small high school and a set of multilevel spaces to accommodate social services, a health clinic and cultural events, all curated between university and community.

THE UCSD-ALACRÁN COMMUNITY STATION

Our fourth and newest station is the UCSD-Alacrán Station, which occupies the most rugged and polluted sub-basin of Los Laureles Canyon. It is a partnership with the faith-based organization Embajadores de Jesús. Our community partners began construction of a refugee camp here a few years ago to provide shelter, food and basic services to hundreds of Haitian and Central American refugees while they navigate unjust asylum procedures in the US and Mexico.

With our partners, we are advancing this Community Station to increase housing capacity for the migrant shelter, embedding migrant housing in spaces of fabrication, training and small-scale economic development co-managed between Embajadores and the University of California San Diego in partnership with local agencies and universities. We have designed spaces and pedagogical programming that integrate the migrant and her children into the civic, social and economic life of this community. As such, the site is fast becoming a nexus for migrant support, research and outreach by many units across the UCSD campus, investigating ecological sustainability, migrant health challenges and the role of social impact investment on incremental housing, job generation and local economy.

With our partners we are rethinking the refugee camp, from a place of short-term habitation and service provision to a durable socio-spatial infrastructure for inclusion. This station expands our research on incremental informal urbanization, on how to develop sequentially in layers, negotiating the ephemeral and the permanent. We conceived the station as housing "scaffolds" that can be incrementally infilled by phased occupancy.

This incremental process is supported by what we are calling a "sanctuary economy." With our partners, we have assembled a model for land acquisition that includes social impact investment leveraged by the sweat equity of migrant labor and programmatic funding from foundations. The UCSD-Alacrán Community Station aspires to economic inclusion, supporting the rights of migrants to migrate, but also to remain. With the support of the PARC Foundation, we have assembled a community-owned business—the Embajadores Construction Cooperative, with a tool library, wood and metal machines, and a couple of trucks and tractors. This migrant-led initiative will complete construction of this site and remain operational for future construction jobs across the informal Los Laureles Canyon settlement.

The UCSD-Alacrán Community Station is the seed for an evolving sanctuary neighborhood. Because of existing environmental damage at the site, we first established an ecological layer comprised of biofiltration systems, gabion wall-terracing and swales, which in turn organize accessibility and pedestrian circulation. The masterplan for the sanctuary neighborhood includes orchards, a farm, economic incubators and health, educational and social spaces to be programmed and managed collaboratively by university and community. Construction of the station began in May 2020.

UNWALLING CITIZENSHIP: CURATING CROSS-BORDER DIALOGUE

Distributed on both sides of the wall, the Community Stations are civic spaces, richly programmed for cross-border dialogue, collaborative research, urban pedagogy, participatory design and cultural production. They are observatories for documenting cross-border flows and circulations through social, ethnographic and scientific research, increasing public awareness of the social and ecological ties between San Diego and Tijuana, between the US and Mexico. The curatorial dimension of the Community Stations is central here—the cultural strategies we employ to circulate knowledges across the border. Sometimes this involves digital infrastructures to support virtual tunnels and bridges that bypass political barriers, enabling transgressive contact and exchange among community activists, researchers, students, youth and designers on both sides of the border wall.

With our partners, we curate "convergences" and "unwalling experiments" supported by visual tools that facilitate the broader recognition of our cross-border citizenship as well as cross-border public knowledge and sentiment. Through these cultural interventions, we work with community leaders and cultural producers to uproot divisive social attitudes and belief systems that have been reinforced by poisonous political rhetoric, making the physical barriers more porous and less definitive.

What makes our approach distinctive is our unconventional cultural strategies that tackle poverty and dramatic social inequality by increasing public knowledge and critical awareness. Whether we are working on issues of environment, urban inequality, race, gender, migration, the border, criminal justice or health, our approach is always focused on exposing injustice, changing hearts and minds, and communicating with wider publics and institutions of power. Our aspiration is to cultivate collaborative, civically engaged communities capable of collective action and influence on public policy.

Through our programming we also introduce university students to the epistemologies, ethics, histories and theories of community-based activism and university-community engagement. Our students arrive from many disciplines, and are interested in a great diversity of social issues—climate change, race, gender equity, migration, criminal justice and policing, environmental health, urbanization and more. Our programming refracts these issues through the lens of social transformation. How can we advance social change through cultural action? How can we change hearts and minds? How can we prompt collective action from the bottom-up, and policy change from the top-down? These are the questions that drive our urban pedagogy. The arts and humanities become tools for community engagement, for exposing injustice and for communicating with wider publics and institutions of power.

In our UCSD Community Stations, the content of cultural programming varies from station to

UNWALLING CITIZENSHIP

The Community Stations are a cross-border observatory for cultivating regional solidarity. We are a region of flows and circulations, shared practices and aspirations, alliances of hearts and minds, regardless of the wall that restricts the movement of our bodies.

station, and from year to year, based on the priorities of all involved. But all the stations seek to increase public knowledge; challenge divisive political narratives; devise strategies to counter exploitation, dispossession, deportation and environmental calamity; foster solidarity and collective agency; and imagine possible futures. To accompany this process, our students learn how to document experiences of injustice through dialogue, workshops, storytelling and nomadic expeditions. They co-develop civic tools with our community partners—diagrams, radical cartographies, storyboards, games, videos—that visualize conflict and render the complex histories and mechanisms of power more accessible. These experiences often become evidentiary material for new cultural strategies that engage hearts and minds and rouse solidarity, including community theater, music, film, dance, exhibition, visual arts and creative writing.

Some examples of our urban pedagogy across the Community Stations include:

Co-production of Evidence
Community activists, residents and researchers assemble bottom-up data and visualizations that are impossible to access through conventional top-down institutional research methods. Our undergraduate student Annika Ullah, a double major in Biology and Visual Arts, was invited to visit the backyard of San Ysidro resident Guillermo Cornejo to see his lemon trees. Every lemon was coated with black silt produced by border traffic. The lemons became powerful bottom-up evidence for a documentary film exploring the intersection of border policy, community health, storytelling and activism. Border Lemons was a cultural strategy for visualizing power, and for mobilizing community awareness and arts activism around air quality—driving home the fact that high rates of lung disease in San Ysidro are not "the way of the world" but an injustice. The lemons also became a tool for dialogue with agencies that govern air quality policy and resources in the border region.

Nomadic Workshops and Urban Games
Another strategy involves the mediation of urban conversations. In the Community Stations, students experiment with the community-workshop format, designing games, objects, images and visualization tools to facilitate dialogue about the complexity of urban processes and policy, and to redraw the territory through narrative, anecdote and everyday practices. Urban anecdotes from the bottom-up can be important tools for communicating historical injustices and for advancing restorative urban practices. The narrativization of urban crisis through everyday life experiences can mobilize evidence to change hearts and minds in ways that hard data cannot.

Indigenous Storytelling
We have partnered closely with leaders of the Kumeyaay Nation to integrate oral histories and Indigenous knowledges into our pedagogic strategies. Students encounter diverse ways of experiencing, constructing and protecting the world, and diverse cosmologies that integrate ecological and social systems. For example, the UCSD-EarthLab Community Station is located in the heart of the Chollas Watershed, a Kumeyaay sacred water environment. The learning stations of the UCSD-EarthLab Community Station promote recognition that Indigenous knowledges and worldviews can contribute to our understanding of climate change and strategies to confront accelerating impacts. At the Restorative Water Garden, for example, students learn about climate adaptation from Kumeyaay approaches to water management, using watershed boundaries to define their territories and to situate and construct community life. This learning station is inspired by Kumeyaay histories that narrate the traditional practice of "rock drop" to confront drought conditions. Piling rocks and brush in drainage zones helps to recharge streams, raise water tables and fortify the boundaries of the wetlands. Wetland restoration is also the key to maintaining supplies of food, medicine and building materials, including reinvigorating the juncus, a root used in traditional basket weaving and a source of local economy. This water environment mobilizes oral histories that reinterpret water as social system, science as an embedded dimension of everyday life and civic participation as central to habitat restoration, cultural sustainability and economy. These multiple literacies, inspired by Indigenous cosmologies, ground a new ecosocial imagination, based on caring for each other and our environment.

Radical Cartographies: Geographies of Coexistence
Our students lead a pedagogic exercise we call Geographies of Coexistence, once again inspired by our desire to build a regional sense of belonging, interdependence and mutual responsibility. Youth on both sides of the border draw cognitive maps of the border region. Can a youth from Tijuana draw her city's main attributes, natural and artificial? Can she name and draw the shape and location of mountains, rivers, valleys, mesas, shores, etc.? Can a youth from San Diego do the same for San Diego? Can each of them draw their immediate walled territory, and beyond the wall? How do we imagine the larger region, regardless of the political artifact

that bisects those geographic features? By drawing and performing the information they draw, they gain consciousness of the meaning and value of their environmental context. The visual cognition of the territory is a requisite for the urban curator.

Often, we use images to organize dialogue. In our UCSD-Alacrán Community Station, for example, participants discuss a map that includes Tijuana, Central America and the Caribbean and are invited to trace their journey. This exercise is more delicate, and requires support of a psychologist trained in PTSD. Almost all migrants in Tijuana come from serious conditions of trauma and violence. We need to ensure that we have tools and resources to adequately support young migrants before we enter into potentially traumatic spaces. Even a simple question like "Why did you migrate?" can be triggering.

The ultimate relations of these visual narratives, the story of one's journey and the cognition of place, can help build confidence, agency, a sense of place and bonds of trust between students and their community partners. These exercises also help us understand the needs and aspirations of our community partners better as we co-develop programming.

Public Scholarship and Creative Writing
Students frequently collaborate with community partners to co-author written work. They begin by identifying a research topic that reflects mutual interests—such as climate change, race, criminal justice, migration, the border, gender, sexuality, environmental health, mental health, urban development and so on—and then co-author a written piece that hybridizes local experiences and specialized research. Co-production has taken the shape of interviews, essays, journalistic pieces, blog entries, fiction, play scripts, lyrics and poetry.

The UCSD Community Stations are curated with a cautious recognition that both communities and institutions might not yet know what they ultimately "want" or what might be possible. For Paulo Freire, it was necessary "to know how to want," which means discovering possibilities shrouded by norms, fears, biases and postcolonial power dynamics. In the UCSD Community Stations, education is a generative framework for citizenship culture—for cultivating tolerance, respect, equity and coexistence in this contested, divided, uneven zone. The UCSD Community Stations consolidate our efforts over many years to mobilize a comprehensive, transgressive urban, architectural and civic project in the border region to mediate the interface between the top-down and the bottom-up.

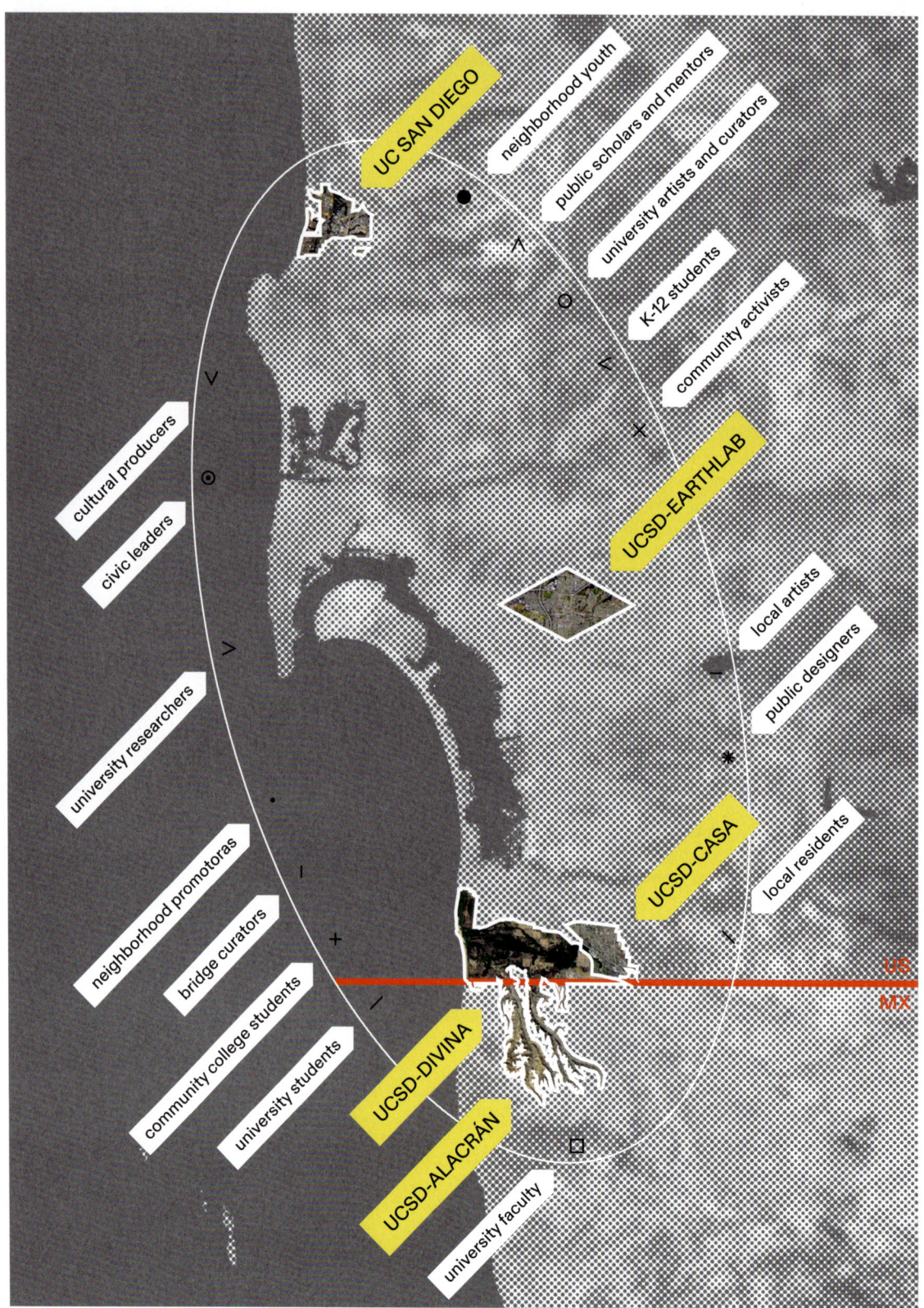

CROSS-BORDER PHYSICAL INFRASTRUCTURE

Over the years, we have partnered with community-based organizations on both sides of the border to co-develop physical and social infrastructure for community-engaged pedagogy and civic participation that transgress the wall.

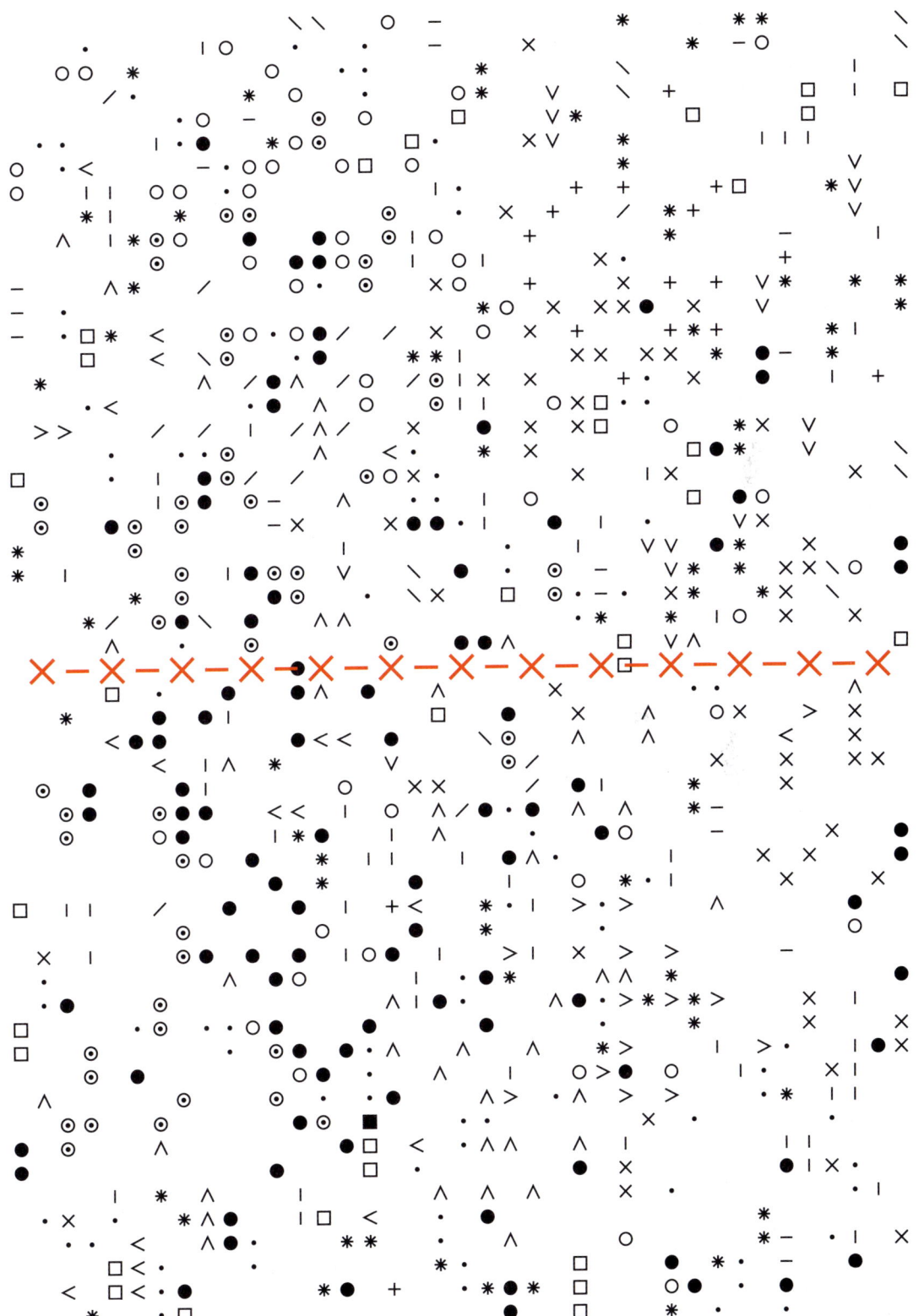

CROSS-BORDER SOCIAL INFRASTRUCTURE

This physical infrastructure is activated by social infrastructure—long-term partnerships and coalitions of knowledge. We are committed to horizontal practices of co-production with communities, to mobilize cross-border citizenship culture through cultural action. Together, we take a long view of resistance, a systemic approach to the drivers of injustice, and we engage in strategic thinking about cultural, institutional and spatial transformation in the border region.

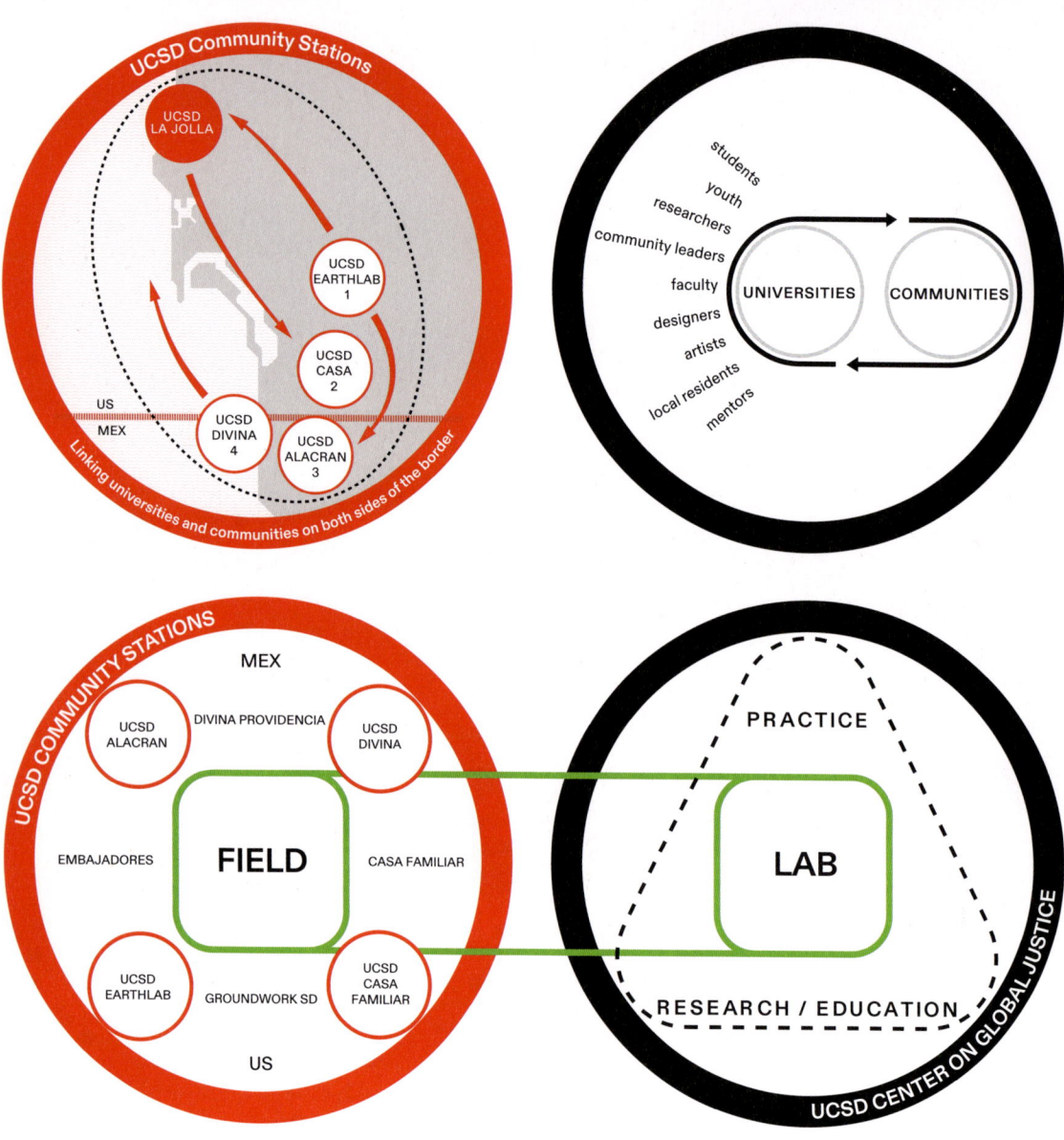

RECIPROCAL KNOWLEDGE PLATFORM

Universities and communities can be meaningful partners to tackle poverty and social inequality. This requires a two-way flow: bringing the knowledges and priorities of communities into university research, and bringing the knowledges and research tools of the university into communities, to increase agency and capacity for political and environmental action. The *UCSD Community Stations* are the field-based social engagement arm of our research-based design practice inside the public university, the University of California, San Diego.

University	Community
Knowledges – Resources	Knowledges – Resources

Research as tool to increase
community capacities for political action

    Existing spaces as
    field-based laboratories

    Access to research areas

PUBLIC SCHOLARSHIP
linking academics and activists
to co-produce knowledge

    Access to public lands

    Channels for new political and
    institutional representation

    Access to parcels for
    co-development

Redirecting purchasing power to communities

    Leveraging programmatic power

    Mediation between state, municipal and
    neighborhood public policy

    Capacity to summon
    diverse publics

Lease guarantees for neighborhood-based
development model

    Community mediation and
    local facilitation

    Fabrication-labs, lab-based research
    and cultural fora

    Meaningful community participation

    Loan Guarantor for community development

    Socio-economic and political
    knowledge on the ground

    Facilitation of civic philanthropy

    Real world challenges in their
    environment to contextualize learning
    and research

University-community foundation development

Facilitation of grants and scholarships for
low-income students

PUBLIC MENTORSHIP
linking university students with
neighborhood youth

    Track record on past project-performance
    that enables assessment of current impact

Leverage for community-led grants

    Opportunities for collaborative research

    Endorsing mentorship circulation
    between campus and neighborhoods

    Attracting funding only available to
    university-community partnerships

    Programs for advancing collaborative education

    Channels for policy-making

13 cross-campus practica internships

    Access to informal knowledges
    embedded in everyday life

    Mediating urban curators to link campus and community

Stipends to support activism and knowledge exchange

    Capacity to gather bottom-up evidence,
    often inaccessible to top-down institutions

    Hundreds of students to neighborhoods

    Summoning elactorate capacity for
    political and social change

HUMANITIES INTERSECTIONS:
Humanities + Public Space
Arts and humanities
Indigenous knowledges
Speculative design
Visual and performing arts
Oral history
Environmental wisdom
Visual literacy
Urban pedagogy
Community-based cultural production

PUBLIC PEDAGOGY
linking university knowledges with
community knowledges

    Co-production of evidence to transform
    public policy

    Access to renewing epistemic languages

    New methods to tackle
    poverty and inequality

    New approaches to equitable urbanization

    Urban anecdotes to recontextualize
    ethnographic assumptions

    Programmatic capacity to connect
    research and community needs

Humanities + Environmental Health
Environmental health and health sciences
Scripps Institution of Oceanography
Institute of Public Health
Climate change and public health communication
Democratizing science and health access

    Hands-on experiences to links
    theory and practice

    Linking educational content to
    social spaces, hybridizing normative
    categorizations of use

    Providing a concrete context for
    understanding 'intersectionality'

    Sources for a new urban pedagogy

Humanities + Social Justice
Social Sciences
Mexican Migration Field Research Program
Education Studies
Ethnography
Migration Law
Informal Learning
K-12 Climate Literacy

    Oral histories to complement
    research agendas

PUBLIC ENGAGEMENT
linking students to civic and
public political processes

    Immediacy of visual context
    to radicalize histories

    Connecting learning and research to
    community-agency social programs

    Performing research through
    action on the ground

DESIGNING PROTOCOLS FOR INCLUSION

Urban justice demands both the redistribution of resources and the redistribution of knowledges. We designed the Community Stations as corridors of reciprocity, to link the resources and knowledges of universities and communities on both sides of the border wall. We curate circulations of programs and activities between the university and border neighborhoods. And we forge channels of political representation to connect bottom-up research with top-down policy-making.

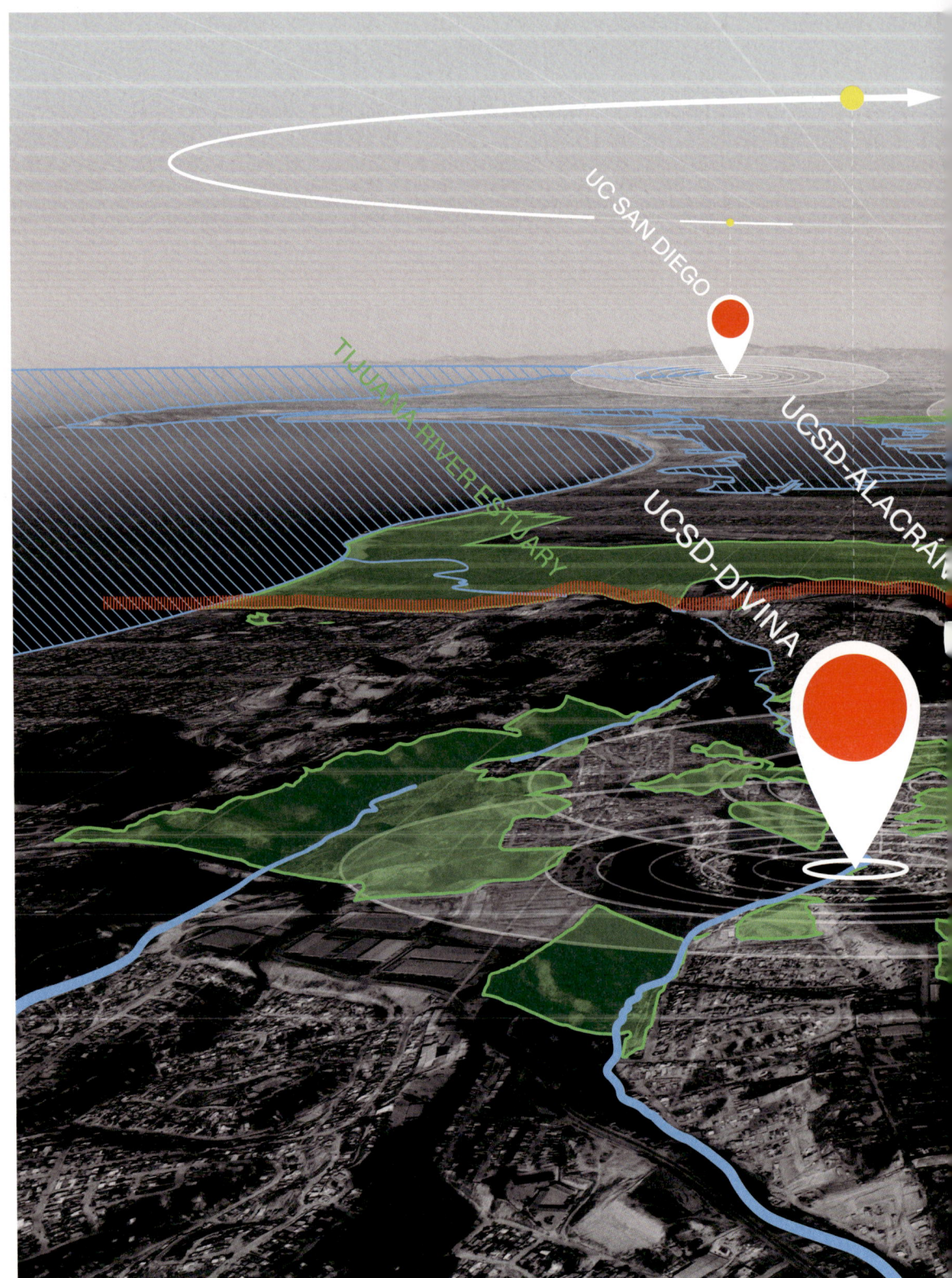

THE UCSD COMMUNITY STATIONS

We designed a network of field stations located in vulnerable neighborhoods across the San Diego–Tijuana border region, where universities and communities meet to share knowledges and resources and co-develop initiatives and projects. The Community Stations are "horizontal" spaces where research and teaching are done collaboratively between researchers, students and communities.

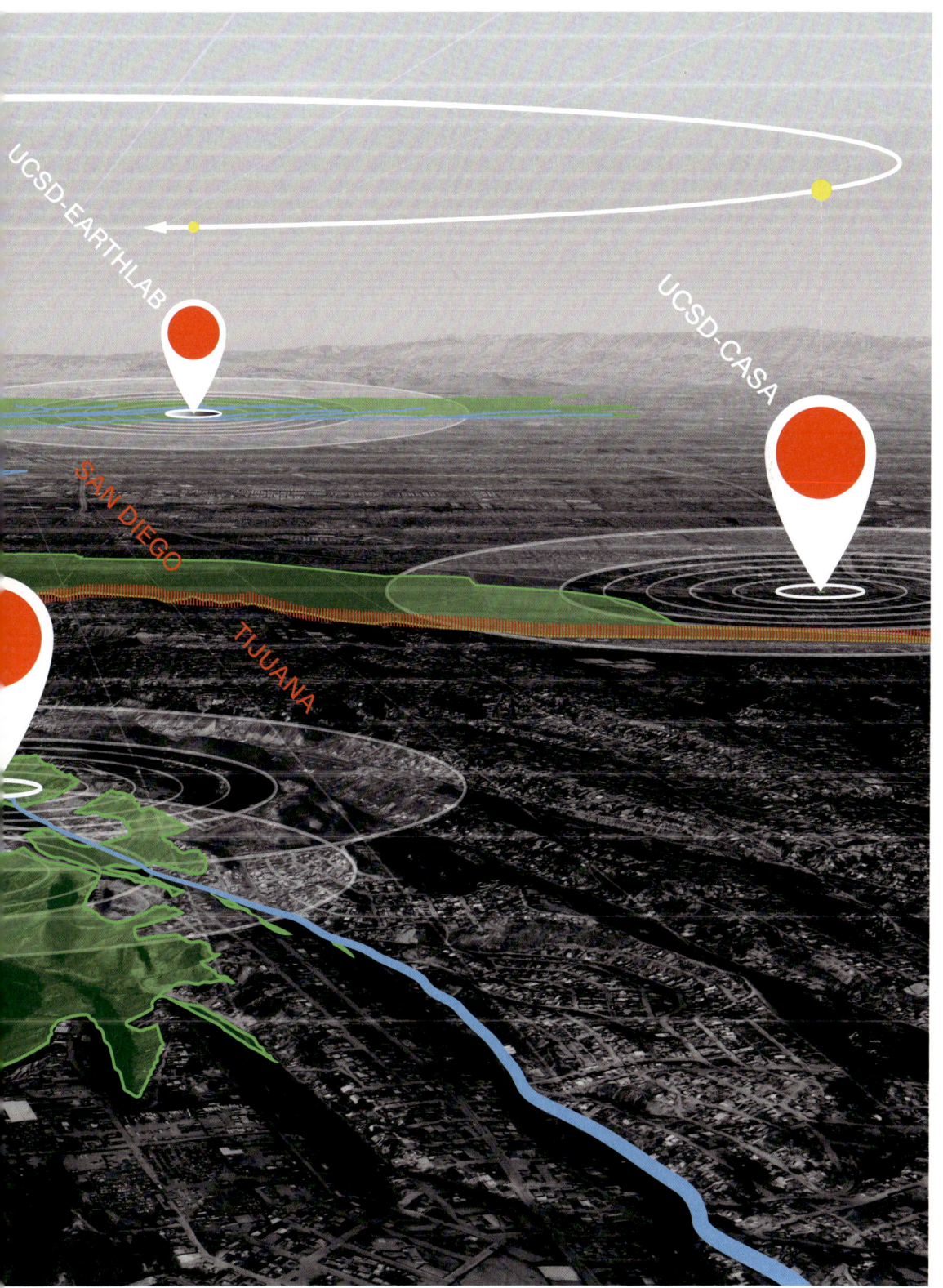

SPATIALIZING SOCIAL JUSTICE
As a distributed system of public spaces transgressing the wall, the Community Stations spatialize social justice. They also illustrate a model of shared urban intervention, where the economic and programmatic power of universities becomes leverage for communities to develop their own public spaces and housing, placing education at the center of community-based economic development. With our community partners, we have co-developed four Community Stations, two in San Diego, two in Tijuana.

WEBSTER ELEMENTARY

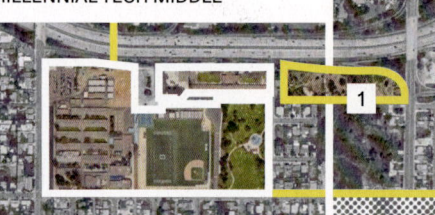

MILLENNIAL TECH MIDDLE

UCSD-EARTHLAB COMMUNITY STATION

Open-Air Classroom: a 4-acre vacant site is co-developed between community, university and school district.

CHOLLAS ELEMENTARY

HORTON ELEMENTARY

LINCOLN SENIOR HIGH

UCSD-EARTHLAB COMMUNITY STATION

In partnership with Groundwork San Diego, an environmental justice nonprofit organization, this station is located 15 miles from the border wall in Encanto, a neighborhood characterized by high unemployment, low educational attainment, food insecurity and cyclical poverty. It occupies a 4-acre parcel, owned by the San Diego Unified School District and granted to our partnership to increase capacity for eight public schools within walking distance, promoting circulation between traditional classroom education and outdoor experiential learning.

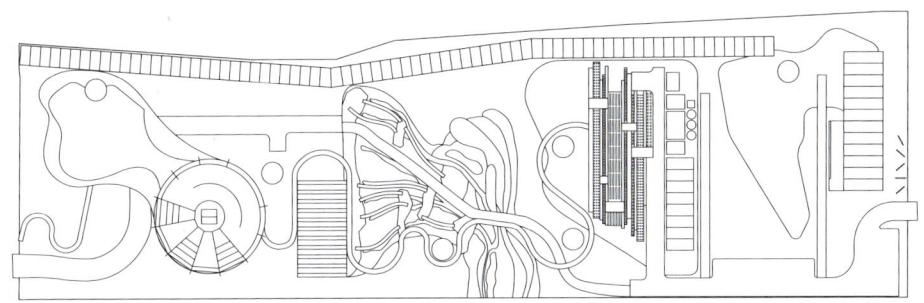

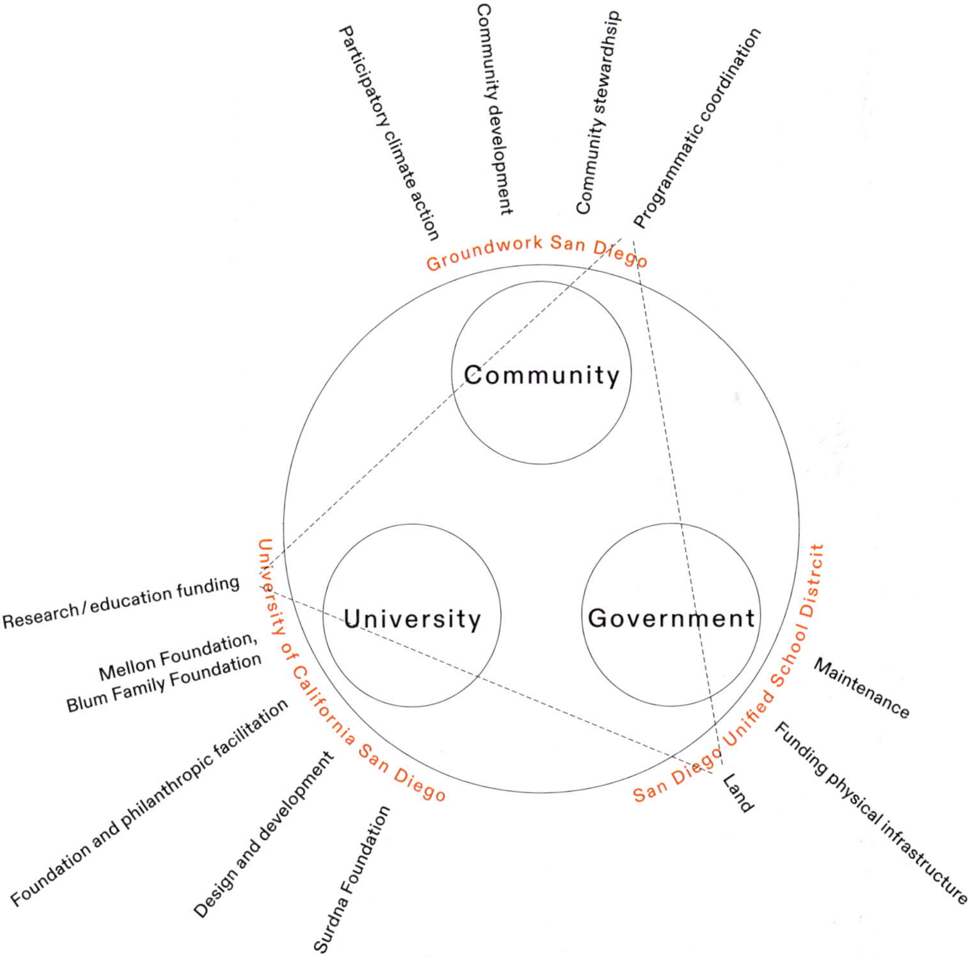

SHARING RESPONSIBILITY FOR PUBLIC SPACE
Access to municipal land gave us leverage to assemble a unique cross-sector collaboration between a major research university, a local school district and a community-based organization to co-develop public space. The San Diego Unified School District (SDUSD) provided the land and the funding for the physical construction of the site; UCSD funds sustainable educational programming, research and management in collaboration with Groundwork San Diego, which stewards community participation.

CHILDREN ARE THE STEWARDS OF THEIR OWN ENVIRONMENT

More than 3,000 kids and their families circulate through the EarthLab each year. During COVID-19 the space continued to operate as an outdoor socially-distanced classroom. When families join their children, the effort becomes a holistic community-based economic development project, opening doors to higher education and vocational training while advancing community-based participatory climate action.

K-12 experiential environmental education

Reason
Technology and science
Improving scientific literacy
To learn like scientists
To reason using evidence

Empathy
Ecology and conservation
Improving conservation literacy
To learn like ecologists
To experience the knowledge of nature

Expression
Arts and Culture
Improving cultural literacy
To learn like artists
To visualize-perform creative processes

Well-Being
Social and emotional
Improving restorative practice
To learn through compassion
To dialogue with others

Connecting formal and informal learning

Extending learning time for low-income students	School-day and after school programs
Linking socio-emotional well-being and environmental empathy	Integrating indigenous cultural practices to tackle climate challenges
Enhancing science standards with a hands-on climate curriculum	Urban-ecological learning stations and environmental design labs
Linkages between academic and vocational knowledges	Participatory community-based climate action
Access to higher education and career pathways	Enhancing conventional STEM with multiple literacies
Opening doors for our children to see themselves reflected in our environment, understanding that the care for nature resembles the care for each other	New interfaces between indoor and outdoor, academic and experiential education, to advance creative interfaces between science, arts, humanities and socio-emotional learning, all mobilized through restorative practices
Motivating family and teacher engagement to accompany these processes	
	Mobilizing community voice to increase collective capacity for climate action
Constructing a new integral person, across multiple literacies, through which social and environmental empathy, moral and ethical standards are reinforced	
	Nurturing a cross-sector learning coalition of school and civic partners
Advancing place-based climate action and neighborhood-based solutions	
	Children are the climate stewards of the future
The healthy social and emotional life of our youth should be the catalyst for a new ecological imagination, defined by interdependence, empathy and coexistence	

COMMUNITY-UNIVERSITY: DESIGNING AN EXPERIENTIAL, INFORMAL EDUCATION

With our partners we have designed an educational method—a portfolio of K-12 programs, lessons and activities that expand learning and experiential environmental education opportunities. This portfolio serves as a model for low-income communities with deficits in green space, to bridge the achievement gap, elevate socio-emotional wellbeing, and develop environmental empathy.

AN OPEN-AIR CLIMATE ACTION PARK

The *UCSD-EarthLab Community Station* is an outdoor civic and environmental classroom, designed for hands-on education and climate justice, and equipped with a variety of landscape-based environments that include energy, water and food learning stations and conservation infrastructure, all wrapped by Indigenous Kumeyaay knowledges and environmental practices. It performs an outdoor environmental design lab:

1. Climate Action Makers Lab building, design and fabrication labs, solar house, 2. Pedagogical Gardens flanking access ramp (threshold into EarthLab), 3. Gathering Plaza—multiuse, design-build, energy temporary installations, 3a. Energy Habitat, 4. Accessibility ramp, 5. Shade Pads for demountable shade structures, water and misting stations, 6. Energy Habitat Circle:

Kumeyaay Universe and Geo-pole garden, 7. Water Habitat-Hydro Stations: pluvial run-off best practices, hydro-ecological, typologies; green hydro-channels and swales, mini-wetlands, hydro-parking stall, 7a. Cooling-pond, related to energy habitat, 7b. Kumeyaay Rock Drop for wetland restoration, 8. Ethno-botanical garden along accessibility ramp, 9. Support shed for botanical gardens, seeding-germination demonstration, shaded area, 10. Pedagogical composting toilets, 11. Mother Oak forum, 12. Creek: reconstructed wetland, the generative epicenter for all habitats, 13. Amphitheater, 14. Food Justice Habitat: Hydroponic Station Shed, 15. Kumeyaay garden for applied industrial practices, 16. Pedagogical Orchard, 17. Community Habitat: Environmental empathy and meditation living room, 18. Native plants garden, 19. Sound mitigation, carbon sequestration landscape berms, 20. Reforestation zone, 21. Kumeyaay trails

A STORY ABOUT CLOSING THE CIRCLE
This is Nashaya Ross. She came to UC San Diego to study Clinical Psychology, with a special scholarship that supports diverse, first-generation college students. This is a story of "closing the circle": as low-income communities experience disinvestment and brain drain, the *UCSD-EarthLab Community Station* in Encanto enabled Nashaya to return to her community to mentor young people. They now see her as a future version of themselves.

CASA FAMILIAR RECREATION CENTER

CASA FAMILIAR CIVIC CENTER

UCSD-CASA COMMUNITY STATION

Casa Familiar acquired a small parcel to anchor a "community campus" across the neighborhood of San Ysidro, including the FRONT art gallery.

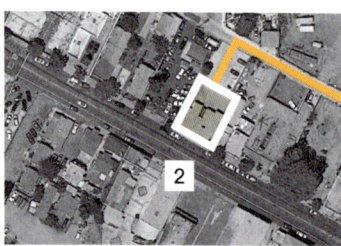
THE FRONT ARTE CULTURA

UCSD-CASA COMMUNITY STATION

In partnership with Casa Familiar, a 30-year-old community-based, social service organization, this station is uniquely located at the busiest land crossing in the Western hemisphere and adjacent to the Tijuana River Estuary. 90% Latinx, with high unemployment, low median household income and dangerous air quality, the border neighborhood of San Ysidro is among the most marginalized neighborhoods in San Diego County.

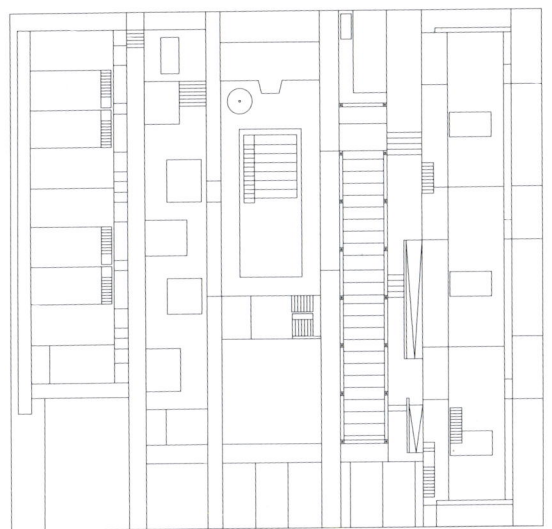

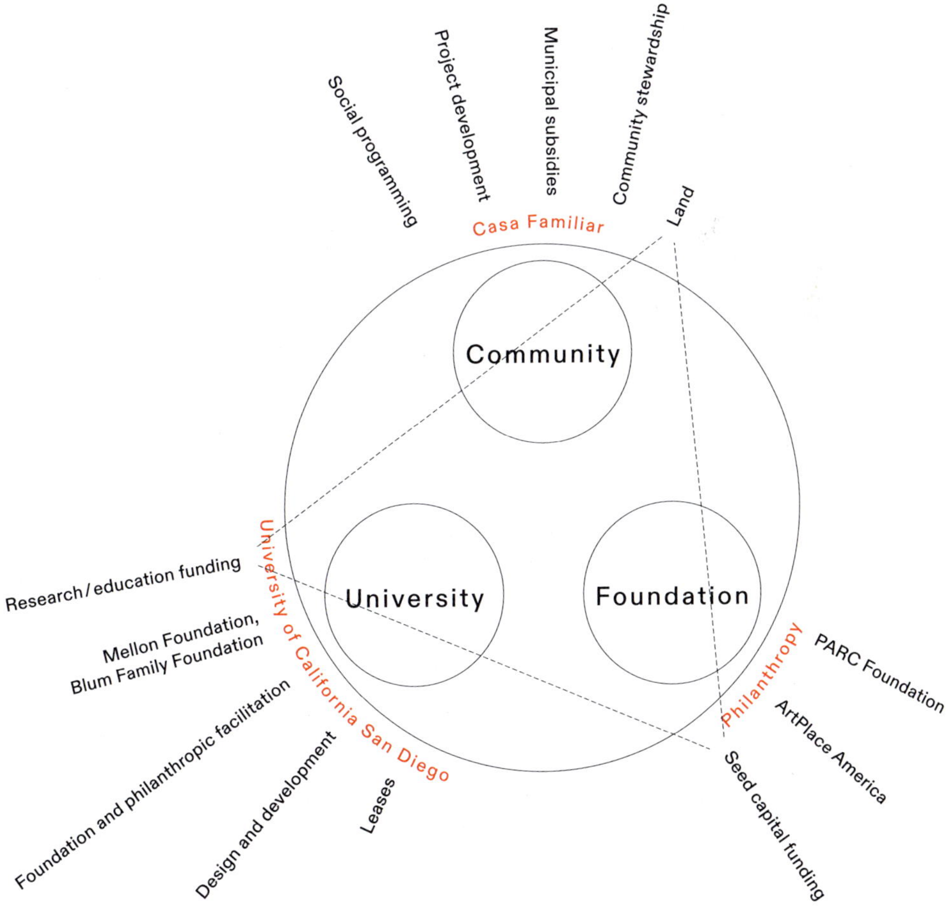

COMMUNITY AS DEVELOPER
Casa Familiar takes a comprehensive approach to improving quality of life for San Ysidro residents, connecting social service programming, education, arts and culture and social housing, empowering residents to take an active role in the planning of their own community. Casa Familiar is emblematic of neighborhood-embedded nonprofits that acquired small parcels in anticipation of developing affordable housing and synergized capacities with universities, foundations and the municipality.

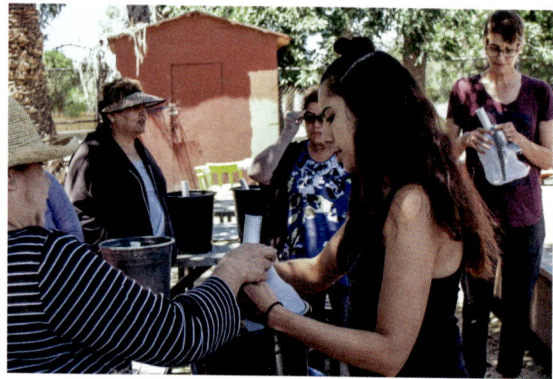

CO-PRODUCING KNOWLEDGE IN ACTION
Students, researchers, community activists and neighborhood youth circulate between the university and the neighborhood, activating arts and cultural programming to increase community capacity for political and environmental action.

Increasing (community-university) capacities for political action

Co-Laboratories
Co-producing cultural-social research on exclusionary urban policy, immigration and environmental injustice through arts, culture and performance

University-Community Arts Coalitions
University students, researchers, neighborhood youth, local artists, promotoras, residents, activists

Parallel Planning
New approaches to community workshops and participatory planning, mobilizing Visual tools to support policy transformation

Co-producing bottom-up evidence towards top-down policy transformation

Documenting, archiving community memory

Intersecting lineages of radical pedagogy and community theater

Visualizing cartographic border archive

Testing neighborhood-scale civic infrastructure

Performing social anecdotes to complement specialized data

Co-producing cross-border social and environmental justice research

Co-developing citizenship culture programming

Organizing community relations through music dialogues

Decolonizing historical analysis through new evidentiary research

Opening doors to accessing the complexity of urbanization processes through new curatorial and visualization tools

Introducing community to the creative processes from which artistic products emerge

Researching the intersection of education, social organization and local economy

Mobilizing arts and culture as tools for community engagement

Promoting border neighborhoods as laboratories for inclusionary public policy, mobilized by social practices

Intersecting affordable housing with public spaces that educate

Elevating the knowledge of community trusts and shared land management

Dialogical processes mobilized through performing arts

COMMUNITY-UNIVERSITY: ARTS FOR POLICY TRANSFORMATION
With our community partners, we develop experimental pedagogical processes to visualize, perform and transform the unrepresented into new forms of political representation. We co-curate community-engaged cultural programming, socio-environmental research and artistic productions rooted in neighborhood stories that become bottom-up evidence to increase public knowledge and influence transformations in public policy.

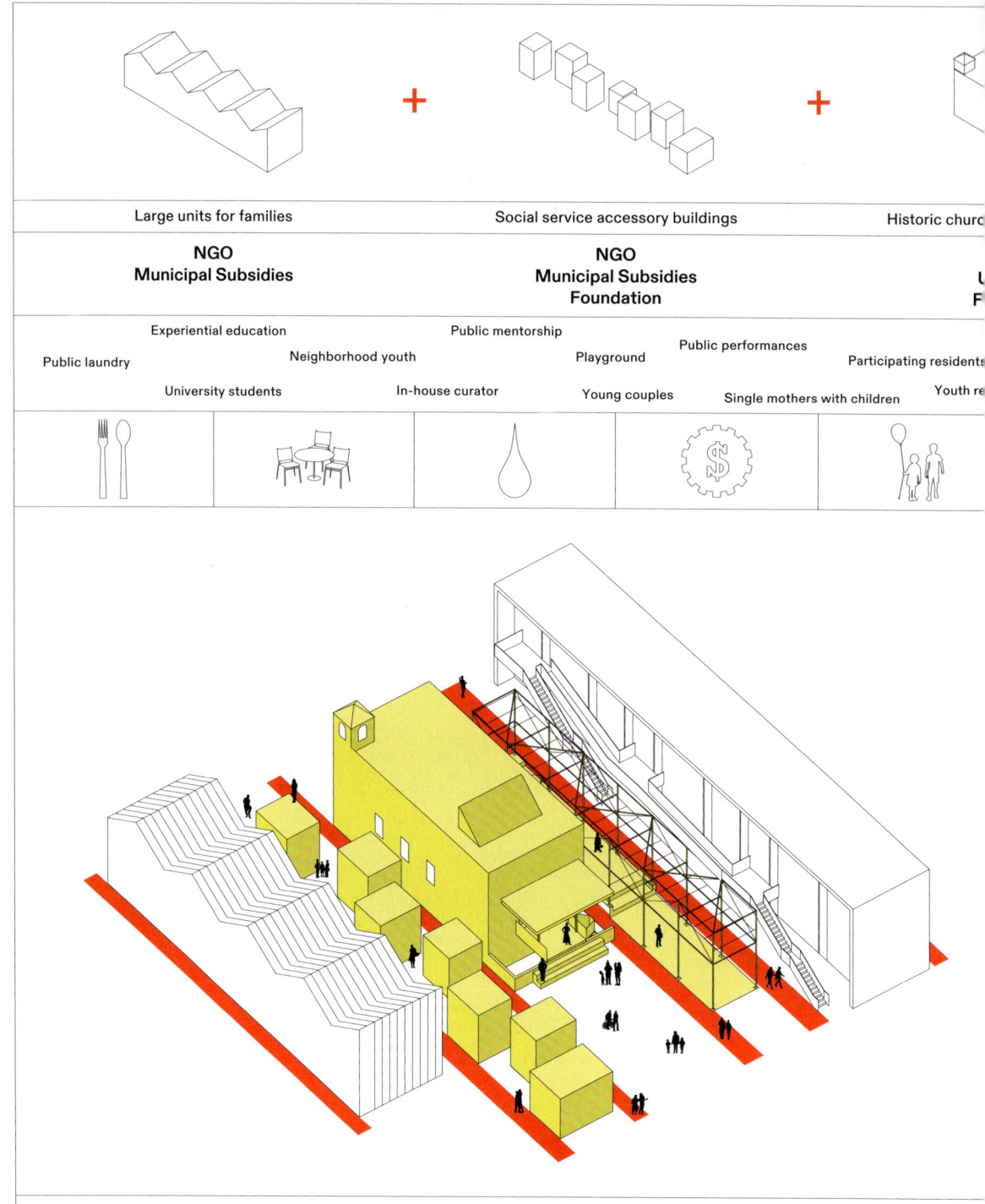

Social Service Infrastructure

INFRASTRUCTURE FOR SOCIAL HOUSING

The Community Station was conceptualized as a parcel-size infrastructure made of cultural and social spaces, anchoring ten diverse units of affordable housing (For *Living Rooms at the Border*, see project cluster 3). It is a collection of small buildings: a community theater, social, immigration and health services, and an open-air civic classroom, led and managed by Casa Familiar and residents. The interface between programmed public space and social housing is essential to assure sustainability and inclusion.

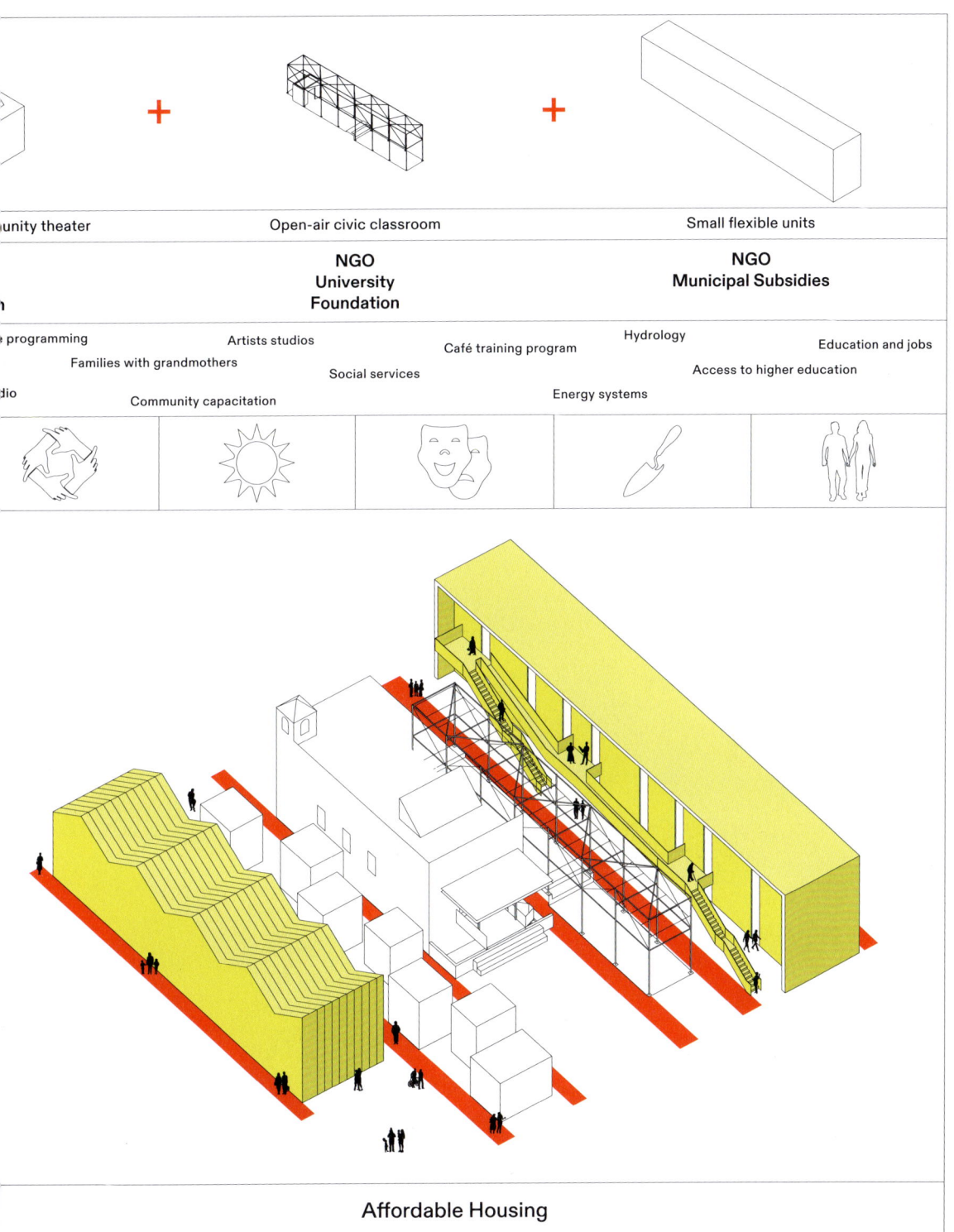

FACILITATING CO-DEVELOPMENT

This Community Station mobilized diverse financial streams to fund the different building typologies. Leveraging programmatic investments by the Mellon Foundation to support the educational and cultural programming between university and community, Casa Familiar and UCSD secured capital investments by the PARC Foundation and ArtPlace America to build the social service infrastructure. Casa Familiar became an alternative housing developer and bundled these resources to qualify for municipal subsidies. Public space was the detonator.

SMALL PARCELS PERFORM
The curatorial programs of the *UCSD-Casa Community Station* summon residents to participate in civic and cultural programming, threading housing into spaces of social and cultural productivity.

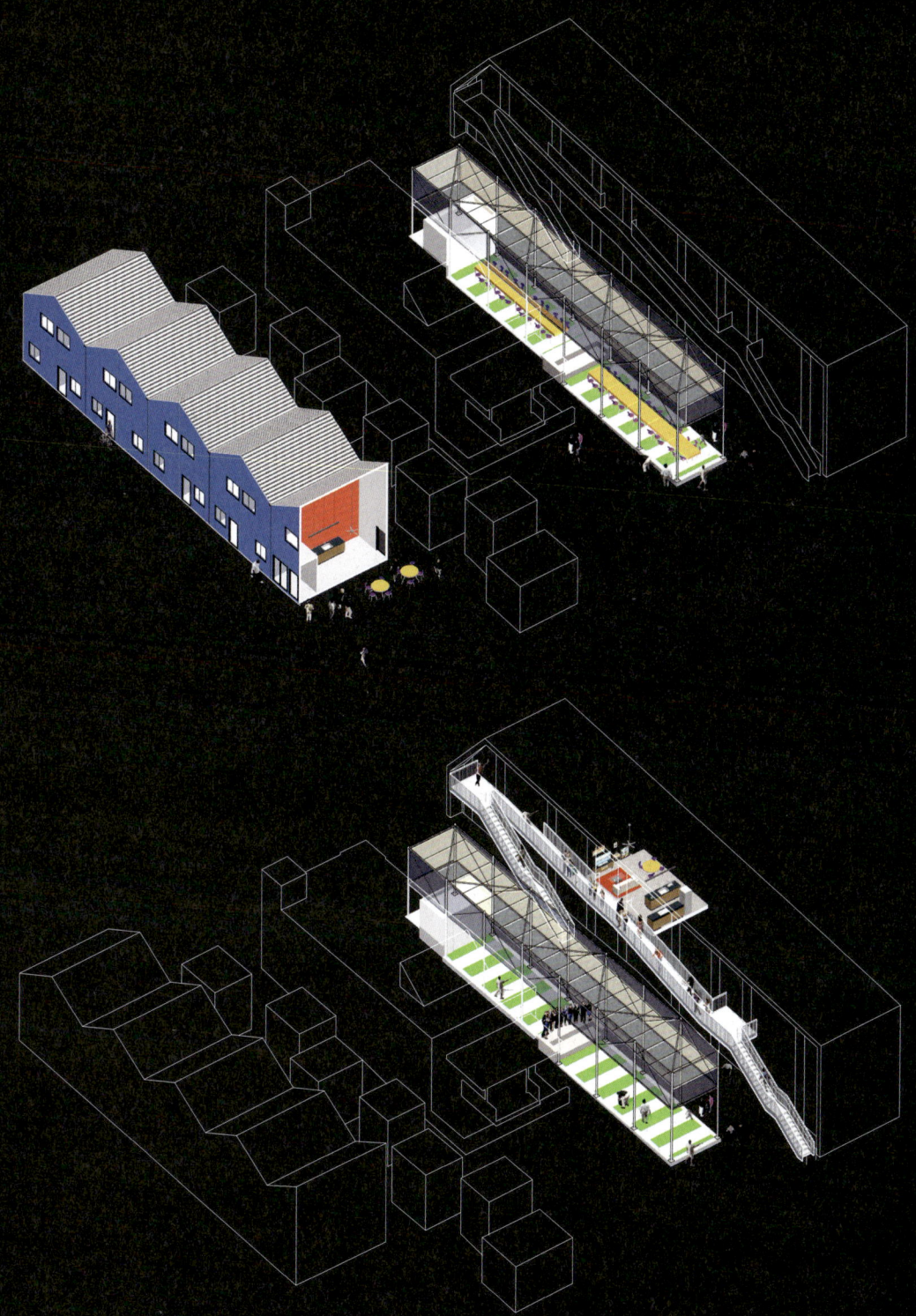

CURATING "ENERGY LOOPS": PEOPLE, PROGRAMS, RESOURCES AND SPACES
Let's imagine a small coalition of local artists, *promotoras*, and neighborhood youth collaborating with university curators, script writers and visual artists, who convene to co-produce a play exploring an urgent issue facing the community that is ultimately performed by local youth in the community theater.

A STORY OF AIR POLLUTION AT THE BORDER

A group of UCSD students, including Anika Ullah, a UC San Diego undergraduate student majoring in Human Biology and Visual Arts, visited the backyard of Anibal Cornejo, a San Ysidro resident. He showed them his lemon trees. Every lemon was coated with black silt, revealing the impact of tens of thousands of cars idling every day, waiting to cross the border a few blocks away.

CO-PRODUCING VISUAL EVIDENCE
The lemons became the subject of an artistic intervention by Andrew Sturm co-produced with the community to explore the intersection of science, air quality, community health and activism. Multimedia story telling can help expose otherwise inaccessible data to publics and institutions, producing bottom-up visual evidence to support community demands for social and environmental justice.

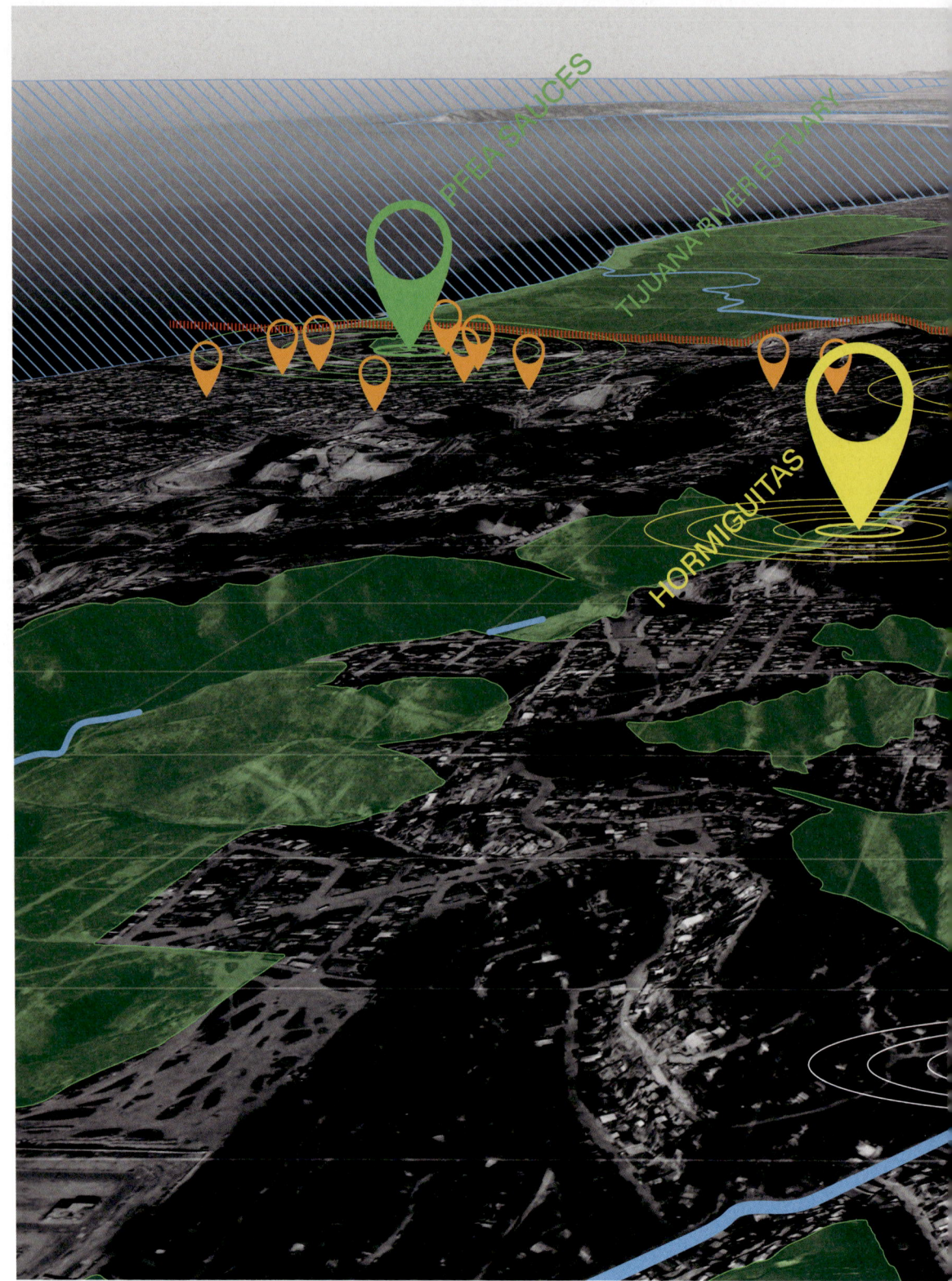

COMMUNITY STATIONS IN TIJUANA

The *UCSD Community Stations* in Mexico are located in Los Laureles Canyon, an informal settlement of 92,000 people on the western periphery of Tijuana. This canyon is part of the Tijuana River Watershed system, whose tributaries crash against the US-Mexico wall before spilling into the Tijuana River Estuary located in San Diego. Our two Community Stations here catalyze a network of hydro-pedagogic public spaces co-developed with community partners to mitigate the impact of pollution on our binational environmental asset.

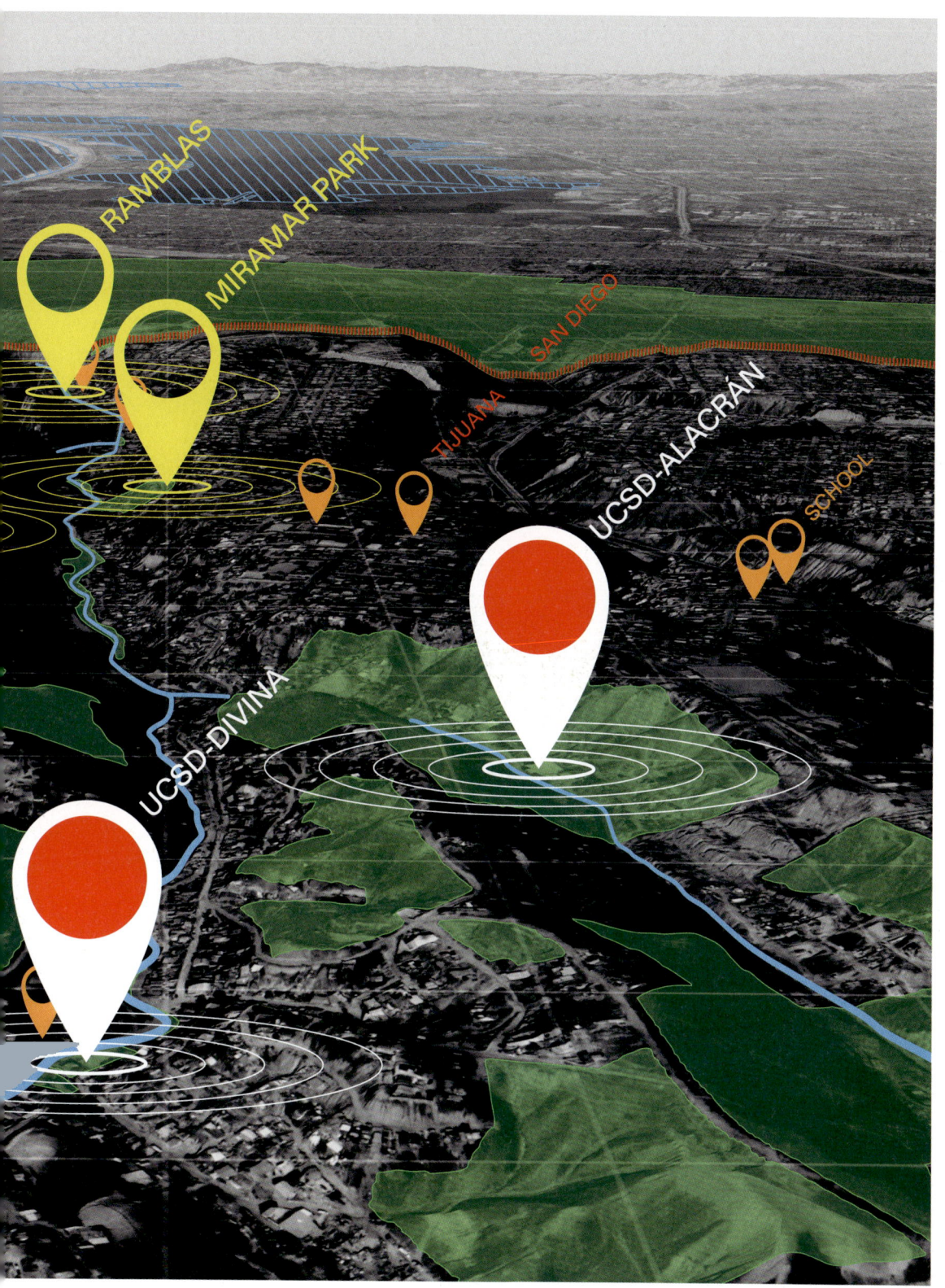

UCSD-DIVINA COMMUNITY STATION
In partnership with Colonos de la Divina Providencia, a Tijuana nonprofit that is rooted in the community of Divina, this Community Station is sited on an "island" of the cross-border conservation commons that we are stewarding in Los Laureles Canyon with local partners (see *The Cross Border Commons* in project cluster 1). Divina Providencia provides social services, including meals for youth and seniors, senior services, medical assistance and youth development through environmental awareness.

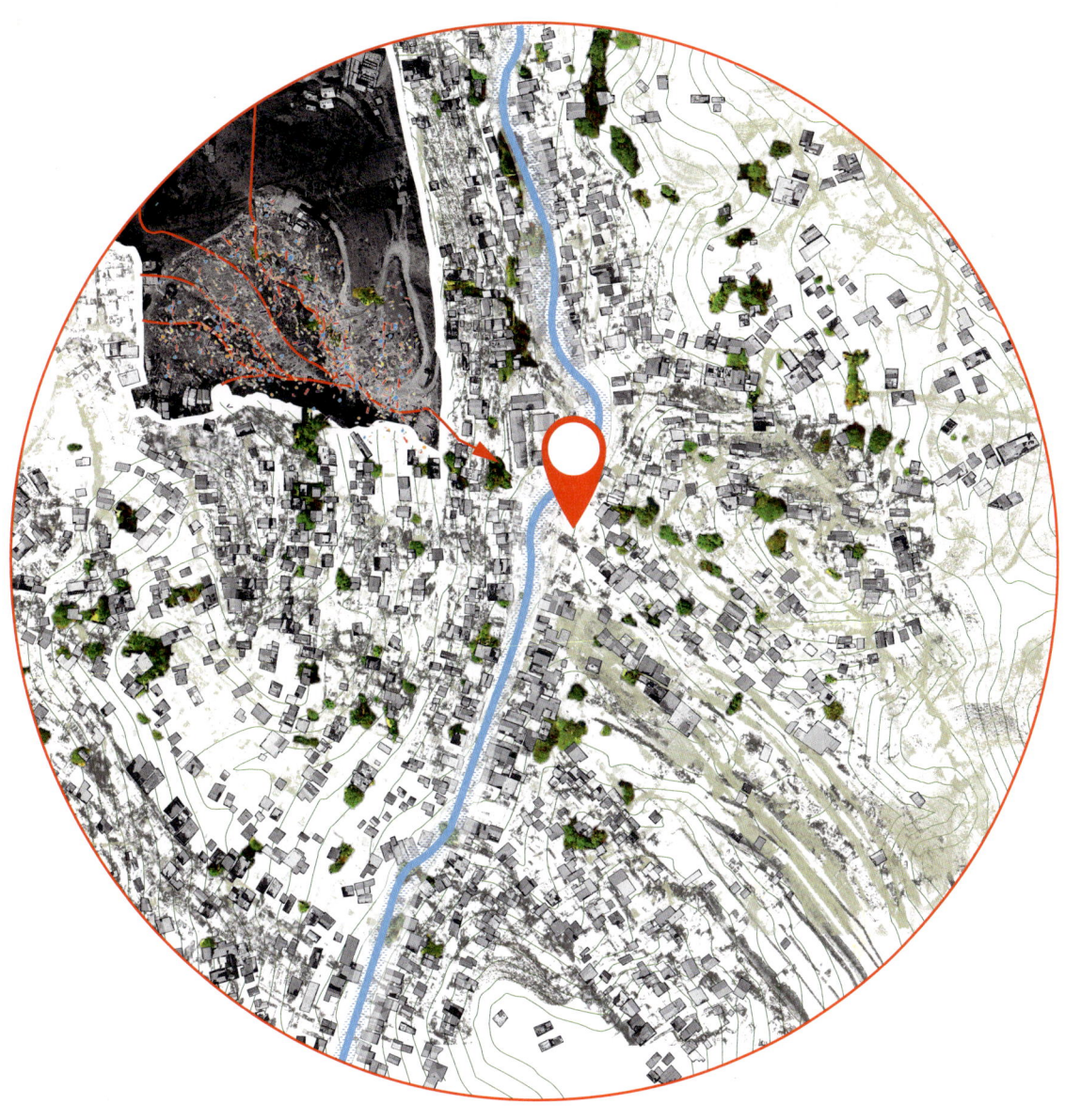

CRITICAL LOCATION
This Community Station is located at a site of conflict that exemplifies the social and environmental crises of Los Laureles Canyon settlement. It sits across the street from a precarious elementary school. Toxic runoff from dump sites passes through the school, crosses the street and ends in an open-air culvert directly in front of Colonos de la Divina Providencia.

ACCESSING INFORMAL PARCELS FOR SOCIAL DEVELOPMENT

Activist Rebeca Ramirez, our Tijuana partner, inherited the land from her mother, who secured it as a public space for her community by sitting on a makeshift basketball court site to protect it from squatting. Access to this parcel was negotiated with the municipality through a special liability transfer that enables our partners to own the site for social purpose, with the assurance of cross-sector resources and management to synergize formal and informal assets.

Programmatic coordination
Community development
Community stewardhsip
Land
Divina Providencia
Community
University
Foundation
Research / education funding
Mellon Foundation,
Blum Family Foundation
Foundation and philanthropic facilitation
Design and development
University of California San Diego
Mecalux maquiladora
Prefabrication subsidy
Philanthropy
Bob Rubin and Stéphane Samuel
Seed capital funding

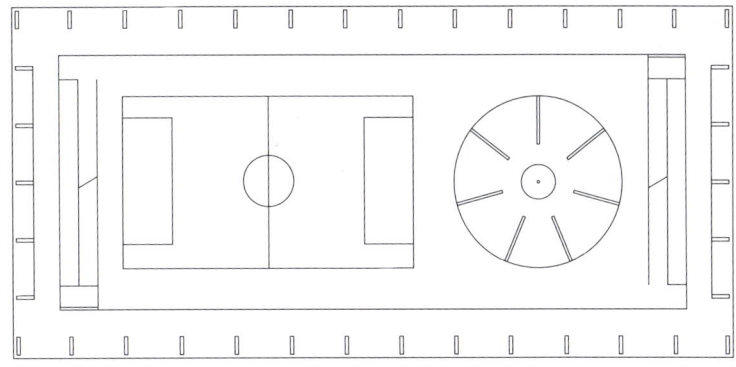

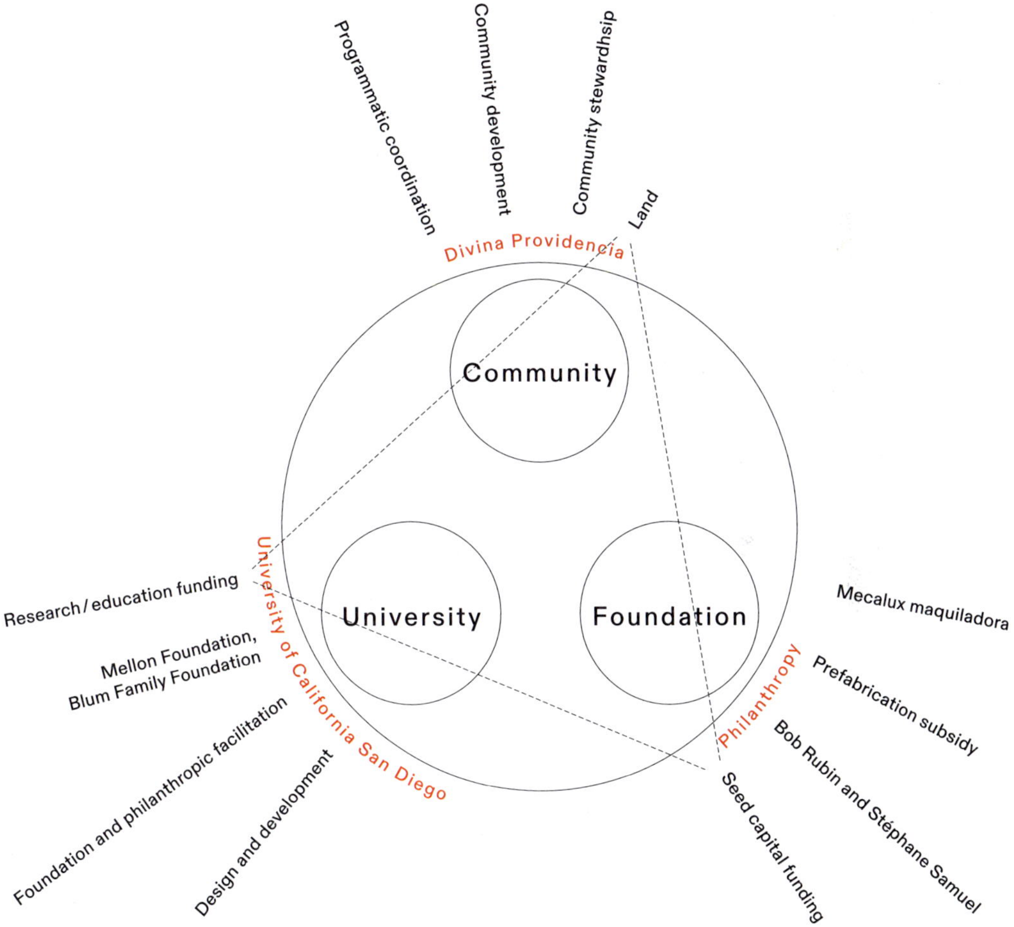

UNDERSTANDING LOCAL IMPACT TO MOBILIZE ACTION

At the Divina Community Station we work with community leaders, students and researchers on social protection from erosion, landslides and floods. We lead educational programming through which young people understand zones of vulnerability in their own neighborhoods, emphasizing ecological conservation of species, reforestation and habitat restoration. We have committed to elevating children here as the "cross-border citizens" of the future.

Recognition of shared environmental assets as building blocks for cross-border citizenship

Cross-border climate vulnerability
Educational strategies for promoting environmental interdependence and health beyond the border wall

Watershed urbanization
Social-ecological programming infrastructure for conservation of species and habitat restoration in informal settlements

Walking as political practice
Nomadic community workshops to recognize ourselves in the immediate environment

Participatory climate action through informal education

Visualizing cross-border environmental flows

Testimonials through radical cartography, oral history and performance

Educational strategies for environmental health and remediation

Bottom-up activities for habitat restoration and reforestation

Researching models for cooperative land ownership and economy

Promoting interfaces between maquiladora industry and community development

Intergenerational education: youth participation through senior programming

Designing community-based visual literacy workshops

Communicational mediation between community and municipality

Online platform capacitation, computer literacy and high school readiness

Connecting food justice and climate literacy

Informal settlements as laboratories for socio-ecological urbanization

Water management as generative tool to summon community

Incentivizing community ownership of public space

Bottom-up protocols to promote co-responsibility between community and government

Mediating the planned and unplanned through environmental awareness

The recognition of local environmental degradation as the catalyst for action

Informal eco-strategies for climate adaptability and resilience

Community brigades transform dumpsites into ecological hubs through education

---

COMMUNITY-UNIVERSITY: PEDAGOGIC STRATEGIES FOR INTERDEPENDENCE

This Community Station's strategic location in Tijuana, and its proximity to the Tijuana River Estuary on the San Diego side makes it a perfect site for advancing strategies for bioregional collaboration across the wall, expanding public awareness of the social-ecological interdependencies between the US and Mexico. We gather community-based data to advocate for responsive binational environmental policy.

HYDRO-PEDAGOGIC PUBLIC SPACES

The Community Station acts as a civic anchor for the neighborhood. Its small scale reinforces the importance of the parcel it occupies, a site of convergence, a node where water and social activity intersect. The Community Station is designed to allow the ground level to flood in times of emergency, blurring the boundaries between the property line and the impacts of storm water runoff, a phenomenon that is occurring with more frequency because of climate change.

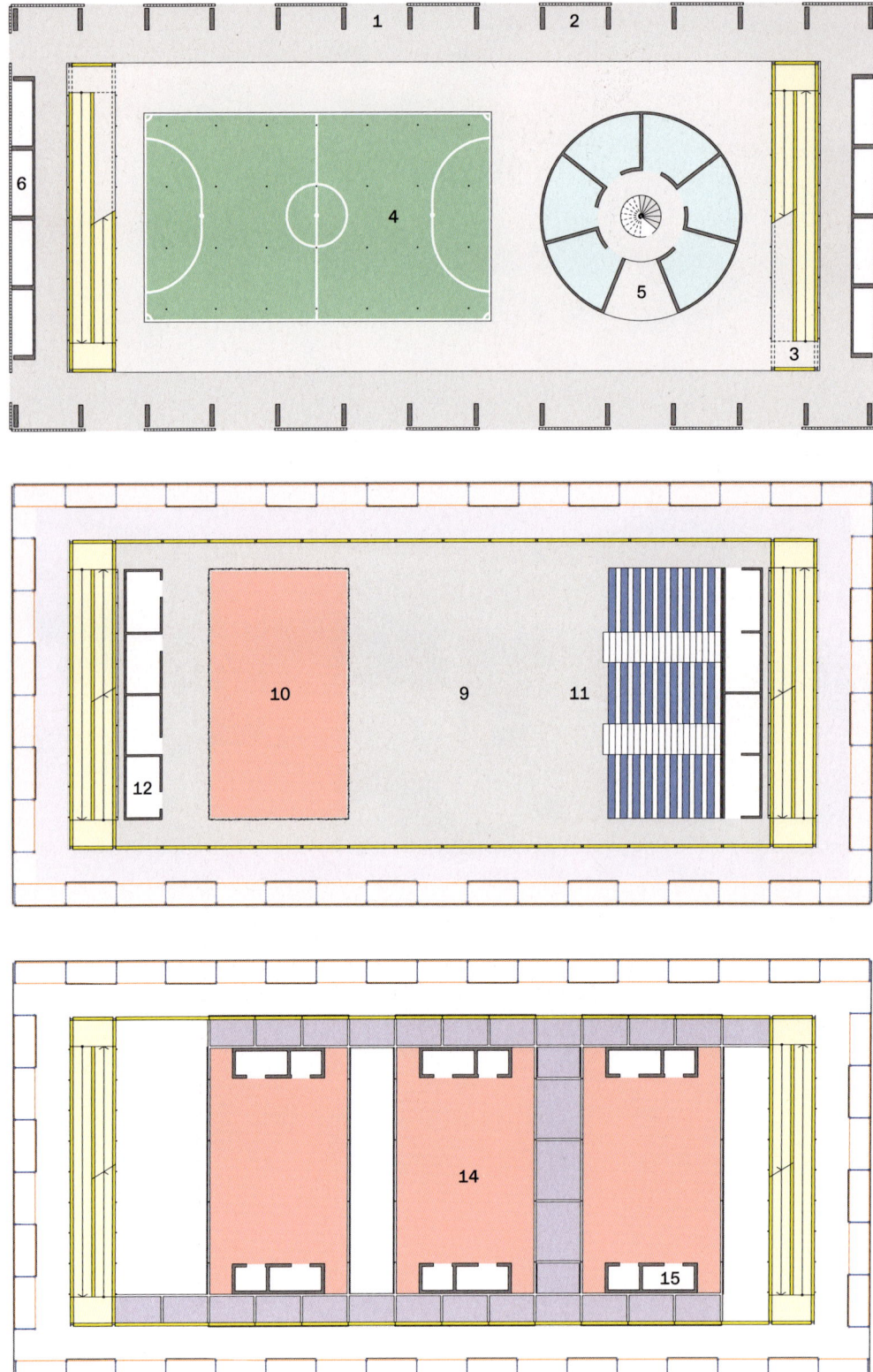

TEMPORALIZING SPACE

A new *UCSD-Divina Community Station* building will be developed in layers as funding becomes available, beginning with a perimeter ambulatorium for vendors and a social garden equipped with movable pavilions for social service. A plinth will be built to support a new flexible sports court and event space, flanked by classrooms and a children's library.

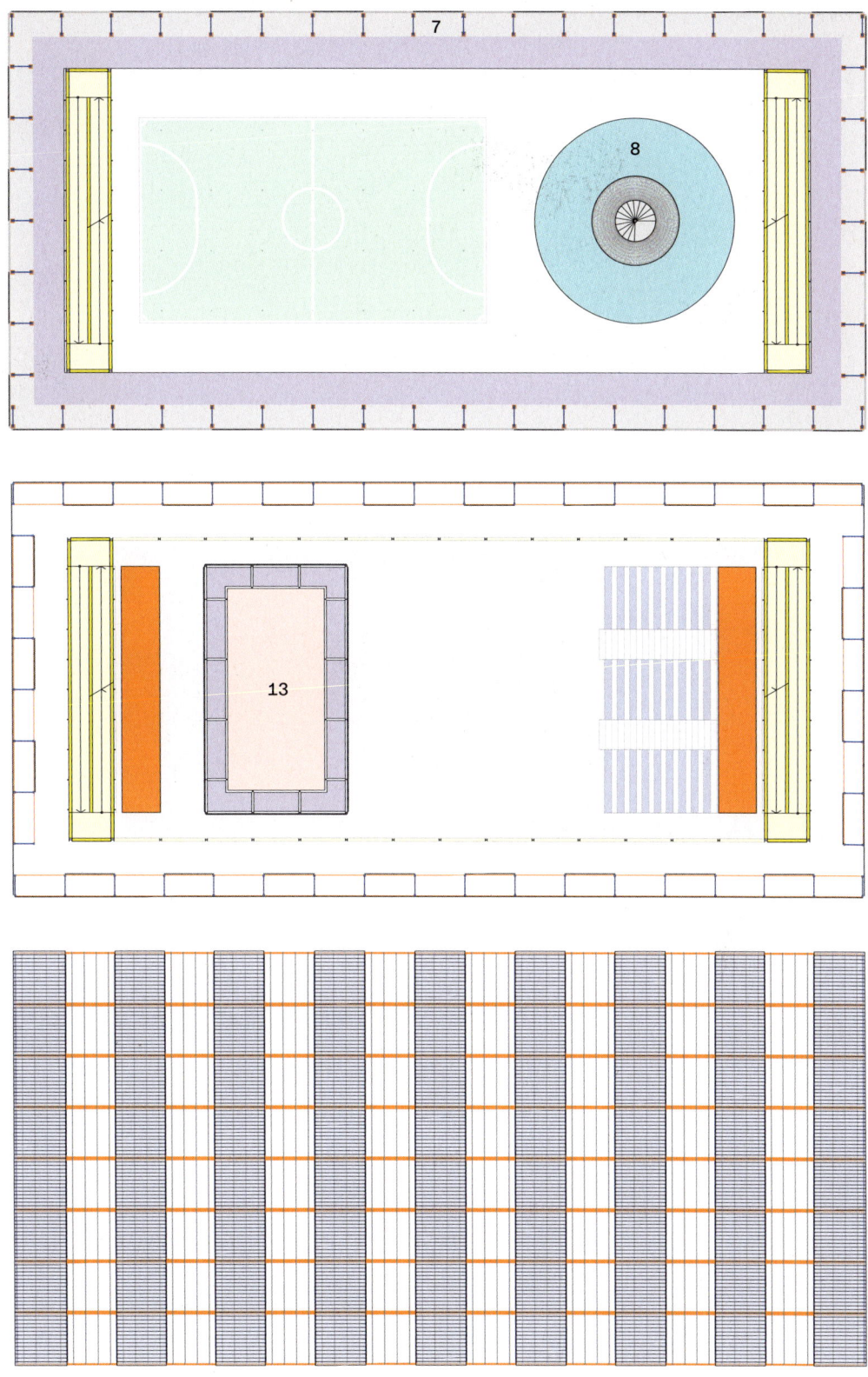

1	Social-economic ambulatorium	6	Support – Restrooms	11	Bleachers
2	Temporary informal economy kiosks	7	Library – Catwalk – Balcony	12	Storage – Restrooms
3	Ramps	8	Social service terrace	13	Catwalk – Support
4	Flexible multiuse court	9	Multiuse platform	14	High school classrooms – multiuse
5	Social service pavilion	10	Flexible classroom-stage	15	Storage – Restrooms

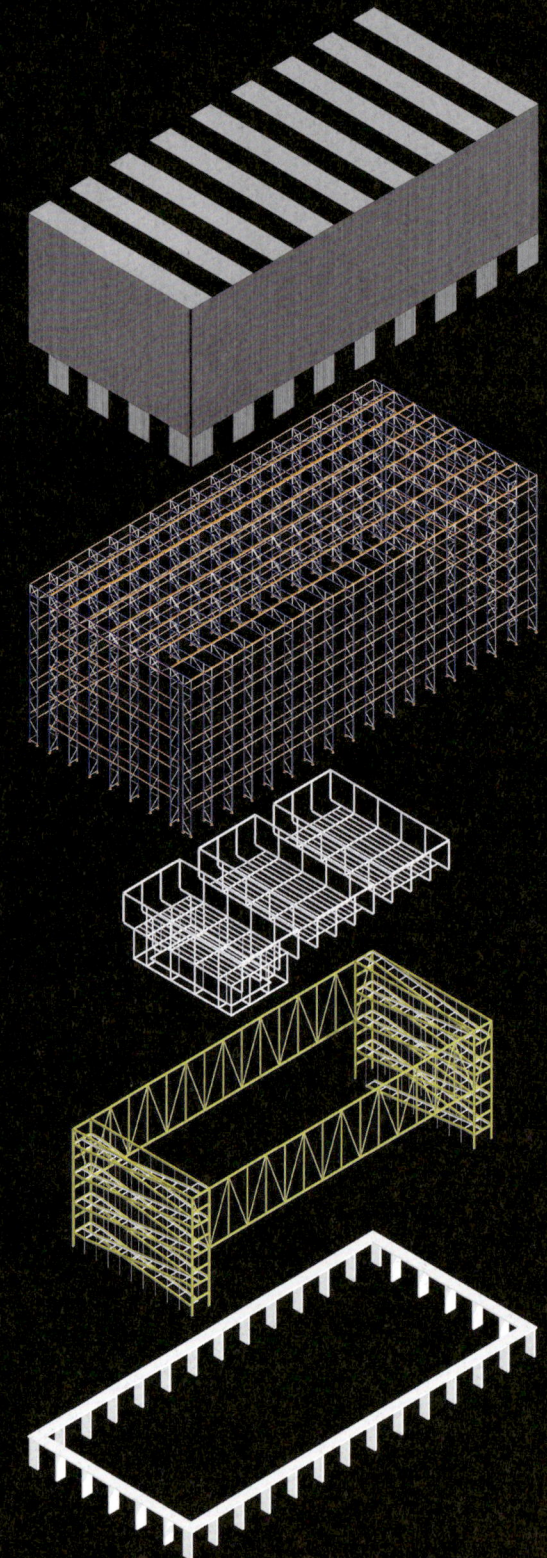

A SOCIAL FACTORY
These porous and multiuse environments will be enveloped by Mecalux trusses and covered with affordable plastic and shading systems.

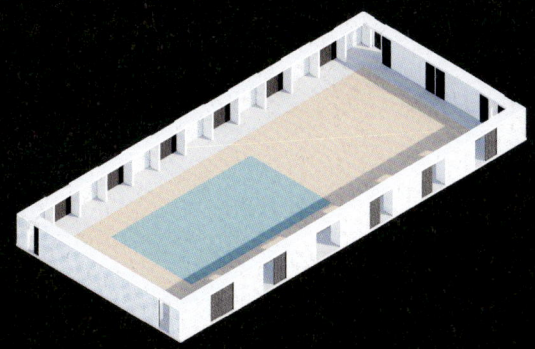

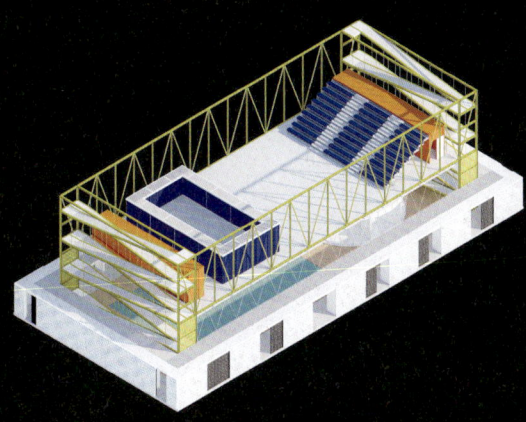

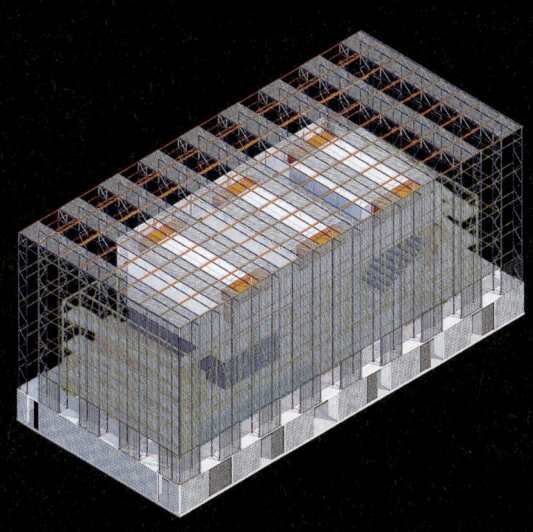

SOCIO-SPATIAL TRANSPARENCY
The *UCSD-Divina Community Station* building is designed as a large scaffold, where the convergence of structural systems and activities transforms the building itself into a pedagogical tool.

ANTICIPATING TRANSFORMATION
The Community Station will accommodate a variety of informal programs, such as weekly neighborhood markets and economic incubators. It will also contain a small high school, and a set of multilevel spaces to accommodate social services, a clinic and cultural events, all curated between university and community.

DECOLONIZING KNOWLEDGE AND DEMOCRATIZING THE CITY: THE UCSD COMMUNITY STATIONS

A STORY OF COEXISTENCE

For Jonathan Padilla, a Tijuana-born UCSD Public Health undergraduate, the *UCSD-Divina Community Station* became an observatory for mutual recognition. Working with local youth, he discovered that the trash from Los Laureles Canyon crossed the border to pollute the US-based estuary—flows that were exacerbated by the border wall. For him and his student collaborators, this became a story of cross-border citizenship and interdependence. Can communities divided by walls collaborate to protect shared social ecologies?

UCSD-ALACRÁN COMMUNITY STATION
In partnership with Embajadores de Jesús, a religious organization led by activist-pastor-economist Gustavo Banda Aceves and activist-pastor-psychologist Zaida Guillen, the *UCSD-Alacrán Community Station* is located in the most vulnerable section of Los Laureles Canyon, ravaged by the impacts of trash and erosion.

UCSD-ALACRÁN COMMUNITY STATION

In addition to a series of informal parcels acquired by our partners, Embajadores de Jesús, we have been able to facilitate land acquisition of adjacent parcels to thread together a community trust.

The site is adjacent to one of the most impactful dumpsites in Los Laureles Canyon.

DUMPSITE

THE STATION AS SANCTUARY

The Community Station sits in *Little Haiti*, a site of arrival for hundreds of migrants escaping violence and climate change in Central America. This site is thirty minutes from the wealthy community of La Jolla in San Diego, where our university is located, illustrating the radical proximity of wealth and poverty in the border region.

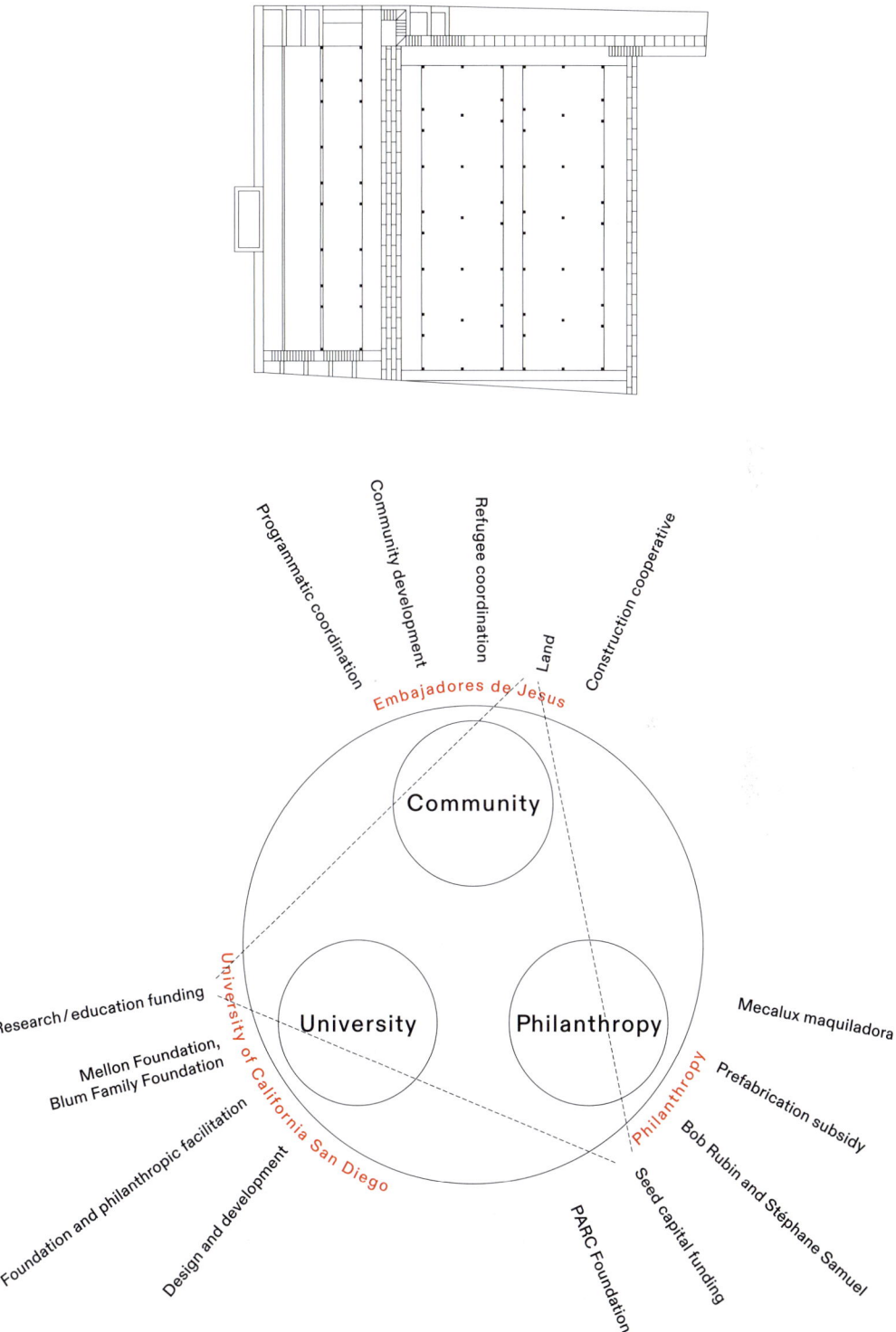

BUNDLING INFORMAL PARCELS
With our partners we have assembled a model for land acquisition that includes social impact investment leveraged by the sweat equity of migrant labor and programmatic funding from foundations.

SPATIALIZING EMPATHY

With limited resources, our partners began construction of a refugee camp to provide shelter for migrants who continue to arrive in Tijuana in waves. With the help of skilled migrants, they began assembling their own emergency housing.

Refugee shelter as socio-ecological infrastructure for inclusion

Sanctuary Ecological Neighborhood
Educational activities to promote social and environmental justice for migrant refugees

Refugee Life and Well-Being
Co-producing awareness programs for promoting health

Capacitation for Circular Economy
Programmatic frameworks for job generation and sanctuary economy

Integrating migrants into the life of the local community

- Asylum educational programming
- Socio-emotional support activities
- Environmental experiential activities
- Computer orientation and communication support
- Basic public health literacy and communicational programming
- Vocational training and capacitation
- Construction workshop management
- Fabrication and construction capacity building
- Financial skills and entrepreneurship
- Recycling, composting and waste management
- Food and farming literacy
- Community gardening and hydroponics
- Children and youth mentorship
- Linking community trust and sanctuary economy
- Expanding skills for promoting trash recycling, bottom-up habitat restoration and informal housing construction
- Habitat and well-being restorative practices
- Connecting migrant housing and green infrastructure
- Clinic as classroom, community communicational strategies for well-being
- Asylum mediation and conflict resolution
- Ethnographic research for migrant orientation guides

COMMUNITY-UNIVERSITY: INFRASTRUCTURE FOR INCLUSION

We design spaces and pedagogical programming that integrate the migrant and her children into the civic, social and economic life of the city. The site is fast becoming a nexus for migrant support, research and outreach by many units across the UC San Diego campus, investigating the public health challenges of precarious human settlements as well as the role social impact investment can play to fortify informal urbanization and support incremental housing, job generation and local economy.

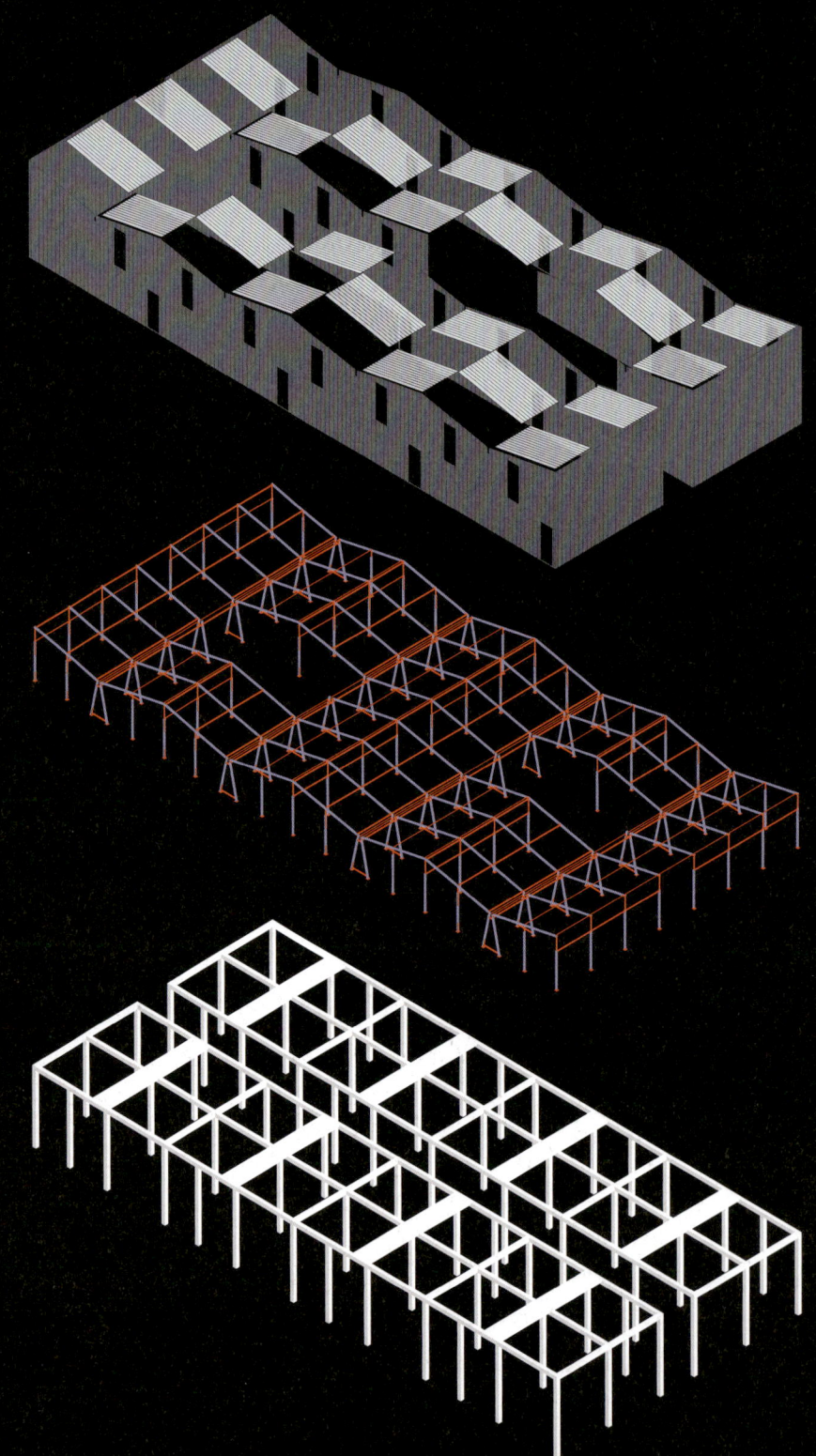

PROGRAMMING SOCIAL SUPPORT SYSTEMS FOR MIGRANT HOUSING

The *UCSD-Alacrán Community Station* is the socioeconomic support infrastructure for the *Santuario Frontera* housing project (see *Tijuana Case Study* in project cluster 3). The housing "scaffolds" are built first with Mecalux maquiladora-made frames, and the Community Station provides spaces of fabrication, training and small-scale economic development to incrementally infill the interiors through phased occupancy.

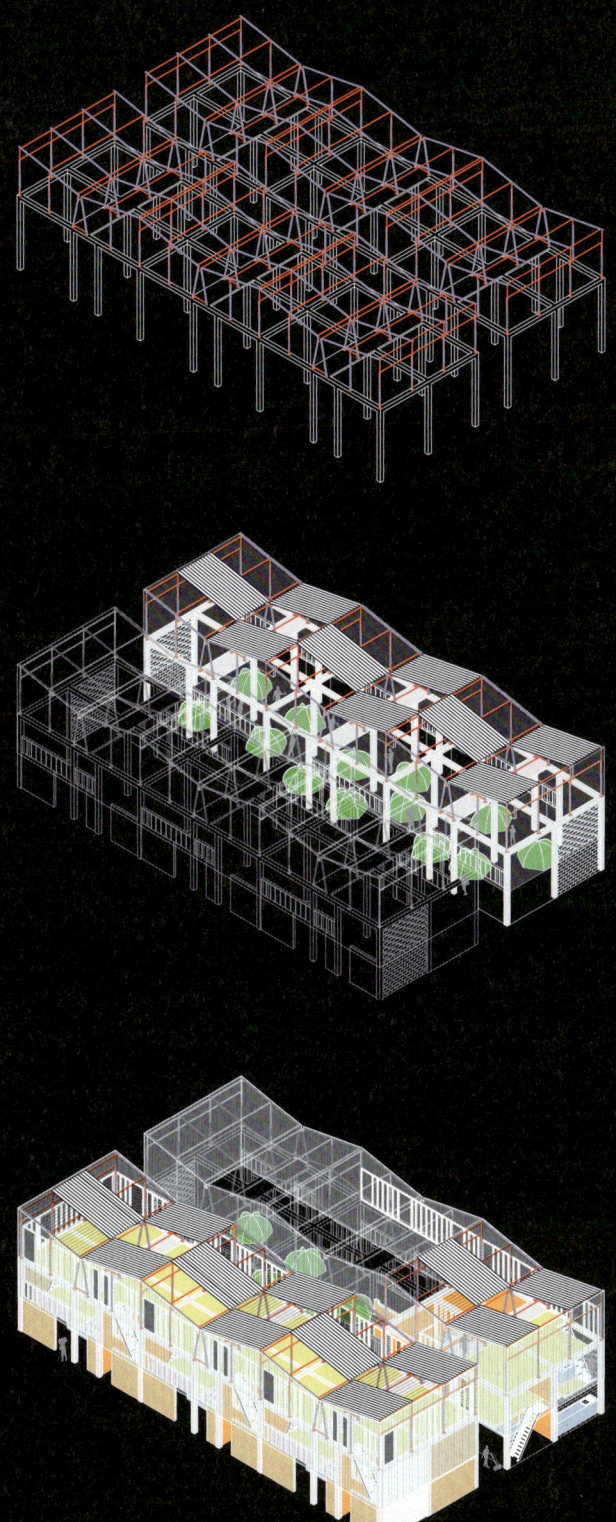

NEGOTIATING TRANSITION
This base infrastructure shapes two large container spaces, one serving as transitional shelter, accommodating migrant tents, and the other the construction workshop. The project will develop sequentially in layers, negotiating the ephemeral and the permanent. One side will finish first, enabling the tents to move into the secure, full-on housing units as the other side begins construction.

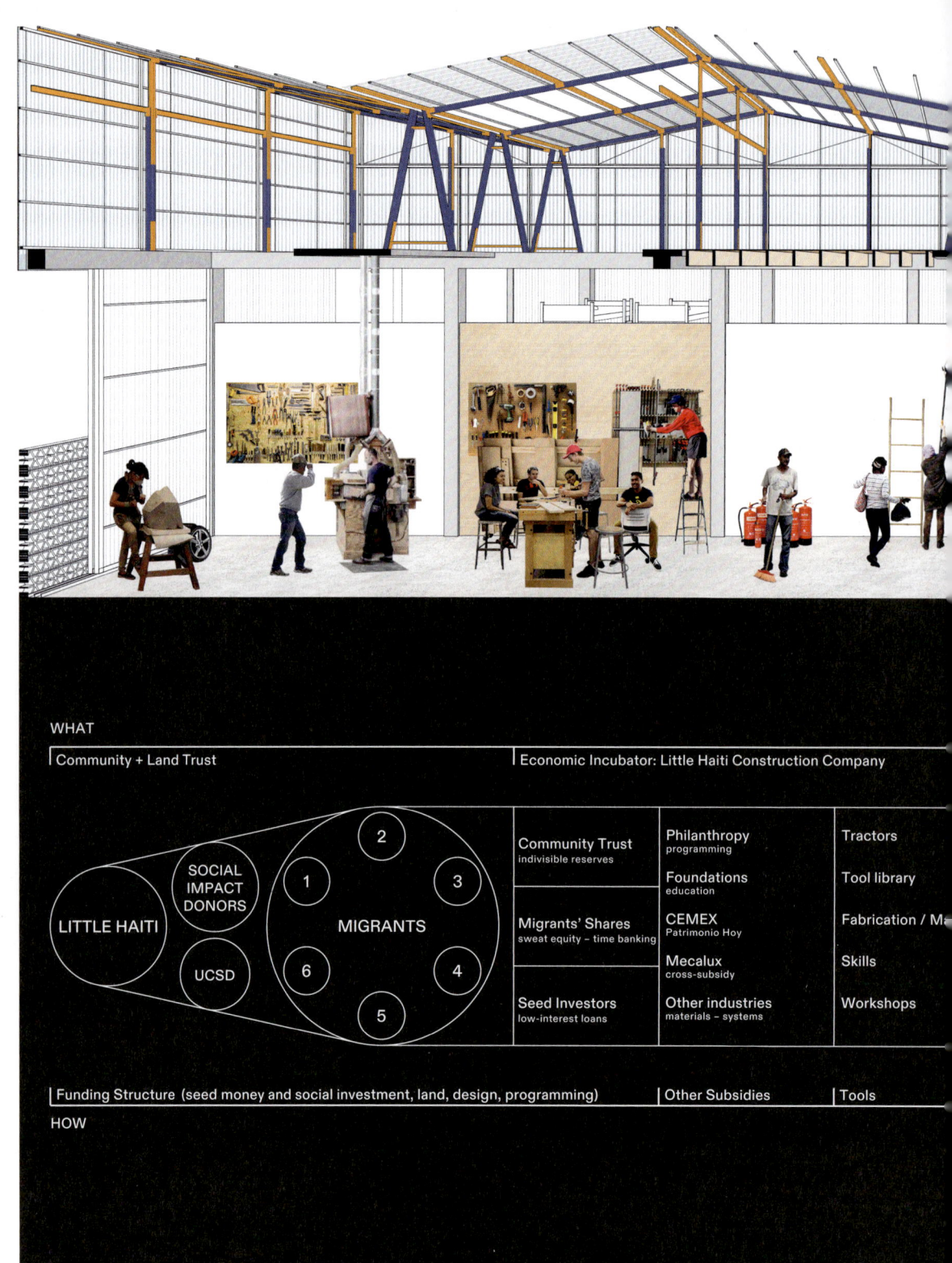

THINKING BEYOND SHELTER

As the needs of refugees become more complex over time, charity is not the appropriate model for building an inclusive society. We need to move from hospitality to inclusion. We are rethinking the refugee camp, from a place of short-term habitation and service provision to a durable socio-spatial infrastructure for inclusion.

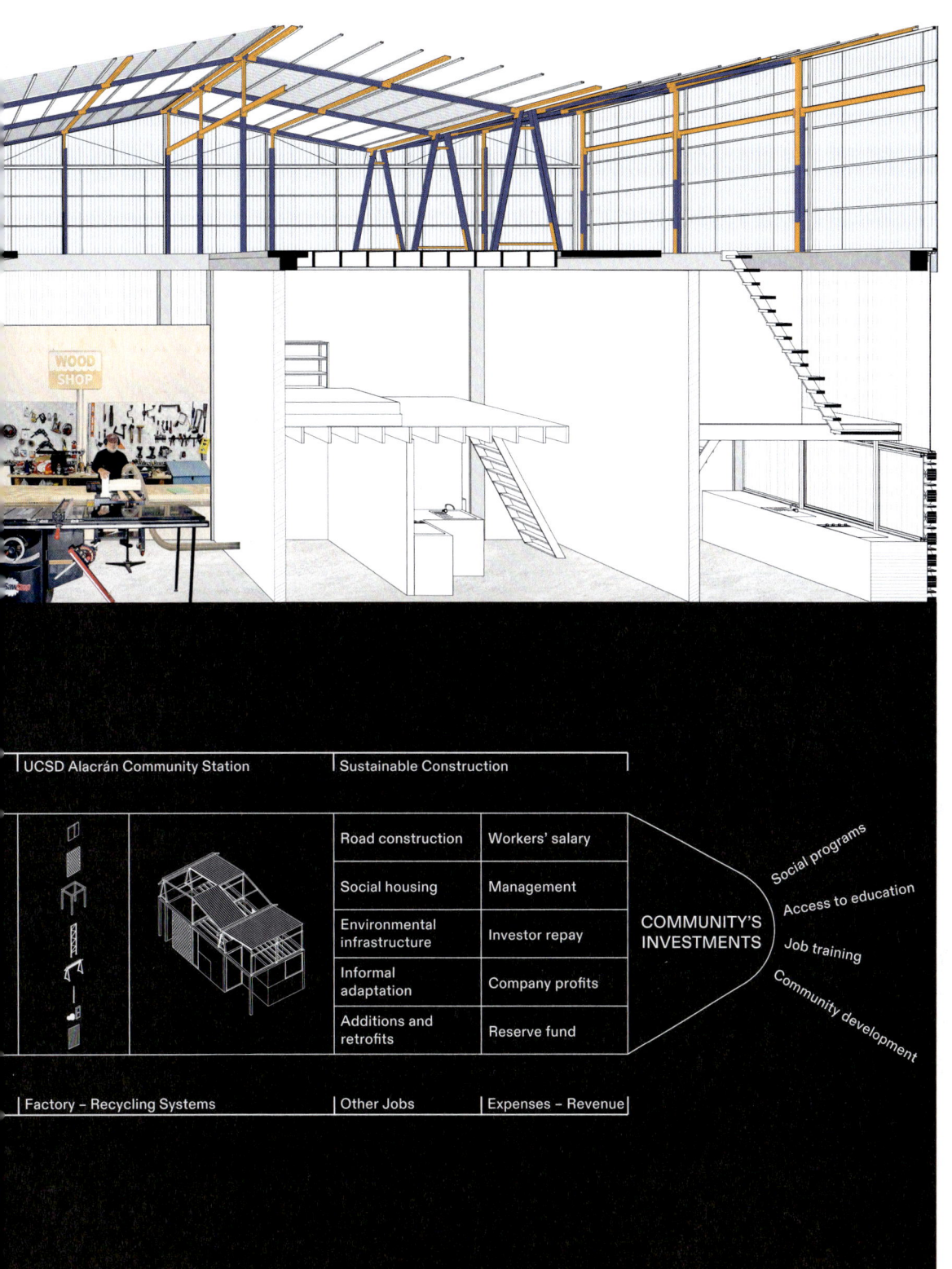

DESIGNING SANCTUARY ECONOMIES

The *UCSD-Alacrán Community Station* aspires to economic inclusion, supporting the rights of migrants to migrate, but also to remain if they choose. With the support of the PARC Foundation, we have assembled a community-owned business—*The Little Haiti Construction Cooperative*, with a tool library, wood and metal machines, and a couple of trucks and tractors. Our partners will complete construction of this site and remain operational for future construction jobs across Los Laureles Canyon.

AN ECOLOGICAL SANCTUARY NEIGHBORHOOD

The Community Station seeds an evolving sanctuary neighborhood. Because of existing environmental damage at the site, the neighborhood is organized by an ecological layer comprised of biofiltration systems, gabion wall-terracing and swales, which in turn organize accessibility and pedestrian circulation. Orchards, a farm, economic incubators and spaces for health, education and social service are programmed and managed collaboratively by the university and the community.

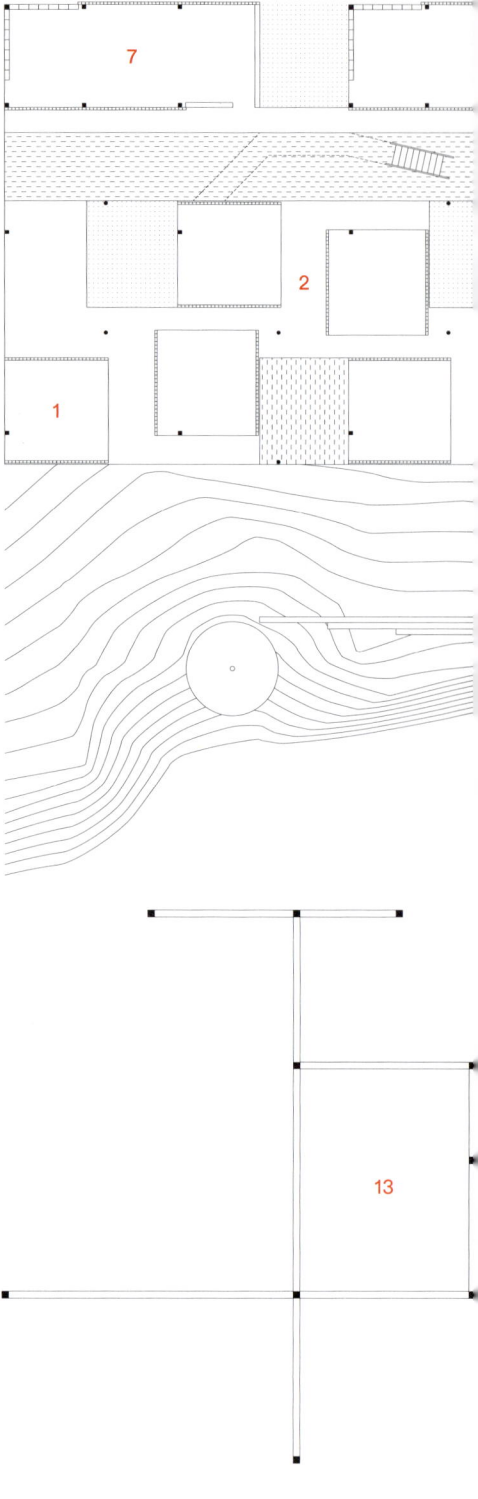

1 Micro-unit with mezzanine, hotplate and bathroom
2 In-between working spaces
3 Working promenade
4 Water-patio
5 Patio-classroom
6 Collective kitchen
7 Classroom, flexible space, storage and bathrooms
8 Industry workshop spaces
9 Hydro-skateboard ramps
10 Reforestation area
11 Mesón del Pueblo: Industrial kitchen and collective dining room
12 Multipurpose event forum
13 Scaffolds to frame existing informal school
14 Stairs and hydro-filtration terraces

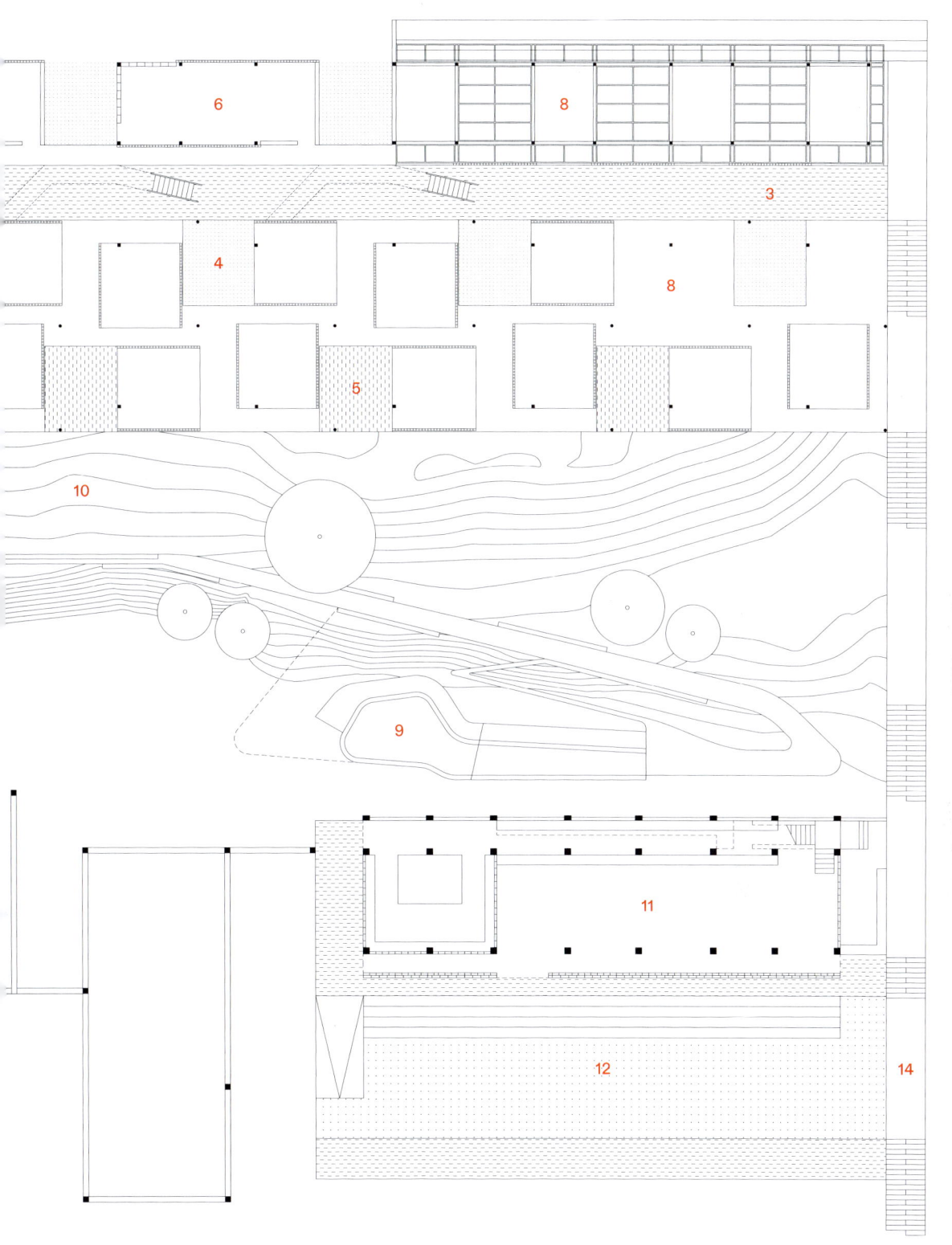

Mesón del Pueblo under construction at the UCSD-Alacrán Community Station: an industrial kitchen, dining and flexible event space for 300 people.

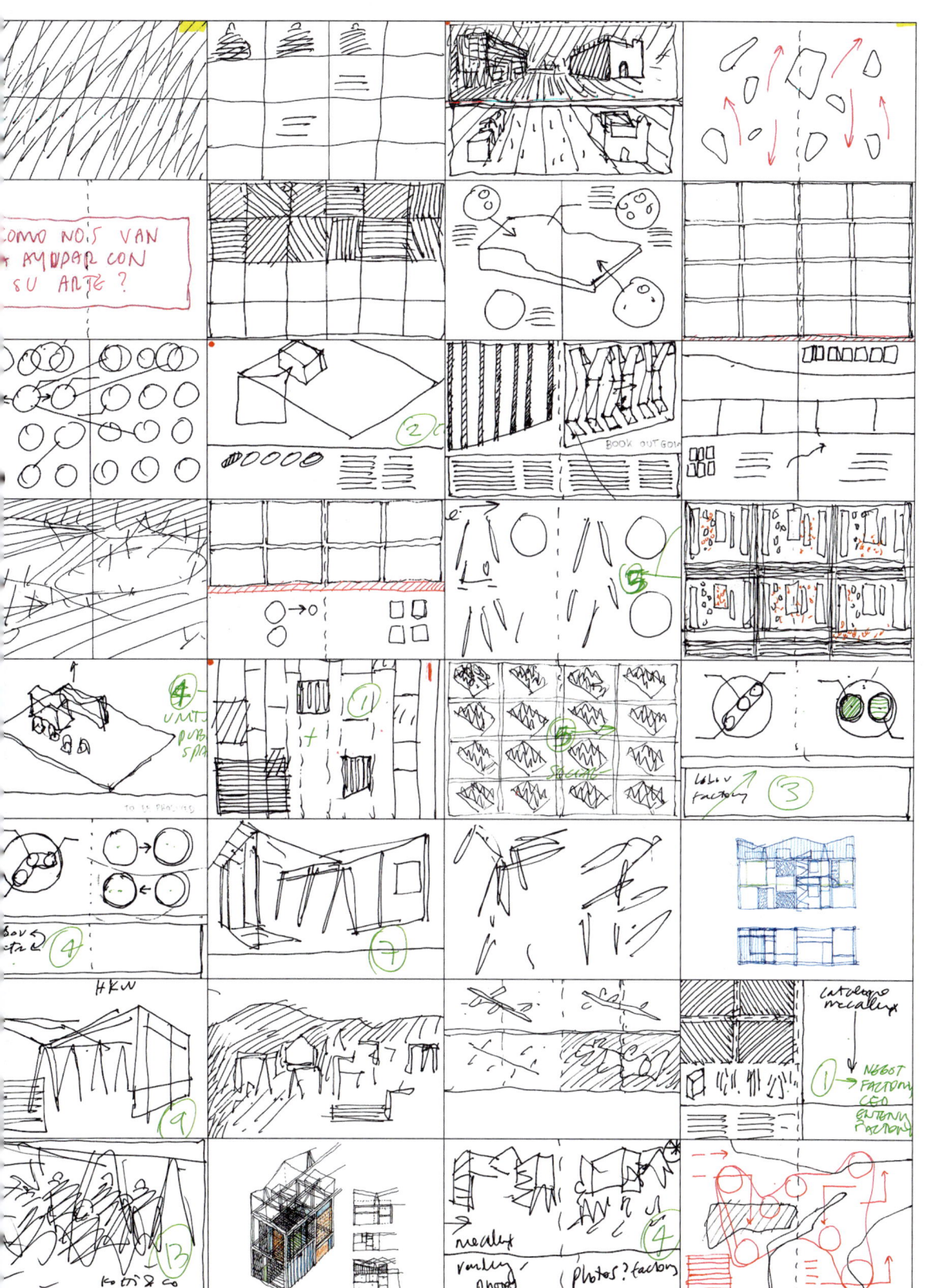

DECOLONIZING KNOWLEDGE AND DEMOCRATIZING THE CITY: THE UCSD COMMUNITY STATIONS

NOTES

1. For more on our ethical and epistemic commitments, see Fonna Forman, "Unwalling Citizenship," in James Tully, Keith Cherry, Fonna Forman, Jeannie Morefield, Joshua Nichols, Pablo Ouziel, David Owen and Oliver Schmidtke, eds., *Democratic Multiplicities: Perceiving, Enacting and Integrating Democratic Diversity* (Cambridge: Cambridge University Press, 2022), pp. 127–51; and Fonna Forman, David Owen and James Tully, "Democratic Coordination and Eco-social Crises," *Citizenship Studies* (July 2022): 26:4–5, pp. 436–446, DOI: 10.1080/13621025.2022.2091225 (25th Anniversary special issue).
2. Mike Davis, *Ecology of Fear* (New York: Knopf, 1999).
3. See Forman, "Unwalling Citizenship," and Brooke Ackerly, Luis Cabrera, Fonna Forman, Genevieve Fuji Johnson, Chris Tenove & Antje Wiener, "Unearthing Grounded Normative Theory: Practices and Commitments of Empirical Research in Political Theory," *Critical Review of International Social and Political Philosophy* (2021), pp. 1–27.
4. For more, see Teddy Cruz and Fonna Forman, "Changing Practice: Engaging Informal Public Demands," in Helge Mooshammer, Peter Mörtenböck, Teddy Cruz and Fonna Forman, eds., *Informal Markets Worlds—Reader: The Architecture of Economic Pressure* (Rotterdam: nai010 Publishers, 2015), pp. 203–65.
5. Christopher Alexander, *A Pattern Language: Towns, Buildings, Construction; House Architecture Plans* (Oxford: Oxford University Press, 1977).
6. Michael Kimmelman, "Hudson Yards Is Manhattan's Biggest, Newest, Slickest Gated Community," *New York Times*, March 14, 2019.
7. Teddy Cruz, "The Architecture of Neoliberalism," in Manuel Schvartzberg, ed., *The Politics of Parametricism: Digital Technologies in Architecture* (London: Bloomsbury, 2015), pp. 189–99.
8. Michael Henry Adams, "The End of Black Harlem," *New York Times*, May 27, 2016.
9. The Richard Florida of *The Rise of the Creative Class and How It's Transforming Work, Leisure, Community, and Everyday Life* (New York: Basic Books, 2002) seems to have tempered his optimism somewhat in *The New Urban Crisis: How Cities Are Increasing Inequality, Deepening Segregation, and Failing the Middle Class—and What We Can Do About it* (New York: Basic Books, 2017).
10. US Census Bureau Quick Facts: https://www.census.gov/quickfacts/fact/table/sandiegocitycalifornia/PST045221
11. Charles Jencks, *The Language of Post-Modern Architecture* (Hoboken: Wiley, 1977).
12. Amanda Kolson Hurley, "One Mayor's Downfall Killed the Design Project that Could've Changed Everything: Public Interest Design's Wild Ride into City Hall," *Next City*, February 23, 2015.
13. For discussion, see Fonna Forman, *Adam Smith and the Circles of Sympathy: Cosmopolitanism and Moral Theory* (Cambridge: Cambridge University Press, 2010); and Fonna Forman, "Adam Smith and a New Public Imagination," in Steven Kautz et al., eds., *Are Markets Moral?*, (Philadelphia: University of Pennsylvania Press, 2018), pp. 167–89.
14. See Thomas Piketty and Emmanuel Saez, "Income Inequality in the United States, 1913–1998," *The Quarterly Journal of Economics* 1 (February 2003).
15. Antanas Mockus, "Building 'Citizenship Culture' in Bogotá," *Journal of International Affairs* 65, no. 2 (2012), pp. 129–32.
16. Fajardo, Sergio, interview by Teddy Cruz and Fonna Forman, Medellín, August 7, 2015.
17. Thomas P. M. Barnett, *The Pentagon's New Map: War and Peace in the Twenty-First Century* (New York: Penguin, 2005).
18. Our friend Michael Sorkin convinced us to think about convergent themes of watershed-based coexistence in Tijuana–San Diego and Gaza-Israel: Teddy Cruz and Fonna Forman, "Interdependence as a Political Tool: Three Building Blocks for

eds., *Open Gaza* (New York: Terreform, American University in Cairo Press, 2020), pp. 302–25.
19 Amartya Sen, *The Idea of Justice* (Cambridge: Belknap, 2009).
20 Chantal Mouffe, *On the Political* (London: Routledge, 2005).
21 Anuradha Mathur and Dilip da Cunha, *Mississippi Floods: Designing a Shifting Landscape* (New Haven: Yale University Press, 2001).
22 Davis, *Ecology of Fear*.
23 Partha Dasgupta and Veerabhadran Ramanathan, "Pursuit of the Common Good," *Science* (September 19, 2014), vol. 345, 6203: 1457–1458.
24 Stan Allen, *Points and Lines: Diagrams and Projects for the City* (Princeton: Princeton University Press, 1999).
25 Richard Marosi, "A Failed Vision: Mexico's Housing Debacle," *Los Angeles Times*, November 26, 2017.
26 Henri Lefebvre, *Le droit à la ville* (Paris: Editions Athropos Paris, 1968).
27 Alastair Gordon, "A Sanctuary Takes Shape, Framed Around Migrants," *New York Times*, September 2, 2021.
28 Olivier Cinqualbre and Robert Rubin, *Jean Prouvé: The Tropical House* (Paris: Editions du Centre Pompidou, April 30, 2011).
29 See "Prouvé in Tijuana: Architect Teddy Cruz and Political Theorist Fonna Forman, with Cultural Historian Robert M. Rubin and Critic Alastair Gordon," *Gagosian Quarterly*, Winter 2020; see also Bob Rubin, "A Rare Prouvé Armchair Sold to Benefit Urgent Housing Initiatives in Tijuana," *Sotheby's 20th Century Design*, November 26, 2019.
30 Antanas Mockus, interview with Teddy Cruz and Fonna Forman, Bogotá, July 24, 2015.
31 Bruno Latour, *Reassembling the Social: An Introduction to Actor-Network-Theory* (Oxford: Oxford University Press, 2007).
32 David Harvey "The Right to the City" *New Left Review* 53 (September 2008), pp. 23–40.
33 James Tully, *Public Philosophy in a New Key*, 2 vols. (Cambridge: Cambridge University Press, 2008).
34 See, for example, Teddy Cruz and Fonna Forman, "Latin America and a New Political Leadership: Experimental Acts of Co-Existence," in Johanna Burton, Shannon Jackson and Dominic Wilsdon, eds., *Public Servants: Art and the Crisis of the Common Good* (Boston, MA: MIT Press, 2017), pp. 71–90; Fonna Forman, "Social Norms and the Cross-Border Citizen: From Adam Smith to Antanas Mockus," in Carlo Tognato, ed., *Cultural Agents Reloaded: The Legacy of Antanas Mockus* (Cambridge, MA: Harvard University Press, 2018), pp. 333–56; and Fonna Forman and Teddy Cruz, "Global Justice at the Municipal Scale: the Case of Medellín, Colombia," in Luis Cabrera, ed., *Institutional Cosmopolitanism* (New York: Oxford University Press, 2018), pp. 189–215.
35 Antanas Mockus, "Bogotá's Capacity for Self-Transformation and Citizenship Building," unpublished paper, 2005.
36 Paulo Freire, *Pedagogy of the Oppressed* (New York: Continuum, 1970).
37 Antanas Mockus, interview by Teddy Cruz and Fonna Forman, Bogotá, July 24, 2015.
38 See the excellent collection edited by Carlo Tognato: *Cultural Agents Reloaded: The Legacy of Antanas Mockus* (Cambridge, MA: Harvard University Press, 2018).
39 Antanas Mockus, interview by Teddy Cruz and Fonna Forman, San Diego, May 26, 2015.
40 Corpovisionarios, in collaboration with the UCSD Center on Global Justice, *Study of Citizenship Culture in San Diego / Tijuana*, Corpovisionarios in collaboration with the UCSD Center on Global Justice (May 2015). See Gregory Scruggs, "New San Diego–Tijuana Survey Holds Mirror Up to Border Cities," *Next City*, February 25, 2015.
41 Douglas Farah, "Record Murder Wave Overwhelms Medellín," *The Washington Post*, March 10, 1991.
42 Fajardo, interview, August 7, 2015.
43 An important but incomplete exception is Francis Fukuyama and Seth Colby, "Half a Miracle: Medellín's Rebirth is Nothing Short of Astonishing," *Foreign Affairs* (May/June 2011). See also Milford

Bateman, Juan Pablo Duran Ortíz and Kate Maclean, "A Post-Washington Consensus Approach to Local Economic Development in Latin America? An example from Medellín, Colombia," *Overseas Development Institute* report (April 2011); John Drissen, "The Urban Transformation of Medellín, Colombia," *Architecture in Development* (August 2012); Joseph Stiglitz, "Medellín's Metamorphosis Provides a Beacon for Cities Across the Globe," *The Guardian*, May 8, 2014. More recently, see chapter 7 of Justin McGuirk, *Radical Cities* (London: Verso, 2011) and Kate Maclean's excellent study, *Social Urbanism and the Politics of Violence: The Medellín Miracle* (London: Palgrave, 2015).

44 Urban Land Institute, "City of the Year," *Wall Street Journal* advertisement, 2012.

45 Tully, *Public Philosophy*.

IMAGE CREDITS

pp. 54–55: *Border Postcards*, LA / LA Workshops, SCI-Arc, 1994–2000.

p. 87 (first row, left): Jesús Blasco de Avellaneda, Melilla, 2014. Reuters Pictures.

p. 87 (first row, right): Oren Ziv, Al-Ram, 2013. Activestills Collective.

p. 87 (second row, left): Channi Anand, Chamliyal, 2014. AP Photo.

p. 87 (second row, right): Joshua Davenport, Panmunjom, 2016. Shutterstock.

pp. 108–11: Tom Harris, La Biennale di Venezia, Italy, 2018.

pp. 116–17: Lorena Branks, Tijuana, 2021.

p. 144: Photos courtesy of the US Pavilion, La Biennale di Venezia, Italy, 2008.

p. 180: Bernard Hoffman, Levittown, 1950. The LIFE Picture Collection/Shutterstock.

pp. 257 (bottom), 278–82, 283 (top), 284–85, 287 (bottom left), 288–91: Stephen Whalen Photography, Living Rooms at the Border, San Diego, 2020.

pp. 283 (bottom), 286, 287 (right), 340–42, 344–46, 347 (bottom): Jesús F. Limón + Prismática, San Diego–Tijuana, 2021.

p. 300: Photos courtesy of MECALUX, S.A., Tijuana, 2022.

p. 314: Bliss Photography, Orange County Museum of Art, Santa Ana, 2017.

pp. 338–39: John Francis Peters, Tijuana, 2021.

pp. 343, 348–49, 558 (first row, right; third row, right; fourth row, left), 566, 570: Daniel Castro Jaramillo, Tijuana, 2021.

pp. 360–63: Photos courtesy of the Washington Street Skateboard Park Collective, San Diego, 1999.

pp. 382–87: Photos courtesy of the Cooperativa Guatemalteca and M7Red, Buenos Aires, 2009.

pp. 394–99: Photos courtesy of Madrid Abierto and M7Red, Madrid, 2010.

pp. 404–09: Photos courtesy of APAP 2010, Youngdoo Moon and M7Red, Anyang, 2010.

pp. 414–15, 418 (fourth row, left), 419 (first row, left): Paul Rivera, Balboa Park, San Diego, 2005.

pp. 421–25: Adrien Le Biavant, Movimiento de Arte y Cultura Latino Americana, San Jose, 2017.

p. 429: Photo courtesy of *Wohnungsfrage*, Haus der Kulturen der Welt, Berlin, 2015.

pp. 449, 458–73: Graphic design by Matthias Görlich and Pawel Wolowitsch, 2022.

p. 476: Medellín. Freepik.

p. 477: Óscar Garcés, Medellín, 2013. Shutterstock.

pp. 488–89: Photos courtesy of the Ontario Museum of Art, Toronto, Canada, 2018.

pp. 490–91: Photos courtesy of the Yerba Buena Center for the Arts, San Francisco, 2017.

p. 531: Andrew Sturm, *Citizen Architect*, San Ysidro, 2018.

Our gratitude to many people and institutions that have supported and partnered with us over many years, and have contributed to the work presented in this book.

BOOK RESEARCH AND DESIGN TEAM
Jonathan Maier, Marcello Maltagliati, Kyle Haines and Ben Notkin.

COMMUNITY STATIONS PARTNERS
Casa Familiar (Andrea Skorepa, Lisa Cuestas, David Flores, Francisco Eme, Andy Sturm); *Colonos de la Divina Providencia* (Rebeca Ramirez, Victor Barragán); *Embajadores de Jesús* (Gustavo Banda Aceves, Zaida Guillén, Hanaeel Banda-Guillén); *Groundwork San Diego-Chollas Creek* (Leslie Reynolds, Patrice Baker, Allie Sifrit, JoAnna Proctor, Bill Ponder, Derryl Williams).

CORE PROJECT RESEARCH AND DESIGN, PAST AND PRESENT
Camille Campion, Giacomo Castagnola, Adriana Cuellar, Andrea Dietz, Cesar Favela, Brendan Finney, Juris Alex Flores, Mark Gusmann, Kyle Haines, Blane Hammerlund, Brian Jaramillo, Maria Leguia, Jesus Limón, Jonathan Maier, Marcello Maltagliati, Brandon Martella, Paúl Moscoso, Ben Notkin, Goyo Ortiz, Erin Ota, Paulina Reyes, Stella Robitaille, Alan Rosenblum, Jota Samper, Bridey Scully, Andy Sturm, Rastko Tomasevic, Megan Willis.

VISITING DESIGNERS AND RESEARCHERS
Farsheed Bazmandegan, Alicia Boswell, Timothée Cachot, Hannah Campi, Elizabeth Chaney, Ivan Cheng, Kate Clark, Rachel Darling, Matthew Draper, Brittany Dutton, Amin Elsokary, Alessandro Falcone, Micah Farver, Benji Forman-Barzilai, Deborah Forster, Emmanuel Fraga, Magnolia Garcia, L'Auné Gergely, Ran Goldblatt, Isabel Gotti, Dario Guazzo, Marta Jankowska, Amy Knight, Tom Kolnaar, Robert Lecusay, Vanessa Lodermeier, Nadia Lopez, Kara Lu, Ethan Ma, Jesus Miramontes, Negin Mirzaeetavana, Sean Morgan, Mike Nicholson, Claire Noyer, Daniel Ochoa, Herman Partida, Juan Pablo Ponce de Leon, John Porten, Natalia Rangel, Ambika Roos, Melissa Rosa, Andres Saavedra, Nikhil Shah, Stephanie Sherman, Natasha Supangkat, Rene Jaime Torrero, Geraldine Wambersie.

Our thanks to the hundreds of graduate and undergraduate students, interns and volunteers who participated in our research and programs over many years.

PROJECT PARTNERS
Centro de Investigaciones Artisticas, Villa 31, Buenos Aires: M7Red (Mauricio Corbalán, Pio Torroja); Cooperativa Guatemalteca (Laura Códega, Leo Estol, Paula Massarutti, Renata Lozupone, Dudu Quintanilla); Centro de Investigaciones Artisticas (Roberto Jacoby).

Civic Innovation Lab, City of San Diego: Bill Fulton, Howard Blackson, Ilisa Goldman, Xavier Leonard, David Saborio.

Cross-Border Citizen: Corpovisionarios (Antanas Mockus, Henry Murrain, Lucía Aguirre), Mario C. Lopez, Matthias Görlich, Pawel Wolowitsch, Tom Wong.

Cross-Border Commons / Miramar Hydro-Pedagogic Park: Proyecto Fronterizo de Educación Ambiental (Laurie Silvan, Margarita Diaz, Delia Castellanos, Manuel Huesca); LandLAB (Neil Hadley, Jon Alarcón, Brian Garrett); Hormiguitas (Jorge Ibañez, Adela Bonilla); the Tijuana River National Estuarine Research Reserve (Kristen Goodrich, Ana Xochilt Eguiarte); The Autonomous University of Baja California (Napoleon Gudino Elizando); 4 Walls International (Steven Wright, Waylon Matson).

EarthLab: Groundwork San Diego-Chollas Creek (Leslie Reynolds, Patrice Baker, Allie Sifrit, Bud Mehan); The San Diego Unified School District (Sharon Whitehurst-Payne, Lee Dulgeroff, Nicola Labas); RNT Architects (Ralph Roesling); LandLAB (Neil Hadley, Jon Alarcón, Brian Garrett); San Diego Canyon-lands (Clayton Tschudy); Kumeyaay Community College (Michael Connolly Miskwish); the office of California State Senator Ben Hueso.

How is Your Art Going to Help us? Madrid: Madrid Abierto; M7Red (Mauricio Corbalán, Pio Torroja); Esgorfera (Iago Carro); Cecilia Andersson, Jorge Díez; Asociación Hasta el Amanecer; Radio Vallecas; AESCO; Asociación Al Alba; Asociación de la Calle; Casa de América.

InfoSite: INSITE (Michael Krichman, Carmen Cuenca, Oswaldo Sanchez); Aaron Gutierrez.

Living Rooms at the Border: Casa Familiar (Andrea Skorepa, Lisa Cuestas, David Flores, Andy Sturm); Studio E Architects (Eric Naslund, Kirsten Blakeman), Allgire Construction; Envision Engineering (Alejandro Barajas); LandLAB (Neil Hadley, Jon Alarcón, Brian Garrett). *The Medellín Diagram:* Alejandro Echeverri (EAFIT); Sergio Fajardo, Matthias Görlich, Pawel Wolowitsch.

Neighborhoods of Coexistence, APAP, Anyang: Kyong Park; Anyang University; M7Red (Mauricio Corbalán, Pio Torroja); Giacomo Castagnola.

Retrofit Gecekondu: Haus der Kulturen der Welt (Jesko Fezer, Christian Hiller, Nikolaus Hirsh, Jessica Paez); Kotti & Co (Sandy Kaltenborn, Ulrike Hamann, Angelika Levi); Envision Engineering (Alejandro Barajas); Mecalux Inc., Tijuana (Angel de Arriba, David Felix Mancera).

Santuario Frontera: Embajadores de Jesús (Gustavo Banda-Aceves, Zaida Guillén); Arq. Lorena K. Branks (Lorena Branks, José Luis Branks, Luis Sauceda); Mecalux Inc., Tijuana (Angel de Arriba, David Felix Mancera, Lluis Fuster Farré); Cultiva YA! (Ricardo Arana); Martin Acosta, Mario Alberto Díaz Cortez, Sergio Contreras; Commonweal (Oren Slozberg, Vanessa Marcotte).

Urban Rooms: Movimiento de Arte y Cultura Latino Americana (Anjee Helstrup-Alvarez); City of San Jose (Mary Rubin).

PROGRAM ADMINISTRATION
Kristen Michener, Carol Hudson, Tim Truitt, Fritz Leader, Ana Minvielle, Ariane Parkes and especially Khushbu Gokalgandhi.

OUR GRATITUDE TO SO MANY WHO HAVE SUPPORTED US AND OUR WORK WITH WISDOM AND RESOURCES
Brooke Ackerly, David Ackerly, Marc Albertin, Stan Allen, Pedro Alonzo, Sean Anderson, Paola Antonelli, the late Hilary Ballon, the late Ben Barber, the late Robert Barros, Bryan Bell, Barry Bergdoll, Deborah Berke, Aaron Betsky, the late Richard C. Blum, Anne Boddington, Denise Bratton, Alfredo Brillembourg, Nathan Brostrom, Gordon Brown, Tania Bruguera, Maria Buhigas, Malin Burnham, Robert Castro, Lifang Chiang, Sherice Clarke, Mike Cole, Mike Connolly, Mauricio Corbalán, Carmen Cuenca, Dana Cuff, Cliff and Delight Curry, Milton Curry, Dilip da Cunha, the late Randy Dalrymple, Mike Davis, Lieven De Cauter, Neil Denari, David Deutsch, Liz Diller, Keller Easterling, Alejandro Echeverri, Julie Eizenberg, Tarek Elhaik, the late Jeff Elman, Vicki Estrada, Ivan Evans, Steve Fagin, Sergio Fajardo, José Falconi, Osvaldo Feinstein, Jesko Fezer, Tom Finkelpearl, Sam Fleischacker, Geraldine Forbes, Andrew Forrest, Deborah Forster, Eva Franch, Christel Fricke, Emiliano Gandolfi, Cathy Gere, Gabriella Gómez-Mont, Coco González, Matthias Görlich, Michael Goodhart, Alastair Gordon, Joseph Grima, Hou Hanru, Dianne Harris, the late Helen Harrison and the late Newton Harrison, Eloisa Haudenschild, the late Marcel Hénaff, Sarah Herda, Catherine Herbst, Sarah Herda, Christian Hiller, Nikolaus Hirsch, Leo Hollis, Robert Horwitz, Ben Hueso, Genevieve Fuji Johnson, Jim Johnson, Tom Keenan, Pradeep Khosla, Inga Kiderra, Michael Kimmelman, Michael Krichman, Laura Kurgan, the late Barbara Lee, Margaret Leinen, Andres Lepik, Aaron Levy, Mario C. Lopez, Rick Lowe, Richard Madsen, Jerry Maldonado, the late Anu Mathur, Richard Matthew, Thom Mayne, Justin McGuirk, Hugh (Bud) Mehan, Rahul Mehrotra, Alejandro Meitin, Carmen Mendoza Arroyo, the late Bill Menkin, Norman Millar, Miodrag Mitrasinovic, Antanas Mockus, Fiamma Montezemolo, Helge Mooshammer, Bill Morrish, Peter Mortenböck, Hussein Munaim, the late Walter Munk, Eric Naslund, Goyo Ortiz, the late Elinor Ostrom, Nicolai Ouroussoff, Pablo Ouziel, David Owen, Sergio Palleroni, Steve Parish, Kyong Park, Rene Peralta, Hector Perez, Keith Pezzoli, Andrea Phillips, the late Nick Phillipson, Edgar Pieterse, Armando Plata, Marty Poirier, Nancy Postero,

Rob Quigley, Hugo Quinto, Ron Rael, Rachael Rakes, Ram Ramanathan, Marcos Ramirez ERRE, Ramesh Rao, Robert Reich, Jana Revedin, Pedro Reyes, Todd Rinehart, Miguel Robles-Durán, Ralph Roesling, Lorenzo Romito, Alan Rosenblum, Andrew Ross, Michael Rotondi, Ananya Roy, Angie Ruano, Bob Rubin, the late Lloyd Rudolph and the late Susanne Hoeber Rudolph, Leslie Ryan, Francisco Sanin, Lucía Sanroman, Saskia Sassen, Steve Schick, Amartya Sen, Richard Sennett, Gershon Shafir, Quentin Skinner, Andrea Skorepa, Cynthia Smith, Ted Smith, the late Ed Soja, the late Ignasi de Solà-Morales, Pau de Solà-Morales, Rebecca Solnit, Gina Solomon, Doris Sommer, the late Michael Sorkin, Andy Spurlock, Matt StClair, Tina Steingräber, the late Leslie Stern, the late Tracy Strong, Andy Sturm, Marcelo Suarez-Orozco, Suresh Subramani, Srinivas Sukumar, Leila Tamari, Pelin Tan, Chris Tenove, the late Jane Teranes, Javier Torres, Billie Tsien, Jim Tully, George Tynan, Nicola Ulibarri, Roberta Uno, Ignacio Valero, Jean-Phillipe Vassal, Ed Wall, Byron Washom, Paul Watson, Barry Weingast, Eyal Weizman, Mariët Westermann, Antje Wiener, Tod Williams, Megan Wurth, the late Daniel Yankelovich, Emily Young, Mimi Zeiger.

Fonna would like to acknowledge especially Ram Ramanathan, Jim Tully and the late Lloyd Rudolph for their inspiration and the countless ways they have supported her in her evolution as a grounded political theorist.

Special gratitude also to Andrea Skorepa for opening the doors to San Ysidro; and to Bob Rubin and Stéphane Samuel, and the late Richard C. Blum, for believing in us and investing in our work over many years.

Our thanks to ArtPlace America; the Blum Family Foundation; Commonweal; the Curry Stone Foundation; the Ford Foundation; Fundación Gonzalo Rio Arronte; the Graham Foundation; Mecalux Inc., Tijuana; the Mellon Foundation; the Minderoo Foundation; David Deutsch and the PARC Foundation; Bob Rubin and Stéphane Samuel; the Surdna Foundation; the Vilcek Foundation; and the San Diego Foundation. Also the California Energy Commission (EPIC: 20163305); and the National Science Foundation (INCLUDES: 2040713; CoPe EAGER: 1940171; SRS-RN: 2115124).

We also acknowledge the generous support of the University of California Office of the President; the University of California, San Diego Office of the Chancellor and the UCSD Center on Global Justice, home of our research-based practice. Our most sincere gratitude to UC San Diego Chancellor Pradeep Khosla, Executive Vice Chancellor Elizabeth Simmons, the late Dean of Social Sciences Jeff Elman and current Dean Carol Padden, and the campus advancement, development and communications offices for their commitment to our work over many years, especially Inga Kiderra, Drew Hunsinger, James Vermillion, Shauna McKenna, Jen Martin, Amanda Estrada and Carol Hobson.

We are grateful to Tina Steingräber for introducing this project to Hatje Cantz, and to Nicola von Velsen at Hatje Cantz and Victoria Hindley at the MIT Press for aligning the stars and co-publishing two volumes of our work. Our deepest thanks to them for their vision and partnership. Thank you to Serge Rompza and Lydia Sachse at NODE Berlin for their inspiring collaboration in the design of these pages. Additionally, our thanks to Dorothee Hahn, Stefanie Kruszyk, Kati Klaeske, Irene Schaudies, Anja Haering, Karen Stein and Claire Cichy at Hatje Cantz and Emma Martin, Kate Elwell, Molly Grote and Matt Badessa at the MIT Press for excellent editorial and production support, and for harmonizing a million moving parts as we brought this project to light.

We feel fortunate every day to work alongside Jonathan Maier and Marcello Maltagliati. We thank them for their brilliant work and their unrelenting commitment to this project.

We thank our families for their love: our parents, Zoraida Cruz, and Narda and Sheldon Forman; and our children, Benji, Sara, Inés and Alexandra.

We close these words with gratitude to our friend David Deutsch for his enduring confidence, guidance and support over many years. Thank you, David, for helping us realize our dreams.

COLOPHON

Editors and Authors
Teddy Cruz and Fonna Forman

Research and Design Team
Jonathan Maier, Marcello Maltagliati,
Kyle Haines and Ben Notkin

Managing Editor
Marcello Maltagliati with Jonathan Maier

Graphic Design
NODE Berlin Oslo
(Serge Rompza, Lydia Sachse)

Project Management
Dorothee Hahn

Copyediting
Matthew Draper, Irene Schaudies

Proofreading
Irene Schaudies

The research and programs of Estudio
Teddy Cruz + Fonna Forman are based in the
Center on Global Justice at the University of
California San Diego.
https://gjustice.ucsd.edu/

David Deutsch and the PARC Foundation
are partners in the production of this book.

Typeface: Diatype, Dinamo Typefaces
Paper: Magno Volume

Production
Stefanie Kruszyk, Kati Klaeske
Hatje Cantz

Reproductions
Repromayer GmbH, Reutlingen

Printing and Binding
Printer Trento s.r.l.

© 2022 for the photographs: see Image
Credits, p. 579

© 2022 Hatje Cantz Verlag, Berlin,
MIT Press, Cambridge, and authors

© 2022 for the designs and drawings:
Estudio Teddy Cruz + Fonna Forman

Library of Congress Control Number:
2022932494

Co-published by

Hatje Cantz Verlag GmbH
Mommsenstraße 27
10629 Berlin
www.hatjecantz.com

A Ganske Publishing Group Company

and

The MIT Press
Massachusetts Institute of Technology
Cambridge, Massachusetts 02142
http://mitpress.mit.edu

The preceding volume *Spatializing
Justice: Building Blocks* was published
in 2022 with the same publishers.

North America, Central America,
and South America:
ISBN 978-0-262-54518-1
E-book: 978-0-262-37347-0
(MIT Press)

Rest of the World:
ISBN 978-3-7757-4322-8
E-book: 978-3-7757-5409-5
(Hatje Cantz Verlag)

Printed in Italy